Core Concepts of Government and Not-for-Profit Accounting

Core Contents of Government and Not-for-Profit Accounting

Michael H. Granof
University of Texas, Austin

Penelope S. Wardlow, PhD, CGFM

JOHN WILEY & SONS, INC.

ACQUISITIONS EDITOR	Mark Bonadeo
MARKETING MANAGER	Keari Bedford
SENIOR PRODUCTION EDITOR	Petrina Kulek
SENIOR DESIGNER	Dawn L. Stanley
ILLUSTRATION EDITOR	Sandra Rigby
COVER PHOTO	©PhotoDisc, Inc.

This book was set in 10/12 Janson by UG / GGS Information Services, Inc. and printed and bound by Hamilton Printing. The cover was printed by Phoenix Color, Corp.

This book is printed on acid free paper. ∞

To order books or for customer service please call 1-800-CALL WILEY (225-5945).
ISBN 0-471-21853-7

Printed in the United States of America

10 9 8 7 6 5 4 3 2 1

We wrote this text to explain the core concepts, principles, and practices of government and not-for-profit accounting and financial reporting for, primarily, students in (1) *graduate and upper-level undergraduate accounting courses* in which the topics are addressed in less than a full semester and (2) *graduate courses in public administration and public affairs* in which the topics are part of a broader course in financial management. Most of the material is drawn from a more comprehensive text: Michael H. Granof, *Government and Not-for-Profit Accounting: Concepts and Practices*, 2nd edition (New York: John Wiley & Sons, Inc., 2001). As such, this text has the same underlying philosophy. We identify the key issues, indicate how and why they have been resolved by current standards, and set forth the strengths and limitations of financial reports. Thus, the text is especially appropriate for students who will eventually be users of government and not-for-profit financial reports, including administrators; financial analysts; members of legislatures, governing boards, and citizen groups; and individual taxpayers and donors.

The text is no less suitable, however, for students preparing for the CPA examination and for careers in professional accounting. The AICPA has indicated that future examinations will be more concerned with fundamental concepts and students' ability to reason than with technical details. Thus, we emphasize the rationale behind current standards and practices and provide the necessary framework for applying the government and not-for-profit accounting models to specific transactions and events. Our approach is consistent with that of the latest pronouncements of the Governmental Accounting Standards Board (GASB) and the Financial Accounting Standards Board (FASB), which focus more on the general concepts and principles of reporting than on detailed rules for specific types of transactions.

Throughout the text, we place accounting and reporting in the larger context of financial analysis and emphasize the importance of using accounting reports in conjunction with other sources of information. We focus as much on the economic substance of events and transactions as on how they are recorded. We hope thereby to enhance students' ability to engage in critical thinking. To that end, we have tried to make the chapter discussions thought provoking and the end-of-chapter materials challenging by requiring students to explain, justify, or criticize current practices.

Our text begins with a thorough exploration, in Chapters 1 and 2, of the environment and objectives of governments and not-for-profits, how they differ from those of businesses, and how and why they affect the recording and reporting of accounting information. We then devote Chapter 3 to the new accounting model for governments, GASB Statement No. 34, its objectives, and the significant changes from the previous accounting model. In Chapters 4 through 11, we fully integrate Statement No. 34, as well as the requirements of Statements Nos. 33 and 35 through 39. We explain how the most common transactions of governments are recorded in the funds and the differences between the fund statements and the government-wide statements in how information is reported and may be interpreted.

To illustrate our discussions in Chapters 3 through 11, we reproduce the financial statements and other information published in the 2001 *Comprehensive Annual Financial Report* (CAFR) of the City of Orlando, Florida, which adopted Statement No. 34 in 1999. Each chapter (and Chapter 14 on financial analysis) includes questions designed to help students explore Orlando's CAFR, find information related to the chapter topics, and discuss the meaning of that information. These assignments can be used discretely or as a continuing problem. Students and instructors can also access Orlando's complete 2001 CAFR (and those of prior years) on the Internet, for further exploration and discussion.

In Chapters 12 and 13, we discuss the philosophy and requirements of FASB Statements Nos. 116 and 117 and related standards for not-for-profits, as well as AICPA and other industry guidance for not-for-profits and issues of special relevance for health care organizations and institutions of higher education. We also highlight key differences between GASB and FASB concepts and requirements for similar transactions.

Building on previous chapters, the text concludes with a full chapter (Chapter 14) on the elements of financial analysis of governments and not-for-profits. We point out the need for a variety of information, in addition to that provided in financial statements, in order to assess the economic condition of these entities.

The text includes extensive end-of-chapter discussion questions, exercises, and problems from two different perspectives: (1) "hands-on" experience with recording and reporting accounting information and (2) discussion of the underlying issues and the meaning of the reported information. We hope that the different perspectives will enable instructors to tailor assignments to the specific needs and interests of their students. A Web site for instructors includes the solutions manual and a test bank.

We thank G. Michael Miller, CPA, CIA, Orlando's Finance Director, for permission to reproduce the City's 2001 financial statements, members of the staffs of the GASB and the FASB for clarification of certain issues discussed in this text, and the reviewers of the initial drafts for their comments and suggestions. We welcome recommendations for improvements to the text. Please send them to michael.granof@bus.utexas.edu or penelopew24@charter.net.

Michael H. Granof
Penelope S. Wardlow

CONTENTS

CHAPTER 1

The Government and Not-For-Profit Environment

Virtually all decisions and events that affect governments and not-for-profit organizations have financial ramifications and are thereby captured in the entities' budgets or financial statements. Government and not-for-profit budgeting, accounting, and reporting are necessarily complex. The financial impact of decisions and events can be measured and reported in any number of ways. So, too, can the financial position of an entity at a particular point in time. As a consequence, all individuals involved with government and not-for-profit entities in a decision-making capacity should have a grasp of the fundamentals of budgeting and accounting. If they do not, they are at the mercy of those who do. The objective of this text is to provide that basic understanding.

Chapters 3 through 11 focus on state and local governments, including government-owned not-for-profits, such as public colleges and universities, county hospitals, and city museums. Chapters 12 and 13 discuss nongovernment not-for-profits, such as private colleges, universities, hospitals, museums, and charities. Chapters 2 and 14 address both governments and not-for-profits. This chapter sets the stage for later chapters by discussing how governments and not-for-profits differ from businesses and why they require unique accounting principles and practices. We also identify the users of government and not-for-profit financial reports, their information needs, and the resultant objectives of financial reporting. The final section spotlights the **Governmental Accounting Standards Board (GASB)** and the **Financial Accounting Standards Board (FASB)**. The GASB sets the accounting and financial reporting standards for state and local governments, whereas the FASB is the standard-setter for all other entities except the federal government. Federal accounting standards are developed by the **Federal Accounting Standards Advisory Board (FASAB)** and are beyond the scope of this text.

HOW DO GOVERNMENTS AND NOT-FOR-PROFITS COMPARE WITH BUSINESSES?

Governments and not-for-profits provide services targeted to groups of constituents who advocate a political or social cause or carry out research or other activities for the betterment of society. The objectives of governments and not-for-profits cannot generally be expressed in dollars and cents and are often ambiguous and not easily quantifiable. Moreover, governments and not-for-profits have relationships with the parties providing their resources that are unlike those of businesses.

DIFFERENT MISSIONS A key objective of financial reporting is to provide information about an entity's performance. The main objective of a typical business is to earn a profit. Financial statements that key on net income are in harmony with that objective because net income is a measure of how well a business achieved its goals. Businesses also may seek to promote the welfare of their executives and employees and improve their surrounding communities. But business accounting and reporting are concerned almost exclusively with the goal of maximizing profits or cash flows.

The financial reports of governments and not-for-profits also can provide information about inflows (revenues) and outflows (expenditures) of cash and other resources. A continuing excess of expenditures over revenues generally signals financial distress or poor managerial performance. However, an excess of revenues over expenditures is not necessarily commendable. It may be achieved, for example, by reducing services, which might be at odds with the entity's objectives.

To report properly on their accomplishments, governments and not-for-profits must augment their financial statements with nonfinancial data relating to their objectives. A school, for example, might include statistics on student test scores or graduation rates. A center for the homeless might present data on the number of people fed or adequately housed.

BUDGETS VERSUS THE MARKETPLACE Governments and not-for-profits are governed mainly by their budgets, not by the marketplace. Revenues and expenditures are controlled or strongly influenced through the budgetary process. A government's revenues may be determined by legislative fiat, so that the government may not be subject to the forces of competition faced by businesses. A not-for-profit's revenues are not established by legal mandate but may be obtained from contributions, dues, tuition, or user charges, none of which are comparable to the sales of a business.

EXPENDITURES AND REVENUES Governments and many not-for-profits establish the level of services they will provide, calculate costs, and then set tax rates and fees to generate the necessary revenues. In sum, expenditures may drive revenues. These organizations cannot, however, simply raise revenues without regard to their services or increase taxes without limit. Governments may be constrained by political forces. Universities may have to keep tuition rates close to those of peer schools. Further, some not-for-profits, such as the United Way or organizations that fund medical research, base their expenditures exclusively on their revenues. The more funds they raise, the more they spend.

PREEMINENCE OF THE BUDGET, NOT THE ANNUAL REPORT For businesses, the annual report is the most significant financial document. An announcement of annual earnings (the preview of the annual report) may make front-page news. By contrast, the annual budget is an internal document seldom made available to investors or the general public.

A government or not-for-profit's release of its annual report is customarily ignored. It seldom contains surprises, for if revenues and expenditures were markedly different from the initial budget, the entity probably was required to amend the budget during the year. By contrast, the budget takes center stage because it is the culmination of the political process. It encapsulates most of the organization's important decisions. It determines which constituents give to the entity and which receive; which activities are supported and which are assessed. As a result, the budget is a source of constituent concern and controversy. Government budget hearings often draw standing-room-only crowds. Church and synagogue budget debates are frequently marked by more intense fervor than worship services.

A government's budget may be backed by the force of law and should not be taken lightly. Government officials are ordinarily prohibited from overspending and can even go to jail for severe violations of budgetary mandates.

IMPORTANCE OF BUDGETS IN ACCOUNTING AND FINANCIAL REPORTING

Constituents want assurance that spending has not exceeded authorized amounts and that revenue and expenditure estimates were reliable. The accounting system and resulting financial reports must be designed to provide that information. Managers need an accounting system that informs them whether they are on target to meet budget projections. Even more critically, they need a system that prevents overspending or warns that it is about to occur. The budget is a control device, but it needs a complementary accounting and reporting system.

Auditors and other evaluators need a basis for assessing an organization's performance. State-of-the-art budgets establish that basis by indicating how much will be spent on a particular activity and what the activity will achieve. A post-period assessment can then focus on whether the entity met its revenue and expenditure projections and whether it achieved expectations. Evaluators can then assess organizational efficiency and effectiveness by comparing *inputs* (such as dollar expenditures) with *outputs* and *outcomes* (results). The accounting system should be designed to facilitate these comparisons, assuring that the organization reports and categorizes revenues and expenditures consistent with the budget. Currently, few organizations have budgetary and accounting systems that will measure and report adequately on nonmonetary performance. However, both standard-setting authorities—the GASB and the FASB—have recognized the importance of performance measures and are taking steps to ensure that eventually they will be provided routinely.

NEED TO ENSURE INTERPERIOD EQUITY Most governments are required by law, and most not-for-profits are expected by policy, to balance their operating budgets. This assures that, in any period, revenues cover expenditures and the entity's constituents, as a group, pay for what they receive. If organizations borrow to cover operating deficits, the cost of benefits enjoyed by today's citizens must be borne by tomorrow's citizens.

The concept that constituents should pay for the services they receive and should not shift the burdens to their children has traditionally been labeled **intergenerational equity**. In recent years, the term **interperiod equity** has been accepted as more appropriate to emphasize that entities should not transfer costs even to future years, let alone to future generations. The accounting systems of governments and not-for-profits must provide information about whether interperiod equity is being maintained. Table 1-1 compares fiscal practices that promote interperiod equity with those that do not.

The concept of interperiod equity applies only to borrowing for operating, not capital, expenditures. A government-constructed highway or university-purchased lab equipment will produce benefits over more than one year. It is only fair to incorporate related debt service costs into the taxes or tuition charges of the citizens or students who will receive the benefits.

REVENUES NOT INDICATIVE OF DEMAND FOR GOODS OR SERVICES For competitive businesses, and if prices are held constant, the greater the revenues, the greater the demand—an indication that the entity is meeting a societal need. For governments and not-for-profits, revenues may not be linked to constituent demand or satisfaction. An increase in tax revenues, for example, tells nothing about the amount

TABLE 1-1
Fiscal Practices that Promote or Undermine Interperiod Equity

Promote	Undermine
1. Setting aside resources for employee pensions during the years in which the employees provide their services.	1. Paying the pensions of retired employees out of current operating funds.
2. Issuing conventional 30-year bonds to finance the purchase of a new building that is expected to have a useful life of 30 years; repaying the bonds, along with appropriate amounts of interest, over the 30-year period.	2. Financing the purchase of the new building with 30-year zero-coupon bonds that permit the entire amount of principal and interest to be paid upon the maturity of the bonds; making no provision to set aside resources for payment of principal and interest on the bonds until the year they mature.
3. Paying the current-year costs of an administrative staff out of current operating funds.	3. Issuing 30-year bonds to finance the current-year operating costs of an administrative staff.
4. Charging payments of wages and salaries made in the first week of the current fiscal year to the previous fiscal year, that in which the employees actually provided their services.	4. Charging wages and salaries applicable to services provided in the last week of the current fiscal year to the following fiscal year, that in which the payments were made.
5. Charging the cost of supplies as expenditures in the year in which they were used rather than when they were purchased.	5. Charging the cost of supplies as expenditures in the year they were purchased, irrespective of the year in which they were used.
6. Recognizing interest on investments in the year in which it is earned, irrespective of when it is received.	6. Recognizing interest in the year in which it is received, irrespective of when it is earned.
7. Setting aside funds each year to pay for an anticipated 20-year renovation of a college dormitory.	7. Paying for an anticipated 20-year renovation of a college dormitory out of current funds in the year the work is performed.

or quality of services provided. Therefore, a conventional statement of revenues and expenditures cannot supply information about the demand for services. Supplementary information is required.

NO DIRECT LINK BETWEEN REVENUES AND EXPENDITURES Further, government and not-for-profit revenues may not be related to expenditures. Donations to a not-for-profit may increase from one year to the next without a corresponding increase in the quantity, quality, or cost of the services provided. Thus, the *matching concept*—business accounting's central notion that expenses must be paired with corresponding revenues—may have a different meaning for governments and not-for-profits than for businesses. Businesses attempt to match the costs of specific goods or services with the revenues they generate. Governments and not-for-profits can sometimes associate only overall revenues with the broad categories of expenditures they are intended to cover.

DIFFERENT ROLE FOR CAPITAL ASSETS Unlike businesses, governments and not-for-profits make significant investments in assets that neither produce revenues nor reduce expenditures. Therefore, conventional business practices for valuing **capital assets**, such as comparing the present values of the asset's expected cash outflows and inflows, may not apply to governments and not-for-profits. A highway being considered by a government will not yield cash benefits—at least not directly to the government. A proposed college library may enrich the community's intellectual life, but not the college's coffers. In fact, some government and not-for-profit "assets" may be more properly interpreted as liabilities because maintaining them will consume rather than provide resources.

RESTRICTIONS ON RESOURCES In contrast to business resources, many government and not-for-profit assets are restricted for particular activities or purposes. For example, if the federal government gives a local government a grant for construction of low-income housing, the award can be used only for that purpose, no matter how worthy other purposes may be.

Taxes and membership dues may also be restricted. A city's hotel tax may be dedicated to financing a local convention center. A cemetery association may have to set aside part of its fees for land acquisition. Governments and not-for-profits must assure the parties that provided restricted funds that they are used properly. Financial reports must show that the restricted resources are unavailable for other purposes. Therefore, the financial statements must either segregate restricted from unrestricted resources or disclose by other means that some resources can be used only for specific purposes.

Slip-ups regarding restrictions carry serious consequences. At the very least they may cause the organization to forfeit past and future awards. The organization must design its accounting system so that management cannot inadvertently misspend restricted resources. To this end, governments and not-for-profits employ a system of accounting known as *fund accounting*. It is described in Chapter 2.

NO DISTINCT OWNERSHIP INTERESTS Unlike businesses, governments and not-for-profits typically cannot be sold or transferred. If they are dissolved, there are no stockholders entitled to receive residual resources. Thus, their financial statements must be prepared for parties other than stockholders. The main groups of statement users will be identified later in this chapter. The lack of ownership interests implies that, unless the entire entity is closed and its assets liquidated, there may be little interest in the market values of its resources. Governments typically cannot sell their highways and sewers. Museums may be required to use the proceeds from selling collection items to acquire similar assets.

LESS DISTINCTION BETWEEN INTERNAL AND EXTERNAL ACCOUNTING AND REPORTING The line between external and internal accounting and reporting is less clear-cut for governments and not-for-profits than for businesses. First, although the external reports of businesses focus on profits, few organizational units are profit centers in which management controls all the key factors that affect profits. Therefore, internal reports present data on other measures of performance, such as total fixed costs (those that do not vary by levels of output) or per-unit variable costs. For governments and not-for-profits, profit is not an appropriate performance measure for either external parties or internal departments. The relevant performance measures must stem from the organizations' unique goals and objectives and are unlikely to be the same for all user groups.

Second, in business the budget is only an internal document. In governments and not-for-profits, it is the key fiscal document and is as important to taxpayers, bondholders, and other constituencies as it is to managers.

Third, the distinction between internal and external parties is more ambiguous in governments and not-for-profits than in business. Taxpayers and organizational members cannot be categorized neatly as either insiders or outsiders. They are not paid managers (and, thus, not traditional *insiders*), but they may nevertheless have the ultimate say as to organizational policies through direct vote or elected officers.

WHAT OTHER CHARACTERISTICS OF GOVERNMENTS AND NOT-FOR-PROFITS HAVE ACCOUNTING IMPLICATIONS?

Several other characteristics of governments and not-for-profits may not distinguish them from businesses but have significant accounting and reporting implications.

MANY DIFFERENT TYPES OF GOVERNMENTS AND NOT-FOR-PROFITS There are approximately 87,000 local governments in the United States. If that number seems surprisingly large, consider how many separate governments have jurisdiction over a typical neighborhood. The neighborhood may be part of a town, and several towns may form a township. The township may be part of a county, which is a subdivision of a state. Further, the neighborhood school, hospital, water supply, and bus system may be administered by, respectively, an independent school district, a hospital district, a utility authority, and a transportation authority. There might also be a community college district and an airport authority. Each category of government will likely differ from others in the services it provides, the types of assets it controls, its taxing and borrowing authority, and the parties to which it is accountable. Even governments in the same category may provide different services. For example, New York and Dallas are among the nation's ten largest cities. But New York operates its own school system, whereas Dallas's schools are under the control of an independent school district.

In addition, more than a million not-for-profit organizations, sometimes referred to as the *independent sector*, offer a wide range of services. Not-for-profits include schools; hospitals; social service organizations; advocacy groups; civic, social, and fraternal organizations; religious and cultural organizations; and foundations.

The diversity of governments and not-for-profits makes it difficult to have a common accounting *model* (set of accounting and reporting principles) that will be suitable for all governments and not-for-profits—or even for any particular type of entity. Assuming that comparability among entities is a desirable characteristic of financial reporting, standard-setting authorities (the GASB and the FASB) face a policy question. Should they adopt common standards for all governments and not-for-profits or only for entities of the same type? When entities are similar, common standards may promote comparability. When entities are not similar, common standards may, like ill-fitting clothes, distort reality. As will be discussed in succeeding chapters, the GASB and the FASB are heading in the direction of one set of common principles for all state and local governments and another set for all nongovernment not-for-profits.

BUSINESS-TYPE ACTIVITIES OF GOVERNMENTS AND NOT-FOR-PROFITS Many governments and not-for-profits engage in business-type activities. Cities, for example, may operate utilities, trash collection services, and golf courses. Universities operate book stores and cafeterias. Environmental organizations publish and sell magazines. These enterprises may, and perhaps should, be managed as if profits were a major objective. If so, their managers and constituents need the same type of financial information as business operators and owners. The appropriate accounting and reporting practices may differ from those suitable for nonbusiness activities. Thus, the challenge of developing accounting and reporting principles for governments and not-for-profits is made more formidable by the potential need for more than one set of standards—even for a single organization.

HOW DO GOVERNMENTS COMPARE WITH NOT-FOR-PROFITS?

In addition to differing from businesses, governments and not-for-profits differ from each other in important ways that affect financial reporting. Governments, unlike not-for-profits, have the authority to command resources—the power to tax, collect license and other fees, and impose charges by legislative action. This ability suggests that a government's balance sheet might not report all of the assets under its control. To obtain a comprehensive picture of a government's financial health, it is necessary to consider not only the resources it actually owns, but also those that it has the power to summon. We return to this point in Chapter 14.

WHAT ARE FINANCIAL REPORTS USED FOR?

How the external financial reports of governments and not-for-profits are used varies from user to user. For the most part, external financial reports should allow users to do the following:[1]

- *Assess financial position and economic condition.* Users need to analyze the entity's past results and current financial position (assets compared with liabilities) and its overall economic condition to determine the entity's ability to meet its obligations and continue to provide expected services. By examining trends, users are better able to predict future financial developments and foresee the need for changes in revenue sources, resource allocations, and capital requirements.
- *Compare actual results with the budget.* Users want assurance that the entity adhered to its adopted budget. Significant variations may signify poor management or unforeseen circumstances that require an explanation.
- *Determine compliance with laws, regulations, and restrictions on the use of resources.* Users want to be assured of compliance with legal and contractual requirements, such as bond covenants, donor and grantor restrictions, taxing and debt limitations, and applicable laws. Violations can have serious financial repercussions and can jeopardize the entity's viability.
- *Evaluate efficiency and effectiveness.* Users want to know whether the entity is achieving its objectives and, if so, how efficiently and effectively. They need to compare accomplishments (outcomes) with service efforts and costs (resource inputs).

WHO ARE THE USERS OF FINANCIAL REPORTS?

The main users of the financial reports of governments and not-for-profits are the parties to whom the organizations are accountable. They include governing boards; investors and creditors; taxpayers, other citizens, and organizational members; donors and grantors; regulatory and oversight agencies; and employees and other constituents.

---

[1]These purposes are drawn from the GASB Concepts Statement No. 1, *Objectives of Financial Reporting* (1987).

The *basic* (or *general purpose*) financial statements and other information in external financial reports are targeted mainly at parties outside the organization. As in business accounting, external reports may not be appropriate for managerial decisions. Executives, agency heads, and other managers should rely on the internal reporting system for the financial information they require. Nevertheless, the information needs of internal and external parties overlap, and internal parties may rely on external financial reports for much of the data they need.

GOVERNING BOARDS In governments and not-for-profits as well as in businesses, the auditors' reports on the financial statements are directed to the organizations' governing boards. The governing board is typically an elected or appointed legislature (such as a city council or board of commissioners) for a government, and a board of trustees or directors for a not-for-profit. Governing boards cannot be neatly categorized as either internal or external users. Customarily, their members come from outside the management team. However, in most organizations, they approve budgets, major purchases, contracts, executive employment agreements, and significant operating policies, thereby not only overseeing managers, but also getting involved in their decisions.

INVESTORS AND CREDITORS Governments and not-for-profits use the same financial markets as businesses to satisfy their debt-financed capital requirements. In 2001, state and local governments had an estimated $1.8 trillion of bonds outstanding, compared with $3.9 trillion for U.S. corporations.[2] The amounts highlight the economic significance of the municipal bond segment. Governments issue bonds primarily to finance long-term assets, such as buildings, roads, highways, and utility systems. Not-for-profits use bond financing for buildings and equipment.

Investors commonly include government and not-for-profit bonds as well as corporate bonds in their investment portfolios. For both kinds of securities, they want assurance that the issuer will meet scheduled interest and principal payments. Most bondholders are only indirect users of financial reports and rely more on the assessments of bond-rating services, such as *Standard & Poor's*, *Moody's*, and *Fitch IBCA*. These services assign to publicly traded bonds a rating (e.g., AAA, AA, A, BBB) reflective of the securities' risk of default.

Governments and not-for-profits also borrow routinely from banks and other financial institutions to finance new facilities or short-term imbalances between cash receipts and disbursements. Lenders use the financial statements of governments and not-for-profits just as they would those of businesses—to help assess the borrowers' credit-worthiness.

CITIZENS AND ORGANIZATIONAL MEMBERS Citizens (or taxpayers) are invariably placed near the top of any list of government financial report users. In reality, few citizens ever see them, perhaps in part because the reports are slow to appear and reporting practices are not user friendly. But citizens are, nevertheless, a significant user group. They obtain financial data through a variety of filters, including civic associations, such as the League of Women Voters, political action groups, and the media. They might not pay attention to the annual report, but they definitely take notice, at any time of the year, of instances of financial mismanagement or other circumstances that may cause unexpected revenue shortfalls or cost overruns.

---

[2]The Bond Market Association, New York, NY, 2001.

How much interest the members of a not-for-profit take in their organization's financial statements or related data depends on the organization's size and the members' involvement. A country club's members may pay more attention to financial affairs than do the members of broader-based organizations, such as the National Geographic Society, because the country club's financial position and performance more directly affect their dues and fees.

DONORS AND GRANTORS Few individuals request financial statements before they drop coins into Salvation Army kettles or Muscular Dystrophy Association canisters. But major donors and grantors, such as the United Way, the Ford Foundation, and federal, state, and local governments, analyze financial reports and other financial information from supplicant associations as carefully as a banker making a loan. Individual donors also should obtain financial information before contributing. Information should be available from the organization or from regulatory authorities about the allocation of resources—the proportion of contributions that goes to programs, as opposed to fundraising and executive salaries.

REGULATORY AGENCIES Local governments usually are required to file financial reports with state agencies; charitable organizations with state or local authorities; and religious and fraternal associations with their national organizations. Recipients use these reports to ensure that the entities are spending and receiving resources in accordance with laws, regulations, or policies; to help assess management's performance; to allocate resources; and to exercise general oversight.

EMPLOYEES AND OTHER CONSTITUENTS Few employees spend their off-hours poring over their organization's financial statements. But officers of their unions or employee associations may examine them, looking for ways to free up resources for salary increases or projects in which they have a special interest. Other constituent or interest groups also use financial reports on an ad hoc basis. Probably few students have seen the financial statements of the college or university they attend. However, students have been known to use budgets and annual reports to support their claims that the college or university need not raise tuition or can afford a new student center.

WHAT ARE THE OBJECTIVES OF FINANCIAL REPORTING?

The overall objective of financial reporting is to meet the information needs of report users. But financial reports cannot possibly satisfy all requirements of all users. Therefore, the GASB and the FASB have established objectives that circumscribe the functions of financial reports. These objectives are the foundation for their financial reporting standards.

GASB OBJECTIVES Because of the unique characteristics of governments and their environment, the GASB established *accountability* as the cornerstone of financial reporting. "Accountability," it says, "requires governments to answer to the citizenry—to justify the raising of public resources and the purposes for which they are used." It "is based on the belief that the citizenry has a 'right to know,' a right to receive openly declared facts that may lead to public debate by the citizens and their elected representatives."[3]

The GASB divided the objective of accountability into three subobjectives:[4]

1. *Interperiod equity*. "Financial reporting should provide information to determine whether current-year revenues were sufficient to pay for current-year services."

2. *Budgetary and fiscal compliance*. "Financial reporting should demonstrate whether resources were obtained and used in accordance with the entity's legally adopted budget; it should also demonstrate compliance with other finance-related legal or contractual requirements."

3. *Service efforts, costs, and accomplishments*. "Financial reporting should provide information to assist users in assessing the service efforts, costs, and accomplishments of the governmental entity."

The GASB established two additional objectives, each of which has three subobjectives. These are set forth in Table 1-2.

TABLE 1-2
Governmental Accounting Standards Board's
Additional Objectives of Financial Reporting

Financial reporting should assist users in evaluating the operating results of the governmental entity for the year.

a. Financial reporting should provide information about sources and uses of financial resources. Financial reporting should account for all outflows by function and purpose, all inflows by source and type, and the extent to which inflows met outflows. Financial reporting should identify material nonrecurring financial transactions.

b. Financial reporting should provide information about how the governmental entity financed its activities and met its cash requirements.

c. Financial reporting should provide information necessary to determine whether the entity's financial position improved or deteriorated as a result of the year's operations.

Financial reporting should assist users in assessing the level of services that can be provided by the governmental entity and its ability to meet its obligations as they become due.

a. Financial reporting should provide information about the financial position and condition of a governmental entity. Financial reporting should provide information about resources and obligations, both actual and contingent, current and noncurrent. The major financial resources of most governmental entities are derived from the ability to tax and issue debt. As a result, financial reporting should provide information about tax sources, tax limitations, tax burdens, and debt limitations.

b. Financial reporting should provide information about a governmental entity's physical and other nonfinancial resources having useful lives that extend beyond the current year, including information that can be used to assess the service potential of those resources. This information should be presented to help users assess long- and short-term capital needs.

c. Financial reporting should disclose legal or contractual restrictions on resources and risks of potential loss of resources.

Source: GASB Concepts Statement No. 1, *Objectives of Financial Reporting* (1987).

---

[3]GASB Concepts Statement No. 1, para. 56.
[4]Ibid., para. 77.

The GASB objectives, taken independently, are unquestionably reasonable. But taken together, do they establish the basis for resolving specific issues and establishing specific standards? Consider the following example:

EXAMPLE *Clash among Reporting Objectives*

In its first year of operations, the Whimsy City Sanitary District (WCSD) prepared a cash-based budget and engaged in the following summary transactions, all of which occurred without variance from the budget.

- It purchased sanitation vehicles having anticipated economic lives of ten years for $10 million cash.
- It billed residents for $9 million, but because bills for the last month of the year were not mailed until early the following year (as planned), it collected only $8.2 million.
- It incurred operating costs, all paid in cash, of $6 million.

Let us prepare a statement of revenues and expenses using accounting standards consistent with the GASB objectives. In a later chapter we will explain the distinction between expenses and **expenditures**, a term commonly used in government accounting. For now consider them to be the same.

Two problems are readily apparent:

1. *Should the WCSD report vehicle-related expenses of $10 million (the amount paid) or $1 million (one-tenth of the assets consumed during the period)?* The broader question is whether governments should charge depreciation.
2. *Should the WCSD recognize as revenues the $9 million billed or the $8.2 million collected?* More generally, should revenues be recognized on a cash basis (i.e., only when cash is collected) or an accrual basis (i.e., when the event giving rise to the revenue occurred, irrespective of when the cash will be received)?

Because the WCSD's budget is on a cash basis, a statement that would fulfill the GASB's objective of budgetary and fiscal compliance would also have to be on a cash basis. The WCSD would recognize revenue as the cash is collected; it would record vehicle-related expenses in the period in which the vehicles are acquired and paid for. Thus (in millions):

Revenues from Customers		$ 8.2
Operating Expenses	$ 6.0	
Vehicle-related Costs	10.0	16.0
Excess of Revenues over Expenses		$(7.8)

Under this cash-basis statement, the entire purchase cost of the vehicles falls on the taxpayers of the year of purchase. In the following nine years, the WCSD would report no expenses related to the purchase or "consumption" of these assets. Thus, management would appear far more efficient in those years than in the first year. Also, if tax rates were set so that revenues would cover expenses, taxpayers would enjoy a rate decrease. However, since the taxpayers of all ten years will benefit from the assets, the reporting objective of interperiod equity would not be served. On the other hand, the WCSD would be credited with only $8.2 million in revenues, even though it provided $9.0 million in services—another, though opposite, violation of the interperiod equity concept.

By contrast, a statement that would fulfill the interperiod equity objective would recognize the WCSD's $10 million in vehicle costs over the ten years of use and the $9.0 in revenues in the year in which the services were provided. Thus:

Revenues from Customers		$9.0
Operating Expenses	$6.0	
Vehicle-related Costs	1.0	7.0
Excess of Revenues over Expenses		$2.0

But this accrual-basis statement cannot readily be compared to the WCSD's adopted budget and therefore cannot, without adjustment, be used to demonstrate its budgetary compliance.

As will be apparent throughout this text, the conflict between the two objectives characterizes many of the issues that government accountants, and the GASB in particular, have to face in assuring that financial statements are informative and useful to the parties that rely on them. In particular, the conflict casts doubt upon whether the objectives can be fulfilled with a single set of financial statements or whether, as an alternative, two sets—one on a full accrual basis, the other on a budget or near-budget basis—may be necessary.

FASB OBJECTIVES FASB objectives for not-for-profits are generally similar to GASB objectives for governments. They are presented in summary form in Table 1-3. Unlike GASB objectives, FASB objectives refer only obliquely to budgetary compliance as information that should be useful in "assessing how managers of a

---

TABLE 1-3
Financial Accounting Standards Board's Objectives of Financial Reporting

- Financial reporting by nonbusiness organizations should provide information that is useful to present and potential resource providers and other users in making rational decisions about the allocation of resources to those organizations.
- Financial reporting should provide information to help present and potential resource providers and other users in assessing the services that a nonbusiness organization provides and its ability to continue to provide those services.
- Financial reporting should provide information that is useful to present and potential resource providers and other users in assessing how managers of a nonbusiness organization have discharged their stewardship responsibilities and about other aspects of their performance.
- Financial reporting should provide information about the economic resources, obligations, and net resources of an organization, and the effects of transactions, events, and circumstances that change resources and interests in those resources.
- Financial reporting should provide information about the performance of an organization during a period, periodic measurement of the changes in the amount and nature of the net resources of a nonbusiness organization, and information about the service efforts and accomplishments of an organization.
- Financial reporting should provide information about how an organization obtains and spends cash or other liquid resources, about its borrowing and repayment of borrowing, and about other factors that may affect an organization's liquidity.
- Financial reporting should include explanations and interpretations to help users understand financial information provided.

Source: FASB Statement of Financial Accounting Concepts No. 4, *Objectives of Financial Reporting by Nonbusiness Organizations* (1980).

nonbusiness organization have discharged their stewardship responsibilities."[5] However, the FASB stresses that external financial statements can "best meet that need by disclosing failures to comply with spending mandates [presumably expressed in budgets] that may impinge on an organization's financial performance or on its ability to provide a satisfactory level of services."[6]

SERVICE EFFORTS AND ACCOMPLISHMENTS SEEN AS A LONG-TERM GOAL

GASB and FASB objectives both endorse the notion, discussed earlier in this chapter, that financial reporting should encompass information on service efforts and accomplishments. This information cannot easily be expressed in monetary units and has not traditionally been included in financial statements. Both boards emphasize that the ability to measure accomplishments is still undeveloped. They see this aspect of performance reporting as a long-term goal rather than an immediate imperative.

DO DIFFERENCES IN ACCOUNTING PRINCIPLES REALLY MATTER?

Financial statements demonstrate what happened to an entity in the past. But they present the evidence from the perspective of the accountant who prepared them. Other accountants might describe the events differently. The underlying accounting principles dictate how the evidence is presented. An important issue is whether differences in accounting principles affect the decisions made on the basis of financial statements.

Just as a witness's explanation of an accident cannot change what actually occurred, neither can an accountant's report on an entity's past transactions change what actually transpired. In the sanitation district example, the district paid $10 million in cash for vehicles, billed its customers $9 million for services, and paid $6 million in operating expenses. Whether the district's financial statements report revenues over expenses of $2 million, expenses over revenues of $7.8 million, or any amount in between is irrelevant to the actual event. Moreover, financial statements, no matter how prepared, do not directly impact the economic worth of an entity. At year-end the district's customers owed it $0.8 million, whether the district reported a receivable of that amount (as it would under an accrual basis of accounting) or of zero (as it would under a cash basis of accounting).

USER ADJUSTMENTS Users of financial statements can be indifferent to how an entity's fiscal story is told, as long as they are given adequate information to reconfigure the statements to a preferred form. Research in the corporate sector provides compelling evidence that stockholders are able to see through differences in accounting practices and adjust financial statements to take the differences into account. Thus, if one firm reports higher earnings than another solely because it employs more liberal accounting principles, the total market value of its shares will be no greater.

The *efficiency* of the municipal bond market—the extent to which it incorporates all public information in pricing securities—has been investigated much less than the efficiency of the stock market. Nevertheless, the available evidence suggests that investors in tax-exempt bonds, like their stock market counterparts, understand the impact of differences in accounting practices.

---

[5]FASB Statement of Financial Accounting Concepts No. 4, *Objectives of Financial Reporting by Nonbusiness Organizations* (1980), para. 40.
[6]FASB Concepts Statement No. 4, para. 41.

ECONOMIC CONSEQUENCES Accounting principles frequently have economic consequences. Important decisions are made based on financial data as presented and without adjustment.

We noted earlier that budgets are governments' paramount financial documents. Most jurisdictions must present balanced budgets (expenditures cannot exceed revenues) in accord with accounting principles that they either select themselves or have imposed upon them by higher-order governments. The choice of accounting principles is critical. Whereas one set of accounting principles may result in a balanced budget, another, which includes identical revenue and expenditure proposals, may not. Most governments budget on a cash or near-cash basis. If they were required to budget on a full accrual basis, their budgets might quickly become unbalanced.

Governments may face restrictions on the amount of debt they can incur. The use of one set of accounting principles in defining and measuring debt (for example, not counting a lease as an obligation) might enable them to issue additional bonds without violating the legal limits. The use of a different set (for example, counting the lease as a liability), might cause them to exceed the limits and be barred from further borrowing.

This text includes many other examples of how specific reporting practices have economic consequences.

WHO ESTABLISHES GENERALLY ACCEPTED ACCOUNTING PRINCIPLES?

Generally accepted accounting principles (GAAP) embrace the rules and conventions that guide the form and content of basic (or general purpose) financial statements. These principles are expressed mainly in pronouncements of the GASB and the FASB for their respective jurisdictions and should be consistent with the objectives that they established. However, in the absence of specific pronouncements, GAAP may also be derived from historical convention and widespread practice.

FUNCTIONS OF THE GASB, THE FASB, AND THE AICPA The GASB and the FASB have each been sanctioned by the **American Institute of Certified Public Accountants (AICPA)** to establish accounting principles for their respective jurisdictions pursuant to Rule 203 of the AICPA's Code of Professional Conduct. Rule 203 provides that a CPA should not express an unqualified audit opinion on financial statements that violate the standards established by the designated authorities. In addition, the AICPA provides accounting guidance through "industry audit guides" and "statements of position" on issues not yet addressed by either the GASB or the FASB.

The FASB was established in 1973 and the GASB in 1984. They are financed and overseen by the Financial Accounting Foundation, a not-for-profit organization governed by trustees drawn from business, professional, and government communities. Thus, standards are set mainly in the private sector, not by any government agency. The GASB has a full-time chairman and six part-time members; the FASB has seven full-time members, including its chairman. Each board has a full-time staff and is supported by an advisory council composed of representatives of constituent groups. GASB and FASB share facilities in Norwalk, Connecticut.

ENTITIES COMMON TO GOVERNMENT AND NOT-FOR-PROFIT SECTORS A controversial and politically sensitive issue arose soon after the GASB was established: Should the GASB or the FASB set standards for entities, such as colleges and universities, that are common to both the government and the not-for-profit sectors? Some constituents asserted that there are few conceptual or operational differences between same-type entities in the two sectors that justify different accounting standards and hence separate standard-setting authorities. Others contended that government hospitals, utilities, and universities have fundamentally different rights, responsibilities, and obligations from their not-for-profit counterparts. For example, they may have the ability to impose taxes and issue tax-exempt debt and may be accountable to the citizenry at large rather than a board of trustees. Concerns over sovereignty made the issue more complex. Some managers of not-for-profits maintained that they had little in common with governments and did not want to be under the GASB's authority. Similarly, government officials refused to yield standard-setting control over any of their component units to the FASB.

In 1989, the Financial Accounting Foundation and the constituents of the two boards agreed on a jurisdictional formula that, in essence, reaffirmed the status quo since the GASB's inception: GASB would have authority over all state and local government entities and the FASB would have authority over all nongovernment entities. Thus, public colleges and universities (such as The State University of New York) are subject to GASB standards; private colleges and universities (such as New York University) come under FASB standards.

If the GASB or the FASB has not issued a pronouncement on a particular issue, then organizations within each of their jurisdictions can look to other sources for guidance. These sources are set forth in two hierarchies that are part of the jurisdiction agreement and were adopted by the AICPA in *Statement on Auditing Standards No. 23*, "The Meaning of Present Fairly in Conformity with Generally Accepted Accounting Principles in the Independent Auditor's Report." As shown in Table 1-4, in the column applicable to the GASB, an FASB pronouncement that has been specifically adopted by the GASB has the same standing (the top category) as one issued by the GASB itself. However, an FASB pronouncement that has *not* been specifically adopted by the GASB is considered "other accounting literature" (the lowest category). The FASB's hierarchy is similar to, but not a mirror image of, the GASB's.

TABLE 1-4
A Summary of The "Hierarchy" of Generally Accepted Accounting Principles

Governmental Entities	Nongovernmental Entities
a. GASB Statements and Interpretations; AICPA and FASB pronouncements specifically made applicable to state and local governments by the GASB	a. FASB Statements and Interpretations; AICPA Accounting Research Bulletins; Accounting Principles Board Opinions
b. GASB Technical Bulletins; AICPA Industry Audit Guides and Statements of Position if specifically made applicable to governments by the AICPA and cleared (not objected to) by the GASB	b. FASB Technical Bulletins; AICPA Industry Audit Guides and Statements of Position if cleared (not objected to) by the FASB
c. AICPA Practice Bulletins if specifically made applicable to governments by the AICPA; consensus positions of a GASB Emerging Issues Task Force if and when established	c. AICPA Practice Bulletins if cleared by the FASB; consensus positions of the FASB Emerging Issues Task Force
d. Implementation guides published by the GASB staff; practices that are widely recognized and prevalent in state and local government	d. Implementation guides published by the FASB staff; AICPA accounting interpretations and implementation guides; practices that are widely recognized and prevalent either generally or in the industry
e. Other accounting literature, including FASB pronouncements not specifically made applicable to state and local governments by the GASB	e. Other accounting literature, including GASB pronouncements

The FASB's influence on government accounting practices is greater than may appear from the hierarchies because governments engage in many business-type activities, such as electric utilities, parking garages, and hospitals. Governments have traditionally accounted for these activities in the same way as their private-sector counterparts, and the GASB requires them to adhere to all FASB standards issued before the 1989 jurisdiction agreement that do not conflict with a GASB standard. Moreover, business-type activities may elect to apply all FASB standards issued after 1989 that do not conflict with GASB standards or to apply none of those standards, unless specifically required by the GASB.

QUESTIONS FOR REVIEW AND DISCUSSION

1. What is the defining distinction between for-profit businesses and not-for-profit entities, including governments? What are the implications of this distinction for financial reporting?

2. Why is the budget a far more important document in both governments and not-for-profits than in businesses?

3. How and why might the importance of the budget affect generally accepted accounting principles for *external* (general purpose) reports?

4. What is meant by *interperiod equity*, and what is its consequence for financial reporting?

5. Why might the *matching concept* be less relevant for governments and not-for-profits than for businesses?

6. What is the significance for financial reporting of the many restrictions that are placed on a government's resources?

7. Why is it difficult to develop accounting principles that are appropriate for governments within the same category (e.g., cities, counties) and even more difficult to develop them for governments within different categories?

8. What is the significance for financial reporting of a government's power to tax? How does it affect the government's overall financial strength?

9. Why has it proven especially difficult to establish accounting principles that enable governments to satisfy all three elements of GASB's first objective (that regarding accountability) of financial reporting in a single statement of revenue and expenditures or balance sheet?

10. Why are measures of "service efforts and accomplishments" of more concern in government and not-for-profits than in businesses?

11. In what key ways does the FASB influence generally accepted accounting principles for governments?

12. Why is it more difficult to distinguish between internal and external users in governments than in businesses?

EXERCISES AND PROBLEMS

1-1

Select the best answer.

1. The traditional business model of accounting is inadequate for governments and not-for-profit organizations primarily because businesses differ from governments and not-for-profits in that
   a. they have different missions
   b. they have fewer assets

   c. their assets are intangible
   d. taxes are a major expenditure of businesses

2. If businesses are governed by the marketplace, then governments are governed by
   a. legislative bodies
   b. taxes
   c. budgets
   d. state constitutions

3. The primary objective of a not-for-profit organization or a government is to

    a. maximize revenues

    b. minimize expenditures

    c. provide services to constituents

    d. all of the above

4. In governments, in contrast to businesses,

    a. expenditures are driven mainly by the ability of the entity to raise revenues

    b. the amount of revenues collected is a signal of the demand for services

    c. there may not be a direct relationship between revenues raised and the demand for the entity's services

    d. the amount of expenditures is independent of the amount of revenues collected

5. The organization responsible for setting accounting standards for state and local governments is the

    a. FASB

    b. GASB

    c. FASAB

    d. AICPA

6. The number of governmental units in the United States is approximately

    a. 870

    b. 8,700

    c. 87,000

    d. 870,000

7. Governments differ from businesses in that they

    a. do not raise capital in the financial markets

    b. do not engage in transactions in which they "sell" goods or services

    c. are not required to prepare annual financial reports

    d. do not issue common stock

8. Interperiod equity refers to a condition whereby

    a. total tax revenues are approximately the same from year to year

    b. taxes are distributed fairly among all taxpayers regardless of income level

    c. current-year revenues are sufficient to pay for current-year services

    d. current-year revenues cover both operating and capital expenditures

9. Which of the following is *not* one of GASB's financial reporting objectives?

    a. providing information on the extent to which interperiod equity is achieved

    b. assuring that budgeted revenues are equal to, or exceed, budgeted expenses

    c. reporting on budgetary compliance

    d. providing information on service efforts and accomplishments

10. Which of the following is *not* one of FASB's financial reporting objectives?

    a. providing information about economic resources, obligations, and net resources

    b. providing information to help resource providers make rational decisions

    c. reporting on budgetary compliance

    d. providing information on service efforts and accomplishments

1-2

Select the best answer.

1. Rule 203 of the AICPA's Code of Professional Conduct pertains to

    a. CPAs' independence

    b. authorities designated to establish accounting standards

    c. standards of competency

    d. solicitation of new clients by a CPA

2. Which of the following rule-making authorities would establish accounting standards for Stanford University (a private university)?

    a. the AICPA

    b. the FASB

    c. the FASAB

    d. the GASB

3. Which of the following rule-making authorities would establish accounting standards for the University of Texas (a public university)?

    a. the AICPA

    b. the FASB

    c. the FASAB

    d. the GASB

4. If the GASB has not issued a pronouncement on a specific issue, then which of the following is true with respect to FASB pronouncements?

    a. they would automatically govern

    b. they could be taken into account but would have no higher standing than other accounting literature

    c. they are irrelevant

    d. they could be taken into account by the reporting entity but only if disclosure is made in notes to the financial statements

5. The FASB is to the GASB as
   a. a brother is to a sister
   b. a father is to a son
   c. a son is to a father
   d. a daughter is to a friend

6. Standards promulgated by the FASB are most likely to be adhered to by which of the following governmental units?
   a. a police department
   b. a public school
   c. an electric utility
   d. a department of highways

7. Which of the following practices is most likely to undermine interperiod equity?
   a. paying for a new school building out of current operating funds
   b. paying the administrative staff of a school out of current operating funds
   c. issuing twenty-year bonds to finance construction of a new highway
   d. recognizing gains and losses on marketable securities as prices increase and decrease

8. The term *independent sector* refers to
   a. states that have opted not to receive federal funds
   b. not-for-profit organizations
   c. churches that are unaffiliated with a particular denomination
   d. universities that are not affiliated with a particular athletic conference

9. Which of the following is not an objective of external financial reporting of either the GASB or the FASB?
   a. to enable the statement user to detect fraud
   b. to disclose legal or contractual restrictions on the use of resources
   c. to provide information about how the organizations meet their cash requirements
   d. to provide information that would enable a user to assess the service potential of long-lived assets

10. Which of the following is the least appropriate use of the external financial statements of a government?
    a. to assess the entity's financial position
    b. to assess whether the compensation of management is reasonable in relation to that in comparable entities
    c. to compare actual results with the budget
    d. to evaluate the efficiency and effectiveness of the entity in achieving its objectives

1-3

Budgeting practices that satisfy cash requirements may not promote interperiod equity.

The Burnet County Road Authority was established as a separate government to maintain county highways. The road authority was granted statutory power to impose property taxes on county residents to cover its costs but it is required to balance its budget, which must be prepared on a cash basis. In its first year of operations it engaged in the following transactions, all of which were consistent with its legally adopted, cash-based, budget:

- Purchased $10 million of equipment, all of which had an anticipated useful life of ten years. To finance the acquisition the authority issued $10 million in ten-year term bonds (i.e., bonds that mature in ten years).
- Incurred wages, salaries, and other operating costs. These expenses were paid in cash, of $6 million.
- Paid interest of $0.5 million on the bonds.
- Purchased $0.9 million of additional equipment, paying for it in cash. This equipment had a useful life of three years.

1. The authority's governing board levies property taxes at rates that will be just sufficient to balance the authority's budget. What is the amount of tax revenue that it will be required to collect?

2. Assume that in the authority's second year of operations, it incurs the same costs, except that it purchases no new equipment. What amount of tax revenue will it be required to collect?

3. Make the same assumption as to the tenth year, when it will have to repay the bonds. What amount of tax revenue will it be required to collect?

4. Comment on the extent to which the authority's budgeting and taxing policies promote interperiod equity. What changes would you recommend?

1-4

The dual objectives of assessing interperiod equity and assuring budgetary compliance may necessitate different accounting practices.

A city engages in the transactions that follow. For each transaction indicate the amount of revenue or expenditure that it should report in 2003. Assume first that the main objective of the financial statements is to enable users to assess *budgetary compliance*. Then, assume that the main objective is to assess *interperiod equity*.

A city prepares its budget on a modified cash basis (that is, it expands the definition of cash to include short-term marketable securities), and its fiscal year ends on December 31.

1. Employees earned $128,000 in salaries and wages for the last five days in December 2003. They were paid on January 8, 2004.

2. A consulting actuary calculated that per an accepted actuarial cost method, the city should contribute $225,000 to its firefighters' pension fund for 2003. However, the city contributed only $170,000, the amount budgeted at the start of the year.

3. The city acquired three police cars for $35,000 cash each. The vehicles are expected to last for three years.

4. On December 1, 2003, the city invested $99,000 in short-term commercial paper (promissory notes). The notes matured on January 1, 2004. The city received $100,000. The $1,000 difference between the two amounts represents the city's return (interest) on the investment.

5. On January 2, 2003, the city acquired a new $10 million office building, financing it with twenty-five-year serial bonds. The bonds are to be repaid evenly over the period they are outstanding—that is, $400,000 per year. The useful life of the building is twenty-five years.

6. On January 1, 2003, the city acquired another $10 million office building, financing this facility with twenty-five-year term bonds. These bonds will be repaid entirely when they mature on January 1, 2028. The useful life of this building is also twenty-five years.

7. City restaurants are required to pay a $1,200 annual license fee, the proceeds of which the city uses to fund its restaurant inspection program. The license covers the period July 1 through June 30. In 2003 the city collected $120,000 in fees for the license period beginning July 1, 2003.

8. The city borrowed $300,000 in November 2003 to cover a temporary shortage of cash. It expects to repay the loan in February 2004.

1-5

Year-end financial accounting and reporting can reveal the economic substance of government actions taken mainly to balance the budget.

Public officials, it is often charged, promote measures intended to make the government "look good" in the short-term, but that may be deleterious in the long-term. Assume that a city's budget is on a cash or near-cash basis. Further assume that

the following actions, designed to increase a reported surplus, were approved by the city council and did indeed reduce budgetary expenditures or increase budgetary revenues:

a. The city reduced its contributions to the employee defined-benefit pension plan from the $10 million recommended by the city's actuary to $5 million. Under a defined-benefit plan the employer promises employees specified benefits upon their retirement, and the level of benefits is independent of when and how much the employer contributes to the plan over the employees' years of service.

b. It reduced by $1 million the city's cash transfer to a rainy-day reserve maintained to cover possible future reductions in tax collections attributable to a downturn in the region's economy.

c. It sold securities that had been held as an investment. The securities had been purchased five years earlier at a cost of $2 million. Market value at the time of sale was $5 million.

d. It delayed until the following year $10 million of maintenance on city highways.

1. Suppose that you were asked to propose accounting principles for external reporting that would capture the true economic nature of these measures—actions that, in substance, did not improve the city's financial performance or position. For each measure, indicate how you would require that it be accounted for and reported.

2. Can you see any disadvantages to the principles that you propose?

1-6

Choice of accounting principles may have significant economic consequences.

In preparing its budget proposals, a city's budget committee initially estimated that total revenues would be $120 million and total expenditures would be $123 million. In light of the balanced budget requirements that the city has to meet, the committee proposed several measures to either increase revenues or decrease expenditures. They included the following:

a. Delay the payment of $0.4 million of city bills from the last week of the fiscal year covered by the budget to the first week of the next fiscal year.

b. Change the way property taxes are accounted for in the budget. Currently, property taxes are counted as revenues only if they are expected to be collected during the budget year. New budgetary principles would permit the city to include as revenues all taxes expected to be collected within the first sixty days of the following fiscal year in addition to those collected during the year. The committee estimates that the change would have a net impact of $1.2 million.

c. Change the way that supplies are accounted for in the budget. Currently, supplies are recognized as expenditures at the time they are ordered. The proposal would delay recognition of the expenditure until they are actually received. The committee estimates a net effect of $0.8 million.

d. Defer indefinitely $1.5 million of maintenance on city roads.

Except as just noted with respect to supplies, the city currently prepares its budget on a cash basis, even though other bases are also legally permissible. It prepares its year-end financial statements, however, on an accrual basis.

1. Indicate the impact that each of the proposals would have on the city's (1) budget, (2) annual year-end financial statements, (3) "substantive" economic well-being. Be sure to distinguish between direct and indirect consequences.

2. It is sometimes said that choice of accounting principles doesn't matter in that they affect only the way the entity's fiscal "story" is told; they have no impact on the entity's actual financial history or current status. Do you agree? Explain.

CHAPTER 2

Fund Accounting

In Chapter 1 we set forth key characteristics that distinguish governments and not-for-profits from businesses and we discussed their implications for accounting and reporting. In particular, we noted that governments and not-for-profits establish their accounting systems on a fund basis. In this chapter we explain the rationale for fund accounting, describe the main types of funds maintained, and examine the relationships among funds. In Chapter 3 we will show how funds are included in a government's financial statements.

WHAT IS A FUND?

In business accounting, *funds* typically refers to working capital (current assets less current liabilities) or selected elements of it (such as cash and investments). But in government and not-for-profit accounting the term **fund** has a different meaning.

Fund accounting is a system in which a government or not-for-profit's resources are divided among two or more **fiscal** and accounting entities known as funds. As a fiscal (or financial) entity, each fund accounts for resources, and the claims against them, that are segregated in accord with legal or contractual restrictions or to carry out specific activities. As an accounting entity, each fund has its own self-balancing set of accounts from which separate financial statements can be prepared. Governments and not-for-profits customarily use several funds to account for their resources and activities. For example, a church may use one fund for general operations, another for resources set aside to construct a new building, and a third for its religious school.

WHAT CHARACTERIZES FUNDS?

As suggested by the earlier reference to a "self-balancing set of accounts," each fund of a government or not-for-profit uses the accounting equation:

$$\text{assets} = \text{liabilities} + \text{fund balance}$$

This is a variation of the business accounting equation (assets = liabilities + owners' equity). The term **fund balance** replaces owners' equity because governments and not-for-profits do not have owners. Fund balance, like owners' equity, is a residual and is often referred to as **net assets**. Fund balance or net assets is the amount left to the parties with rights to the assets after all other claims against those assets have been liquidated.

Because the basic accounting equation is the same, funds can be accounted for by the same double-entry system of bookkeeping as businesses, and their current status and past performance can be summarized by similar financial statements. For example, the balance sheet of a fund can detail the specific assets, liabilities, and elements of fund balance that underlie the accounting equation as of any point in time. A statement of revenues, expenditures (or expenses), and other changes in fund balance can explain the reasons for changes in fund balance during a specified period of time.[1] A statement of cash flows can reconcile the changes in cash between the end and the beginning of a period.

USE OF MULTIPLE FUNDS TO ACCOUNT FOR AN ENTITY Funds may seem similar to business subsidiaries, but they are established for quite different reasons. Businesses generally establish subsidiaries to account for their activities by product or region, to isolate certain business risks, and to minimize their tax obligations. Governments and not-for-profits, on the other hand, most commonly separate resources into funds to assure that they adhere to restrictions placed on them by legislators, grantors, donors, or other outside parties. For example, a university that received a donation to be used only for scholarships would account for it in a special scholarship fund.

Fund accounting promotes control and accountability over restricted resources. To a lesser extent, governments and not-for-profits establish funds to account for certain activities, often those of a business type, that are different from their usual activities. For example, a government might account for its golf course, which operates similarly to a privately owned course, in a fund separate from that used to account for its general operations. By accounting for these types of activities in their own accounting and fiscal entities, governments and not-for-profits are better able to control the activities' revenues and expenditures and to assess their overall performance.

RELATIONSHIPS AMONG FUNDS To appreciate the relationship among two or more funds used to account for a single organization, remember that each fund is a separate accounting entity. Thus, every transaction that affects a fund must be recorded by at least one debit and one credit. Any transaction that affects two or more funds must be accounted for as if it affected two or more independent businesses and must be recorded individually in each fund. Suppose, for example, that a city maintains two funds: a general fund to account for its unrestricted resources and general operations, and a utility fund to account for a utility that sells electricity to city residents and other government departments. The utility bills the other city departments—all accounted for in the general fund—for $10,000. The following entries would be appropriate:

Utility fund

Accounts receivable (from general fund)	$10,000	
Revenue from sale of electricity		$10,000

To record the sale of electricity to general fund

General fund

Electricity expenditure	$10,000	
Accounts payable (to utility fund)		$10,000

To record the use of electricity

---

[1] As will be addressed later in the text, in government accounting, *expenditures* are distinguished from *expenses*. For now, suffice it to note that *expenditures* is used in connection with funds that are not accounted for on a full accrual basis, whereas *expenses* is used in connection with those accounted for on a full accrual basis.

WHAT IS MEANT BY BASIS OF ACCOUNTING AND MEASUREMENT FOCUS?

Basis of accounting determines *when* transactions and events are recognized. For instance, if an entity adopts the full accrual basis of accounting, a transaction is recognized when it has its substantive economic impact, irrespective of when cash is received or paid. If, on the other hand, it adopts the cash basis, the transaction is recognized only as the related cash is received or paid. An entity's **measurement focus** determines *what* is being reported upon—which assets and liabilities will be given accounting recognition and reported on the balance sheet.

The two concepts are closely related; the selection of one implies the selection of the other. For example, if an entity adopts a cash basis of accounting, then its measurement focus will be on cash. Only cash will be reported on its balance sheet. Correspondingly, measurement focus also determines whether the entity reports net profit (the net increase in all economic resources—i.e., both current and noncurrent assets) or merely the net change in selected resource flows (such as current financial resources—e.g., cash, short-term receivables, and short-term investments).

If an entity adopts a full accrual basis of accounting, which is required of businesses, then its measurement focus will automatically be on all economic resources, and its balance sheet will report on all assets and liabilities, both current and noncurrent. Increases or decreases in net **capital assets** (i.e., fixed assets or property, plant and equipment) and long-term obligations are not recognized as revenues or expenses. Suppose, for example, that an organization purchases a vehicle for $25,000 by giving a note for the entire amount. The following entry would be appropriate:

Vehicles	$25,000	
Notes payable		$25,000

To record the acquisition of a vehicle

Because governments and not-for-profits may be primarily concerned with the assets needed to satisfy current-year obligations, they may adopt a **modified accrual basis** of accounting and a measurement focus on mainly short-term financial assets and liabilities for many of their funds.[2] Modified accrual is between the cash and full accrual bases. Under the modified accrual basis used for many of the funds maintained by governments, revenues and some expenditures are recognized on a cash or near-cash basis; other expenditures are recognized on a full accrual basis. Because the measurement focus is on current financial resources, capital assets and long-term liabilities are excluded from the balance sheet and net changes in short-term financial assets and liabilities are recognized as revenues or expenditures. For example, if a government borrows $25,000 (issuing a

---

[2]Although for purposes of internal management and control not-for-profits may adopt a modified accrual basis of accounting, FASB standards require that they prepare their general-purpose external financial statements on a full accrual basis. In contrast, GASB standards require governments to report certain activities on both a modified accrual and a full accrual basis. The modified accrual basis used by governments is discussed in more detail beginning in Chapter 4.

long-term note) and uses the proceeds to purchase a vehicle, the following entries would be proper:

Cash	$25,000	
Proceeds from borrowing		$25,000

To record the issuance of a long-term note

Expenditure for vehicles	$25,000	
Cash		$25,000

To record the purchase of the vehicle

The government would report neither the vehicle nor the long-term note on its fund balance sheet. Instead, it would record both the increase and subsequent decrease in a financial asset (cash) on the fund's statement of revenues and expenditures. From an accounting standpoint, neither the vehicle nor the related liability would be recognized. The vehicle, in effect, would be written off (expensed) at the time acquired. The proceeds from the note would be recorded as proceeds from borrowing, an increase in fund balance that (like a revenue) would be closed to fund balance.

Governments can report their funds on different bases for different purposes. For example, to provide a measure of the full cost of services, a government may report some of its funds on a full accrual basis. To demonstrate compliance with budgetary constraints, it may report other funds on a modified accrual basis. Businesses, of course, also use two or more bases to account for their operations. They prepare their financial statements on a full accrual basis, their tax returns on a basis specified by the IRS, and their reports to state or federal agencies on a basis defined by the relevant regulatory authority.

Irrespective of whether an entity reports capital assets and long-term liabilities on its fund balance sheets, it must still maintain accounting control over them. Management and constituents need to be concerned with all the entity's resources and obligations—not just those given balance sheet recognition. Therefore, the entity must maintain accounting records of all assets and liabilities and must include in its financial statements schedules that summarize them and show the changes that occurred during the year.

Earlier we mentioned that governments and not-for-profits commonly use multiple funds to report their activities. To reinforce the purposes of fund accounting and the relationships among funds, we now present a simple example of a fund accounting system. We use as our illustration a public school district, which accounts for its funds on a modified accrual basis, with a measurement focus on current financial resources. In particular, the illustration is intended to emphasize the following:

- Each fund is a separate accounting and fiscal entity.
- Because the funds are not on a full accrual basis, some economic resources (primarily capital assets) and obligations (primarily those that are long-term) are not recognized on the fund's balance sheet as assets and liabilities (and hence, must be accounted for in off-balance-sheet records).

EXAMPLE   *Fund Accounting in a School District*

A newly formed public school district accounts for its operations on a modified accrual basis, with a measurement focus on current financial resources. It maintains four funds:

1. *A general fund.* This fund accounts for taxes and other unrestricted resources.
2. *A capital projects fund.* This fund accounts for the proceeds of bonds that are restricted for the construction of buildings and similar capital assets.

3. *A debt service fund.* This fund accounts for resources that are to be set aside each year to ensure that the district has the wherewithal to make its required payments of interest and principal on its long-term debt. It may be viewed as a savings account (or sinking fund) for resources restricted by either the debt covenants (agreements) or by policies of the district itself.

4. *A special revenue fund.* This fund accounts for state grants that must be used for specific purposes.

The following is a summary of the district's first year of operations:

1. The district levied $9.0 million of general property taxes of which it actually collected $8.8 million. It expects to collect the balance shortly after year-end. These taxes are unrestricted; they can be used for any legitimate educational purpose. Therefore, the district should record them in its general fund.

General fund

Cash	$8.8	
Property taxes receivable	0.2	
Property tax revenue		$9.0

To record property taxes

2. The district received a state grant of $0.2 million to purchase computers. This grant is restricted for a specific purpose and therefore must be recorded in a restricted fund, the special revenue fund.

Special revenue fund

Cash	$0.2	
Grant revenue		$0.2

To record a state grant restricted for the acquisition of computers

3. The district issued $12 million in long-term bonds to construct a school building. The proceeds must be used for the intended purpose and therefore must be recorded in the capital projects fund. Because the district is on a modified accrual basis of accounting and current financial resources measurement focus, which excludes the recognition of both long-term assets and long-term liabilities, the proceeds from borrowing are recognized in a *revenue*-type account— one that will cause fund balance, rather than a liability, to increase. Of course, the district must maintain a record of both its capital assets and obligations in capital asset and long-term obligation ledgers or other off-balance-sheet lists.

Capital projects fund

Cash	$12.0	
Proceeds from borrowing		$12.0

To record the issuance of bonds

4. The district constructed the school building for $11.0 million. The construction must be accounted for as an *expenditure*, rather than a capital asset. The asset must be recorded in a supplementary ledger or list.

Capital projects fund

Construction of building (expenditure)	$11.0	
Cash		$11.0

To record the costs of constructing the school building

5. The district incurred $6.0 million in general operating expenditures, of which it actually paid $5.5 million.

General fund

General operating expenditures	$6.0	
Cash		$5.5
Accounts payable		0.5

To record general operating expenditures

6. Using its state grant, the district purchased $0.1 million of computers. As with the construction of the building, the district would recognize the acquisition as an *expenditure*, but would record the assets in a supplementary ledger or list.

Special revenue fund

Acquisition of computers (expenditure)	$0.1	
Cash		$0.1

To record the acquisition of computers

7. The district transferred $1.1 million from the general fund to the debt service fund to make the first payments of both principal and interest which are due in the following year. Broken down into its components, this transaction is straightforward, involving simple entries to each of two funds:

General fund

Transfer-out to debt service fund	$1.1	
Cash		$1.1

To record transfer to the debt service fund

Debt service fund

Cash	$1.1	
Transfer-in from general fund		$1.1

To record transfer from the general fund

Tables 2-1 and 2-2 summarize the transactions into balance sheets and statements of revenues and expenditures for the four funds. For convenience, the statements are presented in columnar form. To emphasize that each fund is a separate accounting and reporting entity, combined totals are deliberately omitted.

TABLE 2-1
School District's Funds Balance Sheet
(in millions)

	General	Special Revenue	Capital Projects	Debt Service
Assets				
Cash	$2.2	$0.1	$1.0	$1.1
Property Taxes Receivable	0.2			
Totals	$2.4	$0.1	$1.0	$1.1
Liabilities and fund balances				
Accounts Payable	$0.5			
Fund Balances (net assets)	1.9	0.1	1.0	1.1
Totals	$2.4	$0.1	$1.0	$1.1

TABLE 2-2
School District's Statement of Fund Revenues, Expenditures, and Other Changes in Fund Balances (in millions)

	General	Special Revenue	Capital Projects	Debt Service
Property Tax Revenue	$ 9.0			
Revenue from State Grant		$0.2		
Total Revenues	$ 9.0	$0.2		
Operating Expenditures	$ 6.0			
Construction of Building			$ 11.0	
Acquisition of Computers		$0.1		
Total Expenditures	$ 6.0	$0.1	$ 11.0	
Excess of Revenues over Expenditures	$ 3.0	$0.1	$(11.0)	
Other Increases and Decreases in Fund Balances:				
Transfers in/(out)	$(1.1)			$1.1
Proceeds from Borrowing			$ 12.0	
Net Increase in Fund Balance	$ 1.9	$0.1	$1.0	$1.1

The sections that follow present an overview of the main funds maintained by governments and not-for-profits, respectively. Bear in mind that each fund, like a subsidiary of a corporation, is a separate accounting and fiscal entity for which separate financial statements can be prepared. Just as the financial statements of a corporation can be prepared on different bases (e.g., full accrual, cash, tax, regulatory), so also can those of individual funds (e.g., modified accrual, full accrual). And just as the financial statements of a company's subsidiaries can be combined in different ways (e.g., by region, by product line, by size), so too can those of a government or not-for-profit (e.g., by type, by dollar value, by nature of restrictions). We shall address in Chapter 3 how a government's funds may be aggregated for greater simplicity in financial reporting.

WHAT ARE THE MAIN TYPES OF GOVERNMENTS' FUNDS?

Most general-purpose governments engage in three broad categories of activities:

1. *Governmental activities* are those financed predominantly through taxes and intergovernmental grants.
2. *Business-type activities* are those financed predominantly through user charges.
3. *Fiduciary activities* are those for which the government acts as a trustee or agent for individuals, external organizations, or other governments.

Corresponding roughly to these three kinds of activities, governments classify funds into three broad categories: **governmental funds**, **proprietary funds**, and **fiduciary funds**. As shown in Table 2-3, each category contains several different types of funds, each having a different purpose.

Governmental funds may be characterized as **expendable funds**, in that their resources are received from taxes, grants, or other sources, and then spent. There is no

---

TABLE 2-3
The Fund Structure of State and Local Governments

Governmental Funds
Purpose: To account for governments' operating and financing activities financed predominantly through taxes and intergovernmental grants.
Basis of accounting/measurement focus: Modified accrual/current financial resources
There are five types of governmental funds:

- *General fund*—to account for all resources not legally or contractually restricted or otherwise set aside for specific activities
- *Special revenue funds*—to account for revenues restricted for a specific purpose other than debt service or capital projects (e.g., gas tax revenues required to be used for road repairs)
- *Debt service funds*—to account for the payment of interest and principal on long-term debt of the general government
- *Capital projects funds*—to account for revenues held for the acquisition or construction of major capital facilities, such as buildings and highways
- *Permanent funds*—to account for resources legally restricted in that only the earnings on investments, not the principal, may be used to support specific government programs (e.g., maintenance of a public cemetery or park)

Proprietary Funds
Purpose: To account for governments' activities that are similar to those carried out in the private sector and financed predominantly through user charges.
Basis of accounting/measurement focus: Full accrual/economic resources
There are two types of proprietary funds:

- *Enterprise funds*—to account for business-type activities that serve the public at large (e.g., an electric utility)
- *Internal service funds*—to account for goods and services provided to departments of the same government (e.g., a centralized purchasing function or motor pool).

Fiduciary Funds
Purpose: To account for resources held by governments as trustees or agents for another party or parties.
Basis of accounting/measurement focus: Full accrual/economic resources
There are two kinds of fiduciary funds:

- *Trust funds*
  - *Pension (and other employee benefit) trusts*—to account for resources accumulated to pay pension, healthcare, and other benefits to the government's retired or disabled employees
  - *Investment trusts*—to account for investment pools in which other governments participate (e.g., a state government pool open to local governments within the state)
  - *Private purpose trusts*—to account for resources held for individuals or external organizations (e.g., an escheat fund)
- *Agency funds*—to account for resources held on a short-term basis on behalf of individuals, organizations, or other governments (e.g., taxes collected on behalf of another government). These funds have only assets and liabilities—no revenues or expenses.

---

expectation that the funds will be reimbursed for services rendered to constituents or other departments. By contrast, proprietary funds are said to be **nonexpendable** (or **revolving) funds**. That is, the government may make an initial contribution to establish a proprietary fund, but thereafter the fund is expected to "pay its own way" (at least in part) through customer charges. Fiduciary funds differ from governmental and proprietary funds in that fiduciary fund activities and resources benefit only parties other than the government—not the government itself.

A government should have only one general fund, but it may have any number of the other types of funds. For example a city may maintain a separate special revenue fund for each restricted revenue source, a separate capital projects fund for each major capital project, and a separate debt service fund for each issue of outstanding bonds.

We now take a comprehensive look at each of the types of funds.

WHAT'S NOTABLE ABOUT EACH TYPE OF GOVERNMENTAL FUND?

THE GENERAL FUND The general fund is used to account for all resources that are not legally or contractually restricted or arbitrarily set aside for specific activities. All funds are not created equal; the general fund is more equal than the others. In a city or other general-purpose government, it embraces most major government functions—police, fire, street maintenance, sanitation, and administration.

Why does one single fund cover so many functions? Recall the rationale for fund accounting. Funds are established mainly to assure that governments adhere to resource restrictions. A government's fund structure rarely mirrors its organizational structure. Funds divide a government into categories of resource restriction, not functional departments or operations. To keep their accounting systems as simple as possible, governments should establish only the minimum number of funds necessary to assure legal compliance or efficient administration. Governments finance their general operations mainly with unrestricted resources, such as property taxes. Therefore, they can legally intermingle these resources and can properly account for all activities financed with unrestricted resources in a single fund.

As noted in Table 2-3, the general fund uses a modified accrual basis of accounting and a measurement focus on current financial resources. This basis of accounting and measurement focus are discussed in more detail beginning in Chapter 4. For now, recall that a modified accrual basis falls between the cash basis and the full accrual basis. Thus, the general fund will record and report on its balance sheet not only cash but also other current financial resources, including primarily taxes receivable, accounts receivable, and short-term investments of unrestricted resources. However, it will not record or report capital assets or long-term debt. Obviously a general-purpose government, such as a city, owns police cars, fire equipment, computers, and buildings. Moreover, it probably financed some of its capital assets with long-term debt. Were the general fund accounted for on a full accrual basis (economic resources measurement focus), these assets and liabilities would be reported on the fund's balance sheet. Instead, from the perspective of the general fund, they are written off (recorded as expenditures, not assets) as acquired and are listed only in off-balance-sheet ledgers or other records of capital assets. However, as we shall see in Chapter 3, capital assets and long-term debt associated with the general fund or other governmental funds are reported in financial statements prepared on the full accrual basis for the government as a whole.

SPECIAL REVENUE FUNDS Special revenue funds are established to account for resources legally restricted for specified purposes. Examples of typical restrictions include

- Gasoline tax revenues that must be used for highway maintenance
- Lottery fund proceeds that must be used for education
- A state law-enforcement grant that must be used to train police officers
- Private donations that must be used to maintain parks and other recreational facilities

Special revenue funds use the same basis of accounting and measurement focus as the general fund and, indeed, all governmental funds. Accordingly, almost all of the guidelines set forth in this text for the general fund also apply to special revenue funds and other governmental funds.

DEBT SERVICE FUNDS Debt service funds are maintained to account for resources restricted to the payment of principal and interest on long-term debt. They have much in common with sinking funds (resources set aside to retire debt) maintained by businesses.

The balance sheet of a debt service fund does not include the obligation for the debt being serviced. The purpose of the fund is to account for the resources being accumulated to service the debt—not the debt itself. Also, debt service funds are governmental funds, and no governmental fund gives recognition to long-term obligations. As will be seen in the next chapter, long-term debt for which resources are being accumulated in a debt service fund is reported only in full accrual financial statements for the government as a whole and in supplementary schedules.

The one exception is interest and principal that have matured and are therefore current obligations. They would be reported in a debt service fund as matured interest payable or matured bonds payable. But this exception is of little practical import. On the day the interest or principal matures, it should be paid and the obligation satisfied. Therefore, a liability for interest or principal should be reported in year-end fund financial statements only when payment is due but has been delayed.

Debt service funds derive their resources from other funds (e.g., transfers from the general fund) or from taxes or fees dedicated to debt service. Fund resources are expended to pay principal and interest. Governments commonly invest accumulated resources for debt service in commercial paper, treasury bills, and other financial instruments that, while secure, still provide a reasonable return. Typically, therefore, many debt service fund transactions relate to the purchase and sale of marketable securities and the recognition of investment earnings and related costs.

CAPITAL PROJECTS FUNDS Capital projects funds account for financial resources to be used for the acquisition or construction of major capital facilities. Governments often issue bonds to finance a specific project. The resources received are restricted to that project and must be placed in a restricted fund. Capital projects funds typically derive their resources from the proceeds of bonds. However, they may also receive resources that were initially received by other funds and subsequently earmarked for the acquisition of capital assets.

Just as debt service funds account for resources accumulated to service a debt—but not the debt itself—so, too, capital projects funds account for resources set aside to purchase or construct capital assets, but not the assets themselves. The assets, whether in the form of construction in progress or completed projects, are reported only in the financial statements for the government as a whole and in supplementary schedules. As with the resources accumulated to service their debts, governments must invest any excess cash awaiting expenditure for capital projects. Therefore, many transactions of typical capital projects funds, like those of debt service funds, relate to investment activities.

PERMANENT FUNDS Permanent funds are a type of trust fund, but they are categorized as governmental funds, not fiduciary funds. They are similar to private purpose trusts (fiduciary funds) in that usually only the income from fund investments, not the principal, may be spent. They differ, though, in that permanent funds bene-fit the government itself whereas private purpose trusts—and all fiduciary funds—benefit individuals, private organizations, or other governments.

Suppose, for example, that a government received a donation to support one of its parks. The resources received were to be invested and only the income, not the principal, could be expended. The government would establish a permanent fund to account for the donation. As income is earned, it would be transferred to a special revenue fund, from which it would be used for the intended purpose.

WHAT'S NOTABLE ABOUT EACH TYPE OF PROPRIETARY FUND?

Proprietary funds—enterprise funds and internal service funds—are used to account for activities that are operated in a manner similar to private business enterprises and where a government's intent is to recover costs primarily through user charges. Because a typical objective in providing the service is to at least break even, the government officials responsible for the activity require the same types of financial information as their business counterparts. For example, they need data on the full cost (including depreciation) of the services provided so that they can establish prices. Outsiders, such as tax or rate payers, concerned with the activity's performance or financial position, need the same general information as would corporate shareholders. For this reason, proprietary funds are accounted for in essentially the same manner as private businesses. They employ the full accrual basis of accounting, and their measurement focus is on all economic resources. Therefore, their financial statements, unlike those of governmental funds, report capital assets, long-term debt, and depreciation, as will be discussed further in Chapter 3.

ENTERPRISE FUNDS Enterprise funds account for services provided to the public at large and may include these services:

- utilities, such as electric, gas, and water
- golf courses
- hospitals
- mass transportation
- parking garages
- airport and harbor facilities
- housing authorities

Many government enterprises are financed similarly to businesses. A government enterprise does not sell stock to the general public, but it may issue bonds, called *revenue bonds*. Revenue bond principal and interest are payable exclusively out of revenues of the fund itself—not out of the general revenues of the government at large. Therefore, the fund's resources cannot be commingled with those of other funds.

INTERNAL SERVICE FUNDS Internal service funds account for the provision of goods or services to other departments within the same government (or occasionally to other governments). They bill the receiving departments at rates intended to cover the cost of the goods or services. Although there are no specific guidelines as to which within-government activities should be accounted for in internal service funds, the following are examples:

- A maintenance and repair service for the cars and trucks of the police, fire, and sanitation departments
- A motor pool that acts as a within-government rental car agency

- An electronic data processing department that services other government departments
- A store that sells office supplies to the other government departments
- A print shop that provides government-wide printing services

Internal service funds are typically established with resources contributed from the general fund or another fund and thereafter are expected to be self-sustaining. As such, they use full accrual accounting and the economic resources measurement focus. Most of their transactions are with other funds and their accounting is relatively straightforward, as long as each fund is seen as a separate accounting entity. When an internal service fund bills another department, it recognizes a revenue and a receivable from another fund. Simultaneously, the fund that accounts for the other department records an expenditure or expense and a payable to the internal service fund. Most of the departments to which an internal service fund sells its goods or services are likely to be accounted for in the general fund or an enterprise fund. This is primarily because most government operations (as opposed to accumulations of resources for specific purposes) are accounted for in those funds.

WHAT'S NOTABLE ABOUT EACH TYPE OF FIDUCIARY FUND?

Unlike governmental and proprietary activities, fiduciary activities only benefit parties other than the government itself. They do not result in revenues or expenses to the government—only additions and deductions to the net assets of fiduciary (trust or agency) funds. Therefore, the accounting focus of fiduciary funds is on fund net assets and changes in net assets, which are reported only in fiduciary fund financial statements. They are not included in the financial statements for the government as a whole.

TRUST FUNDS *Kohler's Dictionary for Accountants* defines a trust fund as a "fund held by one person (trustee) for the benefit of another, pursuant to the provisions of a formal trust agreement."[3] There are three types of trust funds:

1. *Pension (and other employee benefit) trust funds* benefit the government's employees by providing retirement income, disability, retiree health care and other benefits for retirees and their beneficiaries.
2. *Investment trust funds* are established when one government, such as a state, maintains an investment pool for other governments. These funds are similar to mutual funds and benefit the parties that have entrusted their resources to the fund.
3. *Private purpose trust funds* encompass all other trust funds that benefit specific individuals, other governments, external organizations, or businesses. A common example is an **escheat** trust fund. *Escheat property* is the name given to property that reverts to a state when a person dies without heirs or other legal claimants. It also includes abandoned and unclaimed property, such as balances in bank accounts that have been inactive for a specified period of time.

---

[3]W. W. Cooper and Yuji Ijiri (eds.), *Kohler's Dictionary for Accountants*, 6th ed. (Englewood Cliffs, N.J.: Prentice-Hall, Inc., 1983), p. 516.

Governments may maintain more than one trust fund of each type. For example, a city may have a pension fund for police officers, another for firefighters and a third for all other employees. Trust funds commonly hold their resources in noncurrent as well as current investments, and fund performance is important to beneficiaries and to fund managers. Therefore, trust funds use full accrual accounting and their measurement focus is on economic resources.

AGENCY FUNDS Agency funds are used to account for assets held, usually for a short period of time, on behalf of other governments, funds, or individuals. Most commonly, they are established to maintain control over the following:

- Taxes collected by one government for the benefit of another
- Special assessments collected to repay debt that the government services but for which it is not responsible
- Refundable deposits
- Pass-through grants—those requiring a government (e.g., a state) to distribute funds to other parties (e.g., school districts or individuals), but for which the government has no financial involvement and for which it performs no significant administrative functions, such as selecting recipients or monitoring performance.

Custodial in nature, agency funds are not used to account for significant government operations. Consequently, agency funds are a student's delight—entities of the utmost simplicity. Their balance sheets show only assets (commonly cash and investments) and liabilities (the amounts owing to the beneficiaries). Assets always equal liabilities, so there are no net assets. Accordingly, governments need not prepare a statement of revenues and expenses.

HOW DO THE FUNDS OF NOT-FOR-PROFITS DIFFER FROM THOSE OF GOVERNMENTS?

Although the GASB mandates fund-based reporting for governments, the FASB imposes no similar requirement on not-for-profits. As stressed earlier, fund accounting is an expedient means of control that helps assure that governments or other organizations use resources only for the purposes for which they have been dedicated. But it is not the only means. After all, private businesses must also account for restricted resources (e.g., income taxes withheld from employees, sales taxes collected from customers, advance payments on government contracts, proceeds from bond issues that must be spent on specific projects). Yet they do not employ fund accounting.

Nevertheless, for purposes of internal accounting and control, most not-for-profits do employ fund accounting, and they maintain funds that are comparable to those of governments. Most not-for-profits maintain a *current* fund, which is like a government's general fund. Similarly, most maintain one or more *current restricted funds*, which are, in essence, special revenue funds. They may also maintain, as needed, funds to account for resources set aside for the acquisition of capital assets and for the repayment of debt. Many colleges and universities categorize all funds having to do with capital assets and the related debt as *plant funds*. These include an *unexpended* plant fund (similar to a capital projects fund), a *retirement of indebtedness* fund (analogous to a debt service fund), and an *investment in plant* fund (which accounts for both capital assets and related long-term debt).

Although the FASB does not require fund accounting, it requires that not-for-profits classify their net assets into these three categories based on the stipulations of *donors*:

- Unrestricted
- Temporarily restricted
- Permanently restricted

Temporarily restricted resources are those that must be used for a specific purpose (e.g., to support donor-designated programs or activities) or that cannot be spent until some time in the future (e.g., when a donor makes good on a pledge). Permanently restricted resources are typically endowments, from which only the income can be spent.

FASB accounting standards for not-for-profits are generally similar to business standards. However, the FASB imposes some accounting and reporting requirements that are unique to not-for-profits. We devote Chapters 12 and 13 to those standards, to the form and content of not-for-profit financial statements, and to other issues that are specific to not-for-profits.

In Chapters 3 through 11 we shall focus entirely on government accounting and financial reporting. In Chapter 14, we shall discuss how the financial statements and other information reported for governments and not-for-profits may be used to help assess their financial position and economic condition.

QUESTIONS FOR REVIEW AND DISCUSSION

1. Distinguish between funds as the term is used in government and not-for-profit accounting as contrasted with business accounting.

2. In what way, if any, does the accounting equation as applied in government and not-for-profit accounting differ from that as applied in business accounting?

3. Upon examining the balance sheet of a large city you notice that the total assets of the general fund far exceed those of the combined total of the city's ten separate special revenue funds. Moreover, you observe that there are no funds for public safety, sanitation, health and welfare, and general administration—all important functions of the government. Why do you suppose the city hasn't attempted to "even out" the assets in the funds? Why does it not maintain funds for each of its major functional areas?

4. Why are there generally no capital assets (work in progress or completed assets) in governments' capital projects funds? Why are there

generally no long-term debts in debt service funds?

5. The balance sheets of both enterprise funds and internal service funds report capital assets and long-term debt. What does that tell you about the funds' measurement focus and basis of accounting? Explain.

6. As will be emphasized later in this text, depreciation is recorded in proprietary funds but not in governmental funds. What is the rationale for recording depreciation in proprietary funds?

7. What are fiduciary funds? What are the two main kinds, and what is the distinction between them?

8. What's permanent about a permanent fund?

9. What is an agency fund? Why is it the easiest fund for which to account?

10. Distinguish among the three categories of restrictiveness into which the net assets of not-for-profit organizations must be separated for purposes of external reporting. Explain. By whom must restrictions be imposed for resources to be considered restricted?

EXERCISES AND PROBLEMS

2-1

The following relate to the town of Coupland (in thousands):

Equipment used in a vehicle repair service that provides service to other departments on a cost-reimbursement basis (The equipment has a 10-year life with no salvage value.)	$1,400
Property taxes levied and collected	6,300
Hotel taxes (restricted for promotion of tourism) collected	1,200
Proceeds of bonds to build a parking garage that must be repaid from user charges	4,000
Proceeds of general obligation bonds to finance construction of a new city hall (The building, which was completed during the year, has a useful life of thirty years with no salvage value.)	9,000
Proceeds of a federal grant to hire additional police officers	1,000
Fees collected from customers by the electric utility	8,000

Match the list that follows with the appropriate amounts. An amount may be selected once, more than once, or not at all.

____ 1. Revenue to be recognized in an enterprise fund

____ 2. Revenue to be recognized in special revenue funds

____ 3. Bonds payable to be recognized in the general fund

____ 4. Bonds payable to be recognized in enterprise funds

____ 5. Depreciation expenditure to be recognized in the general fund

____ 6. Depreciation expense to be recognized in internal service funds

____ 7. Revenue to be recognized in internal service funds

____ 8. Revenue to be recognized in the general fund

____ 9. Capital assets to be recognized in the general fund

____ 10. Capital assets to be recognized in internal service funds

a. 0
b. 140
c. 900
d. 1,260
e. 1,040
f. 1,400
g. 2,200
h. 4,000
i. 6,300
j. 8,000
k. 8,500
l. 10,400

2-2

Select the best answer.

1. Oak Township issued the following bonds during the year:

Bonds to acquire equipment for a vehicle repair service accounted for in an internal service fund	$3,000,000
Bonds to construct a new city hall	$8,000,000
Bond to improve its water utility, which is accounted for in an enterprise fund	$9,000,000

The amount of debt to be reported in the general fund is

a. $0
b. $3,000,000
c. $8,000,000
d. $20,000,000

2. Oak Township should report depreciation in which of the following funds?

a. general fund
b. special revenue fund
c. internal service fund
d. capital projects fund

3. Assuming that Bevo County receives all of its revenues from unrestricted property taxes, in which fund is it most likely to account for the activities of its police department?

a. police department fund
b. police enterprise fund
c. property tax fund
d. general fund

4. The City of Alpine incurred the following costs during the year in its property tax collection department:

Purchase of computer equipment	$ 10,000
Salaries and wages	$400,000
Purchase of electricity from the city-owned electric utility	$ 40,000
Purchase of supplies, all of which were used during the year	$ 10,000

As a consequence of these transactions, the amount that Alpine should report as expenditures in its general fund is

a. $400,000
b. $410,000
c. $450,000
d. $460,000

5. Grove City received the following resources during the year:

Property taxes	$50,000,000
A federal grant to acquire police cars	400,000
Hotel taxes, which must be used to promote tourism	3,000,000
Proceeds of bonds issued to improve the city's electric utility	12,000,000

The amount that the city should most likely report as revenue in its special revenue fund is

a. $400,000
b. $3,000,000
c. $3,400,000
d. $15,400,000
e. $65,400,000

6. The City of Comer issues $20 million of general obligation bonds to improve its streets and roads. In accordance with the bond covenants, it sets aside $1 million to help assure that it is able to meet its first payment of principal and $0.1 million for its first payment of interest. The amount of liability that the city should report in its debt service fund is

a. $0
b. $18.9 million
c. $19 million
d. $20 million

7. During the year, Brian County collects $12 million of property taxes on behalf of Urton Township. Of this amount, it remits $10 million to the township, expecting to remit the balance shortly after the end of its fiscal year. The amount of revenue that the County should report is

a. $0
b. $2 million
c. $8 million
d. $10 million

8. The City of Round Lake receives a contribution of $20 million. The donor stipulates that the money is to be invested. The principal is to remain intact, and the investment proceeds are to

be used to support a city-owned nature center. The city should report the contribution in a

a. special revenue fund
b. permanent fund
c. fiduciary fund
d. agency fund

9. Carver City receives a $30 million contribution. The donor stipulates that the money is to be invested. The principal is to remain intact and the investment proceeds are to be used to provide scholarships for the children of city employees. The contribution should be reported as revenue of a

a. special revenue fund
b. permanent fund
c. fiduciary fund
d. agency fund

10. The Summerville Preparatory School (a private school) receives a donation of $14 million. The donor stipulates that the entire amount must be used to construct a new athletic field house. The school should classify the donation as

a. unrestricted
b. temporarily restricted
c. permanently restricted
d. semi-restricted

2-3

A special district's balance sheet may not capture its economic resources and obligations.

A special district accounts for its general fund (its only fund) on a modified accrual basis. In a particular period it engaged in the following transactions:

a. It issued $20 million in long-term bonds.
b. It acquired several tracts of land at a total cost of $4 million, paying the entire amount in cash.
c. It sold a portion of the land for $1 million, receiving cash for the entire amount. The tract sold had cost $0.8 million.
d. It repaid $2 million of the bonds.
e. It lost a lawsuit and was ordered to pay $9 million over three years. It made its first cash payment of $3 million.

1. Prepare journal entries to record the transactions in the general fund.

2. Based on your journal entries, prepare a balance sheet and a statement of revenues, expenditures, and other changes in fund balance.

3. Comment on the extent to which the balance sheet captures the district's economic resources and obligations. How can you justify such a balance sheet?

4. Comment on the extent to which the statement of revenues, expenditures, and other changes in fund balance captures the district's cost of services. How can you justify such a financial statement?

2-4

Funds are separate fiscal and accounting entities, each with its own self-balancing set of accounts.

The newly established Society for Ethical Teachings maintains two funds—a general fund for operations and a building fund to accumulate resources for a new building. In its first year it engaged in the following transactions:

a. It received cash contributions of $200,000, of which $40,000 was restricted for the acquisition of the new building.

b. It incurred operating costs of $130,000, of which it paid $120,000 in cash.

c. It earned $3,000 of interest (the entire amount received in cash) on resources restricted for the acquisition of the new building.

d. It transferred $17,000 from the operating fund to the new building fund.

e. It paid $12,000 in fees (accounted for as expenses) to an architect to draw up plans for the new building.

1. Prepare journal entries to record the transactions. Be certain to indicate the fund in which they would be made.

2. Prepare a statement of revenues, expenditures, and other changes in fund balances and a balance sheet. Use a two-column format, one column for each of the funds.

2-5

Typical transactions can often be identified with specific types of funds.

Boxer City maintains the following funds:

- general
- special revenue
- capital projects
- debt service
- enterprise
- internal service
- permanent
- agency

For each of the following transactions, indicate the fund in which it would most likely be recorded.

a. The city collects $3 million of taxes on behalf of the county in which it is located.

b. It spends $4 million to pave city streets, using the proceeds of a city gasoline tax dedicated for road and highway improvements.

c. It receives a contribution of $5 million. Per the stipulation of the donor, the money is to be invested in marketable securities and the interest from the securities is to be used to maintain a city park.

d. It collects $800,000 in landing fees at the city-owned airport.

e. It earns $200,000 on investments set aside to make principal payments on the city's outstanding bonds. The bonds were issued to finance improvements to the city's tunnels and bridges.

f. It pays $4 million to a contractor for work on one of these bridges.

g. It pays $80,000 in wages and salaries to police officers.

h. It purchases from an outside supplier $40,000 of stationery that it will "sell" to its various operating departments.

2-6

Each fund must account for interfund activity as if it were a separate accounting entity.

The newly formed Buffalo School District engaged in the following transactions and other events during the year:

a. It levied and collected property taxes of $110 million.

b. It issued $30 million in long-term bonds to construct a building. It placed the cash received in a special fund set aside to account for the bond proceeds.

c. During the year it constructed the building at a cost of $25 million. It expects to spend the $5 million balance in the following year. The building has an estimated useful life of 25 years.

d. It incurred $70 million in general operating costs, of which it paid $63 million. It expects to pay the balance early the following year.

e. It transferred $12 million from its general fund to a fund established to account for resources set aside to service the debt. Of this amount, $10 million was for repayment of the debt; $2 million was for interest.

f. From the special fund established to service the debt, it paid $2 million in interest and $6 million in principal.

g. It collected $4 million in hotel taxes restricted to promoting tourism. Since the resources were restricted they were accounted for in a special restricted fund. During the year, the district spent $3 million on promoting tourism.

h. It established a supplies store to provide supplies to the district's various departments by transferring $4 million from the general fund. It accounted for the store in a proprietary fund. During the year the store purchased (and paid for) $2 million in supplies. Of these, it "sold" $1 million, at cost (for cash), to departments accounted for in the general fund. During the year these departments used all of the supplies that they had purchased.

1. Prepare journal entries to record the transactions and other events in appropriate funds. Assume that governmental funds are accounted for on a modified accrual basis and focus only on current financial resources (and, therefore, do not give balance sheet recognition either to capital assets or long-term debt). Proprietary funds are accounted for on a full accrual basis.

2. Prepare a combined balance sheet—one that has a separate column for each of the funds you established.

3. Prepare a combined statement of revenues, expenditures, and changes in fund balances for all governmental funds—one column for each fund. Prepare a separate statement of revenues, expenses and changes in fund balances for any proprietary funds you established.

2-7

Long-term assets and liabilities are denied recognition on funds statements.

Entrepreneurs Consultants, a state agency, was established to provide consulting services to small businesses. It maintains only a single general fund and accounts for its activities on a modified accrual basis. During its first month of operations, the association engaged in, or was affected by, the following transactions and events:

a. It received an unrestricted grant of $100,000.

b. It purchased five computers at $2,000 each.

c. It paid wages and salaries of $6,000.

d. It borrowed $24,000 from a bank to enable it to purchase an automobile.

e. It purchased the automobile for $24,000.

f. It made its first payment on the note—interest of $200.

g. It destroyed one of its computers in an accident. The computer was not insured.

1. Prepare journal entries in the general fund to record each of the transactions or other events.

2. Prepare a balance sheet and a statement of revenues, expenditures, and changes in fund balance for the general fund.

2-8

The more complete presentation is not always the easier to understand.

Bertram County maintains a fund accounting system. Nevertheless, its comptroller (who recently retired from a position in private industry) prepared the following balance sheet (in millions):

Assets:

Cash	$ 600
Investments	1,800
Construction in Progress	500
Fixed Assets	1,200
Total Assets	$4,100

Liabilities and Fund Balance:

Bonds Payable		$1,700
Fund Balance		
Restricted for Capital Projects	$ 600	
Restricted for Debt Service	200	
Unrestricted	1,600	2,400
Total Liabilities and Fund Balance		$4,100

The fund balance restricted for debt service represents entirely *principal* (not interest) on the bonds payable.

1. Recast the balance sheet, as best you can, into separate balance sheets for each of the funds that are apparently maintained by the county. Assume that the county uses a modified accrual basis of accounting that excludes recognition in its funds of both capital (fixed) assets and long-term debt. Assume, also, that cash and investments are divided among the funds in proportion to their fund balances.

2. In your opinion, which of the two presentations gives the reader a more complete picture of the county's financial status? Why? Which presentation is easier to understand?

CHAPTER 3

Government Financial Reporting

In Chapter 2 we discussed the reasons why governments use fund accounting and we described the purposes of the funds that they maintain. In Chapters 4 through 10 we shall examine the principal transactions of the various types of funds. Our goal in this chapter is to provide a broad understanding of the purpose, form, and general content of the basic financial statements that are required by generally accepted accounting principles (GAAP).

The basic financial statements are the end product of the accounting system. Armed with an overview of the end product, students should find it easier to appreciate the discussions in the next few chapters. Those chapters should fill in the blanks concerning how information is selected and recorded in the various funds and how recorded information is summarized for external reporting.

In Chapter 11 we shall address additional reporting issues, including the scope of the reporting entity (e.g., which affiliated organizations should be included in a government's report) and supplementary information included in a government's comprehensive annual financial report (CAFR). In Chapter 14 we shall discuss the elements of financial statement analysis.

The illustrative financial statements in this and subsequent chapters are from the CAFR of the City of Orlando, Florida, for the fiscal year ended September 30, 2001.[1]

HOW CAN FUNDS BE COMBINED AND CONSOLIDATED?

As discussed in Chapter 2, fund accounting provides accountability for, and control of, public moneys. Each fund is a separate fiscal and accounting entity with its own self-balancing set of accounts. Thus, financial statements, such as a balance sheet and a statement of revenues and expenditures or expenses, can be prepared for each individual fund. However, governments may maintain hundreds of funds. A way is needed to summarize fund information for financial reporting so that the reports are of a manageable size but still provide useful information, including the restrictions on resources that funds represent. One possibility is simply to *combine* or aggregate the funds—add them together without adjusting for interfund activities and balances. Another is to *consolidate* the funds—add them together, but eliminate interfund activities

---

[1]Students can learn more about Orlando and its financial reporting by accessing the city's Web site at *www.cityoforlando.net/admin/accounting/reports.htm* and clicking on "CAFR 2001." The management's discussion and analysis in Orlando's 2001 CAFR provides an introduction to and overview of the financial statements discussed in this and subsequent chapters.

and balances—and prepare financial statements for the government as a single economic entity. Traditionally, government financial reporting standards required the first solution. However, as we shall see, the current standards incorporate both solutions to some extent.

PRE-1999 REPORTING MODEL For many decades, governments prepared financial statements with multiple columns—one for each fund type. For example, a **combined statement** for governmental funds generally included a column for the general fund, a second column for all special revenue funds combined, and other columns for, respectively, all capital projects funds and all debt service funds combined. A combined balance sheet for all fund types included columns for each governmental, proprietary, and fiduciary fund type. It also included additional columns to provide information about general fixed assets and long-term debt, which, as previously discussed, are not recorded in any governmental fund.

Unlike a **consolidated statement**, a combined financial statement does not eliminate activity and balances between funds and fund types, such as interfund receivables, payables, and transfers. Thus, although a "totals" column was provided on most statements, some totals were overstated from the perspective of the government as a single economic entity. As a result, users could not readily obtain a picture of the *government's* financial position and results of operations and were impeded from comparing one government with another. Moreover, because the statements presented combined information for multiple funds of a similar type, information for the more significant funds could be offset or obscured by information for the less significant funds. Thus, comparative analysis was made still more difficult.

WHAT IS GASB STATEMENT NO. 34?

CURRENT REPORTING MODEL Upon its establishment in 1984, the GASB undertook to develop a new reporting model that would address some of the problems of fund-based reporting that had evolved over many decades. After years of considerable and often controversial debate, a final pronouncement (*Statement No. 34, Basic Financial Statements—and Management's Discussion and Analysis—for State and Local Governments*) was issued in June 1999. The statement required governments to implement the new standards for fiscal years beginning after June 15, 2001, 2002, or 2003, depending on the government's size. Thus, by the time this text is in use, most governments should have implemented the new model. Orlando's financial statements, used as illustrations in this text, incorporate most of the requirements of Statement No. 34.

Much of the debate over the new model centered on whether governments should continue to prepare fund-based financial statements or, instead, should present consolidated financial statements for the government as a whole. An important part of this debate was whether the statements should focus on current financial resources (as did the previous model), total financial resources, or all economic resources (including capital assets).

The GASB concluded that the objectives of financial reporting established in Concepts Statement No. 1 could not all be achieved with either fund-based reporting or consolidated financial statements alone; nor could they all be achieved with a single measurement focus and basis of accounting. For example, recall the discussion in Chapter 1 as to the conflict between the objectives of reporting on budgetary and fiscal compliance as opposed to reporting on interperiod equity. Realization of the compliance objective requires financial statements prepared on a budget or near-budget basis (i.e., a cash basis or a modified accrual basis). By contrast, fulfillment of the interperiod equity objective requires financial statements on a full accrual basis with a focus on economic resources.

FISCAL VERSUS OPERATIONAL ACCOUNTABILITY According to Concepts Statement No. 1, the overriding objective of all financial reporting is *accountability*. The GASB concluded that accountability has different forms that reflect variations in users' information needs. Traditionally, governmental funds have focused on *fiscal accountability*, whereas the focus of the proprietary (business-type) funds has been on *operational accountability*. The GASB defines the two types of accountability as follows:

- *Fiscal accountability* is the responsibility of governments to justify that their actions in the current period have complied with public decisions (e.g., the legally adopted budget) concerning the raising and spending of public moneys in the short term (usually one budgetary cycle or one year).

- *Operational accountability* is governments' responsibility to report the extent to which they have met their operating objectives efficiently and effectively, using all resources available for that purpose, and whether they can continue to meet their objectives for the foreseeable future.[2]

The GASB concluded that, to meet users' needs for short-term financial information and budgetary comparisons, the governmental funds should continue to focus on fiscal accountability and that the modified accrual basis of accounting, with a measurement focus on current financial resources, is appropriate for that purpose. Proprietary funds should continue to focus on operational accountability (all economic resources), using the full accrual basis. However, governments should also prepare consolidated financial statements to provide information on the financial position and operating results of the government as a single economic entity. That is, the consolidated financial statements should provide operational accountability information for both governmental and proprietary activities and, therefore, should focus on economic resources, using the full accrual basis of accounting. The GASB also concluded that fiduciary activities (such as pension trust funds) should be excluded from the consolidated statements (but should be reported in fund statements) because trust and agency resources belong to the beneficiaries of the trust or agency relationship. Therefore, they should not be included in assessments of the government's financial position.

WHAT ARE THE REQUIRED BASIC FINANCIAL STATEMENTS?

Statement No. 34 mandates that governments' basic financial statements (those required for compliance with generally accepted accounting principles, or GAAP) include two separate but related sets of financial statements. The first set, the *government-wide statements*, concentrates on the government as a whole. It consolidates

---

[2]GASB Statement No. 34, *Basic Financial Statements—and Management's Discussion and Analysis—for State and Local Governments* (1999), para. 203.

all of a government's own operations (i.e., excluding its fiduciary activities) and includes within its measurement focus all of the government's economic resources, including capital assets. The statements are presented on a full accrual basis.

The second set, the *fund statements*, views the government as a collection of separate funds. Governmental, proprietary, and fiduciary funds are reported on separate statements. The fund statements have multiple columns. However, unlike in the statements of the previous model, the columns do not include combined information by type of fund (e.g., all special revenue funds combined). Instead, the GASB concluded that users' needs would be better served if the statements focused on the major funds, regardless of fund type, within, respectively, the governmental funds and proprietary (enterprise) funds categories. Therefore, instead of one column for each fund type there is one column for each major fund (and one column that combines all the nonmajor funds within the relevant funds category). Thus, for example, the statement that reports governmental funds includes one column for the general fund and one for each of the other major funds—regardless of whether they are special revenue funds, capital projects funds, or debt service funds. Although the fund financial statements contain "totals" columns, they combine, rather than consolidate, the funds. Hence, as was true of the pre–Statement No. 34 model, interfund activities and balances are not eliminated.

To prepare their government-wide statements, governments must adjust the governmental fund statements from the modified accrual to the full accrual basis. Statement No. 34 requires that a summary of the principal adjustments be presented with the financial statements, so that users can more readily understand the relationship between the fund financial statements and the government-wide financial statements.

As illustrated in Figure 3–1, the basic financial statements must include notes and must be followed by required supplementary information, which includes, for example, budget-to-actual comparisons and data relating to pension plans and certain types of risks. Statement No. 34 also requires that governments present with the basic financial statements a management's discussion and analysis (MD&A). Similar in nature to the MD&A that accompanies business financial statements, this narrative presents a brief, nontechnical overview of the government's financial performance during the year and its financial position at year-end.

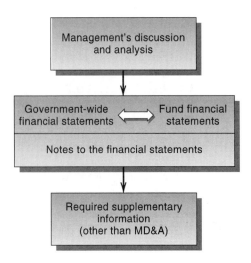

Figure 3–1   Minimum Requirements for Government Financial Reporting

Source: GASB Statement No. 34, *Basic Financial Statements—and Management's Discussion and Analysis—for State and Local Governments*

WHAT ARE THE GOVERNMENT-WIDE FINANCIAL STATEMENTS?

There are just two government-wide statements: a statement of net assets (or a balance sheet) and a statement of activities.

GOVERNMENT-WIDE STATEMENT OF NET ASSETS The statement of net assets (illustrated in Table 3–1) is similar to the balance sheet of a business. However, unlike that of a business, it has separate columns for governmental activities, business-type activities, total primary (reporting) government, and *component units*—entities such as building or housing authorities that are economically intertwined with the government, albeit legally separate (and which are discussed in Chapter 11).

The governmental activities column includes consolidated information (i.e., after eliminating interfund activities and balances) from the governmental funds (and generally also from internal service funds, as discussed later in this chapter and in Chapter 9). The business-type activities column includes consolidated information from the enterprise funds. The column for the total primary government consolidates the information reported in the governmental and business-type activities columns.

The illustrated statement is in the format "assets less liabilities equals net assets." The more traditional format, "assets equals liabilities plus net assets," is also acceptable.

Consistent with the focus on economic resources and the full accrual basis of accounting, the assets section of the statement of net assets includes both capital and financial assets. The capital assets, including infrastructure, such as highways and bridges, as well as land, buildings, and equipment, are generally reported net of accumulated depreciation. (An exception will be discussed in Chapter 7.) Similarly, the liabilities section includes long-term obligations. To highlight the proportion of government resources invested in capital assets, the net assets section of the statement distinguishes between the net capital assets (capital assets less the obligations incurred to construct or purchase them) and the net noncapital assets.

IMPORTANCE OF RESTRICTIONS ON NET ASSETS Governments differ from businesses in that a substantial portion of their resources are restricted for specific purposes, by law or by external parties, such as grantors or donors. It is obviously essential that these resources be distinguished from those that are unrestricted and thereby available to meet all the government's needs. Thus, the GASB requires that net assets be displayed in three separate categories:

1. *Amounts invested in capital assets* (net of related debt, such as mortgages or bonded debt), which obviously cannot be spent unless the assets are sold
2. *Amounts restricted for specific purposes,* such as capital projects or debt service, which, therefore, cannot be used for other purposes
3. *Unrestricted amounts,* which can be used for any purpose.

As shown in Table 3–1, 56 percent of Orlando's reported net assets for governmental activities and 80 percent of its business-type net assets are either tied up in capital assets or are otherwise restricted (not usable to meet general financing needs). Note

TABLE 3–1
Statement of Net Assets

City of Orlando, Florida
Statement of Net Assets as of September 30, 2001

| | Primary Government | | | Component Units |
	Governmental Activities	Business-type Activities	Total	
Assets				
Cash and Cash Equivalents	$239,439,761	$140,375,663	$ 379,815,424	$ 1,522,028
Securities Lending	105,830,638	—	105,830,638	—
Receivables (net)	32,109,079	5,329,340	37,438,419	997,760
Due from Other Governments	10,473,363	1,370,686	11,844,049	1,487,880
Internal Balances	(316,530)	316,530	—	—
Inventories	1,650,031	397,056	2,047,087	32,607
Prepaids	142,032	5,774	147,806	—
Other Assets	955,596	968,753	1,924,349	—
Restricted Assets:				
Cash and Cash Equivalents	4,720,609	18,916,942	23,637,551	844,005
Investments	21,937,931	31,819,341	53,757,272	1,218,035
Capital Assets:				
Non-depreciable	100,030,075	82,491,956	182,522,031	—
Depreciable (Net)	198,024,288	429,799,892	627,824,180	41,506,775
Total Assets	714,996,873	711,791,933	1,426,788,806	47,609,090
Liabilities				
Accounts Payable	21,801,989	6,800,499	28,602,488	233,604
Accrued Liabilities	4,229,127	516,050	4,745,177	23,953
Accrued Interest Payable	3,649,353	3,681,912	7,331,265	93,967
Advance Payments	3,699,502	13,899,722	17,599,224	—
Deferred Revenue	10,342,360	—	10,342,360	13,612
Securities Lending	105,830,638	—	105,830,638	—
Non-Current Liabilities				
Due Within One Year:				
Compensated Absences	1,338,649	238,283	1,576,932	11,132
Loans and Leases Payable	1,165,097	1,488,591	2,653,688	189,691
Bonds Payable	5,325,000	9,275,000	14,600,000	345,000
Due In More Than One Year:				
Compensated Absences	15,394,460	2,740,248	18,134,708	128,014
Loans and Leases Payable	34,507,987	17,375,551	51,883,538	2,813,331
Bonds Payable	166,599,019	171,433,221	338,032,240	2,566,447
Claims Liabilities	29,423,160	—	29,423,160	—
Advances from Orange County	—	—	—	5,959,000
Advances from City of Orlando	—	—	—	14,303,643
Total Liabilities	403,306,341	227,449,077	630,755,418	26,681,394
Net Assets				
Invested in Capital Assets				
(net of related debt)	138,957,233	333,491,749	472,448,982	36,150,385
Restricted for:				
Capital Projects	31,613,959	41,570,562	73,184,521	—
Debt Service	4,171,129	12,000,000	16,171,129	—
Renewal and Replacement	—	3,088,649	3,088,649	207,994
Unrestricted (Deficit)	136,948,211	94,191,896	231,140,107	(15,430,683)
Total Net Assets	$311,690,532	$484,342,856	$ 796,033,388	$20,927,696

that the restrictions for capital projects and debt service do not necessarily coincide with amounts held in governmental funds with those titles. In the Orlando statements, 57 percent of the total amount restricted for capital projects and 74 percent of the amount restricted for debt service are attributable to business-type activities. These assets are not maintained in separate capital projects or debt service funds, even though they are restricted for those purposes.

GOVERNMENT-WIDE STATEMENT OF ACTIVITIES In contrast to the government-wide statement of net assets, which is similar to a business balance sheet, the government-wide statement of activities (illustrated in Table 3–2) bears little resemblance to the income statement of a business. At first glance, it seems quite daunting, but the logic behind it is quite easy to follow. The statement should be particularly useful to users, such as taxpayers and other resource providers, who are interested in how much the government's programs and other services cost.

Unlike a business income statement, the aim of the activities statement is to show the net cost of each of the government's main functions and programs. The net cost is the amount of functional or program expenses that must be covered by taxes and other general revenues, in contrast to fees and charges of the function or program itself. Accordingly, the first column of the statement of activities reports total expenses for each program or function, subdivided, as in the statement of net assets, between governmental and business-type activities of the primary government (and followed by expenses of component units).

The next three columns report revenues that directly help defray the expenses, such as those from charges for services and program-specific grants. Then, two columns (one for governmental activities and one for business-type activities) show the difference between the total expenses for each function or program and the directly attributable revenues (called *program revenues*). The amounts in those two columns indicate the net cost to taxpayers (amounts that must be subsidized from general revenues) of the functions or programs.

CALCULATING THE NET COST TO TAXPAYERS For example, in Table 3–2, Orlando's Community and Youth Service program reports expenses of $14.5 million (column 1), which is partially financed by specific charges for program services ($2.3 million, column 2) and operating grants and contributions to the program ($0.4 million, column 3). This leaves an amount of $11.8 million (column 5) that must be financed from general revenues. Thus, the net cost of the program to the taxpayers is $11.8 million.

The lower portion of the statement summarizes the taxes and other general revenues of the government at large—revenues that cannot be associated directly with specific functions and programs and that can be used to cover the net cost of all of the government's programs. In Table 3–2, the net cost of all programs or functions of the primary government (the City of Orlando) is $213.9 million (total net expense or revenue for the primary government, column 7). This amount was financed from $255.3 million in general revenues (taxes, grants and contributions not restricted to specific programs, and other items reported in column 7 below the net expense figure). After deducting that amount, the net change in the government's net assets is $41.5 million. That amount, when added to the beginning-of-the-year net assets amount of $754.5 million, equals total end-of-the-year net assets of $796 million, as reported for the total primary government in the statement of net assets (Table 3–1).

TABLE 3-2
Statement of Activities

City of Orlando, Florida
Statement of Activities for the Year Ended September 30, 2001

| | | Program Revenues | | |
	Expenses	Charges for Services	Operating Grants and Contributions	Capital Grants and Contributions
Function/Program Activities—Primary Government:				
Governmental Activities:				
General Government	$ 12,233,953	$ 7,178,401	$ 153,750	$ —
Administrative Services	19,310,247	99,422	—	—
Planning and Development	13,291,294	1,850,894	7,378,587	3,000,000
Public Works	29,026,898	5,276,589	1,007,057	1,257,109
Community and Youth Services	14,501,179	2,298,728	372,637	—
Police	73,354,220	10,163,432	4,776,640	—
Fire	36,513,281	339,863	—	—
Community Redevelopment Agency	11,900,678	2,066,558	—	—
Securities Lending	4,341,897	4,580,683	—	—
Lynx/Transit Subsidy	3,419,458	—	—	—
Street Lighting	3,303,344	—	—	—
Payments to Component Units	740,575	—	—	—
Other	15,777,111	—	—	—
Interest on Long-Term Debt	8,870,330	—	—	—
Unallocated Depreciation	1,761,141	—	—	—
Total governmental activities	248,345,606	33,854,570	13,688,671	4,257,109
Business-type Activities:				
Wastewater	60,673,007	47,263,098	—	—
Centroplex	19,984,939	15,866,263	—	—
Parking	11,236,807	9,872,284	—	—
Stormwater Utility	8,389,754	10,304,175	—	—
Solid Waste	15,566,657	15,236,797	—	—
Total business-type activities	115,851,164	98,542,617	—	—
Total primary government	$364,196,770	$132,397,187	$13,688,671	$4,257,109
Component units:				
Downtown Development Board	$ 1,778,975	$ —	$ —	$ —
Civic Facilities Authority	6,247,075	3,691,271	—	—
Total component units	$ 8,026,050	$ 3,691,271	$ -0-	$ —0—

General Revenues:
    Taxes:
        Property taxes, levied for general purposes
        Sales Tax
        Gas Tax
        Occupational Licenses and Franchise Fees
        Public Service Taxes
        Tax Increment Fees
    Grants and contributions not restricted to specific programs:
        Orlando Utilities Commission
        Other
    Impact Fees
    Investment Earnings
    Payment from Primary Government
    Miscellaneous
    Capital Contributions
    Transfers:
        Subsidiary Transfers
        Other Transfers
            Total General Revenues and Transfers
                Change in Net Assets
    Net Assets—Beginning (Restated)
    Net assets—Ending

Net (Expense) Revenue and Changes in Net Assets			
Primary Government			
Governmental Activities	Business-type Activities	Total	Component Units
$ (4,901,802)	$ —	$ (4,901,802)	$ —
(19,210,825)	—	(19,210,825)	—
(1,061,813)	—	(1,061,813)	—
(21,486,143)	—	(21,486,143)	—
(11,829,814)	—	(11,829,814)	—
(58,414,148)	—	(58,414,148)	—
(36,173,418)	—	(36,173,418)	—
(9,834,120)	—	(9,834,120)	—
238,786	—	238,786	—
(3,419,458)	—	(3,419,458)	—
(3,303,344)	—	(3,303,344)	—
(740,575)	—	(740,575)	—
(15,777,111)	—	(15,777,111)	—
(8,870,330)	—	(8,870,330)	—
(1,761,141)	—	(1,761,141)	—
(196,545,256)	—	(196,545,256)	—
—	(13,409,909)	(13,409,909)	—
—	(4,118,676)	(4,118,676)	—
—	(1,364,523)	(1,364,523)	—
—	1,914,421	1,914,421	—
—	(329,860)	(329,860)	—
—	(17,308,547)	(17,308,547)	—
(196,545,256)	(17,308,547)	(213,853,803)	
—	—	—	(1,778,975)
—	—	—	(2,555,804)
—	—	—	(4,334,779)
68,984,150	—	68,984,150	1,048,735
25,117,291	—	25,117,291	—
7,698,638	—	7,698,638	—
25,834,029	—	25,834,029	—
31,827,207	—	31,827,207	—
7,417,664	—	7,417,664	—
32,091,000	—	32,091,000	—
9,586,845	—	9,586,845	—
7,225,526	—	7,225,526	—
14,503,521	15,606,739	30,110,260	382,557
—	—	—	325,000
4,385,131	—	4,385,131	310,084
3,111,512	1,958,392	5,069,904	—
(2,290,772)	2,290,772	—	—
4,113,977	(4,113,977)	—	—
239,605,719	15,741,926	255,347,645	2,066,376
43,060,463	(1,566,621)	41,493,842	(2,268,403)
268,630,069	485,909,477	754,539,546	23,196,099
$311,690,532	$484,342,856	$796,033,388	$20,927,696

The government-wide statements are on a full accrual basis. Therefore, as already noted, the statement of net assets includes both capital assets and long-term debt. Correspondingly, the expenses reported in the statement of activities include charges for depreciation of capital assets, even though they are not broken out separately.

WHAT ARE THE FUND FINANCIAL STATEMENTS?

The three categories of funds necessitate three sets of statements, each containing a slightly different blend of statements. The following are the basic statements required for each fund category (illustrated in the indicated tables):

- Governmental funds:
  - Balance sheet (Table 3–3)
  - Statement of revenues, expenditures, and changes in fund balances (Table 3–5)
- Proprietary funds:
  - Statement of net assets (or a balance sheet) (Table 3–7)
  - Statement of revenues, expenses, and changes in fund net assets (Table 3–8)
  - Statement of cash flows (discussed and illustrated in Chapter 9)
- Fiduciary funds:
  - Statement of fiduciary net assets
  - Statement of changes in fiduciary net assets
    Both statements are discussed and illustrated in Chapter 10.

GOVERNMENTAL FUNDS As illustrated in Tables 3–3 and 3–5, the general fund and each of the government's other major funds are reported in separate columns. **Major funds** are defined as the general fund and other funds in which total assets, revenues, or expenditures/expenses of the fund are at least 10 percent of the corresponding total for the relevant fund category (governmental or enterprise) and also at least 5 percent of the corresponding total for all governmental and enterprise funds combined. The remaining, *nonmajor*, governmental funds are combined into the column captioned *other governmental funds*.

The governmental funds balance sheet is followed by a reconciliation (Table 3–4) of total governmental fund balances ($197.2 million) with the net assets of governmental activities ($311.7 million) per the government-wide statement of net assets. A similar reconciliation (Table 3–6) ties the changes in fund balances per the governmental funds statement of revenues and expenditures ($2.1 million) with the changes in the net assets of governmental activities per the government-wide statement of activities ($43.1 million).

Governmental Funds Balance Sheet In contrast to the government-wide statement of net assets, the governmental funds balance sheet (Table 3–3) uses the more traditional format that presents assets as being equal to liabilities plus fund balances. Recall that, as indicated by the list of long-term items in the reconciliation (Table 3–4), governmental funds focus on current financial resources. (Inventories and prepaid items (such as insurance)—discussed in Chapter 5—are considered current financial resources for reporting purposes.) Therefore, the balance sheet does not include capital or other noncurrent assets. Similarly, all reported liabilities, including compensated absences (e.g., employees' earned vacation pay, discussed in Chapter 5) and deferred revenues (Chapter 4) include only amounts payable or recognizable as revenue within one budgetary cycle or one year.

Reservations of Fund Balances As illustrated in Table 3–3, fund balances are subdivided into amounts that are *reserved* and *unreserved*, rather than restricted and unrestricted, as is the practice in the government-wide statement of net assets. A **reserved fund balance** is similar in concept to resources that are restricted for a specific purpose. However, the term *reserve* is used in governmental fund statements in part because of its long history in governmental fund accounting and reporting and in part because each fund (except the general fund) itself represents a restriction on the use of the resources for which it accounts. A reservation of fund balance is, in essence, an additional restriction on fund resources.

Reserve for Encumbrances A reserve for encumbrances indicates the amount of fund balance that is already committed at year-end related to unfilled purchase orders and other signed contracts and, thus, cannot be used for other purposes. A government establishes, or adds to, a reserve for encumbrances as it orders or contracts for goods or services. It reduces that reserve as it receives the goods or services and either pays for them or records an appropriate liability. At year-end, therefore, the balance in the reserve indicates the amount of goods or services on order, which presumably will be received in the following year. By reporting the reserve for encumbrances, the government informs users that part of the fund balance is already committed and, therefore, cannot be appropriated (included by the legislative body in new expenditure authority) or spent for other fund purposes. As shown in Table 3–3, for example, $10.4 million of Orlando's gas tax revenue fund balance is reserved for goods and services that are on order and is not, therefore, available for other purposes.

Reserve for Inventory and Prepaid Items Fund balance is equal to fund assets less fund liabilities. Like owners' equity in business accounting, fund balance cannot be associated with any particular asset or liability. Thus, it is not the equivalent of cash and is not necessarily indicative of the cash available for distribution or appropriation by the legislative body. Nevertheless, some users of government statements may interpret fund balance as the amount that is available for appropriation. To avoid that misinterpretation, governments have traditionally established reserves for inventory and other prepaid items. These reserves are always equal to the amount reported for inventory and prepaid items in the assets section of the balance sheet. They do nothing more than highlight that the corresponding portion of the fund balance is not available for appropriation.

Governmental Funds Statement of Revenues, Expenditures, and Changes in Fund Balances Similar to the balance sheet, the governmental funds statement of revenues, expenditures, and changes in fund balances is also presented in a more traditional format than the government-wide statement of activities. Statement No. 34 requires revenues (discussed in Chapter 4) to be reported by major source, such as property taxes and licenses and permits. Expenditures (discussed in Chapter 5)

TABLE 3–3
Governmental Funds Balance Sheet

City of Orlando, Florida
Balance Sheet
Governmental Funds
September 30, 2001

	General	Utilities Services Tax	Gas Tax Revenue	Trans- portation Impact Fees
Assets				
Current Cash and Cash Equivalents	$ 66,841,521	$14,290,900	$20,483,988	$31,623,015
Restricted Cash and Cash Equivalents	—	—	—	—
Restricted Investments	—	—	—	—
Securities Lending Collateral	105,830,638	—	—	—
Receivables (Net)				
Accounts	22,851,387	2,922,653	305,805	—
Taxes	497,362	—	—	—
Special Assessments	1,174,200	—	6,629	—
Due from Other Funds	284,737	—	—	—
Due from Other Governments	8,428,121	—	1,325,801	—
Prepaid items	108,286	—	—	—
Inventories	1,033,243	—	—	—
Total Assets	$207,049,495	$17,213,553	$22,122,223	$31,623,015
Liabilities and Fund Balances				
Liabilities:				
Accounts Payable	$ 4,102,792	$ 2,712,650	$ 424,481	$ —
Accrued Liabilities	4,029,850	—	—	—
Advance Payments	2,982,821	—	400	—
Due to Other Funds	—	—	—	—
Short-term Loans from Other Funds	12,851,033	—	—	—
Deferred Revenue	8,065,422	—	1,759,440	9,056
Obligations Under Securities Lending	105,830,638	—	—	—
Accrued Interest Payable	—	—	—	—
Total Liabilities	137,862,556	2,712,650	2,184,321	9,056
Fund Balances:				
Reserved for:				
Debt Service	—	—	—	—
Prepaid Items	108,286	—	—	—
Inventories	1,033,243	—	—	—
Encumbrances	818,546	—	10,358,056	—
Unreserved, reported in:				
General Fund	67,226,864	—	—	—
Special Revenue Funds	—	14,500,903	9,579,846	31,613,959
Capital Project Funds	—	—	—	—
Total Fund Balances	69,186,939	14,500,903	19,937,902	31,613,959
Total Liabilities and Fund Balances	$207,049,495	$17,213,553	$22,122,223	$31,623,015

Community Redevelopment Agency	Capital Improvement	Other Governmental Funds	Total Governmental Funds
$ 8,132,937	$36,168,896	$14,087,575	$191,628,832
4,720,609	—		4,720,609
14,438,953	—		14,438,953
—	—		105,830,638
10,225	291,375	350,292	26,731,737
—	—	—	497,362
—	—		1,180,829
—	—		284,737
—	—	719,441	10,473,363
33,746	—	—	142,032
—	—	50,145	1,083,388
$27,336,470	$36,460,271	$15,207,453	$357,012,480
$ 2,765,125	$ 8,067,955	$ 614,667	$ 18,687,670
13,934	—	50,192	4,093,976
6,734	696,998	12,549	3,699,502
378	—	284,359	284,737
—	—	—	12,851,033
696,615	—	2,261,827	12,792,360
—	—	—	105,830,638
1,618,267	—	—	1,618,267
5,101,053	8,764,953	3,223,594	159,858,183
17,206,486	—	—	17,206,486
33,746	—	—	142,032
—	—	50,145	1,083,388
930	2,240,129	5,673,463	19,091,124
—	—	—	67,226,864
3,209,170	—	5,035,652	63,939,530
1,785,085	25,455,189	1,224,599	28,464,873
22,235,417	27,695,318	11,983,859	197,154,297
$27,336,470	$36,460,271	$15,207,453	$357,012,480

TABLE 3–4
Reconciliation of the Governmental Funds
Balance Sheet to the Government-Wide Statement of Net Assets

City of Orlando, Florida
Reconciliation of the Balance Sheet
to the Statement of Net Assets
Governmental Funds
As of September 30, 2001

Fund balances—total governmental funds		$197,154,297
Amounts reported for governmental activities in the statement of net assets are different because:		
Capital assets used in governmental activities are not financial resources and therefore are not reported in the governmental funds.		
Governmental capital assets	$381,685,797	
Less accumulated depreciation	(109,908,332)	271,777,465
Other assets used in governmental activities are not financial resources and therefore are not reported in the governmental funds.		
Bond costs	579,842	
Less current year amortization	(37,421)	542,421
Long-term receivables applicable to governmental activities are not due and collectible in the current period and therefore are not reported in fund balance in the governmental funds.		
Accounts Receivable		3,606,000
Long-term liabilities, including bonds payable are not due and payable in the current period and therefore are not reported in the governmental funds.		
Governmental bonds payable	(100,690,000)	
Discount	347,882	
Current year amortization	(22,339)	
Compensated Absences	(16,139,660)	
Governmental leases payable	(1,704,789)	
Governmental banking fund debt	(81,486,332)	(199,695,238)
Deferred revenue in governmental funds is susceptible to full accrual on the entity-wide statements.		
Deferred Revenue		2,450,000
Internal service funds are used by management to charge the costs of certain activities to individual funds. The assets and liabilities of internal service funds are not included in governmental activities in the statement of net assets.		35,855,587
Net assets of governmental activities		$311,690,532

should be reported, at a minimum, by function, such as administrative services and public works, similar to the functional breakdown provided in the government-wide statement of activities. As indicated in Table 3–5, Orlando goes beyond the minimum requirements and further groups expenditures by character, such as current operating expenditures and capital improvements.

Revenues and Expenditures versus Other Financing Sources and Uses

Following revenues and expenditures, the statement includes a section for *other financing sources and uses*. Similar to revenues and expenditures, these amounts are inflows and outflows of current financial resources and, therefore, contribute to the net change in fund balances.

However, the terms *revenue* and *expenditure* are generally used only for amounts that increase or decrease the net assets of the government as a whole—not just those of individual funds. In contrast, most other financing sources and uses affect individual fund balances but not the net assets of the government as a whole. Common examples, as illustrated in Table 3–5, include interfund transfers and proceeds of debt. Interfund transfers are essentially nonrepayable subsidies from one fund to another. Proceeds of debt increase a governmental fund balance because they are an inflow of current financial resources. However, they do not increase the government's net assets because the government has incurred a corresponding liability, which is reported in the government-wide statement of net assets. Inasmuch as bond proceeds are recognized as a liability in the government-wide statements but as a financing source in the fund statements, they must be included in the reconciliation between the two sets of statements (as shown in Table 3–6).

The net effect of other financing sources and uses can be to convert a potentially negative change in fund balance, resulting from an excess of expenditures over revenues, to a positive change due to the receipt of transfers or bond proceeds. Correspondingly, transfers-out can convert an excess of revenues over expenditures into a negative change in fund balance. Orlando's general fund, for example, reports a revenue/expenditure deficiency of $5.2 million, but a positive net change in fund balance of $4.3 million. Users should be aware that only revenues and expenditures contribute to a change in the net assets of the government as a whole ($41.5 million for the total primary government in Table 3–2).

PROPRIETARY FUNDS

Proprietary Funds Statement of Net Assets

The net assets statement of proprietary funds (illustrated in Table 3–7) focuses on the major enterprise funds but also includes a column for all nonmajor enterprise funds combined and a column for all internal service funds combined.[3] The measurement focus of proprietary funds is on economic resources. Accordingly, the funds are accounted for on a full accrual basis. Not surprisingly, therefore, the format of the proprietary fund statement of net assets closely resembles that of a business balance sheet. To help users assess liquidity, assets are classified as to whether they are current or noncurrent amounts—just as they are in the balance sheets of businesses. In addition, consistent with the emphasis on restrictions previously described for government-wide and governmental fund financial statements, proprietary fund net assets are subdivided between restricted and unrestricted amounts.

---

[3]Orlando has no nonmajor enterprise funds.

TABLE 3–5
Governmental Funds Statement of Revenues, Expenditures, and Changes in Fund Balances

City of Orlando, Florida
Statement of Revenues, Expenditures, and Changes in Fund Balances
Governmental Funds
For the Year Ended September 30, 2001

	General	Utilities Services Tax	Gas Tax Revenue	Trans-portation Impact Fees
Revenues				
Property Taxes	$ 68,984,150	$ —	$ —	$ —
Intergovernmental:				
Orlando Utilities Commission Contribution	32,091,000	—	—	—
State Sales Tax	25,117,291	—	—	—
Other Intergovernmental	15,644,787	—	8,667,513	—
Occupational Licenses and Franchise Fees	25,834,029	—	—	—
Utilities Services Tax	—	31,827,207	—	—
Other Licenses, Permits and Fees	26,242,387	—	287,862	5,644,016
Fines and Forfeitures	2,407,844	—	—	—
Income on Investments	7,366,440	861,910	1,579,013	2,335,252
Securities Lending Income	4,580,683	—	—	—
Special Assessments	227,691	—	—	—
Other	7,116,402	—	75,000	—
Total Revenues	215,612,704	32,689,117	10,609,388	7,979,268
Expenditures				
Current Operating:				
General Administration	15,193,169	—	—	135,222
Administrative Services	20,797,562	—	—	—
Planning and Development	4,764,363	—	—	—
Public Works	27,189,244	—	—	—
Community and Youth Services	11,061,900	—	—	—
Police	71,727,832	—	—	—
Fire	35,295,129	—	—	—
Other Expenditures	24,952,846	33,431	—	—
Community Redevelopment Agency	—	—	—	—
Capital Improvements	—	—	11,700,898	—
Securities Lending:				
Interest	4,239,463	—	—	—
Agent Fees	102,434	—	—	—
Debt Service:				
Principal Payments	3,565,393	—	1,480,838	—
Interest and Other	1,922,852	—	1,280,617	—
Total Expenditures	220,812,187	33,431	14,462,353	135,222
Excess (Deficiency) of Revenues Over Expenditures	(5,199,483)	32,655,686	(3,852,965)	7,844,046
Other Financing Sources and (Uses)				
Transfers in	32,540,531	—	5,135,203	931,903
Transfers (Out)	(23,211,423)	(34,439,221)	(86,016)	(2,740,284)
Bond and Loan Proceeds	190,064	—	—	—
Total Other Financing Sources and Uses	9,519,172	(34,439,221)	5,049,187	(1,808,381)
Net Change in Fund Balances	4,319,689	(1,783,535)	1,196,222	6,035,665
Fund Balances—Beginning, Restated	64,867,250	16,284,438	18,741,680	25,578,294
Fund Balances—Ending	$ 69,186,939	$14,500,903	$19,937,902	$31,613,959

Community Redevelopment Agency	Capital Improvement	Other Governmental Funds	Total Governmental Funds
$ —	$ —	$ —	$68,984,150
—	—	—	32,091,000
—	—	—	25,117,291
15,417,468	578,234	9,034,274	49,342,276
—	—	—	25,834,029
—	—	—	31,827,207
1,567,896	—	848,500	34,590,661
—	—	—	2,407,844
2,069,840	2,591,856	1,413,998	18,218,309
—	—	—	4,580,683
—	—	—	227,691
1,180,731	3,467,361	605,411	12,444,905
20,235,935	6,637,451	11,902,183	305,666,046
—	—	—	15,328,391
—	—	—	20,797,562
—	—	7,470,767	12,235,130
—	—	7,774,237	34,963,481
—	—	2,264,094	13,325,994
—	—	991,103	72,718,935
—	—	—	35,295,129
—	—	161	24,986,438
10,723,714	—	—	10,723,714
8,397,290	26,567,596	—	46,665,784
—	—	—	4,239,463
—	—	—	102,434
4,412,156	—	—	9,458,387
5,580,211	—	—	8,783,680
29,113,371	26,567,596	18,500,362	309,624,522
(8,877,436)	(19,930,145)	(6,598,179)	(3,958,476)
601,212	23,432,065	1,726,536	64,367,450
(1,494,804)	(2,439,819)	(364,339)	(64,775,906)
5,250,000	—	1,000,000	6,440,064
4,356,408	20,992,246	2,362,197	6,031,608
(4,521,028)	1,062,101	(4,235,982)	2,073,132
26,756,445	26,633,217	16,219,841	195,081,165
$22,235,417	$27,695,318	$11,983,859	$197,154,297

TABLE 3-6
Reconciliation of the Governmental Funds Statement of Revenues, Expenditures, and Changes in Fund Balances to the Government-Wide Statement of Activities

City of Orlando, Florida
Reconciliation of the Statement of Revenues, Expenditures,
and Changes in Fund Balances of Governmental Funds
to the Statement of Activities
Governmental Funds
For the Year Ended September 30, 2001

Net change in fund balances—total governmental funds		$ 2,073,132
Amounts reported for governmental activities in the statement of activities are different because:		
Governmental funds report capital outlays as expenditures. However, in the statement of activities, the cost of those assets is depreciated over their estimated useful lives.		
Expenditures for capital assets	48,034,546	
Less current year depreciation	(14,870,003)	33,164,543
Bond proceeds provide current financial resources to governmental funds, but issuing debt increases long-term liabilities in the statement of net assets. Repayment of bond principal is an expenditure in the governmental funds, but the repayment reduces long-term liabilities in the statement of net assets. This is the amount by which proceeds exceeded repayments.		
Bond and loan proceeds	(6,440,064)	
Bond costs	1,855	
Principal payments	9,458,387	3,020,178
Some revenues reported in the statement of activities do not provide current financial resources and therefore are not reported as revenues in governmental funds.		
Change in accrual of state payments from casualty and property insurance premiums for police and fire pension contributions.	(362,500)	
Change in interest receivable on long term capital lease	(59,441)	(421,941)
Some expenses reported in the statement of activities do not require the use of current financial resources and therefore are not reported as expenditures in governmental funds.		
Amortization of current year bond discount	(22,339)	
Amortization of current year bond costs	(37,421)	
Change in long-term compensated absences	57,430	(2,330)
Internal service funds are used by management to charge the costs of certain activities to individual funds. The net revenue (expense) of the internal service funds is reported with governmental activities.		5,226,881
Change in net assets of governmental activities		$43,060,463

Inasmuch as proprietary funds are accounted for on a full accrual basis in both the government-wide and the fund statements, the net assets section for total enterprise funds (Table 3–7) is identical in content and amounts to the net assets section of the business-type activities column of the government-wide statement of net assets (Table 3–1). Thus, no reconciliation is necessary between the fund financial statements and the government-wide statements, as is required for the governmental funds.

Internal service funds, like enterprise funds, are proprietary and are maintained on a full accrual basis. In the fund statements they are reported as proprietary funds, along with the enterprise funds. However, internal service fund activities typically serve the functional departments (e.g., police, fire, and administration), the operations of which are considered governmental. As a consequence, per Statement No. 34, internal service fund balances generally are included in the *governmental* activities column of the government-wide statement of net assets, rather than in the business-type activities column. To highlight this change in category in the government-wide statements, the internal service funds column in the proprietary funds statement of net assets is reported to the right of the totals column for the enterprise funds and is captioned *governmental activities*.

Proprietary Fund Statement of Revenues, Expenses, and Changes in Fund Net Assets   The format of the operating statement for proprietary funds (illustrated in Table 3–8) is similar to that of a business income statement. It differs, therefore, from the format of the corresponding statement (i.e., the business-type activities column) in the government-wide statement of activities (Table 3–2). The fund statement separates operating revenues and expenses, such as charges and fees for services, from nonoperating revenues and expenses, such as investment income and interest expense on borrowings. Thus, users are provided the information necessary to distinguish between operating income or loss and total income or loss.

Contributed Capital and Transfers   The statement also distinguishes capital contributions (e.g., initial infusions of resources to establish the fund) and transfers to and from other funds from operating and non-operating revenues and expenses. As discussed previously with respect to governmental funds, transfers are separately reported because they do not enhance the *government's* net assets, although they increase *fund* net assets. Also, the separate reporting informs users of the extent to which enterprise funds, which users may expect to be self-supporting, are, in fact, subsidized by other funds.

FIDUCIARY FUNDS Fiduciary activities are excluded from the government-wide statements because the assets of fiduciary funds (per the definition of this fund type) benefit organizations or individuals other than the government itself. Therefore, per Statement No. 34, they should not be included in the financial position or operating results of the government. The government cannot use these funds for its own programs. Nevertheless, the government is accountable for the fiduciary activities that it carries out on behalf of others and for the resources in these funds. Hence, governments are required to include the fiduciary funds in the fund statements, following those of the governmental and proprietary funds. Transactions and reporting requirements for fiduciary funds will be addressed in Chapter 10.

TABLE 3–7
Proprietary Funds Statement of Net Assets

City of Orlando, Florida, Statement of Net Assets
Proprietary Funds, September 30, 2001

	Business-type Activities—Enterprise Funds		
	Wastewater System	Orlando Centroplex	Parking System
Assets			
Current Assets:			
Cash and Cash Equivalents	$109,816,332	$ 1,590,869	$11,036,503
Accounts Receivable (Net)	3,629,929	262,012	133,738
Due From Other Governments	1,309,588	—	60,698
Inventories	330,727	66,329	—
Prepaid Items	—	4,774	—
Total Current Assets	115,086,576	1,923,984	11,230,939
Non-Current Assets:			
Restricted:			
Cash and Cash Equivalents	14,947,591	—	3,969,351
Investments	29,524,326	—	2,295,015
Loans to Other Funds	—	—	—
Capital Assets			
Land	27,523,515	9,214,762	13,004,855
Buildings	156,585,188	77,444,910	59,413,069
Improvements Other Than Buildings	94,388,395	30,098,216	3,497,489
Equipment	104,215,619	5,461,245	1,839,280
Vehicles	—	—	—
Wastewater and Stormwater Lines and			
Pump Stations	202,756,142	—	—
Less Accumulated Depreciation	(273,080,495)	(48,118,602)	(29,544,088)
Construction in Process	30,297,030	—	—
Unamortized Bond Costs	752,680	—	216,073
Total Non-Current Assets	387,909,991	74,100,531	54,691,044
Total Assets	502,996,567	76,024,515	65,921,983
Liabilities			
Current Liabilities:			
Accounts Payable	5,196,419	413,487	470,116
Accrued Liabilities	243,902	102,536	65,546
Accrued Interest Payable	3,207,670	—	474,242
Compensated Absences	123,344	35,792	23,489
Advance Payments	13,186,090	625,514	88,118
Current Portion of Loans Payable	—	1,157,343	331,248
Current Portion of Bonds Payable	7,985,000	—	1,290,000
Total Current Liabilities	29,942,425	2,334,672	2,742,759
Non-Current Liabilities:			
Compensated Absences	1,418,453	411,610	270,122
Arbitrage Rebate Payable	—	—	—
Loans from Other Funds	—	10,716,777	6,658,774
Loans Due After One Year	—	—	—
Bonds Payable After One Year	152,800,240	—	18,632,981
Claims Liabilities	—	—	—
Total Non-Current Liabilities	154,218,693	11,128,387	25,561,877
Total Liabilities	184,161,118	13,463,059	28,304,636
Net Assets			
Invested in Capital Assets, net of related debt	200,161,330	62,226,411	23,808,690
Restricted:			
Debt Service	12,000,000	—	—
Capital Projects	41,570,562	—	—
Renewal and Replacement	883,541	—	2,205,108
Unrestricted	64,220,016	335,045	11,603,549
Total Net Assets	$318,835,449	$62,561,456	$37,617,347

Adjustment to reflect the consolidation of internal service fund activities related to enterprise funds.

Net assets of business-type activities

Stormwater Utility	Solid Waste Management	Total	Governmental Activities Internal Service Funds
$13,435,543	$4,496,416	$140,375,663	$ 47,799,756
44,959	1,258,702	5,329,340	93,151
—	400	1,370,686	—
—	—	397,056	566,643
—	1,000	5,774	—
13,480,502	5,756,518	147,478,519	48,459,550
—	—	18,916,942	—
—	—	31,819,341	7,498,978
—	—	—	117,571,502
654,404	71,165	50,468,701	555,767
—	1,402,289	294,845,456	7,760,098
—	426,850	128,410,950	245,762
222,611	1,155,618	112,894,373	800,467
—	—	—	55,404,202
71,739,296	—	274,495,438	—
(28,107,713)	(1,995,427)	(380,846,325)	(38,478,225)
1,726,225	—	32,023,255	—
—	—	968,753	413,175
46,234,823	1,060,495	563,996,884	151,771,726
59,715,325	6,817,013	711,475,403	200,231,276
354,354	366,123	6,800,499	3,032,153
15,831	88,235	516,050	135,151
—	—	3,681,912	2,031,086
6,389	49,269	238,283	47,476
—	—	13,899,722	—
—	—	1,488,591	660,373
—	—	9,275,000	3,950,000
376,574	503,627	35,900,057	9,856,239
73,469	566,594	2,740,248	545,973
—	—		82,166
—	—	17,375,551	706,599
—	—		37,735,459
—	—	171,433,221	85,709,563
—	—	—	29,423,160
73,469	566,594	191,549,020	154,202,920
450,043	1,070,221	227,449,077	164,059,159
46,234,823	1,060,495	333,491,749	24,921,099
—	—	12,000,000	—
—	—	41,570,562	—
—	—	3,088,649	—
13,030,459	4,686,297	93,875,366	11,251,018
$59,265,282	$5,746,792	$484,026,326	$ 36,172,117
		316,530	
		$484,342,856	

TABLE 3-8
Proprietary Funds Statement of Revenues, Expenses, and Changes in Fund Net Assets

City of Orlando, Florida
Statement of Revenues, Expenses, and Changes in Fund Net Assets
Proprietary Funds
For the Year Ended September 30, 2001

	Business-type Activities Enterprise Funds		
	Wastewater System	Orlando Centroplex	Parking System
Operating Revenues			
User Charges	$ 37,829,255	$11,724,586	$ 2,756,711
Fees	338,929	3,721,004	5,326,116
Parking Fines	—	—	1,667,969
Other	220,278	420,673	121,488
Total Operating Revenues	38,388,462	15,866,263	9,872,284
Operating Expenses			
Salaries, Wages and Employee Benefits	10,476,288	4,429,511	2,750,342
Contractual Services, Materials and Supplies	19,199,716	10,774,796	3,876,467
Depreciation Expense	20,232,764	3,687,016	2,654,679
Insurance and Other Expenses	2,253,994	557,153	648,949
Total Operating Expenses	52,162,762	19,448,476	9,930,437
Operating Income (Loss)	(13,774,300)	(3,582,213)	(58,153)
Non-Operating Revenues (Expenses)			
Income on Investments	12,112,573	216,081	1,324,698
Impact Fees	8,874,636	—	—
Interest Expense	(8,626,511)	(546,217)	(1,315,155)
Gain (Loss) on Sale of Fixed Assets	(6,761)	(1,347)	(7,510)
Total Non-Operating Revenues (Expenses)	12,353,937	(331,483)	2,033
Income (Loss) Before Contributions and Transfers	(1,420,363)	(3,913,696)	(56,120)
Capital Contributions	367,941	—	—
Transfers In	894,837	1,627,847	2,162,925
Transfers (Out)	(2,232,745)	(15,000)	(1,509,093)
	(969,967)	1,612,847	653,832
Changes in Net Assets	(2,390,330)	(2,300,849)	597,712
Net Assets—Beginning	321,225,779	64,862,305	37,019,635
Net Assets—Ending	$318,835,449	$62,561,456	$37,617,347

Adjustment to reflect the consolidation of internal service fund activities related to enterprise funds.

Change in net assets of business-type activities

Stormwater Utility	Solid Waste Management	Total	Governmental Activities Internal Service Funds
$10,297,494	$15,029,345	$77,637,391	$35,902,406
—	147,163	9,533,212	—
—	—	1,667,969	—
6,681	60,289	829,409	896,964
10,304,175	15,236,797	89,667,981	36,799,370
512,949	5,162,940	23,332,030	5,222,261
5,796,530	9,954,512	49,602,021	7,754,524
1,841,813	189,949	28,606,221	5,491,320
246,891	413,516	4,120,503	12,727,739
8,398,183	15,720,917	105,660,775	31,195,844
1,905,992	(484,120)	(15,992,794)	5,603,526
1,555,361	398,026	15,606,739	3,935,633
—	—	8,874,636	—
—	—	(10,487,883)	(6,194,926)
(737)	(2,681)	(19,036)	642,344
1,554,624	395,345	13,974,456	(1,616,949)
3,460,616	(88,775)	(2,018,338)	3,986,577
1,590,451	—	1,958,392	6,350
177,649	210,396	5,073,654	2,432,794
(3,131,365)	(8,656)	(6,896,859)	(882,310)
(1,363,265)	201,740	135,187	1,556,834
2,097,351	112,965	(1,883,153)	5,543,411
57,167,931	5,633,827		30,628,706
$59,265,282	$ 5,746,792		$36,172,117
		316,530	
		$(1,566,621)	

WHAT ARE NOTES AND REQUIRED SUPPLEMENTARY INFORMATION?

As with business financial statements, notes are considered an integral part of the basic financial statements of governments. Voluminous though they may be, notes are too important to be ignored. Per Statement No. 34 and consistent with existing standards, notes should include explanations of the accounting principles used in preparing the financial statements, schedules of changes in capital assets and long-term liabilities, schedules of future debt service requirements, disclosures about contingent liabilities, and other information that might affect users' interpretation of the amounts reported in the statements themselves.

Required supplementary information (RSI) is information that the GASB requires to be presented with, but not as part of, the basic financial statements. It includes the **management's discussion and analysis (MD&A),** which is presented before the basic financial statements, as well as information such as budgetary comparisons and pension schedules, which is presented after the notes. RSI has much in common with notes. Both include GASB-mandated schedules and data. However, whereas notes are considered part of the basic financial statements, RSI is not. Therefore, RSI may be subject to a lower level of auditor scrutiny than notes.

As discussed in Chapter 1, demonstrating compliance with the legally adopted budget is a primary objective of government financial reporting. Accordingly, Statement No. 34 requires that governments include in their annual reports, as RSI, a comparison of actual results with the budget for the general fund and for each special revenue fund for which an annual budget has been adopted.

The GASB specifies the *accounting* principles (GAAP) to which governments must adhere in their external financial reports. It does not have the authority to establish *budgetary* principles, which often differ from GAAP. A comparison between the budget and actual results would not be meaningful unless the two sets of information were calculated using the same principles. Therefore, per Statement No. 34, the GASB requires that governments present their budget versus actual comparisons on a *budgetary* basis and include a schedule that reconciles the actual amounts per the budgetary comparison with the GAAP amounts per the financial statements.

Budget-to-actual comparisons may demonstrate either legal compliance or managerial effectiveness in adhering to budget estimates. One of the major improvements introduced by Statement No. 34 is that it requires governments to present *both* their original and their final appropriated budgets, so that readers can compare the actual results with both budgets. Prior to Statement No. 34, governments could report only their final (amended) budgets. For some governments, their final budgets incorporate changes they authorized only after they were aware of the actual revenues and expenditures of the year. Thus, governments typically reported no significant variance between budgeted and actual amounts.

Table 3–9 shows Orlando's budget-to-actual comparison for its general fund. The column reporting the variances between actual results and the final budget is encouraged but is not required by GASB standards. Governments may also present a column with variances from the original budget.

TABLE 3–9
General Fund Budgetary Comparison Schedule

City of Orlando, Florida
Budgetary Comparison Schedule
General Fund
For the Year Ended September 30, 2001

| | Budgeted Amounts | | Actual Amounts | Variance with Final Budget Positive |
	Original	Final	(Budgetary Basis)	(Negative)
Resources (inflows):				
Property Taxes	$ 66,911,382	$ 66,911,382	$ 68,984,150	$2,072,768
Intergovernmental:				
Orlando Utilities Commission Contribution	25,200,000	31,700,000	32,091,000	391,000
State Sales Tax	25,462,050	25,462,050	25,117,291	(344,759)
Other Intergovernmental	13,425,543	15,522,807	15,644,787	121,980
Occupational Licenses and Franchise Fees	23,083,089	24,483,089	25,834,029	1,350,940
Other Licenses, Permits and Fees	28,667,726	28,852,699	26,242,387	(2,610,312)
Fines and Forfeitures	2,226,400	2,226,400	2,407,844	181,444
Income on Investments	3,471,595	5,159,170	7,366,440	2,207,270
Special Assessments	25,000	25,000	227,691	202,691
Other	5,362,537	5,790,388	7,116,402	1,326,014
Bond and Loan Proceeds	—	190,064	190,064	—
Transfers from Other Funds	31,672,629	32,069,045	32,540,531	471,486
Amounts Available for Appropriation	225,507,951	238,392,094	243,762,616	5,370,522
Charges to appropriations (outflows)				
General Administration	15,808,458	16,319,253	15,252,047	1,067,206
Administrative Services	21,342,778	21,370,607	20,806,493	564,114
Planning and Development	4,650,838	4,934,344	4,793,605	140,739
Public Works	28,974,131	29,429,774	27,375,622	2,054,152
Community and Youth Services	11,181,460	11,704,745	11,078,064	626,681
Police	70,597,888	73,744,580	71,986,491	1,758,089
Fire	35,792,238	35,834,251	35,357,720	476,531
Nondepartmental:				
Miscellaneous	22,552,027	22,552,027	25,150,549	(2,598,522)
Debt Service	5,359,693	5,359,693	5,488,245	(128,552)
Transfers to other funds	13,709,094	23,209,094	23,211,423	(2,329)
Total Charges to Appropriations	229,968,605	244,458,368	240,500,259	3,958,109
Excess (Deficiency) of Resources Over Charges to Appropriations	(4,460,654)	(6,066,274)	3,262,357	9,328,631
Fund Balance Allocation	4,460,654	6,066,274	—	(6,066,274)
Excess (Deficiency) of Resources Over Charges to Appropriations	$ —0—	$ —0—	$ 3,262,357	$3,262,357

Explanation of Differences between Budgetary Inflows and Outflows and GAAP Revenues and Expenditures

Sources/inflows of resources

Actual amounts (budgetary basis) "available for appropriation" from the budgetary comparison schedule	$243,762,616
Differences—budget to GAAP:	
Securities lending income is not budgeted as a source of resources.	4,580,683
Bond and loan proceeds are inflows of budgetary resources but are not revenues for financial reporting purposes.	(190,064)
Transfers from other funds are inflows of budgetary resources but are not revenues for financial reporting purposes.	(32,540,531)
Total revenues as reported on the statement of revenues, expenditures, and changes in fund balances—governmental funds.	$215,612,704

Uses/outflows of resources

Actual amounts (budgetary basis) "total charges to appropriations" from the budgetary comparison schedule	$240,500,259
Differences—budget to GAAP:	
Securities lending expenditures are not budgeted as a use of resources.	4,341,897
Encumbrances for supplies and equipment ordered but not received are reported in the year the order is placed for budgetary purposes, but in the year the supplies are received for financial reporting purposes.	(818,546)
Transfers to other funds are outflows of budgetary resources but are not expenditures for financial reporting purposes.	(23,211,423)
Total expenditures as reported on the statement of revenues, expenditures, and changes in fund balances—governmental funds.	$220,812,187

WHAT ADDITIONAL INFORMATION DO GOVERNMENTS TYPICALLY REPORT?

In addition to the basic financial statements and RSI, many governments include in their CAFRs **combining statements** for the nonmajor funds—that is, financial statements that present each of the nonmajor funds in a separate column. Governments also provide statistical information relating to trends in revenues and expenditures, population, employment, and property values. This expanded approach to reporting helps users better assess the government's financial position and its economic condition—its ongoing ability to provide services and meet its obligations—by providing information that will have a direct bearing on both the demand for the government's services and the government's ability to finance them. The statistical information that governments typically include in their financial reports is discussed in Chapters 11 and 14.

QUESTIONS FOR REVIEW AND DISCUSSION

1. Distinguish between a financial statement that *combines* funds with one that *consolidates* them.

2. What is the rationale of the GASB for requiring *two* sets of financial statements, each with a different measurement focus and basis of accounting for governmental activities?

3. How many government-wide statements are required? What are they?

4. In what key ways does the format of the government-wide statement of activities differ from that of a traditional income statement?

5. What are the three categories of fund statements?

6. What is the purpose of a reserve for encumbrances? When do governments add to the reserve? When do they subtract from it?

7. What are internal service funds? Why are they classified differently in government-wide than in fund statements?

8. What are major funds? In what key ways are major funds reported differently than nonmajor funds?

9. What are fiduciary funds? Why are they not reported in the government-wide statements?

10. How does required supplementary information differ from notes to the financial statements?

11. What is the advantage of basing budgetary comparisons on the original budget, as opposed to the amended budget? What is the advantage of basing budgetary comparisons on the amended budget?

EXERCISES AND PROBLEMS

3–1

Select the best answer.

1. Which of the following best describes government-wide statements?

   a. combined on a full accrual basis

   b. combined on a modified accrual basis

   c. consolidated on a full accrual basis

   d. consolidated on a modified accrual basis

2. How many government-wide statements is a major city, such as New York, required to prepare?

   a. two

   b. three

   c. four

   d. six

3. The net assets section of a government-wide statement of net assets would typically not

have a separate category to show amounts invested in

a. capital assets

b. unrestricted assets

c. restricted assets

d. current assets

4. Which of the following funds would not be incorporated into the government-wide statements?

a. enterprise funds

b. permanent funds

c. internal service funds

d. fiduciary funds

5. Which of the following funds is least likely to be separately reported in the governmental funds balance sheet?

a. a general fund

b. a nonmajor special revenue fund

c. a major capital projects fund

d. a major permanent fund

6. Which of the following items is least likely to be reported on Midlake County's governmental funds balance sheet?

a. the county courthouse

b. amounts due to the internal service fund

c. a reserve for encumbrances

d. amounts invested in federal securities

7. A reserve for encumbrances is generally decreased when goods are

a. ordered

b. received

c. paid for

d. used

8. The year-end balance of a reserve for inventory is generally equal to the

a. market value of inventory on hand

b. cost of inventory on hand

c. amount of inventory on order

d. amount of inventory purchased but not yet paid for

9. Which of the following would not be shown as a revenue of the function "public safety" on Millburg Township's government-wide statement of activities?

a. a grant from the federal government to acquire radar equipment

b. amounts charged to local funeral homes to provide police escorts

c. an appropriation from the town council to pay police officers

d. fees charged to the surrounding county to provide services outside of township limits

10. Which of the following would be most likely to be reported among restricted net assets on a city's government-wide statement of net assets?

a. the balance in the city's debt service fund

b. the amount owed to city employees for services rendered since they received their last paychecks

c. the actuarial liability of the city's pension fund

d. the cost, less accumulated depreciation, of the city's highway system

3–2

Select the best answer.

1. Internal service funds are reported as

a. business-type activities in government-wide statements and governmental funds in fund statements

b. proprietary funds in fund statements and governmental activities in government-wide statements

c. business-type activities in government-wide statements and proprietary funds in fund statements

d. governmental funds in fund statements and governmental activities in government-wide statements

2. In which of the following statements would depreciation *not* be reported?

a. internal service fund statement of revenues, expenses, and changes in fund net assets

b. government-wide statement of activities

c. capital projects fund statement of revenues, expenditures, and changes in fund balance

d. enterprise fund statement of revenues, expenses, and changes in fund net assets

3. Which of the following is "required supplementary information"?

a. explanation of accounting principles used in preparing the financial statements

b. schedule of changes in capital assets

c. budgetary comparison

d. ten-year trend of assessed property values

4. Which of the following is not required to be incorporated into the budgetary comparison?

   a. expenditures per the originally adopted budget

   b. expenditures per the amended budget

   c. actual expenditures

   d. variance between the actual expenditures and those per the amended budget

5. The management's discussion and analysis (MD&A) is most likely to include information on

   a. service efforts and accomplishments

   b. market values of government-owned capital assets

   c. the condition of infrastructure assets

   d. financial performance during the period covered by the financial statements

6. Which of the following is not one of the three main categories of funds?

   a. governmental funds

   b. permanent funds

   c. proprietary funds

   d. fiduciary funds

7. "Major" funds include

   a. all governmental funds plus proprietary funds that have fund balances greater than 10 percent of those of all proprietary funds combined

   b. the general fund, special revenue funds, capital projects funds, and debt service funds

   c. the general fund plus all funds that have assets greater that 50 percent of those of the general fund

   d. the general fund plus other funds in which total assets, revenues, or expenditures/expenses of the fund are at least 10 percent of the corresponding total for the relevant fund category (governmental or enterprise) and also at least 5 percent of the corresponding total for all governmental and enterprise funds combined

8. The assets and liabilities of nonmajor governmental funds would be

   a. aggregated and reported in the governmental funds balance sheet in a single column

   b. excluded from the government-wide statement of net assets

   c. shown only in notes to the financial statements

   d. reported as required supplementary information

9. Which of the following would *not* be reported on a government-wide statement of activities?

   a. a transfer of cash from the general fund to a debt service fund

   b. costs incurred by the recreation department for electricity purchased from the city-owned electric utility

   c. depreciation on traffic lights

   d. interest on bonds issued by the electric utility department

10. Which of the following is *not* required to be included in a government's basic financial statements or required supplementary information?

   a. a reconciliation between proprietary fund financial statements and the business-type activities column of the government-wide financial statements

   b. a reconciliation between governmental fund financial statements and the governmental activities column of the government-wide financial statements

   c. a reconciliation between revenues reported on the basis of GAAP and those reported on a budgetary basis

   d. a comparison between actual expenditures and expenditures per the amended budget

3–3

Even at this early stage of the course it is possible to reconstruct journal entries from a balance sheet.

The Sherill Utility District was recently established. Here is its balance sheet, after one year.

Sherill Utility District Balance Sheet as of End of Year 1 (in millions)				
	General Fund	**Capital Projects Fund**	**Debt Service Fund**	**Totals**
Assets:				
Cash	$30			$ 30
Investments	___	$90	$20	110
Total Assets	$30	$90	$20	$140
Liabilities and Fund Balances:				
Fund Balances	$30	$90	$20	$140

Note the following additional information:

   a. The general fund received all of its revenue, $150 million, from taxes (all collected). It had operating expenditures, excluding transfers to other funds, of $100 million (all paid for).

b. The general fund transferred $20 million to the debt service fund. Of this, $15 million was to repay the principal on bonds outstanding; $5 million was for interest.

c. The district issued $130 million in bonds to finance construction of plant and equipment. Of this, it expended $40 million.

1. Prepare journal entries to summarize these activities in the appropriate funds. You need not make closing entries. Do not be concerned as to the specific titles of accounts to be debited or credited (e.g., whether a transfer from one fund to another should be called a "transfer," an "expense" or an "expenditure," or whether proceeds from bonds should be called "bond proceeds" or "revenues.")

2. Comment on how the district's government-wide (full accrual) statement of net assets would differ from the balance sheet presented.

3–4

Funds can be consolidated, but only at the risk of lost or misleading information.

The balance sheet below was adapted from the financial statements of the Williamsburg Regional Sewage Treatment Authority (dates have been changed).

Williamsburg Regional Sewage Treatment Authority
Balance Sheet
October 31, 2003

	General Fund	Capital Projects Fund
Assets:		
Cash	$ 751	$ 5,021
Time Deposits		16,398
Due on Insurance Claim	9,499	
Due from General Fund		9,000
Due from Participants	66,475	4,414
Total Assets	$76,725	$34,833
Liabilities and Fund Balance:		
Accounts Payable	$17,725	
Due to Capital Projects Fund	9,000	
	26,725	
Fund Balance	50,000	34,833
Total Liabilities and Fund Balance	$76,725	$34,833

The transactions of the authority are accounted for in the following governmental fund types:

- *General fund*—To account for all revenues and expenditures not required to be accounted for in other funds.

- *Capital projects fund*—To account for financial resources designated to construct or acquire capital facilities and improvements. Such resources are derived principally from other municipal utility districts to which the Williamsburg Regional Sewage Treatment Authority provides certain services.

1. Recast the balance sheets of the two funds into a single *consolidated* balance sheet. Show separately, however, the restricted and the unrestricted portions of the consolidated fund balance account (not each individual asset and liability). Be sure to eliminate interfund payables and receivables.

2. Which presentation, the unconsolidated or the consolidated, provides more complete information? Explain. Which presentation might be seen as misleading? Why? What, if any, advantages do you see to the presentation that is less complete and more misleading?

3–5 bonus pt. Net Assets

Consolidated balances are not substitutes for individual fund balance sheets.

The combined governmental fund balance sheet of the town of Paris is presented on next page.

Per schedules included in the notes to the financial statements, the town had $1,450 of capital assets (net of accumulated depreciation) and $1,315 in long-term liabilities associated with the capital assets.

1. Recast the balance sheets in the form of a single consolidated, full accrual balance sheet.

2. Put yourself in the place of an analyst. The town mayor presents you with the consolidated balance sheet. He asserts that the town's financial position is excellent, as measured by the exceedingly "healthy" fund balance. Based on your having seen the combined balance sheet that shows the individual fund types, why might you be skeptical of his claim?

3. Comment on why a consolidated balance sheet is no substitute for a combined balance sheet that reports on major funds.

	General Fund	Special Revenue Fund	Capital Projects Fund	Debt Service Fund	Permanent (Endowment) Fund	Totals
	**Town of Paris**					

	General Fund	Special Revenue Fund	Capital Projects Fund	Debt Service Fund	Permanent (Endowment) Fund	Totals
Assets:						
Cash	$ 38	$ 20	$ 35	$340	$ 10	$ 443
Investments	105	60	480	136	960	1,741
Due from Other Funds	—	120	46	39	—	205
Total Assets	$143	$200	$561	$515	$970	$2,389
Liabilities and Fund Balances:						
Accounts Payable	$ 8	–	–	–	–	$ 8
Due to Other Funds	205	–	–	–	–	205
Fund Balances	(70)	$200	$561	$515	$970	2,176
Total Liabilities and Fund Balances	$143	$200	$561	$515	$970	$2,389

3–6

Exploring Orlando's financial report

Refer to the financial statements of the City of Orlando that are included in this chapter.

1. Per the government-wide statement of activities, how much did the city incur in expense for police? Of this amount, how much had to be covered from general tax and other unrestricted revenues?

2. Per the governmental funds statement of revenues, expenditures, and changes in fund balances, how much did the city incur in expenditures for police? How do you account for the difference between this amount and your response to question 1?

3. Per the government-wide statement of activities, what was the ending balance in net assets associated with governmental activities? Is this consistent with the government-wide statement of net assets?

4. How much was transferred (net) from business-type to governmental activities during the year?

5. How much in taxes did the city direct to the support of business-type activities?

6. As noted in the text, government-wide statements are on a full accrual basis and therefore the statement of activities includes charges for depreciation. Orlando's government-wide statement of activities reports $1.8 million of unallocated depreciation (i.e., not allocated to specific functions or programs) for governmental activities. How much depreciation did Orlando allocate to specific functions or programs of governmental activities? How can you tell?

7. Orlando's statements include a schedule (Table 3–6) that reconciles its statement of revenues, expenditures, and changes in fund balances of governmental funds to the statement of activities, governmental activities. However, it does not include a corresponding reconciliation of the statement of revenues, expenses, and changes in fund net assets of proprietary funds to the statement of activities, business-type activities. Why not?

3–7

Exploring Orlando's financial report

Refer to the financial statements of the City of Orlando that are included in this chapter.

1. How much of the city's governmental activities assets are classified as capital? How much of the city's governmental activities liabilities were used to finance those capital assets?

2. How much of the city's net assets associated with governmental activities are restricted for capital projects? What is the combined fund balance of the city's capital projects funds (per the governmental funds balance sheet)? How do you account for the difference between these two amounts?

3. In the city's governmental funds balance sheet, some funds are reported in separate columns, whereas others are combined into a single column captioned "other governmental funds." How do you think the city determined which funds to report in a separate column and which to aggregate with other funds?

4. How much did the city report as the total actual amount available for appropriation in the gen-

eral fund per the budgetary comparison? How much did it report as revenues of the general fund per the statement of revenues, expenditures, and changes in fund balances? What item is the principal cause of the difference?

5. What are the main types of transactions, and in what amounts, that account for the differences between the change in fund balances of governmental funds, per the statement of revenues, expenditures, and changes in fund balances, and the change in net assets of governmental activities, per the government-wide statement of activities?

6. Over 60 percent of the total amount of capital assets reported in the government-wide statement of net assets are devoted to business-type activities. What is the most likely explanation as to why the proportion of capital assets directed to business-type activities is greater than that devoted to governmental activities?

CHAPTER 4

Governmental Activities— Recognizing Revenues

In Chapter 3 we discussed the basic financial statements and other minimum financial reporting requirements for governments. In this chapter and the next six chapters, we examine the principal transactions that underlie the basic financial statements.

This chapter and Chapter 5 address what are probably the most difficult issues in accounting for governmental activities (those supported primarily by taxes and intergovernmental revenues):

- When should revenues and expenditures be recognized in the governmental funds and in the government-wide statement of activities (governmental activities column) and
- How should the related assets and liabilities be measured?

Most of the fund-accounting examples in these two chapters will implicitly be directed toward the general fund. However, the discussion also applies to the other governmental funds (special revenue, capital projects, debt service, and permanent funds). In Chapter 9 we examine similar issues for business-type activities and the proprietary funds used to record their transactions.

WHY AND HOW DO GOVERNMENTS USE THE MODIFIED ACCRUAL BASIS OF ACCOUNTING?

RATIONALE FOR THE MODIFIED ACCRUAL BASIS As discussed in Chapter 3, GASB Statement No. 34 requires two sets of financial statements to meet two key but potentially conflicting objectives of financial reporting:

- Providing information about interperiod equity (i.e., whether an entity's current-year revenues were sufficient to pay for its current-year services)
- Demonstrating whether the entity obtained and used its resources in accordance with its legally adopted budget

The government-wide statements are consolidated and use the full **accrual basis** of accounting, thereby demonstrating whether current-year revenues were sufficient to pay for current-year services. The fund statements, by contrast, present governmental funds—whose activities are generally governed by a legally adopted budget—on a modified accrual basis, thereby facilitating budgetary comparisons.

The **modified accrual basis** is far more budget oriented than the full accrual basis in that the budgets of most governments focus on either cash or cash plus selected short-term financial resources. The budgetary measurement focus of governments is determined by applicable state or local laws. Except for governments that elect or are required to budget on a modified accrual basis as defined by GAAP, the revenue and expenditure principles that underlie their governmental fund statements may differ from those of their legally adopted budgets. Hence, as discussed in Chapter 3, the budgetary comparisons (budget versus actual amounts) that governments are required to present with their financial statements must include a reconciliation and explanations of differences between the budgetary and the GAAP basis. In developing Statement No. 34, the GASB opted to retain the modified accrual basis (with some refinements) from its previous reporting standards, rather than to require the government's budgetary basis for governmental fund financial statements. This approach assures that all governments present those statements on the same basis. It thereby facilitates comparisons among entities, which would be difficult if each entity reported on its own particular budgetary basis.

RELATIONSHIP BETWEEN MEASUREMENT FOCUS AND BASIS OF ACCOUNTING

The criteria an entity uses to determine when to recognize revenues and expenditures stem from its measurement focus and basis of accounting. As pointed out in Chapter 2, **measurement focus** refers to *what* is being reported upon—which assets and liabilities are being measured. **Basis of accounting** refers to *when* transactions and other events are recognized. The two concepts obviously are closely linked. If an entity opts to focus on cash, then it will necessarily adopt a **cash basis** of accounting. Correspondingly, if it elects to focus on *all economic resources* (both current and long-term assets and liabilities), then it will adopt a *full accrual basis of accounting*.

Many versions of modified accrual accounting are possible, each of which lies somewhere on a continuum between cash and full accrual accounting. Statement No. 34 requires a particular version of modified accrual accounting for compliance with GAAP. A government's budgetary basis may lie elsewhere on the continuum. Therefore, the fact that a government budgets on a "modified accrual" basis does not necessarily mean that it budgets on a GAAP basis.

OVERVIEW OF THE MODIFIED ACCRUAL BASIS Statement No. 34 reaffirms that governmental funds should be accounted for on a modified accrual basis, with a measurement focus on current financial resources. **Current financial resources** has been made operational as encompassing *expendable financial resources*—cash and other items that can be expected to be transformed into cash in the normal course of operations. The "other items" include investments and receivables but *not* capital assets.

As noted in Chapter 3 (see Table 3–3) and discussed in Chapter 5, inventories and prepaid items (e.g., insurance) are also reported on governmental fund balance sheets, even though they are not, strictly speaking, financial resources. However, although these assets will not ordinarily be transformed into cash (e.g., inventories will be consumed, not sold for cash), they generally will result in short-term cash savings because the entity will not have to expend additional cash to acquire them.

A government's current claims against financial resources include wages and salaries payable, accounts payable, and deferred revenues (e.g., property taxes collected in advance of the period they are intended to finance). Current claims exclude long-term obligations such as the noncurrent portions of bonds payable and of liabilities for compensated absences. Consistent with conventional relationships between balance sheet and operating statement accounts, governmental fund revenues and expenditures include only those amounts that result in increases or decreases in net *current financial* resources (as opposed to all increases or decreases in net *economic* resources, as would be true under the full accrual basis).

WHAT TRIGGERS REVENUE RECOGNITION FOR NONEXCHANGE VERSUS EXCHANGE TRANSACTIONS?

A thorny issue, under both the modified accrual and the full accrual basis of accounting, is *when* revenues should be recognized. What key economic event in the revenue generation process should trigger the recognition of revenue and the corresponding increase in net assets?

The revenue-recognition issues facing governments are more difficult to resolve than those of businesses. Businesses derive their revenues mainly from **exchange transactions**—those in which each party gives and receives consideration of equivalent value. The occurrence of an economic exchange is the foundation of revenue recognition for businesses and, by extension, for the business-type activities of governments. However, the governmental activities derive their revenues mainly from **nonexchange transactions**—those, such as property-taxes and most intergovernmental grants, in which one party gives or receives value without directly receiving or giving equivalent value in exchange. When there is no exchange, it is more difficult to determine when revenue should be recognized.

STATEMENT NO. 33 GASB Statement No. 33, *Accounting and Financial Reporting for Nonexchange Transactions* (1998), governs the recognition of nonexchange revenues on both the modified accrual basis (in the governmental fund financial statements) and the full accrual basis (in the government-wide statements and the statements of proprietary and fiduciary funds). The recognition requirements are the same for both bases, except that, when the modified accrual basis is used, revenues are subject to an additional, extremely significant, stipulation. They cannot be recognized until they are both *measurable and available to finance expenditures of the fiscal period*. The need for revenue to be "measurable" should be intuitive. For example, if a local government does not know and cannot reasonably estimate the amount of sales taxes it is entitled to receive from the state government, it cannot recognize an amount for sales tax revenue in the financial statements. But what does "available to finance expenditures of the fiscal period" mean?

MEANING OF, AND RATIONALE FOR, "AVAILABLE TO FINANCE EXPENDITURES OF THE FISCAL PERIOD" The nonexchange revenues of governments are intrinsically associated with expenditures; they are generated solely to meet expenditures. Budgets are formulated so that each period's estimated revenues are sufficient to cover appropriated expenditures (those authorized by the legislative body for that period). Expenditures of a fiscal period may either require cash outlays during the period or create liabilities that have to be satisfied shortly after the end of the period. For example, goods or services that a government receives toward the end of one year would ordinarily not have to be paid for until early the next year. **Available**, therefore, means "collected within the current period or expected to be collected soon enough thereafter to be used to pay liabilities of the current period."[1]

The liabilities referred to are only *current liabilities*. Recall that long-term liabilities are outside of the measurement focus of governmental funds and hence are not recorded by them. As discussed in the next chapter, under the modified accrual basis, transactions that result in long-term liabilities are not recorded as expenditures of governmental funds.

How many days after the close of the year must revenues be received to satisfy the criteria of having been received "soon enough" to pay the liabilities of the current period? With respect to *property taxes only*, existing standards provide that, except in unusual circumstances, revenues should be recognized only if cash is expected to be collected within sixty days of year-end.[2]

Because existing standards provide no specific guidance as to time periods for the recognition of other revenues, this *sixty-day rule* has become widely used to define *available* for all types of revenues, not just property taxes. However, many governments have established other time periods, such as thirty days, ninety days, or even one year for revenues other than property taxes. The period used to define *available* must be disclosed in the notes to the financial statements.[3]

WHAT ARE THE MAIN TYPES OF NONEXCHANGE REVENUES?

Statement No. 33 divides nonexchange revenues into four classes:

1. **Imposed nonexchange revenues.** These are assessments imposed on individuals and business entities—mainly property taxes and fines.

2. **Derived tax revenues.** These are taxes derived (i.e., that result) from assessments on exchange transactions of taxpayers. They include sales taxes (derived from sales transactions), and income and other taxes on earnings or assets (derived from various income-producing commercial transactions).

3. **Government-mandated nonexchange transactions.** These occur when a government at one level provides resources to a government at another level and requires the recipient to use the resources for a specific purpose. For example, a state may grant funds to a county stipulating that the resources be used for road improvements. Acceptance and use of the resources are mandatory.

4. **Voluntary nonexchange transactions.** These result from legislative or contractual agreements entered into willingly by two or more parties. They include grants given by one government to another and contributions from individuals (e.g., gifts to public universities). Often, the provider imposes restrictions on the use of the funds. Unlike government-mandated nonexchange transactions, the recipient government is not required to accept the awards, but if it does, it must observe the accompanying spending restrictions.

Statement No. 33 establishes standards for each class of transactions. The standards for government-mandated and voluntary nonexchange transactions apply to both

---

[1]GASB Statement No. 33, *Accounting and Reporting for Nonexchange Transactions*, footnote 16.

[2]GASB Interpretation No. 5, *Property Tax Revenue Recognition in Governmental Funds*.

[3]GASB Statement No. 38, *Certain Financial Statement Note Disclosures*, para. 7.

revenues and expenditures. Thus payments from one government to another should be accounted for using the same criteria.

Statement No. 33 also identifies two types of limitations that constrain when or how a government may use the resources it receives in nonexchange transactions:

1. *Time requirements.* These *specify the period* in which resources must be used or when use may begin. For example, local governments typically levy property taxes to finance a particular fiscal year. Similarly, state governments may require that their grants to local school districts be used during the state's fiscal year.

2. *Purpose restrictions.* These *specify the purpose* for which the resources must be used. For example, states may require that sales taxes be used for road improvements. Property taxes may be reserved for the payment of debt. Certain grants or private donations may be restricted by the donor or grantor to finance specific acquisitions or services.

According to Statement No. 33, governments should *not* recognize revenue, expenditures, or expenses for nonexchange transactions until time requirements have been met (e.g., the start of the specific period in which resources may or must be used). By contrast, the existence of purpose restrictions does *not* justify a deferral of revenue recognition. Revenue should be recognized but governments must specifically identify the resources that are subject to purpose restrictions by reporting a reservation of fund balance in their governmental fund financial statements and restricted net assets in their government-wide statements. The requirement to report a reservation and restriction continues in force until the related amounts are spent for the specified purpose.

How Should Property Taxes and Other Imposed Nonexchange Revenues Be Accounted For?

FUNDAMENTALS OF PROPERTY TAXES Property taxes are the bread and butter of local governments. Although increasingly being supplemented by other taxes and fees, they still account for more than one-fourth of local government revenues.

Classified as *ad valorem taxes* (based on value), property taxes are most typically levied against real property (land and buildings). However, many jurisdictions also include personal property, such as automobiles, boats, business inventories, and intangible assets (such as securities and bank deposits), within the tax base.

Property taxes are levied against the **assessed value** of taxable assets. Most jurisdictions are required to assess property at 100 percent of its *appraised* fair market value. Many, however, assess property at a fraction of its appraised value (perhaps in the hope of discouraging taxpayer protests) and then adjust the tax rate upward to offset the reduction in the tax base.

Most governments establish the property tax rate by dividing the amount of revenue needed from property taxes by the assessed value of the property subject to tax. For example, if a government needs $400 million in property tax revenue and its jurisdiction has $22 billion in taxable property, then the property tax rate would be $400 million divided by $22 billion—1.818 percent, or 18.18 *mils* (dollars per thousand).

In reality the computation is somewhat more complex, as allowances have to be made for discounts, exemptions, and taxes that will be delinquent or uncollectible. Most jurisdictions experience a low rate of bad debts on property taxes, since they are able to impose a **lien** (right to seize and sell) on the taxed property. However, it may be several years before the government can actually collect from a property owner or seize and sell the property.

Many jurisdictions grant discounts for early payment. For example, taxpayers may be allowed discounts of 1 to 3 percent for paying, respectively, one to three months before the due date. Payments after the due date are generally subject to interest and penalties.

Property held by other governments (e.g., a federal building in a city) and religious institutions is ordinarily exempt from property taxes. In addition, many jurisdictions grant *homestead* exemptions to homeowners on their primary residences. These exemptions include basic allowances, often of a fixed dollar amount (e.g., $5,000), that are available to all taxpayers, and supplementary amounts to senior citizens or members of other designated classes. Thus, if a residence were assessed at $200,000 but the homeowner were granted a $5,000 exemption, the property's net assessed value would be $195,000. If the tax rate were 18.18 mils, the tax would be $195,000 multiplied by .01818, or $3,545.

SIGNIFICANT EVENTS IN THE REVENUE GENERATION PROCESS Several events in the property tax timeline have potential accounting significance:

- The legislative body levies the tax, establishing the tax rate and estimating the total amount to be collected.
- Administrative departments determine the amount due from the individual property owners, enter the amounts on the *tax roll* (a subsidiary ledger that supports the taxes receivable control account), and send out tax notices (bills) to property owners.
- The taxes are collected, most prior to the due date, some afterward.
- The taxes are due and the government has the right to impose a lien on the property for which taxes have not been paid.

The *stated* due date for property taxes must be distinguished from the *substantive* due date. Some jurisdictions establish a due date but do not impose interest, penalties, or a lien until a later date. The later date is the substantive due date.

The question facing governments is which of the many events in a property-tax calendar warrants revenue recognition, subject (on the governmental fund statements) to the "available" constraint?

DESIGN OF CHAPTER EXAMPLES In this and subsequent chapters, we spotlight accounting issues by using short examples followed by journal entries. We also highlight the authoritative standards that relate to the topic. In many of the examples, we use a single entry to summarize what in practice would be many individual entries. The illustrated entry is intended to show the net effect of the described events on the year-end *governmental fund* (modified accrual) financial statements. Conversions from the modified accrual amounts to full accrual amounts for the government-wide statements can be made at year-end using worksheets that will support the reconciliations presented with the financial statements. (See Chapter 3, Tables 3–4 and 3–6 for examples of reconciliations.) Governments are *not* required to maintain two sets of books to support their government-wide (governmental activities) versus their governmental fund statements.

In most of the examples we assume, for convenience, that the entity's fiscal year ends on December 31, even though the fiscal year of most governments ends on the last day of June, July, August, September, or October.

EXAMPLE   *Property Taxes*

• •

In January 2003 a city levies property taxes of $515 million for the year and collects $410 million during the year. It collects another $30 million during each of the first three months of 2004 and estimates that the $15 million balance will be uncollectible. In addition, in 2003 it collects $20 million in taxes applicable to 2004. Taxes are due on May 31 of each year and the government has the right to impose a lien on the taxed property if it has not received payment by that date.

GASB Standards

Per GASB Statement No. 33, governments should recognize *assets* from property taxes and other imposed nonexchange revenues in the period in which they first have an enforceable claim to the assets or when they receive the assets, whichever comes first. For property taxes, the date when they have an enforceable claim is specified in the legislation authorizing or imposing the tax. It is frequently referred to as the *lien date*, but sometimes as the *assessment date*.

Governments should recognize *revenue* from property taxes in the *period for which the taxes are levied* (i.e., the period that the taxes are expected to finance). Therefore, governments must delay revenue recognition for taxes collected in advance, in both their fund and their government-wide statements, until the period that the taxes have been budgeted to finance, thereby satisfying the time requirement established by Statement No. 33. In addition, as previously discussed, in the governmental fund statements, the property taxes must be *available*—that is, collected in the current period or within sixty days of year-end.

If property taxes are collected prior to the period for which they are budgeted, or will not be collected in time to pay liabilities of the current period, the government should report an asset (e.g., cash or property taxes receivable) and a deferred revenue (e.g., taxes collected in advance or deferred property tax revenue.)

In the example, the total revenue to be recognized in 2003 on a modified accrual basis would be $470 million—the $410 million due and collected during the year and applicable to it, plus the $60 million collected in the first sixty days of the next year. The $30 million to be collected after sixty days would be recognized as deferred revenue. The following entries for 2003 would give effect to the current guidance:

Property taxes receivable	$515	
Deferred property tax revenue		$500
Allowance for uncollectible property taxes		15
To record the property tax levy		

Cash	$410	
Property taxes receivable		$410
To record the collection of cash in 2003		

Deferred property tax revenue	$410	
Property tax revenue		$410
To recognize revenue on the taxes collected		

Deferred property tax revenue	$60	
Property tax revenue		$60
To recognize revenue on the taxes to be received in the first sixty days of 2004		

(Since this entry would be made as of year-end, it might appear to recognize only an *estimate* of the tax receipts of the first sixty days of 2004. In reality, the government would record its actual collections. Few governments are able to close their books and prepare financial statements within sixty days of year-end. Therefore, by the time they do so, they are able to determine exactly how much revenue from collections subsequent to year-end must be recognized.)

Cash	$20	
Deferred property tax revenue		$20

To record collection of property taxes received in advance of the year to which they are applicable

(The advance collections are intended to cover 2004 expenditures. Hence, they should be recognized as revenue in 2004 and thereby matched with the expenditures.)

The example solution follows the practice of many governments that initially defer all property-tax revenue and then recognize revenue as it becomes *available* to meet current-period expenditures. An alternative approach used by many governments is to recognize revenue initially and then, at year-end, reduce the revenue account and record deferred revenue equal to the amount that will not be collected in time to meet the available criterion (or that had been collected in advance of the applicable fiscal year). The amounts reported as, respectively, revenue and deferred revenue on the year-end financial statements would be the same under either approach.

DELINQUENT PROPERTY TAXES At year-end, overdue taxes receivable should be reclassified as *delinquent*, so that they are not intermingled with the current receivables of the following year. The journal entry would look like this:

Property taxes receivable—delinquent	$105	
Property taxes receivable		$105

To reclassify uncollected taxes as delinquent

This entry has no impact on revenues or governmental fund balances (and hence on the government's net assets). However, it provides statement readers with additional information as to the status of property taxes receivable. An increase in delinquent taxes relative to tax revenues should warn of a possible economic downturn in the jurisdiction or of ineffective tax collection practices.

As the delinquent property taxes are collected, they would be recorded as follows:

Cash	$60	
Property taxes receivable—delinquent		$60

To record the tax collections of the first two months of 2004, which had been recognized as revenue of 2003

Cash	$30	
Deferred property tax revenue	30	
Property taxes receivable—delinquent		$30
Property tax revenue (2004)		30

To record the tax collections of the third month of 2004, which had not been recognized as revenue of 2003

PROPERTY-TAX WRITE-OFFS Despite their powers to enforce claims against recalcitrant taxpayers, governments are not always able to collect the full amount of property tax levies. In some instances, seized property cannot be sold at prices sufficient to cover outstanding balances. In others, the costs of recovery would be more than the expected yield, so the governments elect not to exercise all available legal options.

As a government writes off (eliminates from the accounts) uncollectible taxes, it should offset the reduction in property taxes receivable with a corresponding reduction in the allowance for uncollectible property taxes. Thus, if $15 million of taxes (now classified as delinquent) were written off, the journal entry would look like this:

Allowance for uncollectible property taxes $15
   Property taxes receivable—delinquent $15
To write off delinquent taxes

This entry has no impact on revenues, expenditures, governmental fund balance, or the government's net assets. The government gave substantive accounting recognition to the potential uncollectible taxes in the period in which it established the allowance for uncollectible property taxes.

Governments may accrue interest charges and penalties on delinquent property taxes as they impose them. However, on their fund statements they should recognize revenue only when it is measurable and available. Until those criteria are satisfied, they should offset interest and penalties receivable with deferred revenue, rather than revenue.

DIFFERENCES IN GOVERNMENT-WIDE STATEMENTS

The general rules of revenue recognition for fund statements also apply to government-wide statements, except for the available criterion applicable to the governmental funds. Thus, in its government-wide statement of activities, a government can recognize property tax revenue as soon as it either has an enforceable claim or has collected the taxes (whichever comes first)—subject, of course, to the time requirement that the taxes not be recognized as revenue prior to the period for which they were budgeted.

In the example, the city would report the following in its 2003 financial statements:

Government-wide statements (governmental activities)

Revenue	$500	($410 of 2003 taxes collected in 2003 plus the remaining $90 that the government expects to collect)
Deferred revenue	$ 20	(taxes collected in 2003 but applicable to 2004)

Governmental fund statements

Revenue	$470	($410 of 2003 taxes collected in 2003 plus $60 collected during the sixty-day window after year-end)
Deferred revenue	$ 50	($30 of 2003 taxes collected after the sixty-day window plus $20 of taxes collected in 2003 but applicable to 2004)

For most governments, the difference between the property taxes recognized as revenues in the governmental fund statement of revenues, expenditures, and changes in fund balances and those recognized in the government-wide statement of activities is small. As long as the ratio of taxes levied to taxes collected remains fairly constant, the government-wide "gains" owing to the year-end accruals of taxes to be collected beyond the sixty-day window will be offset by the "losses" attributable to the taxes collected in the current year but recognized as revenues in the previous year. However, the difference in the deferred taxes to be reported, respectively, on the governmental fund balance sheet and the government-wide statement of net assets will be more pronounced, because the available criterion affects the governmental fund balance sheet but not the government-wide statement of net assets. The full amount of the deferrals due to the available criterion will be reported on the governmental fund balance sheet as additions to liabilities (and hence reductions in the fund balance).

OTHER IMPOSED NONEXCHANGE REVENUES The recognition requirements of Statement No. 33 for fines, penalties, and other imposed nonexchange transactions are the same as for property taxes in both the fund and the government-wide statements. However, the window for satisfying the available criterion in the fund statements is not specified and may be more or less than sixty days, at the government's discretion. The government should disclose the number of days used.

HOW SHOULD SALES AND INCOME TAXES AND OTHER DERIVED TAX REVENUES BE ACCOUNTED FOR?

Sales and income taxes are categorized as *derived tax revenues*. They are derived (result) from impositions on the exchange transactions of taxpayers.

Sales taxes are imposed on customers that purchase goods or services. The seller or merchant is responsible for collecting the taxes and for reporting and transmitting them to the government. Unlike property taxes, which are government assessed, sales taxes are taxpayer assessed; parties other than the beneficiary government determine the tax base. Thus, the government has to rely upon merchant tax returns to become aware of the proceeds to which it is legally entitled.

SIGNIFICANT DATES FOR SALES TAXES Three significant dates underlie sales tax transactions:

1. The date of the sales transaction and the collection of the tax by the merchant
2. The date the merchant is required to file the tax return and transmit the taxes (generally the same)
3. The date the merchant actually files the return and transmits the taxes

The sale date is arguably the most significant date, since that is when the transaction producing the tax takes place, the amount of the tax is established, and the merchant's liability to transmit the tax is created. However, the government is not entitled to the tax until the date the return is to be filed and the tax paid. Moreover, except for unusual circumstances, such as when a merchant files a return but fails to make timely payment, the government does not know what the amount will be until it actually receives the tax.

EXAMPLE   *Sales Taxes*

In December 2003 merchants collect $20 million in sales taxes. Of this amount, $12 million is collected prior to December 15 and must be remitted by February 15, 2004; the remaining $8 million must be remitted by March 15, 2004.

GASB Standards

Statement No. 33 requires that *revenue* from sales taxes and other derived tax revenues be recognized at the time the underlying exchange transaction takes place. For sales taxes, that is the date of the sale.

In the governmental fund statements, the sales taxes must also satisfy the available test to be recognized as revenue. Current standards do not provide guidance as to how soon after the end of the fiscal year resources must be received in order to be considered available. Hence, governments must exercise their own judgment. However, they must be consistent from year to year and disclose the period used.

Statement No. 33 stipulates that governments should recognize *assets* from derived tax transactions in the period in which the underlying transaction takes place. Thus, a government should recognize an asset, "sales taxes receivable," for taxes imposed in the current year, even if they will not be collected in time to pay the current liabilities of that year.

Assuming that the government adopts sixty days as the available window, then it could recognize as 2003 revenue only the $12 million in taxes that it expects to collect within sixty days of year-end. The $8 million balance must be deferred until $2004:

Sales taxes receivable	$20	
Sales tax revenue		$12
Deferred sales tax revenue		8

To summarize December sales tax activity

Suppose, instead, that sales taxes are imposed only on motor fuels and have to be used to construct and maintain roads. Would this *purpose restriction* affect the recognition of revenue?

Because the revenues are restricted, they should be reported in a special revenue fund, which, like the general fund, is a governmental fund. GASB standards (and the discussion in this chapter and in the following chapter on expenditures) apply to all governmental funds. Per Statement No. 33, purpose restrictions should not affect the *timing* of revenue recognition. If the underlying transaction has taken place and the resources are measurable and available, then the government has benefited from an increase in net assets and should recognize the increase as revenue. The increase in net assets also should be reported as a reservation of fund balance until the resources are used for the purpose indicated by the restriction.

DIFFERENCES IN GOVERNMENT-WIDE STATEMENTS

The same general principles of revenue recognition for governmental fund statements apply to the government-wide statements, except for the available criterion.

Hence, in the example, the government would recognize as revenue in its *government-wide statements* the entire $20 million of taxes derived from the sales of December. (If there is a purpose restriction, the $20 million should be included in restricted net assets in the statement of net assets.) In contrast, in its *governmental fund statements* the government would recognize $12 million of revenue and $8 million of deferred revenue.

INCOME TAXES—THE COLLECTION PROCESS Forty-six states and a few major cities, such as New York, Philadelphia, and Detroit, impose personal or corporate income taxes.[4] Some of these states impose what they call a "franchise" tax on businesses, but they base the tax on income.

Income taxes present especially vexatious issues of revenue recognition, owing to their multistage administrative processes. Consider, for example, the following:

- The tax is based on income of either a calendar year or a fiscal year elected by the taxpayer that may not coincide with the government's fiscal year.

- Taxpayers are required to remit tax payments throughout the tax year, through either payroll withholdings or periodic payments of estimated amounts. Within three or four months after the close of the year, they are required to file a tax return in which they inform the government of the actual amount of tax owed. At that time, they are expected to make a final settlement with the government, by either paying additional taxes due or requesting a refund of overpayments. Thus, the taxes received by the government during the year may be more or less than the amount to which it is entitled.

- Governments review all tax returns for reasonableness and select a sample for audit, which may result in additional taxes due. Moreover, some taxpayers are delinquent on their payments. Thus, taxes continue to trickle in for several years after the due date. Although governments can reliably estimate the amount of late collections based on historical experience, they may not have a legal claim to the taxes until taxpayers either file their returns or agree to the adjustments resulting from an audit.

EXAMPLE   *Income Taxes*
. . . .

A state imposes an 8 percent tax on personal income. Employers are required to withhold taxes from payroll and remit withholdings on a monthly basis, and taxpayers are required to make quarterly tax payments on income from sources other than salaries and wages. Taxpayers must file a tax return with the state by April 15 of the year following the tax year (calendar year) and must pay the remaining tax owed (or claim a refund) at that time.

---

[4]U.S. Bureau of the Census, *State Government Finances: 1999.*

In concept, the state should recognize the taxes as revenue in the period in which taxpayers earn the income. Nevertheless, the GASB recognizes in Statement No. 33 that it is impractical to determine precisely the amount of taxable income that taxpayers earned during the tax year. Therefore, the state may base the amount to be recognized on the remitted withholdings and estimated tax payments, adjusted for the April 15 payments and refunds, on both its governmental fund and government-wide statements.

HOW SHOULD GRANTS AND SIMILAR NONEXCHANGE REVENUES BE ACCOUNTED FOR?

State and local governments receive grants and similar forms of financial assistance from both other governments and private sources. Some grants are *mandated* by a higher-level government; the lower-level government has no choice but to accept them (as when the federal government requires states to undertake environmental clean-up efforts and provides resources for them to do so). Most grants, however, are *voluntary*; the government can choose not to accept the resources if it is unwilling to comply with the attached conditions or to carry out the programs the grant is intended to finance.

TYPES OF INTERGOVERNMENTAL REVENUES Typical intergovernmental grants and similar nonexchange revenues include the following:

- **Reimbursement grants.** The most common form of grants, these are payments intended to reimburse specific types of expenditures for designated purposes, projects, or activities. They may be mandated or voluntary.

- **Unrestricted grants.** These are payments that are unrestricted as to purpose, project, or activity.

- **Contingent grants.** These are grants contingent upon a specified occurrence or action on the part of the recipient (e.g., the ability of the recipient to raise "matching" resources from other parties).

- **Entitlements.** These are payments, usually from a higher-level government, to which a lower-level government is automatically entitled in an amount determined by a specified formula. Entitlements are often designated for a broad functional activity, such as education.

- **Shared revenues.** These are revenues raised by one government, such as a state, but shared on a predetermined basis with other governments, such as cities.

Rec. Rev. when Coll. is assured →

- **Payments in lieu of taxes.** These are amounts paid by a government in place of property taxes that it is not required to pay. Such payments are an important revenue source for governments having within their jurisdiction substantial facilities of other governments. For example, the federal government, whose property is tax exempt, may make payments to school districts in which military bases are located to compensate them for educating military dependents.

PRIVATE CONTRIBUTIONS Examples of voluntary nonexchange revenues from nongovernment sources include private donations to school districts and universities, contributions of land from developers (often tied to a project they are undertaking), and gifts of collectible items to museums or cultural centers. Some donations are endowments—gifts that stipulate that the contribution must be invested and only the income from the investments can be spent.

GASB Standards

Recipients of grants and contributions, whether mandatory or voluntary, inter-governmental or private, should recognize both revenue and related receivables only when all eligibility requirements, including *time requirements*, have been met (plus, of course, the available criterion in the governmental fund statements). Resources received in advance should be reported as deferred revenue.

Reimbursement grants have an inherent eligibility requirement—the recipient is eligible only if and when it incurs allowable costs. Hence, recipients typically must recognize revenue in the period in which they make reimbursable expenditures.

Endowment contributions that stipulate that only the income from investing the contributions can be spent are subject to infinite time requirements. Does that mean that the recipients can never recognize revenue from the gift? No. The GASB makes an exception to the general rule that revenue from contributions cannot be recognized until all time requirements have been satisfied. Per Statement No. 33, governments can recognize revenue from endowments and similar gifts in which the main benefit to the recipient is from the derived income, not the gift itself, as soon as they receive the resources. Similar rules apply to gifts of historical treasures and art works that the recipient agrees it will hold rather than sell.

EXAMPLES OF ACCOUNTING FOR GRANTS AND CONTRIBUTIONS The following six examples illustrate the accounting for different kinds of grants and private contributions. Note that, as discussed in the preceding sections, the specific features of a grant or contribution might or might not determine the timing of revenue recognition and other reporting requirements in the governmental fund and government-wide statements.

EXAMPLE *Unrestricted Grant with Time Requirement*

In October 2003 a school district is notified that, per legislative-approved formulas, the state has awarded it $15 million in assistance. The resources are transmitted in December 2003 and may be used to supplement teachers' salaries, acquire equipment, and support educational enrichment programs. They can be used only in the year ending December 31, 2004.

The grant is unrestricted. The stipulations concerning the use of the resources are not purpose restrictions. They are requirements in form, not substance, because the state is demanding nothing that the district would not otherwise do. However, the grant is subject to a time requirement—the resources must be used in 2004. Hence, the school district must defer recognizing grant revenue until 2004 in both its government-wide and its governmental fund financial statements:

Cash	$15	
Deferred grant revenue		$15

To record the receipt of state funds in 2003

Deferred grant revenue	$15	
Grant revenue		$15

To recognize grant revenue in 2004

EXAMPLE   *Grant with Purpose Restriction*

In October 2003 a school district is notified that, per legislated formulas, the state has granted it $15 million to enhance its technological capabilities. The resources are transmitted in December 2003. They must be used to acquire computers, but may be spent at any time.

   This grant is subject only to a purpose restriction. Purpose restrictions do not affect the timing of revenue recognition in either the government-wide or the fund financial statements. Thus, the district should recognize the revenue as soon as the grant is announced. However, owing to the purpose restriction the district should record the grant in a special revenue fund and report a reservation of fund balance (and a restriction on net assets in its government-wide statements).

EXAMPLE   *Reimbursement (Eligibility Requirement) Grant*

In December 2003 a city is awarded a reimbursement grant of $400,000 to train social workers. The grant is subject to an eligibility requirement in that to be eligible for the grant the city must first incur allowable costs. During the year the city spends $300,000 in allowable costs and is reimbursed $250,000. It expects to be reimbursed for the $50,000 balance in January 2004 and to expend and be reimbursed for the remaining $100,000 during 2004.

   In this example, the city can recognize the grant only as it incurs allowable costs. Thus, in 2003 it can recognize $300,000 in both revenue and increases in assets (amounts in thousands):

Expenditures to train social workers	$300	
Cash (or payables)		$300
To record allowable costs		

Cash	$250	
Grants receivable	50	
Grant revenue		$300
To recognize grant revenue		

The city should recognize grant revenue of $300,000 in both its government-wide and its governmental fund statements. In contrast, if payment were not expected within the available period, the fund statements should defer revenue (credit deferred revenue, instead of revenue, in the second entry), whereas the government-wide statements should recognize revenue.

EXAMPLE   *Unrestricted Grant with Contingency Eligibility Requirement*

In January 2004, a private foundation agrees to match all private cash contributions up to $20 million received by a state-owned museum during its 2004–2005 fund drive. In 2004 the museum receives $14 million in private cash contributions.

   The museum is eligible for the foundation's matching contribution only insofar as it receives funds from other sources. Thus, in 2004 it can recognize only $14 million of matching foundation revenue (debit receivable, credit revenue) in both its government-wide and its fund statements.

If the contribution is not expected to be collected in time to meet the museum's 2004 current liabilities, then the museum should credit deferred revenue, rather than revenue, and report deferred revenue in its governmental fund statements. (The government-wide statements should report $14 million of revenue.)

EXAMPLE   *Endowment Gift*

A private citizen donates $1 million to a city to maintain and repair historical monuments. He stipulates that the principal should remain intact permanently and that only the income should be used for the intended purpose.

Endowments intended to support a government's activities and thereby benefit the public are accounted for in a permanent (governmental) fund. Inasmuch as the gift is intended to provide an on-going source of income, the city should recognize the $1 million as revenue upon receipt, in both its government-wide and its fund statements. It should also reserve fund balance for $1 million and report restricted (government-wide) net assets in that amount to indicate that the gift cannot be expended.

EXAMPLE   *Pledges*

A private citizen pledges $10,000 to a county to help maintain a park. Park activities are accounted for in the general fund. The government is confident that the promised donation will actually be made.

Governments should recognize revenue from pledges as soon as they meet all eligibility requirements. Thus, if the county has to do nothing further to receive the donation, it should recognize revenue at the time the pledge is made, in both the government-wide and the fund statements. Of course, if receipt of the donation is not expected to meet the available criterion, the county should report the pledge as a deferred revenue in the fund statements.

HOW SHOULD PASS-THROUGH GRANTS BE ACCOUNTED FOR?

For some types of grants, the recipient is required to distribute the resources to other parties, or payment is made directly to a third party for the benefit of the recipient. For example, a state might receive federal funds earmarked for each of its local school districts. Should the state record the receipt of the funds as a revenue and the disbursement as an expenditure? Or should it omit the grant from its budget and its accounts on the grounds that it is merely acting as an agent of the federal government?

Grants that a government must transfer to, or spend on behalf of, a secondary recipient are referred to as **pass-through grants**. In the past, some governments opted to exclude pass-through funds from both revenues and expenditures. Instead, they accounted for the funds *off the budget*—often in agency (fiduciary) funds in which only assets and liabilities are reported. (Accounting for agency funds is discussed in Chapter 10.)

In 1994 the GASB stated that governments should generally recognize cash pass-through grants as revenue and expenditures or expenses in governmental, proprietary, or trust funds.[5] An agency fund should be used only when the government

---

[5]GASB Statement No. 24, *Accounting and Financial Reporting for Certain Grants and Other Financial Assistance*, para. 5.

merely serves as a "cash conduit"— that is, it simply transmits the funds without having administrative involvement. *Administrative involvement* would be indicated if the government selected the secondary recipients of the funds (even based on grantor-established criteria) or monitored compliance with grant requirements.

As a result of these requirements, governments should account for most pass-through grants as revenues and expenditures or expenses in accordance with the requirements of Statement No. 33 for government-mandated nonexchange transactions.

HOW SHOULD SALES OF GENERAL CAPITAL ASSETS BE ACCOUNTED FOR?

Governments sell capital assets for the same reasons as businesses—the services provided by the assets can be provided more economically by another means or by replacement assets. The unique accounting problem for governments that sell general capital assets is that the financial resources received are accounted for in a governmental fund, but the assets that are sold are not.

EXAMPLE *Sales of General Capital Assets*

On December 31, 2003, a city purchases a new police car for $30,000. On January 2, 2004, the vehicle is nearly demolished in an accident. It is uninsured. The city sells it for $5,000.

Current standards for modified accrual accounting require the following, seemingly odd, entry:

Cash	$5,000	
Other financing sources—sale of vehicle		$5,000

To record the sale of general capital assets

It is "seemingly odd" because, as discussed in Chapter 3, an other financing source is reported on a governmental fund statement of revenues, expenditures, and changes in fund balance (below the revenues and expenditures). Although not a revenue, it is similar to one in that it may be budgeted as a revenue and results in an increase in fund balance.

From an accounting perspective, therefore, the accident that destroyed a $30,000 vehicle left a governmental fund $5,000 better off, even though the government's capital assets were reduced. This outcome is inevitable because the measurement focus of governmental funds excludes capital assets.

DIFFERENCES IN GOVERNMENT-WIDE STATEMENTS

In their government-wide statements, governments should report their general capital assets in the governmental activities column at historical cost, less accumulated depreciation (except for nondepreciable assets, as discussed in Chapter 7). When a capital asset is sold, governments should recognize a gain or loss for the difference between sale proceeds and book value. Hence, in the example, assuming that no depreciation had yet been charged, the government-wide statements should recognize a loss of $25,000 (cost of $30,000 less sale price of $5,000).

How Should Investment Gains and Losses Be Accounted For?

The investment portfolios of governmental funds generally contain mainly short-term debt securities. Because they are short-term, their values are not greatly influenced by swings in interest rates. However, some portfolios also include longer-term instruments that are considerably more sensitive to changes in interest rates. In recent years, some governments—sometimes in violation of both accepted standards of sound fiscal management and common sense—have speculated in "derivatives" and other instruments that are extremely sensitive to interest rate changes.

Until 1997, GASB standards (established by its predecessor, the National Council on Governmental Accounting, or NCGA) required that investments of governmental funds be reported at cost or amortized cost. However, many constituents, especially the financial community, believe that most investments should be reported at fair (market) value, primarily for the following reasons:

- For virtually all decisions involving investments, fair value is more relevant than historical cost.

- Investments are often held as cash substitutes. They can be liquidated with a phone call to the entity's broker or a quick computer entry.

- Fair values are objective; up-to-the-minute prices are available from computer and telephone information services.

- The performance of investment managers, and their employer governments, is measured by total return—dividends, interest, and changes in fair values.

- Although prices that go up can also come down, financial statements report on performance within specified periods. An increase (or decrease) in the value of a security in a particular year is indicative of sound (or poor) investment performance in that year. Government portfolio managers are expected to achieve specified investment goals and statement users are entitled to the information needed to assess how well they have done.

EXAMPLE   *Investment Income*

The following table summarizes the 2003 investment activity in a county's general fund (all amounts in thousands):

	Cost	Fair Value on Jan. 1	Purchases	Sales (Proceeds)	Fair Value on Dec. 31
Security A	$120	$120	—	—	$140
Security B	520	540	—	—	540
Security C	200	200	—	$250	0
Security D	90	—	$90	—	75
	$930	$860	$90	$250	$755

GASB Standards

In 1997 the GASB determined that governments should state their investments as fair value. GASB Statement No. 31, *Accounting and Financial Reporting for Certain Investments and for External Investment Pools*, requires that changes in fair value should be included in investment income in the operating statement or other statement of activities of all entities and funds.

The Board made a notable exception for short-term securities that are not subject to the same volatility as long-term instruments. Governments are permitted to report money-market investments having a remaining maturity at time of purchase of one year or less at amortized cost rather than market value. These investments would include certificates of deposit, commercial paper, and U.S. Treasury obligations.

Per Statement No. 31, the investments should be reported on the county's December 31, 2003, statements at their fair value—$755. The gain or loss (net change in fair value) to be reported on the county's 2003 operating statements can be determined by subtracting investment inputs from outputs. The inputs ($950) are the securities on hand at the start of the year ($860, stated at fair value as of the beginning of the year) plus the $90 of purchases during the year. The outputs ($1,005) are the securities on hand at year-end ($755, stated at fair value as of year-end) plus the $250 of proceeds from the sale of securities during the year. Thus, in the example, the net gain is $55 ($1,005 less $950). The following entry would therefore be appropriate:

Investments	$55	
Revenue—increase in fair value of investments		$55

To record the increase in the fair value of the investments

Note that the recognition as revenue of an increase in the fair value of investments applies to governmental fund statements as well as to the government-wide statements, even though the amount may not be available to finance current-period liabilities. Thus, the modified accrual available criterion for governmental funds does not apply to investment valuation—a notable exception to the philosophy and most standards underlying accounting for governmental funds.

HOW SHOULD EXTERNAL INVESTMENT POOLS BE ACCOUNTED FOR?

Many local governments invest what would otherwise be idle cash in investment pools maintained by their states or other government entities. Investment pools are similar to mutual funds. Each participant purchases shares in the underlying portfolio. Statement No. 31 specifies that governments should state their investments in a pool at the fair value per share of the pool's underlying portfolio. Each period they should recognize the change in the fair value of their shares as an investment gain or loss.

The government that maintains the pool would report its own shares in the pool, and resulting gains or losses, in both its governmental fund statements and its government-wide statements, because its investment in the pool supports its own programs. By contrast, other entities' shares in the pool do not support the programs of the administering government. The administering government would account for them in an investment trust (fiduciary) fund and, therefore, would not report them in its governmental funds or government-wide statements.

How Should Interest on Investments Be Accounted For?

Governmental funds ordinarily do not hold investments that have a **stated** or **coupon rate** of interest (i.e., a nominal rate of interest stated on the face of the instruments, as is the case for many long-term bonds). However, if they do, the stated interest amount should be recognized as revenue in the year that the interest accrues, subject to the available criterion for governmental funds. More common for governmental funds are investments in discounted debt securities. By recording the changes in fair value of those instruments, governments automatically accrue interest as it is earned.

EXAMPLE   *Interest Income on a Discounted Note*

On December 1, a town purchased a $1,000, two-year discounted note for $873, a price that reflects an annual yield of approximately 7 percent. As a discounted note, the security provides no periodic payments of interest. However, assuming no change in prevailing interest rates or other factors that would also affect fair value, the note's fair value can be expected to increase by approximately $5 the first month. On December 31, if the fair value of the note were $878, the government would adjust the security by $5 and recognize interest revenue (debit investments, credit revenue) of $5, which, in economic substance, is earned interest.

If, on the other hand, the investment were a short-term Treasury note (one-year or less) the government need not look to fair value to adjust the security. Instead, it would amortize the initial discount over the life of the note by a debit to the discount account (or the investment account) and a credit to interest revenue.

The impact of the two approaches on the change in both government-wide net assets and the governmental fund balance is the same. Both approaches would give recognition to the interest earned and the resultant change in the value of the underlying security.

The GASB approach to investments has been extremely controversial and unpopular among many government officials. It is easy to see why. To the extent that Statement No. 31 requires reporting investments at fair value, it widens the gap between financial reporting and budgeting. The investment portfolios of many governments are dominated by notes and other securities having a fixed maturity date. If a government holds its securities to maturity, year-to-year changes in market value have no impact on the cash that is available for expenditure. Yet increases in market value must be reported as revenues (increases in net assets) and decreases must be reported as expenditures (decreases in net assets). Imagine the difficulty of having to explain to governing board members why an increase in net assets is only a paper gain that cannot be spent. Or try telling a TV reporter in thirty seconds why a decline in the value of a government's portfolio will have no impact on the amount for which the securities will eventually be sold.

How should licenses, permits, and other exchange or "exchange-like" transactions be accounted for?

Governments issue licenses (or permits) that allow citizens and businesses to carry out regulated activities over a specified time period. However, the license period may not coincide with the government's fiscal year.

The primary issue relating to licenses is whether the revenue should be recognized when a license is issued and cash is received (usually concurrently) or whether it should be spread out over the period covered by the license. In other words, is the significant economic event the collection of cash (suggesting that cash basis accounting is appropriate) or is it the passage of time (supporting accrual basis accounting)?

The issue is by no means clear-cut in light of the following characteristics of licenses:

- Some license fees are intended to cover the cost of services provided to the licensee or related to the activity in which the licensee engages. Thus, they have the characteristics of *exchange* transactions because the licensee pays cash and receives value in exchange. For example, the charge for restaurant licenses may be calculated to cover the cost of inspecting restaurants, thereby assuring customers that the restaurants meet minimum standards of cleanliness. Other fees, however, may bear little relation to the cost of services provided and may be imposed mainly as a source of general revenues. They are more in the nature of *nonexchange* revenues.

- Generally, license fees are not refundable. Therefore, unless a license fee is tied to specific services (not just a time period), once the government receives the fee, it has no further obligation, either actual or contingent, to the licensee.

E X A M P L E   *License Fees*

In June 2003 a city imposed license fees on barber and beauty shops for the first time. It collected $360,000. The fees are intended to cover the cost of health inspections. The licenses cover the one-year period from July 1 to June 30.

GASB Standards

In Statement No. 33, the GASB acknowledges that license fees and permits may not be pure exchange transactions. They may not be paid voluntarily and rarely is the amount paid reflective of the fair value of benefits received by the licensee. Still, the GASB maintains that they are "exchange-like" in nature and should be accounted for as if they were true exchange transactions. Therefore, they are not covered in Statement No. 33, which addresses only nonexchange transactions.

GASB standards with respect to miscellaneous exchange revenues are those of its predecessor (the NCGA) and state simply: "*Miscellaneous Revenues.* Golf and swimming fees, inspection charges, parking fees and parking meter receipts, and the vast multitude of miscellaneous exchange revenues are best recognized when cash is received."[6] Therefore, the 2003 activity can be summarized by a debit to cash and a credit to revenue from license fees for $360,000.

Because this standard recognizes miscellaneous revenues on a cash basis, it is inconsistent with the accrual basis of accounting that would suggest that the fees be recognized over the period covered by the license. However, it is a pragmatic approach to recognizing revenues that for most governments are not of major consequence.

In the spirit of Statement No. 34, exchange revenues of governmental activities should be accounted for in the government-wide statements on the accrual basis. However, mainly because these miscellaneous types of revenue are not of great significance, the GASB has not yet indicated whether governments should accrue them in their government-wide statements or whether they may report them on a cash basis, as they do in their governmental fund statements (the pragmatic approach).

HOW SHOULD GOVERNMENTS REPORT REVENUES IN THEIR GOVERNMENT-WIDE STATEMENTS?

A primary objective of the government-wide statement of activities is to show the relative financial burden to the taxpayers of each function or program—the amount that has to be financed out of general revenues. As discussed in Chapter 3, the government-wide statement of activities reports the net cost (or net revenue) of each of the government's main functions or programs. (See Chapter 3, Table 3–2, for an illustration.) The net cost of a function or program is its expenses less any revenues that are reported as **program revenues**—that is, those generated by the function or program itself (e.g., user charges or fees) or directly attributed to it by external grantors or donors. As a consequence, governments must determine which revenues should be classified as program revenues and which as **general revenues**. General revenues is

---

[6]NCGA Statement No. 1, *Governmental Accounting and Financial Reporting Principles*, para. 67.

the default classification; all revenues that cannot be classified as program revenues are considered general revenues.

As a rule, revenues from charges or fees imposed on parties that benefit from specific activities are classified as program revenues because they are generated by the program. So also are grants from other governments or outside parties that must be used for specific purposes of the function or program. By contrast, taxes that are imposed on the reporting government's citizens are considered general revenues, even if they are restricted to specific programs. Thus, for example, a general sales tax would be classified as general revenue even though it might be dedicated to education or road construction. Interest and other earnings from investments, as well as other nontax revenues such as grants and contributions, would be counted as general revenues unless explicitly restricted (by law or external parties) for specific programs.

As illustrated in Table 3–2, the government-wide statement of activities reports the program revenues of each function or program in three separate columns:

TABLE 4–1
Summary of Asset and Revenue Recognition for Governmental Activities

Transaction Class	Recognition Requirement
Imposed nonexchange revenues Examples: property taxes, fines	*Revenue*: In the period in which the revenue is intended to be used *Asset*: When the government has an enforceable legal claim or when resources are received, whichever comes first
Derived taxes Examples: sales taxes, income taxes, hotel taxes, fuel taxes	*Revenue*: In the period of the underlying transaction *Asset*: In the period of the underlying transaction or when resources are received, whichever comes first
Government-mandated nonexchange transactions Example: a federal grant for a federally mandated drug prevention program	*Revenue*: When all eligibility requirements (including time requirements) have been met *Asset*: When all eligibility requirements have been met, or when resources are received, whichever comes first
Voluntary nonexchange transactions Examples: entitlements, federal grants for general education, donations	Same as for government-mandated nonexchange transactions
Exchange and "exchange-like" transactions Examples: license fees, permits, inspection charges	*Revenue:* When cash is received *Asset:* When cash is received
Examples: investment gains and losses, shares in investment pools	*Revenue:* As securities increase in value *Asset:* As securities increase in value (i.e., should be "marked to market")

Note: These guidelines apply to both the government-wide and governmental fund statements. However, in the governmental fund statements, an additional criterion applies (except for investment valuation): Revenues should be recognized no sooner than the period in which the resources to be received are measurable and available to pay liabilities of the current period.

Source: Nonexchange transaction information adapted from GASB Statement No. 33, *Accounting and Financial Reporting for Nonexchange Transactions* (1998), para. 103.

1. *Charges for services.* These would include fees for services such as garbage collection, licenses and permits, and special assessments for roads or other capital projects. This column would also include program-specific fines and penalties such as speeding tickets generated by the police function.

2. *Program-specific operating grants and contributions.* These would include federal or state grants for specific operating purposes, such as law enforcement, education, and recreation.

3. *Program-specific capital grants.* These would include grants for the purchase and construction of capital assets directly associated with specific functions or programs, such as buses, jails, and roads.

Some government grants are for multiple purposes. If the amounts can be identified as generated by specific programs (either through the grant application or the grant notification), they should be apportioned appropriately. If they cannot, they should be reported as general revenues.

Table 4–1 summarizes the principles of revenue and asset recognition as they apply to the main types of revenue-producing transactions recorded in governmental funds, as set forth in Statement No. 33 and other GASB pronouncements. As discussed in this chapter, the same requirements apply for recognition in the government-wide statements, except that the available criterion for recognition in governmental funds does not apply. Therefore, some revenues may be recognized earlier in the government-wide (full accrual) statements than in the governmental fund (modified accrual) statements.

QUESTIONS FOR REVIEW AND DISCUSSION

1. Why is a choice of *basis of accounting* inexorably linked to *measurement focus*?

2. What are the measurement focus and basis of accounting of governmental funds? What is the rationale for this basis of accounting—as opposed, for example, to either a full accrual basis or a budgetary basis?

3. What is the difference between an *exchange* and a *nonexchange* transaction?

4. What are the main categories of nonexchange revenues per GASB Statement No. 33, *Accounting and Financial Reporting for Nonexchange Transactions*?

5. What criteria must be met before revenues can be recognized on a modified accrual basis? What is the rationale for these criteria?

6. What is the general rule for recognizing property taxes as revenues? How would property taxes be accounted for differently in the governmental fund statements, as opposed to the government-wide statements?

7. What is the earliest point in the sales tax collection process that revenue may be recognized?

How can you justify recognizing revenue on the basis of this event?

8. Explain the distinction between *reimbursement grants* and *entitlements*. How does this distinction affect the way each type of grant is accounted for?

9. A private citizen makes an unrestricted pledge of $5 million to a city's museum. The city is confident that the donor will fulfill her pledge. However, the cash will not be received for at least two years. How will the amount of revenue reported in the governmental fund statements differ from that reported in the government-wide statements? Explain.

10. What are pass-through grants? Under what circumstances must a recipient government report a pass-through grant as both a revenue and an expenditure?

11. A student comments: "A government destroys a recently acquired car, sells the remains for scrap, and its general fund surplus for the year increases. That's ridiculous. Government account-

ing makes so much less sense than private-sector accounting." Explain why the situation described by the student arises. Considering the economic value of capital assets compared with their reported values, does government accounting, in fact, differ so much from business accounting?

12. Until recently, governments were not permitted to recognize increases in the value of investments as revenue. What arguments might you present in support of the current position that investments be stated at fair value and that changes in fair value be recognized as either revenues or expenditures? What arguments might you present against the current position?

EXERCISES AND PROBLEMS

4–1

Select the best answer.

1. Under the modified accrual basis of accounting, revenues cannot be recognized
   a. until cash has been collected
   b. unless they will be collected within sixty days of year-end
   c. until they are subject to accrual
   d. until they are measurable and available

2. *Available* (as in "measurable and available") means
   a. available to finance expenditures of the current period
   b. subject to accrual
   c. collectible
   d. available for appropriation

3. Property taxes are an example of
   a. an imposed exchange transaction
   b. an imposed nonexchange transaction
   c. a derived tax transaction
   d. a government-mandated nonexchange transaction

4. To be considered available, property taxes must have been collected either during the government's fiscal year or within
   a. the time it takes for the government to liquidate its obligations from the prior year
   b. thirty days of year-end
   c. sixty days of year-end
   d. the following fiscal year

5. For its fiscal year ending September 30, 2003, Twin City levied $500 million in property taxes. It collected taxes applicable to fiscal 2003 as follows (in millions):

June 1, 2002 to September 30, 2002	$ 20
October 1, 2002 to September 30, 2003	440
October 1, 2003 to November 30, 2003	15
December 2003	4

The city estimates that $10 million of the outstanding balance will be uncollectible. For the fiscal year ending September 30, 2003, how much should Twin City recognize in property tax revenue (in millions) in its general fund?
   a. $440
   b. $460
   c. $475
   d. $490

6. Assume the same facts as in the previous example. How much should Twin City recognize in property tax revenue (in millions) in its government-wide statement of activities?
   a. $440
   b. $460
   c. $475
   d. $490

7. Central City was awarded two state grants during its fiscal year ending September 30, 2003: a $2 million block grant that can be used to cover any operating expenses incurred during fiscal 2004 and a $1 million grant that can be used any time to acquire equipment for its police department. For the year ending September 30, 2003, Central City should recognize in grant revenue in its governmental fund statements (in millions)
   a. $0
   b. $1
   c. $2
   d. $3

8. Assume the same facts as in the previous example. How much should the city recognize in grant revenue in its government-wide statements?
   a. $0
   b. $1
   c. $2
   d. $3

9. Assuming that a government will collect its sales taxes in sufficient time to satisfy the available criterion, it would ordinarily recognize revenue from sales taxes in its governmental fund statements
   a. when the underlying sales transaction takes place
   b. on the date the merchant must remit the taxes to the government
   c. on the date the merchant must file a tax return
   d. when the taxes are received by the government

10. Assuming that a government will collect its sales taxes in sufficient time to satisfy the available criterion, it would ordinarily recognize revenue from sales taxes in its government-wide statements
   a. when the underlying sales transaction takes place
   b. on the date the merchant must remit the taxes to the government
   c. on the date the merchant must file a tax return
   d. when the taxes are received by the government

4–2

The following information relates to Hudson City for its fiscal year ended December 31, 2003:

- On January 31, 2003, the city purchased as an investment for its debt service fund a three-year, 6 percent, $1 million bond, for $998,000. During the year it received $3,000 in interest. At year-end the market value of the bond was $999,500.
- On December 31, 2002, the Foundation for the Arts pledged to donate $1, up to a maximum of $1,000,000, to finance construction of the city-owned art museum for each $3 that the museum is able to collect from other private contributors. During 2003, the city collected $600,000. In January and February 2004 it collected an additional $2,400,000.
- During the year the city imposed license fees on street vendors. All vendors were required to purchase the licenses by September 30, 2003. The licenses cover the one-year period from October 1, 2003, through September 30, 2004.

During 2003, the city collected $240,000 in license fees.
- The city sold a fire truck for $40,000 that it had acquired five years earlier for $250,000. At the time of sale the city had charged $225,000 in depreciation.
- The city received a grant of $2 million to partially reimburse costs of training police officers. During the year the city incurred $1,500,000 of allowable costs and received $1,200,000. It expects to incur an additional $500,000 in allowable costs in January 2004 and to be reimbursed for all allowable costs by the end of February 2004.

Select an answer from the list of amounts below. An amount may be selected once, more than once, or not at all.

____ 1. amount of investment income that the city should recognize in its debt service fund
____ 2. reported value of the bond in the government-wide statements at year-end
____ 3. amount of investment income that the city should recognize in its government-wide statements
____ 4. contribution revenue from Foundation for the Arts to be recognized in the governmental fund statements
____ 5. contribution revenue from Foundation for the Arts to be recognized in the government-wide statements
____ 6. revenue from license fees to be recognized in the governmental fund statements
____ 7. increase in general fund balance owing to the sale of the fire engine
____ 8. increase in net assets (government-wide statements) owing to the sale of the fire engine
____ 9. revenue in the governmental fund statements from the police training grant
____ 10. revenue in the government-wide statements from the police training grant

a. 0
b. 1,500
c. 3,000
d. 4,500
e. 15,000
f. 40,000
g. 60,000
h. 200,000
i. 225,000
j. 240,000
k. 600,000
l. 998,000
m. 999,500
n. 1,000,000
o. 1,200,000
p. 1,500,000
q. 2,000,000

4–3

Property taxes are not necessarily recognized as revenue in the year collected.

Duchess County had the following property tax transactions in 2003 and 2004. Its fiscal year ends on December 31. Property taxes are due March 31 of the year they are levied and intended to finance.

a. January 15, 2003, the county levied property taxes of $170 million for the year ending December 31, 2003. Officials estimated that 1 percent would be uncollectible.

b. During 2003 it collected $120 million.

c. In January and February 2004, prior to preparing its 2003 financial statements, it collected an additional $45 million in 2003 taxes. It reclassified the $5 million of 2003 taxes not yet collected as delinquent.

d. In January 2004, the county levied property taxes of $190 million to finance activities of 2004; officials estimated that 1.1 percent would be uncollectible.

e. During the remainder of 2004, the county collected $2.5 million more in taxes relating to 2003, $160 million relating to 2004, and $1.9 million (in advance) applicable to 2005.

f. In December 2004, it wrote off $1 million of 2003 taxes that it determined would be uncollectible.

1. Prepare journal entries (excluding closing entries) in the general fund (modified accrual basis) to record the 2003 and 2004 property-tax transactions.

2. What amount of property tax revenue would the county report in its government-wide (full accrual) statements for 2003 and 2004? Explain.

4–4

Nonexchange revenues can be of four types.

The GASB has identified four classes of nonexchange revenues:

- Derived tax
- Imposed
- Government-mandated
- Voluntary

1. For each of the following revenue transactions involving a city, identify the class in which the revenue falls and prepare a journal entry for a governmental fund for the current year (2004), as necessary. Provide a brief explanation or justification for your entry.

a. In December 2004, the state in which the city is located announced that it would grant the city $20 million to bring certain public facilities into compliance with the state's recently enacted disability laws. As of year-end the city had not yet received the funds and it had not yet expended any funds on the state-mandated facility improvements.

b. The city imposes a $100 tax on all sales of real estate. The tax is collected by the title companies that process the sales and must be forwarded to the state within thirty days of the transaction. In December, there were 600 sales of real estate. As of year-end the city had collected $40,000 of the $60,000 that it was owed.

c. In December 2004, the state announced that the city's share of state assistance for the calendar year 2005 would be $120 million.

d. The city imposes a tax on all boats owned by residents. The tax is equal to 1 percent of the assessed value of a boat (determined by the city by taking into account the boat's original cost and its age). The tax is payable on the last day of the year prior to the year which the tax is intended to finance. In 2004 the city levied $640,000 of 2005 boat taxes of which it collected $450,000.

e. A local resident sends to the city a copy of her will, in which she bequeaths $3 million to the city museum upon her death.

f. The U.S. Justice Department announces that it will reimburse the city, up to $400,000, for the purchase of telecommunications equipment. As of year-end the city had incurred only $200,000 in allowable expenditures.

g. A resident donates $10 million in securities to the city to support a cultural center. Only the income from the securities, not the principal, can be spent.

2. What amount of revenue would the city recognize in its government-wide statement of activities for 2004 for each of the above transactions? Explain.

4–5

Grants are not necessarily recognized as revenue when awarded.

Columbus City was awarded a state reimbursement grant of $150,000 to assist its adult literacy program. The following were significant events relating to the grant:

a. The city, which is on a calendar year, was notified of the award in November 2003.

b. During 2004 it expended $30,000 on the literacy program and was reimbursed for $20,000. It expected to receive the balance in January 2005.

c. In 2005 it expended the remaining $120,000 and was reimbursed by the state for the $10,000 owing from 2004 and the amount spent in 2005.

1. Prepare journal entries to record the events in a governmental fund.

2. Suppose instead that the city received the entire $150,000 in cash at the time the award was announced in 2003. How much revenue should the city recognize in its governmental fund statements in each of the three years? Explain.

3. Suppose that, instead of a reimbursement grant, the state awarded the city an unrestricted grant of $150,000, which the city elected to use to support the adult literacy program. The city received the entire $150,000 in cash at the time the award was announced in 2003. How much revenue should the city recognize in its governmental fund statements in each of the three years? Explain.

4. Using the information provided for questions 1, 2, and 3, how much revenue should the city recognize in its government-wide statements for each of the three years? Explain.

4–6

Sales taxes should be recognized when the underlying event takes place.

A state requires "large" merchants (those with sales over a specified dollar amount) to report and remit their sales taxes within fifteen days of the end of each month. It requires "small" merchants to report and remit their taxes within fifteen days of the end of each quarter.

In January 2004, large merchants remitted sales taxes of $400 million owing to sales of December 2003. In February 2004, they remitted $280 million of sales taxes owing to sales of January 2004. In January 2004, small merchants remitted sales taxes of $150 million owing to sales of the fourth quarter of 2003.

1. Prepare a journal entry to indicate the impact of the transactions on the state's governmental fund financial statements for the year ending December 31, 2003.

2. Suppose, instead, that 10 percent of the taxes received by the state were collected on behalf of a city within the state. It is the policy of the state to remit the taxes to the city thirty days after it receives them. Prepare a journal entry to indicate the impact of the transactions on the city's governmental fund financial statements for the year ending December 31, 2003.

3. Suppose, instead, that it were the policy of the state to remit the taxes to the city ninety days after it receives them. How would your response to question 2 differ? Explain. Would your response be the same with respect to the city's government-wide statements?

4–7

The amount of revenue to be recognized from grants depends on the type of grant.

The following information relates to three grants that the town of College Hills received from the state during its fiscal year ending December 31, 2003:

a. A cash grant of $200,000 must be used to repair roads.

b. $150,000 in cash is received out of a total grant of $200,000 intended to reimburse the town for actual expenditures incurred in repairing roads. During the year, the town incurred $150,000 in allowable repair costs.

c. A cash entitlement grant of $200,000 is intended to supplement the town's 2004 budget and must be expended in that year.

1. Prepare journal entries to record the three grants in a governmental fund.

2. What amount of revenue would be reported for each grant in the town's government-wide statement of activities for 2003? Where on that statement would these revenues be most likely to be reported?

4–8

Unrealized investment gains and losses may be difficult to explain to legislators and constituents.

A government held the securities shown below (all of which are either bonds that mature in more

	Beginning Balance		Transactions during the year		Ending Balance	
	Cost	Fair Value	Purchases	Sales	Cost	Fair Value
A	$100	$100	—	—	$100	$120
B	520	540	—	—	520	510
C	200	240	—	250	—	0
D	—	—	330	—	330	315
	$820	$880	$330	$250	$950	$945

than one year or stocks) in one of its investment portfolios.

1. Ignoring dividends and interest, what amount of gain or loss should the government recognize during the year?
2. What was the government's "realized" gain or loss (sales proceeds less cost) for the year? Which gain or loss—that which would have to be reported on the financial statements (as computed in question 1) or the realized gain or loss—would be more indicative of the change in resources available for future expenditure?
3. Suppose that Security B is a long-term bond that the government intends to hold to maturity. What is the most probable reason for the decline in fair value during the year? In what sense is the reported loss indicative of an economic loss?

4–9

A change to the full accrual basis may have little impact upon reported revenues.

A city levies property taxes of $4 billion in June 2004 for its fiscal year beginning July 1, 2004. The taxes are due by January 31, 2005. The following (in millions) indicates actual and anticipated cash collections relating to the levy:

June 2004	$ 100
July 2004 to June 2005	3,600
July 2005 to August 2005	80
September 2005 to June 2006	150

The city estimates that $30 will eventually have to be refunded, owing to taxpayer appeals as to the assessed valuation of their property, and $70 will be uncollectible.

1. Prepare a journal entry for a governmental fund that summarizes the city's property tax activity for the fiscal year ending June 30, 2005.

2. Indicate the differences in the amounts that would be reported on the government-wide statement of net assets and the statement of activities.
3. Suppose that, in the following year, the tax levy and pattern of collections were identical to those of the previous year. What would now be the differences in the amounts reported on the government-wide statements?

4–10

Exploring Orlando's financial report

Refer to the financial statements of the City of Orlando in Chapter 3.

1. Per the government-wide statement of activities, how much revenue did the city recognize from property taxes?
2. What amount of property-tax revenue did the city recognize in the funds? Where is this amount reported?
3. Per the statement of activities, how much revenue did the city recognize from state sales taxes?
4. Per the fund statements, how much revenue did the city recognize from state sales taxes? If the amount is the same as is reported in the statement of activities, would this always be the case? Explain.
5. What amount did the city recognize in the general fund as proceeds of bonds and loans? This amount increased the fund balance. Did it also increase the city's net assets on the statement of net assets? Explain.
6. What is the total fund balance in the general fund? Can this amount be appropriated and spent for any purpose? Explain.
7. Per the government-wide statement of activities, is the Community and Youth Service self-supporting? Explain.

CHAPTER 5

Governmental Activities—Recognizing Expenditures and Expenses

In the previous chapter, our discussion centered on *nonexchange* revenues, as most revenues of governmental activities are of that type. By contrast, most expenditures result from *exchanges*—the acquisition of goods and services for cash or other assets. To be sure, governments also incur nonexchange expenditures—principally, grants to other governments, not-for-profits, and individuals (e.g., assistance payments). However, we need direct only minimal attention to them because, per GASB Statement No. 33, nonexchange expenditures should be accounted for as the mirror image of nonexchange revenues (except, of course, that the available criterion for revenues recognized on a modified accrual basis does not apply to expenditures).

Exchange expenditures are accounted for on a modified accrual basis on the governmental fund statements and on a full accrual basis on the government-wide statements. GASB Statement No. 34 states that governments should generally look to FASB standards (and those of its predecessors) issued before November 30, 1989, for guidance on when to recognize exchange expenditures of governmental activities on a full accrual basis.[1] This chapter, therefore, is devoted mainly to the modified accrual basis, although we also note how expenditures would be accounted for differently on the full accrual basis.

HOW IS THE ACCRUAL CONCEPT MODIFIED FOR EXCHANGE EXPENDITURES?

THE DISTINCTION BETWEEN EXPENDITURES AND EXPENSES Under the modified accrual basis of accounting governmental funds are concerned with **expenditures** rather than **expenses**. Expenditures are decreases in net *financial* resources, whereas expenses are reductions in overall net assets. Expenditures are generally recognized when resources are acquired; expenses when resources are consumed.

MODIFICATIONS TO THE ACCRUAL BASIS Owing to the importance of the budget, governmental fund expenditures are closely tied to cash flows and near-cash flows, rather than to flows of economic resources. In addition, governmental funds report only current, not long-term, liabilities. Therefore, although the general principles of

---

[1]GASB Statement No. 34, *Basic Financial Statements—and Management's Discussion and Analysis—for State and Local Governments*, para. 17.

accrual accounting apply to governmental fund expenditures, they are applied differently in key respects. Under the modified accrual basis, governmental fund expenditures are decreases in *net current financial resources*—current assets less current liabilities. However, governmental fund liabilities are considered current only when they must be liquidated with expendable available financial resources—not, as in businesses and in the government-wide statements, when they must be paid within a year.

A government should recognize an expenditure in a governmental fund when the fund's net expendable available financial resources are reduced—that is, when the government either pays cash for goods or services upon receipt or it *accrues* (gives accounting recognition to) a governmental fund liability. Under the modified accrual basis a government should, as a general rule, *accrue* a liability in the period in which it *incurs* (becomes obligated for) the liability. This general rule, however, does not by itself distinguish the modified accrual basis from the full accrual basis. Rather, the distinction results from several *exceptions* set forth by the GASB.

These exceptions permit governments to delay recording both a governmental fund liability and its associated expenditure until the period in which the liability must be paid—that is, when the payment will reduce expendable available financial resources. Until that period, the government need report the liability only in its government-wide statements and in a schedule of long-term obligations.

HOW SHOULD WAGES AND SALARIES BE ACCOUNTED FOR?

Most governments pay their employees on a specified day of a week or month. When the end of a pay period does not coincide with the fiscal year-end, the government must carry over wages and salaries until the next year. Should these amounts be reported as expenditures in the period earned or in the period paid?

EXAMPLE   *Wages and Salaries*

A city pays its employees for the two-week period ending January 4, 2004, on January 9, 2004. The portion of the payroll applicable to December 2003 is $40 million, an amount included in the city's 2003 budget.

GASB Standards

GASB Interpretation No. 6, *Recognition and Measurement of Certain Liabilities and Expenditures in Governmental Fund Financial Statements*, states that "In the absence of an explicit requirement to do otherwise, a government should accrue a governmental fund liability and expenditure in the period in which the government incurs the liability. Governmental fund liabilities and expenditures that should be accrued include liabilities that, once incurred, normally are paid in a timely manner and in full from current financial resources—for example, salaries, professional services, supplies, utilities, and travel. To the extent not paid, such liabilities generally represent claims against current financial resources and should be reported as governmental fund liabilities."[2] Hence, wages and salaries should be recognized in the period in which the employees earn them.

---

[2]GASB Interpretation No. 6, *Recognition and Measurement of Certain Liabilities and Expenditures in Governmental Fund Financial Statements*, para. 12

In the example, the following entry would be made in December 2003, corresponding to the amount earned before year-end (ignoring payroll-related taxes, withholdings, and benefits):

Payroll expenditures	$40	
Accrued wages and salaries		$40

To record the December payroll (in 2003)

The entries in this chapter designate an **object** classification (such as payroll or insurance). Alternatively, they could designate an *organizational unit* (such as a police or fire department) or a *function or program* (such as public safety or general government). Statement No. 34 requires governments to report expenditures at a minimum by function on both the governmental fund and the government-wide statements. However, they are typically charged initially to an object account.

DIFFERENCES IN GOVERNMENT-WIDE STATEMENTS

Wages and salaries are recognized in the governmental funds on an accrual basis; no change would be required for the government-wide statements.

HOW SHOULD COMPENSATED ABSENCES BE ACCOUNTED FOR?

ACCOUNTING FOR VACATIONS Governments compensate employees for time off for vacations, holidays, sick leave, and other reasons. The accounting issues are similar to those for wages and salaries earned in one period but paid in another, but there are differences. Most significantly, compensated absences earned in one period may not be paid until several periods later. Hence, the liability is not current. Also, the amount to be paid is not always certain. Some employees may leave before they take all the time off to which they are entitled. Also, the amount paid is generally based on the pay rate in effect when the time off is taken, not when it is earned.

EXAMPLE *Vacation Leave*

In 2003, city employees earn $8 million in vacation leave and take (are paid for) $6 million. They defer the balance until future years. The unused leave *vests* (i.e., employees are legally entitled to it, even if they resign or are discharged) and can be taken at any time up to and including the retirement date.

GASB Standards

GASB standards state that vacation leave and comparable compensated absences should be accrued as a *liability* as the benefits are earned by the employees if *both* of the following conditions are met:

- The employees' rights to receive compensation are attributable to services already rendered.

(continued)

> ## GASB Standards (*continued*)
>
> • It is probable that the employer will compensate the employees for the benefits through paid time off or some other means, such as cash payments at termination or retirement.
>
> The compensation should be based on the wage or salary rates in effect at the balance sheet date, and employers should adjust for benefits that are expected to lapse.[3]

Although this guidance appears to sanction the accrual of vacation pay, compensated absences are one of the exceptions mentioned earlier. The GASB explains that compensated absences liabilities are normally liquidated with expendable available financial resources when the payments are made. Therefore, the vacation pay expenditures and related fund liabilities should be recognized in the periods in which the payments are due.[4] Until then, the liabilities should be reported only in the government-wide statements and in a schedule of long-term obligations.

The following entry would give effect to the GASB standards:

Vacation pay expenditure $6
   Cash (or wages payable) $6
To record vacation pay (e.g., in general fund)

The $2 million deferred until future periods should be recognized as an expenditure in the years the vacations are taken and paid for.

DIFFERENCES IN GOVERNMENT-WIDE STATEMENTS

The government-wide statements are on a full accrual basis. Accordingly, the city should report vacation pay expense of $8 million in 2003 and a long-term liability (accrued vacation pay) for the $2 million of earned but unused vacation.

ACCOUNTING FOR SICK LEAVE Like vacations, sick leave is a compensated absence, but there are critical distinctions that result in different accounting requirements. First, unlike vacation leave, the timing of sick leave is beyond the control of the employer and the employee. Second, most organizations permit only a portion of sick leave, or none of it, to vest. That is, employees can store sick days not taken in a particular year until they need them. However, if they resign or are terminated, they are not entitled to compensation for all of their unused leave.

---

[3]GASB Statement No. 16, *Accounting for Compensated Absences*, para. 7, and GASB Interpretation No. 6, para. 11.

[4]GASB Interpretation No. 6, para. 11.

EXAMPLE   *Sick Leave*

A city allows employees one sick day a month and permits them to accumulate any days they do not take. If they terminate after at least ten years of service, they will be paid for unused sick leave up to thirty days. In 2003, employees earned $12 million of sick leave that they did not take during the year. The city estimates that, of this amount, $8 million will be paid to employees in future years as sick leave, $1 million will be paid to ten-year employees upon their termination, and $3 million will not be paid.

GASB Standards

Per GASB standards, sick leave should be recognized as a liability and an expenditure only insofar as it is expected to be paid to employees upon their discharge, resignation, or retirement.[5] The standards are grounded in the rationale that sick leave, other than the portion that vests, is contingent upon an employee getting sick. The key economic event, therefore, is not the employee's service, but rather his or her illness.[6]

In the example, the city would recognize a liability only for the $1 million to be paid at termination.[7] However, as with vacation pay, only the portion of the liability expected to be liquidated with expendable available financial resources may be recorded in a governmental fund. Assuming, therefore, that none of the termination benefits will be paid with funds budgeted for the current year, no entry is required in the general or other governmental fund. The obligation would be reported only in a schedule of long-term obligations.

DIFFERENCES IN GOVERNMENT-WIDE STATEMENTS

Recognition of sick leave on a full accrual basis would not affect the measurement of the obligation, only when it is reported. As with vacation pay, both the expense and the liability (the $1 million to be paid upon termination) would be reported in the government-wide statements in the period the sick leave is earned. The balance, the wages to be paid to employees who miss work because of actual illnesses, would be recognized as both an expense and a liability in the periods of the employee absences.

---

[5]GASB Statement No. 16, para. 8.

[6]FASB Statement No. 43, *Accounting for Compensated Absences*, draws a similar distinction between sick leave and other types of compensated absences. Whereas employers are required to accrue the costs of other types of compensated absences, they are not required to accrue a liability for nonvesting sick leave.

[7]GASB Statement No. 16 provides detailed guidance as to how government entities should estimate the amounts to be paid upon termination.

HOW SHOULD PENSIONS BE ACCOUNTED FOR?

Pensions are sums of money paid to retired or disabled employees owing to their years of employment. Under a typical defined benefit plan (one that specifies the benefits to be paid in the future), an employer makes a series of contributions to a special fund over the working lives of its employees. Under most plans the employees also contribute.

Calculating the employer's required contribution to a defined benefit plan is complex and based on a number of estimates such as employee life expectancy and turnover, and anticipated earnings of fund investments. In its simplest form, the required contribution is the employer's share of the total expected cost of pension benefits attributable to a particular period (i.e., the benefits earned by the employees in that period). If the government makes its required contribution in full, it will record an expenditure equal to the contribution. But what if the government contributes less or more than the required contribution per generally accepted accounting principles (GAAP) because of legal requirements or budgetary constraints? Should the expenditure be the required contribution, which is indicative of the economic value of the pension benefits earned by the employees during the period? Or should it be the actual contribution, which is likely to be indicative of the amount budgeted for pension payments in that period?

EXAMPLE   *Pension Contributions*

A city is informed by its actuary that it should contribute $55 million to its pension fund, an amount calculated in accordance with GAAP. However, the city contributes only $45 million.

GASB Standards

The standards set forth in GASB Statement No. 27, *Accounting for Pensions by State and Local Governmental Employers*, are consistent with those for compensated absences. The pension expenditure should be the amount that will be liquidated with expendable available financial resources.

Although, in the example, the economic cost of employee pension benefits earned during the period is $55 million, the city would report a governmental fund expenditure of only $45 million. It would disclose the balance in notes and reflect it as a liability in its schedule of long-term obligations.

DIFFERENCES IN GOVERNMENT-WIDE STATEMENTS

In their government-wide statements, governments would report pension expenses equal to their required contribution, irrespective of the amount actually contributed. This approach also is required by Statement No. 27 for proprietary funds, which are accounted for on a full accrual basis. Thus, in the example, the government would report pension expense of $55 million and a liability of $10 million.

HOW SHOULD CLAIMS AND JUDGMENTS BE ACCOUNTED FOR?

Common examples of claims and judgments against governments include those arising from

- injuries to employees (e.g., workers' compensation)
- negligence of government employees (e.g., medical malpractice in city hospitals, failure to properly repair streets, auto accidents, wrongful arrests)
- contractual disputes with suppliers
- employment practices (e.g., civil rights violations, sexual harassment, wrongful discharge)

The key accounting questions are when and in what amounts expenditures and liabilities should be reported. These questions arise, first, because of the considerable length of time between when an alleged wrong takes place and when the claim is ultimately resolved and, second, because of the uncertainties as to the likelihood and dollar amount of a required payment.

In governmental funds, the major constraint is identical to that faced in accounting for compensated absences. The event causing the claim or judgment usually precedes by one or more years the disbursement of financial resources, and governmental funds do not recognize long-term obligations.

EXAMPLE   *Claims and Judgments*

A county is sued for personal injuries caused by the negligence of a road maintenance crew. The county attorney estimates that the case will be settled for $400,000, but due to the slow pace of the judicial process, it will be at least five years before payment must be made.

GASB Standards

Per GASB Statement No. 10, *Accounting and Financial Reporting for Risk Financing and Related Insurance Issues*, a liability for claims and judgments should be recognized when information available before the issuance of the financial statements indicates that

- it is probable that an asset has been impaired or a liability has been incurred at the date of the financial statements, *and*
- the amount of the loss can be reasonably estimated.[8]

However, as with compensated absences, a governmental fund would report only the portion of the total liability that will be paid with expendable available financial resources. The balance would be reported in a schedule of long-term obligations. Thus, the expenditure would be reported in the period that the liability is liquidated, not when the offending incident took place or a settlement was agreed upon or imposed.

---

[8]GASB Statement No. 10, *Accounting and Financial Reporting for Risk Financing and Related Insurance Issues*, para. 53. These are the same criteria that are set forth in FASB Statement No. 5, *Accounting for Contingencies*.

In the example, the city would not recognize an expenditure or a liability until the year that it expects to liquidate the liability, because no portion of it is expected to be liquidated with expendable available financial resources before that year. However, the estimated liability would be reported in the schedule of long-term obligations, beginning with the year in which the estimated loss met the criteria of Statement No. 10.

DIFFERENCES IN GOVERNMENT-WIDE STATEMENTS

As with compensated absences and pensions, the full accrual basis would require that the city recognize an expense and a liability (of $400,000 or its discounted present value)[9] in the year that the loss liability first satisfies the Statement 10 criteria.

HOW SHOULD THE ACQUISITION AND USE OF MATERIALS AND SUPPLIES BE ACCOUNTED FOR?

The acquisition and use of materials and supplies (and the related issue of prepaid expenditures, to be discussed in the next section) present unique accounting problems in governmental funds. These items are not strictly *expendable available financial resources*, in that they will neither be transformed into cash nor used to satisfy governmental fund obligations. However, having supplies on hand obviates the need to purchase the items in the future.

Governments do not generally acquire inventories for resale or for use in manufacturing. However, they maintain inventories of office supplies, road maintenance and construction materials, spare parts, and other items needed for day-to-day operations. Accounting issues include:

- *The timing of the expenditure*. Specifically, should governmental funds recognize an expenditure when they *acquire* the materials and supplies, when they *pay for* them, or when they *use* them?
- *The reporting of the asset*. Specifically, should inventory be reported as a governmental fund asset, even though it is not strictly an expendable available financial resource?

EXAMPLE   *Supplies*

During the year, a city purchases $3.5 million of supplies, pays for $3 million, and uses $3.3 million. At the start of the year it had no inventory on hand. Hence, at year-end it has $0.2 million of supplies available for future use.

---

[9]GASB Statement No. 10, para. 24, neither mandates nor prohibits discounting claims except in specific circumstances that do not apply to the example.

GASB Standards

GASB standards permit governments to recognize inventory items as expenditures either when purchased (the *purchases* method) or when consumed (the *consumption* method). However, irrespective of the method used, significant amounts of inventory on hand should be reported on the governmental funds balance sheet.[10] Governments may *not* account for inventories on a payment (cash) basis.

PURCHASES METHOD Using the **purchases method**, the city would record the *purchase* of the inventory as an *expenditure*. Thus, in the example:

Supplies expenditure	$3.5	
Accounts payable		$3.5

To record the acquisition of supplies

Although the accounting is seemingly unambiguous, there's a complexity. Current standards state that significant amounts of inventory must be reported on the balance sheet. This is accomplished by reporting year-end inventory on hand as an asset offset by a fund balance reserve. (See the discussion of reserves in Chapter 3 and Orlando's governmental funds balance sheet in Table 3-3.) The following entry would do the trick:

Supplies inventory	$0.2	
Fund balance—reserve for supplies inventory		$0.2

To record the inventory on hand at year-end

This entry increases reported assets and reserved fund balance. It has no impact on either expenditures or unreserved fund balance. In subsequent years, the supplies inventory and the reserved fund balance would be adjusted to reflect the change in inventory during the year. If, for example, at the conclusion of the following year, the city had only $150,000 of inventory on hand, then both supplies inventory and the reserve would be reduced (debit reserve, credit inventory) by $50,000.

CONSUMPTION METHOD Using the **consumption method**, the city would record the inventory as an *asset* when purchased:

Supplies inventory	$3.5	
Accounts payable		$3.5

To record the acquisition of supplies

Then, as it *uses* the inventory, it would record an expenditure and reduce the inventory account:

Supplies expenditure	$3.3	
Supplies inventory		$3.3

To record the consumption of inventory

At year-end, the inventory account balance would be $0.2 million—the amount of supplies on hand. The reported expenditure would be $3.3 million—the amount of supplies consumed. A reservation of fund balance generally is not required when the consumption method is used. However, some governments elect to reserve a portion

---

[10]NCGA Statement No. 1, *Governmental Accounting and Financial Reporting Principles*, para. 73.

of fund balance—an amount equal to the inventory on hand. The reserve is intended to emphasize that such portion of fund balance represents inventory (as opposed to all cash or other more liquid assets) and is thereby unavailable for future appropriation.

DIFFERENCES IN GOVERNMENT-WIDE STATEMENTS

The purchases method is inconsistent with full accrual accounting. Hence, inventory expense should be reported on a consumption basis.

HOW SHOULD PREPAYMENTS BE ACCOUNTED FOR?

Prepaid expenditures are comparable in economic substance to inventories. For example, a government purchases an insurance policy covering more than one period. As with materials and supplies, it will consume a portion in one period and the balance in the following periods. Or, by prepaying rent in one period, it acquires the right to use property in a subsequent period.

GASB Standards

As with inventories, GASB standards permit governments to use either the purchases or the consumption method in accounting for prepaid expenditures.[11] In contrast to the standards for inventories, however, the GASB does *not* prescribe that governments using the *purchases* method report material amounts of prepayments on the balance sheet.

GASB standards do not distinguish between current and long-term prepayments. Thus, under the consumption method, the unused portion of a three-year insurance policy would be reported as a governmental fund asset—the same as a one-year policy.

DIFFERENCES IN GOVERNMENT-WIDE STATEMENTS

The use of the purchases method on full accrual government-wide statements is as inappropriate for prepayments as it is for inventories. Only the consumption method should be used.

HOW SHOULD CAPITAL ASSETS BE ACCOUNTED FOR?

The accounting issues for capital assets are comparable to those of each of the costs addressed so far in this chapter. Just as a three-year insurance policy benefits a government over the period covered by the policy, whether it is paid for before, during,

---

[11]NCGA Statement No. 1, Appendix A.

or after the policy period, so a computer with a three-year useful life benefits the government over three years regardless of the timing of payments. Many statement users and accountants have suggested that governmental funds should account for capital assets in the same way as businesses and proprietary funds do. That is, the cost of the asset should be recorded on the fund balance sheet when the asset is acquired and then allocated as depreciation expense in future periods, thereby matching the asset's cost to the revenues it helps generate.

However, governmental fund accounting aims to provide information as to the inflows and outflows of current financial resources and whether they were used in accordance with the entity's legally adopted budget. Governments must budget and appropriate the resources for capital assets in the periods when they are to be paid for, not those in which they will be used. Therefore, accounting practices in which capital asset expenditures are tied to services rather than to payments may not provide the sought-after budget-related information.

EXAMPLE   *Capital Assets*

A village purchases for cash $90,000 of road maintenance equipment expected to have a useful life of three years.

GASB Standards

General capital assets are the capital assets of governments that are not specifically related to activities reported in proprietary or fiduciary funds. Most often they result from the expenditure of governmental fund financial resources. Per GASB standards, governments do not report general capital assets or depreciation in governmental funds. Instead, they record expenditures in the period that requires the outflow of expendable available financial resources. The capital assets are reported on the government-wide statement of net assets (governmental activities column) and in a schedule of capital assets.

In the example, the following entry in a governmental fund would be appropriate when the assets are acquired:

Capital assets—expenditure $90,000
   Cash $90,000
To record the acquisition of equipment

Many capital assets are acquired with debt. The main accounting issue is that the purchase of the asset does not coincide with the repayment of the debt—or, therefore, with the outflow of the cash or other expendable resources required to obtain the asset. Thus, it is not obvious when the expenditures associated with the acquisition of the asset and the repayment of the debt should be recorded. For example, should the cost of the asset be recognized at the time of purchase, even in the absence of a cash outflow, or only as the debt is repaid?

When governments issue debt to acquire capital assets, they often account for the debt proceeds in a capital projects fund. However, they may also use the general fund or a special revenue fund. The debt may take the form of bonds, conventional notes, installment notes, or capital leases. The accounting for capital projects funds is discussed in Chapter 6. However, the general principles of accounting are the same for all governmental funds.

EXAMPLE   *Installment Notes*

As in the previous example, a village purchases road maintenance equipment for $90,000. This time, however, the equipment is acquired with three annual installments of $36,190—the amount required to liquidate a loan of $90,000 over three periods at an interest rate of 10 percent.

Inasmuch as long-term obligations are not reported in governmental funds, GASB standards require that the proceeds of long-term debt be reflected as other financing sources in the recipient fund's operating statement.[12]

Thus, were the village to *borrow* $90,000 cash and then use the proceeds to purchase the equipment, the following entries would be appropriate:

Cash	$90,000	
Other financing sources—installment		
note proceeds		$90,000

To record a loan

Capital assets—expenditure	$90,000	
Cash		$90,000

To record the acquisition of equipment

In the example at hand, however, the government effectively borrowed the purchase price and acquired the asset, but at the time of acquisition did not actually receive or pay cash. Hence, it could properly make the following combining entry that eliminates the debit and credit to cash:

Capital assets—expenditure	$90,000	
Other financing sources—installment		
note proceeds		$90,000

To record the acquisition of equipment

The related accounting question is how the loan repayment should be recorded. Specifically, to what type of account should the payment be charged, since no long-term liability is reported on the governmental fund balance sheet?

Current practice requires that the repayment be charged as an expenditure. Thus, the following entry would recognize the first payment of principal and interest:

Debt service expenditure (note principal)	$27,190	
Debt service expenditure (interest)	9,000	
Cash		$36,190

To record the first payment of installment note interest (10 percent of $90,000) and principal

---

[12]NCGA Statement No. 1, para. 73.

Subsequent payments would be recorded in the same way, with only the division of the payment between principal and interest changing from period to period. The equipment and long-term debt would be reported in, respectively, a schedule of capital assets and a schedule of long-term obligations (as well as in the government-wide statements).

The series of entries results in the asset being recorded as an expenditure twice—once when acquired and again as the loan is repaid. However, fund balance is not misstated, because the acquisition expenditure is offset by other financing sources—a credit to fund balance that adds back the amount of the charge.

Goverments also acquire capital assets through capital leases, which are, in economic substance, purchase-borrow transactions. Accordingly they are accounted for just as other transactions in which the government finances the acquisition of long-term assets with long-term debt. Capital leases are addressed in more detail in Chapter 8.

HOW SHOULD INTEREST AND PRINCIPAL ON LONG-TERM DEBT BE ACCOUNTED FOR?

Interest on long-term debt is a major expenditure for many governments. Most typically, government debt takes the form of bonds, which pay interest twice per year. Many governments accumulate the resources to pay debt interest and principal in a debt service (governmental) fund. However, the necessary resources are likely to be transferred to the debt service fund from the general fund or a special revenue fund.

Because governmental funds do not record long-term liabilities, the increase in (debit to) cash when debt is issued is offset by a credit to *bond proceeds*—an other financing source (operating statement) account—rather than to *bonds payable*. Therefore, when the bonds are repaid, the offset to the reduction of cash cannot be to a liability, but must be to an expenditure or comparable operating statement account.

The key accounting issues with regard to long-term debt interest and principal arise because an interest payment may cover some months in one year and some in another, and a principal repayment covers the entire time the debt has been outstanding. Should the expenditures be allocated proportionately among the years (i.e., accrued) or should they be recognized entirely in the year of payment?

Proportionate allocation would capture the economic substance of the transaction. However, taxpayers obviously prefer to provide resources only as they are required to satisfy current obligations. Most governments budget (appropriate) resources for principal and interest only for the period in which a payment is due—not for future payments. Therefore, the budgetary compliance objective, in contrast to the interperiod equity objective, would suggest that the expenditures be recognized entirely in the year the payments are due.

EXAMPLE   *Long-Term Debt*

On August 1, 2003, a state issues $100 million of twenty-year, 6 percent bonds for $89.3 million, a price that reflects a semiannual yield of 3.5 percent. Interest ($3 million per semiannual period) is payable on January 31 and July 31, beginning January 31, 2004.

GASB Standards

GASB standards specify that interest and principal on long-term debt should not be accrued in governmental funds until the period in which they are due. Until then, they are not current liabilities; they will not require the liquidation of expendable available financial resources.

In the example, the government would make *no entry* in 2003 to accrue either interest or principal payments on the debt. On January 31, 2004, when the first interest payment is due, it would accrue interest expenditure and record a corresponding liability in the fund that will pay the interest:

Debt service, interest—expenditure	$3	
Matured interest payable		$3

To record obligation for interest due

When the bonds mature in July 2023 the government would make a comparable entry to record the obligation for repayment of principal:

Debt service, principal—expenditure	$100	
Matured bonds payable		$100

To record obligation for matured bonds payable

ADVERSE CONSEQUENCES OF FOCUS ON CASH PAYMENTS Consistent with the standards that neither interest nor principal should be accrued until due, current standards for governmental funds make no provision for recognizing and amortizing bond discounts or premiums. As a result, the reported interest expenditure fails to capture the true economic cost of using borrowed funds. Instead, it indicates merely the required interest payments. In the example, the state had the use of $89.3 million (the amount of the proceeds), not $100 million (the face value). Its true economic cost of using the borrowed funds in the six months ending January 31, 2004, was $3.1 million ($89.3 million times the effective interest, or yield, rate of 3.5 percent per period), not $3.0 million (the required payment). Nevertheless, as illustrated, the state would record an interest expenditure equal to the $3.0 million required payment.

The failure of current standards to recognize premiums and discounts in governmental funds may not be particularly serious when the difference between a bond's **coupon rate** and its **yield rate** is small. But large differences result in fund financial statements that seriously distort borrowing costs. Consider an extreme case. A government issues $100 million of twenty-year **zero coupon bonds**. The bonds are sold for $25.26 million, a price that provides an annual yield of 7 percent. As implied by their name, these bonds pay zero interest each period. Instead, they are sold at a deep discount, in this case a discount of $74.74 million. Upon maturity, the investor, who loaned the government $25.26 million, would receive $100 million. Inasmuch as $25.26 million is the present value of $100 million discounted at a rate of 3.5 percent for forty periods, the bonds provide a return of 3.5 percent (compounded) per semiannual period.

Under current standards for governmental funds the government would record *no* interest or principal costs until the bonds mature. In the period of maturity it would recognize the entire $100 million as a debt service expenditure. Fortunately, users are informed of the economic costs through the government-wide statements in which long-term debt is accounted for on a full accrual basis.

ACCRUAL OF INTEREST AND PRINCIPAL WHEN RESOURCES ARE TRANS-FERRED GASB standards make one exception to the general rule that neither interest nor principal be accrued in governmental funds. If resources to service the debt are transferred from one fund to a debt service fund in a current year for payment of principal and interest due early the next year (within no more than a month), then both the expenditure and related liability *may* be (are not *required* to be) recognized in the recipient fund.[13]

Suppose that, in the example, in 2003 the government transferred from the general fund to the debt service fund $2.5 million of the $3 million interest payment due on January 31, 2004. The government would, of course, recognize the cash received by the debt service fund as a fund asset and would record a corresponding increase in the debt service fund balance. Per current standards, to avoid reporting a misleadingly high fund balance in the debt service fund, it would be permitted also to accrue the related interest expenditure. Thus:

Debt service, interest—expenditure $2.5
    Accrued interest payable $2.5
To accrue interest in the amount of resources received from the general fund

---

DIFFERENCES IN GOVERNMENT-WIDE STATEMENTS

In the government-wide statements, long-term debt must be reported at face value plus any unamortized premiums or less any unamortized discounts. Interest must be accrued; the timing of cash payments is irrelevant to the period in which the expense is recognized.

Thus, when the bonds are issued, the state would have a liability for bonds payable of $100 million less unamortized discount of $10.7 million. In the 2003 year-end financial statements, the statement of activities would report interest expense of $2.6 million (5/6 of $89.3 million times 3.5 percent effective interest). Interest expense would consist of $2.5 million of interest payable (5/6 of $100 million times the 3 percent coupon rate) and $0.1 million of amortization of bond discount (interest expense less interest payable). The statement of net assets would therefore report bonds payable of $100 million less unamortized discount of $10.6 million ($10.7 million original discount less $0.1 million amortized to interest expense in the last five months of 2003).

Table 5-1 summarizes the seven differences that we have discussed in the previous sections of this chapter in the way the accrual concept is applied in the governmental funds compared with the government-wide statements.

---

[13]NCGA Statement No. 1, para. 108.

TABLE 5-1
Seven Exceptions to the Accrual of Expenditures in Governmental Funds

GASB standards require that most expenditures of governmental funds be recognized on the accrual basis. However, the standards identify these seven exceptions.

1. *Vacations, sick leave, and other compensated absences* are not accrued unless they will be liquidated with current financial resources.
2. *Pension expenditures* are reported equal to the governmental fund's actual contribution for the year, not, as in the government-wide statements and the notes, equal to a required contribution that may be more or less than the cash contribution.
3. *Claims and judgments* are reported as expenditures only insofar as they will be paid out of current financial resources.
4. *Inventory* may be accounted for using either the purchases method or the consumption method, but significant amounts must be reported in the governmental fund balance sheet, regardless of the method used.
5. *Prepaid expenses* such as insurance may be accounted for using either the purchases or the consumption method. Unlike inventory, significant amounts generally need not be reported on the balance sheet.
6. *Capital asset costs* are reported as expenditures when the assets are acquired. Depreciation is not recorded in governmental funds.
7. *Repayments of long-term debt* are reported as expenditures as the payments are made; interest on the debt is ordinarily not accrued.

How should nonexchange expenditures be accounted for?

As previously noted, this chapter is directed mainly to *exchange* expenditures because, unlike revenues, few types of expenditures of governmental activities result from nonexchange transactions. Governments do not typically pay taxes or fines (nonexchange transactions), but they do make grants (most of which are nonexchange transactions) to other governments, not-for-profits, and individuals.

GASB Standards

Statement No. 33 indicates that nonexchange expenditures should generally be recognized symmetrically with their revenue counterparts. Thus, grant providers should recognize an expenditure when the recipient has satisfied all eligibility requirements, including time requirements. The eligibility requirements are those discussed in Chapter 4 for nonexchange revenues. As with revenues, purpose restrictions (i.e., constraints placed by grantors on the purposes for which the grants may be used) do not affect the timing of recognition of nonexchange expenditures.

Absent time requirements, a grantor government should accrue an expenditure as soon as it awards the grant, irrespective of when the grant will be paid. That is, the grant would be recognized on an accrual basis in both the governmental fund statements and the government-wide statements. Statement No. 33 states that the timing of recognition of expenditures, assets, and liabilities for nonexchange transactions is identical for the accrual and the modified accrual basis of accounting; only revenues are affected by the available criterion applicable to governmental funds.

HOW SHOULD INTERFUND ACTIVITIES BE ACCOUNTED FOR?

As stressed in Chapter 2, each of a government's funds is an independent fiscal and accounting entity. When the focus is on individual funds, many types of activity between funds create revenues and expenditures. Yet when the government is viewed as a whole, most of these activities are nothing more than intragovernmental transfers. If certain types of activities were classified as revenues of one fund and expenditures of another, then the revenues and the expenditures of the government as a whole would be overstated. On the other hand, for other activities, the failure to recognize an expenditure (or expense) in both funds could result in an understatement of the operating costs of each fund. Consider the following examples, which illustrate two different situations.

EXAMPLE *Interfund Transfer*

A government transfers $3 million from its general fund to a debt service fund for payment of interest. When the debt service fund pays the interest, it will record the payment as an expenditure.

Should the general fund record the payment to the debt service fund as an expenditure and the debt service fund record the receipt as a revenue? As independent entities, both funds incur expenditures and earn revenues. Yet if each fund recognized an expenditure, the government as a whole would recognize the interest cost as an expenditure twice (once in the general fund when the resources are transferred to the debt service fund and again when the interest is paid out of the debt service fund).

EXAMPLE *Interfund Purchase/Sale*

A government department (general fund) acquires $30,000 of supplies from a supply center (internal service fund).

The internal service fund will report the cost of the supplies "sold" as an expense. Should the general fund also report an expenditure? If it does not, then its reported expenditures—the measure of the cost of general government operations—would be less than if it had purchased the same supplies from outside vendors.

GASB Standards

Statement No. 34 differentiates between two types of interfund activities: reciprocal and nonreciprocal.

Reciprocal interfund activities are the internal equivalent of *exchange* transactions (those in which the parties receive and surrender consideration of approximately equal value). They include the following:

- *Payments for the purchase of goods and services at a price that approximates their external fair value.* An example would be when the general fund acquires goods from an internal service fund. These activities should be reported as *revenues* (called *interfund services provided*) in the seller fund and *expenditures*, or expenses (called *interfund services used*) in the purchasing fund.

(continued)

GASB Standards *(continued)*

- *Loans and repayments of loans*. Loans that are expected to be repaid within a reasonable period of time should be reported by the lending fund as a receivable and by the borrowing fund as a payable. However, if the loans are not expected to be repaid within a reasonable period of time (and hence are not really bona fide loans) then the activity should be accounted for by both funds as nonreciprocal activities.

  Nonreciprocal interfund activities are the internal equivalent of *nonexchange* transactions. They represent transfers of cash for which goods or services of equivalent value have not been received in return. Typical examples are cash transfers from the general fund to a debt service fund for principal or interest payments on long-term debt or to a new internal service fund for "start-up capital." These types of interfund activities should be accounted for as *nonreciprocal transfers-out* by the disbursing fund and a *nonreciprocal transfers-in* by the receiving fund.

  Statement 34 also notes that interfund reimbursements (repayments from a fund responsible for an expenditure to the fund that initially paid for it) should *not* be reported in the financial statements. Thus, for example, if the general fund paid for a cost that was the responsibility of a capital projects fund, the expenditure and the corresponding reduction in cash should be reported only in the capital projects fund—as if that fund had paid the bill itself. The capital projects fund should not report a transfer-out to the general fund; the general fund should report neither a payment to the vendor nor a transfer-in from the capital projects fund.

In the first example, the transfer would be recorded by the two funds as *nonreciprocal* interfund activity:

Nonreciprocal transfer-out to debt service fund	$3	
Cash		$3
To record transfer to debt service fund (in general fund)		
Cash	$3	
Nonreciprocal transfer-in from general fund		$3
To record transfer from general fund (in debt service fund)		

By contrast, in the second example (the purchase/sale), the payment by the general fund to the internal service fund would be considered a *reciprocal* interfund activity and hence recorded as if it were an exchange transaction:

Supplies expenditure	$30,000	
Cash		$30,000
To record the purchase of supplies (in the general fund)		
Cash	$30,000	
Sales revenue		$30,000
To record the sale of supplies (in the internal service fund)		

DIFFERENCES IN GOVERNMENT-WIDE STATEMENTS

Government-wide statements present revenues and expenses from the perspective of the government, not of individual funds. Reported expenses are those of the government as a whole (with separate sections for governmental versus business-type activities), not of individual funds. Therefore, to avoid double-counting, interfund activities must be eliminated.

Special provisions of Statement No. 34 direct how interfund activities involving internal service funds should be eliminated. Internal service fund residual balances (those remaining after the interfund activities have been eliminated) are included in the governmental activities column because internal service funds provide services mainly to governmental activities. The reporting of internal service funds was introduced in Chapter 3 and is addressed further in Chapter 9.

WHAT CONSTITUTE OTHER FINANCING SOURCES AND USES?

Governmental funds receive or use resources from transactions that, under a full accrual basis, would affect long-term asset or liability accounts. For example, if a business issued long-term debt, it would establish a long-term liability. However, the measurement focus of governmental funds excludes capital assets and long-term liabilities. Therefore, resources received from the issuance of bonds cannot be recorded as fund liabilities. Although similar to revenues in that they increase fund balance, the proceeds of debt issues lack the characteristics of conventional revenues in that they will need to be repaid. Similarly, the proceeds from the sale of equipment can neither reduce a reported asset nor be interpreted as a revenue.

Generally accepted accounting principles direct that certain governmental fund resource flows that would otherwise affect long-term assets or liabilities be classified on statements of revenues, expenditures, and changes in fund balances as *other financing sources and uses*. The main types are as follows:

- proceeds of long-term debt
- proceeds from the sale of fixed assets
- present value of assets and liabilities created by capital leases
- payments to bond escrow agents who maintain accounts for the eventual repayment of long-term obligations
- nonreciprocal transfers

HOW SHOULD GOVERNMENTAL FUND OPERATING SYSTEMS BE FORMATTED?

In light of the variety of activities and transactions in which the multitude of different entities engage, governments need flexibility as to the form and content of their financial statements. At the same time, though, a certain degree of uniformity is required if statement users are to make meaningful comparisons among governments.

Therefore, Statement 34 sets forth the general framework of the governmental fund statement of revenues, expenditures, and changes in fund balances.[14]

GASB Standards

Revenues, expenditures, and changes in fund balances should be reported in governmental funds in a statement that takes the following form (amounts assumed for illustration):

Revenues (detailed)	$100
Expenditures (detailed)	90
Excess of Revenues over Expenditures	10
Other Financing Sources and Uses, Including	
Transfers (detailed)	(5)
Special and Extraordinary Items (detailed)	8
Net Change in Fund Balance	13
Fund Balance, Beginning of Period	11
Fund Balance, End of Period	$24

Expenditures would generally be shown by function (e.g., public safety, recreation, administration) rather than by object (e.g., salaries, travel, rent).

The governmental fund statement of revenues, expenditures, and changes in fund balances of Orlando is illustrated in Chapter 3, Table 3-5.

WHAT IS THE SIGNIFICANCE OF THE GOVERNMENTAL FUND FINANCIAL STATEMENTS?

The ultimate question faced by governmental fund financial statement readers is, "What does it all mean?" A governmental fund balance sheet presents the fund's net current financial resources at a particular point in time; its operating statement accounts for the net change in those resources during a particular period of time. All measurements are in accord with GAAP, thereby enabling users to compare similar operations of different governments. However, the governmental fund statements do not fully meet either the budgetary compliance or the interperiod equity objective. For example:

- Revenues and expenditures may be recognized on different bases than they are in the government's budget.
- Fund balance, inasmuch as it is derived from revenues and expenditures, may not be indicative of amounts legally available for future appropriation.
- The balance sheet may not capture all economic resources and obligations. Conspicuously missing may be certain long-term receivables, as well as capital assets and long-term obligations.

---

[14]GASB Statement No. 34, para. 86.

The limitations of the governmental fund statements do not, by themselves, imply criticisms of either the statements or the GASB. As suggested in Chapter 1, it is questionable whether a single set of financial statements can satisfy each of the key accounting and reporting objectives. It is for that reason that the complete governmental reporting model established by Statement No. 34 encompasses two sets of financial statements—fund and government-wide.

QUESTIONS FOR REVIEW AND DISCUSSION

1. What is the distinction between *expenditures* and *expenses* as the terms are used in governmental accounting?

2. A government expects to pay its electric bill relating to the last month of its current fiscal year sometime in the following year. An official of the government requests your advice as to whether the anticipated payment should be charged as an expenditure of the current or the following year. How would you respond?

3. Under pressure to balance their budgets, governments at all levels have resorted to fiscal gimmicks, such as delaying the wages and salaries of government employees from the last day of the month to the first day of the following month. In the year of the change they thereby had one fewer pay periods. How would the change affect the reported expenditures of a governmental fund under GAAP?

4. GAAP require that, if specified conditions are satisfied, the costs of compensated absences be accrued as a liability as the benefits are earned by employees. Yet even if a government adheres to these standards, it might not necessarily have to record a governmental-fund expenditure indicative of the amount accrued and the liability recognized. How can that be? Explain and justify.

5. A government permits its employees to accumulate all unused vacation days and sick leave. Whereas (in accord with current standards) it may have to "book" a liability for the unused vacation days, it may not have to record an obligation for the unused sick leave. Explain and justify the applicable standards.

6. A government accounts for inventory on the purchases basis. Why *must* it offset its year-end inventory balance with a fund balance reserve?

7. A government sells a building that it had acquired the previous year. When acquired, the building had an expected useful life of thirty years. The sales price exceeded the amount that the city had paid for the building. How would the sales transaction affect revenues and fund balance (or net assets) of the government's fund statements and government-wide statements?

8. Governments are not required to accrue interest on long-term debt in governmental funds even if the interest is applicable to a current period and will be due the first day of the following year. Explain and justify the standards that permit this practice.

9. A school district accounts for its pension costs in a governmental fund. In a particular year the district's actuary calculates the required contribution for the year to be $18 million. The district, however, had only budgeted $15 million and chooses to contribute only what was budgeted. What should the district report as its pension expenditure for the year? Explain.

10. A city's electric utility transfers $40 million to its general fund. Of this amount, $30 million is a return of the general fund's initial contribution of start-up capital. The balance is a payment in lieu of property taxes that a private utility operating in the city would have had to pay. Explain how each element of the transfer would be reported in the general fund's operating statement.

11. True or false? A government's unreserved general fund balance at year-end is ordinarily indicative of the amount that the government has available for appropriation in future years. Explain and provide an example to support your answer.

Exercises and Problems

5-1

Assume that Nolanville's fiscal year ends on December 31 to answer the following questions.

1. Nolanville's payroll for one of its departments is $15,000 per week. It pays its employees on the Thursday of the week following that in which the wages and salaries are earned. In 2003, December 31 fell on a Wednesday. For the workweek beginning Monday, December 29, 2003, and ending Friday, January 2, 2004, employees were paid on Thursday, January 8, 2004. For fiscal 2003, what amount should the city recognize as wage and salary expenditure/expense pertaining to the week ending Friday, January 2, 2004, in its fund statements and its government-wide statements?

	Fund Statements	*Government-wide Statements*
a.	$ 0	$ 0
b.	$9,000	$9,000
c.	$ 0	$9,000
d.	$9,000	$ 0

2. In its fund financial statements, the city would recognize the receipt of a new computer (to be used for general administrative purposes) that it had ordered the previous year as an
   a. encumbrance
   b. expense
   c. expenditure
   d. asset

3. In 2003, city employees earned $1.4 million in sick leave. The city estimates that of this amount, $0.8 million will actually be paid to employees who take sick leave. Of the balance, $0.1 million will be paid to employees upon their retirement or resignation and $0.5 million will not have to be paid (since employees are limited in the number of sick days that they can carry over from one year to the next). The amount that the city should add to a fund-statement liability account as of year-end 2003 is
   a. $0
   b. $0.1 million

c. $0.8 million
   d. $0.9 million

4. Assume the same facts as in question 3. The amount that the city should add to a government-wide statement liability account as of year-end 2003 is
   a. $0
   b. $0.1 million
   c. $0.8 million
   d. $0.9 million

5. In 2003, city employees earned $3.6 million in vacation pay that they did not use during the year. The city estimates that of this amount, $2.8 million will be paid in 2004 (out of amounts budgeted for that year), $0.6 million will be paid in subsequent years, and the balance of $0.2 million will not have to be paid. The amount that the city should add to a fund-statement liability account as of year-end 2003 is
   a. $0
   b. $2.8 million
   c. $3.4 million
   d. $3.6 million

6. Assume the same facts as in question 5. The amount that the city should add to a government-wide statement liability account as of year-end 2003 is
   a. $0
   b. $2.8 million
   c. $3.4 million
   d. $3.6 million

7. Nolanville starts fiscal 2003 with $25,000 in supplies. During the year it orders $180,000 in supplies, receives $170,000, and uses $190,000. It accounts for inventories on the purchases basis. In its 2003 governmental fund financial statements it should report

	Expenditure	*Fund Balance Reserve*
a.	$180,000	$ 0
b.	$170,000	$5,000
c.	$190,000	$ 0
d.	$190,000	$5,000

8. Assume the same facts as in question 7. In its 2003 government-wide financial statements it should report

	Expense	*Restricted Net Assets*
a.	$170,000	$ 0
b.	$170,000	$15,000
c.	$190,000	$ 0
d.	$190,000	$15,000

9. On December 1, 2003, Nolanville issued $10 million of thirty-year, 8 percent bonds for $9.78 million, a price that reflects a semiannual yield of 4.1 percent. Interest ($400,000 per semiannual period) is payable on May 31 and November 30, beginning May 31, 2004. In its 2003 fund and government-wide statements, Nolanville should report an interest expenditure/expense of

	Fund Statements	*Government-wide Statements*
a.	$ 0	$ 0
b.	$66,667	$66,667
c.	$66,830	$66,830
d.	$ 0	$66,830

10. In May 2006, Nolanville repaid $2 million of the bonds that it had issued in 2003. In its 2006 fund and government-wide statements, Nolanville should report an expenditure/expense relating to the repayment of the bonds of

	Fund Statements	*Government-wide Statements*
a.	$ 0	$ 0
b.	$2 million	$ 0
c.	$ 0	$2 million
d.	$2 million	$2 million

5-2

During its fiscal year ending August 31, 2003, the Eaton School District engaged in the transactions that follow.

● It established a purchasing department, which would be accounted for in a new internal service fund to purchase supplies and distribute them to operating units. To provide working capital for the new department it transferred $1.7 million from its general fund to the internal service fund.

● During the year, operating departments that are accounted for in the general fund acquired supplies from the internal service fund, for which they were billed $300,000. Of this amount the government transferred $200,000 from the gen-

eral fund to the internal service fund, expecting to transfer the balance in the following fiscal year. The supplies had cost the purchasing department $190,000. During 2003, the operating departments used only $220,000 of the supplies, for which they were billed. They had no supplies on hand at the start of the year.

● The school district transferred $150,000 from its general fund to its debt service fund to make its required March 31, 2003, interest payment. This amount was paid from the debt service fund when due. It represented interest on $8 million of bonds that were issued, at par, on September 30, 2002. The next interest payment of $150,000 is due on September 30, 2003. The district also transferred $75,000 from the general fund to the debt service fund to provide for the eventual repayment of principal.

● The district transferred $4.5 million from the general fund to its pension fund (a fiduciary fund) in partial payment of its actuarially required contribution of $5.0 million for the year.

● On August 31, the district acquired school buses at a cost of $900,000. The district gave the supplier installment notes that required the district to make three annual payments of $361,903. The first payment is due in August 2004. The buses have a useful life of ten years, with no salvage value.

Select an answer from the list of amounts on the next page. An amount may be selected once, more than once, or not at all.

____ 1. Amount that the general fund should recognize as supplies expense, assuming that inventory is accounted for on a purchases basis.

____ 2. Amount that the district should recognize as a pension expenditure in its general fund.

____ 3. Amount that the district should recognize as a pension expense in its government-wide statements.

____ 4. Amount that the general fund should recognize as nonreciprocal transfers-out.

____ 5. Amount that the district should recognize as total debt service expenditures in its governmental funds.

____ 6. Amount that the government should recognized as total debt service expense in its government-wide statements.

____ 7. Amount that the district should recognize as other financing sources in its general fund financial statements.

___ 8. Amount that the district should recognize as capital-related expenditures (including depreciation) pertaining to its buses in its governmental fund financial statements. The district recognizes a full year's depreciation on all capital assets in the year of acquisition.

___ 9. Amount that the district should recognize as capital-related expenses (including depreciation) pertaining to its buses in its government-wide financial statements. The district recognizes a full year's depreciation on all capital assets in the year of acquisition.

___ 10. Amount that the district should recognize as fund-balance reserves in its governmental fund statements.

a. 0		i. 300,000	
b. 75,000		j. 900,000	
c. 80,000		k. 1,925,000	
d. 90,000		l. 4,500,000	
e. 137,500		m. 5,000,000	
f. 150,000		n. 8,000,000	
g. 220,000		o. 8,900,000	
h. 275,000			

5-3

The purchases method differs from the consumption method.

The Boyd School District began a recent fiscal year with $3,000 of supplies in stock. During its fiscal year, it engaged in the following transactions relating to supplies:

a. It purchased supplies at a cost of $22,000.
b. It paid for $19,000 of the supplies.
c. It used $20,000 of the supplies and therefore had $5,000 in supplies inventory at year-end.

The district establishes inventory reserves as required.

1. Record the transactions, assuming that the district uses the purchases method.

2. Record the transactions, assuming that the district uses the consumption method.

3. Comment on any differences between the two as they would affect the district's general fund financial statements.

5-4

Inventory transaction amounts during the year can be derived from year-end balances.

The following amounts relate to a city's supplies inventory for the year ended December 31, 2004:

Inventory on hand, 1/1/2004	$ 54,000
Expenditures	315,000
Inventory on hand, 12/31/2004	81,000

All purchases during the year were paid in cash.

Prepare journal entries to record the supplies purchased and consumed during the year.

1. Assume the city used the *consumption* method.

2. Assume the city used the *purchases* method.

5-5

Paid time off may not all be the same.

A city has adopted the following plan as to compensated time off:

- City employees are entitled to a specified number of days each year for holidays and vacation. The number depends on length of service (e.g., 20 days for employees with fewer than five years of service, twenty-five days for employees with between five and ten years, thirty days for employees with more than ten years). Employees may accumulate up to forty days, which they can either carry over to future years or be compensated for upon termination.

- Employees are also entitled to seven sick days per year. They may carry over to future years up to sixty sick days. However, upon termination they can be paid for no more than twenty unused days.

During 2004, the city paid employees $4.2 million for holidays and vacations during the year. Of this amount, $0.4 million was for days carried over from previous years. In addition, employees earned $0.5 million in time off that they expect to use, and be paid for, in the future.

The city also paid $1.5 million in sick leave, none of which was paid to employees upon termination. Of this amount, $0.3 million was carried forward from previous years. The city estimates that employees earned an additional $0.8 million in unused sick leave. Of this, $0.5 million will eventually be paid for as time off, $0.2 million will be paid upon termination, and $0.1 million will lapse.

1. Prepare a general fund journal entry to record the holiday and vacation compensation. Indicate the amount of any other liability that would be recorded on both the government-wide statements and the schedule of long-term obligations.

2. Do the same for the sick leave.

3. Justify any differences between the two sets of entries.

5-6

The manner in which a transfer is accounted for depends on its nature.

Prepare general fund journal entries to record the following cash transfers that a city made from its general fund to other funds. Be sure your entry reflects the nature of the transfer.

1. $4,000,000 to provide start-up capital to a newly established internal service fund that will account for the city's data processing activities.
2. $50,000 to pay for data processing services provided by the data processing internal service fund.
3. $38,000 to reimburse the capital projects fund for equipment rental costs that it incurred on behalf of activities accounted for in the general fund.
4. $300,000 to pay the electric utility fund for four months of electric service.
5. $600,000 to enable the debt service fund to make timely payments of principal and interest on outstanding general obligation debt.

5-7

Irrespective of how capital assets are acquired, they are recorded differently in governmental funds than in businesses.

In a recent year, Ives Township acquired six police cars at a total cost of $200,000. The vehicles are expected to have a useful life of four years.

1. Prepare the journal entries that the township would make in its general fund in the year of acquisition, assuming that:
   a. It paid for the cars in cash at the time of acquisition.
   b. It leased the cars agreeing to make four equal payments of $63,095, starting in year of acquisition, an amount that represents the annuity required to liquidate a loan of $200,000 at 10 percent interest. The lease would satisfy the criteria necessary to be accounted for as a capital lease (purchase-borrow transaction).
   c. It issued $200,000 in installment notes to the car dealer, agreeing to repay them in four annual payments of $63,095, starting in the year of acquisition.
2. Comment on how any assets or obligations that are not included in the governmental fund balance sheet would be reported.
3. Comment on any adjustments that would have to be made to report the assets on the government-wide statements.

5-8

Accounting practices for interest expenditures may neither reflect actual economic costs nor mirror those for interest revenues.

A town plans to borrow about $10 million and is considering three alternatives. A town official requests your guidance on the *economic cost* of each of the arrangements and advice as to how each would affect the town's *reported expenditures*. The alternatives are:

(1) The town would issue $10 million of twenty-year, 6 percent coupon bonds on September 1, 2004. The bonds would be issued at par. The town would be required to make its first interest payment of $200,000 on January 1, 2005.
(2) The town would issue $10 million of twenty-year, 6 percent bonds on July 1, 2004. The bonds would be sold for $9,552,293, a price that reflects an annual yield (effective interest rate) of 6.4 percent. The town would be required to make its first interest payment of $300,000 on December 31, 2004.
(3) The town would issue $32,071,355 of twenty-year, zero coupon bonds on July 1, 2004. The bonds would be sold for $10 million, an amount that reflects an annual yield of 6 percent. The bonds require no payment of principal or interest until June 30, 2024.

1. For each of the town's three alternatives, what would be the town's economic cost of using the funds in the year ending December 31, 2004? What would be the amount of interest expenditure that the town would be required to report for the year ending December 31, 2004 in its governmental funds?
2. Suppose that the town elects the first option and issues $10 million of twenty-year, 6 percent coupon bonds at par on September 1, 2004. The town establishes a debt service fund to account for resources that it sets aside to pay principal and interest on the bonds. On December 31, 2004, the town transfers $200,000 from the general fund to the debt service fund to cover the first interest payment that is due on January 1, 2005.
   a. How would the transfer be reported in the general fund?
   b. How would the transfer be reported in the debt service fund? What options are available to the town to record 2004 interest in the debt service fund?
3. Suppose that the town borrowed $10 million on September 1, 2004, and temporarily invested the proceeds in two-year, 6 percent Treasury

notes. The first payment of debt interest, $200,000, is payable on January 1, 2005.

a. What would be the town's economic gain from investing the funds in the year ending December 31, 2004? Ignore borrowing costs.

b. How much investment revenue should the town report for the year ending December 31, 2004? Assume there was no change in prevailing interest rates.

5-9

Fund balance deficits may not be all bad.

These are the balance sheet and statement of revenues, expenditures, and changes in fund balance for Boulder, Colorado's Parks and Recreation Fund, a special revenue fund, for the year ending December 31, 2004 (dates changed).

Boulder, Colorado Statement of Revenues, Expenditures, and Changes in Fund Balance Year Ended December 31, 2004 (in thousands)	
Revenues:	
General Property Taxes	$855
Other Taxes—Development Excise	663
Development Fees	13
Golf Expansion Fees	138
Interest Earnings	42
Lease/Rent From Land	24
Other	209
Total Revenues	1,944
Expenditures:	
Culture and Recreation	1,881
Interest	119
Total Expenditures	2,000
Excess (Deficiency) of Revenues	
Over Expenditures	(56)
Other Financing Uses:	
Transfers-Out	(123)
Net Change in Fund Balance	(179)
Fund Balance, Beginning of Year	(367)
Fund Balance, End of Year	$(546)

Balance Sheet as of December 31, 2004 (in thousands)	
Assets:	
Cash and Equivalents	$ 3
Investments at Cost or Amortized Cost	902
General Property Taxes Receivable	938
Accrued Interest	8
Other	9
Due From Other Funds	14

Balance Sheet *(continued)* as of December 31, 2004 (in thousands)	
Restricted Asset—Cash for	
Special Purposes	4
Total Assets	$1,878
Liabilities and Fund Balance:	
Liabilities:	
Vouchers and Accounts Payable	$ 120
Salaries and Wages Payable	9
Advances from Other Funds	1,357
Deferred Revenue—	
General Property Taxes	938
Total Liabilities	2,424
Fund Balance:	
Reserved For:	
Encumbrances	112
Special Purposes	24
Unreserved	(682)
Total Fund Balance	(546)
Total Liabilities and Fund Balance	$1,878

A note to the financial statements states the following:

Fund Deficits

The Parks and Recreation Fund has a fund balance deficit of $546,539. This deficit is the result of the Parks and Recreation Fund expenditures: one-half of the cost of a central irrigation system for city parks and the acquisition of Roper fields for soccer fields. The cost of the central irrigation system was shared with the Water Utility Fund to improve water conservation. The Parks and Recreation Fund has funded these projects through interfund loans with December 31, 2004, balances of: Water Utility Fund ($52,870), and Flood Control Utility Fund ($1,274,524).

1. Suppose that you are the chief accountant of the Parks and Recreation Department. A member of the city council accuses you and your department of mismanagement, as evidenced by the substantial fund deficit. How would you defend yourself? What is the significance of the fund deficit?

2. Prepare journal entries (as best you can with the information provided) in the Parks and Recreation Fund to record:

a. the acquisition of the central irrigation system and the Roper fields (assuming that the cost of the assets is equal to the December 31, 2004, interfund loan balances even though the acquisition was, in fact, made prior to 2004 and a portion of the balances had already been repaid by December 31, 2004)

b. the interfund loans

3. A schedule of changes in general capital assets by function and activity indicates the following with respect to parks and recreation:

General Capital Assets as of January 1, 2004	$24,100
Additions, 2004	1,291
Deductions, 2004	(373)
General Capital Assets as of December 31, 2004	$25,018

How are the additions (which are other than the irrigation system and the soccer fields) and deductions most likely reflected in financial statements of the Parks and Recreation Fund?

4. Another note to the financial statements indicates that the Boulder city council levies property taxes by December 15 of each year. The taxes are payable in full by April 15, or in two installments by June 15 of the following year. Prepare the 2004 property tax entries (in summary form) most likely made in the Parks and Recreation Fund.

5-10

Some transactions are reported differently in fund versus government-wide statements, others are not.

The State Department of Highways engaged in the following transactions or was affected by the following events during its fiscal year ending on December 31, 2004.

a. It signed a two-year lease for office space for the period June 1, 2004, through May 31, 2006. Rent was to be $20,000 per month. Upon signing the lease, it paid one year's rent of $240,000 in advance. It accounts for prepayments on a purchases basis.

b. In December, it settled accident-related litigation by agreeing to pay the injured party $2.5 million. The payment was to be made in June 2005.

c. In November, it announced $145 million in reimbursement grants to counties within the state. The grants are to cover road improvements to be made in the years 2005 and 2006.

d. In December, it announced a $5 million grant to a city to install computerized traffic signals. The

department expects to make payment in January but did not specify the year in which the funds can be expended.

e. On July 1, it issued $10 million of 6 percent, 20-year bonds, receiving proceeds of $10,234,930. The bonds were sold to yield of 5.8 percent (2.9 percent per semi-annual period). On December 31, it made its first semi-annual interest payment of $300,000.

Prepare journal entries to reflect how the transactions and events would be recorded for (1) governmental fund statements and (2) government-wide statements.

5-11

Exploring Orlando's Financial Report

Refer to the financial statements of the City of Orlando in Chapter 3.

1. Wages and salaries are often a large proportion of a general purpose government's expenditures. Why, then, are these amounts not separately reported in Orlando's government-wide and governmental fund financial statements?

2. The notes to Orlando's financial statements state that inventories are accounted for using the consumption method. What does this mean?

3. What amount does Orlando report for inventories related to governmental activities in its government-wide statement of net assets?

4. Does Orlando report a reservation of governmental fund balances for inventory? If so, how should users of the financial statements interpret the reservation?

5. What amounts does Orlando report in its governmental fund statements as expenditures for repayment of debt principal? Are the same amounts reported as expenses in the government-wide statements? Explain.

6. What types of other financing sources and uses does Orlando report in the general fund?

7. What effect did the other financing sources and uses have on the net change for the year in the general fund balance?

CHAPTER 6

Governmental Activities— Accounting for Capital Projects and Debt Service

In this chapter we discuss accounting for the *resources* to acquire general capital assets and service general long-term debt. Accounting for the assets and liabilities themselves will be addressed in Chapters 7 and 8. The resources to acquire the assets, especially those financed with debt, are generally accounted for in **capital projects funds**. However, they may also be accounted for in the general fund or special revenue funds, particularly if their costs are relatively low. Because all three fund-types are governmental, the accounting entries and issues are similar. The resources to service debts are typically accounted for in **debt service funds**.

First, we discuss capital projects and debt service funds. Then we address the related issues of special assessments, arbitrage, and debt refunding.

HOW DO GOVERNMENTS ACCOUNT FOR CAPITAL PROJECTS?

Governments establish capital projects funds to account for resources dedicated to the purchase and construction of capital facilities (other than those to be financed by proprietary and trust funds). They may maintain a separate fund for each major project or combine two or more projects in a single fund. Capital facilities include buildings, infrastructure (such as roads, bridges, airports, and sewer systems), and plant and equipment.

REASONS FOR MAINTAINING CAPITAL PROJECTS FUNDS Governments *must* maintain capital projects funds for resources that are *legally restricted* for the acquisition of general capital assets. Some governments also maintain capital projects funds for resources they have set aside for capital purposes at their own discretion. This practice may mislead users of the fund financial statements into assuming that the resources are legally restricted when they are not. However, resources that are not restricted by law or external parties would be reported as *unrestricted* net assets in the government-wide statements.

Major capital projects are most commonly financed with bonds or other forms of long-term debt, but they may also be funded by grants, special tax levies, or assessments. Restrictions on capital project resources usually stem from debt covenants or from legislation authorizing the taxes or assessments. Generally the restrictions are exceedingly specific as to how the resources may be used. For example, they may be used only for the construction of a particular bridge or the purchase of a narrowly defined type of equipment.

BASIS OF ACCOUNTING Like all governmental activities, capital projects are accounted for on the modified accrual basis in the fund statements and on a full accrual basis in the government-wide statements. Accordingly, the principles of revenue and expenditure or expense recognition spelled out in Chapters 4 and 5 for all governmental activities are applicable to capital projects.

FUND FINANCIAL STATEMENTS Per GASB Statement No. 34, the requirements for reporting capital projects funds are similar to those for special revenue funds. Each major fund should be reported in a separate column in the governmental funds balance sheet and statement of revenues, expenditures, and changes in fund balances; nonmajor capital projects funds should be combined in a single column with other nonmajor governmental funds.

Statement No. 34 does not require a budgetary comparison statement for capital projects funds as it does for the general fund and for each major special revenue fund that has a legally adopted annual budget. This is because governments generally budget capital expenditures on the basis of projects rather than periods. Therefore, many governments do not prepare an annual budget for capital projects funds.

REPORTING BOND PROCEEDS AND ISSUE COSTS Government long-term obligations can take many forms. The most common form is bonds, which are formal certificates of indebtedness. However, the discussion in this section can be generalized to other forms of debt, such as leases and certificates of obligation, which often differ from bonds more in legal form than in economic substance.

Capital projects funds do not report long-term obligations. Therefore, when the proceeds of bonds or other long-term obligations are received, they must be accounted for as other financing sources.

When governments issue bonds, the cash they receive is seldom equal to the bonds' face value, for at least two reasons:

- *Issue costs.* The bond underwriters (the brokers and dealers who will distribute the securities to other brokers and dealers or sell them directly to investors) will withhold a portion of the gross proceeds as fees for their services. These fees are called **issue costs**.
- *Premiums and discounts.* The bond **coupon rate** (the stated interest rate) is rarely equal to the market rate or yield rate at the time of sale. Bonds may be printed with a coupon rate days or weeks prior to the issue date. Market rates fluctuate constantly, and the rate that will prevail at the time of issue cannot be determined accurately in advance. The exact rate that the bonds will yield is established by issuing the bonds at a price greater or less than face value. A bond sold to yield an interest rate *greater* than the coupon rate will be sold at a *discount*. Because the prevailing rate is greater than the coupon rate, the bond is of less value to an investor than a bond with a comparable face value paying the prevailing rate; hence, the investor will pay less than the face value for it. Conversely, a bond sold to yield an interest rate *less* than the coupon rate will be sold at a *premium*. Because the prevailing rate is less than the coupon rate, the bond is of greater value than a bond with a comparable face value paying the prevailing rate.

Whenever they can separate the underwriting and other issue costs from the discounts or premiums, governments should report the issue costs as an expenditure.

Bond premiums and discounts become an accounting issue only insofar as there is uncertainty as to how the "excess" cash will be disposed of and the manner of compensating for any cash deficiency.

EXAMPLE   *Bond Premiums and Discounts*

A government authorizes two highway construction projects, Project #1 and Project #2, each to cost no more than $50 million. To finance the projects, it issues two series of bonds, Series #1 and Series #2, each with a face value of $50 million. Both mature in thirty years (60 semiannual periods) and pay interest at an annual (coupon) rate of 6 percent (semiannual rate of 3 percent). Owing to the prevailing interest rate of 5.9 percent on the issue date, Series #1 is issued for $50.699 million (a *premium* of $0.699 million). However, as a consequence of subsequent increases in prevailing interest rates to 6.1 percent, Series #2 is issued for $49.315 million (a *discount* of $0.685 million).

The initial entries to record both bond issues are straightforward:

Cash	$50.699	
Other financing sources—bond proceeds (face value)		$50.000
Other financing sources—bond proceeds (bond premium)		0.699

To record the issue of Series #1

Cash	$49.315	
Other financing sources—bond proceeds (bond discount)	0.685	
Other financing sources—bond proceeds (face value)		$50.000

To record the issue of Series #2

Each project was authorized to cost no more than $50 million. Therefore, the $0.699 million premium should not be used to add unauthorized frills to the planned highway. Instead, it should be applied to future interest payments. The bonds were printed with a coupon rate of 6 percent. Owing to favorable market conditions, the government was able to borrow funds at only 5.9 percent. Still, its annual cash interest payments will be $3.0 million (6 percent of $50 million)—not $2.95 million (5.9 percent of $50 million). The $0.699 million premium can be seen as interest that investors paid the government up front to receive extra interest of $0.1 million each year over the life of the bonds. Accordingly, the government should transfer the $0.699 premium to the *debt service fund*—the fund that will be used to accumulate the resources required to pay the interest and principal on the bonds. The following entry would give effect to this policy:

Other financing use—nonreciprocal transfer-out of bond premium to debt service fund	$0.699	
Due to debt service fund		$0.699

To record the premium payable to the debt service fund

Accounting for the discount is generally not the mirror image of that for the premium. A bond discount, like a bond premium, adjusts the bond issue price so as to align the coupon rate with the prevailing rate. Because of the unfavorable market conditions, the government had to pay interest at a rate greater than the bond coupon rate. Therefore, it received less than the face value of the bonds; less than it apparently planned to spend on the capital project.

When the bonds are issued at a premium, the capital projects fund can transfer resources to the debt service fund. However, when the bonds are issued at a discount, the debt service fund would not have resources available for transfer to the capital projects fund. Therefore, the government has a choice. It can either reduce the scale of the project or make up the deficiency by some other means. If it elects to reduce the scale of the project, then no further journal entries are required. If it opts to fund the shortfall by other means, then the source of the funds will dictate the additional accounting entries. For example, if the government were to appropriate $0.685 million of general fund resources, then the following capital projects fund entry would be necessary:

Due from general fund	$0.685	
Other financing sources—nonreciprocal		
transfer-in from general fund		$0.685

To record anticipated transfer from the general fund to compensate for the bond discount

COMPREHENSIVE EXAMPLE
Main Types of Transactions Accounted for in Capital Projects Funds

The voters of New City authorize the issuance of $20 million in general obligation bonds to finance the construction of a new highway. The project is expected to cost $30 million (including bond issue costs), with the additional $10 million to be financed with a state grant. Although the grant may be paid in advance, it is intended to reimburse the city for actual costs incurred. The city is required to account for the resources in a fund dedicated exclusively to this project.

Issuing the Bonds   The city issues $20 million of bonds. Owing to favorable market conditions, the bonds are sold for $20.2 million. After deducting issue costs of $0.15 million, the sale nets $20.05 million.

Cash	$20.05	
Issue costs (expenditures)	0.15	
Other financing sources—bond proceeds		
(face value)		$20.00
Other financing sources—bond proceeds		
(bond premium)		0.20

To record the issuance of bonds

Transferring the Premium to the Debt Service Fund   The city transfers the premium to the debt service fund.

Other financing use—nonreciprocal transfer-out		
of bond premium to debt service fund	$0.05	
Cash		$0.05

To transfer the bond premium, net of issue costs, to the debt service fund

Encumbering Available Resources   The city signs several construction-related contracts for goods and services expected to cost $16 million. As discussed in Chapter 3, governments can avoid overspending fund resources by encumbering the fund balance in the amount of purchase orders and similar commitments.

Encumbrances	$16.00	
Reserve for encumbrances		$16.00

To encumber $16 million for contracts signed

Recording Grants   The city receives $8 million of its state grant. As discussed in Chapter 4 for general and special revenue funds, the recognition of reimbursement grant revenue should be expenditure driven. Hence, the city should record the advance payment from the state as deferred revenue.

Cash	$8.00	
Deferred revenue (grants)		$8.00

To record the advance from the state

Recording Expenditures   The city receives and pays contractor invoices of $15 million for construction and related services.

Expenditures—construction related	$15.00	
Cash		$15.00

To record construction and related expenditures

Capital projects funds are maintained to account for resources that will be expended on capital projects, not for the capital projects themselves. Therefore, construction outlays are charged as *expenditures*, not construction in process (an asset). The government should report the construction in process in its schedule of capital assets and its government-wide statements, as discussed further in Chapter 7.

When it records the expenditures, the city must also reverse the related encumbrance account entries and recognize the revenue that was previously deferred.

Reserve for encumbrances	$15.00	
Encumbrances		$15.00

To reverse the encumbrance entry upon receipt of services

Deferred revenue (grants)	$8.00	
Revenue from grants		$8.00

To recognize grant revenue upon incurring allowable costs

This entry assumes that the government recognizes grant revenue as soon as it has incurred any costs that the grant is permitted to cover. Hence, it does not divide its costs between those applicable to the bonds and those applicable to the grant.

Recognizing Investment Earnings   The city invests $5 million in U.S. Treasury notes so as to earn a return on temporarily available cash.

Marketable securities	$5.00	
Cash		$5.00

To record the purchase of Treasury bills

As of year-end, the city has earned $0.15 million in interest. Although it does not expect to receive the interest until the notes mature, the accrued interest is reflected in the market price of the notes. As observed in Chapter 4, GASB pronouncements require that appreciation in the fair value of investments be recognized as revenue.

Marketable securities	$0.15	
Investment revenue		$0.15

To recognize appreciation in investments

Table 6-1 presents an operating statement and balance sheet for New City's capital projects fund.

TABLE 6-1
New City
Capital Projects Fund—Construction of Highway
Statement of Revenues, Expenditures, and Changes in Fund Balance
(in millions)
For the City's Fiscal Year

Revenues:	
Grant from State	$ 8.00
Investment Revenue	0.15
Total Revenues	8.15
Expenditures:	
Bond Issue Costs	0.15
Construction Related	15.00
Total Expenditures	$15.15
Excess of Revenues over Expenditures	(7.00)
Other Financing Sources (Uses):	
Proceeds of Bonds (Including Premium)	20.20
Nonreciprocal Transfer-out of Premium to Debt Service Fund	(0.05)
Total Other Financing Sources (Uses)	20.15
Net Change in Fund Balance	13.15
Fund Balance, Beginning of Year	0
Fund Balance, End of Year	$13.15

Balance Sheet
As of the End of the City's Fiscal Year

Assets:	
Cash	$ 8.00
Marketable Securities	5.15
Total Assets	$13.15
Fund Balance:	
Reserved for Encumbrances	$ 1.00
Unreserved	12.15
Total Fund Balance	$13.15

HOW DO GOVERNMENTS ACCOUNT FOR RESOURCES DEDICATED TO DEBT SERVICE?

Debt service funds are maintained to account for *resources* accumulated to pay interest and principal on *general* long-term debt—that is, long-term debt associated primarily with governmental activities. Debt service funds do *not* record a liability for the debt principal, unless it has matured but payment has been delayed.

REASONS FOR MAINTAINING DEBT SERVICE FUNDS GASB standards, continued from its predecessor the National Council on Governmental Accounting (NCGA), direct that debt service funds be established when they are legally required and financial resources are being accumulated for principal and interest payments maturing in future years.[1]

Legal mandates are commonly incorporated into agreements associated with debt issuance. Lenders want assurance that the funds will be available to make timely payments of interest and principal. They may require that the borrower maintain a specified amount, perhaps one year's interest, in a *reserve* fund, similar to the way a landlord requires a tenant to deposit one month's rent.

Debt service funds may receive their resources from several sources:

- Transfers from the general fund
- Special taxes restricted to the payment of debt (e.g., a school district may dedicate a portion of its property tax to the repayment of bonds issued to construct a new high school)
- Special assessments (charges to an identifiable group of residents who will receive a disproportionate share of the benefits of a project for which long-term debt was issued).

As with capital projects funds, governments may be required to maintain several independent debt service funds or may be permitted to combine some or all of them into common funds.

BASIS OF ACCOUNTING Like all governmental funds, debt service funds are accounted for on the modified accrual basis. As discussed in Chapter 5, GASB standards stipulate that, unlike the general rule of expenditure accrual, unmatured principal and interest on general long-term debt are *not* considered current liabilities of the debt service fund, as they do not require the expenditure of existing fund assets. Moreover, governments are unlikely to appropriate the resources required for payment and transfer them to the debt service fund until the period in which the interest and principal actually must be paid.

It has been argued that it would be confusing to accrue a debt service fund expenditure and liability in one period and record the transfer of financial resources for debt service purposes in a later period, and it would overstate debt service fund expenditures and liabilities and understate fund balance. The standards make clear, however, that when the general fund appropriates resources for debt service in one year for payment early (within one month) in the next year, then the government *may*

---

[1]NCGA Statement No. 1, *Governmental Accounting and Financial Reporting Principles*, para. 30.

(but is not required to) accrue the expenditure and related liability in the debt service fund.[2]

In contrast to the accounting for debt service fund expenditures, the interest *revenue* on bonds held as investments is, in effect, accrued as earned. This is because investments must be stated at fair value, and interest earned but not yet paid affects fair value.

COMPREHENSIVE EXAMPLE
Main Types of Transactions Accounted for in Debt Service Funds
••

In January 2003, Carver City establishes a debt service fund to account for a serial issue of $100 million, 6 percent bonds sold at a premium of $200,000. Principal is to be repaid evenly over a period of twenty years beginning on December 31, 2003. Interest is payable semiannually, beginning June 30, 2003. Of the bond proceeds, $2 million is to be retained in the debt service fund as a reserve for payment of interest and principal.

The debt is to be repaid from a voter-approved addition to the property tax, plus earnings from debt service fund investments. Any revenue shortage is to be made up by a general fund appropriation. The revenues generated by the property tax are expected to increase over time. However, the city estimates that in 2003 it will collect only $8 million, not the $11 million required interest and principal payments.

Serial bonds, as distinguished from term bonds, which mature on a single specified date, are repaid in installments over the life of the issue. The first installment may be delayed for several years after the bonds have been issued, and uniform payments may not be required. Also, the amount of principal repaid with each installment, although established in advance, may vary from year to year. Serial bonds are, in essence, a collection of term bonds, each of which matures at a different time.

Transferring-in the Bond Premium and the Amount to Be Held as a Reserve   The bonds are issued and the proceeds are placed in a capital projects fund. The premium of $200,000 and the $2 million to be held in reserve are transferred from the capital projects fund to the debt service fund.

Cash	$2,200,000	
Other financing source—nonreciprocal transfer-in		
from the capital projects fund		$2,200,000

To record the transfer-in of the bond premium and the amount to be placed in reserve

The debt itself would be recorded only in the government-wide statements and in a schedule of long-term obligations, not in the debt service fund.

Recognizing Investment Earnings   The city purchases as an investment $1 million (face value) of long-term U.S. Treasury bonds. Acquired in the secondary market, the bonds pay interest at a rate of 6 percent annually (3 percent each semiannual period) and mature in seven years. They are purchased for $894,369—a price that provides an effective yield of 8 percent annually (4 percent semiannually).

Investment in bonds	$894,369	
Cash		$894,369

To record purchase of bonds as an investment

---

[2]GASB Interpretation No. 6, *Recognition and Measurement of Certain Liabilities and Expenditures in Governmental Fund Financial Statements*, para. 13.

As discussed previously, investments will be carried at fair value. Therefore, the bond discount should not be reported separately from the bonds.

During the year the city receives two semiannual interest payments of $30,000 (3 percent of $1 million). At the same time, the fair value of the bonds increases by $5,775 in the first period and by $6,006 in the second period. Even in the absence of changes in prevailing interest rates, the fair value of the bonds can be expected to increase each period by the amount by which the discount would otherwise be amortized. In that way, their fair value at maturity would be equal to their face value. In this instance, the increases in value can be attributed entirely to the amortization of the discount.

Cash	$30,000	
Investment in bonds	5,775	
Investment revenue		$35,775
To record the first period's interest		

Cash	$30,000	
Investment in bonds	6,006	
Investment revenue		$36,006
To record the second period's interest		

Recognizing Tax Revenue   During the year, the city collects $7.5 million of the $8.0 million in dedicated property taxes due during the period. It expects to collect the balance within sixty days of year-end.

Cash	$7,500,000	
Property taxes receivable	500,000	
Property tax revenue		$8,000,000
To record property taxes		

Property taxes are recognized as revenue on the same basis as if recorded in the general fund or a special revenue fund. Taxes restricted for a specific purpose may be recorded initially in the general fund, especially if, as in this situation, they are part of a larger tax levy. However, it is generally preferable that they be reported directly in the fund to which they are dedicated.

Recording the Transfer from the General Fund   To service the debt, the city transfers $2,940,000 during the year from the general fund to the debt service fund:

Cash	$2,940,000	
Other financing source—nonreciprocal transfer-in		
from the general fund		$2,940,000
To record the transfer from the general fund		

Recording the Payment of Interest and Principal   The city makes its first payment of interest on the $100 million of bonds, as due, on June 30:

Expenditure—debt service, interest	$3,000,000	
Matured interest payable		$3,000,000
To record the obligation for the first payment of interest		

Matured interest payable	$3,000,000	
Cash		$3,000,000
To record the first payment of interest		

Many governments use a bank or other fiscal agent to distribute payments of interest and principal to bondholders. Any cash transferred to a fiscal agent should be reported as an asset *cash with fiscal agent*. This account, along with the liability *matured interest (or principal) payable*, should be reduced as the fiscal agent reports that it has made the required payments to the bondholders.

Although the second interest payment and the first principal payment are due on December 31, 2003, the city does not actually mail the checks until January 2, 2004. Nevertheless, the expenditure and related obligation must be recognized when the payments are due:

Expenditure—debt service, interest	$3,000,000	
Expenditure—debt service, principal	5,000,000	
Matured interest payable		$3,000,000
Matured bonds payable		5,000,000

To record the obligation for the second payment of interest and the first payment of principal

Table 6-2 presents the 2003 financial statements for Carver City's debt service fund.

TABLE 6-2
Carver City
Debt Service Fund
Statement of Revenues, Expenditures, and Changes in Fund Balance
For the Year Ending December 31, 2003

Revenues:	
Property Taxes	$ 8,000,000
Investments	71,781
Total Revenues	8,071,781
Expenditures:	
Debt Service, Interest	6,000,000
Debt Service, Principal	5,000,000
Total Expenditures	11,000,000
Excess (Deficiency) of Revenues over Expenditures	(2,928,219)
Other Financing Sources:	
Nonreciprocal Transfer-in from the General Fund	2,940,000
Nonreciprocal Transfer-in from the Capital Projects Fund	2,200,000
Total Other Financing Sources	5,140,000
Net Change in Fund Balance	2,211,781
Fund Balance, Beginning of Year	0
Fund Balance, End of Year	$ 2,211,781

Balance Sheet as of December 31, 2003

Assets:	
Cash	$ 8,805,631
Property Taxes Receivable	500,000
Investment in Bonds	906,150
Total Assets	$10,211,781
Liabilities and Fund Balance:	
Matured Interest Payable	$ 3,000,000
Matured Bonds Payable	5,000,000
Total Liabilities	8,000,000
Fund Balance	2,211,781
Total Liabilities and Fund Balance	$10,211,781

HOW DO GOVERNMENTS HANDLE SPECIAL ASSESSMENTS?

Governments sometimes construct capital projects or provide services that primarily benefit a particular group of property owners, rather than the general citizenry, and assess (i.e., charge) those taxpayers all or a substantial share of the cost. Generally, a majority of the affected property owners must approve the project and the assessments. They can ordinarily pay the assessments in installments over several years, with interest on unpaid balances.

REASONS FOR SPECIAL ASSESSMENTS Cities and towns often levy special assessments when taxpayers in areas beyond their jurisdiction want to benefit from certain municipal services, such as trash collection, snow plowing, or a professional fire department. Also, special assessments are often levied for specific projects within a city or town, such as parks, recreation centers, or infrastructure improvements, including expanded water and sewer lines, sidewalks, roads, and street lights. Sometimes the area to be assessed is designated a special purpose government district (such as a local improvement district), and it may be authorized to levy and collect the assessments.

Alternatively, the assessments are levied and administered by the city or town itself. Because the enhancements in infrastructure or services may provide at least some benefits to the citizenry at large (for example, improved roads are not for the exclusive use of the taxpayers who live along them), governments may share in the cost of the improvements. Therefore, the projects may be financed in part by direct government contributions, general obligation debt, or revenue debt (debt to be repaid from user fees, such as water and sewer charges).

Assessments for services should be accounted for in the fund that best reflects the nature of the assessment and the services to be provided—usually the general fund, a special revenue fund, or an enterprise fund. Governments assure collectibility of the assessments by attaching liens against the affected properties. Thus, they can foreclose upon delinquent property owners and can prevent the properties from being sold or transferred until the assessments are current.

ACCOUNTING FOR SPECIAL ASSESSMENT CAPITAL PROJECTS AND THE RELATED DEBT Capital improvement special assessments involve two distinct, albeit overlapping, phases—the construction and financing phase and the debt service phase. In the first phase, a project is authorized and the government assesses the property owners, issues long-term debt to finance the project, and undertakes the construction. In the second phase, the property owners pay their assessments and the debt is serviced. The first phase is usually fairly short—the time required to complete the project; the second phase may extend over many years.

A government should account for the proceeds of special assessment debt, bond issue costs, bond premiums and discounts, and construction costs in a capital projects fund, in the same manner as discussed earlier in this chapter for other capital projects. It should recognize the special assessment levies, contributions from the general fund and other sources, and interest and principal payable on special assessment debt in a debt service fund.

Special assessments are imposed nonexchange transactions, similar to property tax levies. Like property taxes, they should be recorded as assets in the period in which the government has an enforceable legal claim to the resources and as revenues when the resources become available for expenditure. Therefore, when a government imposes the special assessments, it should report the assessments receivable as *deferred* revenue.

Only as it collects the assessments (or as they become available to meet current-year expenditures) should it recognize them as revenues. It should report contributions from the general fund or other sources just as if they were for other types of projects. The government also should account for interest and principal payable on special assessment debt in the debt service fund no differently than for other project-related debt. Thus, it should recognize expenditures (and a corresponding liability) only when the payment is actually due. It should not accrue either interest or principal.

GOVERNMENT OBLIGATIONS AS TO PROPERTY OWNERS' DEBT The key accounting issue pertaining to special assessments is if, and under what circumstances, a government should report the special assessment debt as its own debt. In economic substance, though not necessarily in legal form, special assessment debt is usually an obligation of the property owners on whom the assessments are levied, not the government. Arguably, therefore, the government need not report the debt on its own financial statements. In most circumstances, however, the government is linked to the debt in some manner. For example, the government may issue the debt as **general obligation debt** or otherwise guarantee it to make it more marketable and lower the interest rate, or it may agree to share in the project cost and be responsible for a specified portion of the debt.

GASB Standards

GASB standards require that a government account for special assessment debt as its own as long as it is "obligated in some manner" to assume responsibility for the debt in the event of property owner default. A government is obligated in some manner unless one of the following is true:

- It is *prohibited* (by constitution, charter, contract, or statute) from assuming the debt in the event of property owner default.
- It is not legally liable for assuming the debt and makes no statement, or gives no indication, that it will, or may, honor the debt in the event of default.[3]

A government that is obligated in some manner for special assessment debt should record the debt service phase of a special assessment project in a debt service fund, as just described. It should report the special assessment debt as if it were its own—that is, in a schedule of long-term obligations and in the government-wide statement of net assets.

A government that is *not* obligated in any manner for the debt, but simply collects the assessments from property owners and forwards them to the bondholders, should record the debt service transactions in an *agency* fund (reflecting the government's role as a mere agent). It should also disclose in notes to the financial statements the amount of debt and the government's role as an agent of the property owners. It need *not* report the debt in either its schedule of long-term obligations or its government-wide statements.[4]

Irrespective of whether it is responsible for the debt, a government should record the construction phase of a special assessment project in a capital projects fund and should report the capital assets in a schedule of capital assets and in its government-wide statement of net assets.

---

[3]GASB Statement No. 6, *Accounting and Financial Reporting for Special Assessments*, para. 16.
[4]Statement No. 6, paras. 19 and 20.

ACCOUNTING FOR SPECIAL ASSESSMENTS IN ENTERPRISE FUNDS Governments sometimes assess property owners for projects that they would ordinarily account for in enterprise funds. These projects typically involve infrastructure associated with utilities, such as water, sewer, and electric power lines and related facilities.

If special assessment debt is related to, and is expected to be paid from, an enterprise fund, then the government should account for all transactions related to both the debt and the improvements financed by the debt in an enterprise fund. It should account for the special assessment revenues and receivables on a full accrual basis and should capitalize improvements financed with the assessments in the same manner as other capital improvements.

In some situations, the government is not responsible in any manner for the related special assessment debt. Instead, the debt is an obligation exclusively of developers, property owners, or other outside parties. If so, then the government should report a *capital contribution* (in a section of its enterprise fund operating statement that follows nonoperating revenues) equal to the amount of the property that it capitalized.[5]

DIFFERENCES IN GOVERNMENT-WIDE STATEMENTS

In their government-wide statements, governments would combine their capital projects funds and debt service funds with all other governmental funds in the governmental activities column, and include the related general capital assets and long-term debt. Because the resources of the capital projects and debt service funds may be restricted by the bond indentures for asset acquisition or debt service, the existence and nature of the restriction should be clearly conveyed by including the net assets in the appropriate component of the net assets section of the statement of net assets. As discussed in Chapter 3, the three components are: *invested in capital assets; net of related debt; restricted net assets;* and *unrestricted net assets.*

In the governmental activities column, the invested-in-capital-assets component would include the government's general capital assets (including construction in process), less its capital-related debt. The restricted component would show the net financial resources that are restricted by law or external parties and set aside in capital projects funds, debt service funds, and other restricted funds. The unrestricted component would include all unrestricted net financial resources, irrespective of the governmental fund used to account for them. The City of Orlando's Statement of Net Assets (Chapter 3, Table 3-1) provides an example of this presentation.

As was emphasized in Chapters 4 and 5, revenues and expenses would be accounted for on a full accrual basis in the statement of activities. Revenues would be subject to the same standards as applicable to the governmental fund (modified accrual) statements except that the available test would not have to be met. Expenses would also be subject to the same standards, except that the exceptions that transform the full accrual basis into the modified accrual basis would not be pertinent.

(continued)

---

[5]Statement No. 6, para. 23.

> Some of the more consequential differences from the governmental fund statements are that in the government-wide statements:
>
> - Interest expense on long-term debt would be accrued as a function of time, irrespective of when payment is due.
> - Discounts and premiums on bonds payable would be amortized over time— just as they currently are on the financial statements of businesses and the enterprise funds of governments.
> - Property taxes dedicated to debt service would be recognized as revenues in the year for which they are levied, even if they will not be collected within sixty days of year-end.
> - The present value of special assessments would be recognized as both assets and *revenues*, not deferred revenues, in the period in which the government has a legal claim to the resources, irrespective of when they will be received. Also, the total debt incurred to construct the capital assets would be reported as a liability and the construction costs would be capitalized as assets (construction in process) as they are incurred.

WHAT IS ARBITRAGE, AND WHY IS IT OF CONCERN TO GOVERNMENTS?

Arbitrage, as it applies to state and local governments, refers to the issuance of debt at relatively low, tax-exempt rates of interest and the investment of the proceeds in taxable securities yielding a higher return. Arbitrage is of major concern to governments and can have important financial and accounting consequences for both capital projects and debt service funds.

The interest paid on debt issued for *public* purposes by state and local governments is not subject to federal taxation. The federal government draws the distinction between public and private purposes so as to restrict governments from assisting private corporations by substituting their own low-interest, tax-exempt debt for that of the corporations.

State and local governments can issue bonds for public purposes at lower interest rates than either the federal government or private corporations. Taking into account the required taxes on the taxable bonds, the tax-exempt bonds can provide a return equivalent to that on taxable bonds. For example, a 6 percent tax-exempt bond provides a return to an investor in a 30 percent tax bracket equal to that of an 8.571 percent taxable bond [$6.0 \div (1 - .30) = 8.571\%$].

Arbitrage subverts the federal government's rationale for exempting municipal debt from federal taxation—that of indirectly subsidizing state and local governments by enabling them to save on interest costs. At one time it was argued that the federal government did not have the constitutional right to regulate the issuance of municipal debt or tax the interest on it. Today the federal government does regulate the issuance and it is widely believed that a tax on the interest could withstand constitutional challenges.

Were governments permitted to engage in arbitrage, they could generate virtually unlimited earnings by investing the proceeds of their own bond issuances in higher yielding, risk-free federal government securities. Using those securities as collateral for their own bonds, they could assure that their debt was also risk free. To prevent municipalities from reaping the benefits of arbitrage, the federal government has added restrictions to the Internal Revenue Code and accompanying regulations.

COMPLEXITY OF FEDERAL REGULATIONS As previously discussed, governments typically spend bond proceeds over the period of project construction, which may take several years to complete. Moreover, governments may transfer a portion of the proceeds from a capital projects fund to a debt service fund, either because the proceeds include a premium or because the debt covenants stipulate that they must maintain a reserve fund to guard against default. Sound fiscal management dictates that proceeds held for anticipated construction costs, for future debt service, or as bondholder-required reserves be invested in interest-earning securities, such as those issued by the U.S. government.

The tax provisions are complex because they must allow for legitimate temporary investment of funds while preventing arbitrage abuse. To achieve this objective, the federal government has produced a highly complex set of regulations. In essence, they are of two types:

- *Arbitrage restrictions.* Primarily developed in 1969, these provisions establish a general rule prohibiting arbitrage, with several exceptions. For example, issuers can invest construction funds and reserve funds for limited periods of time (e.g., 85 percent of the proceeds must be spent within three years).
- *Arbitrage rebates.* Regulations under the Tax Reform Act of 1986 require that all arbitrage earnings, with some exceptions (e.g., the proceeds are spent within six months, or 75 percent of the proceeds are spent on construction within two years), be remitted to the federal government.

By failing to comply with these mandates a government can compromise the tax-exempt status of its bonds, thereby subjecting itself to bondholder litigation and political embarrassment.

ACCOUNTING PROBLEMS The main accounting problems arise because the regulations permit issuers to calculate and remit their required rebates as infrequently as every five years. Moreover, the arbitrage earnings may be measured over multiyear, rather than annual, periods. At the conclusion of any one year, the government might be unable to determine its expenditure and related liability for that year. Thus, although the GASB has not yet issued a pronouncement pertaining to arbitrage, it is clear that governments must estimate their rebate obligations and recognize an appropriate expenditure/expense and liability.

HOW CAN GOVERNMENTS BENEFIT FROM DEBT REFUNDINGS?

Governments retire debt prior to maturity for a variety of reasons. For example, owing to greater revenues than anticipated, they may be able to pay off bonds earlier than planned. Or, they may elect to sell facilities financed by the debt and use the proceeds to liquidate the obligations.

In this section, however, we will be concerned with **bond refundings**—the early retirement of existing debt so that it can be replaced with new debt. Governments refund—that is, **refinance**—their debt to take advantage of more favorable (lower) interest rates, to shorten or lengthen the debt payout period, or to rid themselves of restrictive bond covenants (such as those that prevent them from incurring new debt).

GENERAL RULE AS TO POTENTIAL FOR ECONOMIC GAINS As a general rule, if a government must retire outstanding debt by repurchasing it in the open market and paying a price reflective of current interest rates, then there would be no benefit to refunding—even in the face of prevailing interest rates that are substantially lower than those on the existing debt. There would be no economic gain because the premium to retire existing bonds would exactly offset the present value of the future interest savings. A simple example will demonstrate the point.

EXAMPLE *Debt Refundings*
• •

A government has bonds outstanding that pay interest at an annual rate of 8 percent (4 percent per semiannual period). The bonds mature in ten years (twenty periods). In the years since the bonds were issued, annual interest rates on bonds with similar risk characteristics have decreased to 6 percent. Owing to the decline in interest rates, each of the government's bonds ($1,000 face value) is selling in the secondary market for $1,148.78.

The **economic cost** to the government of the debt, assuming that it will remain outstanding until maturity in ten years, is $1,148.78—the same as its market value. Economic cost is the *present value of all future payments*, based on the *prevailing* interest rate of 6 percent (3 percent per period). Hence, the economic cost is the twenty semiannual interest payments of $40 each and a single principal payment of $1,000:

Present value, at 3 percent, of $1,000 principal (a single sum) to be paid at the end of 20 periods (present value of $1 = $.55368)	$ 553.68
Present value, at 3 percent, of $40 interest (an annuity) to be paid at the end of each of 20 periods (present value of an annuity of $1 = $14.87748)	595.10
Total economic cost of existing bonds	$1,148.78

Were the government to retire the debt, it would have to pay the market value of $1,148.78. Assuming that it still needs the funds initially borrowed, it would have to issue new bonds to obtain the required $1,148.78. Because current market rates have fallen to 6 percent, it could reduce its semiannual interest payments from $40 to $34.46 (3 percent of $1,148.78). The present value of all future payments on the new debt at 6 percent (3 percent per period) would also be $1,148.78:

Present value, at 3 percent, of $1,148.78 principal (a single sum) to be paid at the end of 20 periods (present value of $1 = $.55368)	$ 636.07
Present value, at 3 percent, of $34.46 interest (an annuity) to be paid at the end of each of 20 periods (present value of an annuity of $1 = $14.87748)	512.68
Total economic cost of new bonds	$1,148.75

The three cents discrepancy is attributable to rounding. It is, of course, no coincidence that the economic cost of the new bonds is the same as their face value. The present value of bonds issued at par is always the same as their face value. The economic cost of the new bonds is the same as that of the existing bonds. Hence, there is no economic gain to refunding.

REALIZING ECONOMIC GAINS—EXCEPTIONS TO THE GENERAL RULE There are exceptions to the general rule that there is no benefit to refunding. First, *yield curves* (the relationship between interest rates and time to maturity) may be such that by refunding the existing bonds with new bonds having a different maturity (and thus different prevailing interest rates and prices) the government can obtain true economic savings. Second, bonds are often issued with specified **call prices**. These give the issuer the opportunity to redeem (call) the bonds at a pre-established price, irrespective of the current market price. The call price places a ceiling on the bond's market price. After all, why would an investor pay more for a bond than its call price, knowing that the government could, at its discretion, buy back the bond at the call price? If a government can redeem a bond at a call price less than the economic value of the existing bonds (i.e., what the market price of the bonds would be in the absence of a call provision), then it could realize an economic saving.

Suppose that, in the example, the bonds contained a call provision allowing the government to redeem the bonds at a price of $1,050. The government refunds the existing debt, issuing $1,050 of new bonds at 6 percent for ten years—an obligation having a present economic value of $1,050. The government would thereby realize an economic gain of $98.78—the existing bonds' economic cost of $1,148.78 less the new bonds' economic cost of $1,050.00.

Most call provisions do not become effective until a specified number of years after the bonds have been outstanding. By delaying the effective date, an issuer is able to assure investors that they will receive their agreed-upon return for the indicated period and thereby enhance the marketability of its bonds.

Even if a call provision is not yet effective, the government can still lock in the savings that would result from a decline in prevailing interest rates. It can do this through a process known as an **in-substance defeasance**—an advance refunding in which the borrower *economically*, although not legally, satisfies its existing obligations. The government issues new debt and places in trust sufficient funds to make all required interest payments on the old debt through the earliest call date and to redeem the debt on that date.

EXAMPLE   *In-Substance Defeasance*

A government has outstanding the same 8 percent, ten years to maturity bonds described in the previous example. The call provision permits the government to redeem the bonds at a price of $1,050 per bond, but the earliest call date is five years (ten semiannual periods) in the future. Prevailing interest rates are 6 percent (3 percent per period).

To defease the bonds in substance the government would have to place $1,122.51 with a trustee. This amount, determined as follows, is based on an assumption that the bond proceeds will be invested in securities earning the prevailing annual interest rate of 6 percent (3 percent per period):

Present value, at 3 percent, of the $1,050 (a single sum) required to redeem the bonds after 10 periods (present value of $1 = $.74409)	$ 781.30
Present value, at 3 percent, of the $40 interest to be paid at the end of each of 10 periods (present value of an annuity of $1 = $8.53020)	341.21
Total economic cost of redeeming the bonds in 5 years (10 periods)	$1,122.51

The government would borrow the required $1,122.51 at an annual rate of 6 percent, an obligation that would have an economic cost of $1,122.51. This amount, if invested in securities earning 6 percent, would be just sufficient to make the required ten interest payments of $40 and the single principal payment of $1,050.

Most commonly (though not necessarily), the maturity date of the new bonds would be the same as those on the existing bonds. If so, the government would have the same amount of time to repay the debt as it had originally planned.

The total economic cost of taking no action is that of the existing bonds, determined previously to be $1,148.78. Therefore, the economic saving from defeasing the bond, in substance, is $26.27 for each $1,000 of existing bonds outstanding—$1,148.78 less $1,122.51.

Reporting the In-Substance Defeasance in Governmental Funds The in-substance defeasance would generally be reported in the debt service fund. The accounting is straightforward:

Cash	$1,122.51	
Other financing source—proceeds of refunding bonds		$1,122.51

To record the issuance of the refunding (the "new") bonds

Other financing use—payment to trustee	$1,122.51	
Cash		$1,122.51

To record the transfer of cash to the trust responsible for servicing and redeeming the existing bonds

---

GASB Standards

Assuming that an in-substance defeasance transaction satisfies certain conditions intended to assure that the government has, in economic substance, no further responsibility for the existing debt, then the government may remove the existing bonds from its schedule of long-term obligations (and its government-wide statements) and replace them with the new bonds. The conditions include:

- The debtor irrevocably places cash or other assets with an escrow agent in a trust to be used solely for servicing and retiring the debt.
- The possibility of the debtor having to make future payments on the debt is remote.
- The assets in the escrow fund must be essentially risk-free, such as U.S. government securities.[6]

In addition, the government must detail the transaction in notes to the financial statements, indicating the resultant economic gain or loss.

The more controversial question involves how refundings should be accounted for on a full accrual basis in government-wide or proprietary fund statements. The issue arises because on a full accrual basis long-term liabilities are reported on the statement of net assets; they are not shunted off to the schedule of long-term obliga-

---

[6]GASB Statement No. 7, *Advance Refundings Resulting in Defeasance of Debt*, para. 4.

tions. Hence, when a debt is refunded and must be removed from the statement of net assets, a gain or loss may have to be recognized.

RECOGNIZING THE GAIN OR LOSS IN PROPRIETARY FUNDS AND IN GOVERN-MENT-WIDE STATEMENTS Suppose the bonds described in the previous example were issued at par and are thereby reported in an enterprise fund at a face value of $1,000. Were the bonds to be defeased by placing $1,122.51 in trust, then the following entry would be in order to remove the existing debt from the books:

"Loss" (past, present, or future?)	$ 122.51	
Bonds payable	1,000.00	
Cash		$1,122.51

To record the in-substance defeasance of the existing bonds

As demonstrated previously, the government realizes an economic *gain* by defeasing the debt prior to maturity. Yet because the book value of the debt is less than the reacquisition price, the government is forced to recognize an *accounting loss*. As implied by the parenthetical question in the entry, the salient accounting issue relates to the disposition of the loss. There are at least three possibilities:

1. *Recognize the loss over the prior years in which the debt has been outstanding.* This approach is impractical, because several years of previous financial statements would need to be restated.

2. *Recognize the loss at the time of defeasance.* This approach would distort the operating results of the period. In addition to reporting a loss when, in economic substance, it realized a gain, the government would be forced to recognize the entire loss in a single period.

3. *Defer the loss, and amortize it over future years.* This approach is grounded on the assumption that the defeasance is merely a substitution of new debt for existing debt with a corresponding adjustment in interest rates.

GASB Standards

The GASB opted for the third method. It requires that the difference between the book value of the existing debt and the reacquisition price be deferred and amortized over the *remaining life of the existing debt or the new debt, whichever is shorter.*[7] This amortization period is consistent with an interpretation that the new debt is merely a restructured version of the old. The GASB does not permit the amortization to extend past the maturity date of the existing debt, because it sees any debt outstanding beyond that date as essentially a new borrowing for an additional period of time.

By contrast, in 1996 the FASB ruled that a debtor can "derecognize" a liability only if it has either paid the obligation or has been legally released from it. Therefore, the debtor must report on its balance sheet both the debt that it in-substance defeased and the assets set aside to refund it. Correspondingly, it must include on its statement

---

[7] GASB Statement No. 23, *Accounting and Financial Reporting for Refundings of Debt Reported by Proprietary Activities*, para. 4.

of revenues and expenses both the interest expense on the defeased debt and the investment revenue on the assets that it has set aside.[8] Thus, nongovernmental not-for-profits must account for defeasances differently than governments.

What needs to be emphasized is that the *reported* gain or loss from defeasance, whether amortized over several periods or recognized as once, may be counter to the *economic* gain or loss. Entities may be tempted, therefore, to defease debt at an economic loss just so they can report a gain.

QUESTIONS FOR REVIEW AND DISCUSSION

1. Although many governments prepare budgets for both capital projects and debt service funds, the GASB does not mandate budgetary comparisons for these funds as it does for other types of governmental funds. How can you justify this apparent discrepancy?

2. When bonds are issued for capital projects, premiums are generally not accounted for as the mirror image of discounts. Why not?

3. It is sometimes said that in debt service funds the accounting for interest revenues is inconsistent with that for interest expenditures. Explain. What is the rationale for this seeming inconsistency?

4. Until recently governments maintained a unique type of fund to account for special assessments. This fund recorded the construction in process, the long-term debt and the assessments receivable. Explain briefly how governments account for special assessments today.

5. Special assessment debt may be, in economic substance and/or legal form, an obligation of the assessed property owners rather than a government. Should the government, therefore,

report it in its statements as if it were its own debt? What are the current standards as to when a government should recognize special assessment debt as its own obligation?

6. How should governments report their capital projects and debt service activities in their government-wide statements?

7. A government issues bonds at a discount. Where would the government report the discount on its (a) fund statements and (b) government-wide statements?

8. What is *arbitrage*? Why does the Internal Revenue Service place strict limits on the amount of arbitrage that a municipality can earn?

9. Under what circumstances can a government refund outstanding debt and thereby take advantage of a decline in interest rates?

10. What is meant by an *in-substance defeasance*, and how can a government use it to lower its interest costs? How must it recognize a gain or loss on defeasance if it accounts for the debt in a proprietary fund? How do the GASB standards pertaining to in-substance defeasances differ from those of the FASB?

EXERCISES AND PROBLEMS

6-1

Select the *best* answer.

1. A government opts to set aside $10 million of general fund resources to finance a new city hall. Construction is expected to begin in sev-

eral years, when the city has set aside an additional $90 million. Which is true?

a. The government *must* account for the $10 million in a capital projects fund, and in its government-wide statements it *must* report the $10 million as "restricted."

---

[8]FASB Statement No. 125, *Accounting for Transfers and Servicing of Financial Assets and Extinguishments of Liabilities*.

b. The government *may* account for the $10 million in a capital projects fund, and in its government-wide statements it *may* report the $10 million as "restricted."

c. The government *may not* account for the $10 million in a capital projects fund, and in its government-wide statements it *may not* report the $10 million as "unrestricted."

d. The government *may* account for the $10 million in a capital projects fund but in its government-wide statements it *may not* report the $10 million as "restricted."

2. If a government can distinguish underwriting and other issue costs from bond premiums and discounts it should

a. report them as expenditures

b. add them to the face value of the bond

c. report them in a separate account and amortize them over the life of the bond

d. deduct them from the bond premiums or add them to the bond discounts

3. When a government issues bonds at premiums or discounts and records the proceeds in a capital projects fund, what else should it do?

a. Transfer an amount equal to the premiums from the capital projects fund to a debt service fund, and an amount equal to the discounts from a debt service fund to the capital projects fund.

b. Transfer an amount equal to the premiums from the capital projects fund to a debt service fund, but make no transfer of an amount equal to the discounts from a debt service fund to the capital projects fund.

c. Make no transfers between the capital projects fund and a debt service fund.

d. Transfer an amount equal to the discounts from a debt service fund to the capital projects fund, but make no transfer of an amount equal to the premiums from the capital projects fund to the debt service fund.

4. A city holds U.S. Treasury notes as an investment in a capital projects fund. During the year, the market value of the notes increases by $50,000. Of this amount $14,000 can be attributed to a decline in prevailing interest rates and $36,000 to interest that has been earned but not yet received. As of year-end, the city should recognize as revenue

a. $0

b. $14,000

c. $36,000

d. $50,000

5. Which of the following accounts is least likely to be shown on the balance sheet of a debt service fund?

a. bonds payable

b. investments (at market value)

c. cash

d. special assessments receivable

6. Special assessment debt need not be reported on the government-wide statement of net assets of a city if the debt is to be paid from assessments on property owners and

a. the city has not guaranteed payment of the debt

b. the city has guaranteed payment of the debt but the probability of the city having to make good on the guarantee is remote

c. the city serves only as a collection agent with no substantive responsibility other than to transfer the funds collected to a bond trustee

d. none of the above

7. In its fund statements, a government should recognize revenue from special assessments

a. entirely in the year in which the assessment is imposed

b. in the years in which the assessments are paid

c. in the years in which the assessments are due

d. in the years in which the assessments become available for expenditure

8. In the year it imposes a special assessment, a government should recognize in its government-wide statements

a. the full amount of the assessment as both revenue and an asset

b. the present value of the assessment as both revenue and an asset

c. only the amount of the assessment due in the current year as revenue but the full amount of the assessment as an asset

d. only the amount of the assessment due in the current year as both revenue and an asset

9. Under existing federal statutes, *arbitrage* as it applies to state and local governments

a. is illegal

b. is illegal unless the government can demonstrate a just cause for engaging in it

c. is legal in some circumstances, but the government may be required to remit arbitrage earnings to the federal government

d. is illegal unless there is no more than a 2 percent difference between interest earned and interest paid

10. Bond refundings are most likely to result in an economic gain when

a. the bonds are subject to arbitrage

b. there is an inverted yield curve

c. the bonds were initially issued at a premium

d. the bonds are subject to a call provision

6-2

Select the *best* answer.

1. Which of the following items is least likely to appear on the balance sheet of a capital projects fund?

a. cash

b. investments

c. construction in process

d. reserve for encumbrances

2. The fund balance of a debt service fund is most likely to be incorporated into a government's government-wide statement of net assets as

a. net assets, invested in capital assets, net of related debt

b. net assets, restricted

c. net assets, unrestricted

d. capital assets

3. The repayment of bond principal should be reported in the fund statements of a debt service fund as

a. an expenditure

b. an other financing use

c. a reduction of bonds payable

d. a direct charge to fund balance

4. A state issues bonds, at a premium, to finance road construction projects. The premium would affect

a. interest expenditure in the state's debt service fund

b. nonreciprocal transfers-out in the state's general fund

c. capital assets in the state's government-wide statement of net assets

d. net assets invested in capital assets, net of related debt, in the state's government-wide statement of net assets

5. In the period that a government issues bonds at a discount, either all or a portion of the discount should be reported as

a. a reduction of fund balance in the balance sheet of a capital projects fund

b. an expenditure in the statement of revenues, expenditures, and changes in fund balance of a capital projects fund

c. an expense in the government-wide statement of activities

d. an asset in the government-wide statement of net assets

6. A city issued bonds on July 1. Interest of $600,000 is payable the following January 1. On December 31, the city transfers the required $600,000 from its general fund to its debt service fund. On its December 31 debt service fund statement of revenues, expenditures, and changes in fund balance, the city

a. must report interest expenditure of $0

b. must report interest expenditure of $600,000

c. must report interest expenditure of $500,000

d. may report interest expenditure of either $0 or $600,000

7. A city issues $10 million of debt that it uses to acquire an office building. In the year that it issues the debt and acquires the building, the city neither charges depreciation on the building nor repays any of the debt principal. Assume that the city accounts for all capital acquisitions in a capital projects fund and all payments of interest in a debt service fund. The transaction would

a. increase expenditures of the capital projects fund

b. increase other financing sources of the debt service fund

c. increase fund balance of the capital projects fund

d. increase expenditures of the debt service fund

8. A city assesses property owners $50 million to extend sewer lines to their neighborhood. By year-end, however, it has not yet begun construction of the new lines and has not yet collected any of the assessments. It accounts for its waste-water services in an enterprise fund. In its year-end enterprise fund financial statements the government should

a. recognize the assessments as assessments receivable and deferred revenue

b. recognize the assessments as assessments receivable and revenue

c. recognize the assessments as assessments receivable and a liability for future construction costs

d. should not recognize the assessments until they will be available for expenditure

9. A county engages in an in-substance defeasance of its bonds. The transaction results in an economic gain but an accounting loss. In its government-wide statements the county should

a. recognize the loss entirely in the year of the defeasance

b. amortize the loss over either the remaining life of the existing debt or the new debt

c. report the loss as a direct charge to net assets

d. not recognize the loss, but instead continue to report the defeased bonds (as well as the new bonds) as liabilities

10. A government issued, at par, $10 million of twenty-year, 6 percent bonds. The bonds do not contain a call provision. Ten years later, prevailing interest rates have fallen to 5 percent. The government is considering whether to purchase the outstanding bonds at their market price and retire them. It would acquire the necessary funds by issuing new ten-year, 5 percent bonds. The transaction would most likely result in

a. an economic gain but an accounting loss

b. an economic loss but an accounting gain

c. an economic gain and an accounting gain

d. neither an economic gain or loss but an accounting loss

6-3

Capital projects funds account for construction expenditures, not for the assets that are being constructed.

The Wickliffe City Council approves a budget of $9,027,000 to restore the city library. The project is to be funded by the issuance of $6 million of general obligation bonds, a $2.5 million state grant, and $527,000 from general fund property taxes. The city estimates that construction costs will be $8,907,000 and bond issue costs $120,000.

1. Prepare journal entries in the capital projects fund to reflect the following events and transactions.

a. The city issues 9 percent, 15-year bonds that have a face value of $6,000,000. The bonds are sold for $6,120,000, an amount reflecting a price of $102. The city incurs $115,000 in issue costs; hence, the net proceeds are $6,005,000.

b. The city transfers the net premium of $5,000 to its debt service fund.

c. It receives the anticipated $2,500,000 from the state and it transfers in $527,000 from the general fund.

d. It signs an agreement with a contractor for $8,890,000.

e. It pays the contractor $8,890,000 upon completion of the project.

f. It transfers the remaining cash to the debt service fund.

2. Prepare appropriate closing entries.

6-4

The accounting for bond premiums is not the mirror image of that for bond discounts.

Pacific Independent School District issued $100 million of general obligation bonds to finance the construction of new schools. The bonds were issued at a premium of $0.6 million.

1. Prepare the capital projects fund journal entries to record the issue of the bonds and the transfer of the premium to an appropriate fund.

2. Suppose, instead, that the bonds were issued at a discount of $0.6 million but that the project will still cost $100 million. Prepare the appropriate entries.

a. Contrast these entries with those of question 1.

b. Indicate the options available to the school district and tell how they would affect the entries required of the district.

c. Suppose the government chose to finance the balance of the project with general revenues. Prepare the appropriate capital projects fund entry.

6-5

Debt service funds account for resources accumulated to service debt, not the debt itself.

On July 1, a city issued, at par, $100 million of 6 percent, twenty-year general obligation bonds. It established a debt service fund to account for the resources set aside to pay interest and principal on the obligations.

In the year it issued the debt, the city engaged in the following transactions involving the debt service fund:

a. Upon issuing the bonds, the city transferred $1 million of the bond proceeds from the capital projects fund to the debt service fund. It invested $977,254 of these funds in twenty-year, 6-percent Treasury bonds that had a face value of $1 million. The bond discount of $22,746 reflected an effective yield rate of 6.2 percent.

b. On December 31, the city received $30,000 interest on the Treasury bonds. This payment represented interest for six months. Correspondingly, the market value of the bonds increased by $294, reflecting the amortization of the discount.

c. On the same day the city transferred $2.97 million from the general fund to pay interest on the bonds that it had issued. It also transferred $0.5 million for the eventual repayment of principal.

d. Also on December 31, it made its first interest payment of $3 million to bondholders.

1. Prepare appropriate journal entries in the debt service fund, including closing entries.

2. The bonds issued by the city pay interest at the rate of 6 percent. The bonds in which the city invested its reserve have an effective yield of 6.2 percent. Why might the difference in rates create a potential liability for the city?

6-6

The construction and financing phase of a special assessment project is accounted for in a capital projects fund; the debt service phase in a debt service fund (see the next problem).

Upon annexing a recently developed subdivision, a government undertakes to extend sewer lines to the area. Estimated cost is $10 million. The project is to be funded with $8.5 million in special assessment bonds and a $1.0 million reimbursement grant from the state. The balance is to be paid by the government out of its general fund. Property owners are to be assessed an amount sufficient to pay both principal and interest on the debt. The government estimated that, during the first year of the project, it would earn $0.20 million in interest on the temporary investment of bond proceeds, an amount that would reduce the required transfer from the general fund. It also estimated that bond issue costs would be $0.18 million.

During the year, the government engaged in the following transactions, all of which would be recorded in a capital projects fund.

a. It issued $8.5 million in bonds at a premium of $0.30 million and incurred $0.18 million in issue costs. The premium, net of issue costs, is to be transferred to a newly established debt service fund.

b. It received the $1 million grant from the state, recognizing it as deferred revenue until it incurred at least $1 million in construction costs.

c. It invested $7.62 million in short-term (less than one-year) securities.

d. It issued purchase orders and signed construction contracts for $9.2 million.

e. It sold $5 million of its investments for $5.14 million, the excess of selling price over cost representing interest earned. By year-end, the investments still on hand had increased in value by

$0.06 million, an amount that also could be attributed to interest earned.

f. It received invoices totaling $5.7 million. As permitted by its agreement with its prime contractor, it retained (and recorded as a payable) $0.4 million pending satisfactory completion of the project. It paid the balance of $5.3 million.

g. It transferred $0.12 million to the debt service fund.

h. It updated its accounts, but did not close them, inasmuch as the project is not completed and its budget is for the entire project, not for a single period.

1. Prepare appropriate journal entries for the capital projects fund.

2. Prepare a statement of revenues, expenditures, and changes in fund balance, in which you compare actual and budgeted amounts.

3. Prepare a year-end balance sheet.

4. Does your balance sheet report the construction in process? If not, where might the construction in process be recorded?

6-7

The debt service phase special assessment bonds are accounted for in a debt service fund (see the previous problem).

As indicated in the previous problem, a government issued $8.5 million of special assessment bonds to finance a sewer-extension project. To service the debt, it assessed property owners $8.5 million. Their obligations are payable over a period of five years, with annual installments due on March 31 of each year. Interest at an annual rate of 8 percent is to be paid on the total balance outstanding as of that date.

The bonds require an annual principal payment of $1.5 million each year for five years, due on December 31. In addition, interest on the unpaid balance is payable twice each year, on June 30 and December 31, at an annual rate of 8 percent.

The government agreed to make up from its general fund the difference between required debt service payments and revenues.

At the start of the year, the government established a debt service fund. It estimated that it would collect from property owners $1.3 million in special assessments and $0.5 million of interest on the unpaid balance of the assessments. In addition, it expected to earn interest of $0.08 million on temporary investments. It would be required to pay interest of $0.68 million and make principal payments of $1.7 million on the outstanding debt. It anticipated transferring $0.5 million from the general fund to cover the revenue shortage.

During the year, the government engaged in the following transactions, all of which would affect the debt service fund.

a. It recorded the $8.5 million of assessments receivable, estimating that $0.2 million would be uncollectible.

b. The special assessment bonds were issued at a premium (net of issue costs) of $0.12. The government recognized the anticipated transfer of the premium to the debt service fund.

c. During the year the government collected $2.0 million in assessments and $0.4 million in interest (with a few property owners paying their entire assessment in the first year). During the first sixty days of the following year it collected an additional $0.1 million in assessments and $0.01 in interest, which were due the previous year.

d. It transferred in $0.12 million (the premium) from the capital projects fund.

e. It purchased $0.8 million of six-month Treasury bills as a temporary investment.

f. It made its first interest payment of $0.34 million.

g. It sold the investments for $0.85 million, the difference between selling price and cost representing interest earned.

h. It recognized its year-end obligation for interest of $0.34 million and principal of $1.7 million, but did not actually make the required payments.

i. It prepared year-end closing entries.

1. Prepare appropriate journal entries for the debt service fund.

2. Prepare a statement of revenues, expenditures, and changes in fund balance.

3. Prepare a year-end balance sheet.

4. Does your balance sheet report the balance of the bonds payable? If not, where might it be recorded?

6-8

Governments can seldom realize an economic gain by refunding bonds in the absence of call provisions.

A government has outstanding $100 million of twenty-year, 10 percent bonds. They were issued at par and have sixteen years (32 semiannual periods) until they mature. They pay interest semiannually.

1. Suppose current prevailing interest rates had decreased to 8 percent (4 percent per period). What amount would you estimate the bonds were trading at in the open market? (Present value at 4 percent of $1 paid at the end of 32 pe-

riods is $.28506; present value at 4 percent of an annuity of $1 paid at the end of each of 32 periods is $17.87355.)

2. Suppose the government elected to purchase the bonds in the market and retire them. To finance the purchase it issued sixteen-year 32 semiannual periods bonds at the prevailing rate of 8 percent (4 percent per period). What would be the *economic cost* (i.e., the present value of anticipated cash flows) of issuing these bonds? Would the government realize an economic gain by retiring the old bonds and issuing the new?

3. Suppose a call provision permitted the government to redeem the bonds for a total of $101 million. Could the government realize an economic gain by recalling the bonds and financing the purchase by issuing $101 million in new, 8 percent, sixteen-year bonds?

6-9

Governments may report substantially different amounts of interest on their government-wide and fund financial statements.

Charter City issued $100 million of 6 percent, twenty-year general obligation bonds on January 1, 2003. The bonds were sold to yield 6.2 percent and hence were issued at a discount of $2.27 million (i.e., at a price of $97.73 million). Interest on the bonds is payable on July 1 and January 1 of each year.

On July 1, 2003, and January 1, 2004, the city made its required interest payments of $3 million each.

1. How much interest expenditure should the city report in its debt service fund statement for its fiscal year ending December 31, 2003? During 2003, the city did not transfer resources to the debt service fund for the interest payment due on January 1, 2004.

2. How much interest expense should the city report on its government-wide statement for the year ending December 31, 2003? (It might be helpful to prepare appropriate journal entries.)

3. On January 1, 2023, the city repaid the bonds. How would the repayment be reflected on the city's (1) fund statements and (2) government-wide statements?

6-10

Debtors may be able to realize an economic gain by defeasing their debt in substance.

A hospital has outstanding $100 million of bonds that mature in twenty years (40 periods). The debt was issued at par and pays interest at a rate of 6 percent (3 percent per period). Prevailing rates on comparable bonds are now 4 percent (2 percent per period).

1. What would you expect to be the market price of the bonds, assuming that they are freely traded? Would there be an economic benefit for the hospital to refund the existing debt by acquiring it at the market price and replacing it with new, low-cost debt? (Present value at 2 percent of $1 paid at the end of 40 periods is $.452890; present value at 2 percent of an annuity of $1 paid at the end of each of 40 periods is $27.35548.)

2. Assume the bonds contain a provision permitting the hospital to call the bonds in another five years (ten periods) at a price of $105 and that any invested funds could earn a return equal to the prevailing interest rate of 4 percent (2 percent per period). What would be the economic saving that the hospital could achieve by defeasing the bonds in substance? (Present value at 2 percent of $1 paid at the end of 10 periods is $.820348; present value at 2 percent of an annuity of $1 paid at the end of each of 10 periods is $8.98258)

6-11

Exploring Orlando's financial report

Refer to the financial statements of the City of Orlando in Chapter 3.

1. In which governmental fund or funds does Orlando report capital projects?

2. How would capital improvements expenditures be reported in the government-wide statements?

3. Were revenues, as reported in the capital improvements fund, sufficient to cover expenditures? If not, where did the additional needed resources come from?

4. Orlando does not maintain a debt service fund. In which governmental fund or funds does the city report debt service? How is debt service reported in the government-wide statements?

5. The governmental funds balance sheet reports special assessments receivable of $1.2 million in the general fund. However, special assessment revenue of the general fund is only $0.2 million. Do you think Orlando has a significant problem collecting special assessments? Explain.

CHAPTER 7

Governmental Activities— Capital Assets and Investments in Marketable Securities

In Chapter 6 we discussed the *resources* used to acquire general capital assets— those that serve the government as a whole and are financed primarily by governmental, rather than business-type, activities. In this chapter we discuss the assets themselves.

General capital assets are a key component of many government services. They include police cars, administrative buildings, roads, streets, and street lighting. If these and other capital assets are inadequate to meet the citizens' demands for services, then the government will have to reduce its services or come up with the financial resources to enhance the assets. At the same time, existing capital assets require an ongoing commitment of financial resources to maintain or replace them. Also, constituents generally want, and are entitled to, assurance that their government is using its assets efficiently and effectively.

Capital asset reporting is evolving and is controversial. This is particularly true with respect to whether and how governments should report their **infrastructure assets**, such as highways, roads, bridges, and tunnels, and with respect to reporting depreciation or another measure of capital asset use or consumption.

The last section of the chapter addresses marketable securities held for *investment*. Investments are at the opposite end of the liquidity spectrum from capital assets and present contrasting issues of disclosure and control. Unlike capital assets, they are subject to significant risks of declines in market values as well as of fraud and mismanagement by the financial institutions with whom governments deal and by governments' own employees. Governments need to inform financial statement users of these risks and to establish policies and procedures to manage and control them.

WHAT ACCOUNTING PRACTICES DO GOVERNMENTS FOLLOW FOR GENERAL CAPITAL ASSETS?

In its *Objectives of Financial Reporting*, the GASB set forth the purpose of capital asset reporting and laid the foundation for the current provisions:

> Financial reporting should provide information about a governmental entity's physical and other nonfinancial resources having useful lives that extend beyond the current year, including information that can be used to assess the service potential of these resources.

This information should be presented to help users assess long- and short-term capital needs.[1]

MAINTAINING ACCOUNTING CONTROL OVER CAPITAL ASSETS General capital assets—capital assets that, by definition, are associated with the government as a whole, rather than with any specific fund—are distinguished from the capital assets of proprietary funds (enterprise funds and internal service funds) and of fiduciary funds (pension and other trust funds in which land, buildings, and other capital assets are, for the most part, held as investments).

Nonfinancial in character, capital assets are excluded from governmental funds because of the funds' measurement focus (current financial resources). Therefore, in governmental funds, the capital asset costs are reported as *expenditures* when the assets are acquired. They are not capitalized as assets and subsequently written off (depreciated) as the assets are consumed, as would be the case in a proprietary fund or a business. However, governments must maintain records of their general capital assets so that they can prepare their government-wide statements and the required schedule of capital asset activity.

The most common classes of general capital assets are

- land
- buildings
- equipment
- improvements other than buildings
- construction in progress
- infrastructure

However, "softer" assets, such as library books and recordings, purchased (as opposed to internally developed) computer software, and intangibles (e.g., easements and water rights) may also be capitalized.

DIFFERENCES IN GOVERNMENT-WIDE STATEMENTS

General capital assets, including infrastructure, should be reported on the government-wide statement of net assets (governmental activities column) at historical cost, net of accumulated depreciation, if applicable. Accumulated depreciation may be reported on the face of the statement or disclosed in the notes. Most assets should be depreciated over their estimated useful lives in a manner that is "rational and systematic" (i.e., using one of the methods commonly used by businesses). However, governments, like businesses, do not have to depreciate inexhaustible assets, such as land, works of art, or historical treasures. Moreover, as is addressed in a section to follow, governments do not have to depreciate infrastructure assets if they can demonstrate that they are preserving them in a specified condition.

(continued)

---

[1]GASB Concepts Statement No. 1, para. 79.

DIFFERENCES IN GOVERNMENT-WIDE STATEMENTS *(continued)*

A government does not have to include a separate line item for depreciation on its government-wide statement of activities. The statement will typically report expenses by function (e.g., public safety, recreation, health), and the government may aggregate the depreciation charge and other expenses applicable to each function. However, the notes to the financial statements must include information as to each of the major classes of general capital assets, including the beginning and ending balances; acquisitions and retirements; and current period depreciation, including the amount charged to each of the functions reported on the statement of activities. Table 7–1 presents Orlando, Florida's schedule for the year ended September 30, 2001. (See Table 3–1 in Chapter 3 for the related reporting of the year-end balances of Orlando's general capital assets in the statement of net assets.)

PLACING A VALUE ON GENERAL CAPITAL ASSETS   When a government acquires a general capital asset, it should follow the same general guidelines used by businesses to determine the costs to be capitalized in the government-wide statements and reported in the schedule of capital assets in the notes. Thus, capitalized value should include all costs necessary to bring the asset to a serviceable condition. For purchased assets, the capitalized cost would include the purchase price (less any discounts, such as those for prompt payment or for favored customers), plus transportation and installation costs. For land, the capitalized cost would include legal fees, title fees, appraisal costs, closing costs, and costs of demolishing existing structures that cannot be used (less recoveries from salvage).

For constructed assets, the capitalized cost would include direct labor and materials, overhead costs, architect's fees, and insurance premiums during the construction phase. However, unlike businesses, governments should *not* capitalize interest on general capital assets that they construct themselves.[2] This is because, per Statement No. 34, interest expense on general long-term liabilities should be treated as an indirect expense, rather than being attributed to specific functions or programs, such as public works.

Governments should report donated capital assets at their estimated fair value (plus ancillary charges, if any) at the time of donation. If the assets are exhaustible, they should be depreciated over their remaining useful lives in the government-wide statements.

HOW SHOULD GOVERNMENTS ACCOUNT FOR COLLECTIBLES?   Like their private not-for-profit counterparts, government museums, universities, libraries, and historical centers own collections of works of art, rare books, and historical artifacts. These **collectibles** often have considerable monetary value and for some entities may be their most significant assets. However, many entities have opposed capitalizing their collectibles and recognizing contributions of collectibles as revenue, for several

---

[2]GASB Statement No. 37, *Basic Financial Statements—and Management's Discussion and Analysis—for State and Local Governments: Omnibus, an amendment of GASB Statements No. 21 and No. 34*, paras. 6 and 7.

TABLE 7-1
City of Orlando, Florida
Information about General Capital Assets

Capital asset activity for the year ended September 30, 2001 was as follows (in thousands):

	Primary Government			
	Beginning Balance	Additions	Retirements	Ending Balance
Governmental Activities:				
Non-Depreciable Assets:				
Land	$ 50,397	$ 1,384	$(25)	$ 51,756
Artwork	1,592	2,935	(*)	4,526
Infrastructure in Progress	37,476	22,177	(33,928)	25,726
Construction in Progress	1,493	21,918	(5,390)	18,022
Depreciable Assets:				
Buildings	107,441	1,458	(132)	108,766
Improvements	92,185	2,016	—	94,200
Equipment	27,802	6,544	(3,432)	30,913
Motor Vehicles	50,173	10,402	(5,171)	55,404
Infrastructure	25,631	31,496	—	57,127
Totals at historical cost	394,190	100,330	$(48,078)	446,441
Less accumulated depreciation for:				
Buildings	(33,913)	(3,560)	189	(37,283)
Improvements	(43,498)	(5,995)	*	(49,492)
Equipment	(19,509)	(4,172)	1,353	(22,327)
Motor Vehicles	(36,729)	(5,206)	4,721	(37,214)
Infrastructure	(641)	(1,429)	—	(2,069)
Total accumulated depreciation	(134,289)	(20,361)	6,263	(148,387)
Governmental activities capital assets, net	$259,901	$ 79,968	$(41,815)	$298,054

*Less than $1,000.

Depreciation expense was charged to governmental functions as follows:

General Administration	$ 235
Executive Offices	928
Planning and Development	823
Administrative Services	5,390
Public Works	2,814
Community and Youth Services	1,115
Police	2,311
Fire	907
Community Redevelopment Agency	2,180
Unallocated—Governmental Funds	1,761
Unallocated—Internal Service Funds (assets not assigned to a governmental function)	1,896
Total depreciation expense	$20,361

Source: City of Orlando, Florida, *Comprehensive Annual Financial Report* for the year ended September 30, 2001, page 55.

reasons. They believe that the value of such objects, like their beauty, may be in the eye of the beholder, and only the most Philistine of accountants would place a dollar sign beside a "priceless" work of art. Moreover, they believe that works of art are not assets than can be associated with future cash receipts unless and until they are sold. Rather, while they are held they are a drain upon resources because they require ongoing protection. To report them as assets, it can be argued, would result in financial statements that are as surrealistic as some of the art itself.

GASB Standards

The GASB's treatment of collectibles in Statement No. 34 follows the FASB's lead on the same issues in its Statement No. 116, *Accounting for Contributions Received and Contributions Made*. Thus, governments are not required to capitalize their art and similar assets (although capitalization is encouraged) as long as they meet the following conditions:

- They are held for public exhibition, education, or research in furtherance of public service, rather than for financial gain.
- They are protected, kept unencumbered, cared for, and preserved.
- They are subject to an organizational policy that requires the proceeds from sales of collection items to be used to acquire other items for collections.

Works of art and other collectibles that do *not* meet these conditions (e.g., a work of art held purely as an investment or acquired for an administrator's office that is not accessible to the public or for research purposes) must be capitalized.

If governments capitalize their art or historical collections, then they should depreciate the assets that are exhaustible but not those that do not necessarily decline in value with time. Governments should recognize contributions of collectibles as revenue, just as they should when other assets are received (i.e., per the guidelines discussed in Chapter 4). However, if the items are to be added to noncapitalized collections, then the governments should offset the revenue with a charge to a program expense rather than to an asset. In contrast, per FASB Statement No. 116, nongovernmental not-for-profits are not allowed to recognize revenue for items contributed to noncapitalized collections.

WHY AND HOW SHOULD GOVERNMENTS REPORT INFRASTRUCTURE?

A government's infrastructure is its capital assets that are immovable and can be preserved for a significantly longer period than most other assets. They include roads, sidewalks, drainage systems, bridges, tunnels, and lighting systems. Although many citizens take the nation's infrastructure for granted, public officials, investors, and economists are expressing serious concern over it. In the past thirty years, spectacular failures have called attention to the deteriorating condition of much of the country's public physical plant. For example, in the 1970s, New York City was forced to close a portion of its West Side Highway, a scenic drive along the Hudson River, because the road had become unsafe and the city was unable to come up with the cash to repair it. In 1982, the residents of Jersey City, New Jersey, had to go without water for three days owing to a breakdown in the city's aqueduct system. Then in 1983, Connecticut's Mianus River Bridge on Interstate 95, the main east coast highway, collapsed, killing three people. Numerous research studies have confirmed that there is an increasing gap between the nation's infrastructure requirements and its ability to pay for them.

Infrastructure may be a national problem, but it must be solved mainly at the state and local level. After all, most roads and highways (apart from those that are part of the Interstate system), bridges, drainage, water and public power systems are the responsibility of state and local governments.

Governments are accountable for infrastructure assets, and it is difficult to see how the objectives of financial reporting can be fulfilled without comprehensive information, not only as to the expenditures for infrastructure but also on their status. For example, data on infrastructure are essential if government financial reports are to achieve the following general goals set forth in the GASB's *Objectives of Financial Reporting*:[3]

- To help users assess the economy, efficiency, and effectiveness with which government used the resources within its command
- To determine whether the entity's financial position improved or deteriorated during the reporting period
- To provide information about a government's physical and other nonfinancial resources having useful lives that extend beyond the current year, including information that can be used to assess the service potential of those resources
- To help users assess long and short-term capital needs.

Until the GASB issued Statement No. 34, governments provided virtually no information as to most of their infrastructure. Although infrastructure (such as sewer and power lines) accounted for in proprietary funds was capitalized, as required by the accrual basis of accounting applicable to those funds, infrastructure assets associated with the government as a whole (roads, streets, bridges, etc.) were not. Rather, they were charged as governmental fund expenditures as the assets were constructed. Governments were not required even to describe infrastructure assets in the notes to the financial statements. Governments thereby treated their infrastructure as a "sunk cost," and many governments, in violation of existing accounting requirements, did not even maintain records of their infrastructure.

GASB Standards

Statement No. 34 requires that, in general, governments should account for infrastructure assets just as they do other capital assets. That is, in their governmental fund statements, they should report the costs of infrastructure associated with the government as a whole (general infrastructure assets) as expenditures when the assets are acquired or as they are constructed. In their government-wide statements, governments should capitalize the costs of infrastructure assets and depreciate them over their estimated useful lives.

However, in Statement No. 34 the GASB acknowledges the limitations of depreciation as a measure of the cost of using infrastructure assets. It permits a government not to charge depreciation on infrastructure assets—including those reported in proprietary funds as well as general infrastructure assets—if the government meets certain conditions. If the government can demonstrate

(continued)

---

[3]Concepts Statement No. 1, paras. 77–79.

GASB Standards *(continued)*

that it satisfies those conditions, then it can elect to report as period expenses in its government-wide statements all costs of preserving eligible infrastructure assets *except* costs that result in additions or improvements. It need not charge depreciation expense or report accumulated depreciation on the capitalized cost of these assets.

To use this *modified approach* on all or some of its infrastructure assets, a government must assess the condition of its infrastructure at least every three years. As part of this assessment it must estimate the annual amount necessary to preserve the assets at a specified "condition level" (established by the government itself) and must document that the assets are, in fact, being preserved at or above that level.

Although the modified approach may be at odds with conventional business practice, it is consistent with the theoretical underpinning of depreciation accounting. Properly preserved infrastructure assets may, like land, have infinite useful lives; they need not decline in economic value. Indeed, as evidenced by Roman aqueducts and Chinese great walls, properly cared for assets can last well beyond the number of years that are of concern to financial statement users.

THE MODIFIED APPROACH COMPARED WITH STANDARD DEPRECIATION
Under the modified approach, preservation costs (outlays that extend the useful life of an asset beyond the originally expected useful life) are expensed as incurred. By contrast, under the standard (depreciation) approach, preservation costs are capitalized and depreciated over an asset's expected useful life.

Suppose, for example, that to preserve a road at a specified condition level, a government must repave it every five years at a cost of $200,000. Under the modified approach, the government would report the $200,000 as an expense when incurred. Under the standard approach, it would capitalize the $200,000 and depreciate it over five years. Thus, for this road, the modified approach would result in a charge of $200,000 every five years, whereas the standard approach would result in a charge of $40,000 per year.

A government that elects the modified approach must disclose (as required supplementary information) the assessed condition of the assets and the basis on which it made that assessment. The basis would ordinarily be an engineering measurement scale, such as one that ranks pavements from 0 (unsafe) to 100 (perfect). The government must also report, for the latest five years, the estimated cost of maintaining the assets at the specified condition, as compared to the amounts actually expensed. Table 7–2 illustrates disclosures consistent with GASB standards for the hypothetical City of Morse.

RETROACTIVE CAPITALIZATION OF EXISTING INFRASTRUCTURE Recognizing the difficulty of establishing the original cost of existing general infrastructure assets (those already in place when a government implements Statement No. 34), Statement No. 34 exempts governments from capitalizing general infrastructure assets acquired in fiscal years ending before July 1, 1980. It also permits them to estimate the original

TABLE 7–2
Infrastructure Note
Condition Rating of the City of Morse's Street System

Percentage of Lane-Miles in Good or Better Condition

	2003	2002	2001
Main arterial	93.2%	91.5%	92.0%
Arterial	85.2%	81.6%	84.3%
Secondary	87.2%	84.5%	86.8%
Overall system	87.0%	85.5%	87.3%

Percentage of Lane-Miles in Substandard Condition

	2003	2002	2001
Main arterial	1.7%	2.6%	3.1%
Arterial	3.5%	6.4%	5.9%
Secondary	2.1%	3.4%	3.8%
Overall system	2.2%	3.6%	3.9%

Comparison of Needed-to-Actual Maintenance/Preservation (in Thousands)

	2003	2002	2001	2000	1999
Main arterial:					
Needed	$2,476	$2,342	$2,558	$2,401	$2,145
Actual	2,601	2,552	2,432	2,279	2,271
Arterial:					
Needed	1,485	1,405	1,535	1,441	1,287
Actual	1,560	1,531	1,459	1,367	1,362
Secondary:					
Needed	990	937	1,023	960	858
Actual	1,040	1,021	972	911	908
Overall system:					
Needed	4,951	4,684	5,116	4,802	4,290
Actual	5,201	5,104	4,863	4,557	4,541
Difference	250	420	(253)	(245)	251

Note: The condition of road pavement is measured using a pavement management system, which is based on a weighted average of six distress factors found in pavement surfaces. The pavement management system uses a measurement scale that is based on a condition index ranging from 0 for a failed pavement to 100 for a pavement in perfect condition. The condition index is used to classify roads in good or better condition (70–100), fair condition (50–69), and substandard condition (less than 50). It is the city's policy to maintain at least 85 percent of its street system at a good or better condition level. No more than 10 percent should be in a substandard condition. Condition assessments are determined every year.

cost of the assets that they retroactively capitalize by applying a price-level index to the current replacement cost of the assets.

Assume, for example, that a road, constructed in 1991, is to be recorded in 2005. Were the road to be constructed in 2005, the cost would be $10 million. A road construction price-level index is 90 for 1991 and 120 for 2005. The road would be recorded at an initial cost of $7.5 million ($10 million times 90/120), less accumulated depreciation, if the standard approach rather than the modified approach were elected. If the road had an expected useful life of thirty years, and therefore, should be 50 percent depreciated, its net book value would be $3.75 million (initial cost of $7.5 million, less accumulated depreciation of $3.75 million).

NEW INFRASTRUCTURE All governments are required to capitalize general infrastructure assets acquired or constructed on or after the effective date of Statement No. 34. (Of course they must also continue to capitalize infrastructure accounted for in proprietary funds.) However, in further acknowledgment of the difficulty of *retroactively* capitalizing general infrastructure assets (i.e., assets already in service), the GASB permitted large and middle-sized governments three years beyond the effective date to capitalize them. Moreover, it permanently exempted small governments from the retroactive capitalization requirement.

A CONTROVERSIAL PRONOUNCEMENT Because of its provisions on general infrastructure, Statement No. 34 has proven to be the most controversial pronouncement that the GASB has ever issued. Critics of the statement have presented several arguments as to why its general infrastructure provisions are flawed:

- Statement users have given no indication that they want or would use data on the historical cost of infrastructure. In fact, a 1986 research study published by the GASB presented a sample of users, including investors, managers, and legislators, with six types of information that governments could provide about their infrastructure: historical cost, replacement cost, constant dollar cost, budget-to-actual data, financial plans, and engineering information. The users ranked engineering and financial plan information first and second as most useful. They ranked historical cost data last.[4]

- A key reason for maintaining accounting control over assets is to prevent fraud or abuse. But infrastructure assets cannot be stolen or misused. Therefore, there is no reason to capitalize them.

- Another important reason for reporting assets is to enable statement users to assess whether the assets have been used efficiently. Governments are not expected to earn a monetary return on general infrastructure. Therefore, a comparison between a measure of output (performance) and any monetary value that might be assigned to the assets in the financial statements is not likely to be meaningful.

- Another rationale for reporting assets is to enable statement users to consider alternative uses for them. However, infrastructure assets generally cannot be moved or sold; they seldom have alternative uses.

- The cost of infrastructure assets constructed in the past is of no significance. Many infrastructure assets have evolved over time, rather than being constructed as part of a single project. For example, a government does not typically construct a four-lane highway through virgin fields or forests. More likely, the high-

---

[4]Relmond P. Van Daniker and Vernon Kwiatkowski, *Infrastructure Assets: An Assessment of User Needs and Recommendations for Financial Reporting* (Norwalk, CT: Governmental Accounting Standards Board, 1986).

way began as a footpath and metamorphosed over generations to an unpaved road, a paved road, and a two-lane highway.

In brief, critics of Statement No. 34 have argued that the information about general infrastructure that must be reported on the face of the government-wide statement of net assets facilitates no decisions and, therefore, the cost of recording and reporting general infrastructure assets is not justified.

The GASB, of course, took note of these criticisms in its deliberations. Its position, however, is not that the historical cost of infrastructure is, by itself, useful for decision making. Rather, the GASB believes that if the government-wide statements are to provide a measure of the cost of services, then they must be on a full accrual basis and, therefore, cannot ignore the costs associated with a class of assets as significant as infrastructure. After all, how credible can a balance sheet be if it excludes an entity's most prominent (and costly) assets?

DEFERRED MAINTENANCE As pointed out earlier in the text, a government's assets, especially its infrastructure, can be seen as liabilities as much as assets. Infrastructure assets must be maintained and, like an individual's car, home, and college-age children, are a continuing drain upon fiscal resources.

Governments can postpone asset upkeep costs, but they cannot avoid them. For some assets, engineers have developed sophisticated maintenance schedules that minimize long-term costs by, for example, recommending that streets and highways be resurfaced after a specified number of years. If governments delay beyond that period, then the costs to repair the further deterioration are expected to outweigh the financial benefits of having put off the expenditures.

Deferred maintenance costs are defined as "delayed repair, or upkeep, measured by the outlay required to restore a plant or individual asset to full operating characteristics."[5] They can be measured as the amount necessary to bring the assets up to their expected operating condition. Deferred maintenance costs may be interpreted as a potential call upon government resources—an obligation that is being passed on to taxpayers of the future. They are an indication that taxpayers of the past or present have not paid for the maintenance costs applicable to the services received.

In the GASB infrastructure study, at least 84 percent of the academic, investor, legislator, and citizen groups were in favor of including information on deferred maintenance in annual financial reports. Managers (who would be responsible for providing the data) were less enthusiastic, with only 52 percent advocating inclusion.[6]

Statement No. 34 goes a long way toward providing the information that users want. Governments that do not depreciate their infrastructure assets must demonstrate that they are, in fact, maintaining them at, or above, a specified condition level. In addition, they must disclose, for a five-year period, their actual maintenance costs as compared to the amounts needed to maintain the assets at the specified condition level. (See Table 7–2 for an example.)

---

[5]W. W. Cooper and Y. Ijiri (eds). *Kohler's Dictionary for Accountants*, 6th edition (Englewood Cliffs, N.J.: Prentice-Hall, 1983), p. 155.

[6]Van Daniker and Kwiatkowski, p. 112.

What Are the Limitations of Information Reported About General Capital Assets?

Statement No. 34 elevated the level of governments' general capital asset reporting and accountability to that of businesses and proprietary funds. However, *improved* reporting should not be mistaken for *adequate* reporting. In reality, readers can learn very little from financial statement data on a government's capital assets—any more than they can from financial statement data on a business's net assets. Consider, for example, typical questions relating to capital assets that city officials or external parties might ask:

- *Should the city sell an asset and replace it with another?* For this decision the recorded amount, indicative of the initial cost of the asset, is irrelevant. It is a **sunk cost**—an unrecoverable amount—and has no bearing on cash flows of the future. By contrast, the current market price of the asset—that for which it could be sold—is of direct concern, but is not required to be reported.

- *Are assets being used efficiently?* Again, the historical cost of the assets is irrelevant. Suppose that the city owns two parcels of land, which it uses as sports fields. Both have the same market value. It would make no sense to assume that one is being used more efficiently than the other merely because it was acquired earlier and at a lower price.

- *Is the city replacing assets that it sells or retires?* A comparison between capital asset additions and the book value of retirements sheds little light on whether the city is maintaining its asset base, since it relates assets at current prices to assets at past prices.

- *Are the city's assets adequately insured?* The adequacy of insurance should be assessed by comparing the amount of coverage with the cost of replacing the assets, but the replacement cost is not required to be reported.

In recent years, it has become widely acknowledged that the financial statements of businesses, especially those in high-tech industries, fail to capture a firm's intangible assets, such as intellectual capital, internally developed software, marketing skills, and brand names. The most notable evidence of this deficiency is the wide disparity between the book and stock market values of many of our leading companies (e.g., Microsoft and Dell).

Governments, too, have intangible assets, and as we advance further into the electronic age, these will become an increasingly large proportion of their total assets. The failure of financial statements to incorporate them will become increasingly significant.

What Issues Are Critical as to Investments in Marketable Securities?

In previous chapters we have discussed the standards for valuing investments in marketable securities, such as stocks, bonds, and notes, and for recognizing interest, dividends, and gains and losses (both realized and unrealized). However, the concerns of governments and their constituents with regard to investments extend beyond purely accounting issues. Investments in marketable securities and related financial instruments, such as commodity options, allow organizations to enhance their revenues and, in some cases, to better manage their risks. But they also present special hazards. In this section of the chapter we discuss the reasons why governments purchase marketable securities and we identify some of the associated perils.

REASONS FOR PURCHASING MARKETABLE SECURITIES Governments may have large pools of cash available for investments. The following are among the major sources:

- Governments periodically receive large amounts of cash—from tax collections, tolls, fees, charges for services, and so on.
- Governments maintain reserve funds to repay debt or to save for a particular purpose or for a "rainy day."
- They accumulate resources in pension funds.
- They—especially universities and hospitals—maintain permanent endowments, which are established to generate investment revenues.

A fundamental rule of cash management is "the less cash on hand, the better." As long as the cash is not needed to meet required expenditures of the same day, it should be placed in short-term—even overnight—securities. Governments invest in marketable securities for much the same reason that businesses do—to earn a return on cash that would otherwise be unproductive.

Many governments invest their funds directly in stocks, bonds, notes, and other financial instruments. Others, especially smaller units, participate in **investment pools** maintained by other governments. For example, most states operate investment pools for their cities, counties, and school districts to enable them to gain the benefits of increased portfolio size—lower trading costs, greater opportunity to diversify, and ability to pay for sophisticated investment advice.

CAUSES FOR SPECIAL CONCERN Until recently, governments generally were satisfied with "conservative securities" that provided steady, if relatively modest, returns. Accordingly, their risks of loss were low.

Now, however, treasurers and other officials responsible for their governments' investments are under considerable pressure to increase their portfolio yields. In part, the demands can be attributed to the need for governments to maintain or enhance services in the face of increasing costs. Also, though, the treasury function has become more professional. No longer can treasurers simply divide their available resources among local banks or friendly brokerage houses. Today, their performance—and, consequently, their salary increases and opportunities for advancement—are more likely to be tied to the yields on the portfolios they control. Given these incentives, it is easy for portfolio managers to ignore a fundamental concept of finance: the greater the returns, the greater the risk.

At the same time, the range of investment products offered by Wall Street has increased dramatically. Succumbing to aggressive sales tactics from brokers and dealers, many treasurers purchase securities that they do not understand and that are clearly unsuited to their governments' investment objectives.

When governments restricted their portfolios to conventional financial instruments, the accounting issues of asset classification (e.g., current or noncurrent), asset valuation (cost or market), and revenue recognition (upon change in value or only upon sale) were far more tractable than they are today. The new financial instruments are often multifaceted and extremely difficult to value. In addition, identical types of financial instruments can be held for diametrically opposed purposes (e.g., to increase risk or to decrease risk).

SPECIAL RISKS OF REPURCHASE AGREEMENTS In the mid-1980s it became clear that existing reporting requirements were inadequate to ensure that investors of all types (governments, private not-for-profits, and businesses) fully disclosed their investment risks. One main problem centered around repurchase agreements. A **repurchase agreement** (referred to as a **repo**) is a short-term investment in which an investor (a lender) transfers cash to a broker-dealer or other financial institution (the counterparty) in exchange for securities. The broker-dealer or other financial institution promises to repay the cash, plus interest, in exchange for the same (or in some cases different) securities.

Repurchase agreements usually have either short-term (sometimes overnight) maturities or open-ended maturities in which the interest rates may be changed daily and the agreement may be terminated at any time by either party. To facilitate the transactions, the investor may not actually take custody of the securities (in effect, the collateral) that back its investment. Instead the securities may be retained by the counterparty (perhaps in its trust department) or by its agent. Moreover, the securities may be held in the name of the counterparty rather than the investor.

The major risks to the government (or other investor) from a repurchase transaction are that the counterparty will be unable to repay cash and that either the government will be unable to obtain the securities or that the securities will have decreased in value. As might be expected, for some governments the risks became the reality.

Governments and other entities may also enter into **reverse repurchase agreements**. A **reverse repo** is one in which the government or other party is a borrower rather than an investor. The broker-dealer or other financial institution transfers cash to the government in exchange for securities, and the government agrees to repay the cash plus interest and return the securities.

SPECIAL RISKS OF DERIVATIVES In the 1980s and 1990s many governments and other entities invested in derivatives. A **derivative** is a security whose value depends on (is *derived* from) that of some underlying asset (such as a share of stock), a reference rate (such as a prevailing interest rate), or an index (such as the Standard & Poor's index of stock prices). Derivatives embrace many types of securities, ranging from the ordinary to the esoteric. For example, they include ordinary stock options (such as puts and calls), debt instruments that are backed by pools of mortgages, and interest-only or principal-only *strips* (bond-like securities in which the obligations to pay principal and interest are traded separately). Most derivatives are highly volatile instruments and can enable an investor to achieve gains, or cause it to incur losses, greatly out of proportion to the change in the value of the securities or assets to which they are linked.

Ironically, many types of derivatives were developed to *reduce* overall investment risks. Hence, they may have a legitimate place in the portfolios of even the most conservative entities. However, they have been widely misused by some governments (and not-for-profits and businesses) as a means of speculation.

GASB Standards

Recognizing that the then-current standards of providing information on investments were inadequate, the GASB in 1986 issued Statement No. 3, *Deposits with Financial Institutions, Investments (including Repurchase Agreements), and Reverse Repurchase Agreements.* Statement No. 3 mandates extensive note disclosures, not only as to repurchase agreements but also as to all investments and deposits with banks and other financial institutions. Most prominently, it requires governments to classify their bank balances and other investments into three categories of **credit risk** (the risk that the other party to an investment transaction will not fulfill its obligations). For bank balances the required classifications are

1. Insured or collateralized, with securities held by the government or by its agent in the government's name
2. Collateralized, with securities held by the pledging financial institution's trust department or agent in the government's name
3. Uncollateralized

For other investments, including repurchase agreements, the three categories are

1. Insured, registered in the government's name, or held by the government or its agent in the government's name
2. Uninsured and unregistered, with securities held by the other party's trust department or agent in the government's name
3. Uninsured and unregistered, with securities held by the other party or its agent but not in the government's name[7]

In addition, Statement No. 3 requires governments to indicate both the reported value and the fair value of their investments.[8]

In 1994, the GASB issued a technical bulletin reaffirming previous standards that governments must disclose their accounting policies as to investments and must provide any other information to ensure that the financial statements are not misleading. The technical bulletin, however, also interprets existing provisions as implying that a government must reveal any violations of legal, regulatory, or contractual provisions caused by investing in derivatives. Further, it says, the government must explain the nature of derivative transactions, indicate the reasons why they were entered into, and include a discussion of its exposure to credit risk (that of the other party defaulting), market risk (that of changes in interest rates or market prices), and legal risk (that of the transaction being determined to be prohibited by law, regulation, or contract).[9]

Table 7–3 presents excerpts from the notes to the financial statements of Orlando, Florida, for the year ended September 30, 2001. The excerpts include the city's investment policy and disclosures required by GASB Statement No. 3 and Technical Bulletin 94–1.

---

[7]As this book went to press, the GASB had outstanding for public comment a proposal (exposure draft) to amend Statement No. 3. The proposal would eliminate the requirement to disclose deposits and investments in categories 1 and 2, as a result of federal banking reforms enacted since Statement No. 3 was issued. However, new disclosures would be required related to credit risk, interest rate risk, foreign currency risk, and deposit and investment policies.

[8]This requirement is now moot for most investments because, as discussed in Chapter 4, Statement No. 31 requires governments to report them at fair value. However, governments should continue to disclose the fair value of any short-term securities reported at cost.

[9]GASB Technical Bulletin No. 94–1, *Disclosures about Derivatives and Similar Debt and Investment Transactions.*

TABLE 7–3
City of Orlando, Florida
Excerpts from Investment Notes
September 30, 2001

Investments. All investments, including Pension Funds, are stated at fair value, which is either a quoted market price or the best available estimate.

. . . . . .

. . . . . .

The City's investment (cash management pool) guidelines, except for pension fund and deferred compensation assets and the Trustee Accounts, are defined by City ordinance and written investment policies which are approved by the City Council. The policy specifies limits by instrument and institution (within instrument) and establishes a diversified investment strategy, minimum credit quality and authorized institutions available as counterparties. Implementation and direction of investment strategies, within policy limits, are established by an internal Investment Committee and managed by either internal or external money managers.

. . . . . .

. . . . . .

The City's investment policy requires transactions to meet "payment versus delivery" perfection with securities being held by the City's third party custodian on behalf of and in the name of the City. The exceptions to this policy are overnight repurchase agreements with the City's primary banking institution, mutual funds, investments held by a broker/dealer under a reverse repurchase agreement and investments with Florida's State Board of Administration (SBA). In accordance with GASB Statement #31, the SBA has reported that the Local Government Investment Trust, which it operates, is a "2A-7 like" pool and, thus, these investments are valued using the pooled share price.

. . . . . .

. . . . . .

The Ordinance allows the City to enter into reverse repurchase agreements; that is, a sale of securities with a simultaneous agreement to repurchase them in the future at the same price plus a contract rate of interest. The fair value of the securities underlying reverse repurchase agreements normally exceeds the cash received, providing the dealers a margin against a decline in fair value of the securities. If the dealers (which are limited to primary dealers) default on their contractual obligations to resell these securities to the City, or provide securities or cash of at least equal value, the City would suffer an economic loss equal to the difference between the fair value plus accrued interest of the underlying securities and the repurchase agreement obligations, including accrued interest. There were no holdings in reverse repurchase agreements at September 30, 2001.

The City's investment policy (a) authorizes the use of options, puts, forwards and futures, (b) establishes a minimum total portfolio duration of nine months, (c) establishes the maximum total portfolio duration of five years and (d) allows limited use of high-yield corporate, long duration treasuries, international investment grade and emerging market bonds.

. . . . . .

. . . . . .

Investment portfolios are reported and normally classified in three credit risk categories as follows:
(1) Insured or registered, or securities held by the entity or its agent in the entity's name.
(2) Uninsured and unregistered, with securities held by the counterparty's trust department or agent in the entity's name, and
(3) Uninsured and unregistered, with securities held by the counterparty, or by its trust department or agent but not in the entity's name. This includes the portion of the carrying amount of any repurchase agreements that exceeds the fair value of the underlying securities.

TABLE 7-3 *(continued)*
City of Orlando, Florida
Excerpts from Investment Notes
September 30, 2001

Investments in the SBA, mutual funds, closed-end real estate trusts and indexed (passively managed) pension accounts are not required to be categorized since the investments are not evidenced by securities that exist in physical or book entry form. All classifiable investments in the Operating, Trustee and Pension Portfolios are classified as Category 1, both at year end and throughout the year.

All investments are made based on reasonable research as to credit quality, liquidity and counterparty risk prior to the investment being acquired.

......

......

Source: City of Orlando, Florida, *Comprehensive Annual Financial Report* for the year ended September 30, 2001, pages 44, 48, 49, and 53 (cross-references to more detailed notes omitted).

QUESTIONS FOR REVIEW AND DISCUSSION

1. Why are general capital assets not recorded in either the general fund or any other governmental fund?

2. What are the key differences in how general capital assets are reported on government-wide as opposed to fund statements?

3. A city establishes an art museum. What options does it have in accounting for its collection of paintings?

4. Although Statement No. 34 requires that infrastructure assets be accounted for similarly to other capital assets, it allows for a major exception with regard to depreciation. What is that exception?

5. Why have many government officials objected to Statement No. 34's requirement that general infrastructure assets be accounted for similarly to other capital assets?

6. What are *deferred maintenance costs*, and how must a government report them (as they relate to infrastructure) in its financial statements?

7. What is a *repurchase agreement*, and what are its special risks to a government that invests in one?

8. What are *derivatives*? Why may they be especially high risk securities?

9. A government with which you are familiar has earned a return on its pension fund portfolio that far exceeds the average earned by other governments. Why might the high return be of concern? What might motivate the pension fund manager to adopt the policies that generated that high return?

10. What is meant by credit risk? To what extent are governments required to disclose the credit risk they have assumed?

EXERCISES AND PROBLEMS

7–1

Select the *best* answer.

1. Which of the following would be least likely to be classified as a city's *general* capital assets?
   a. roads and bridges
   b. electric utility lines
   c. computers used by the police department
   d. computers used by the department that collects the city's sale tax, which is dedicated to debt service on general obligation bonds

2. A city should not report on its general fund balance sheet an office building constructed over a hundred years ago because
   a. the building would likely be fully depreciated

b. it would be too difficult to determine the historical cost of the building as measured in current dollars

c. the measurement focus of the general fund is on current financial resources and the building is not a current financial resource

d. the building would be considered an infrastructure asset and infrastructure assets are excluded from governmental funds

3. Which of the following costs should *not* be capitalized and reported on a city's government-wide statement of net assets?

a. computer software that the city developed internally

b. computer software that the city purchased from outsiders

c. paintings acquired for display in the city's art museum

d. legal fees incurred in acquiring land to be used for a city park

4. Which of the following collectibles need *not* be capitalized and reported on a city's government-wide statement of net assets?

a. a statue donated to the city, which it intends to sell and use the proceeds from the sale to fund a children's art center

b. a series of books that the city intends to place in its library's general circulation collection

c. an abstract painting that the city purchased to decorate the mayor's office

d. an early twentieth century impressionist painting that the city's art museum purchased for its permanent collection

5. Per GASB Statement No. 34, roads and bridges should be capitalized and reported as assets on

a. both a government-wide statement net of assets and a general fund balance sheet

b. neither a government-wide statement of net assets nor a general fund balance sheet

c. a government-wide statement of net assets but not a general fund balance sheet

d. a general fund balance sheet but not a government-wide statement of net assets

6. Which of the following conditions does a government *not* have to satisfy to use the modified approach to reporting infrastructure assets?

a. It must assess the condition of its infrastructure at least once every three years.

b. It must estimate the annual amount necessary to preserve the assets at a specified condition level.

c. It must document that the assets are, in fact, being preserved at or above the specified condition level.

d. It must use the modified approach for all of its infrastructure assets.

7. Per the modified approach, a government need not

a. capitalize infrastructure assets

b. depreciate infrastructure assets

c. report in its fund statements expenditures to acquire or construct infrastructure assets

d. record maintenance costs as expenditures

8. A government constructed a bridge twenty years ago but does not have reliable records of the cost. However, the cost to construct a comparable bridge today would be $30 million. A bridge construction index has a value today of 200 and a value for twenty years ago of 80. The bridge has a useful life of sixty years. The government should record the bridge at a value, net of accumulated depreciation, of

a. $8 million

b. $12 million

c. $30 million

d. $75 million

9. Recognizing the difficulty of implementing the provisions of GASB Statement No. 34 pertaining to the *retroactive* capitalization of general infrastructure, the GASB

a. exempted "small" governments from having to apply them

b. gave all governments an additional six years from the effective date of Statement No. 34 to apply them

c. exempted special purpose governments, such as public schools, from having to apply them

d. permitted governments to capitalize general infrastructure only prospectively—i.e., only those assets constructed or acquired after the statement's implementation date

10. Per GASB Statement No. 34, deferred maintenance costs

a. must be estimated and reported in notes to the financial statements

b. must be reported in the government-wide statement of net assets but not in fund statements

c. must be estimated and reported in the management's discussion and analysis

d. need not be explicitly measured or reported when capital assets are depreciated

7–2

Select the *best* answer.

1. A government repaves a section of highway every four years at a cost of $2 million so as to preserve it at a specific condition level. How much should it report in depreciation charges under alternative assumptions as to whether it adopts the modified approach to accounting for infrastructure?

	Modified Approach	*Standard Approach*
a.	$0	$0
b.	$500,000	$500,000
c.	$500,000	$0
d.	$0	$500,000

2. States typically maintain *investment pools* for their towns and counties primarily to
   a. provide the participants with the benefits of increased portfolio size
   b. assure that the participants adhere to all state investment laws and policies
   c. enable the participants to enhance internal and administrative controls over their investments
   d. spread the risk of losses among the participants

3. When a city enters into a repurchase agreement, it will typically
   a. give an investor the opportunity to repurchase equity securities that it will sell to the investor
   b. borrow cash from a bank with the understanding that it will use the cash to repurchase bonds that the city previously issued
   c. sell securities to an investor guaranteeing that it will repurchase them at a higher price
   d. buy securities from a third party with the promise that the third party will repurchase the securities at a higher price

4. A government would typically enter into a reverse repurchase agreement in order to
   a. borrow cash for a short period of time
   b. invest cash overnight or for some other short period of time
   c. diversify its investment portfolio
   d. hedge its investments against fluctuations in interest rates

5. Derivatives are
   a. variable interest-rate bonds, the interest rate on which is derived from (based on) the prime rate of interest
   b. shares of common stock, the value of which is derived from (based on) the market value of the underlying assets (typically investments in subsidiaries) of the issuing corporation
   c. investments, the value of which is derived from (based on) some underlying asset or reference rate
   d. investment pools, the value of which is derived from (based on) the pools' investments

6. Which of the following statements is true with respect to derivatives?
   a. They are highly speculative instruments and therefore are suitable only for governments that are willing to accept a high degree of investment risk.
   b. Their market values are typically less volatile than those of the underlying assets.
   c. GASB standards require that governments explain in their annual reports the reasons why they invested in derivatives.
   d. They need not be reported on governments' financial statements; they need only be disclosed in notes to the financial statements.

7. GASB Statement No. 3 requires governments to classify their repurchase agreements and other investments into three categories of
   a. credit risk
   b. market value risk
   c. interest rate risk
   d. physical loss

8. Investments would generally be considered subject to the least credit risk if they are
   a. registered in the government's name but in the possession of a broker-dealer
   b. registered in the government's name and in the physical possession of the government itself
   c. registered in the broker-dealer's name and in the possession of the broker-dealer
   d. registered in the broker-dealer's name but in the possession of the government itself

9. A city needs to determine whether it should sell its downtown administrative facility and move to an outlying location. The value of the facility that is most relevant to this decision is
   a. historical cost
   b. current market value
   c. historical cost less accumulated depreciation
   d. assessed value

10. Which of the following costs should *not* be included in the cost of a highway that a county constructed itself?

    a. insurance premiums paid while the project was under construction

    b. interest incurred on debt used to finance the project while it was under construction

    c. overhead costs of the construction department

    d. fees paid to consultants to determine the highway's optimum route

7–3

General capital assets are accounted for differently in fund and government-wide financial statements.

A city engaged in the following transactions during a year.

a. It acquired computer equipment at a cost of $40,000.

b. It completed construction of a new jail, incurring $245,000 in new costs. In the previous year the city had incurred $2.5 million in construction costs. The project was accounted for in a capital projects fund.

c. It sold for $16,000 land that it had acquired three years earlier for $28,000.

1. Prepare journal entries to reflect the transactions in an appropriate governmental fund (e.g., a general fund or a capital projects fund).

2. Prepare journal entries to reflect the transactions in the city's government-wide statements.

7–4

Capital assets are accounted for in government-wide statements on a full accrual basis.

The following events summarize the history of Sharp Hall, the main foreign language classroom building at a state university. The university bases its accounting on the reporting model applicable to cities and other general purpose governments.

1. In 1978, the university constructed the building at a cost of $1.5 million. Of this amount, $1 million was financed with bonds and the balance from unrestricted university funds.

2. In the ten years from 1978 through 1987 the university recorded depreciation (as appropriate) based on an estimated useful life of thirty years.

3. In the same period, the university repaid $750,000 of the bonds.

4. In 1988, the university renovated the building at a cost of $3 million. The entire amount was financed with unrestricted university funds. The renovation was expected to extend the useful life

of the building so that it would last twenty-five more years—that is, until 2013.

5. In the fifteen years from 1988 through 2002, the university recorded depreciation (as appropriate). Depreciation was calculated by dividing the undepreciated balance of the original cost, plus the costs of renovation, by the anticipated remaining life of twenty-five years.

6. In the same period, the university repaid the $250,000 balance of the debt.

7. In 2003, the university demolished the building so that the land on which it was situated could be converted into a practice field for the women's soccer team.

Prepare journal entries to summarize the history of Sharp Hall, as it would be reported in the university's government-wide statements.

7–5

Capital assets are accounted for in governmental fund statements on a modified accrual basis.

Refer to the transactions in the previous exercise.

1. Prepare the journal entries that the university would make in its governmental funds (e.g., its general fund or a capital projects fund).

2. How would you recommend that the university maintain accounting control over the capital assets themselves—those that you did not record as assets in the governmental funds?

7–6

Estimating the cost of old infrastructure is one of the most challenging problems facing governments as they implement Statement No. 34. Fortunately the GASB permits an alternative to reconstructing old records.

In 1993, a city constructed a park but has inadequate records of its cost. Engineers estimate that in 2005 the cost of replacing that park would be $3 million. They have also determined that the park has a total useful life of thirty years. An appropriate construction price index had a value of 108 in 1993 and 180 in 2005.

1. What value (estimated initial cost less accumulated depreciation) should the city assign to the park in 2005?

2. Suppose that the city opted to report only an annual maintenance charge for the park; it would not report a depreciation charge. At what value would it report the park?

3. In your opinion, does the depreciation charge add significant information to the financial statements? Explain and justify your response.

7–7

If governments don't preserve their infrastructure assets they must depreciate them.

1. In 2003, Bantham County incurred $80 million in costs to construct a new highway. Engineers estimate that the useful life of the highway is twenty years. Prepare the entry that the county should make to record annual depreciation (straight-line method) to facilitate preparation of its government-wide statements.

2. What reservations might you have as to the engineers' estimate of useful life? Why might any estimate of a highway's useful life be suspect?

3. In 2004, the engineers determined that the county would have to incur $1 million in resurfacing costs every four years to preserve the highway in the same condition as it was when the road was completed. In 2004, the county spent $1 million to resurface the highway. Prepare the entries, including that for first-year depreciation, that the county should make.

4. Assume instead that, as permitted by Statement No. 34, the county opts to report a road preservation charge in lieu of depreciation. Prepare the entry the county should make in 2004.

5. Suppose that in 2005 the county added a new lane to a portion of the highway. The cost was $1.5 million. Prepare an appropriate journal entry to facilitate preparation of the government-wide statements, regardless of whether the county takes the depreciation or the modified approach.

7–8

Positive revenue to expenditure ratios may not always be as favorable as they appear.

In the management's discussion and analysis accompanying its 2003 financial statements, Tiber County reported that "for the fifth consecutive year revenues exceeded expenditures." However, a note included in required supplementary information indicated the following:

County Roads and Highways:
Comparison of Needed to Actual Maintenance/
Preservation Costs (in thousands)

	Actual	*Needed*
2003	$3,400	$4,200
2002	3,000	4,000
2001	2,900	3,000
2000	3,100	3,100
1999	2,800	2,700

The county has not been depreciating its infrastructure system.

1. What reservations might you have as to the significance of the county's excess of revenues over expenditures in 2003?

2. Suppose that you were the county's independent auditor. What reservation might you have as to the county's reporting practices?

3. Suppose that the county was required to depreciate its roads. As of year-end 2003, the estimated initial cost of the roads was $100 million and their estimated useful life was forty years. How would the change from the modified approach to the standard approach affect the county's general fund excess of revenues over expenditures? How would it affect the county's government-wide statements?

7–9

Similar collectibles may be accounted for quite differently.

The City of Allentown recently received a donation of two items:

- A letter written in 1820 by James Allen, the city's founder, in which he sets forth his plan for the city's development. Independent appraisers have valued the letter at $24,000.

- A 1920 painting of Allentown's city hall. Comparable paintings by the same artist have recently been sold for $4,000.

The city intends to place the letter on public display in its city hall. It plans to sell the painting and use the proceeds to redecorate the city council's meeting chambers. The city's policy is to capitalize collectibles only when required by GASB standards to do so.

1. Prepare journal entries, as necessary, to reflect how each of the contributions should be reported on the city's government-wide financial statements. Briefly explain and justify any apparent inconsistencies in the entries.

2. Suppose that the city had purchased each of the items. Would that affect whether you capitalized each of the assets?

3. Suppose that when the city accepted the painting it agreed that, if it sold the painting, it would use the proceeds only to acquire other works of art. Would that affect how you accounted for the painting?

4. Suppose that the city operated a museum. The museum's building, furniture, and fixtures had cost $10 million and, on average, were midway through their useful life. They had a replacement cost of $12 million. The art collection had a market value of $300 million. Consistent with your response to question 1, what value would

you place on the art collection? What value would you place on the building, furniture, and fixtures? Briefly justify your response, commenting specifically on whether you think the resultant statement of net assets would provide useful information to statement users.

7–10

Investment notes provide only limited information on investment risks.

Use Table 7–4, an excerpt from a note included in the annual report of the City of Minneapolis, to answer these questions.

1. By what types of risk are the securities categorized? Which category of risk (1, 2, or 3) is the most risky? Why?

2. What other major risks does the city accept when it invests in securities?

3. Suppose that the U.S. Federal Agency Obligations held by the city have an average maturity of one year, whereas the commercial paper has an average maturity of only thirty days. Which investment is likely to be the more risky? Why?

4. Another note indicates that the city may invest in repurchase agreements. What are repurchase agreements? What risks does the city assume in investing in them?

7-11

Exploring Orlando's financial report

Refer to the City of Orlando's capital asset disclosures in Table 7–1.

1. What are the principal classes of capital assets associated with governmental activities that Orlando reports in the financial statements?

2. Some analysts use the accumulated depreciation amount reported for capital assets to assess roughly how close they are to needing replacement, which will require an outflow of financial resources, possibly financed by the incurrence of new debt. (Of course, other factors, such as changes in technology and programs, also contribute to replacement decisions.) Orlando uses straight-line depreciation. Based on the information reported in Table 7–1, which classes of capital assets are closest to needing replacement?

3. As shown in Table 7–1, Orlando reports assets of $57.1 million for (completed) infrastructure—roughly the same as the amount reported

---

TABLE 7–4
City of Minneapolis
Deposits and Investments

Investments are categorized into three categories of custodial credit risk as follows:

(1) Insured or registered, or securities held by the City or its agent in the City's name.

(2) Uninsured and unregistered, with securities held by the counterparty's trust department or agent in the City's name.

(3) Uninsured and unregistered, with securities held by the counterparty, or by its trust department or agent but not in the City's name.

Investments at December 31 (in thousands):

Security type	Custodial Credit Risk Category 1	2	3	Fair Value
U.S. Treasury Obligations	$ 42,632	$ 559	$1,129	$ 44,320
U.S. Federal Agency Obligations	110,147	2,046	468	112,661
Municipal Bonds	20,263	21,045	—	41,308
Corporate Bonds	—	—	476	476
Commercial Paper	172,590	—	161	172,751
Common Stock	—	—	2,856	2,856
	$345,632	$23,650	$5,090	
Mutual Fund				944
Money Market				4,203
Insurance Annuities—Trustee				680
Guaranteed Investment Contracts				45,855
Total				$426,054

for motor vehicles. Why do you think the amount reported for infrastructure assets is not substantially larger?

4. A fellow student looks at Table 7–1 and comments that Orlando must be substantially increasing its capital assets because the amounts reported for additions generally are much larger than those reported for retirements. Do you agree with her assessment? Explain.

5. Table 7–1 shows that Orlando does not depreciate artwork. What is the justification for that decision?

7–12

Exploring Orlando's financial report

Refer to the financial statements of the City of Orlando in Chapter 3 and to Table 7–3 in this chapter.

1. What amount does Orlando report on its government-wide statement of net assets for investments of governmental activities? Where are these investments reported in the fund financial statements?

2. Orlando, like many governments, participates in an externally managed investment pool. Who manages the pool? How would Orlando's investments in the pool be valued?

3. Does Orlando's investment policy permit investments in repurchase agreements and derivatives? Does Orlando have any reverse repurchase agreements?

4. As discussed in the text, GASB Statement No. 3 requires that governments categorize their investments in one of three categories of credit risk. How much does Orlando report in each of the three categories?

CHAPTER 8

Governmental Activities— Long-Term Obligations

This chapter is directed to *general* long-term obligations—that is, those of the government at large that are associated primarily with governmental activities. General long-term obligations include liabilities, such as bonds, that are recognized in the government-wide statement of net assets, as well as other commitments, such as loan guarantees, that may be disclosed only in notes. General long-term liabilities may be viewed as negative long-lived assets. They present comparable issues of valuation and reporting and, for the most part, are accounted for as mirror images of their capital asset counterparts, which were discussed in Chapter 7.

WHY IS INFORMATION ON LONG-TERM DEBT IMPORTANT TO STATEMENT USERS?

The issues addressed in this chapter are closely tied to a key objective of financial reporting. As stated by the GASB:

> *Financial reporting should provide information about the financial position and condition of a governmental entity.* Financial reporting should provide information about resources and obligations, both actual and contingent, current and noncurrent. The major financial resources of most governmental entities are derived from the ability to tax and issue debt. As a result, financial reporting should provide information about tax sources, tax limitations, tax burdens, and debt limitations.[1]

Information on long-term debt is especially important to statement users because a government's failure to make timely payments of interest and principal can have profound repercussions, for both its creditors and itself. Creditors will obviously incur losses. But insofar as governments rely on debt to finance acquisitions of infrastructure, buildings, and equipment, a loss of credit standing can seriously harm their ability to provide the services expected of them.

A key message of this chapter is that statement users must look beyond the basic financial statements to understand the amount and nature of a government's debt burden. The financial statements cannot be relied upon to disclose all of a government's obligations or to provide sufficient data to assess their economic value. Hence, users must pay particular attention to note disclosures, supplementary data in the annual report's statistical section, and, if necessary, public data available outside the annual report.

---

[1]GASB Concepts Statement No. 1, para. 79.

CAN GOVERNMENTS GO BANKRUPT?

A government's failure to satisfy claims against it can produce dire results, including bankruptcy. In such a situation governments can seek protection under the Federal Bankruptcy Code—just as can individuals, businesses, and nongovernmental not-for-profits.

Bankruptcy filings by major governments are rare, but those of smaller units, especially utility districts, are much more common, particularly in years of economic downturn. In the past few decades several cities, including New York, Yonkers (New York), Bridgeport (Connecticut), Philadelphia, Washington, D.C., and Camden (New Jersey), avoided bankruptcy only by being brought under the authority of financial control boards by higher-level governments.

The concept of municipal bankruptcy is elusive. Governments have the power to tax and, in return, are expected to provide certain essential services. In a sense, their access to resources is limited only by the wealth of their populations. Correspondingly, their expenditures can be reduced to zero by cutting back on services. In reality, however, there are practical limits to both their taxing authority and the extent to which they can eliminate services. Raise taxes above a certain level and both residents and businesses flee the jurisdiction, thereby reducing overall revenues. Reduce services beyond a certain point and the safety and overall well-being of the community are impaired.

When a court declares a government bankrupt, it temporarily transfers control over the government's affairs to an independent trustee. The eventual outcome, with the court's approval, is generally a settlement with creditors and a reorganization, sometimes with the jurisdiction being permanently incorporated into another government.

Bankruptcy represents the ultimate fiscal failure, resulting in almost certain losses to creditors. But creditors can also experience losses, even in the absence of bankruptcy. New York City, for example, responded to its mid-1970s financial crisis by obtaining creditor agreement to a voluntary debt restructuring. Even though creditors may have eventually received the full face value of their loans, payments were delayed and interest was reduced. Thus, the economic loss was as real (if not necessarily as great) as if the city had filed for bankruptcy.

HOW DO GOVERNMENTS ACCOUNT FOR GENERAL LONG-TERM OBLIGATIONS?

General long-term debt has been defined as:

> *the unmatured principal* of bonds, warrants, notes, special assessment debt for which the government is obligated in some manner, or other forms of noncurrent or long-term *general obligation* debt that is not a specific liability of any proprietary fund or trust fund.[2]

General obligation (long-term) **debt** is the obligation of the government at large and is thereby backed by the government's general credit and revenue-raising powers. It is distinguished from **revenue debt**, which is secured only by designated

---

[2]GASB *Codification of Governmental Accounting and Financial Reporting Standards, as of June 30, 2001*, Section 1500.103.

revenue streams, such as from utility fees, highway tolls, rents, receipts from student loans, or patient billings.

The long-term debts of governments by no means include *all* their financial obligations—any more than do those of businesses. As a general rule, only debts resulting from past transactions for which the government *has already received a benefit* are recognized. Reported obligations thereby exclude commitments for payments of interest when the government has not yet enjoyed the use of the borrowed funds; the salary of a city manager that, although contractually guaranteed, has not been earned; future rent payments that are established by a noncancelable operating lease; and amounts owing under long-term service contracts when the promised services have not yet been provided.

ACCOUNTING FOR LONG-TERM OBLIGATIONS IN GOVERNMENTAL FUNDS As previously emphasized, governmental funds focus on current financial resources. A long-term obligation, by definition, does not have to be repaid in the current year and does not require current-year appropriation or expenditure of fund resources. Therefore, "to include it as a governmental fund liability would be misleading and dysfunctional to the current period management control (for example, budgeting) and accountability functions."[3]

When the proceeds of long-term debt are received by a governmental fund, the debit to cash (or other assets) is offset by *other financing sources—bond proceeds*, or a comparable account signifying an inflow of resources, *not* by a liability. Just as the existence of buildings, vehicles, and other long-term assets is ignored in governmental funds, so also are long-term debts, including the portion of bonds, notes, claims and judgments, and obligations for sick-leave and vacations for which payment is not required out of resources appropriated for the current year. As a consequence, long-term debt includes amounts arising out of operating as well as capital transactions. As emphasized in previous chapters, the expenditures relating to these operating transactions will be charged in the periods in which the resources are appropriated for payment—in effect, when the long-term debts are liquidated—not necessarily in the periods in which the government reaped the benefits.

Because governments do not report long-term obligations in governmental fund balance sheets, they do not record them in the accounts for those funds. However, in order to prepare government-wide statements, governments must keep track of their long-term obligations through subsidiary ledgers or other records.

DIFFERENCES IN GOVERNMENT-WIDE STATEMENTS

In their government-wide statements, governments should account for their general long-term obligations as do businesses. They should record debt at face value or, if the debt is issued at a premium or discount, at the unamortized issue price. They may account for bond issue costs as an adjustment to the premium or discount. Each period they must amortize the premium or discount, offsetting the unamortized premium or discount with a decrease or increase, respectively, in interest expense.

(continued)

---

[3]NCGA Statement No. 1, *Governmental Accounting and Financial Reporting Principles*, para. 44.

As discussed in Chapter 6, a bond premium or discount represents the difference between the face value of a bond and the amount for which it is issued. A bond is sold at a premium whenever its specified interest rate (its stated or coupon rate) is greater than interest rates prevailing at the time of issuance (the yield rate). It is sold at a discount whenever the specified rate is less than the prevailing rate. The greater the difference between the coupon rate and the yield rate and the greater the number of years to maturity, the greater is the premium or discount.

Governments must include in notes to their financial statements a schedule of changes in long-term obligations showing the beginning and ending balances and the increases and decreases during the year. The schedule should incorporate not only debts, such as bonds, notes and leases, but also other liabilities such as those for compensated absences and claims and judgments. The schedule for Orlando, Florida, is presented in Table 8–1.

As with general capital assets (discussed in Chapter 7), the GASB recognizes that when governments first adopt Statement No. 34, they might not have adequate records to make the adjustments that it requires. Therefore, except for deep-discount or zero coupon debt, they may report debt issued prior to the implementation of Statement No. 34 at face value; they need not adjust it for premiums or discounts.

TABLE 8–1
City of Orlando, Florida
Schedule of Long-term Liabilities
(Governmental Activities only)

Long-term liability activity for the year ended September 30, 2001, was as follows (in thousands):

	Beginning Balance	Additions	Reductions	Ending Balance	Amounts Due within One Year
Governmental Activities					
Bonds, loans, and leases payable:					
Redevelopment agency bonds	$ 24,665	$ —	$(1,305)	$ 23,360	$1,375
Special assessment bonds	79,080	—	(1,750)	77,330	—
Capital improvement bonds	79,820	—	(3,840)	75,980	3,950
General obligation loans	10,244	5,860	—	16,104	—
Leases payable	2,933	—	(1,229)	1,705	1,165
Long-term loans	18,100	—	—	18,100	—
	214,843	5,860	(6,124)	212,579	6,490
Less bond discount and deferred amount on refunds	(5,386)	—	(404)	(4,982)	—
Total bonds, loans, and leases payable	209,457	5,860	(7,720)	207,597	6,490
Other liabilities:					
Compensated absences	16,697	37	—	16,733	1,339
Claims and judgments	25,028	13,724	(9,329)	29,423	—
Total other liabilities	41,725	13,761	(9,329)	46,156	1,339
Governmental activities long-term liabilities	$251,182	$19,620	$(17,049)	$253,753	$7,829

Source: City of Orlando, *Comprehensive Annual Financial Report* for the year ended September 30, 2001, page 77.

EXAMPLE   *Accounting for Bonds in Government-wide Statements*

A city issues $10 million of 6 percent, twenty-year term bonds at a price of $10,234,930 (i.e., a premium of $234,930). The issue price provides an effective yield of 5.8 percent per year (2.9 percent per semiannual period).

In the year of issuance, the city would report in its government-wide statement of net assets (governmental activities column) the cash received ($10,234,930) and a long-term liability in the same amount (bonds payable of $10 million plus the premium of $234,930).

Upon making its first semiannual interest payment of $300,000, the city would report interest expense of $296,813 in its government-wide statement of activities. This amount represents the yield rate of 2.9 percent times $10,234,930, the book value of the liability (bonds payable plus unamortized bond premium). The first interest payment would reduce the unamortized premium by $3,187 ($300,000 of interest paid less $296,813 of interest expense) to $231,743. Therefore, the interest expense to be reported when the second semiannual interest payment is made would be only $296,721 (2.9 percent of $10,231,743, the bonds payable plus the adjusted unamortized premium). The unamortized premium would thereby be reduced by $3,279 ($300,000 less $296,721) to $228,464. Thus, after the second interest payment, the book value of the liability to be reported in the statement of net assets would be $10,228,464:

	Interest Payment	Interest Expense	Reduction of Premium	Unamortized Bond Premium	Book Value of Liability
Upon issuance				$234,930	$10,234,930
First interest payment	$300,000	$296,813	$3,187	231,743	10,231,743
Second interest payment	300,000	296,721	3,279	228,464	10,228,464

In contrast to what is reported in the government-wide statement of net assets, no liability would be recognized in the city's governmental fund statements (capital projects fund or whichever governmental fund received the proceeds of the bond issuance); the cash received would be offset by other financing sources—bond proceeds. The periodic interest expenditures in the debt service fund (or whichever governmental fund paid the interest) would be in the amount of the required cash payment—not the cash payment less the amortization of the premium.

LIMITATIONS OF CURRENT STANDARDS: PRESENT VALUES VERSUS MARKET VALUES Per Statement No. 34, governments generally should report their bonds, notes, and comparable long-term obligations at present value.[4] Present values, as currently reported, are firmly rooted in historical cost traditions. They represent the future cash flows (both principal and interest) associated with an obligation dis-

---

[4]GASB Statement No. 34 incorporates the requirements of Accounting Principles Board Opinions No. 12, *Omnibus Opinion—1967*, and No. 21, *Interest on Receivables and Payables*, which contain provisions concerning the reporting of information at present value, except when a GASB standard would be contradicted. For example, GASB Statement No. 10, *Accounting and Financial Reporting for Risk Financing and Related Insurance Issues*, para. 24, states that governments are neither required nor precluded from discounting most claims liabilities to present value.

counted by a rate established when the obligation was first recorded. This rate is not adjusted over the life of the obligation to take into account changes in prevailing interest rates.

Present values capture more faithfully the economic substance of transactions than do face values. Like the carrying (book) values of capital assets, however, they are based on transactions and prices of the past and are thereby not as decision-useful as *market values*.

Corresponding to market values of assets, market values of obligations point to the amount for which liabilities can be liquidated. Market values of outstanding debt securities are driven mainly by prevailing interest rates but are influenced by other factors, such as the issuer's economic condition. At the same time, however, the issuer's economic condition may be affected by the market value of its debts.

Virtually all decision models relating to bond retirements and refundings incorporate market, not historical, values as their parameters. Suppose, for example, that a hospital issues thirty-year, 4 percent, bonds for $10 million (at par). Five years later interest rates increase to 8 percent and, as a consequence, the market value of the bonds decreases to $5.7 million.

In assessing the fiscal health of the hospital, the market value of $5.7 million may be more relevant than the historical value of $10 million. As of the date that the value is determined, the hospital can liquidate the entire $10 million liability for $5.7 million by purchasing the bonds in the secondary markets. Indeed, in deciding whether it should purchase the bonds, it should compare the cash flows to be received and paid in the future with the $5.7 million to be paid out immediately. It need not take into account the original issue price. That value, the equivalent of a sunk cost, will not affect any future cash flows. Over time, the effectiveness of the hospital's debt management should be assessed, at least in part, by measuring the changes in the market value of outstanding debt. Declining market values would imply that the hospital correctly forecast interest rate trends and was able to lock in low-cost financing prior to interest rate increases.

The case in favor of reporting liabilities at market values has become increasingly compelling now that both the FASB and GASB require entities within their purview to report investments at fair value. If a government has long-term debt outstanding and, at the same time, holds long-term bonds as an investment, then the market values of both are affected by prevailing interest rates—albeit in opposite directions. It would be inconsistent and misleading to show changes on one side of the statement of net assets while ignoring those on the other side.

The primary argument in favor of historical, rather than market price-based, reporting of debt is that the market value information will not be used. This contention is most convincing when the entity has no intention of retiring the debt until it matures, and therefore is not concerned with period-to-period fluctuations. This is the same argument that was made with respect to valuing the corresponding assets—investments in long-term bonds or other debt securities.

Accounting standard-setters have not responded uniformly to this argument with respect to the assets. In its Statement No. 115, *Accounting for Certain Investments in Debt and Equity Securities*, the FASB recognized the legitimacy of the argument by allowing businesses to report "held-to-maturity" debt securities at cost (or amortized cost), whereas all other investments must be reported at market. However, per FASB Statement No. 124, *Accounting for Certain Investments Held by Not-for-Profit Organizations*, nongovernmental not-for-profits must report *all* investments at market value, including those intended to be held to maturity. For governments, the GASB, per its Statement No. 31, *Accounting and Financial Report-*

ing for Certain Investments and for External Investment Pools, requires all investments, including those intended to be held to maturity, to be reported at fair value, except for certain money market securities with a remaining maturity of one year or less at the purchase date.

WHAT CONSTITUTES LONG-TERM DEBT OF GOVERNMENTAL ACTIVITIES?

As previously discussed, whereas governments account for short-term liabilities of governmental activities—those expected to be liquidated with currently available assets—in governmental funds, they report long-term liabilities only in the government-wide statements. If assets are held constant, short-term debt reduces a government's general fund (or other governmental fund) balance, whereas long-term debt does not. Thus, whether a liability is short-term or long-term is a significant issue for governments and for users of their fund financial statements.

DEMAND BONDS: CURRENT OR LONG-TERM LIABILITIES? **Demand bonds** are obligations that permit the holder (the lender) to demand redemption within a specified period of time, usually one to thirty days after giving notice. Although they may have maturity periods of up to thirty years, their redemption date is uncertain and beyond the issuer's control. The issuer cannot confidently classify them as long-term obligations because it may have to redeem them at any time. Yet classifying them as short-term obligations may be too conservative, because the issuer may not have to redeem them until maturity.

One apparent solution would be to estimate the proportion of bonds likely to be called within the short term (similar to estimating the proportion of receivables that will be uncollectible). The issuer would classify these bonds as governmental fund liabilities and the balance as nonfund liabilities. However, this solution fails to consider the inherent characteristics of the bonds and the reasons for redemption.

Inherent Characteristics and Reasons for Redemption   Demand bonds are issued to permit the borrower to take advantage of the lower interest rates paid on short-term obligations. If prevailing short-term rates increase, then the lenders (the bondholders) will no longer find them attractive. They will demand redemption so that they can use the funds to purchase higher-yielding bonds. Since the economic conditions motivating redemption are common to all bondholders, the issuer should expect that, if some bonds are presented for redemption, they all will be. In substance, therefore, demand bonds, taken by themselves, are short-term, not long-term, instruments, because the lender has made no long-term commitments and has assumed no long-term risks.

Most issuers provide for the possibility of redemption by arranging with a financial institution to convert the bonds to long-term notes. In a contract called a *take-out agreement*, the financial institution promises to lend the issuer sufficient funds to repay the bonds. The payback period on the notes is usually long-term, sometimes ten years or more. Thus, the demand bonds, together with the take-out agreement, can rightfully be viewed as long-term instruments.

GASB Standards

In a 1984 interpretation, the GASB tied the classification of demand bonds to the take-out agreement. It said that demand bonds that are exercisable within one year of the balance sheet date should not be reported as governmental fund liabilities as long as the entity has entered into a take-out agreement that satisfies the following criteria:

- It does not expire within one year.
- It is not cancelable by the lender or prospective lender during that year.
- The lender or prospective lender is financially capable of honoring the take-out agreement.[5]

If the demand bonds satisfy these criteria, then, per Statement No. 34, the issuer should report them as *long-term* liabilities only in its government-wide statement of net assets (governmental activities column). In the governmental fund that receives the resources—usually a capital projects fund—the issuer should report only the proceeds of the sale (debit *cash* and credit *proceeds of sale of demand bonds*—an other financing source). In contrast, if the demand bonds do *not* satisfy the criteria, they should be reported as liabilities of the governmental fund receiving the resources (debit *cash* and credit *demand bonds payable*) as well as in the government-wide statement of net assets.

BOND ANTICIPATION NOTES Bond anticipation notes (BANs) are short-term notes issued by the lender with the expectation that they will soon be replaced by long-term bonds. Governments issue BANs after obtaining necessary voter and legislative authorization to issue long-term bonds. The BANs enable them to postpone issuing the bonds in the hope of obtaining more favorable long-term interest rates, or to begin work on construction projects without having to wait until they have cleared the lengthy administrative and legal hurdles to issue the bonds.

If a government can, as planned, refund the BANs with long-term bonds, then the notes are, in essence, long-term obligations; the government will not have to repay them with current financial resources. However, if it is unable to refund them, then it must repay them when due—and must have on hand the requisite cash.

GASB Standards

A government may recognize BANs as long-term obligations if, by the *date the financial statements are issued*, it has taken all legal steps to refinance the BANs and is able to refinance the short-term notes on a long-term basis.[6] Evidence of

(continued)

---

[5]GASB Interpretation No. 1, *Demand Bonds Issued by State and Local Governmental Entities*, para. 10. The interpretation does not specify the interest rate to be paid by the borrower on loans resulting from the take-out agreement. Thus, in the event the bonds had to be redeemed, the issuer might have to pay a considerably higher interest rate on the new loan than on the old loan.

[6]NCGA Interpretation No. 9, *Certain Fund Classifications and Balance Sheet Accounts*, para. 12.

GASB Standards (continued)

this comes through meeting the conditions set forth by the FASB in Statement No. 6, *Classification of Short-Term Obligations Expected to Be Refinanced:*

- The entity has already refinanced the BANs; or
- It has entered into a financing agreement that does not expire within one year of the balance sheet date and is noncancelable by the lender, has not been violated as of the balance sheet date, and is capable of being honored by the lender.

As with demand bonds, governments would report the BANs as liabilities in their government-wide statements, regardless of whether they report them in a governmental fund as an other financing source (proceeds from the sale of bond anticipation notes) or as fund liabilities. They must, however, be sure to properly describe their obligations and classify them—for example, as BANs or bonds; short- or long-term obligations.

TAX ANTICIPATION AND REVENUE ANTICIPATION NOTES Governments usually do not receive their taxes or other revenues evenly throughout the year. Property taxes, for example, may not be due until three or more months after the start of a fiscal year. To meet cash needs earlier in the year, governments can issue **tax anticipation notes (TANs)** and **revenue anticipation notes (RANs)**—short-term notes that are payable out of specified streams of revenues.

Like BANs, TANs and RANs are a means of borrowing against expected cash proceeds. But unlike BANs, they will *not* be converted into long-term instruments. Therefore, they must be reported as liabilities of the governmental funds in which the related revenues will be reported (debit *cash*, credit *tax anticipation notes payable* or *revenue anticipation notes payable)*, as well as in the government-wide statements.

CAPITAL VERSUS OPERATING LEASES Governments, like businesses, may enter into both **operating leases** and **capital leases.** Operating leases are conventional rental agreements, such as daily automobile rentals and long-term rentals of office space. They give a **lessee** (renter) the right to use property of a **lessor** (owner) for a portion of its useful life, but they do not confer ownership in the property. Governments enter into operating leases for the same reasons as do individuals and businesses:

- They need an asset for only a small part of its useful life.
- They wish to avoid risks of ownership, such as declines in market value and technological obsolescence.
- They have neither available cash nor credit to purchase the asset.

Accounting for operating leases is straightforward. The rental payments should be recognized as expenditures in a governmental fund (debit *expenditures—operating lease*, credit *cash* or *accounts payable)* and as expenses in the government-wide statement of activities in the periods to which they apply. In addition, basic information about an operating lease and a schedule of future lease payments should be disclosed in the notes, so that users of the financial statements can assess the effect of the lease on future cash flows. The government has no liability for the lease, other than for rental payments due but not yet paid.

CAPITAL LEASES In contrast to operating leases, capital leases are, in essence, financing arrangements. The lessee effectively "purchases" an asset in exchange for a long-term note (liability). The accounting and reporting requirements are correspondingly more complex than for operating leases. Thus, it is important that governments and users of their financial statements distinguish between the two forms of leases.

GASB Standards

The GASB has adopted the criteria of FASB Statement No. 13, *Accounting for Leases,* to distinguish between a capital lease and an operating lease.[7] A capital lease is a lease that meets *any one* of the following four conditions:

1. The lease transfers ownership of the property from the lessor to the lessee by the end of the lease term.
2. The lease contains an option permitting the lessee to purchase the property at a bargain price (i.e., an amount substantially less than market value).
3. The lease term is equal to or greater than 75 percent of the estimated economic life of the leased property.
4. The present value of rental and other minimum lease payments equals or exceeds 90 percent of the fair value of the leased property.

A lease that does not meet any of these four conditions is an operating lease.

Similarities and Differences from Other Long-term Financing Arrangements
A capital lease may be structured like an ordinary mortgage note or a coupon bond. The *lessor* (the owner-lender) may be a manufacturer, retailer, or financing institution. If it were a financing institution, it would first purchase the property from the retailer or manufacturer on behalf of, and for lease to, the ultimate user (the purchaser/borrower). The financing institution may even sell shares in the lease to investors for whom the shares would be an alternative to bonds or notes. If the lessee were a government, then the investors' shares might be exempt from federal taxation, just as if they were the government's bonds. Assets commonly acquired under capital leases include heavy equipment, communications systems, motor vehicles, and buildings.

Collateral   Capital leases are almost always secured only by the leased assets, not by the lessee's full faith and credit. The leased assets, however, are often inadequate as collateral. First, if seized by the lessor, they may have only limited value. If a government were to abrogate its lease, it might do so for the very reason that the property is of less value than anticipated (e.g., it has become technologically obsolete). Second, seizing government property may be extremely costly in terms of bad publicity and public ill will. What local bank or finance company would like to be shown on the six o'clock news repossessing a city's ambulance or emergency communications equipment?

Nonappropriation and Nonsubstitution Clauses   Government leases characteristically contain what is known as either a **nonappropriation** or a **fiscal funding clause.** This provision, by stipulating that the payments for each year must be separately appropriated by the legislative body, permits the government to cancel the lease at the

---

[7]GASB *Codification*, Section L20.103 and L20.109.

end of each year. However, to mitigate this clause, a lessor might add provisions to the lease agreement that would make it economically impractical for the lessee to cancel. For example, the contract might contain a *nonsubstitution clause* prohibiting the lessee from replacing the leased property with similar property. Thus, the government would be unable to invoke the nonappropriation clause without impairing its ability to maintain essential services.

Rationale for Capital Leasing   Why would governments opt for capital leases rather than conventional buy-and-borrow arrangements? Owing to the nature of the collateral and the inclusion of nonappropriation clauses, capital leases are decidedly less attractive to lenders than comparable full faith and credit instruments. Therefore, they invariably bear higher effective interest rates.

However, capital leases may be an effective means of circumventing debt limitations. Restrictions on state and local government borrowing were first imposed in the 1840s. During a period of rapid growth between 1820 and 1837, many states financed public works, such as railroads and canals, with general obligation debt. They invested the bond proceeds in the stock of private rail and canal companies, with the expectation that resulting dividends would be sufficient to service the debt. When the economy collapsed in 1837, many companies failed and governments were forced to default on their bonds.

To ensure fiscal discipline in the future, state governments limited the amount of debt that they or their subdivisions could incur. Today, these limits are generally set as a percentage of the assessed value of the jurisdiction's property. Alternatively, the limits can be established indirectly through restrictions on tax increases, balanced budget mandates, or requirements that voters approve either all debt or debt above a specified amount.

The extent to which capital lease obligations are considered as debt, and thereby subject to debt limitations, has been the object of extensive litigation. The outcomes vary by state, but in at least twenty-six states the courts have upheld capital leases as being beyond the purview of debt restrictions. As might be expected, the court decisions have often run counter to prevailing accounting and financial wisdom. For example, in some states the courts have keyed their opinions to the nonappropriation clauses, asserting that, because the lease payments are subject to annual authorization, capital leases lack the characteristics of long-term debts.

Capital leasing is especially popular in municipalities in which the debt limitations take the form of voter approvals. It is a convenient means of acquiring assets that public officials might consider more essential to the public welfare than does the electorate.

GASB Standards

Per both GASB and FASB standards, capital leases are accounted for by the lessee as if it had purchased an asset and issued long-term debt. If a lease meets the criteria for a capital lease, then the entity would record both the acquired asset and the incurred debt at the *present value* of the required lease payments— an amount that would ordinarily be equal to the fair market value of the prop-

(continued)

GASB Standards (*continued*)

erty. The discount rate would be agreed by the lessor and lessee in establishing the lease payments (and could be derived mathematically from the market price of the property and the schedule of lease payments).

A government would account for the leased asset and the related lease liability just as it would an installment purchase. In a governmental fund, such as the general fund or a capital projects fund, it would debit an expenditure for the acquisition of the asset and credit *other financing sources—capital leases*. As it made each lease payment it would report the outlay as a governmental (usually debt service) fund expenditure, dividing it between *debt service expenditure— interest* (the discount rate times the remaining principal balance) and *debt service expenditure—principal*.

In its government-wide statements, consistent with FASB Statement No. 13, a government would record both the leased asset and the corresponding liability as if it had purchased the asset and borrowed the required funds. It would depreciate the asset over the term of the lease (or the economic life of the property, if it expects to receive ownership upon the expiration of the lease). It would charge a portion of each lease payment to interest (the discount rate times the remaining principal balance) and the remainder to principal.

EXAMPLE   *Capital leases*

A municipality agrees to lease an office building with a remaining economic life of twenty years. The building has a fair market value of $3 million. Based on an interest rate of 6 percent, annual lease payments are set at $261,554 (the amount required to liquidate a $3 million, twenty-year, 6 percent loan in equal annual installments).

The municipality would record the lease as follows in an appropriate governmental fund:

Governmental fund

Capital assets expenditure	$3,000,000	
Other financing sources—capital lease		$3,000,000

To record the acquisition of equipment under a capital lease

Of the first payment of $261,554, $180,000 would be for interest (6 percent of $3 million); the balance of $81,554 would be for principal. Thus:

Governmental fund

Debt service expenditure (lease principal)	$ 81,554	
Debt service expenditure (lease interest)	180,000	
Cash		$261,554

To record the first lease payment

In its government-wide statements the municipality would record the transaction as if it had purchased the building in exchange for an interest-bearing note:

Government-wide statements

Building held under lease	$3,000,000	
Capital lease obligations		$3,000,000

To record the acquisition of equipment under a capital lease

It would divide its first interest payment between principal and interest:

Government-wide statements

Capital lease obligations (lease principal)	$ 81,554	
Interest expense (lease interest)	180,000	
Cash		$261,554

To record the first lease payment

Correspondingly, it would also recognize annual depreciation (assuming an asset life of twenty years):

Government-wide statements

Depreciation expense	$150,000	
Accumulated depreciation—building held under lease		$150,000

To record the first year's depreciation ($3 million divided by 20 years)

Governments are required to disclose the specifics of their capital and operating lease obligations, including the future minimum payments for each of the next five fiscal years and in five-year increments thereafter.[8] (See, for example, the lease disclosures of Orlando, Florida in Table 8–2.)

TABLE 8–2
City of Orlando, Florida
Note Disclosures as to Leases

Lease Obligations

Operating—On April 2, 1973, the City entered into a long-term lease agreement with the Orange County Civic Facilities Authority (CFA) for the Tinker Field and the Florida Citrus Bowl facilities. The lease is for an initial term of thirty years and is accounted for as an operating lease. The lease also includes a twenty-year renewal option.

On September 27, 1976, the City entered into a turnover agreement with the Greater Orlando Aviation Authority (GOAA), which authorized the GOAA to operate the Herndon Airport and Orlando International Airport for a term of fifty years commencing October 1, 1976.

Amendment 1 of that agreement allowed the City to acquire a portion of the land for $586,500 and the right to use the land for the site of the Conserv I plant. Amendment 2 of the agreement provided for a land lease on which the plant's effluent disposal system was constructed. After a five-year period of fixed payments between 1986 and 1991, annual payments increase 25 percent on each fifth anniversary of the May 1, 1986, date. The term of the original agreement does not change and expires on October 1, 2026.   *(continued)*

---

[8]GASB Statement No. 38, *Certain Financial Statement Note Disclosures*, para. 11.

TABLE 8–2 *(continued)*
City of Orlando, Florida
Note Disclosures as to Leases

The following schedule reflects the operating lease obligations for the next five years and for each five-year period thereafter:

Year Ending September 30	Lease Payments
2002	$ 499,848
2003	499,848
2004	499,848
2005	499,848
2006	551,918
Total	$2,551,310
2007–2011	$3,189,165
2012–2016	3,986,455
2017–2021	4,983,055
2022–2026	6,228,820

The lease allows the GOAA, for certain aviation–related reasons, to require the City to relocate all or a portion of its Rapid Infiltration Basins (RIBs) and, for nonaviation relocation, for the City and the GOAA to share in the associated costs.

Total rent expense incurred by the City for the year ended September 30, 2001, was $1,836,912.

Capital—On March 24, 2000, the City entered into a capital lease agreement with Koch Financial Corporation. Property being acquired under this agreement consists of computer equipment with an asset value of $3,463,715. Future minimum payments under the agreement and the present value of the minimum payments, as of September 30, are as follows:

Fiscal Year Ending	Amount
2002	$1,227,547
2003	548,322
Total Minimum Lease Payments	1,775,870
Less Amount Representing Interest	71,081
Present Value of Minimum Lease Payments	$1,704,789

The implied interest rate was 5.46 percent.

Source: City of Orlando, Florida, *Comprehensive Annual Financial Report* for the year ended September 30, 2001, pages 72 and 73 (cross-references to other notes omitted).

LINKS BETWEEN REVENUE BONDS AND GENERAL OBLIGATION BONDS General obligation (GO) bonds are debt of the government at large and are backed by the government's full faith and credit (all revenue sources). Revenue bonds, in contrast, are backed only by specific revenues—usually those, such as utility charges, from a government's business-type activities. Revenue bonds are generally reported in enterprise funds (as well as in the government-wide statements), and are thereby accounted for as if they were issued by a business. Nevertheless, revenue bonds are integrally linked to GO bonds and the government's debt burden cannot be assessed without taking both into account.

Even if a government is legally responsible for servicing its revenue debt only out of designated revenues, fiscal reality might dictate that it back the bonds with its full faith and credit. Were a government to default on the revenue debt of one of its component units (e.g., a utility, convention center, or airport), the fiscal community would be likely to view the failure as one of the government at large. Thus, the credit standing of the entire government would be severely diminished and the government would either be denied access to the credit markets or would be admitted only by paying a substantial interest penalty.

Governments generally have a choice whether to finance revenue-generating activities with GO or revenue bonds. Because revenue bonds are not backed by the government's full faith and credit, they almost always bear higher interest rates than comparable GO bonds. Why, then, would a government issue the more costly revenue bonds? At least two reasons can be cited, both of which point to the interrelationship between the two types of securities:

- Revenue bonds, because they are not obligations of the government at large, are usually not subject to voter approvals or other forms of voter oversight. Therefore, they are a means of circumventing constitutional or legislative constraints on GO borrowing.

- By using revenue bonds, the government can readily incorporate debt service costs into user fees. Thus, the facilities financed by revenue bonds will be paid for out of user charges, not taxes or other general revenues. The costs will be shared among the constituents of the government based on the benefits they receive, rather than on the factors on which taxes and other general revenues are based. Revenue-bond financing may be especially appropriate when parties residing outside of the government's property-tax jurisdiction are to be the major users of the facilities. These parties might otherwise escape paying for the assets.

It should also be noted that, whereas any single incremental issue of revenue bonds is likely to be more costly than a comparable issue of GO bonds, the choice between the two types of debt might not affect the issuer's total borrowing costs. A government's total revenues and other resources available to service its debt are not changed by the type of debt issued. Accordingly, its overall risk of default remains the same, irrespective of whether it issues GO or revenue bonds. The bond mix affects only the distribution of the risk among the bondholders. By issuing revenue bonds, the government shifts a portion of the risk—and the attendant interest costs—to the revenue bondholders, who are in a less secure position than the GO bondholders. Were the government to issue only GO bonds, however, the same risk and interest costs would have to be assumed by the GO bondholders and the interest rates on the GO bonds would then increase.

OVERLAPPING DEBT **Overlapping debt** refers to the obligations of property owners within a particular government for their proportionate share of debts of other governments with overlapping geographic boundaries. Concern for overlapping debt arises because the property located in one government's jurisdiction may serve as the tax base for one or more other governments.

Suppose, for example, that a town is located within a surrounding county. The town's taxable property is assessed at $600 million; that of the county (including the town) is assessed at $800 million. The town's outstanding debt is $30 million; the county's is $50 million.

Based on the ratio of the value of the property within the town to that within the entire county, the town supports 75 percent ($600 million/$800 million) of the county's debt. Thus, the town's overlapping debt would be $37.5 million (75 percent of $50 million). The town's taxable property also supports 100 percent of the town's own direct debt of $30 million. Its combined overlapping and direct debt would be $67.5 million—overlapping debt of $37.5 million plus direct debt of $30 million.

Insofar as property taxes are the mainstay revenue of local governments, financial analysts look to the ratio of assessed value of property to total debt outstanding as a primary measure of ability to sustain both existing and proposed liabilities. They obviously would run the risk of overestimating the town's **fiscal capacity** (the economic base it can draw upon) if they considered only the town's direct debt and ignored that of the county—which will be repaid from taxes on the same property as that of the town.

The computation of overlapping debt may be more complicated than is suggested by the previous illustration because governments may be overlapped by several taxing authorities. The governments' boundaries may not be concentric; instead, only a portion of one entity may lie within the geographic boundaries of another. The general principle of computing overlapping debt is the same as in the simple example, however. A government's share of the debt of one or more other entities' is determined by the percentage of each entity's property that is within that government's boundaries.

Because overlapping debt is not an actual liability of the reporting government, that government cannot report it on its own financial statements. Owing to its analytical significance, however, a government should include a schedule of overlapping debt as supplementary information in the statistical section of its annual report.

EXAMPLE   *Overlapping Debt*

A city's property is located within a total of five governmental units, as shown in the following schedule and in Figure 8–1 on the next page.

	Outstanding Debt	Assessed Valuation of Taxable Property
	(in Millions)	
County	$320	$2,000
School District	160	2,000
Library District	12	2,400
Hospital District	40	4,000
City	400	1,800

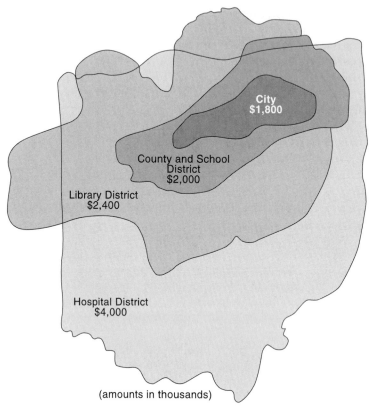

(amounts in thousands)

FIGURE 8–1   Diagram of Overlapping Jurisdictions and Assessed Value of Property

The city's *direct* debt is $400 million. Its share of the debt of the overlapping jurisdictions is based on the ratio of the assessed value of the city's own property to that of each of the other jurisdictions. Thus:

	Debt	City's Share Proportion	City's Share Percent	City's Share Amount
		(Dollar Amounts in Millions)		
Direct Debt				
City	$400	$1,800/$1,800	100%	$400
Overlapping Debt				
County	320	$1,800/$2,000	90%	288
School District	160	$1,800/$2,000	90%	144
Library District	12	$1,800/$2,400	75%	9
Hospital District	40	$1,800/$4,000	45%	18
Total Overlapping Debt				459
Total Direct and Overlapping Debt				$859

The schedule indicates that the city's property (assessed at $1,800 million) supports $400 million of the city's own debt and $459 million of the debt of other governments with overlapping geographic boundaries.

CONDUIT DEBT **Conduit debt** refers to obligations issued in the name of a government on behalf of a nongovernmental entity, such as a business or not-for-profit organization. The debt is expected to be serviced entirely by the nongovernmental entity and usually takes the form of revenue bonds or certificates of participation. Often the government retains title to the property financed by the obligations and leases it back to the beneficiary. Other times, it simply loans the resources to the beneficiary. The lease or loan payments are typically established so as to match the payments on the debt. The bonds are payable exclusively from the lease or loan payments. Generally the debt is secured by the property financed by the bonds and, in the event of default, the bondholders have claims only on the property and the lease or loan payments. Therefore, conduit debt is also referred to as **no-commitment debt**.

Conduit debt is a form of government assistance to the beneficiary organizations in that it enables them to obtain financing at lower rates than if they issued the debt themselves. The lower rates can be obtained because interest on debt issued by a government is exempt from federal income taxes, whereas interest on debt issued by the beneficiary may be taxable. Bonds issued by a government to attract a private corporation to its jurisdiction are known as **industrial development bonds**. Although the bonds benefit, and will be repaid by, the corporation, they nevertheless qualify as tax-exempt municipal debt. The federal government imposes strict limitations on the dollar amount of industrial development bonds that can be issued within each state. These limitations constrain municipalities from transferring to corporations the interest-rate subsidies that Congress intended for governments.

The key reporting question relating to conduit debt is the extent to which the issuing government should account for the obligations as if they were its own.

GASB Standards

Although governments may elect to report conduit obligations in their government-wide and proprietary fund statements, the GASB has ruled that note disclosure is sufficient. The following information must be provided in the notes:

- A general description of the conduit debt transactions

- The aggregate amount of all conduit debt obligations outstanding

- A clear indication that the issuer has no obligation for the debt beyond the resources provided by related leases or loans[9]

WHAT OTHER INFORMATION DO USERS WANT TO KNOW ABOUT OUTSTANDING DEBT?

The magnitude and nature of a government's obligations, each with its own unique characteristics and risks, is obviously of major concern to the entity's creditors as well as other statement users. As might be expected, governments devote a substantial portion of their annual financial reports to long-term debt, and their debt disclosures

---

[9]GASB Interpretation No. 2, *Disclosure of Conduit Debt Obligations.*

are far more comprehensive than those relating to long-term assets. They typically include not only technical features of the debt, such as interest rates, payout schedules, and collateral, but also selected financial ratios that incorporate debt.

The economic burden of long-term debt is dependent on the issuer's ability to pay. Ability to pay is tied to a wide range of financial, social, economic, political, and administrative factors, only some of which are reported in financial statements. This section will focus on some of these factors, but will be limited to those tied directly to the debt itself. Broader measures of ability to pay will be considered in Chapter 14, which is directed to financial analysis.

CREDIT ENHANCEMENTS A government can enhance the security of its bonds by acquiring bond insurance or obtaining the moral obligation of another government to back its debt.

Bond Insurance   Bond insurance guarantees the timely payment of both interest and principal. It is purchased by the bond issuers, but is intended to protect the bondholders. It is written mainly by American Municipal Bond Assurance Corp. (AMBAC), Municipal Bond Insurance Association (MBIA), and a small number of other specialized companies. Bond insurance may appear costly; premiums range from 0.1 percent to 2.0 percent of principal and interest, depending on the risk. However, bond insurance often results in net savings to the issuer in that the leading bond rating services automatically raise the rating of any covered issue to AAA (the highest). The higher the bond rating, the lower the interest cost.

Moral Obligation Debt   Bonds or notes issued by one entity (usually a state agency) but backed by the promise of another entity (usually the state itself) to make up any debt service deficiencies are referred to as **moral obligation debt**. The debt is described as moral when the promise of the backer is not legally enforceable.

Moral obligation debt is motivated mainly by a state's intent to avoid the need for voter approvals or to circumvent debt limitations. To issue debt that would otherwise be proscribed, a state, with legislative approval, borrows in the name of a state agency—sometimes one formed specifically to issue the debt—that is not subject to the same voter approvals or debt limitations as the state itself. To enhance the creditworthiness of the agency, the state supports the bonds with a promise to cover debt service shortages.

The state does not typically place its full faith and credit behind its pledge. Rather, it promises only to seek future appropriations for any required debt service payments. This promise may be of dubious value. When New York State issued moral obligation bonds, for example, the promise took the form of a so-called moral makeup clause, wherein the state budget director was required to ask for an appropriation to make up any shortfall in its debt service reserve fund. However, the legislature was not committed to honoring the budget director's request.

Moral obligation bonds obviously are not as secure as the state's general obligation bonds, and rating agencies typically assign them a rating at least one grade below that of the state's general obligation bonds. Still, the rating is likely to be significantly higher than if the bonds were issued by the state agency without the backing of the state.

DEBT MARGIN As discussed earlier, governments may be limited in the amount of GO debt that they can incur. The difference between the amount of debt outstanding (computed according to applicable legal provisions, not necessarily as reported on the issuer's financial statements) and the amount of debt allowed is described as **debt margin**. For example, assume that a government's GO bonded debt is legally limited to 6 percent of the assessed value of taxable property within its jurisdiction. The assessed value of the property is $10 billion. Therefore, the government can issue a maximum of $600 million in debt. If the government currently has $450 million of debt outstanding, then its legal debt margin is $150 million (25 percent of its limit).

PAYOUT SCHEDULES Payout schedules can take a variety of forms, ranging from those in which a substantial portion of principal is repaid early in the bond's life to those in which it is paid entirely at the end. A typical payout schedule is one in which 50 percent of the debt is retired in ten years. Often, this is accomplished through a twenty- to twenty-five-year serial bond issue with an equal proportion of the issue maturing each year. Usually lenders see a faster retirement schedule as positive, as long as it does not place too great a fiscal strain upon the issuer. Schedules in which the payout is strung out over thirty to forty years, while not uncommon, are viewed as negative.

Sound fiscal policy dictates that the payout schedule correspond to the useful life of the property being financed. Indeed, the very rationale for borrowing is that the burden of paying for long-lived assets should be borne by the parties who will use them. When the schedule is shorter than the useful life, then only the early-year users will pay for the assets. When it exceeds the useful life, then parties beyond the period of use will be required to pay for the assets and, in effect, a portion of the debt will be financing operations rather than capital assets.

RESERVE FUNDS As discussed in Chapter 6 on debt service funds, to ensure that an issuer keeps current on its principal and interest payments, lenders commonly stipulate that it maintain a reserve fund. Usually, the amount to be set aside is based on principal and interest payments—for example, the highest year's debt service. A reserve fund can generally be dipped into only for the final year's debt service or in the event that the issuer is otherwise unable to make its required payments. From the perspective of a lender, the reserve fund provides a cushion against difficult fiscal times and thereby makes the bond a more attractive investment.

COMMON RATIOS AND PAST HISTORY Investors and other statement users look to a variety of bond-related ratios and other data to assess ability to pay and risk of default. The most notable of these are:

- *Debt service costs as a percentage of total general fund and debt service fund expenditures.* Similar to the times-interest-earned ratio that is widely used in business, this ratio is usually considered high if it exceeds 20 percent of total general and debt service fund expenditures.
- *Debt per capita and debt as a percentage of taxable property.* Both of these ratios are measures of *fiscal capacity.* They relate the bonded debt, not to resources or resource flows within the government, but to the ultimate sources of a government's revenues. As with most ratios involving long-term obligations, debt can be expressed with varying degrees of inclusiveness. For example, debt could be limited to GO debt or could include revenue debt. Moreover, it could incorporate only the issuer's direct debt or both direct and overlapping debt.
- *Past history.* As any banker will testify, character dominates all quantifiable measures in capturing a borrower's credit standing. Users want information as to whether past payments were made on time. Whereas the bond community may forgive borrowers for unintentionally missing or being late on payments, it may be less tolerant of an issuer who evades payments through bankruptcy or comparable legal maneuvers.

Ratios pertaining to revenue bonds are discussed in the following chapter dealing with business-type activities. The long-term debt of utilities, hospitals, universities, and other special-purpose governments is often of this type.

WHAT ARE BOND RATINGS, AND WHY ARE THEY IMPORTANT?

The leading bond rating agencies, *Standard & Poor's (S&P)*, *Moody's Investors Service*, and *Fitch's IBCA* will assign a quality rating to the debt instruments of any issuer (government, not-for-profit, or business) that requests it.

The agencies base their ratings on a comprehensive review of all factors affecting the issuer's ability to pay. A review would include analyses of the debt instrument itself, the issuer's financial reports and budgets, key demographic data, and a range of economic statistics. It would also incorporate interviews with city officials and assessments of their competence.

The rating services continue to monitor an issuer even after they have assigned an initial rating, and they expect the issuer to update them continually with current information. A rating generally remains in effect until the issuer's next offering of comparable securities. Sometimes, however, as a result of new developments the agencies will change their initial classification.

The classification scheme of Standard & Poor's for municipal debt (which includes that of not-for-profits as well as governments) is presented in Table 8–3.

Debt ratings are of critical concern to both issuers and investors because they affect the debt's marketability and hence its interest rate. In fact, many institutions are legally prohibited from investing in securities classified by a specified rating service as less than *investment grade*. A rating service downgrade, even though it generally does nothing more than spotlight information that was already widely known, can be a

---

TABLE 8–3
Debt Rating Definitions of Standard and Poor's

Investment Grade

AAA	Debt rated AAA has the highest rating assigned by S&P. Capacity to pay interest and repay principal is extremely strong.
AA	Debt rated AA has a very strong capacity to pay interest and repay principal and differs from the highest rated issues only in a small degree.
A	Debt rated A has a strong capacity to pay interest and repay principal, although it is somewhat more susceptible to adverse effects of changes in circumstances and economic conditions than debt in higher-rated categories.
BBB	Debt rated BBB is regarded as having an adequate capacity to pay interest and repay principal. Whereas it normally exhibits adequate protection parameters, adverse economic conditions or changing circumstances are more likely to lead to a weakened capacity to pay interest and repay principal for debt in this category than in higher-rated categories.

Speculative Grade

Debts rated BB, B, CCC, CC, and C are regarded as having significant speculative characteristics with respect to capacity to pay interest and repay principal. BB indicates the least degree of speculation and C the highest. While such debt will likely have some quality and protective characteristics, these may be outweighed by large uncertainties or major risk exposures to adverse conditions.

Source: Summarized from *Standard & Poor's Public Finance Criteria* (New York: Standard & Poor's, 2000), p. 6.

traumatic fiscal event for an issuer. Almost always, it increases the issuer's interest costs, thereby adding to its fiscal anguish.

Despite the significance attached to bond ratings, investors should no more rely solely on them than they should on a report of a stock brokerage firm. The rating agencies are neither prophets nor seers; their ratings are merely opinions, not guarantees. The information on which they base their ratings—all of which is in the public domain—is subject to varying interpretation, and an independent analysis may provide insights in addition to, or at variance with, those of the agencies.

QUESTIONS FOR REVIEW AND DISCUSSION

1. What unique issues arise when a government, as opposed to a business, is declared bankrupt?

2. What is the distinction between *general obligation* debt and *revenue* debt? Which one is likely to bear higher interest rates?

3. At what value would a government report bonds payable on its government-wide statements? Why might this value differ from the bonds' face value? Why might it differ from their market value?

4. A government's interest expenditure as reported in its debt service fund differs significantly from its interest expense as reported in its government-wide statements. What is the most likely explanation for the difference?

5. What are *demand* bonds? When can they be reported as long-term, rather than current, obligations?

6. If, under GAAP, capital leases are considered long-term obligations, why, in many jurisdictions, are they not subject to debt limitations?

7. What is *overlapping debt*, and why is it of significance to financial analysts and other users of a government's financial statements?

8. What are *BANs* and *TANs*? Why are they accounted for differently?

9. What distinguishes *moral obligation* bonds from other types of debt? Why would one government assume a moral obligation for another government's bonds?

10. Why are bond ratings of vital concern to bond issuers?

EXERCISES AND PROBLEMS

8–1

Select the *best* answer.

1. Which of the following is true with respect to bankruptcy?

   a. Per the federal bankruptcy code, a municipality can be declared insolvent but not bankrupt.

   b. Many major cities have avoided bankruptcy by being placed under the control of financial control boards by their state governments.

   c. The concept of bankruptcy does not apply to governments because they have the authority to increase taxes and reduce services.

   d. Municipalities that are declared bankrupt by a court are brought under the control of independent trustees whose primary objective is to assure that obligations to bondholders are satisfied in full.

2. A government issues $1 million in thirty-year, 6 percent coupon bonds at a discount of $50,000. At what amount would the bonds be reported (net) in the government-wide statement of net assets and governmental fund balance sheet immediately upon issuance?

	Government-wide	Fund
a.	$1,000,000	$1,000,000
b.	950,000	950,000
c.	950,000	0
d.	950,000	1,000,000

3. The government issues the bonds described in question 2. It makes its first semi-annual interest payment of $30,000. How much interest expense/expenditure should it report in its government-wide and governmental fund statements?

	Government-wide	Fund
a.	$30,000	$30,000
b.	28,500	28,500
c.	28,500	0
d.	28,500	30,000

4. The government makes subsequent interest payments. Reported interest expense/expenditure in the government-wide and governmental fund statements will

	Government-wide	Fund
a.	Increase	Remain the same
b.	Increase	Increase
c.	Remain the same	Remain the same
d.	Decrease	Remain the same

5. Suppose a government issues $1 million in bonds at a premium of $50,000. It temporarily invests the proceeds of $1,050,000 in U.S. Treasury bonds having a face value of $1 million (i.e., at a premium of $50,000). At what value would the government report the bonds payable and the investment in bonds in its government-wide statements subsequent to the date of the transactions?

	Bond Payable	Investment in Bonds
a.	Amortized cost	Market value
b.	Market value	Market value
c.	Amortized cost	Amortized cost
d.	Market value	Amortized cost

6. Which of the following is true of demand bonds?
   a. They give the issuer the right to call the bonds at a pre-established price.
   b. They give the issuer the right to demand that the bondholders purchase additional bonds at a pre-established price.
   c. They give the bondholder the right to demand repayment prior to maturity.
   d. They give the bondholder the right of first refusal with respect to any additional bonds sold by the issuer.

7. Demand bonds should be reported as governmental fund liabilities
   a. if the government has not entered into a take-out agreement

   b. if prevailing interest rates are higher than the interest rate on the bonds
   c. if prevailing interest rates are lower than the interest rate on the bonds
   d. if the government, by the time it issues its financial statements, has neither refinanced the bonds nor entered into an agreement to do so

8. A city issues bond anticipation notes on October 21, 2002. It refunds the notes with thirty-year bonds in January 2003. In its financial statements for the year ending December 31, 2002, which are issued in April 2003, it should report the bond anticipation notes as obligations
   a. in both its government-wide statement of net assets and a governmental fund balance sheet
   b. in its government-wide statement of net assets but not its governmental fund balance sheet
   c. in its governmental fund balance sheet but not its government-wide statement of net assets
   d. in neither its governmental fund balance sheet nor its government-wide statement of net assets

9. A city issues revenue anticipation notes on October 21, 2002. It repays the notes in January 2003. In its financial statements for the year ending December 31, 2002, which are issued in April 2003, it should report the revenue anticipation notes as obligations
   a. in both the government-wide statement of net assets and a governmental fund balance sheet
   b. in the government-wide statement of net assets but not a governmental fund balance sheet
   c. in a governmental fund balance sheet but not the government-wide statement of net assets
   d. in neither a governmental fund balance sheet nor the government-wide statement of net assets

10. Which of the following conditions would not automatically classify a lease as a capital lease?
   a. Ownership is transferred to the lessee at the end of the lease term.
   b. The term of the lease is 80 percent of the useful life of the property.
   c. The lease contains an option permitting the lessee to purchase the property at a bargain price.

d. The present value of rental and other minimum lease payments equals or exceeds 50 percent of the fair value of the leased property.

8–2

Select the *best* answer.

1. A town signs a ten-year capital lease by which it acquires equipment with a market value of $1 million. The lease incorporates an implicit interest rate of 8 percent per year. Accordingly, annual lease payments are $149,029. When the town make its *second* annual lease payment, it would report in its government-wide statements
   a. interest expense of $80,000
   b. rent expense of $149,029
   c. interest expense of $74,478
   d. rent expense of $100,000

2. State courts that have held that capital leases do not qualify as long-term debt subject to debt limitations commonly base their decision on the inclusion in the lease agreement of a
   a. nonsubstitution clause
   b. nonappropriation clause
   c. nonparticipation clause
   d. forward funding clause

3. Revenue bonds, compared with general obligation bonds, generally
   a. are paid out of property or sales tax revenues
   b. bear lower interest rates
   c. are subject to the same debt limitations
   d. are not backed by the full faith and credit of the issuing government

4. A town is located within both a school district and a county. The assessed property valuations and bonded debts of the three governments are as follows (in millions):

	Assessed Valuation	*Bonded Debts*
Town	$ 800	$40
School district	1,600	90
County	2,400	18

The combined direct and overlapping debt of the town is
   a. $40 million
   b. $51 million
   c. $91 million
   d. $148 million

5. Clifford City has issued $10 million of revenue bonds to help fund a factory for Travis, Inc., a private manufacturing company. The city owns the factory and leases it to the company. The bonds are payable exclusively from the lease payments. In the event the company defaults on its lease payments, the bondholders have claims only on the factory. The city has no obligation for the bonds other than to transmit to the bondholders the lease payments that it receives from the company. In its annual financial statements the city should report the bonds
   a. on its government-wide statement of net assets but not in any fund statements
   b. only in notes
   c. only as required supplementary information
   d. both on its government-wide statement of net assets and in its proprietary funds balance sheet

6. Which of the following is *not* a common reason for issuing revenue bonds rather than general obligation bonds?
   a. to obtain lower interest rates
   b. to incorporate debt service costs into user fees
   c. to avoid debt limitations or voter approvals
   d. to shift a portion of the burden of paying for the project to parties who reside outside the issuer's jurisdiction but nevertheless benefit from the project

7. On December 1, 2003, a city issued $20 million in BANs and $6 million in RANs. By April 15, 2004, the date the city issued its financial statements for the year ending December 31, 2003, the city had not yet converted the BANs into long-term bonds. However, the city repaid the RANs on February 28, 2004. The amount that the city should report as an obligation of its general fund in its December 31, 2003, financial statements is
   a. $0
   b. $6 million
   c. $20 million
   d. $26 million

8. A state agency issues moral obligation debt. This debt
   a. is probably backed by the full faith and credit of the state
   b. is probably subject to the same debt limitations as if it had been issued by the state itself
   c. probably bears a lower interest rate than if there were no moral obligation associated with it

d. imposes greater pressure upon the agency to repay the debt than if there were no moral obligation associated with it

9. Certificates of participation have the most in common with
   a. revenue bonds
   b. pension annuities
   c. participating preferred stock
   d. operating leases

10. A city issues the following bonds:

Revenue bonds to fund
  improvements to the
  town-owned electric utility $50 million
Conduit bonds issued to assist
  a fast food franchisee to
  construct a restaurant $ 7 million

The amount that the city should report as an obligation in its government-wide statement of net assets and its proprietary funds balance sheet is

	Government-wide	Proprietary Fund
a.	$57 million	$57 million
b.	$57 million	$ 0
c.	$50 million	$50 million
d.	$ 0	$ 0

8–3

Both the reported value of long-term debt and periodic interest charges should be based on unamortized issue price (plus or minus unamortized premiums or discounts) and initial yield.

The City of Fairfield issued $100 million of twenty-year, 6 percent coupon bonds (3 percent per semiannual period) for $89.322 million. The price reflected a yield of 7 percent (3.5 percent per semiannual period).

1. Prepare entries to reflect how the following would be reported in the city's government-wide statements:
   a. The issuance of the bonds
   b. The first semiannual payment of interest
   c. The second semiannual payment of interest

2. Prepare entries to account for the same transactions in an appropriate governmental fund.

8–4

The accounting for BANs depends on events subsequent to year-end.

In anticipation of issuing long-term bonds, a state issues $200 million of sixty-day BANs to finance highway construction. It expects to roll over

the BANs into long-term bonds within sixty days. Its fiscal year ends on May 31.

1. Prepare a journal entry in a governmental fund (such as a capital projects fund) to record the issuance of the $200 million, 60-day BANs on May 1, 2004.

2. Prepare a journal entry, if required, to record the conversion of the BANs to long-term bonds on June 18, 2004.

3. Prepare a journal entry, if required, to adjust the accounts as of year-end May 31, 2004, assuming that the state was unable to convert the BANs to long-term bonds.

4. Comment on how the BANs would be reported on the government-wide statements as of May 31, 2004, assuming first that they were converted and second that they were not converted.

8–5

Debt is accounted for differently in fund and government-wide statements.

The following transactions affected a city's general fund. Prepare a table in which you indicate for each transaction the expenditure/expense and change in liabilities that the city would report in its (a) general fund and (b) government-wide statements.

1. City employees earned $7.7 million in vacation pay during the year, of which they took only $6.6 million. They may take the balance in the following three years.

2. The employees were paid $0.5 million for vacations that they had earned in previous years.

3. The city settled a claim brought against it during the year by a building contractor. The city agreed to pay $10 million immediately and $10 million at the end of the following year.

4. The city issued $100 million in general obligation bonds at a price of $99.7 million—that is, a discount of $0.3 million.

5. It paid $4 million in debt service. Of this, $3 million was for the first payment of interest; the balance was for repayment of principal.

8–6

Capital leases create both assets and liabilities.

Pearl City leases an emergency communications system. The term of the lease is ten years, approximately the useful life of the equipment. Based on a sales price of $800,000 and an interest rate of 6 percent, the city agrees to make annual payments of $108,694. Upon the expiration of the lease, the equipment will revert to the city.

1. Prepare an appropriate entry in the city's government-wide statements to reflect the signing of the lease.

2. Prepare appropriate entries to record the first payment on the lease. The city charges depreciation using the straight-line method.

3. Will your entries to record the final payment on the lease be the same as for the first payment? Explain.

4. Comment briefly on how the lease transactions would be recorded in the city's general fund or other appropriate governmental fund.

8–7

Government-wide statements are on a full accrual basis; fund statements are on a modified accrual basis.

The East Eanes School District engaged in, or was affected by, the following events and transactions during its fiscal year ending June 30, 2004.

a. Teachers and other personnel earned $350,000 in vacations and other compensated absences that they did not take but for which they expect to be paid in the future.

b. The district settled a suit brought by a student, agreeing to pay $3 million by December 31, 2005.

c. The district issued $8 million in GO bonds to finance an addition to its high school. By year-end, it had expended $1 million in construction costs.

d. The district signed a three-year lease for office space. Annual rent is $40,000.

e. It acquired school buses and other vehicles, financing them with an eight-year capital lease. Annual lease payments are $140,000. Had the district purchased the equipment outright, the price would have been $869,371, reflecting an interest rate of 6 percent.

f. The district transferred $500,000, representing the final year's principal payment, to a reserve fund required by the bond indenture.

g. To smooth out cash flows, the district issued ninety-day tax anticipation notes of $950,000.

h. The district paid teachers and other personnel $150,000 for compensated absences earned in previous years.

1. Prepare the entries (as required) to record the transactions in the general fund or whatever other governmental fund seems most appropriate.

2. Prepare the entries that would be needed to reflect the transactions and events in the district's government-wide statements.

8–8

Demand bonds may provide the issuer with the disadvantages, but not the advantages, of long-term debt.

On January 1, 2004, a city issues $2 million in 7 percent demand bonds. Although the bonds have a term of ten years, they contain a put option permitting the holder to present the bonds for redemption, at par, any time after December 31, 2005. The bonds pay interest semiannually.

1. Prepare journal entries in the city's general fund or other governmental fund to record the bonds, assuming:

   a. The city has entered into a qualifying take-out agreement

   b. The city has not entered into a qualifying take-out agreement

2. Suppose that on January 1, 2006, prevailing interest rates for bonds of similar credit risk had fallen to 4 percent. A bondholder needed immediate cash for personal reasons. Assuming that the bonds were publicly traded, do you think the bondholder would redeem his bonds? Do you think that any other bondholders would redeem their bonds? Explain.

3. Suppose, instead, that prevailing interest rates had increased to 9 percent. Do you think that the bondholder needing cash would redeem the bonds? Do you think that the other bondholders would redeem their bonds?

4. Suppose that the city has entered into a take-out agreement that does not specify the interest rate at which the financing institution would provide the funds necessary for the city to redeem its bonds. If prevailing rates have increased to 9 percent, at approximately what rate is it likely that the financing institution would loan the city the required funds?

5. Comment on the extent to which the demand bonds provide the city with one of the primary benefits of issuing long-term debt—the guarantee of a fixed interest rate over the life of the bond. To what extent does it burden the city with the corresponding disadvantage—being required to pay no less than the stated rate over the life of the bond (or otherwise retire the bonds at market prices)?

8–9

BANs, TANs, and RANs may sound alike, but they are not necessarily accounted for alike.

In August 2003, voters of Balcones, a medium-sized city, approved a $15 million general obligation bond issue to finance the construction of recreational facilities. So as to begin construction immediately, without waiting to complete the lengthy process of issuing long-term bonds, the city issued $4 million in bond anticipation notes (BANs). The notes matured in March 2004, but the city had the right to prepay them at any time prior to maturity.

On February 15, 2004, the city issued $15 million of 6 percent, twenty-year GO bonds. Upon receiving the proceeds, it repaid the BANs, along with $80,000 in interest.

1. Prepare a journal entry to indicate how the city should report the BANs in its December 31, 2003, governmental fund financial statements, assuming that it issued the statements after February 15, 2004.

2. Suppose that the city did not refinance the BANs prior to the date the financial statements were issued. What other evidence must the city present to justify reporting the BANs as long-term obligations? Prepare a journal entry to indicate how the city should report the BANs in its governmental fund financial statements if it is unable to provide this evidence.

3. Assume, also, that the city experienced a cash flow shortage in November 2003. Anticipating tax collections in January 2004, it issued $2 million in tax anticipation notes (TANs) due February 2004. In February 2004, instead of repaying the notes, it rolled them over for an additional six months. Should the city report the TANs in its governmental fund financial statements? Explain.

4. Assume further that, in July 2003, the city was awarded a $1 million reimbursement grant. It expected to receive the grant funds in January 2004. Inasmuch as it expected to incur many of the expenditures covered by the grant in 2003, it issued $1 million in six-month revenue anticipation notes (RANs). As of December 31, the city had not repaid the notes but had secured the written agreement of the lender that they could be extended for an additional six months. How should the city report the RANs in its December 31, 2003, governmental fund financial statements? Explain.

8–10

Overlapping debt can significantly alter key measures of debt capacity.

Use the following information, taken from the City of Wyoming, Michigan's, schedule of direct and overlapping debt, to answer the questions.

Name of Governmental Unit	Net Debt Outstanding	Percent Applicable to City
City of Wyoming	$ 22,863,510	100.00%
Kent County	125,653,951	13.40
Kent County Intermediate School District	1,766,795	13.55
Wyoming Public Schools	3,956,922	99.24
Godwin Heights Public Schools	1,338,501	85.96
Kelloggsville Public Schools	2,363,037	61.97
Grandville Public Schools	10,734,809	13.58
Kentwood Public Schools	25,502,958	0.55
Godfrey Lee Public Schools	3,204,362	100.00

1. The schedule does not indicate the origin of the percentages of the debt applicable to the city. What is the most likely way these percentages were derived?

2. Compute the total amount of the City of Wyoming's direct and overlapping debt.

3. Another schedule in the city's annual report indicates that the city's ratio of net direct debt to assessed value of property is 1.861 percent and that net debt per capita is $354.47. The schedule reports that the assessed value of property is $1,228,774,900, and the population is 64,500. What would be the ratio of total net direct debt and overlapping debt to assessed value of property? What would be the total net direct and overlapping debt per capita?

4. Why might a statement user be at least as concerned with the ratios that include overlapping debt as with those limited to direct general obligation debt?

8–11

Exploring Orlando's financial report

Refer to the financial statements of the City of Orlando in Chapter 3 and to Tables 8–1 and 8–2 in this chapter.

1. What amount did Orlando report in its government-wide statements for bonds payable associated with governmental activities?

2. Did Orlando issue capital improvement bonds in the year ending September 30, 2001? What amount of outstanding capital improvement bonds did it repay during the year?

3. In addition to bonds payable, what other kinds of long-tem debt for governmental activities did Orlando report in its statement of net assets?

4. How much of the amount reported in Orlando's statement of net assets for loans and leases payable is for leases? Is this amount for capital leases or operating leases? Explain.

5. What did Orlando acquire under the lease reported in the statement of net assets? What was the acquisition value of this item? Is this amount included in the financial statements? If so, where is it reported?

CHAPTER 9

Business-Type Activities and Internal Services

Governments engage in a variety of functions that are similar to those carried out by businesses. They range in size from small community health centers to multi-billion-dollar regional power authorities. These "business-type activities," as well as certain internal services of governments, such as motor pools, data processing, and self-insurance, are accounted for and reported similarly to corresponding private sector enterprises.

In both the fund statements and the government-wide statements, business-type activities and internal services are on a full accrual basis, and their measurement focus is on all economic resources. Thus, we shall direct relatively little attention to the general principles (such as those of revenue and expense recognition) of accounting for them. These principles are similar to those covered in other courses dealing with financial (business) accounting. Instead, we shall focus on issues and concepts that are specific to government enterprises and internal services.

WHY DO GOVERNMENTS ENGAGE IN BUSINESS-TYPE ACTIVITIES?

Governments engage in a wide variety of activities that are also carried out by for-profit businesses. For example:

- Governments provide waste removal, electric, and other utility services; maintain hospitals; and operate swimming pools, tennis courts, and golf courses, often in competition with similar for-profit entities.
- Universities sell computers, books, and clothing; sponsor professional-like sports teams; operate cafeterias and restaurants; and maintain dormitories.
- Hospitals, museums, and zoos sell gifts, posters, and books.

In the United States, prevailing political and economic doctrine dictates that goods and services should be provided mainly by the business sector. Why, then, do governments engage in similar activities? Several reasons can be cited:

- *To provide resources that would otherwise have to be raised by taxes, contributions, tuition, or other means.* Gift shops, for example, may be major sources of revenue for hospitals; utilities may generate cash as well as electricity.

- *To complement and support the government's main mission.* For example, cafeterias, book stores, and sports programs are an integral part of a university environment.
- *To control the activity.* Thus, universities operate dormitories not necessarily because they can do so at less cost than a private contractor, but so they can maintain authority over them.
- *To provide the services more cheaply or efficiently than can a private firm.* Public housing authorities, for example, have an inherent cost advantage over private landlords in providing apartments to low-income families in that their properties are not subject to property taxes.
- *To ensure that the goods or services are available at less than market rates.* Thus, a city might maintain a bus service or a public golf course, even though it is unprofitable.

In recent years, governments have come under attack for operating activities that critics believe should be carried out in the private sector. Opponents of large government have urged the **privatization** of services, claiming that, lacking the profit motive, governments are inherently inefficient. Merchants have charged tax-exempt universities and museums with unfair competition in selling books, computers, and other items to the public at less than prevailing prices.

The issue of whether governments should engage in business-type activities is beyond the scope of this text. But the reasons they do so are directly pertinent to the questions of how to distinguish business-type from governmental activities and how to account for them.

WHAT ARE PROPRIETARY FUNDS?

Business-type activities and internal services are often referred to as *proprietary* (similar to for-profit) activities and governments use two types of **proprietary funds** to account for them.

- **Enterprise funds** account for business-type activities—those in which goods or services are provided to the general public for a fee.
- **Internal service funds** account for operations in which goods or services are provided by one government department to other departments within the same government, or to other governments, on a cost-reimbursement basis.

We shall discuss accounting and reporting issues that are common to both enterprise and internal service funds at the same time. However, we shall also devote a separate section to each fund type to discuss its unique features.

Governments account for both enterprise and internal service funds on a full accrual basis. They recognize exchange revenues as earned and *expenses* (rather than expenditures) as incurred, irrespective of when cash is received or paid. They recognize capital assets and long-term debt in the fund statements of net assets, and they depreciate the capital assets and amortize any premiums or discounts on long-term debt.

SHOULD GOVERNMENTS ACCOUNT FOR PROPRIETARY FUNDS DIFFERENTLY THAN GOVERNMENTAL FUNDS?

A fundamental question pertaining to proprietary funds (both enterprise and internal service funds) is whether and why governments should account for and report them differently than governmental funds. In particular, why should governments account for them on a full rather than a modified accrual basis of accounting?

Key reasons cited for using full accrual accounting for proprietary funds include the following:

- The full accrual basis of accounting captures all the resources and obligations, including capital assets and long-term obligations, associated with the services provided. It thereby provides a more complete picture of financial position and operating results.

- The measurement focus on all economic resources is more consistent with the GASB's objectives that financial reporting should provide information to determine whether current-year revenues were sufficient to pay for current-year services and should assist users in assessing service efforts, costs, and accomplishments.

- Full accrual accounting provides information on depreciation, which is an essential cost of operations that use capital assets to provide services.

- Full accrual accounting facilitates comparisons with similar private enterprises. For example, users might wish to compare a county hospital with a similar for-profit hospital, or the cost of providing centralized data processing internally versus contracting out for similar services.

At the same time, there are cogent arguments against different accounting principles for proprietary versus governmental funds:

- Two separate measurement focuses and bases for accounting within the same set of fund financial statements are confusing and add complexity to the reporting process.

- Despite many similarities, a government's operations cannot—and should not—be compared to those carried out in the private sector. A government should have sound political and economic reasons—other than merely earning a profit—for conducting a particular activity. If it does not, then the activity should be privatized. These reasons, by themselves, suggest that all government operations should be assessed by criteria other than comparisons between fund revenues and expenses.

- Surveys of enterprise fund statement users indicate that information on depreciation is not a high priority. They are concerned mainly with the ability of revenues to cover debt service rather than depreciation. This applies especially to users interested in toll roads, tunnels, and bridges.

Closely tied to the issue of whether proprietary funds should use different accounting principles from governmental funds is that of whether proprietary activities should even be accounted for in separate funds. A key rationale for fund accounting and reporting in general is that legally restricted resources (e.g., for debt service) should be reported apart from those that are unrestricted (e.g., general fund resources). The resources directed to proprietary activities, especially those accounted for in internal service funds, are often not legally restricted. They can be used for all purposes of government and are subject to the claims of general creditors. Moreover, although governments must present restricted proprietary fund assets (usually owing to revenue bond covenants) separately from those that are unrestricted, both are presented within the same fund.

Obviously, there are compelling reasons to account *internally* for different activities in different funds. Separate funds facilitate budgeting, planning, and control. However, when proprietary resources that are not legally restricted are reported on apart from other unrestricted resources, statement users may have difficulty determining the total resources available for future appropriation or payment to creditors. They may be misled into thinking that unrestricted proprietary fund resources are, in fact, restricted.

Nevertheless, the arguments in favor of reporting on proprietary fund activities apart from governmental fund activities are also persuasive. Up to the point of information overload, more information is better than less. If managers need separate reports to assess the performance and fiscal status of proprietary fund activities, so too do citizens, investors, and other statement users. Insofar as statement users are concerned with the total amount of unrestricted resources, they can readily add the unrestricted amounts reported in the proprietary funds to those reported in the general fund and other governmental funds.

WHAT ARE THE THREE BASIC FINANCIAL STATEMENTS OF PROPRIETARY FUNDS?

Similar to businesses, governments are required to prepare three basic financial statements for proprietary funds:

1. Statement of net assets (or balance sheet)
2. Statement of revenues, expenses, and changes in fund net assets
3. Statement of cash flows

The amounts reported in proprietary fund statements are generally the same as those reported in the government-wide statements because both sets of statements are on a full accrual basis of accounting. Therefore, unlike the governmental fund statements, no reconciliation is required.

The Statement of Net Assets and the Statement of Revenues, Expenses, and Changes in Fund Net Assets for Orlando's proprietary funds were presented in Chapter 3 (Tables 3-7 and 3-8). Orlando's Statement of Cash Flows for its proprietary funds is presented in Table 9-1.

STATEMENT OF NET ASSETS (OR BALANCE SHEET) Similar to the option that it grants at the government-wide level, the GASB permits governments to present proprietary fund assets and liabilities either in a net assets format: *assets less liabilities equal* *net assets*, or in a balance sheet format: *assets equal liabilities plus net assets*. In either case, net assets should be displayed in three components:

1. Invested in capital assets, net of related debt (i.e., the total capital assets, less the remaining debt used to acquire, construct, or improve them)
2. Restricted net assets
3. Unrestricted net assets

In addition to segregating restricted net assets, proprietary fund statements should also segregate restricted *assets*. Suppose, for example, that a government holds in a separate bank account cash that is legally restricted for debt service. To classify that cash as a current asset would suggest that it is available for general use. Therefore, it should be reported as a restricted asset, apart from the other current assets.

STATEMENT OF REVENUES, EXPENSES, AND CHANGES IN FUND NET ASSETS (INCOME STATEMENT) The statement of revenues, expenses, and changes in fund net assets is comparable to the income statement of a business, except that it is all inclusive. That is, in addition to operating and nonoperating revenues and expenses, it reports capital contributions and it incorporates a reconciliation of beginning and ending net assets. The key elements may be summarized as follows.[1] (See Chapter 3, Table 3-8, for a detailed illustration.)

Operating Revenues	
Fees and Charges	$10,000
Others (detailed)	2,000
Total Operating Revenues	12,000
Operating Expenses	
Wages and Salaries	8,000
Others (detailed)	1,500
Total Operating Expenses	9,500
Operating Income (loss)	2,500
Nonoperating Revenues and Expenses	
State Operating Grants	2,400
Others (detailed)	500
Total Nonoperating Revenues and Expenses	2,900
Income Before Other Revenues, Expenses,	
Gains, Losses, and Transfers	5,400
Capital Contributions and Other Changes in Net Assets	
Federal Capital Grant	800
Others (e.g., additions to permanent and term	
endowments, special and extraordinary items,	
and transfers)	300
Total Capital Contributions	1,100
Increase (decrease) in Net Assets	6,500
Net Assets—Beginning of Period	20,000
Net Assets—End of Period	$26,500

---

[1]GASB Statement No. 34, *Basic Financial Statements—and Management's Discussion and Analysis—for State and Local Governments*, para. 101.

The distinction between operating and nonoperating revenues and expenses is not always clear and is subject to management discretion. In general, the classification scheme should follow that adopted for the statement of cash flows. Capital contributions will be discussed after the statement of cash flows.

STATEMENT OF CASH FLOWS Governments are required to prepare a statement of cash flows for proprietary funds (see Table 9-1), but not for governmental funds. There is less need for a statement of cash flows for governmental funds in that the statement of revenues and expenditures is on a modified accrual basis. It, therefore, focuses on cash and near-cash resources that are currently available for disbursement.

The preparation of a statement of cash flows can be complex and tedious, but it presents few, if any, conceptual problems. In essence, the statement is a summary of an entity's cash account. The issues that both the FASB and the GASB have had to address pertain mainly to transaction classification.

Different Standards for Governments than for Businesses The GASB and FASB standards for statements of cash flows establish differing classification schemes. FASB Statement No. 95, *Statement of Cash Flows*, which does not apply to governments, requires that cash transactions be classified into three categories:

1. *Cash flows from operating activities*, such as receipts from sales of goods and services, interest, and dividends, and disbursements for goods and materials, interest, and taxes

2. *Cash flows from financing activities*, such as proceeds from issuing stocks and bonds, and payments for dividends and repayments of loans

3. *Cash flows from investing activities*, such as receipts and disbursements from the sale and purchase of marketable securities and long-lived assets

These categories have obvious limitations if applied to governments. Governments typically characterize their activities as either operating or capital. Capital activities—those involving the acquisition and financing of capital assets—are often both budgeted and accounted for apart from operating activities. Yet the FASB classification scheme draws no distinction between the two.

To remedy this deficiency, the GASB issued its Statement No. 9, *Reporting Cash Flows of Proprietary and Nonexpendable Trust Funds[2] and Governmental Entities That Use Proprietary Fund Accounting*, which provides for a classification scheme with *four* categories:

1. *Cash flows from operating activities*, such as receipts from sales of goods or services and grants for activities considered operating activities by the grantor government (e.g., a grant to provide services); and disbursements for materials, employee compensation, operating grants to other governments, and taxes, fines, and penalties

2. *Cash flows from noncapital financing activities*, such as proceeds from issuing debt not clearly attributable to the acquisition, construction, or improvement of capital assets, grants not specifically restricted for capital purposes or for activities considered operating activities by the grantor government (e.g., a grant to finance an operating deficit); and repayments of borrowings for noncapital purposes, interest on noncapital borrowings, and grants or subsidies provided for activities considered operating activities by the grantor

---

[2]Statement No. 34 eliminated nonexpendable trust funds as a fund type and reclassified them as, primarily, permanent funds, which, like other governmental funds, are not required to present a statement of cash flows.

TABLE 9-1
City of Orlando, Florida
Statement of Cash Flows—Proprietary Funds
For the Year Ended September 30, 2001

	Business-type Activities		
	Wastewater System	Orlando Centroplex	Parking System
Increase (Decrease) in Cash and Cash Equivalents:			
Cash Flows from Operations:			
Receipts from Customers	$ 37,941,871	$14,366,828	$ 9,864,421
Repayment of Loans from Other Funds	—	—	—
Repayment of Loans from Component Units	—	—	—
Loans to Other Funds	—	—	—
Payments to Suppliers	(20,497,675)	(11,446,022)	(4,172,980)
Payments to Employees	(7,707,808)	(3,523,440)	(2,122,844)
Payments to Internal Service Funds and Administrative Fees	(3,598,777)	(760,402)	(813,192)
Net Cash Provided by (Used in) Operating Activities	6,137,611	1,363,036	2,755,405
Cash Flows from Noncapital Financing Activities:			
Transfers In	894,837	1,627,847	2,162,925
Transfers (Out)	(2,232,745)	(15,000)	(1,509,093)
Principal Paid on Bonds and Loans	—	—	—
Interest Paid on Bonds and Loans	—	—	—
Net Cash Flows from Noncapital Financing Activities	(1,337,908)	1,612,847	653,832
Cash Flows from Capital and Related Financing Activities:			
Additions to Property, Plant and Equipment	(20,605,490)	(249,915)	(77,544)
Principal Paid on Bonds, Interfund Loans, Loans & Leases	(11,006,412)	(1,081,630)	(2,460,577)
Interest Paid on Bonds, Interfund Loans, Loans and Leases	(7,955,228)	(546,217)	(1,327,212)
Capital Contribution Other Governments, Developers and Funds	367,941	—	—
Impact Fees Received	11,474,241	—	—
Proceeds from Sale of Property, Plant and Equipment	—	—	—
Net Cash Flows from Capital and Related Financing Activities	(27,724,948)	(1,877,762)	(3,865,333)
Cash Flows from Investing Activities:			
Purchases of Investments	(119,276,256)	—	(13,639,723)
Proceeds from Sales and Maturities of Investments	118,770,594	—	13,519,347
Interest on Investments	12,127,187	216,081	1,324,698
Net Cash Flows from Investing Activities	11,621,525	216,081	1,204,322
Net Increase (Decrease) in Cash and Cash Equivalents	(11,303,720)	(1,411,870)	748,226
Cash and Cash Equivalents at Beginning of Year	136,067,643	3,002,739	14,257,628
Cash and Cash Equivalents at End of Year	$124,763,923	$ 1,590,869	$15,005,854
Classified As:			
Current Assets	$109,816,332	$ 1,590,869	$11,036,503
Restricted Assets	14,947,591	—	3,969,351
Totals	$124,763,923	$ 1,590,869	$15,005,854

	Enterprise Funds			Governmental Activities Internal Service Funds
	Stormwater Utility	Solid Waste Management	Total	
	$10,302,430	$15,216,101	$87,691,651	$37,103,753
	—	—	—	12,036,486
	—	—	—	176,142
	—	—	—	(13,812,917)
	(6,101,393)	(7,016,145)	(49,234,215)	(12,938,931)
	(502,240)	(3,590,106)	(17,446,438)	(5,015,245)
	(422,485)	(4,745,564)	(10,340,420)	(1,669,021)
	3,276,312	(135,714)	10,670,578	15,880,267
	177,649	210,396	5,073,654	2,432,794
	(3,131,365)	(8,656)	(6,896,859)	(882,310)
	—	—	—	(3,840,000)
	—	—	—	(5,889,912)
	(2,953,716)	201,740	(1,823,205)	(8,179,428)
	(6,295,495)	(457,603)	(27,686,047)	(10,802,980)
	—	—	(14,548,619)	(1,178,164)
	—	—	(9,828,657)	(86,650)
	1,590,451	—	1,958,392	6,350
	—	—	11,474,241	—
	—	—	—	954,348
	(4,705,044)	(457,603)	(38,630,690)	(11,107,096)
	—	—	(132,915,979)	(9,566,622)
	—	—	132,289,941	9,418,689
	1,555,361	398,026	15,621,353	3,935,633
	1,555,361	398,026	14,995,315	3,787,700
	(2,827,087)	6,449	(14,788,002)	381,443
	16,262,630	4,489,967	174,080,607	47,418,313
	13,435,543	4,496,416	159,292,605	47,799,756
	$13,435,543	$ 4,496,416	$140,375,663	$47,799,756
	—	—	18,916,942	—
	$13,435,543	$ 4,496,416	$159,292,605	$47,799,756

(*continued*)

TABLE 9-1 *(continued)*
City of Orlando, Florida
Statement of Cash Flows—Proprietary Funds
For the Year Ended September 30, 2001

	Business-type Activities		
	Wastewater System	Orlando Centroplex	Parking System
Reconciliation of Operating Income (Loss) to Net Cash Provided by (Used In) Operating Activities:			
Operating Income (Loss)	$(13,774,300)	$ (3,582,213)	$ 58,153
Adjustments Not Affecting Cash:			
Depreciation	20,232,764	3,687,016	2,654,679
Amortization	101,369	—	35,753
(Increase) Decrease in Assets and Increase (Decrease) in Liabilities:			
Accounts Receivable	7,258	15,704	1,703
Due from Other Governments	(453,849)	—	(12,227)
Inventory	(109,265)	39,464	—
Prepaid Items	—	(4,774)	—
Loans to Other Funds	—	—	—
Loans to Component Units	—	—	—
Accounts Payable	(410,528)	(106,765)	59,937
Accrued Liabilities	9,285	2,920	10,273
Arbitrage Rebate Payable	—	—	—
Compensated Absences	534,877	100,751	60,779
Claims Payable	—	—	—
Advance Payments	—	(1,515,139)	2,661
Total Adjustments	19,911,911	2,219,177	2,813,558
Net Cash Provided by (Used in) Operating Activities	$ 6,137,611	$ (1,363,036)	$ 2,755,405

3. *Cash flows from capital and related financing activities,* such as proceeds of debt clearly attributable to the acquisition, construction, or improvement of capital assets, capital grants, sales of capital assets, and special assessments and property taxes levied to finance capital assets; and disbursements to acquire, construct, or improve capital assets, repayments of capital debt, and interest on capital debt

4. *Cash flows from investing activities,* such as receipts from sales of marketable securities, interest and dividends, collections of loans, and withdrawals from investment pools; and disbursements for purchases of marketable securities, loans, and deposits into investment pools

In addition to the number of categories, the GASB and FASB standards also differ in how interest should be reported. Whereas the FASB classifies interest paid and interest received as operating activities, the GASB requires that governments classify interest paid as financing activities and interest received as investing activities. Whether interest paid is classified as a capital or a noncapital financing activity would

| Enterprise Funds | | | Governmental Activities |
Stormwater Utility	Solid Waste Management	Total	Internal Service Funds
$1,905,992	$(484,120)	$(15,992,794)	$ 5,603,526
1,841,813	189,949	28,606,221	5,491,320
—	—	137,122	42,179
(1,745)	(20,296)	2,624	262,204
—	(400)	(466,476)	—
—	—	(69,801)	(150,234)
—	—	(4,774)	—
—	—	—	(1,776,431)
—	—	—	176,142
(363,858)	(74,403)	(895,617)	1,656,513
(1,396)	9,222	30,304	4,052
—	—	—	82,166
(104,494)	244,334	836,247	94,033
—	—	—	4,394,797
—	—	(1,512,478)	—
1,370,320	348,406	26,663,372	10,276,741
$3,276,312	$ (135,714)	$ 10,670,578	$15,880,267

depend on how the underlying debt is classified. The GASB maintains that by classifying interest received and disbursed in the same categories as purchases and sales of the underlying securities, governments provide a more complete picture of the cash flows associated with financing and investing activities.

In another significant difference from FASB requirements, GASB Statement No. 34 mandates that governments report their cash flows using the direct method. The direct method explicitly reports the operating cash flows in a way that makes clear their source or use (e.g., cash receipts from customers, cash payments to employees). The indirect method, by contrast, reconciles operating cash flows to operating income. Thus, the reporting entity would add to, or subtract from, operating income any differences between cash flows (e.g., cash receipts from customers, cash payments to employees) and the related revenues or expenses (e.g., sales revenues, wage and salary expense). The FASB encourages but does not mandate use of the direct method, and the overwhelming majority of businesses use the indirect method.

WHAT ACCOUNTING ISSUES ARE UNIQUE TO ENTERPRISE FUNDS?

Although governments have adopted the business accounting model for their enterprise funds, they nevertheless face several unique issues. Two basic issues are: When should an activity be accounted for in an enterprise fund, and should enterprise fund accounting follow FASB or GASB pronouncements? Other, more specific, issues relate to budgetary reporting, capital contributions, and landfills.

CRITERIA FOR ESTABLISHING AN ENTERPRISE FUND Almost all government departments engage in some form of entrepreneurial activity. Accordingly, there is no obvious way to distinguish activities that should be accounted for in enterprise funds rather than governmental funds, and in the past there has been considerable diversity of practice. To reduce this diversity, GASB Statement No. 34 establishes general criteria as to when a government *may*, and when it *must*, account for an activity in an enterprise fund.

GASB Standards

Statement No. 34 prescribes that a government *may* account for an activity in an enterprise fund as long as it charges fees to external users for goods and services. It *must* account for an activity in an enterprise fund if the activity satisfies one of the following criteria:

- The activity is financed solely with revenue debt (which is secured merely by the revenues from a specific activity), as opposed to general obligation debt (which is backed by the full faith and credit of the entire government).

- Laws or regulations require that the activity's costs of providing services (including capital costs) be recovered by fees and charges, rather than by general purpose taxes or similar charges.

- The activity's pricing policies establish fees and charges designed to recover its costs, including capital costs (such as depreciation or debt service).[3]

These criteria should be applied to an activity's principal sources of revenue—not to insignificant sources. Thus, even if a police department charges fees for escorting funeral processions or for controlling traffic at charitable fun runs, it need not be accounted for in an enterprise fund because the department's principal revenue sources are taxes and intergovernmental grants.

ACCOUNTING STANDARDS Traditionally, enterprise funds were accounted for like businesses and applied the pronouncements of the FASB and its predecessors, except when the GASB had specifically prohibited their application (often referred

---

[3]Statement No. 34, para. 67.

to as a *negative standard*). However, on November 30, 1989, the Board of Trustees of the Financial Accounting Foundation (which oversees the FASB and the GASB) issued a "Jurisdiction Determination." The key feature of this agreement was a new hierarchy of generally accepted accounting principles. It established that the GASB has the final standard-setting authority for all activities of state and local governments, including the activities of government hospitals, universities, utilities, and other proprietary activities. Thus, GASB pronouncements must be followed by all entities within its jurisdiction. However, the GASB requires or accepts the use of certain FASB standards for proprietary funds and governement-wide statements.

GASB Standards

Statement No. 34,[4] requires governments to apply all pronouncements of the FASB and its predecessors issued on or before November 30, 1989, to the government-wide statements (both governmental and business-type activities) and the proprietary fund statements (both enterprise and internal service funds), unless those pronouncements conflict with or contradict GASB pronouncements (in which case, the GASB pronouncements apply).

In addition, governments have the *option* to apply *to business-type activities only* (those that are reported in the business-type activities columns of the government-wide statements and are accounted for and reported as enterprise funds in the fund statements) either *all* FASB pronouncements issued after November 30, 1989, except those that conflict with or contradict GASB pronouncements, or *none* of those pronouncements. This option is *not* available for governmental activities or for internal service funds.

Note that the option for business-type activities is "all or none" of the FASB pronouncements issued after the cut-off date. Governments cannot cherry-pick the most appealing statements and reject the others. Moreover, the GASB encourages governments to make the same election for all of their business-type activities.

BUDGETS Government enterprises are disciplined by the marketplace rather than by their budgets. Their revenues and expenses, unlike those of governmental funds, are determined by "customer" demand, not by legislative fiat. Principles of sound management dictate that governments, like businesses, prepare annual budgets. These budgets would usually include a *cash budget* to facilitate cash management, a *capital budget* to expedite the acquisition of capital assets, and a *flexible budget* indicating **fixed costs** and **variable costs** at different levels of output, to help control costs.

However, unlike governmental fund budgets, enterprise fund budgets are not the equivalent of either spending authorizations or tax levies. Accordingly, governments generally do not have to get formal legislative approval for enterprise fund budgets or

---

[4]Statement No. 34, paras. 17, 93, and 94.

incorporate them into their accounting systems. Moreover, governments need not compare the budgeted amounts with actual results in their annual reports.

CAPITAL CONTRIBUTIONS Enterprise funds receive capital contributions from other funds and from new customers, developers, and other governments. Examples include contributions of capital assets, grants restricted for the acquisition of capital assets, and permanently restricted financial assets. The key issues are how to present capital contributions on the financial statements and how to distinguish them from ordinary revenues. Consider these examples of nonroutine receipts:

- *Tap (system development) fees.* A city's electric or water utility charges a **tap fee** to hook up new customers to an existing system. The fee may exceed the cost of connecting the customer to the system; part may cover the customer's share of the capital cost of the system already in place.
- *Impact fees.* A municipal utility district charges developers a fee for anticipated improvements, such as new water and sewer lines, that will be required because of new development. Unlike tap fees, these **impact fees** cannot necessarily be associated with specific projects or improvements.
- *External subsidies.* A municipal transit authority receives a federal grant to purchase new buses and defray operating costs.
- *Internal subsidies.* A county hospital receives transfers from the county's general fund, based on the number of indigent patients served, to cover operating expenses and acquire new equipment.
- *Debt forgiveness.* A state provides a loan to state-operated liquor stores. The stores have historically been unprofitable and the loan is unlikely to be repaid.

GASB Standards

Prior to the issuance of Statement No. 34, governments reported capital contributions in the financial statements as balance-sheet only transactions—i.e., as direct additions to fund balance or net assets—and not as revenues on the statement of revenues and expenses. In Statement No. 34, however, the GASB switched to an "all inclusive, change in net assets" approach. This approach dictates that the statement of revenues, expenses, and changes in fund net assets (and the government-wide statement of activities) report on *all* changes in net assets, including capital contributions. However, the GASB determined that capital contributions should be presented separately from other revenues. Accordingly, as illustrated earlier in this chapter and in Chapter 3, Table 3-8, governments should present capital contributions after nonoperating revenues and expenses but before the change in net assets for the year.

The GASB recognizes that tap fees, impact fees, and similar types of charges may be, at least in part, nonvoluntary capital contributions. Nevertheless, it directs, in Statement No. 33 pertaining to nonexchange revenue recognition, that these types of charges should be accounted for as if they were "pure" exchange transactions. The GASB does not provide guidance as

(continued)

GASB Standards *(continued)*

to whether mixed grants, such as those to both acquire capital equipment and to cover operating expenses, should be classified as operating revenues or capital contributions. However, because capital contributions must now be reported as revenues, rather than as a direct increase in net assets, the distinction between operating revenues and capital contributions is less significant than it was before the issuance of Statement No. 34.

LANDFILL COSTS One of the most pressing economic and political issues of the foreseeable future will be how to maintain—and pay for—a clean environment. Governments and private industry will face billions of dollars of costs to dispose of wastes, to prevent additional pollution, and to clean up messes that have been made in the past. The associated accounting issues are complex because the costs are large and the timing, specific amounts, and distribution of cash outlays are uncertain. So far, the GASB has addressed only one aspect of the issues—accounting for landfill costs.[5]

Governments can account for landfills in either governmental or enterprise funds, depending mainly on whether they charge user fees. Because most governments charge a fee, they generally use an enterprise fund. The choice of fund does not affect GASB standards with regard to the calculation of the *amount* of the landfill liability to be reported. However, because governmental and enterprise funds use different measurement focuses and bases of accounting, the standards differ as to *where* the liability should be reported and *when* the related expenditure must be charged.

Landfills provide benefits over the period that they accept waste, often thirty or forty years. However, state and federal regulations make landfill operators responsible for properly closing their landfills and subsequently caring for and monitoring them. Operators incur sizable expenditures when they close their landfills and for a period as long as twenty years thereafter.

The accounting problems pertaining to closure and postclosure costs are comparable to those of pensions. The benefits are received over the years when the landfill accepts the waste (or, in the case of pensions, when employees provide their services). Although some closure-related expenditures (pension payments) are made prior to closure (retirement), most are made in the years of closure and beyond. Moreover, the actual expenditures that will be required are subject to unpredictable factors.

GASB Standards

Consistent with pension accounting principles in both industry and government, the GASB has directed that enterprise funds allocate estimated closure and postclosure costs to the years in which the landfill accepts waste rather than when they are paid. Therefore, in each year of a landfill's useful life, the government should recognize, as both an expense and an increase in a liability, an appropriate portion of the estimated total costs for closure and postclosure care.

---

[5]GASB Statement No. 18, *Accounting for Municipal Solid Waste Landfill Closure and Postclosure Care Costs.*

GASB Standards (continued)

Total costs would include:

- Cost of equipment expected to be installed and facilities expected to be constructed near or after the date that the landfill stops accepting waste (e.g., gas monitoring and collection systems, storm water management systems, ground water monitoring wells, and so on)
- Cost of final cover
- Cost of monitoring and maintaining the landfill during the postclosure period

The amount to be added to a liability account at the end of each year would be based on the percentage of the landfill actually used up to that point. It would equal the percentage of the landfill used during the year times the total estimated costs. At any point during the life of the landfill, the balance in the liability account would equal the sum of the yearly amounts added to the account less any expenditures for closure-related costs.

From a slightly different perspective, the amount to be added to a liability each year—and to be charged as the expense for that year—would be the total amount that should have been recognized as an expense (added to the liability) up to the date of computation, less the amount that has actually been recognized so far. Thus, the amount to be added each year (the current-year expense) equals:

$$\frac{\text{Estimated}}{\text{total cost}} \times \frac{\text{landfill capacity}}{\text{used to date}} \quad less \text{ Amounts recognized in the past}$$
$$\overline{\text{Total landfill capacity}}$$

Both costs and capacity would be based on *current* conditions at the time of the computation. Each year the government would reestimate both the total landfill capacity and the total closure and postclosure costs, thus taking into account inflation, new regulatory requirements, and technological improvements since the previous computation.

The GASB does *not* deal with the issue of when governments should *finance* closure and postclosure costs. Therefore, a government does not necessarily have to "fund" the costs during the landfill's useful life; it merely has to report both an expense and a liability for them. Moreover, in contrast to the manner in which it would compute its pension liability, it need not explicitly take into account the time value of money in making its calculations.

The example that follows illustrates how a government would account for a landfill in an *enterprise fund* (as well as in its government-wide statements). If it accounted for the landfill in a governmental fund, only the journal entries would differ, not the total liability or the amount to be added each year. Inasmuch as governmental funds do not report long-term obligations, the liability for the closure and postclosure costs would be reported only in the government-wide statements, not in the fund itself. Correspondingly, the governmental fund would not report an annual expenditure for the amount added to the liability account. As with other long-term obligations, a fund expenditure would be charged only in the period that the liability is to be liquidated with currently available financial resources. The result, therefore, is that with respect to the governmental fund expenditures, the government is on a pay-as-you-go basis.

EXAMPLE   *Landfill Costs in an Enterprise Fund*

At the start of year 1, a government opens a landfill, which it elects to account for in an enterprise fund. It estimates that total capacity will be 4.5 million cubic feet, that the site will be used for thirty years, and that total closure costs will be $18 million.

Year 1   During year 1, the government uses 90,000 cubic feet of the landfill. At year-end, it estimates that total capacity will still be 4.5 million cubic feet but that closure-related costs will now be $18,036,000. The required expense addition to the liability would be computed as follows:

Total Estimated Costs	$18,036,000
Proportion of Landfill Used (90,000/4,500,000)	.02
Required Expense (addition to liability)	$360,720

Journal Entry

Landfill expense	$360,720	
Liability for landfill costs		$360,720

To record the landfill liability and expense for year 1

The end-of-year balance in the liability account would be $360,720.

Year 2   In year 2, the government uses 120,000 cubic feet of the landfill. At year-end, it estimates that total closure-related costs have increased to $18,526,600 and that landfill capacity has decreased to 4,275,000 cubic feet. During the year the government also spends $277,221 on closure-related costs.

Total Estimated Costs	$18,526,600
Proportion of Landfill Used to Date (90,000 + 120,000)/4,275,000	.049122
Amount that Should Have Been Added to the Liability to Date (Cumulative Expense)	910,079
Less: Amount Recognized Previously	360,720
Required Expense (Addition to Liability)	$549,359

Journal Entry

Landfill expense	$549,359	
Liability for landfill costs		$549,359

To record the increase in the landfill liability and the expense for year 2

As the government actually makes the closure-related expenditures of $277,221, it would record the payment as follows:

Liability for landfill costs	$277,221	
Cash		$277,221

To record the payment of closure or postclosure costs

It would not matter if these payments were made for the acquisition of capital assets (e.g., earth-moving equipment) or for operating purposes (e.g., salaries). When the government makes the payments, it reduces the previously established liability. It does *not* record the closure-related equipment and facilities as capital assets. The end-of-year balance in the liability account would be $360,720 + $549,359 − $277,221 = $632,858.

WHAT ARE INTERNAL SERVICE FUNDS, AND HOW ARE THEY ACCOUNTED FOR?

Internal service funds are used to account for departments that provide goods or services to other departments, or to other governments, on a cost-reimbursement basis. Most commonly, the accounting entities correspond to related organizational units, such as data processing or vehicle repair centers. Sometimes, however, an internal service fund may be established to account for an activity for which there is no parallel organizational unit—for example, to account for self-insurance, which may be administered by a finance or accounting department.

The range of activities that some governments account for in internal service funds is far-reaching:

- supplies stores
- legal, accounting, auditing, and personnel services
- maintenance and janitorial services
- insurance
- capital asset leasing

REASONS FOR ESTABLISHING INTERNAL SERVICE FUNDS Internal service funds are intended to promote efficiency in the acquisition, distribution, and use of goods and services. The department providing the goods or services is, in effect, a profit center. Therefore, it is expected to keep its costs in line with its revenues and to satisfy the requirements of its customers. At the same time, the customers are charged for the goods or services that they receive and thereby have incentives to demand only what they can optimally use. Internal service funds also are a means of allocating the costs of functions and activities to the departments that are the ultimate beneficiaries.

Statement No. 34 permits, but does not require, governments to establish internal service funds when the reporting government is the main participant in the activity. Because the resources assigned to internal service funds are generally not legally restricted, it would usually be as proper for a government to account for them in the general fund. When the reporting government is not the main participant, it should report the activity in an enterprise fund.[6]

REVENUE AND EXPENSE RECOGNITION Internal service funds may provide services to a large number of different departments. However, most of their revenues are generally earned from a small number of funds—typically, the general fund and

---

[6]Statement No. 34, para. 68.

the enterprise funds. Revenues and expenses are recognized on a full-accrual basis. Internal service funds ordinarily recognize revenue as they deliver the goods or services. However, they might also recognize revenue uniformly over time—as would be appropriate for a fund that leases assets or underwrites insurance. Expenses include all costs incurred to produce the goods and services, including depreciation on capital assets and amortization of bond premiums and discounts. Correspondingly, internal service funds report capital assets and long-term debt on their statements of net assets.

The example that follows highlights the key features of internal service fund accounting.

EXAMPLE *Internal Service Fund Accounting*

Establishment of Fund A government establishes an internal service fund to account for a new data processing department. It transfers $0.6 million from its general fund to the internal service fund as an initial contribution of capital.

Cash	$0.6	
Nonreciprocal transfer-in from general fund		$0.6

To record the capital contribution from the general fund

The general fund would record a corresponding nonreciprocal transfer-out.

Issuing Long-term Debt The government issues $1.0 million in general obligation bonds to support the new department. It intends to service the debt entirely from the revenues of the data processing fund.

Cash	$1.0	
Bonds payable		$1.0

To record the long-term debt

Even though the bonds are general obligation bonds, they can be recorded as a fund liability as long as the government intends to repay them from the internal service fund.

Acquisition of Capital Assets The department acquires buildings, computers, and furniture for $1.4 million.

Capital assets (specified in detail)	$1.4	
Cash		$1.4

To record the acquisition of capital assets

Billings to Other Departments For services rendered during the year, the department bills the utility (enterprise) fund for $0.3 million, and the police department, the fire department and all other departments accounted for in the general fund for $0.8 million.

Due from general fund	$0.8	
Due from utility fund	0.3	
Operating revenues		$1.1

To record billings to other departments

Correspondingly, the general fund would report an expenditure, and the utility fund an expense, for the amounts billed. The two funds would recognize expenditures or expenses, rather than intragovernmental transfers, since these transactions qualify as **interfund services used**—costs that would be characterized as expenditures or expenses if the services were provided by outside vendors. (See the discussion of reciprocal interfund activities in Chapter 5.)

Depreciation and Other Expenses   The data processing department incurred $0.2 million in depreciation and $0.7 million in other operating expenses. In addition, it acquired $0.1 million in supplies inventory that remained on hand at year-end.

Depreciation expense	$0.2	
Other operating expenses (specified in detail)	0.7	
Supplies inventory	0.1	
Accounts payable		$0.8
Accumulated depreciation		0.2

To record depreciation and other expenses

Other transactions, such as those involving purchases of investments, the use of materials and supplies, and the accrual of interest, would be accounted for in the same manner as they would in a comparable business.

BASIS FOR BILLING RATES Internal service funds are used to account for goods and services provided to other government departments on a *cost reimbursement basis*. This implies that billing rates should be established so as to cover costs. However, *cost* can have several different meanings: full cost, incremental cost, opportunity cost, and direct cost.

In practice, for internal service funds, cost has been interpreted to mean **full cost**. They are expected, over time, neither to earn profits nor to incur losses. Thus, their billing rates should reflect all operating costs, including depreciation, interest, and other indirect costs.

The accumulation of unrestricted net asset surpluses or deficits may suggest that billing rates either exceed or are less than actual costs. However, governments may intentionally establish rates that exceed cost. This enables them to accumulate the resources required either to replace existing assets or to expand the asset base to meet anticipated increases in demand.

Ironically, the practice of establishing billing rates at full cost may subvert a key objective of internal service funds—that the supplying and receiving departments each provide or take an optimal quantity of goods and services. Full cost prices do not reflect the cost of providing incremental amounts of goods or services. Therefore, they may encourage departments to purchase either more or fewer goods or services than is optimal from the perspective of the government as a whole.

RAMIFICATIONS FOR OTHER FUNDS The accounting and operating practices of departments accounted for in internal service funds have critical implications, not only for the internal service funds themselves but also for the other funds with which they interact.

Duplicate Reported Expenses   Costs reported by internal service funds are reported twice within the same set of financial statements: once by the internal service fund providing the goods and services and a second time by the fund that is billed for them. Correspondingly, revenues are also reported twice: once by the fund receiving them from outside parties (as taxes or fees) and again when earned by the internal service fund.

Fortunately, as is explained in a section that follows on proprietary fund reporting requirements, the duplications are largely eliminated in the consolidated, government-wide financial statements.

Transfer of Depreciation to Governmental Funds   Governmental funds do not report capital assets or charge depreciation. However, insofar as an internal service fund incorporates depreciation expense into its billing rates, the depreciation charge is transferred, along with all other costs, to the funds that it bills.

The impact on reported expenditures of a governmental fund can be telling. Suppose that one government accounts for a motor pool in an internal service fund; another in its general fund. The motor pool of each government serves only other departments that are accounted for in the government's general fund. The general fund of the government maintaining the internal service fund will record the cost of the motor pool vehicles over their useful lives (through the depreciation expense incorporated into the billing rates). The general fund of the other government will record the cost as the vehicles are acquired or paid for.

Detract from Objectivity of Financial Statements   An internal service fund should establish its billing rates so it covers its costs. Yet cost is an elusive concept. It depends on estimates (such as the useful life of assets), choices among accounting methods (as to expense recognition, depreciation, inventory), and bases of overhead allocation. Although generally accepted accounting principles establish broad guidelines for cost determination, they leave considerable latitude for individual companies or governments. Thus, neither the billing rates nor the total revenues of an internal service fund are objective. And if its revenues are not objective, then neither are its changes in net assets for the year or its total net assets.

The inevitable subjectivity of individual internal service fund financial statements might be of only minor concern to statement users if the impact were limited to the internal service fund statements. However, the revenues of an internal service fund are the expenditures and expenses of other funds. Thus, if the revenues of an internal service fund are subjective, then so also are the expenditures of the general fund and all other funds to which the internal service provides goods or services. And if their expenditures are subjective, then so, too, are their annual excess of revenues over expenditures, their fund balances, and their assets or liabilities.

By controlling billing rates, government officials can fine-tune the reported excess of revenues over expenditures of the general fund—the fund most subject to balanced budget requirements and public scrutiny. For example, faced with pressure to hold down general fund expenditures, a government can delay imposing rate increases that would otherwise be warranted. Or, with an eye to maximizing cost recovery under a state or federal grant, it can increase the internal service fund charges to the programs whose costs are eligible for reimbursement.

Obscure Fund Balance Surpluses or Deficits   By adjusting the billing rates, government officials can transfer surpluses or deficits (i.e., positive or negative fund balances) from the general fund to the internal service fund. These surpluses or deficits might be prohibited if they remained in the general fund. Suppose, for example, that government officials see a need to set aside resources for the replacement of capital assets or for a rainy day. They recognize, however, that if the general fund were to report a surplus, legislators would seek either to increase spending or to reduce taxes.

The officials could achieve their objective by increasing the billing rates of an internal service fund, thereby transferring resources from the general fund to the internal service fund. The reserve would be maintained in the internal service fund rather than the general fund. To be sure, the reserve would be reflected in the net assets of the internal service fund. But the internal service fund might not be as carefully examined as the general fund. Since net assets includes a conglomeration of cumulative earnings for many years and many purposes, the reserve could readily be obscured.

WHAT SPECIAL PROBLEMS ARE CREATED IN ACCOUNTING FOR SELF-INSURANCE?

Many governments elect to *self-insure* all or a portion of their risks, especially those for less than catastrophic losses. Independent insurance companies set premiums to cover anticipated claims, administrative costs, and capital costs. For the portion of its policy applicable to routine losses, such as from automobile accidents or worker injuries, an insured entity's premiums are almost always based on the entity's own claims history. **Self-insurance** may provide an opportunity for the government to reduce the portion of the premium that covers the administrative and capital costs.

GASB permits governments to account for their self-insurance activities in either an internal service fund or the general fund.[7] Either way, the insurance "department" (which may be only an accounting entity rather than an organizational unit) operates as if it were an independent insurance company. It periodically bills other departments for premiums and it pays their claims as losses are incurred.

Self-insurance presents intriguing and controversial issues of accounting. The term self-insurance is an oxymoron. The essence of insurance is the transfer of risk to an outsider. When a government self-insures, it retains the risk itself. Therefore, self-insurance is no insurance.

The key accounting issues pertain to when, and in what amount, the insured departments should recognize expenditures or expenses for premiums paid, and the insurance department should recognize revenues for the insurance premiums received.

USING AN INTERNAL SERVICE FUND Suppose a government accounts for its insurance activities in an internal service fund and all the departments that it insures are accounted for in the general fund. The general fund, therefore, pays annual premiums to the internal service fund.

If the general fund paid these premiums to an outside insurance company, the premiums would be recorded as an expenditure. Consistent with the principles that *interfund services used* be accounted for as expenditures, it might appear that premiums paid to the internal service fund should also be accounted for as an expenditure. However, the general fund does not actually transfer risk to the internal

---

[7]GASB Statement No. 10, *Accounting and Financial Reporting for Risk Financing and Related Insurance Issues.*

service fund. Except for the portion of the premiums that covers losses actually incurred, it simply sets aside funds to provide for possible losses in the future. In that regard the transaction is comparable to a transfer of resources to a debt service fund for the future repayment of bonds. Therefore, it has been argued that only the portion of the premium that covers actual losses should be reported as an expenditure in the general fund. The excess should be accounted for as a nonreciprocal transfer-out. Correspondingly, only the portion of the premium that represents a reimbursement for actual losses should be recognized as a revenue in the internal service fund.

GASB Standards

The GASB has held that as long as specified criteria are satisfied, an internal service insurance fund can recognize revenues, and the insured funds (departments) can recognize expenditures or expenses, for the full amount of the premiums billed. The government can use any basis that it considers appropriate to establish the internal service fund's premiums, as long as they satisfy either of the following conditions:

- The total charge covers the actual losses incurred by the internal service insurance fund.
- The total charge is based on an actuarial method or historical cost method and adjusted over time so that internal service fund revenues and expenses are approximately equal.

The premiums can also include a provision for expected catastrophe losses.

If the premiums satisfy either of these criteria, then the internal service insurance fund may recognize revenue upon billing the insured funds and the insured funds may recognize an expenditure. If, however, the premiums exceed the amount that satisfies these criteria, the excess should be reported as a nonreciprocal transfer-out from the insured funds to the internal service fund. If the premiums are less, the resultant deficit in the internal service fund should be charged back to the insured funds and reported as an expenditure in those funds.

Consistent with FASB Statement No. 5, *Accounting for Contingencies*, the internal service insurance fund should recognize its expenses for claims expenses and liabilities when two conditions hold:

- It is probable that an asset has been impaired or a liability incurred.
- The amount of loss can be reasonably estimated.

EXAMPLE   *Insurance Premiums*

A government maintains an internal service fund to insure all government vehicles for loss and damage and for liability to third parties. It establishes premiums using actuarial techniques intended to ensure that over time the premiums will cover claims, administrative expenses, and catastrophic losses. In a particular year, the internal service fund bills the general fund $260,000 and the utility (enterprise) fund $130,000—a total of $390,000. Of this amount, $25,000 is for potential catastrophes. During the year it incurs $360,000 in claims losses, none of which resulted from catastrophes.

The internal service fund would recognize as revenues the entire $390,000 in premiums:

Cash	$390,000	
Revenues—insurance premiums		$390,000

To record premium revenue

At the same time, the general fund would recognize an expenditure of $260,000 and the utility fund an expense of $130,000.

The internal service fund would also recognize claims expenses for the actual $360,000 of losses:

Expenses—claims	$360,000	
Claims liability (or cash)		$360,000

To record losses incurred

As a consequence of closing the revenue and expense accounts at year-end, net assets will increase by $30,000. Of this sum, $25,000 is attributable to the premiums for the potential catastrophes. GASB standards direct that this amount should be designated, in the notes to the statements, as intended for catastrophes.

USING THE GENERAL FUND Suppose that, instead of using an internal service fund, the government accounts for its self-insurance activities in the general fund. How would the accounting differ?

GASB Standards

The GASB stipulates that when self-insurance activities are accounted for in a general fund, the amount of premium revenue recognized by the general fund should be limited to actual claims expenditures (i.e., those losses that satisfy the criteria of FASB Statement No. 5). Correspondingly, total expenditures and expenses recognized by the general fund and any other insured funds should be limited to the same amounts. Any amounts charged to the other funds (including the general fund itself) in excess of the actual claims should be accounted for as nonreciprocal transfers. The differences in accounting principles are justified according to the GASB, because the general fund transfers neither risk nor actual resources to either an outside party or to a separate fund.

E X A M P L E   *Self-Insurance in a General Fund*
• •

Assume the same facts as in the previous example, except that the insurance activities are accounted for in the general fund. The general fund would recognize the $360,000 of claims, as would an internal service fund (except that the amount would be recorded as an expenditure rather than an expense). In contrast, the maximum that the insurance department could recognize as premium revenues from the other departments would now be $360,000—the amount of the actual claims. Of this, one-third ($130,000/$390,000), or $120,000, would be attributable to the utility fund and the remaining two-thirds ($240,000) to the insured general fund departments.

However, the utility fund was billed for $130,000, not $120,000. The general fund would report the additional $10,000 as a nonreciprocal transfer-in, rather than as a revenue. Correspondingly, the utility fund would recognize a premium expense of $120,000 and a nonreciprocal transfer-out of $10,000.

The insurance department would also record the billings to the insured departments accounted for in the general fund. Because the insurance department is also accounted for in the general fund, there would be no impact on the financial statements. Intrafund revenues and expenditures would net out.

HOW ARE PROPRIETARY FUNDS REPORTED?

The reporting of enterprise funds is relatively straightforward. That of internal service funds is more complex.

ENTERPRISE FUNDS: GOVERNMENT-WIDE STATEMENTS Recall from Chapter 3 that the government-wide statement of net assets contains two columns under the heading primary government. (See Table 3-1 for an illustration.) One is for governmental activities, and the other for business-type activities. The balances of the various enterprise funds are consolidated and reported in the column for business-type activities.

The government-wide statement of activities reports on revenues and expenses by functions. As discussed and illustrated in Chapter 3 (Table 3-2), the first column of the statement lists the expenses for each function in separate sections for governmental and business-type activities. The expense column is followed by one or more columns for the program revenues—those, such as fees for goods or services and restricted grants, that are directly associated with the functions. The net expenses or revenues (the differences between the expenses and the program revenues) are shown in one of two columns—one for governmental activities, the other for business-type activities. The net expenses or revenues of enterprise funds are, of course, shown in the column for business-type activities.

The government-wide statements consolidate the government's funds and report on the government as a whole—not as a series of independent funds. Therefore, interfund revenues, expenses/expenditures, transfers, receivables, and payables generally must be eliminated.

Suppose, for example, that a city's electric utility sold electricity to departments accounted for in its general fund. At year-end, the utility (enterprise) fund had a receivable of $100,000 from the general fund—and correspondingly, the general fund had a payable of $100,000 to the utility fund. From the perspective of the government as a whole, both the receivable and the payable would have to be eliminated on the government-wide statement of net assets. The government cannot owe money to itself. Nevertheless, the government-wide statements distinguish between business-type and governmental activities and report them in separate columns. The enterprise fund does have a receivable from the general fund, and the general fund does have a payable to the enterprise fund. These must be shown in the columns for each activity, yet they cannot be shown in the "total" column—that which presents the balances for the government as a whole. How can a government show the receivables and payables in the individual columns but not in the totals column?

GASB Standards

Interfund receivables and payables may be reported either on a single line—with one a positive amount and the other a negative amount—or on separate lines with the amounts being excluded from the "total" column. Thus, for example, if shown on a single line the amounts might be reported among the assets as follows:

	Governmental Activities	Business-type Activities	Total
Internal balances	($100,000)	$100,000	—

If shown on two lines (one in the asset section, the other in the liability section) they would be presented as:

	Governmental Activities	Business-type Activities	Total
Interfund receivable		$100,000	—
Interfund payable	$100,000		—

In concept, the sales of a utility fund and resulting purchases by a general fund should also be eliminated. However, the units or departments accounted for in the general fund are usually but a few of many customers of the utility department, and they acquire electricity that they would otherwise have purchased from outside parties. Thus to eliminate the sales and purchases would understate both the operating costs of the governmental activities and the revenues of the business-type activities. Per the GASB, therefore, interfund services provided and used between functions need not be eliminated.

ENTERPRISE FUNDS: FUND STATEMENTS In the section of the basic financial statements containing the fund statements, the three required statements of proprietary funds (statement of net assets; statement of revenues, expenses, and changes in fund net assets; and statement of cash flows) are presented separately, after the statements of governmental funds. Each major enterprise fund is reported in a separate column, as if it were an independent entity. Hence, no eliminations are necessary. Correspondingly, in the statements of the funds that received the services, the interfund activities would be accounted for as if they were transactions with external parties.

INTERNAL SERVICE FUNDS: GOVERNMENT-WIDE STATEMENTS The government-wide statements present an overview of the government as a whole and, hence, consolidate the various individual funds. Inasmuch as internal service funds exist to service departments that are accounted for in other funds, interfund receivables, payables, as well as the related revenues and expenses, must be eliminated in the consolidation process.

EXAMPLE *Eliminating Interfund Balances and Transactions of Internal Service Funds*
. . . .

Suppose that a data processing internal service fund provided service to other departments, all of which were accounted for in the general fund or other governmental funds. The data processing fund billed the other funds for $10 million, the full cost of providing its services. At year-end it had uncollected receivables of $2 million from the other funds. These transactions would have been reflected in the data processing fund and the various governmental funds as follows:

	Data Processing Internal Service Fund	Various Governmental Funds	Total
Sales revenues	$10		$10
Expenses/expenditures	10	$10	20
Accounts receivable	$2		$2
Accounts payable		$2	2

From the perspective of the government as a whole, the cost of providing the data processing services was only $10 million—not the total of $20 million that is reported in the "total" column above. Correspondingly, the government as a whole had zero revenue from the interfund "sales" and no receivables and payables from the amounts that one department owed to another. Therefore, both the sales revenues and the expenses/expenditures must be reduced by $10 million, and both the receivables and payables must be reduced by $2 million.

Internal service funds do not exist to earn a profit; their billings to other departments should reflect actual costs. Accordingly, their revenues should equal their expenses, and both can be eliminated in their entirety in the consolidation process. In fact, even if the rates were not set to equalize revenues and expenses, they should be retroactively adjusted so that the internal service funds just break even. The end result will be that all the costs of operating the internal service funds can be *charged back to*, and reported as expenditures or expenses by, the funds that were the consumers of the internal service funds' goods and services.

By contrast, the assets and the liabilities other than interfund receivables and payables would not be eliminated in the consolidation process. These include cash, capital assets, and obligations to outsiders. A question arises, therefore, as to whether these assets and liabilities (and the resultant net assets) should be classified as governmental or business-type activities in the government-wide statements. Internal service funds are proprietary funds. Nevertheless, they typically provide services mainly to departments that are accounted for in the general fund or other governmental funds.

GASB Standards

In Statement No. 34,[8] the GASB has prescribed that internal service fund balances that are not eliminated in the consolidation process ordinarily should be reported in the *governmental activities* column of the government-wide statement of net assets. However, if the internal service fund provides services solely or mainly to enterprise funds, then the government should report the balances in the business-type activities column.

The consequence of these standards is that, in the government-wide statements, the revenues of the internal service fund and the offsetting expenses/expenditures of the service recipient funds are eliminated in the consolidation process. The expenses of the internal service fund are charged back to the service recipient funds and are thereby aggregated with their applicable functional expenses. In the usual situation, that in which the internal service fund provides services mainly to departments accounted for in governmental funds, internal service fund activities are considered governmental activities. Therefore, any receivables from, and payables to, *governmental funds* are eliminated in the consolidation process. By contrast, because business-type activities are reported in a separate column, receivables from, and payables to, *enterprise funds* are not eliminated. They are included, as appropriate, in either the governmental or the business-type activities column but excluded from the "total" column. That is, they are reported in a manner similar to that in the earlier illustration in which a utility fund had a receivable from the general fund. At the same time, internal service fund assets and liabilities, such as capital assets and payables to outsiders, that are not eliminated in the consolidation process are reported in the governmental activities column.

INTERNAL SERVICE FUNDS: FUND STATEMENTS In the funds statements, internal service funds are categorized as proprietary funds. In each of the three required proprietary fund statements, data for all internal service funds are aggregated into a single column. (See Tables 3-7 and 3-8 in Chapter 3 and Table 9-1 in this chapter for illustrations.) The internal service funds column is presented after the totals column for enterprise funds. However, even though internal service funds are incorporated into the proprietary fund statements, they appear under a heading "Governmental Activities—Internal Service Funds." Moreover, owing to the different characteristics of enterprise and internal service funds, the proprietary fund statements do *not* include a total column for all proprietary funds.

---

[8]Statement No. 34, para. 62.

WHAT DO USERS WANT TO KNOW ABOUT REVENUE DEBT?

In Chapter 8 we highlighted some of the data that investors and other statement users look to in assessing a government's ability to repay its general obligation debt. In this section we do the same as to revenue debt.

Revenue bonds encompass the debt that will be paid from a dedicated revenue stream produced by the assets that the debt financed. These assets typically include utilities, convention centers, toll roads, hospitals and other health care centers, university dormitories, stadiums, parking facilities, and similar fee-generating projects.

In light of the vast array of entities that issue revenue bonds, it is difficult to generalize as to the data needed by users. The salient fiscal characteristics of a small community health center, for example, may differ considerably from those of a large state university. Nevertheless, some types of information are central to the evaluation of any revenue-backed security. Among the types identified by Standard & Poor's, a leading bond rating service, are the following:[9]

- *Security Provisions.* Revenue bonds are secured by specific fees or taxes. These may include user charges (such as highway tolls, college tuition, and hospital billings) or dedicated taxes (such as a sales tax restricted for debt service or a gasoline tax restricted for highway improvements).
- *Competition.* Revenue bonds, unlike general obligation bonds, are often used to support activities that are competitive. For example, hospitals, universities, airports, parking garages, and museums compete with other public and private institutions that provide similar services. Whereas general obligation bonds are backed by the full faith and credit of the government—and thus, by its power to tax—revenue bonds are backed only by specified revenues. Competition introduces a credit risk not normally associated with general obligation bonds.
- *Service area.* Projects financed by revenue bonds do not necessarily serve areas that are within predetermined geographic boundaries. For example, a university may attract students from throughout the world. A hospital may compete statewide for patients. The broader the geographic base of a revenue stream, the less likely it is to be affected by local economic downturns.
- *Revenue-raising flexibility.* Some user charges can be raised more easily than others. For example, a city may be constitutionally prohibited from increasing a restricted sales tax, whereas a hospital may have considerable flexibility in increasing patient charges. The greater the revenue-raising flexibility, the less the credit risk.

The specific information needed depends, of course, on the nature of the institution. Table 9-2 outlines the factors that Standard & Poor's deems important in evaluating the revenue debt of municipal parking facilities. The list is especially notable for the prominence of nonfinancial factors. It shows that even to assess the ability of the bond issuer to service its debt—the primary concern of a rating service—users must look beyond conventional financial statements.

---

[9]The information requirements presented in this section were drawn from *Standard & Poor's Public Finance Criteria 2000* (New York: Standard & Poor's Ratings Services, 2000), page 106.

TABLE 9-2
Factors Focused on (and documents required) by Standard & Poor's in Evaluating the Revenue Bonds of Municipal Parking Facilities

Basic documents
- Official statement
- Bond resolution or trust indenture
- Five years financial audits
- Consultants' feasibility studies
- Capital program
- Current budget

Operational data
- Description of existing facilities
- Service area
- Occupancy rates
- Description of type of use (monthly, daily, or hourly)
- History of rates and rate increases
- Proposed rate schedule
- Rate setting procedure
- Competing facilities (location, number of spaces, and rates)
- Collection and enforcement procedures

Economic data
- Description of area economy, including:
  - Leading employers
  - Employment and labor force trends
  - Wealth and income indicators
  - Retail sales activity
  - Building activity

Source: *Standard & Poor's Public Finance Criteria 2000* (New York, Standard & Poor's, 2000), page 134.

QUESTIONS FOR REVIEW AND DISCUSSION

1. You are the independent CPA for a medium-sized city. The city manager asks your guidance as to whether, according to generally accepted accounting principles, the municipal golf course should be accounted for in an enterprise fund. What would be your response?

2. How would you compare the accounting for enterprise funds with that of (a) businesses and (b) governmental funds? Summarize the reasons both for and against accounting for enterprise funds differently than governmental funds.

3. Business accounting is governed by the pronouncements of the Financial Accounting Standards Board. Enterprise funds are generally accounted for using the accounting principles applicable to businesses. Must, therefore, a government adhere to all pronouncements of the FASB in accounting for its enterprise funds? Explain.

4. Although proprietary fund accounting is similar to business accounting, there are considerable differences in standards pertaining to the statement of cash flows. What are the main differences?

5. A government accounts for a municipal landfill in an enterprise fund. How will it determine how much to charge as an expense (and add to a liability) each year that the landfill is in use? Suppose, instead, that it accounts for the landfill in a governmental fund. What will be the amount charged as an expenditure?

6. For what types of activities are internal service funds used to account? Provide several examples. Is a government *required* to account for the activities you cite in an internal service fund, or may it account for them instead in its general fund?

7. Self-insurance, it is often said, is an oxymoron. Why? If it is, what are the implications as to whether a government should be permitted to recognize self-insurance premiums as a general fund expenditure when paid to an internal service fund?

8. In what way must a government account for premium revenue differently if it accounts for self-insurance in an internal service fund rather than its general fund?

9. You have been given the responsibility of assigning a bond rating to a municipal parking garage. Indicate the type of information that you would consider essential to your assessment, but which is unlikely to be reported on in the facility's fund financial statements.

10. In government-wide statements enterprise funds are reported differently than internal service funds. Explain and justify.

11. Enterprise funds are also reported differently than internal service funds in the proprietary fund statements of net assets and of revenues, expenses, and changes in fund net assets. Explain.

EXERCISES AND PROBLEMS

9-1

Select the *best* answer.

1. What basis of accounting do enterprise and internal service funds use?

	Enterprise	Internal Service
a.	Modified accrual	Modified accrual
b.	Modified accrual	Full accrual
c.	Full accrual	Modified accrual
d.	Full accrual	Full accrual

2. Which of the following is *not* a GASB-required statement for proprietary funds?

   a. Statement of net assets
   b. Statement of revenues, expenses, and changes in fund net assets
   c. Statement of cash flows
   d. Statement of changes in fund net assets

3. A government need not necessarily account for an activity in an enterprise fund even though it

   a. charges fees for the activity and those fees are material in amount
   b. finances the activity solely with revenue debt
   c. is required by law or policy to recover the cost of the activity by fees
   d. opts to establish pricing policies so as to recover its costs, including capital costs

4. Except for FASB pronouncements that have been overridden by specific GASB pronouncements, governments, in their enterprise funds, must

   a. apply all FASB pronouncements, irrespective of when issued
   b. apply all FASB pronouncements issued prior to November 30, 1989, and either all or none of the pronouncements issued after that date
   c. apply all FASB pronouncements issued subsequent to November 30, 1989
   d. apply all FASB pronouncements issued prior to November 30, 1989, and may apply pronouncements of their choosing issued after that date

5. Tap fees should be accounted for as

   a. capital contributions
   b. ordinary revenues
   c. a combination of capital contributions and ordinary revenues
   d. extraordinary items

6. Landfill closure and postclosure costs should be recognized as expenses

   a. in the periods incurred
   b. in the period that the landfill is closed
   c. in the periods that the landfill is in operation
   d. in the period that the landfill is opened

7. Which of the following would *not* be included in the computation of the amount to be recognized as a landfill closure expense?

   a. the total estimated closure costs
   b. the capacity of the landfill
   c. the proportion of capacity used in prior years
   d. an appropriate discount rate

8. A city maintains a staff of internal auditors. It may properly account for its internal audit costs in an internal service fund only if

   a. it is required to do so by state or city statutes or regulations

   b. the internal audit activity is carried out in a discrete organizational unit

   c. it charges a fee to the city departments for which it provides service

   d. a GASB pronouncement specifies that internal audit activity is eligible for internal service fund accounting

9. A government accounts for its self-insurance activities in an internal service fund. Per GASB guidelines, the premiums charged to other funds

   a. must, in total and over time, cover the actual losses incurred by the fund

   b. cannot include a provision for catastrophic losses

   c. must be competitive with what an independent insurer would charge

   d. must be at least as great as the losses incurred each year

10. If a government accounts for self-insurance activities in its general fund, then premiums charged in excess of actual claims should be accounted for as

   a. ordinary revenues

   b. an offset against claims expenditures

   c. an increase in claims reserves

   d. a nonreciprocal transfer-in

9-2

Select the *best* answer.

1. A city's general fund has an outstanding payable to its electric utility, which is accounted for in an enterprise fund. The utility has a corresponding receivable from the general fund. In the city's government-wide statement of net assets, which would be correct?

   a. The payable and the corresponding receivable would be eliminated in the consolidation process and thus not reported.

   b. The payable may be aggregated with payables to an internal service fund and reported as "payables to proprietary funds."

   c. The payable should be reported in the governmental activities column and the receivable in the business-type activities column.

   d. The payable and the receivable would each be reported in the "totals" column, but would not be reported in either the governmental activities column or the business-type activities column.

2. A city's general fund has an outstanding payable to its vehicle repair internal service fund, which has a corresponding receivable from the general fund. In the city's government-wide statements, which would be correct?

   a. The payable and the corresponding receivable would be eliminated in the consolidation process and thus not reported.

   b. The payable may be aggregated with payables to an enterprise fund and reported as "payables to proprietary funds."

   c. The payable would be reported in the governmental activities column and the receivable in the business-type activities column.

   d. The payable and the receivable would each be reported in the "totals" column, but would not be reported in either the governmental activities column or the business-type activities column.

3. Which of the following projects is a state university most likely to finance with revenue bonds rather than general obligation bonds?

   a. a football stadium

   b. an outdoor swimming pool

   c. an intramural field house

   d. a boathouse for its rowing team

4. In what way would the statement of cash flows of a government-owned electric utility differ from that of a privately owned counterpart?

   a. It would not include a category for operating activities.

   b. It would have separate categories for cash flows from noncapital financing activities and cash flows from capital and related financing activities.

   c. It would not include a category for cash flows from investing activities.

   d. It would include a category for cash flows from other nonoperating activities.

5. A government is considering whether to account for a vehicle repair service in an internal service fund or in its general fund. In a year in which the vehicle repair service did not acquire any capital assets, the amount charged as expenses or expenditures for vehicle repair-related costs would likely

a. be the same, irrespective of which fund is used

b. be greater if the general fund were used

c. be greater if an internal service fund were used

d. be the same, irrespective of which fund is used, as long as the internal service fund adopted all FASB pronouncements issued prior to November 30, 1989

6. A school district's internal service fund has cash on hand at year-end of $2 million. On its government-wide financial statements, this amount would be reported as an asset in the

a. governmental activities and total columns

b. business-type activities and total columns

c. total column only

d. business-type activities column only

7. In its first year of operations, a self-insurance internal service fund billed the general fund $500,000 for premiums. Of this amount, $75,000 was intended for catastrophes. During the year, the insurance fund paid out $380,000 in claims, none of which was for catastrophes. As a consequence of these transactions, the insurance fund would report on its statement of net assets

a. net assets of $120,000

b. net assets of $45,000

c. reserve for catastrophes of $45,000

d. claims reserves of $120,000

8. A city makes an interest payment of $6 million on its utility fund revenue bonds. In the utility fund statement of cash flows, the payment would be reflected as a cash flow from

a. operating activities

b. noncapital financing activities

c. capital and related financing activities

d. investing activities

9. A utility fund temporarily invests the proceeds from the issuance of revenue bonds in U.S. Treasury bills and receives interest of $300,000. In the utility fund statement of cash flows, the receipt would be reflected as a cash flow from

a. operating activities

b. noncapital financing activities

c. capital and related financing activities

d. investing activities

10. A city's transportation service, which is accounted for in an enterprise fund, has outstanding $10 million in revenue bonds. The bonds are also guaranteed by the city itself.

These bonds should be reported as a liability in

a. both the governmental fund statements and the proprietary fund statements, as well as both the business-type activities column and the governmental activities column of the government-wide statements

b. only the proprietary fund statements and the business-type activities column of the government-wide statements

c. only the governmental fund statements and the governmental activities column of the government-wide statements

d. only the proprietary fund statements

9-3

Internal service funds are accounted for similarly to businesses.

William County opted to account for its duplication service center in an internal service fund. Previously the center had been accounted for in the county's general fund. During the first month in which it was accounted for as an internal service fund, the center engaged in the following transactions.

a. Five copiers were transferred to the internal service fund from the government's general capital assets. At the time of transfer they had a book value (net of accumulated depreciation) of $70,000.

b. The general fund made an initial cash contribution of $35,000 to the internal service fund.

c. The center borrowed $270,000 from a local bank to finance the purchase of additional equipment and renovation of its facilities. It issued a three-year note.

d. It purchased equipment for $160,000 and paid contractors $100,000 for improvements to its facilities.

e. It billed the county clerk's office $5,000 for printing services, of which the office remitted $2,500.

f. It incurred, and paid in cash, various operating expenses of $9,000.

g. The fund recognized depreciation of $1,500 on its equipment and $900 on the improvements to its facilities.

1. Prepare journal entries in the internal service fund to record the transactions.

2. Comment on the main differences resulting from the shift from the general fund to an internal service fund in how the center's assets and liabilities would be accounted for and reported.

9-4

Cash flows of a government must be presented in four categories, rather than the three categories used by businesses.

The following list was taken from the statement of cash flows of Grand Junction's internal service fund. All amounts are in thousands.

Cash on hand at beginning of year	$122
Interest from investments	45
Wages and salaries paid	(3,470)
Purchases of supplies	(1,650)
Collections (for services) from other funds	6,380
Interest on long-term debt	(150)
Repayment of loans to other funds	(880)
Purchase of capital assets	(900)
Proceeds of revenue bonds	800
Purchases of investments	(440)
Proceeds from sale of capital assets	23
Proceeds from sale of investments	33
Loans from other funds	600

Recast the list into a statement of cash flows, adding a line for cash on hand at the end of the year.

9-5

The insurance expense recognized by an enterprise fund depends on the type of carrier.

The water and waste-water utility (enterprise) funds of three cities each paid $1 million in casualty insurance premiums. City A is insured by a small independent insurance company. City B is self-insured and accounts for its insurance activities in an internal service fund. City C is self-insured and accounts for its insurance activities in its general fund.

Each of the insurers collected a total of $10 million in premiums from all of the parties that it insures, including the city utility funds. Of this amount, each paid out $8 million in actual claims. The balance was held in reserve for major catastrophes.

Prepare the journal entry that each of the three utility funds should make to record its insurance payment and expense for the year. Comment on any differences.

9-6

The differences in accounting for an activity in an internal service fund rather than the general fund may be striking.

A school district establishes a vehicle-repair shop that provides service to other departments, all of which are accounted for in its general fund. During its first year of operations, the shop engages in the following transactions.

- It purchases equipment at a cost of $24 million and issues long-term notes for the purchase price. The useful life of the equipment is eight years, with no residual value.
- It purchases supplies at a cost of $4 million. Of these, it uses $3 million. In its governmental funds, the district accounts for supplies using the purchases method.
- It incurs $13 million in other operating costs.
- It bills other departments for $19 million.

For purposes of external reporting, school district officials are considering two options:

- Account for the vehicle-repair shop in an internal service fund.
- Account for the vehicle-repair shop in the general fund.

1. For each of the following items, indicate the amounts that would be reported in the year-end financial statements of (1) the internal service fund, assuming that the school district selected the first option and (2) the general fund, assuming that it selected the second option.
   a. Billings to other departments (revenues)
   b. Cost of supplies (expense or expenditure)
   c. Expenses or expenditures relating to the acquisition or use of equipment
   d. Other operating costs
   e. Equipment (asset)
   f. Accumulated depreciation
   g. Inventory (asset)
   h. Notes payable
   i. Reserve for inventory

2. What would be the total expenses reported in the internal service fund, assuming that the school district selected the first option?

3. What would be the total amount of expenditures reported in the general fund, assuming that the school district (1) selected the first option; (2) selected the second option?

4. What would be the reported revenue and expenses relating to the vehicle-repair shop in the district's government-wide statements? Would it matter whether the district accounted for the shop in an internal service fund or the general fund?

9-7

Internal service funds can be used to reduce general fund expenditures.

A city maintains an internal audit department and accounts for it in its general fund. In the coming year, the department will purchase $300,000 of computer and other office equipment, all of which will be paid for out of current resources (i.e., not with debt).

City officials have given top priority to reducing general fund expenditures. To that end, the city comptroller has proposed accounting for the internal audit department in an internal service fund rather than the general fund.

As envisioned by the comptroller, the audit department would bill each of the city's departments (all of which are accounted for in the general fund) for each audit performed. Fees would be established so that they would cover all audit department costs. The fund would be established by a nonreciprocal transfer of $300,000 from the general fund to cover the cost of the new equipment.

The city estimates that, for the coming year, the audit department's operating costs, excluding any costs relating to the new equipment, will be $1,600,000. The equipment is expected to have a useful life of five years.

1. Assume that the city accepts the comptroller's suggestion. Prepare journal entries in the internal service fund to record the following:
   a. the transfer-in of the $300,000
   b. the acquisition of the equipment
   c. the operating and other costs
   d. the billings to, and collection of cash from, the general fund

2. Prepare journal entries in the general fund to record:
   a. the transfer-out of the $300,000
   b. the billings from, and payment of cash to, the internal service fund

3. Would the establishment of the internal service fund result in a decrease in overall government costs (e.g., cash outflows)? Would it result in a reduction in reported general fund expenditures? Explain.

4. Suppose that in the following year, the city does not plan to acquire additional capital assets. Comment on whether reported general fund expenditures would be greater if the internal service fund were established than if it were not.

9-8

A city's financial statements and related disclosures as to one of its internal service funds raise intriguing questions.

The statements of net assets and of revenues, expenses, and changes in fund net assets of a medium-sized city's "Support Services" internal service fund are as follows.

Support Services Fund
Statement of Fund Net Assets

Assets

Pooled Investments and Cash	$ 546,463
Prepaid Expenses	239,582
Total Current Assets	786,045
Property, Plant, and Equipment	3,587,524
Less Accumulated Depreciation	(2,007,684)
Net Property, Plant, and Equipment	1,579,840
Total Assets	$2,365,885

Liabilities

Accounts Payable	$ 39,034
Accrued Payroll	854,956
Accrued Compensated Absences	291,470
Due to Other Funds	89,876
Total Current Liabilities	1,275,336
Bonds Payable	1,049,902
Total Liabilities	$2,325,238

Net Assets

Invested in Capital Assets, Net of Related Debt	529,938
Unrestricted	(489,291)
Total Net Assets	$ 40,647

Statement of Revenues, Expenses, and Changes in Fund Net Assets

Billings to Other Departments	$20,340,426
Operating Expenses	
Operating Expenses before Depreciation	32,228,281
Depreciation	122,544
Total Expenses	32,350,825
Operating Income (loss) before Transfers	(12,010,399)
Transfers-in	9,083,006
Increase (decrease) in Net Assets	(2,927,393)
Net Assets, Beginning of Year	2,968,040
Net Assets, End of Year	$ 40,647

The notes to the financial statements provide a limited amount of additional information as to the Support Services Fund:

- The fund includes the activities of the various support service departments.
- The fund provides services exclusively to departments accounted for in the general fund.
- The transfer-in was from the general fund.

The city's general fund reported the following (in millions):

Revenues	$196
Expenditures	227
Excess (deficiency) of Revenues over Expenditures	(31)
Transfers-in	43
Transfers-out	(9)
Net Transfers-in	34
Net Change in Fund Balance	3
Fund Balance, Beginning of Year	25
Fund Balance, End of Year	$ 28

1. The financial statements do not provide additional information as to what constitute support services. What are some likely activities that support services could include?

2. What is the significance of the deficit in "unrestricted net assets" on the internal service fund's statement of net assets? What concern might the deficit raise as to the proper application of accounting principles?

3. What is the significance of the internal service fund's operating loss as it relates to the general fund?

4. If you were the city's independent auditor, what changes in the billing practices of the internal service fund might you propose that the city consider?

5. In the city's government-wide statements, how would the revenues and expenses of the internal service fund be reported? Which of the revenues and expenses or expenditures of the internal service fund and the general fund would be eliminated?

6. Suppose that the city accounted for the support services in its general fund, instead of an internal service fund.

a. Approximately how much more or less would the general fund's net change in fund balance have been?

b. Which of the internal service fund's expenses would not be reported as general fund expenditures?

c. Which of the internal service fund's assets and liabilities would not be reported as general fund assets or liabilities?

9-9

Landfill costs must be reported as expenses during the periods of use—but only if an enterprise fund is used.

In 2005, a city opens a municipal landfill, which it will account for in an enterprise fund. It estimates capacity to be 6 million cubic feet and usable life to be twenty years. To close the landfill, the municipality expects to incur labor, material, and equipment costs of $3 million. Thereafter, it expects to incur an additional $7 million of costs to monitor and maintain the site.

1. In 2005, the city uses 300,000 cubic feet of the landfill. Prepare the journal entry to record the expense for closure and postclosure costs.

2. In 2006, it again uses 300,000 cubic feet of the landfill. It revises its estimates of available volume to 5.8 million cubic feet and of closure and postclosure costs to $10.2 million. Prepare the journal entry to record the expense for closure and postclosure costs.

3. In 2024, the final year of operation, it uses 350,000 cubic feet of the landfill. The actual capacity has proven to be only 5 million cubic feet and closing costs are now estimated to be $15 million. Through the year 2023, the municipality had used 4,650,000 cubic feet and had recorded $14.2 million in closure and postclosure costs. In 2024, it actually incurs $5 million in closure costs, the entire amount of which is paid in cash.

a. Prepare the journal entry to record the 2024 expense for estimated closure and postclosure costs.

b. Prepare the journal entry to record the actual closure costs paid in 2024.

4. Suppose, instead, that the landfill was accounted for in the general fund. Indicate how the entries would differ from those in the enterprise fund.

9-10

Financial statements must be adjusted to assure proper accounting of internal service fund activities.

Sun City accounts for its telecommunication services in an internal service fund. In a recent year, its records indicated the following:

Billings to units accounted for in governmental funds	$400,000

Billings to units accounted for in
proprietary funds   100,000

Year-end accounts receivable
from units accounted for in
governmental funds   25,000

Year-end accounts receivable
from units accounted for in
proprietary funds   10,000

Per city policy, the telecommunications department bills other departments for the actual cost of providing its services.

1. How would each of the following be reported in the city's government-wide statement of net assets and statement of activities?

   a. the billings of the internal service fund (and offsetting purchases of services by other funds)

   b. the year-end accounts receivable and payable

2. How would each of the following be reported in the balance sheets and statements of revenues and expenditures or expenses of the individual governmental and proprietary funds to which the internal service fund provided services and of the internal service fund itself?

   a. The billings from the internal service fund

   b. The year-end accounts payable and receivable

3. Internal service funds are classified as proprietary funds. Yet in the government-wide statements, their assets and liabilities that have not been eliminated in the consolidation process are generally reported in the governmental activities column. How can you justify this apparent inconsistency?

9-11

Exploring Orlando's financial report

Refer to the financial statements of the City of Orlando in Chapter 3 and to Table 9-1 in this chapter.

1. What kinds of business-type activities does Orlando engage in? Are these activities accounted for in major or nonmajor enterprise funds?

2. Orlando's government-wide statement of activities reports that the police function and the Stormwater Utility each had approximately the same amount of revenues ($10 million) from charges for services. Why, then, is the police function reported as a governmental activity, whereas the Stormwater Utility is reported as a business-type activity?

3. Answer the following questions about the Orlando Centroplex.

   a. What was the reported amount of cash and cash equivalents (e.g., demand deposits)? How much of this amount is classified as restricted assets?

   b. What was the principal cash inflow? What was the principal cash outflow?

   c. Did cash and cash equivalents increase or decrease during the year? By how much?

   d. Which of the four categories of cash flows required per GASB Statement No. 9 resulted in net cash inflows? Which resulted in net cash outflows?

4. The proprietary funds statement of revenues, expenses, and changes in fund net assets reports that the Orlando Centroplex incurred interest expense of $546,217. How much of this amount was for debt related to capital assets? How can you tell?

5. Based on the information reported in the proprietary funds financial statements, what kinds of activities do you think Orlando accounts for in internal service funds?

6. The proprietary funds statement of net assets reports arbitrage rebate payable in the amount of $82.2 million as a liability of internal service funds. To whom is this amount owed? How was the liability incurred? (*Hint*: Refer to the discussion of arbitrage in Chapter 6.)

CHAPTER 10

Permanent Funds and Fiduciary Funds

When one thinks of government assets, it is natural to conjure up images of highways, buildings, and police cars. In fact, however, governments are some of the nation's largest holders of stocks, bonds, and similar securities. Government pension funds, public university and hospital endowments, and state investment pools are among the most powerful and influential of corporate investors.

This chapter is directed to **permanent funds** and **fiduciary funds**. Permanent funds are used to account for *nonexpendable* resources (endowments) that benefit activities of the government itself (i.e., are held for public purposes), rather than activities of outside parties. Related *expendable* resources (i.e., the income generated by permanent fund investments) would generally be accounted for in a special revenue fund or the general fund, depending on whether the income is restricted or unrestricted.

Fiduciary funds, by contrast, are maintained to account for both expendable resources and endowments that governments hold as trustees or agents for individuals, private organizations, or other governments. Fiduciary funds are often referred to as trust funds. **Trust fund** is a generic term for any fund in which one party (a trustee) holds resources for the benefit of another party, usually under the terms of a formal agreement.

Permanent and fiduciary (trust) funds are of critical concern to both statement preparers and statement users, not only because they may contain vast amounts of resources, but also because their assets are typically liquid and therefore subject to risk of loss both through fraud and reduction in value. Moreover, the resources may be relied upon by the governments themselves as well as their employees and other constituents as a main source of current and future income.

WHAT ARE ENDOWMENTS?

Endowments are assets donated to a government (or not-for-profit) with the stipulation that only the income earned from the assets can be expended. Typically, the gift principal must be preserved in perpetuity. However, in some endowments, called *term endowments*, the principal can be expended after a specified number of years. The income earned from investing endowed assets may be restricted by the donors for specific programs or activities or it may be unrestricted.

The following are a few examples of endowments maintained by governments:

- University endowments are major sources of operating revenues. Some take the form of *chairs* or *professorships* and support the teaching and research activities of specific faculty members. Other endowments help to finance scholarships, teaching awards, research, or general operations.

- Public school endowments provide support for specific activities, such as a school band or science enrichment programs.
- Municipal endowments support museums, nature centers, performing arts centers, and parks.

A government endowment is accounted for in either a permanent fund or private-purpose trust (fiduciary) fund, depending on whether it supports activities of the government itself or those of outsiders.

WHAT ARE PERMANENT FUNDS, AND HOW ARE THEY DISTINGUISHED FROM FIDUCIARY FUNDS?

PERMANENT FUNDS Permanent funds are used to account for *nonexpendable* resources (endowment principal) provided by a donor to support the reporting government's own programs—those that benefit either the government itself or its citizenry in general. Only the income of permanent funds can be spent. The principal must be preserved intact, generally in perpetuity. Permanent funds

- support government-owned museums, nature centers, or zoos
- provide for perpetual care of public cemeteries
- supplement the compensation of public university faculty
- provide student financial aid
- fund research at government-owned hospitals

Governments may accumulate earnings from permanent fund investments in the permanent fund until they are to be used for their intended purposes. However, it is preferable that legally expendable earnings be accounted for in an *expendable* fund—generally a special revenue fund. Otherwise, users of the financial statements may conclude that the earnings are permanently unavailable for expenditure when, in fact, they may be available for immediate expenditure.

Per Statement No. 34, permanent funds are classified as *governmental* funds. Accordingly, their measurement focus is on current financial resources and they use a modified accrual basis of accounting. However, as discussed in a subsequent section, given that permanent funds commonly include only financial assets, their revenues and expenditures generally do not differ from those that would be obtained using the full accrual basis of accounting.

Governments report their permanent funds as they do other governmental funds. In the government-wide statements they are included with other governmental funds in the governmental activities columns. In the governmental fund statements, permanent funds are shown in a separate column only if they are considered major funds; otherwise they are included with other nonmajor governmental funds in the "other funds" column.

FIDUCIARY FUNDS Fiduciary funds are used to account for resources held by a government in a trustee or agent capacity, for parties *other than* the government itself. These outside parties include employees, when the resources are held in trust for them individually or their dependents or survivors (e.g., pension funds), other governments, corporations, not-for-profits, and individual citizens. There are four major types of fiduciary funds:

1. **Pension (and other employee benefit) trust funds.** These are used to account for the assets of both defined benefit and defined contribution plans (defined later in this chapter).

2. **Investment trust funds.** These are used to account for *investment pools*—mutual fund-type arrangements in which a sponsoring government (such as a state or county) holds and invests the cash of other governments (such as the cities and towns within the sponsoring government's jurisdiction).

3. **Private-purpose trust funds.** These are trust funds, other than investment pools and pension funds, in which resources are held for the benefit of outsiders. Examples include:

   ● Funds used to account for **escheat property**—inactive bank accounts and the property of the deceased, which are temporarily held by the state until they are either claimed or revert to the state

   ● Scholarship funds to benefit a specific narrowly defined class of students (e.g., those with a specified family name)

   ● Endowments held to benefit needy employees or their families (e.g., a fund for children of slain police officers)

4. **Agency funds.** These are used to account for resources held by a government in a purely custodial capacity (such as when one government collects taxes on behalf of another), ususally for one year or less.

Unlike permanent funds, private-purpose trust funds account for expendable as well as nonexpendable resources. Expendable resources, such as investment earnings, are both accumulated in and expended from the trust fund itself. All resources of the other three types of fiduciary funds are expendable for the purposes defined in the trust or agency agreement.

Fiduciary funds focus on all economic resources and use a full accrual basis of accounting. Inasmuch as their assets are not assets of the government but are held for the benefit of outside parties, fiduciary funds are *excluded* from the government-wide statements. However, fiduciary fund statements should be reported as part of the fund financial statements, following those of the governmental and proprietary funds.

WHY SHOULD ALL ENDOWMENTS BE ACCOUNTED FOR ON A FULL ACCRUAL BASIS—AND WHY AREN'T THEY?

Prior to the issuance of Statement No. 34, governments had traditionally accounted for all endowments in fiduciary funds, whether they were intended to support the activities of the government itself or those of outside parties. All endowments were accounted for on a full accrual basis—and for valid reasons. The full accrual basis helps to assure that endowed assets are not dissipated by inappropriately basing distributions of resources on cash flows rather than economic earnings. For governments this means using the same accounting principles as for their proprietary funds. Most of the transactions in endowment funds involve investments in stocks, bonds, and similar types of securities. Consistent with the accrual basis of accounting, interest and dividends are recognized as earned, not necessarily when cash is received.

Governments may also invest their resources in nonliquid assets, such as commercial real estate or equity securities of nonpublic corporations. The rationale for using the full accrual basis of accounting can best be demonstrated with an illustration that focuses on a depreciable asset.

EXAMPLE *Charging Depreciation*

An endowment receives a contribution of a commercial office building having a fair market value of $20 million. The donor stipulates that only the income, not the principal, may be used to carry out the purposes of the gift. The estimated useful life of the building is twenty years (with no residual value). The endowment expects to earn $1 million per year in rent revenue, net of cash operating expenses. Consistent with the wishes of the donor, the endowment will each year distribute all of its reported income, but none of its principal.

If the endowment were not to charge depreciation, then its reported earnings would be $1 million per year—the rent revenue net of cash operating expenses. It would therefore distribute $1 million per year. By contrast, if it were to charge depreciation, its reported earnings would be zero per year—net rent revenue of $1 million less depreciation of $1 million ($20 million divided by 20 years).

Irrespective of whether the endowment charges depreciation, the economic value of the building at the end of its twenty-year life can be expected to be zero (i.e., it would generate no additional cash receipts), assuming that the initial estimate of useful life were correct.

The following table compares the consequences of charging, and not charging, depreciation over the period of twenty years (in millions):

	Do Not Depreciate	Depreciate
Total assets (building), beginning of period 1	$20	$20
Net cash receipts ($1 million per year)	20	20
Depreciation expense ($1 million per year)	0	20
Net income and hence total cash distributions	20	0
Cash balance, end of period 20	0	20
Market value of building, end of period 20	0	0
Total assets (cash and building), end of period 20	0	20

By charging depreciation, the endowment reduces its reported income—and thus its cash distributions—to reflect the ongoing decline in the value of the building. It thereby preserves the principal at $20 million, consistent with the expectations of the donor. At the end of the twenty-year period, it no longer has a building of value, but it has $20 million in other assets; in this example, cash.

By not charging depreciation, the endowment is, in effect, distributing not only its cash earnings, but also a portion of the building. At the end of the twenty-year economic life of the building it is left with neither a building nor any compensating assets.

Donors may explicitly stipulate that depreciation need not be charged against revenues in determining expendable income. Moreover, in some jurisdictions, in the absence of donor stipulations, the endowment is not required to charge depreciation. Even so, inasmuch as capital assets lose economic value over time, sound accounting would dictate that depreciation be charged and that any distributions in excess of net income (after depreciation) be explicitly reported as distributions of principal.

GASB Standards

Consistent with both tradition and the rationale implied by the depreciation example, GASB requires that governments account for their *fiduciary funds on a full accrual basis*. At the same time, however, it directs that they account for their *permanent funds on a modified accrual basis*.

Why the discrepancy? The resources held in permanent funds generally benefit governmental activities, such as cemeteries, libraries, museums, parks, and scholarships. For that reason, it makes sense to account for them in governmental, rather than proprietary funds (the only other alternative, since accounting for them as fiduciary funds is precluded). If they are to be classified as governmental funds, then, like all other governmental funds, they must be accounted for on a modified, rather than full, accrual basis.

Moreover, the assets accounted for in permanent funds are typically financial assets, mainly marketable securities. Relatively few permanent funds hold depreciable assets. Financial assets are accounted for identically under both the full and modified accrual bases. Interest and dividends are recognized as revenue when they are earned; changes in market values are recognized as they take place. Therefore, in practice, the measurement of earnings remains the same whether the funds are accounted for under the full accrual or the modified accrual basis of accounting.

SHOULD INVESTMENT GAINS BE CONSIDERED NET ADDITIONS TO ENDOWMENT PRINCIPAL OR EXPENDABLE INCOME?

A significant issue pertaining to endowments—whether they are accounted for in permanent funds or in private-purpose trust funds—relates to whether, in the absence of specific donor or legal stipulations, investment gains and losses, including unrealized appreciation, should be included in expendable income or added to nonexpendable principal. The issue has economic consequences that reach far beyond the content of financial reports; it affects the amount of resources available to support the endowment's purpose and is likely to influence the government's investment policies.

Whether gains on the sale of investments (capital gains) or gains from appreciation should be accounted for as income or as an adjustment to endowment fund principal is as much a *legal* question as an accounting one. If a particular policy is required either by donor stipulation or by law, then that policy will dictate accounting practice.

Parties establishing endowments often stipulate that gains from the sale of investments be added to the endowment principal and not incorporated into income. Thus, the gains will not be expendable; they will be available only for reinvestment. However, in the absence of donor stipulations or other applicable legal provisions, the government is generally free to appropriate investment gains for current use.

The widespread practice of accounting for gains as adjustments to endowment principal rather than to income is grounded in the need to protect endowment principal from inflation. In the long term, owing to inflation, the market value of a corporation's common stock can be expected to increase, even in the absence of substantive changes in supply and demand relationships. Thus, when an endowment sells that stock, the gain may represent nothing more than a decrease in the purchasing power of a dollar.

Although it can protect an endowment from inflation, a policy of automatically assigning investment gains to principal rather than income might have the perverse consequence of encouraging governments to adopt less than optimum investment strategies. Consider the following example.

EXAMPLE   *Investment Gains of an Endowment*

A state university's policies require that all investment gains, both realized and unrealized, be added to endowment principal. The university has to choose between one of two stock portfolios as an investment for a $1 million endowment. The first portfolio contains the common stock of high-tech companies that pay either no, or very small, dividends. The returns will be almost entirely from appreciation. The second portfolio contains an extremely conservative mix of bonds, preferred stocks, and the common stocks of well-established industrial firms, all of which pay high dividends or interest. The endowment fund managers estimate that the first portfolio will provide a total return (appreciation plus dividends) of 14 percent per year; the second only 6 percent per year (almost all interest and dividends).

Assuming that the university needs the income to be generated by the endowment, it has little choice but to select the second portfolio; the first provides no accessible resources. Yet the first provides the greater returns and—were the university to periodically liquidate a portion of the portfolio—the greater cash flows.

GASB Standards

GASB pronouncements do not specify whether investment gains should be added to endowment principal or should be made available for expenditure. Therefore, in the absence of specific donor or legal stipulations, the gains should be accounted for in accordance with the decision of the endowment trustees or governing board. If the endowment is in a permanent fund and the gains are considered expendable, then they could be reported initially in the permanent fund and then transferred to a special revenue fund, or they could be reported directly in the special revenue fund. In the government-wide statements, the gains would be included in restricted net assets, unless the donor has not placed restrictions on the use of endowment income. If the endowment is in a private-purpose trust fund, the gains would be reported in that fund, whether considered expendable or added to the endowment principal.

In its Statement No. 34, the GASB requires that governments disclose whether they are permitted to expend the net appreciation on investments of donor-restricted endowments.[1]

---

[1]Statement No. 34, para. 121.

HOW SHOULD PERMANENT FUND INVESTMENT LOSSES BE ACCOUNTED FOR?

The issue of accounting for net investment losses (realized losses and unrealized losses due to market value changes) is the same as the issue for gains, if the endowment is accounted for in a private-purpose trust fund. However, if the endowment is in a permanent fund, the issue of losses is intriguing because investment losses are not the mirror image of investment gains. Whereas a permanent fund's investment gains can be distributed to other funds, investment losses cannot always be recovered from them.

E X A M P L E   *Investment Losses of a Permanent Fund*

At the start of a year, a government has a permanent fund to which donors had contributed $1 million in securities. In addition, as a result of previous investment gains, it has $10,000 of securities that are restricted for programs specified by the endowment donor. These are reported in a special revenue fund. Thus, the total value of its investment portfolio, all of which is restricted, is $1,010,000. During the year, owing to losses on the sale of securities, the value of the portfolio declines by $25,000 to $985,000.

The key question is whether, in the absence of specific legal requirements or donor stipulations, the government should reduce the stated value of permanent fund principal to an amount below the $1 million original contribution or whether it should compensate for the loss from other sources, such as restricted or unrestricted net assets.

As noted previously, in the absence of specific provisions to the contrary, most governments report all types of investment income initially in the permanent fund. If they are permitted to appropriate the gains for expenditure, they then transfer resources to, generally, a special revenue fund. Therefore, if all of the losses were applicable to securities held in the permanent fund, they would reduce the fund by the amount of the losses. If some of the losses were applicable to securities held in the special revenue fund, then they would reduce the balance in that fund. Thus, in the event of losses, the balance in the permanent fund could be reduced below the amount contributed by the donors—the amount they expected to be preserved in perpetuity.

In the example, if the $25,000 in losses were uniform across the portfolio, then $24,752 [$25,000 × ($1,000,000/$1,010,000)] would be assigned to the (nonexpendable) permanent fund and $248 [$25,000 × ($10,000/$1,010,000)] to the (expendable) special revenue fund.

HOW ARE ENDOWMENT TRANSACTIONS RECORDED AND REPORTED?

Governments account for their permanent funds (governmental funds) on a modified accrual basis and their private-purpose trust funds (fiduciary funds) on a full accrual basis. However, in the absence of depreciable assets, the accounting entries would be similar for most transactions of either fund type. Nevertheless, the financial statements would be significantly different. Thus, we shall first present the entries required for a permanent fund and the resulting financial statements for both the permanent fund and its related special revenue fund. We shall then describe the differences in the accounting entries and illustrate the required financial statements if the endowment were accounted for in a private-purpose trust fund.

PERMANENT FUND

EXAMPLE   *Recording Transactions in a Permanent Fund*
....

Establishing the Permanent Fund   A town receives a bequest of $12 million in cash to support its zoo. The donor stipulates that the bequest must be maintained intact in perpetuity. The income from investing the bequest may be expended, but only to support the activities of the zoo. Investment gains, such as gains on the sale of investments and unrealized appreciation in the market value of the investments, must be added to the endowment in an amount sufficient to protect it from declines in the value of the dollar. Gains in excess of that amount may be appropriated for zoo use as if they were ordinary income. The town accounts for zoo operations in a special revenue fund. However, as required by GASB standards, the bequest is accounted for in a permanent fund.

Cash	$12,000,000	
Endowment contributions		$12,000,000

To record the bequest of cash to endow the town zoo

Purchases of Securities   The town purchases common stock for $2 million and bonds having a face value of $10 million. The bonds are twenty-year, 9 percent bonds that yield 10 percent and pay interest annually. They are acquired for $9,149,000. Both securities are recorded at cost.

Common stock	$2,000,000	
Bonds	9,149,000	
Cash		$11,149,000

To record the purchase of stocks and bonds

Interest Revenue   The town collects its first payment of bond interest, $900,000.

Cash	$900,000	
Interest revenue		$900,000

To record collection of the first payment of interest

The interest to be recognized as revenue is based on the cash received. Inasmuch as the bonds will be reported in the financial statements at fair value, the amortization of the bond discount will be incorporated implicitly into the revenue from appreciation. Therefore, no journal entry is required to record the amortization.

Unrealized Appreciation   Owing mainly to decreases in prevailing interest rates, the market value of the bonds increases by $751,000 to $9,900,000. The market value of the stock increases by $200,000 to $2,200,000. The town recognizes the changes in value.

Bonds	$751,000	
Stocks	200,000	
Investment income—appreciation		$951,000

To record appreciation in the value of the securities

The town sells the bonds for $9,900,000, the amount to which the carrying value of the bonds had been adjusted immediately prior to sale.

Cash	$9,900,000	
Bonds (face value)		$9,900,000
To record the sale of bonds		

Investment Management Costs   The town incurs $20,000 of costs in managing the investments.

Investment management expenditures	$20,000	
Cash		$20,000
To record investment management costs		

Closing Revenue and Expenditure Accounts   The town closes its revenue and expenditure accounts, other than gains on investments.

Interest revenue	$900,000	
Investment management expenditures		$ 20,000
Income available for transfer to a special revenue fund		880,000
To close revenue and expenditure accounts		

"Income available for transfer" is a temporary account, similar to "income summary" in a business. It is established mainly to show the distributable income in a single account. Because of the donor restriction, the income should be transferred to a special revenue fund.

Distribution of Investment Gains between Principal and Income   The town determines that the prevailing inflation rate is 4 percent. Per the donor's stipulations, any annual investment gains greater than the inflation rate are expendable. Thus, the amount available for transfer to a special revenue fund is calculated as follows.

Investment income—appreciation (per unrealized appreciation entry)		$951,000
Beginning of year balance in the permanent fund	$12,000,000	
Inflation rate	$\times$ .04	
Amount to be retained in the permanent fund		(480,000)
Amount of investment income—appreciation available for transfer to a special revenue fund		$471,000

The following entry would accomplish the distribution of the investment gains between principal and income:

Investment income—appreciation	$951,000	
Fund balance		$480,000
Income available for transfer to a special revenue fund		471,000
To close the investment income—appreciation account and distribute the balance between		
fund balance and income available for transfer		

Transfer to Special Revenue Fund   The town transfers the distributable income ($880,000 + $471,000) to a special revenue fund restricted for zoo operations.

Nonreciprocal transfer-out to special revenue fund	$1,351,000	
Cash		$1,351,000

To transfer available income to special revenue (zoo operations) fund

Correspondingly, of course, the special revenue fund records a nonreciprocal transfer-in of the same amount.

Closing Remaining Accounts   To complete the bookkeeping process, the government closes both the transfer account and the income available for transfer account ($880,000 + $471,000).

Income available for transfer to special revenue fund	$1,351,000	
Fund balance		$1,351,000

To close the income available for transfer account

Fund balance	$1,351,000	
Nonreciprocal transfer-out to special revenue fund		$1,351,000

To close the transfer account

Table 10-1 presents summary statements of revenues, expenditures, and changes in fund balances and balance sheets for both the permanent fund and the special revenue fund.

In the town's government-wide statements, the expendable income from the permanent fund would be shown as revenue in the same function or program (e.g., parks and recreation) as that in which the zoo's operating expenses and any other of its program revenues are reported.

PRIVATE-PURPOSE TRUST FUND   Suppose, instead, that the zoo was operated by an independent not-for-profit organization, but that the city was nevertheless responsible for administering the zoo endowment. In that case the city would account for the endowment as a private-purpose trust fund—a fiduciary fund, not a governmental fund. Inasmuch as the endowment holds no long-term depreciable assets, most of the journal entries in the example of a permanent fund would be the same, although the trust fund would record investment management *expenses*, rather than expenditures.

However, the distributable income of $1,351,000 would be paid to the not-for-profit organization, rather than being transferred to a special revenue fund of the town. Therefore, the private-purpose trust fund would record an *expense* ("Benefits") for the payment to the not-for-profit, rather than a nonreciprocal transfer-out to another fund of the same government.

Table 10-2 shows how the statements of the zoo endowment would appear if it were a private-purpose trust fund.

TABLE 10-1
Governmental Zoo Funds
Statements of Revenues, Expenditures, and Changes in Fund Balances

	Expendable Zoo Fund (Special Revenue)	Nonexpendable Zoo Fund (Permanent)
Revenues		
Contributions		$12,000,000
Interest		900,000
Investment Income—Appreciation		951,000
Total Revenues		13,851,000
Expenditures		
Administrative Expenditures		20,000
Excess of Revenues over Expenditures		13,831,000
Other Financing Sources (Uses)		
Transfer to Expendable Fund	$1,351,000	(1,351,000)
Net Change in Fund Balances	1,351,000	12,480,000
Beginning Fund Balance	0	0
Ending Fund Balance	$1,351,000	$12,480,000

Governmental Zoo Funds
Balance Sheets

	Expendable Zoo Fund (Special Revenue)	Nonexpendable Zoo Fund (Permanent)
Assets		
Cash	$1,351,000	$10,280,000
Common Stock		2,200,000
Total Assets	$1,351,000	$12,480,000
Fund Balance	$1,351,000	$12,480,000

WHAT FINANCIAL STATEMENTS ARE REQUIRED FOR FIDUCIARY FUNDS?

As illustrated in Table 10-2 for a private-purpose trust fund (and in the next section for a pension trust fund), GASB requires two statements for fiduciary funds: a statement of fiduciary net assets and a statement of changes in fiduciary net assets (not applicable for agency funds). These statements differ from those required for proprietary funds, as well as those for governmental funds. The statement of fiduciary net assets focuses on the amount of net assets that is held in trust for the beneficiaries of the trust and on the composition of the assets (e.g., the major classes of investments). The statement of changes focuses on the sources of the additions to net assets (e.g., contributions from donors versus investment earnings) and the reasons for deductions from net assets (e.g., payments to trust beneficiaries versus administrative expenses not related to the management of investments).

TABLE 10-2	
Zoo Endowment Fund (Private-Purpose Trust)	
Statement of Changes in Fiduciary Net Assets	
Additions	
Contributions of Donor	$12,000,000
Investment Earnings:	
Interest	900,000
Investment Income—Appreciation	951,000
Total Investment Earnings	1,851,000
Less: Administrative Expenses	(20,000)
Net Investment Earnings	1,831,000
Total Additions	13,831,000
Deductions	
Benefits	1,351,000
Change in Net Assets	12,480,000
Net Assets—Beginning of Year	0
Net Assets—End of Year	$12,480,000

Zoo Endowment Fund (Private-Purpose Trust)	
Statement of Fiduciary Net Assets	
Assets	
Cash	$10,280,000
Common Stock	2,200,000
Total Assets	12,480,000
Liabilities	0
Net Assets—Held in Trust for Benefit of Zoo	$12,480,000

The concept of *major* versus *nonmajor* funds does not apply to fiduciary funds, as it does to governmental and proprietary funds. Rather, all fiduciary funds of similar types (e.g., all private-purpose trust funds or all pension trust funds) should be consolidated and reported in separate columns in the fiduciary fund statements.

Fiduciary funds are not reported in government-wide statements, because their assets are not assets of the administering government; they benefit outside parties rather than the government itself.

WHAT ARE PENSIONS, AND WHY ARE THEY IMPORTANT?

Pensions are sums of money paid to retired or disabled employees from a pension plan sponsored by their employer or by the state. The plan is financed by contributions that an employer (and usually the employees as well) makes while the employees are working and by earnings on plan investments.

In essence, pensions are deferred compensation for employee services. While employees are in active service, part of their compensation is paid to them in the form of wages or salaries; part is deferred until they retire or become disabled. Although the employees earn their pensions—and employers receive the benefit of their services—during their years of employment, the actual cash payments do not have to be made to the employees until their years of retirement. Thus, the earning of benefits and the cash payments of benefits may be mismatched by many years. Nevertheless, most governments are required by state law to set aside resources, including withholdings from employees' salaries or wages, while employees are in active service to meet future pension payment obligations. These resources are generally held in trust for the employees and, once paid in, cannot be withdrawn by the employer. The plan trustees are responsible for investing the pension fund assets and for making the required payments to retirees.

The resources held by public pension funds can be gargantuan. For example, on June 30, 2001, the assets of CalPERS, the California Public Employees Retirement System, totaled more than $174 billion; those of the New York State Teachers Retirement System were more than $85 billion. These and similar pension funds face pressures like those of large mutual funds and other institutional investors to maximize earnings while protecting against investment losses. Moreover, because of the magnitude of their stock holdings, public pension funds can have considerable influence on business corporations' decisions about their operations and, thus, on the nation's economy.

HOW SHOULD AN EMPLOYER ACCOUNT FOR ITS PENSION CONTRIBUTIONS?

Employers generally account for their contributions to pension plans in the general fund or a proprietary fund, depending on the fund used to record salaries and wages. In Chapter 5, we briefly discussed how a government should record pension expenditures or expenses. In this section we examine further the issues involved in determining the amount of the employer's expenditures or expenses and liabilities as well as how and when they should be recorded. In a subsequent section we shall address accounting and financial reporting for a pension trust fund—a fiduciary fund used to account for the assets, liabilities, and changes in net assets of the pension plan itself.

DEFINED CONTRIBUTION VERSUS DEFINED BENEFIT PLANS The type of pension plan—whether it is a **defined contribution plan** or a **defined benefit plan**—affects accounting for the employer's contributions. In a defined contribution plan, the employer is obligated only to make annual contributions in the amount specified in the plan terms. The retirees are entitled only to the accumulated contributions in their accounts, adjusted by investment gains and losses. Thus, accounting for the employer's contributions is straightforward. The employer records each year an expenditure or expense and a reduction in cash for the amount of the required contribution. It has no liability other than for its required contributions that are due but not yet paid to the pension plan. If investment losses reduce employees' retirement accounts below their expectations, the employer is not required to make up the difference.

Most public plans, however, are defined benefit in nature. In this type of plan, the plan terms specify the benefits that the employees will receive after retirement, based on a formula that takes into account years of employment and salary levels. For example, a college might promise to pay faculty members 2.5 percent of their average annual salaries during their last three years of service for each year of employment. If a faculty member with thirty years of service earned an average of $100,000 during the three years prior to retirement, he or she would be guaranteed an annual pension of $75,000 (2.5 percent × 30 years × $100,000).

Thus, in a defined benefit plan, in contrast to a defined contribution plan, the employer, not the employees, bears the risks that contributions and investment earnings may not be sufficient to meet expected pension payments. The employer guarantees the outputs (the payments to the retirees), not the contributions to the pension fund.

For plan financing (*funding*) purposes, the employer's **annual required contribution** to a defined benefit plan is calculated so that the amounts contributed each year, together with the employees' own contributions and investment earnings, will be sufficient to pay the promised benefits after the employees retire. If the amounts in the pension trust fund should prove to be insufficient (e.g., because of investment losses) to make all the promised benefit payments when they become due, the employer (or the state) would be required to make up the difference. Thus, in contrast to its participation in a defined contribution plan, an employer may have a liability to a defined benefit plan other than for its annual required contributions, depending on the future financial health of the plan.

CALCULATING THE ANNUAL REQUIRED CONTRIBUTION Simply stated, the annual required contribution is the employer's share of the total expected cost of pension benefits attributable to a particular year of employee service. The amount that must be contributed each year can be calculated actuarially. Actuaries are statisticians who compute pension and insurance risks and premiums. They have also been described as "accountants with no sense of humor."

Precisely how the required contribution for a particular year is determined is beyond the scope of this text. However, it usually consists of two actuarially calculated components. The first component corresponds to the amount of pension benefits earned by the employees for that year's service, based on the plan formula, and is commonly referred to as the *normal cost*, or *current service cost*. The second is a "catch-up" amount. It is calculated to gradually reduce any difference between the assets set aside in the pension trust fund and the **actuarial accrued liability**—that is, the amount of benefits earned to date by the plan members (retirees, their survivors, and employees still in active service). This difference is generally called an **unfunded actuarial accrued liability** (or, simply, unfunded liability), although sometimes the assets exceed the actuarial accrued liability. Either way, unfunded liabilities are generally reduced (or *amortized*), for both actuarial funding and accounting purposes, gradually over a predetermined number of years, rather than immediately after they are identified, to avoid sudden increases or decreases in the employer's required contributions.

Unfunded liabilities occur basically for two reasons. First, when an employer establishes a pension plan, or subsequently decides to increase benefits, it may decide to apply the new benefits retroactively (i.e., to past service as well as to future service). If so, past contributions were not sufficient to pay for the now increased benefits attributable to past service. Second, to calculate annual required contributions, actuaries need to make assumptions about the probability of future events, such as the number of years the employees will work, their future salary levels, how long they or their beneficiaries will live, and the investment return on plan assets.

Actuaries, though trained to assess probabilities, are not seers. Thus, the actual results for any year (e.g., how many employees actually left service without qualifying for benefits and the actual return on plan assets) might be different from previous assumptions. If so, to compensate for those differences, the employer might need to contribute more (or less) than the normal cost in current and future periods.

ACCOUNTING ISSUES As indicated, the employer's annual required contribution is generally determined using actuarial methods and assumptions. Several different calculation approaches are acceptable according to the principles set forth by the Actuarial Standards Board-—the equivalent for the actuarial profession of the FASB and the GASB for accounting and financial reporting. The annual required contribution will vary, depending on the approach used to determine it. Thus, a significant accounting issue is whether the annual required contribution should be measured in the same way for accounting as for funding purposes, or whether all governments should use a specific method for accounting, irrespective of the methods used for funding (financing) the plan.

An equally important issue is how much of the annual required contribution should be recorded as an expenditure or expense. Obviously, if the contribution is made in full, the government will record an equal amount of expenditures or expenses. But suppose the government contributes less (or more) than the annual required contribution because of legal requirements or budgetary considerations. Should the recorded expenditure or expense be the actuarially calculated amount, which is indicative of the economic value of the pension benefits attributed to that year of employee service? Or should it be the contribution actually made, which is indicative of the amount budgeted for pension contributions?

EXAMPLE *Pension Contributions*

Based on an actuarial valuation, a city's annual required contribution to its pension fund for the current year is $80 million, an amount calculated in accordance with generally accepted accounting and actuarial principles. Due to budget constraints, the city contributes only $75 million. In the past, the city has always paid its annual required contributions in full. Thus, it has no liability for past required contributions. The city records pension contributions in the general fund.

GASB Standards

Because of the differences between accrual and modified accrual accounting, the GASB, in its Statement No. 27, *Accounting for Pensions by State and Local Governmental Employers*, distinguishes between how an employer's annual required contributions should be *calculated and disclosed* and how much of that amount should be *recorded* in the financial statements as an expenditure or expense.

GASB requires governments to *calculate* their annual required contributions on an accrual basis, using the same methods and assumptions as the actuary uses for plan funding purposes, provided that the actuary's methods and assumptions meet certain requirements set forth by the GASB. If they do not, then governments must nevertheless use the GASB-sanctioned methods for accounting purposes, and the funding and accounting amounts would likely be different.

When pension contributions are made from governmental funds (modified accrual basis), governments would record pension expenditures in the amount that will be liquidated with expendable available financial resources. However,

(continued)

GASB Standards (*continued*)

the full amount of the annual required contribution would be disclosed in the notes, irrespective of whether the reported expenditures are lower or higher. Any difference, called a **net pension obligation (NPO)** (or asset), between the two amounts would be disclosed in the notes. Also, an NPO would be included as a liability in the schedule of long-term obligations.

Governments would report pension expenses in their government-wide (and proprietary fund) statements equal to the annual required contribution. The statement of net assets would report a liability—NPO—or an asset— prepaid pension expense—for any difference between the reported pension expense and the actual contribution. A government may incur a prepaid pension expense if the amount that it is required to contribute by law exceeds the amount of the annual required contribution per accounting and actuarial principles.

In the example, although the annual required contribution (economic cost of providing employees with pension benefits) is $80 million, the city would report a governmental fund expenditure of $75 million, equal to the cash contribution. However, it would disclose the $80 million requirement and an NPO of $5 million in the notes and it would include the obligation in its schedule of long-term obligations. In its government-wide statements, the city would report pension expenses of $80 million and an NPO to the pension plan of $5 million.

The NPO would be increased in future years by the accrual of interest on its outstanding balance and by any additional shortfalls in meeting the annual required contributions; it would be decreased by payments in excess of pension expenses.

LIMITATIONS In truth, the pension information disclosed in the body of an employer's financial statements may not provide adequate insight into an employer's pension costs and obligations. Users also must look to the required disclosures. The following are some limitations of the amounts displayed in the financial statements:

- Insofar as employment costs and obligations are divided among several funds, so too may be the pension expenditures and liabilities. Even in the government-wide statements they may be divided between governmental and business-type activities. Nevertheless, the government's total pension expenses and the NPO, irrespective of the funds used to record them, are disclosed as single amounts in the notes.

- The NPO may not be the full economic obligation to current and future pensioners; it is merely the difference between the cumulative pension expenses and actual contributions. An additional economic obligation may exist if the plan has an unfunded liability—that is, if the assets set aside in the pension fund are less than the benefits earned to date by the employees and retirees.

- Since employers have considerable flexibility in choosing actuarial methods and assumptions, as long as they meet the GASB's requirements, the reported pension expenses and obligations may not be readily comparable among employers.

To compensate for these limitations, the GASB directs that employers provide extensive information about their pension expenses and NPOs and about the funded status (fiscal condition) of the underlying pension plan. The required disclosures include the following:

- A detailed description of the pension plan, including the types of benefits provided
- The employer's funding policy, including employer and employee contribution rates for the current and past two years
- The components of pension expenses and the changes in the NPO
- Key assumptions used in determining the annual required contributions, including the actuarial cost method and the future inflation rate, projected salary increases, and rate of return on plan investments
- The actuarial values of plan assets and liabilities for the current and past two years
- Significant ratios, such as the **funded ratio** (actuarial value of plan assets to actuarial accrued liability for benefits earned to date) and the ratio of the unfunded actuarial accrued liability to annual covered payroll, for the current and past two years

HOW SHOULD A DEFINED BENEFIT PENSION PLAN BE ACCOUNTED FOR?

ACCOUNTING FOR THE PENSION PLAN As discussed in the previous section, GASB Statement No. 27 sets forth how the employers' annual required contributions to pension plans should be calculated and reported. In this section, we address how the government should report on the pension plan itself, as set forth in GASB Statement No. 25, *Financial Reporting for Defined Benefit Pension Plans and Note Disclosures for Defined Contribution Plans.*

Almost all governments contribute to one or more defined benefit pension plans. These plans are generally set up under state law as trusts—legally separate entities from the governments that sponsor them. Most state government plans, as well as the larger plans of local governments, issue financial reports. Nevertheless, GASB standards require that, with rare exceptions, defined benefit pension plans also be included as pension trust funds in the sponsoring government's financial reports, because the sponsor generally has fiduciary responsibility for the plan.

Governments may sponsor one or more plans—for example, a plan for all employees, or separate plans for police officers, firefighters, and general employees— or they may participate in multiple-employer plans set up by another government, such as a state, for all local governments within the state. Some plans are administered by the sponsoring government. Others are administered by a legally separate entity, usually set up by a state government, that is often referred to as a *public employee retirement system (PERS)*. Depending on the terms of the plan and the extent of the employer's legal responsibility for financing its employees' benefits, employers that participate in a pension plan sponsored by another government may be required to present financial statements for their respective shares of the plan, even though the plan sponsor presents financial statements for the plan as a whole.

As a consequence, almost all governments include pension trust fund financial statements in their financial reports for at least one of the plans in which they participate. These statements should be included in the government's fiduciary fund statements. However, they should be *excluded* from the government-wide statements.

Pension plan assets are not assets of the sponsor or participating employers and, by law, are not accessible by the government's general creditors. Rather, they are held in trust exclusively for the plan members.

GASB Standards

Statement No. 25 requires, for each defined benefit pension plan, two financial statements and two schedules of required supplementary information, as well as explanatory notes:

- Statement of plan net assets
- Statement of changes in plan net assets
- Schedule of funding progress, covering at least six years, reporting the plan's funded status and progress toward full funding (assets equal to earned benefits)
- Schedule of employer contributions, covering at least six years, comparing the employer's actuarially determined required contributions with the contributions actually made

The calculation of the amounts reported in the required schedules requires the use of actuarial methods and assumptions. As previously discussed with respect to the employer's annual required contributions (Statement No. 27), the GASB allows governments to select from among several methods that are acceptable under pronouncements of the Actuarial Standards Board, within limits set by GASB standards. The same provision applies to plan reporting, under Statement No. 25. Moreover, the GASB requires governments to use the same methods and assumptions for similar or related information reported, respectively, for pension trust funds (in the required schedules) and for governmental and proprietary funds (annual required contributions and net pension obligations).

Tables 10-3 and 10-4 illustrate the required financial statements and supplementary schedules for a defined benefit pension plan.[2]

STATEMENT OF PLAN NET ASSETS Plan assets consist mainly of cash, securities, and other income-producing assets. Although investments in stocks and bonds are most common, many PERS and large individual plans also invest in commercial real estate, such as shopping centers, and provide venture capital.

The pension trust is liable only for benefits and refunds due but not yet paid. As a result, benefits earned by employees who have not yet retired, and benefits earned by retirees that are not yet due and payable, are not included in plan liabilities on the financial statement. Instead, these amounts are included in the actuarial accrued liability reported in the required schedule of funding progress. Consequently, the statement of net assets focuses on reporting the amount and composition of net assets available for future benefit payments. The note following "net assets held in trust" is required by Statement No. 25 and refers users to the required schedule of funding progress for information on the plan's funded status.

---

[2]Statement No. 25, para. 153.

TABLE 10-3
Statements of Plan Net Assets and Changes in Plan Net Assets as Illustrated by the GASB

Statement of Plan Net Assets as of June 30, 20X2 (in thousands)

Assets:

Cash and Short-Term Investments	$ 66,129
Receivables	
Employer	16,451
Employer—Long-Term	—
Interest and Dividends	33,495
Total Receivables	49,946
Investments, at Fair Value	
U.S. Government Obligations	541,289
Municipal Bonds	33,585
Domestic Corporate Bonds	892,295
Domestic Stocks	1,276,533
International Stocks	461,350
Mortgages	149,100
Real Estate	184,984
Venture Capital	26,795
Total Investments	3,565,931
Properties, at Cost, Net of Accumulated Depreciation	6,351
Total Assets	3,688,357

Liabilities:

Refunds Payable and Other	4,212
Net Assets Held in Trust for Pension Benefits	**$3,684,145**

(A schedule of funding progress is presented on page ___ of this report.)

Statement of Changes in Plan Net Assets
for the Year Ending June 30, 20X2 (in thousands)

Additions:

Contributions	
Employer	$ 137,916
Employer—Long-Term	—
Plan Member	90,971
Total Contributions	228,887
Investment Income	
Net Appreciation (Depreciation) in Fair Value of Investments	(241,408)
Interest	157,371
Dividends	123,953
Real Estate Operating Income, Net	10,733
	50,649
Less Investment Expense	54,081
Net Investment Income	(3,432)
Total Additions	225,455
Deductions:	
Benefits	170,434
Refunds of Contributions	15,750
Administrative Expense	4,984
Total Deductions	191,168
Net increase	34,287
Net Assets Held in Trust for Pension Benefits	
Beginning of Year	3,649,858
End of Year	$3,684,145

TABLE 10-4
Schedules of Funding Progress and Employer Contributions as Illustrated by the GASB

Schedule of Funding Progress (Dollar Amounts in Thousands)

Actuarial Valuation Date	Actuarial Value of Assets (a)	Actuarial Accrued Liability (AAL)— Entry Age (b)	Unfunded AAL (UAAL) (b − a)	Funded Ratio (a/b)	Covered Payroll (c)	UAAL as a Percentage of Covered Payroll ((b − a)/c)
12/31/W6	$2,005,238	$2,626,296	$621,058	76.4%	$ 901,566	68.9%
12/31/W7	2,441,610	2,902,399	490,789	83.1	956,525	51.3
12/31/W8	2,709,432	3,331,872	622,440	81.3	1,004,949	61.9
12/31/W9	3,001,314	3,604,297	602,983	83.3	1,049,138	57.5
12/31/X0	3,366,946	3,930,112	563,166	85.7	1,093,780	51.5
12/31/X1	3,658,323	4,284,961	626,638	85.4	1,156,346	54.2

Schedule of Employer Contributions (Dollar Amounts in Thousands)

Year Ended June 30	Annual Required Contribution	Percentage Contributed
20W7	$100,729	100%
20W8	106,030	100
20W9	112,798	100
20X0	118,735	100
20X1	124,276	100
20X2	137,916	100

All plan investments are required to be reported at fair value. Capital assets used in administering the plan ("properties")—for example, buildings, equipment, and furniture—are stated at cost less accumulated depreciation.

STATEMENT OF CHANGES IN PLAN NET ASSETS Additions to plan assets are subdivided into the three main sources: contributions from employers, contributions from employees, and investment income, including the net investment appreciation or depreciation. Reported contributions are those actually received or receivable by the plan. The amount reported as contributions from employers is not affected by the amount of pension expenses (or the net pension obligation) reported by the employer in its government-wide and proprietary fund statements and disclosed in the notes, which reports the employer's economic cost, rather than the amount actually contributed.

Plan expenses are required to be subdivided to the extent possible between those related to investment activities (shown as a reduction of income in the additions section, so that users are informed of investment income net of all related expenses) and those related to administrative activities other than investment management (shown in the deductions section). Corresponding to the policy for the net assets statement, the amounts reported for benefits and refunds are only those that became due and payable in the year reported on.

The notes to the financial statements should include a description of the plan terms, classes of employees covered, funding policy, employee contribution rates, and other information useful in interpreting the financial position of the pension trust fund.

SCHEDULE OF FUNDING PROGRESS Whereas the statement of net assets focuses on pension fund resources held in trust to pay benefits, the schedule of funding progress presents the plan's funded status (the actuarial value of plan assets compared with the actuarial accrued liability for benefits earned to date). A minimum of six years is required because, given the long-term nature of public pension plans and the inherent volatility of actuarial calculations, the GASB believes that users are better informed by observing the trend in the funded status (whether it is improving or deteriorating) than by focusing on the results of a single actuarial valuation.

The actuarial value of assets is based on market values but may not be identical to plan assets reported in the statement of net assets. The methods used to calculate it generally spread year-to-year fluctuations in market values over a three- to five-year period, to avoid large single-year effects on the funded status and, therefore, on the employer's contribution rates.

The actuarial accrued liability is the amount of benefits earned by retirees and current employees that are not yet due and payable. The unfunded actuarial accrued liability is the current shortfall between the actuarial assets and liabilities. Sometimes, there is a surplus: actuarial assets exceed the liabilities. Either way, the difference will be reduced through increases or decreases in future employer contribution requirements.

The funded ratio (actuarial value of assets divided by the actuarial accrued liability) is a statistic commonly used to assess a plan's funding progress. If the funding policy is sound and the employer is making its required contributions, the ratio should be increasing over time. Conversely, the ratio of the unfunded actuarial accrued liability to covered payroll should be decreasing over time.

SCHEDULE OF EMPLOYER CONTRIBUTIONS Perhaps the single most influential factor affecting a plan's funding progress is whether the employer is making its required contributions. Even the most soundly conceived funding policy will fail if the employer does not comply. Thus, this schedule is intended to supplement the schedule of funding progress. For example, if the funded ratio is not increasing, the schedule of employer contributions may show that at least part of the reason is that the employer is contributing less than the required amounts. Conversely, if the ratio is not increasing, even though the employer is making its required contributions, then users should look to other factors, such as the investment policy, asset mix, or increases in benefits without corresponding increases in contribution rates.

Statement No. 25 requires governments to disclose in notes to the required schedules the actuarial methods and assumptions used, significant changes in benefits, and other information that may affect users' interpretation of the reported trend in the plan's funding progress.

HOW SHOULD RETIREE HEALTH CARE BE ACCOUNTED FOR?

We now focus our attention, albeit only briefly, on postemployment benefits other than pensions, often referred to as OPEB (other postemployment benefits). These benefits include primarily health care benefits for retirees, whether provided through a pension plan or another vehicle. However, OPEB also include other retiree benefits provided outside pension plans, such as life insurance and housing assistance.

Retiree health care benefits present all of the issues associated with pension benefits—and then some. In addition to the uncertainties surrounding the computation of pension benefits—mortality rates, investment return rates, turnover rates, and so on—the cost of health care for retirees will depend on medical technology and the institutional and economic structure of health care—factors difficult to predict five years into the future, to say nothing of the potential sixty to eighty years between the start of an employee's career and the end of his or her life.

The GASB has underway a project on how retiree health care and other OPEB costs should be measured and recognized by employers, and how the plans should be reported. Pending completion of that project, governments are permitted to account for benefits as they have in the past—that is, on a pay-as-you-go basis.

GASB Standards

GASB allows (but does not require) employers to apply the requirements of Statement No. 27 to retiree health care benefits as well as pension benefits. Employers that choose not to do so and those that offer other kinds of OPEB should apply the disclosure requirements of Statement No. 12, *Disclosure of Information on Postemployment Benefits Other Than Pension Benefits by State and Local Governmental Employers*. The required disclosures include a description of the benefits provided, employee groups covered, employer and employee obligations to contribute, funding policy, and expenditures or expenses recognized for the period.

Per its Statement No. 26, *Financial Reporting for Postemployment Healthcare Plans Administered by Defined Benefit Pension Plans*, GASB requires a pension plan or PERS that administers a retiree health care plan to present separate fiduciary fund financial statements for that plan, in addition to those required for the pension trust fund. These statements are not illustrated in this chapter. They would be virtually identical to the statements for pension trust funds.

The plan or PERS need not present schedules of funding progress and employer contributions for a retiree health care plan comparable to those required for the pension trust, inasmuch as the GASB has not yet specified how these amounts should be measured. Moreover, Statement No. 26 does not apply to retiree health care plans administered separately from pension plans or to other OPEB plans. Thus, until the GASB issues a final pronouncement on OPEB, financial reports will provide only minimal information on the fiscal status of a retiree health care or other OPEB plans and the employer's related costs and obligations.

Even though the GASB has so far provided only limited guidance on accounting and financial reporting for retiree health care and other OPEB, the potential significance of these benefits should not be underestimated. Most governments that offer these benefits fund them on a pay-as-you-go basis. Therefore, they have neither set aside the resources nor reported the expenditure/expense or liability for the benefits being earned today. But the bills will eventually be presented and will have to be paid.

WHAT ACCOUNTING ISSUES DO INVESTMENT TRUST FUNDS PRESENT?

Governments, especially states and counties, may sponsor investment pools as a service to the other governments within their jurisdiction. They operate the pools like mutual funds. Governments are permitted to invest temporarily available cash in these pools and thereby earn a return on their assets without having to incur the costs and risks of either managing an investment portfolio themselves or giving their assets over to private money managers.

Sponsoring governments must account for their investment pools in accord with the provisions of Statement No. 31, *Accounting and Financial Reporting for Certain Investments and for External Investment Pools*. Most of the requirements are the same as those for investments in securities that are not included in the pool, which are discussed in Chapter 4. Most notably, both equity and debt securities of investment pools must be *marked to market*, and changes in market values must be recognized as gains or losses as they occur.

Statements No. 31 and 34 require governments that sponsor investment pools to include in their fund financial statements a statement of fiduciary net assets and a statement of changes in fiduciary net assets similar to those discussed previously for all fiduciary funds and illustrated for pension and private-purpose trust funds. The investment trust statements should *exclude* assets of the sponsoring government. Inasmuch as the sponsoring government acts in a fiduciary capacity (i.e., as a trustee) only for pool participants other than itself, the fiduciary fund statements should include only the assets of the outsiders. The sponsoring government should report its own assets in the fund (e.g., the general fund or a capital projects fund) with which they are associated.

WHAT ACCOUNTING ISSUES DO AGENCY FUNDS PRESENT?

Agency funds are the fourth type of fiduciary funds. They are used to account for resources held by one government acting as an agent (representative) of another government, usually on a temporary basis (one year or less). Agency funds are the simplest of all funds to account for. They are custodial in nature. Assets always equal liabilities. There are no fund balances—and therefore no changes in fund balances—upon which to report.

GASB Standards

In Statement No. 34, GASB requires governments to include agency funds in a separate column of the fiduciary funds statement of net assets. However, because agency fund assets should always equal liabilities, agency funds should not be included in the fiduciary funds statement of changes in net assets. As is true for all fiduciary funds, agency funds should *not* be reported in the government-wide statements.

The journal entries of an agency fund present few problems. An increase in assets is generally offset with a liability to the party on whose behalf the assets are being held. When assets are distributed to the beneficiary, the government would reduce agency fund liabilities and assets in the same amount.

More challenging—and sometimes controversial—questions than accounting for agency funds relate to when an agency fund should be established. Consider, for example, two issues: special assessments and pass-through grants.

Special Assessments   A government issues debt that is to be serviced entirely from special assessments. The government collects the assessments from the assessed property owners, temporarily invests any funds on hand, and makes the required payments to the bondholders or the bond trustee. Although it anticipates that it will service the debt entirely from the assessments, the government may, to a variety of degrees, be liable for any shortages. For example, it may formally guarantee the debt, it may be required to cover delinquencies until foreclosure proceeds are received from defaulting property owners, or it may explicitly indicate that in the event of default, it *may* cover delinquencies even if not legally obligated to do so.

As discussed in Chapter 6, a government should account for special assessment resources in an agency fund only when it is not obligated for the related debt *in any manner*. "Any manner" would include any indication that it is either legally obligated for the debt or may assume responsibility for it, even if not legally obligated. If the government *is* obligated in some manner, then it should account for the resources in the appropriate governmental or proprietary fund or funds.[3]

Pass-Through Grants   Governments routinely receive grants that they are required to *pass through* to secondary recipients. For example, the federal government may distribute money to state governments with the requirement that it be passed through to school districts to fund programs for the prevention of drug and alcohol abuse.

Although the assets may be used only to benefit the secondary recipients, the governments may have varying responsibilities for administering the grants. For example, some grants require the government to disburse funds to parties named by the grantor. Others require the government to select the recipients and subsequently monitor their performance. Thus, in some circumstances the government may be a mere agent for the grantor; in others the government may have substantive control over the funds.

As discussed in Chapter 4, per GASB Statement No. 24, *Accounting and Financial Reporting for Certain Grants and Other Financial Assistance*, a government may account for the proceeds of a pass-through grant in an agency fund only when it serves as a *cash conduit*. A government serves as a cash conduit when it merely transmits funds to the recipients without having any administrative involvement in the grant program. Administrative involvement includes monitoring compliance with grant requirements, selecting recipients, or exercising discretion in how the funds are allocated.[4] When a government has administrative involvement, it should account for grant receipts and subsequent outlays as revenues and expenditures or expenses, respectively, in an appropriate governmental, proprietary, or private-purpose trust fund.

QUESTIONS FOR REVIEW AND DISCUSSION

1. What is the distinction, as drawn by the GASB, between a fiduciary fund and a permanent fund?
2. What is the rationale for accounting for (non-expendable) endowment funds on a full, rather than a modified, accrual basis? Why is it important that depreciation be charged on capital assets held as endowment fund investments?
3. Why, despite your response to the previous question, does the GASB direct that permanent funds be accounted for on a modified accrual basis?
4. How should governments report permanent fund and fiduciary fund balances and income in their government-wide statements? Explain.
5. You are the sole contributor to a government's endowment fund. You must specify whether investment gains should be expendable or nonexpendable. Present the key arguments in

[3]GASB Statement No. 6, *Accounting and Financial Reporting for Special Assessments*, para. 19.
[4]Statement No. 24, para. 5.

favor and against permitting the gains to be expendable.

6. A government has an endowment which is accounted for in a permanent fund. At the start of the year, the fund had a value of $1 million— the amount initially contributed to establish the fund. In a previous year, the organization had added $100,000 of endowment fund investment gains to a special revenue fund. Of this amount, $20,000 has already been spent. The investments of both the permanent fund and the special revenue fund are in a common pool. In the current year, the investment pool lost $50,000 in market value. How should the $50,000 of investment losses be accounted for? More specifically, what amounts should be charged to the permanent fund and to the special revenue fund?

7. Distinguish between a defined benefit pension plan and a defined contribution plan. Why does a defined benefit plan present far more complex accounting issues than a defined contribution plan?

8. Why may a government's reported pension expenditure in a governmental fund differ from its annual required contribution?

9. Why do the basic financial statements (statement of plan net assets and statement of changes in plan net assets) of a pension plan provide inadequate information to assess the plan's funded status? Where would a statement user look for more comprehensive information?

10. Why are the problems of accounting for postemployment health care benefits even more intractable than those of accounting for pensions? Do you believe that current reporting standards ensure that statement users have sufficient information to assess whether government employers have adequately funded their postemployment health care benefits?

11. Why do the balance sheets of agency funds contain only assets and liabilities, but no fund balances? Why is it often unclear whether the resources relating to a particular activity should be accounted for in an agency fund or a governmental fund?

EXERCISES AND PROBLEMS

10-1

Select the *best* answer. Items 1 though 5 refer to Riverview City.

1. Riverview City received a gift of $1 million. The sum is to be maintained as an endowment, with income used to preserve and improve the city's jogging trails. The $1 million should be reported in
   a. a governmental fund
   b. an agency fund
   c. a fiduciary fund
   d. a proprietary fund

2. Riverview City collected $80 million in property taxes on behalf of the Riverview Independent School District. The $80 million should be reported in
   a. a governmental fund
   b. an agency fund
   c. a fiduciary fund
   d. a proprietary fund

3. The $80 million collected by Riverview City would be reflected in statements of the appro-priate fund as an increase in cash and an offsetting increase in
   a. a liability
   b. a reserve
   c. fund balance
   d. none of the above

4. In the city's government-wide statements the $80 million would be reported as
   a. a liability
   b. a reserve
   c. net assets
   d. none of the above

5. The city maintains a $1 million endowment to provide financial assistance to needy retired employees and their families. In its government-wide statements, the $1 million would be reported as an asset in the column for
   a. governmental activities
   b. business-type activities
   c. totals, but not in the column for either governmental or business-type activities
   d. none of the above

b. could answer
be an answer too

6. As of year-end, a city's pension plan had $1.5 million in current obligations to retired employees. The city would report this amount as a liability on
   a. the pension trust fund statements only
   b. the pension trust fund statements and the government-wide statements
   c. the government-wide statements only
   d. neither the pension trust fund statements nor the government-wide statements

7. Depreciation on capital assets would never be reported in which of the following funds?
   a. fiduciary
   b. permanent
   c. internal service
   d. enterprise

8. Which of the following would *not* be reported on a pension plan's statement of plan net assets?
   a. long-term investments at fair value
   b. capital assets used in plan operations at cost less accumulated depreciation
   c. net assets held in trust for pension benefits
   d. actuarial accrued liability to current and retired employees

9. A city maintains a $10 million endowment fund to preserve and improve its parks. During the year, the fund had investment gains from the sale of securities of $1 million. These investment gains should be
   a. added to the endowment principal and thereby not be expendable
   b. added to the fund that accounts for dividends and interest and thereby be expendable
   c. either added to the endowment or added to the fund that accounts for dividends and interest, depending on the stipulations of the donor that established the endowment or, absent donor stipulations, on the decision of the endowment's trustees
   d. added to the endowment to the extent necessary to cover losses due to inflation; the balance would be added to the fund that accounts for dividends and interest

10. In a particular year, the Haynes Independent School District collects $100 million in property taxes. State law requires that property-rich school districts contribute 2 percent of all property taxes that they collect to a state pool, which will be divided among property-poor districts. Upon receipt of the taxes, the Haynes district, which the state considers a property-rich district, should account for
    a. $100 million in an agency fund
    b. $98 million in a governmental fund and $2 million in an agency fund
    c. $100 million a governmental fund
    d. $98 million in a governmental fund and $2 million in a fiduciary fund other than an agency fund

10-2

Select the *best* answer.

1. A city's annual required contribution (as distinguished from its pension expenditures) represents the city's
   a. required contribution to a pension trust fund as determined on the accrual basis by an appropriate actuarial method
   b. actual cash contribution to the pension trust fund
   c. required payments to retired employees per the terms of the pension plan
   d. normal cost, as determined by an appropriate actuarial method

2. A city's annual required contribution to a pension trust fund
   a. must be no less than the actual payments to retirees
   b. must consist of normal cost plus an amount for amortizing the pension plan's unfunded actuarial accrued liability
   c. must consist of normal cost plus an amount for amortizing the city's actuarial accrued liability
   d. is the amount that the city should report as its pension expenditure in a governmental fund

3. Per its actuary, Carlin City's annual required contribution for a particular year is $2.5 million. Of this amount, $2 million is applicable to employees whose compensation is accounted for in its general fund and $500,000 is applicable to employees whose compensation is accounted for in a utility (enterprise) fund. For that year, the city contributes to the pension plan $1.8 million from its general fund and $450,000 from its utility fund. How much should the city record as an expenditure in its general fund and an expense in its utility fund?

	General Fund	Utility Fund
a.	$2,000,000	$500,000
b.	$1,800,000	$450,000
c.	$1,800,000	$500,000
d.	$2,000,000	$450,000

4. Assume the same facts as in the previous item. The amount by which the city's total pension liability (net pension obligation) would increase in its government-wide statements is

   a. $0
   b. $50,000
   c. $200,000
   d. $250,000

5. A pension plan's actuarial accrued liability refers to

   a. the difference between the plan's assets and its obligations, computed by an appropriate actuarial method, to current and retired employees
   b. the total amount to be paid to current and retired employees computed by an appropriate actuarial method
   c. the proportion of the total amount to be paid to current and retired employees, computed by an appropriate actuarial method, that has been earned by those employees to date
   d. the difference between the total amount to be paid to current and retired employees, computed by an appropriate actuarial method, and the amount that has actually been paid to them

6. Which of the following would *not* be reported on the statement of plan net assets of a city's pension plan?

   a. actuarial accrued liability
   b. plan investments at fair value
   c. obligations to retired employees that are past due
   d. contributions receivable from employers

7. Which of the following is a city *not* required to disclose in its notes or required supplementary information pertaining to its pension trust fund?

   a. unfunded actuarial accrued liability as a percent of covered payroll
   b. difference between cost and fair value of plan investments
   c. percentage of annual required contribution actually contributed
   d. ratio of plan assets to actuarial accrued liability

8. A city is notified by its actuary that its actuarially determined required contribution to its postemployment health care plan is $800,000. Of this amount, the city contributes only $600,000. The compensation cost of all covered employees is accounted for in the general fund. Assuming that the city does not apply Statement No. 27 in accounting for retiree health care, the city should report an expenditure in its general fund and an expense in its government-wide statements of

	General Fund	Government-Wide
a.	$800,000	$800,000
b.	$800,000	$600,000
c.	$600,000	$800,000
d.	$600,000	$600,000

9. A city maintains a defined contribution plan to which it agrees to contribute 6 percent of employee wages and salaries. During the year, employees earned $10 million in wages and salaries but the government contributed only $500,000 to the plan. The city accounts for the compensation of all employees in the general fund. The amount that the city should report as an expenditure in its general fund and an expense in its government-wide statements is

	General Fund	Government-Wide
a.	$500,000	$500,000
b.	$500,000	$600,000
c.	$600,000	$500,000
d.	$600,000	$600,000

10. A defined benefit plan is one in which

    a. the employer promises specified payments to employees upon their retirement
    b. the specific provisions are defined by the Internal Revenue Code
    c. the specific provisions are defined by the Uniform Code of Retirement Plans
    d. the employee can specify the mix of benefits (e.g., health, pension, insurance, etc.) that will be received upon retirement

11. Elton City contributes to a pension plan for its firefighters. The city makes contributions to the pension trust fund from its general fund. As of year-end, the pension plan owed $2 million to retired employees. The city would report this amount as a liability on

    a. its general fund statements and government-wide statements
    b. its permanent fund statements and government-wide statements
    c. its government-wide statements only
    d. neither its governmental fund statements nor its government-wide statements

12. The funded ratio of a pension plan compares

    a. the actuarial value of plan assets to the actuarial accrued liability

b. employer contributions to the actuarial value of plan liabilities

c. employer contributions to the unfunded actuarial liability

d. employer contributions to the annual required contribution

10-3

Fiduciary funds are accounted for differently than permanent funds, even though both may account for nonexpendable resources.

Christopher City received a contribution of $520,000 to provide scholarships to the children of deceased city employees. The donor stipulated that all income, including both realized and unrealized investment gains, should be used to support the beneficiaries.

1. Record journal entries for the following, assuming that the gift is to be accounted for in a private-purpose trust (fiduciary) fund.

    a. The gift was composed of
    - cash of $20,000
    - marketable securities with a fair market value of $100,000
    - a building with a fair market value of $400,000 and an estimated useful life of 40 years

    b. The city leased the building as office space to Brooks Law Firm. It collected $46,000 in rent and it incurred expenses, other than depreciation, of $15,000. The city records depreciation on the straight-line basis.

    c. The city sold $20,000 of the marketable securities for $26,000. At year-end, the remaining securities had a market value of $97,000.

    d. It earned and received dividends of $5,000.

2. The city closed the fund's revenue and expense accounts and distributed to beneficiaries the total amount available for distribution. It then closed the distribution account. Prepare the entries to make the distribution and close the accounts.

3. Prepare the fund's year-end statement of fiduciary net assets.

4. How would the fund be reported in the city's government-wide statements? Explain.

5. Suppose the trust was established to benefit programs and activities of the city itself. In what type of fund would it be accounted for? What would be the main differences in accounting principles? How would it be reported in the city's government-wide statements?

10-4

Investment gains and losses may have to be accounted for differently in nonexpendable than in expendable funds.

The McCracken County Humane Society (MCHS), a county government agency, established a permanent fund to provide support for its pet neutering program. As of the start of the year, the fund had a balance of $600,000, composed of both cash and marketable securities.

The program itself, which is accounted for in a special revenue fund, is funded by both direct contributions and the income from the permanent fund.. At the start of the year, the special revenue fund had assets (all investments) of $26,000.

The following transactions and events occurred during the year.

a. The MCHS conducted a "walk your pet day" fund-raising drive. The event raised $120,000, of which $20,000 was in pledges expected to be collected shortly after year-end.

b. The society acquired food and medicine at a cost of $60,000 (cash). During the year, it used $30,000 of these supplies. The society accounts for supplies on a consumption basis. It incurred other operating costs (all paid in cash) of $85,000.

c. The society earned interest of $45,000 on investments accounted for in the permanent fund.

d. During the year, the market value of the investments held by the permanent fund increased by $30,000. Per the terms of the agreement establishing the endowment, all capital gains, both realized and unrealized, must be added to principal.

e. During the year, the value of investments held by the special revenue fund increased by $3,000.

f. The society transferred cash from the permanent fund to the special revenue fund in the amount of the earnings of the permanent fund.

1. Prepare journal entries to record the events and transactions. Be sure you indicate the fund in which they would be recorded.

2. In your opinion, should the unrealized gains on the investments held in the special revenue fund be considered expendable or nonexpendable? Explain.

3. How would the transfer from the permanent fund to the special revenue fund be reported in the government-wide statements?

10-5

The accounting for trusts is dependent upon donor stipulations.

To promote computer education, a leading computer manufacturer donates $4 million to the Kerrville Independent School District. The donor stipulates that the district is to establish an endowment, from which only income is expendable. Income is defined to include interest, dividends, and investment gains. All income is to be recorded initially in a (nonexpendable) permanent fund. Each year the district is to transfer to an expendable endowment fund (i.e., a special revenue fund) all income of the year that exceeds the rate of inflation, as measured by the consumer price index times the beginning fund balance. The expendable funds are to be used exclusively to acquire computer-related materials and to provide computer training for teachers.

In the year the contribution was received, the district

a. Purchased bonds having a face value of $3 million for $2.97 million and common stock for $1 million

b. Received $180,000 in interest and recognized an increase of $3,000 in the fair value of the bonds

c. Sold $500,000 of the common stock at a gain of $50,000 and used the proceeds to purchase additional common stock

d. Transferred expendable income to a newly established special revenue fund (During the year the consumer price index increased by 5 percent.)

1. Prepare journal entries, including closing entries, in the permanent fund to record the year's transactions.

2. Prepare a statement of revenues, expenditures, and changes in fund balance and a balance sheet for the permanent fund.

3. Some donors stipulate that no investment gains are expendable. What is the most probable purpose of that restriction? What is its limitation? In what way is the approach taken by the donor in this example preferable?

4. How would the permanent fund be reported in the school district's government-wide statements?

10-6

Expendable funds may be different in character than nonexpendable funds.

On January 1, 2004, the balance sheet of a city's funds for the acquisition of library books showed the following (in thousands):

	Permanent (Nonexpendable) Fund	Special Revenue (Expendable) Fund
Cash	$ 1,400	$120
Marketable securities	10,000	160
Total assets	$11,400	$280
Fund balance	$11,400	$280

The endowment was established in 1996 with a contribution of cash, securities, and real estate (a building) having a total market value of $24 million. The endowment agreement stated that *income only* (excluding both realized and unrealized investment gains, and deducting depreciation on a straight-line basis) could be used to acquire library books.

The building has a useful life of forty years with no expected salvage value. It had a market value of $20 million when acquired.

The following table provides information about cash transactions and other events (excluding depreciation) during 2004 (in thousands):

	Permanent Fund	Special Revenue Fund
Interest and dividends received (in cash)	$ 760	$60
Rent received (in cash)	1,800	
Cash expenditures for building maintenance	400	
Sales price of securities sold	800	20
Book value of securities sold	200	15
Increase during the year in market value of securities on hand at year-end	150	12

As of January 1, 2004, all prior-year earnings of the permanent fund had been transferred to the special revenue fund and are therefore available for expenditure.

1. Prepare in good form a schedule in which you calculate the total amount available on December 31, 2004, for the acquisition of books.

2. Did you account for the gains on the sale of investments of the special revenue fund in the same way as those of the permanent fund? If not, justify any differences.

3. Why is the building not reported on the balance sheet of the permanent fund? How would the building be reported on the city's government-wide statements?

10-7

Pension plan contributions might be reported differently in governmental than in proprietary funds.

Pebble City maintains a defined benefit pension plan for its employees. In a recent year, the city's consulting actuary calculated that the city's annual required contribution for the year was $6 million. Its determination was consistent with the GASB's requirements. The city records 50 percent of its payroll in its general fund and 50 percent in an enterprise fund.

1. During the year the city contributed the entire $6 million to the pension plan. Prepare the journal entries that the city should make to record its pension contribution (cash), expenditure or expense, and net pension obligation (if any) in the applicable funds (excluding the pension trust fund).

2. Assume, instead, that the city contributed only $5.6 million. Prepare the appropriate journal entries.

3. How can you justify the differences in the reported expenditures/expense between the two funds?

10-8

The financial statements of a defined benefit pension plan provide only limited information as to its economic condition.

The following information relates to the Lincoln County Firefighters Pension Plan (dollar amounts in thousands):

Beginning-of-Year Balances

Cash and cash equivalents, January 1	$ 67
Marketable securities and other investments at fair value, January 1	3,180
Current liabilities to retirees, January 1	4
Actuarial accrued liability, January 1	3,430

Transactions During the Year

Contributions received during the year from employers and employees	138
Benefits that retirees were entitled to receive during the year	120
Benefits actually paid to retirees, including amounts owed from prior year	122
Interest and dividends earned during the year	145
Net appreciation in fair value of marketable securities and other investments (i.e., realized and unrealized gains) during the year	36

Investment management costs	10
Administrative expenses	35

End-of-Year Balances

Cash on hand, December 31	92
Marketable securities and other investments at fair value, December 31	3,307
Current liabilities to retirees, December 31	2
Actuarial accrued liability, December 31	3,690

1. Prepare a statement of plan net assets as of January 1. You may not have to include all of the data provided.

2. Prepare a statement of changes in plan net assets for the year.

3. Prepare a statement of plan net assets as of December 31.

4. Comment on the significance of the data provided that you did not include in your statements. Where in the plan's financial report would this information be reported?

5. Determine the amount of the unfunded actuarial accrued liability as of December 31, assuming that the actuarial value of the plan assets is the same as their fair value. (Sometimes actuaries use average values over several years rather than point-in-time values as of the date of the financial statements.)

10-9

A pension plan's financial statements provide useful, but limited, information as to the plan's fiscal condition.

The following are the statements of plan net assets for 2004 and 2003 and the statement of changes in plan net assets for 2004 for Rockville School District Teachers Retirement Plan. All dollar amounts are in millions.

Statements of Plan Net Assets As of December 31		
	2004	**2003**
Assets:		
Cash	$ 210	$ 440
Contributions Receivable from Employer	39	46
Interest and Dividends Receivable	87	81
Investments in Stocks and Bonds (at Fair Value)	9,176	8,831
Total Assets	$9,512	$9,398
Liabilities		
Benefits Payable	6	37
Net Assets Held in Trust for Pension Benefits	$9,506	$9,361

Statement of Changes in Plan Net Assets For the Year Ended December 31, 2004

Additions:

Employer Contributions	$ 541
Interest and Dividends	630
Net Depreciation in Value of Investments	(621)
Total Additions	$ 550

Deductions:

Benefits to Which Retirees are Entitled during Year	$ 394
Administrative Expenses	11
Total Deductions	$ 405
Net Increase	$ 145
Plan Net Assets, January 1, 2004	9,361
Plan Net Assets, December 31, 2004	$9,506

1. Prepare a summary journal entry to record the employer contributions recognized during the year, the cash actually received from the employer during the year, and the change in the contributions receivable from previous years.
2. Prepare a journal entry to record the benefits paid to retirees.
3. Should the net depreciation in the value of investments include unrealized as well as realized gains and losses? Why?
4. Based on the data provided, are you able to determine the obligation of the plan attributable to benefits earned to date by current and retired employees? Are you able to determine whether the financial health of the plan has improved or deteriorated in 2004? If not, where could you find this information?

10-10

Required supplementary schedules provide the actuarial information necessary to assess a plan's fiscal status.

The following information was reported in the schedule of funding progress of a state's Police Officers Pension Plan. Dollar amounts are in millions.

Valuation Date December 31		
	2004	2003
Value of Assets (a)	$2,411	$2,005
Actuarial Accrued Liability (b)	$2,902	$2,626
Unfunded Actuarial Accrued Liability (b − a)	$491	$621
Funded Ratio (a/b)	83%	76%
Covered Payroll (c)	$957	$902
Unfunded Actuarial Accrued Liability as a Percent of Covered Payroll ((b − a)/c)	51%	69%

The plan's schedule of employer contributions indicated that the employer's annual required contribution was $106 million in 2004 and $100 million in 2003. In both years, the employer contributed 100 percent of those amounts.

1. Based on the limited data available, do you think that the fiscal health of the plan improved in 2004? Explain, citing the specific factors you took into account and telling why they are significant.
2. Suppose you were asked to prepare a schedule explaining the change in the value of assets. What factors might account for increases and decreases in this amount?
3. Suppose you were asked to prepare a schedule explaining the change in the actuarial accrued liability. What factors might account for increases and decreases in this amount?
4. What is the total amount that the employer should report as pension expenditures in 2004?

10-11

The major issue relating to agency funds is when they should be established.

Consider each of the following situations. Indicate whether (and why or why not) you think that the government should account for the transactions and resources in an agency fund, some other type of fiduciary fund, or a governmental fund. Not all the situations have been explicitly addressed in the text. Therefore, you may have to generalize from those that have been discussed.

1. A city extended sewer and water lines to a recently annexed community. Per agreement with the community, the improvements are to be paid for entirely by local residents. To finance the improvements, the city issued ten-year notes on behalf of the residents. It assessed the residents for the amount of the debt, plus interest. The city guaranteed the notes and agreed to collect the assessments from the residents and make appropriate payments to the noteholders. However, the city's role is primarily one of an intermediary. The residents, not the city, are expected to service the debt.
2. A state receives a federal law-enforcement grant intended to assist local communities in hiring additional police officers. The federal granting agency selects the cities and counties that are to receive the awards and determines the amounts they are to receive. The federal government, not the state, is responsible for monitoring grant compliance. The state's only responsibility is to write the checks to the cities and counties.
3. A state receives a federal educational grant intended to assist local school districts in hiring additional teachers. The federal granting agency

establishes the criteria that the state is to use in determining which school districts are to receive the awards and the amounts they are to receive. The district has no discretion in selecting recipients other than to apply the specified criteria.

4. A county collects sales taxes that it distributes among itself and the towns within its jurisdiction. The taxes are levied by the county and are divided among the recipient governments in accordance with a formula set forth in the legislation that authorized the tax.

10-12

Exploring Orlando's financial report

Refer to the financial statements of Orlando in Chapter 3 and to Tables 10-5 and 10-6.

1. Does Orlando have any major permanent funds? How can you tell?

2. What kinds of fiduciary funds does Orlando have? Are these funds required to be included in Orlando's basic financial statements? Are they included in the government-wide statements? Explain.

3. Is Orlando's agency fund included in the statement of changes in fiduciary fund net assets? Explain.

4. Orlando's statement of fiduciary net assets reports $762 million of pension fund assets. However, it does not report a liability for plan members' accrued pension benefits. Why not? Where would a user of the financial statements find this information?

5. Per the statement of changes in fiduciary net assets, what were the major sources of resources for Orlando's pension plans? What was the principal use of resources?

TABLE 10-5
City of Orlando, Florida
Statement of Fiduciary Net Assets
as of September 30, 2001

	Employee Retirement Funds	Agency Fund
Assets		
Cash and Cash Equivalents	$ 20,010,128	$64,548
Accounts Receivable	1,060	—
	20,011,188	$64,548
Investments, at Fair Value		
U.S. Government Obligations	135,479,083	—
Domestic Corporate Bonds	74,980,753	—
Foreign Sovereign Bonds	1,037,980	—
Domestic Stocks	206,357,495	—
International Stocks	39,324,266	—
Short-term Investments	34,945,280	—
Mortgages	49,309,833	—
Real Estate	8,938,111	—
Accrued Income	3,425,763	—
Defined Contribution Investments	62,923,939	—
Total Investments	616,722,503	—
Securities Lending Collateral	120,897,402	—
Participant Loans	4,622,518	—
Total Assets	762,253,611	64,548
Liabilities		
Obligations Under Securities Lending	120,897,402	—
Accounts Payable	529,839	64,548
Total Liabilities	121,427,241	$64,548
Net Assets		
Held in Trust for Pension Benefits and Other Purposes	$640,826,370	

TABLE 10-6 *City of Orlando, Florida* **Statement of Changes in Fiduciary Net Assets** **For the Year Ended September 30, 2001**	Employee Retirement Funds
Additions	
Contributions:	
Employer	$ 9,757,926
State	3,221,036
State in Excess of 1997 Frozen Amounts	127,024
Plan Members	6,466,958
Plan Members Buybacks	39,004
Total Contributions	19,611,948
Investment Earnings:	
Net Decrease in Fair	
Value of Investments	(71,890,641)
Interest	20,585,744
Dividends	3,488,206
Securities Lending	6,417,690
Total Investments Earnings	(41,399,001)
Less Investment Expenses:	
Investment Management Fees	2,304,409
Custodian Fees	128,667
Securities Lending Expenses:	
Interest Expense	5,930,714
Agent Fees	146,416
Net Investment Income	(49,909,207)
Total Additions	(30,297,259)
Deductions	
Benefits	34,870,022
Refunds of Contributions	183,851
Administrative Expense	305,666
Salaries, Wages, and Employee Benefits	50,517
Total Deductions	35,410,056
Net Decrease	(65,707,315)
Net Assets—Beginning of Year as Restated	706,533,685
Net Assets—End of Year	$640,826,370

6. Would you say that the pension fund investments had a "good year"?

7. One of the pension plans reported in the fiduciary fund statements is for police officers. The schedule of funding progress (not illustrated) for the police pension fund reports the following funded ratios:

10/1/96	84.8
10/1/97	88.9
10/1/98	94.9
10/1/99	96.7
10/1/00	103.1
10/1/01	100.8

How is a funded ratio calculated? What do the reported funded ratios suggest to you about the financial health of the police pension plan? What does the ratio for 10/1/01 tell you?

CHAPTER 11

Issues of Reporting
and Disclosure

In this chapter we present an overview of a government's annual financial report. We first consider the *reporting entity*—what related entities a government must incorporate into its report. Thereafter, we highlight the structure of the report and the need for statistical information to supplement the financial statements. We conclude by addressing reporting by public colleges and universities and other special purpose governments. We shall return to the annual report in Chapter 14 when we discuss financial analysis for governments and not-for-profits.

WHY IS THE REPORTING ENTITY AN ISSUE FOR GOVERNMENTS?

The composition of the **reporting entity** has proven one of the least tractable issues for both the GASB and the FASB. An organization's legal entity may differ from its economic entity. For example, if a company controls another company, then its economic entity comprises the company itself plus its subsidiaries. Yet satisfactory definitions of *control* or other criteria for including related enties have proven elusive. Neither the FASB nor the GASB has yet developed standards that meet the challenges of today's complex organizational relationships without legitimate criticism.

The reporting entity issue for governments can be delineated by the example and subsequent variations to it that follow.

EXAMPLE   *The Reporting Entity*

A city operates a facility that supplies electricity exclusively to its subway system. Owing to debt limitations, the city cannot borrow the funds needed for capital improvements. To circumvent the limitations, the city forms a new unit of government, a public power authority, to which it transfers the facility. City council members will form the authority's board of directors. The authority will issue city-backed bonds and repay them from revenues earned from the sale of electricity to the city.

In this example, the power authority is an independent legal entity, but it is within the city's economic and political control no less than if it were a city department. City council members govern the authority and the city is obligated for its debt and is the sole beneficiary of its resources. Therefore, if the city's financial statements were to include all of its economic assets and liabilities, they would have to encompass the assets and liabilities of the authority.

Consider, however, a continuum of modifications to the example:

- The authority's governing board, rather than being composed of city council members, is appointed by the city's mayor.
- The authority's governing board is independently elected, but the city retains the right to approve the authority's budget.
- The governing board is independently elected, and the city has no right to approve the authority's budget.

In this sequence of variations, the city's ability to control the authority is gradually reduced and the economic borders between the city and the authority become more pronounced. Consequently, with each variation the rationale for including the authority within the city's reporting entity is diminished. But where should the GASB draw the line?

The problem is oversimplified in that it focuses exclusively on whether the city *controls* the authority. In fact, the notion of control may be inadequate for assessments of economic interdependence. Interdependence may be influenced by whether one organization shares geographic boundaries with the other, is responsible for its debts, must fund its deficits, can benefit from its surpluses, and is a major source of its revenues. The GASB has had to develop multidimensional standards that are appropriate for the over 80,000 U.S. governments, all of which are tied to at least one other government.

The following are but a small sample of common intergovernmental relationships:

- Housing authorities established by cities to provide low-cost financing for city residents
- Turnpike commissions established by states to finance and operate toll roads
- Volunteer fire departments partially funded by counties or towns
- Universities that receive state funds but are controlled by independently elected boards of regents

WHAT CRITERIA HAVE BEEN ESTABLISHED FOR GOVERNMENT REPORTING ENTITIES?

GASB standards are set forth primarily in its Statement No. 14, *The Financial Reporting Entity*. This statement established the criteria for determining which units should be included in a reporting entity and how they should be reported.

TYPES OF UNITS COMPOSING THE REPORTING ENTITY Per Statement No. 14, a financial reporting entity should consist of a **primary government** and its **component units**.

A *primary government* can be a state government, a general purpose local government, such as a municipality or a county, or a special purpose government. Statement No. 14 explicitly states that general purpose local governments are primary governments. Without that provision, virtually all municipalities would be component units of their states rather than primary governments, inasmuch as local governments are subunits of the states and are subject to their control. To qualify as a primary government, a special purpose government, such as a school district, utility district, or transportation authority, must be a legally separate government, have a separately elected governing body, and be **fiscally independent** of other governments. Fiscal independence means that it has the authority, without another government's approval, to determine its budget, levy taxes and set rates, and issue bonds.

A *component unit* is a legally separate entity for which the primary government has **financial accountability**. It might also be an entity whose exclusion would cause a primary government's statements to be *misleading or incomplete* because of the relationship between the two. For example, to help New York City out of its financial difficulties in the mid-1970s, the State of New York established the Municipal Assistance Corporation (known as Big MAC) to supervise the city's fiscal affairs and issue bonds on its behalf. Since the city was financially accountable to the corporation, not the other way around, the corporation would not qualify as a component unit, were it not for this "misleading or incomplete" provision.

MEANING OF FINANCIALLY ACCOUNTABLE COMPONENT UNITS The key criterion as to whether a primary government is financially accountable for another entity (which thereby qualifies as a component unit) is that either the primary government *appoints a voting majority of the governing body* or a majority is composed of primary government officials. In addition, the relationship between the two entities must satisfy either of two criteria:

1. The primary government can *impose its will* upon the other entity.
2. The other entity can *provide specific financial benefits to*, or *impose specific financial burdens on*, the primary government.

Indicators that the primary government can *impose its will* include the following (of which only one need be met). The primary government can

- Remove appointed members of the other entity's governing board
- Modify or approve its budget
- Approve or modify its fees or charges
- Veto, overrule, or modify the governing board's decisions
- Appoint, hire, reassign, or dismiss the managers responsible for the other entity's day-to-day operations

The ability to *provide specific financial benefits to*, or *impose specific financial burdens on*, a primary government exists if the primary government is

- Entitled to the other entity's financial resources
- Legally obligated for, or has assumed the obligation to finance, the other entity's deficits or is otherwise obligated to support its operations
- Obligated "in some manner" for the other entity's debt, whether that obligation is express or implied

EXAMPLE *Financially Accountable Component Units*

The Jefferson Hospital District, located entirely within Jefferson County, was established to furnish medical aid and hospital care to indigent county residents. The county's commissioners' court appoints the district's board of trustees and has the authority to approve its budget. The trustees set policy and oversee day-to-day operations.

The hospital district is a component unit of the county. It satisfies the two criteria of financial accountability in that

- The county appoints the voting majority of the district's governing board
- The authority to approve the district's budget gives it the ability to impose its will on the district

FISCAL DEPENDENCY As a general rule, a primary government is financially accountable for another entity *only* if the government controls the appointment of its governing board. However, per Statement No. 14, even if the board is independently elected, financial accountability may be indicated by *fiscal dependency*. An entity is fiscally dependent on a primary government if it is unable to determine its own budget, levy taxes or set rates, or issue bonds without the primary government's approval. Suppose, for example, that a school district has an independently elected governing board, but the county board of supervisors must approve the district's budget and tax rates. The district would be financially accountable to, and thus a component unit of, the county because it is fiscally dependent upon it.

REPORTING COMPONENT UNITS Governments must report their component units in either of two ways:

- *Discrete presentation* Reporting one or more component units in a single column, apart from the data of the primary government. This is the default means of reporting.
- *Blending* Combining the component unit's transactions and balances with those of the primary government—that is, reporting the unit's funds as if they were funds of the primary government. Reporting this way is appropriate only when, despite their legal separation, the two entities are so closely related that they are substantively the same. Either of two circumstances would indicate that two entities should be blended:
  - They have the same governing boards (e.g., the city council serves as the component unit's board of directors).
  - The component unit provides services solely or almost entirely to the primary government (not just to the primary government's citizens). A common example is when a financing authority acquires property exclusively for lease to the primary government.

Governments must incorporate their blended component units into both the fund and the government-wide statements. By contrast, they must report their discretely presented component units only in the government-wide statements. The rationale for this distinction is that, as indicated by the criteria for blending, the activities of blended component units are as much a part of the primary government as those that it accounts for in its own funds. Component units that are fiduciary in nature should be reported only in the fiduciary fund financial statements.

Discrete Presentation In their government-wide statements, governments should report their discretely presented component units to the right of the "totals" columns of the primary government. However, they have several options:

- They may combine all the component units in a single column. (See Chapter 3, Table 3-1, for an illustration.)
- They may report each component unit in a separate column.
- They may combine component units into any number of columns based on the characteristics of the component units (e.g., all power authorities into one column, all housing authorities into another).

Blending When a primary government blends component units into its financial statements, it reports the funds of the component units as if they were its own funds. Thus, it accounts for the component units' special revenue funds as if they were its own special revenue funds; its debt service funds as if they were its own debt service funds, and so on. However, owing to the significance of the primary government's general fund, there is an exception. A primary government should report only one general fund. It should report the general funds of its component units as if they were its own special revenue funds. In determining whether these and other component unit funds are major or nonmajor funds, the government should apply the same criteria as it does to its own funds. (Chapter 3, Table 3-3, shows how Orlando reports its Community Redevelopment Agency, which meets the criteria for blending, as a major fund on the city's governmental funds balance sheet.)

Required Disclosures   Irrespective of how it reports its discretely presented component units, the primary government must disclose detailed information as to each *major* component unit. This information can be shown in any of these locations:

- The government-wide statements (i.e., by presenting the component unit in a separate column)
- Notes to the financial statements or
- Combining financial statements (one column for each major component unit). These statements would be presented as part of the government's basic financial statements in a section following the fund financial statements.

The data that must be disclosed should include key accounts drawn from the totals columns of the component units' own government-wide statements. The decision as to whether a component unit is major or nonmajor should be based on the judgment of the government officials as to the significance of its relationship to the primary government.

In addition, the primary government should include in the notes a brief description of both the blended and the discretely presented component units, their relationship to the primary government, and how they are reported. The government also should provide information about how to obtain the component units' separately issued financial statements.

Table 11-1 contains excerpts from the City of Orlando's note on its component units.

REPORTING OTHER TYPES OF UNITS

Joint Ventures   A **joint venture** is a contractual arrangement, whereby two or more participants agree to carry out a common activity and share its risks and rewards. For example, two cities (e.g., Dallas and Fort Worth) may jointly construct and operate an airport.

In its government-wide statements, a government should report its investment in a joint venture as an asset and should account for gains and losses on the *equity* basis (the same as a corporation accounts for unconsolidated subsidiaries in which it has a 20 percent or more interest). If it made the investment with proprietary fund resources, it would also report the asset and record gains and losses on the equity basis in a proprietary fund. However, if it made the investment from a governmental fund, it would report the investment in its schedule of capital assets, not in the fund itself. It would recognize governmental fund revenue on a modified accrual basis, as the venture declares dividends and they satisfy the available criterion.

Related Organizations   Per Statement No. 14, a **related organization** is an entity that satisfies the key criterion of financial accountability (i.e., the primary government appoints a voting majority of its governing board) but does not meet either of the other two criteria for a component unit. That is, the primary government cannot

---

TABLE 11-1
City of Orlando, Florida
September 30, 2001
Note re: Reporting Entity (excerpt)

The City is a Florida municipal corporation with a seven-member City Council comprised of the Mayor (elected at large) and six district Commissioners. In evaluating the City as a reporting entity, management has addressed all potential component units (traditionally separate reporting entities) for which the City may or may not be financially accountable and, as such, be includable within the City's financial statements. The City (the primary government) is financially accountable if it appoints a voting majority of the organization's governing board and (1) it is able to impose its will on the organization or (2) there is a potential for the organization to provide specific financial benefit to or impose specific financial burden on the City. Additionally, the primary government is required to consider other organizations for which the nature and significance of their relationship with the primary government are such that exclusion would cause the reporting entity's financial statements to be misleading or incomplete.

The financial statements are formatted to allow the user to clearly distinguish between the primary government and its component units. Because of the closeness of their relationship with the primary government (the City), some component units are blended as though they are part of the primary government; however, GASB suggests that most component units will be discretely presented.

1. Blended Component Units:

Community Redevelopment Agency (CRA)—The City Council serves as the CRA board. Although legally separate, the CRA is appropriately blended as a governmental major fund component unit into the primary government. The CRA has responsibility for three specifically separate tax increment districts (which have specific debt obligation and related revenues), which are disclosed in segment-like information.

2. Discretely Presented Component Units:

Downtown Development Board (DDB)—The DDB has a separate five-member board appointed by the City Council. Staff is shared with the CRA as the CRA defined area encompasses all of the DDB area.

Civic Facilities Authority (CFA)—Although the City does not appoint the board (which is appointed by Orange County), in accordance with a 1976 tri-party agreement (between City, County and the CFA), the City is primarily responsible for the budget, debt, deficit, and management of the CFA.

The component unit major fund statements reflect these discretely presented units. Separate financial statements for the CRA districts are only produced as necessary, upon request. Separate financial statements for the DDB and CFA are not presently developed.

Source: City of Orlando, *Comprehensive Annual Financial Report* for the year ended September 30, 2001, pages 38 and 39 (cross-references to related notes omitted).

---

impose its will upon the organization, and there is no potential for the organization to provide specific financial benefits to, or impose specific financial burdens on, the primary government. An example would be a housing authority, the governing board of which is appointed by a city's mayor, but the city has no other influence over the authority, receives no direct benefits from it, and has no direct obligations to it. A related organization cannot be incorporated into the primary government's statements. Nevertheless, the government should describe in the notes each of its related organizations and the nature of the relationship.

"Certain Organizations"   Governments may be closely tied to other legally separate entities that meet neither the criteria of Statement No. 14 for component units nor the definition of a related organization. Nevertheless, to exclude them from the primary government's reporting entity might render its financial statements misleading or incomplete. Many of these organizations qualify as tax-exempt, not-for-profit organizations under the Internal Revenue Code, Section 501(c)(3), and their purpose is to provide financial and other types of assistance to the government with which they are associated. An example is a state university's development foundation whose main mission is to raise funds for the university. Its officers might work closely with university administrators, but the foundation would be governed by an independent board of trustees. The university would have no direct or indirect control over the foundation.

Governments may have a wide variety of relationships with numerous organizations of this kind, ranging from university and hospital foundations to public school parent–teacher associations and sports booster clubs. Consequently, the GASB has found it extraordinarily difficult to define precisely the types of organizations that governments should report on and how they should present information about them.

In its Statement No. 39, the GASB amended Statement No. 14 to require governments to report "certain organizations" as discretely presented component units if they are *legally separate* from the primary government, are *tax-exempt*, and meet *all three* of the following conditions:

1. The economic resources of the separate organization are entirely or almost entirely for the direct benefit of the primary government, its component units, or its constituents.
2. The primary government or its component units are entitled to, or have the ability to otherwise access, a majority of the economic resources of the separate organization.
3. The economic resources of an *individual organization* that the primary government is entitled to, or has the ability to otherwise access, are significant to that primary government.[1]

The last provision is expected to exempt most small organizations, such as parent–teacher associations and booster clubs. If an organization does not meet the three criteria, governments should nevertheless report it in accord with Statement No. 14 if its exclusion would render the primary government's financial statements misleading or incomplete.

EXAMPLE   *Summary of Statement No. 14*

A legally separate state financing authority was created to enhance the availability of low and moderate income housing by providing mortgage loans to purchasers of residential homes according to guidelines included in the authority's enabling legislation. The governor appoints the authority's governing board. The authority determines its budget, holds title to property in its own name, controls its own day-to-day operations, and is permitted to issue debt, subject to a statutory limitation. All bonds issued are secured by first mortgages on the related properties and are payable from the

---

[1]GASB Statement No. 39, *Determining Whether Certain Organizations Are Component Units* (an amendment of GASB Statement No. 14), para. 5.

proceeds of mortgage repayments. If the authority determines that funds will not be sufficient to pay the bond principal and interest during the next state fiscal year, the governor must include these amounts in the state budget. However, the legislature has no obligation to appropriate funds for the authority.[2]

A series of questions and answers can be used to assess whether the financing authority qualifies as a component unit of the state and, if so, how it should be incorporated into the state's financial statements:

- Does the financing authority qualify as a component unit of the state?
  - Is the financing authority legally separate? *Yes.*
  - Does the state appoint a voting majority of its board? *Yes.*
  - Is the state able to impose its will on the financing authority? *There is no evidence of this.*
  - Is there a financial benefit/burden relationship? *Yes, the state is obligated, in "some manner," for the authority's debt. It must include the debt in its budget. Therefore, the agency would qualify as a component unit.*
- How should the authority be reported?
  - Are the governing boards of the state and the authority the same? *No.*
  - Does the authority provide services entirely or almost entirely to the state government? *No. Therefore, the state would report the component unit, in the government-wide statements only, using discrete presentation.*

Had the answer to either of the last two questions been yes, then the authority would be blended with the state's own units in both the government-wide and the fund statements.

CONTROVERSY SURROUNDING STATEMENT NO. 14 The GASB's objective in promulgating Statement No. 14 was to ensure that a government's financial statements include information on all organizations for which it is accountable. Yet in the eyes of critics, the statement requires governments to cast out nets that are both too wide and too fine, thereby drawing into their reporting entities organizations for which they are only remotely accountable.

In the summary illustration the state would have to include the financing authority in its reporting entity even if, in reality, it had only a minimal degree of accountability for its activities and obligations. For example, if the governor's appointees to the board served for nonrenewable terms and could not be removed from office except for cause, then the governor might have little ability to influence them. Similarly, if it were highly improbable that the authority would default on its obligations, and, even if it did, that the legislature would appropriate the funds to make up the deficiencies, then the state would bear little financial risk.

Nevertheless, the GASB believed that the voting majority criterion, coupled with the other requirements (i.e., imposition of will or financial benefit/burden) provided reasonable assurance that governments would have to include in their reporting entity only those governments for which they were legitimately accountable.

Critics of Statement No. 14 have also charged that when a government aggregates two or more component units into a single column for discrete presentation, the information loses significance. This is especially true, they note, when the aggregated units engage in totally dissimilar activities (e.g., a power authority and a housing authority).

---

[2]Drawn from a GASB "implementation guide," *Guide to Implemenation of GASB Statement No. 14 on the Financial Reporting Entity*, Case 16, page 48.

WHAT IS INCLUDED IN A GOVERNMENT'S CAFR?

The complete annual report of a government, known as a **comprehensive annual financial report (CAFR)**, consists of more than the basic financial statements and required supplementary information that we have discussed in previous chapters. Indeed, the CAFRs of states, cities, counties, and other general purpose governments are notable for their bulk. Those of medium to large cities may exceed 200 pages, few of which contain pictures or other touches of frivolity. Government accountants are not typically compensated by the page. Why, then, are the reports so lengthy?

As pointed out in Chapter 1, the fiscal wherewithal of a government cannot be assessed in isolation of the community to which it must provide services and from which it must draw its resources. As a consequence, in addition to the basic financial statements and required supplementary information, the complete CAFR includes statements for individual funds and an array of statistical data on both the government itself and its jurisdiction.

The CAFR is divided into three main sections: the *introductory section*, the *financial section*, and the *statistical section*.

INTRODUCTORY SECTION The introductory section consists of

- table of contents
- letter of transmittal
- any other material deemed appropriate by management, such as the Government Finance Officers Association's certificate of achievement

Traditionally, the letter of transmittal, usually from the government's chief financial officer (often cosigned by the city manager or other chief executive officer) and addressed to the governing board and the citizenry, has served as a written "state of the government" address, describing local economic conditions, providing an overview of the government's financial status, setting forth major initiatives, and summarizing key budgetary and accounting practices. Per Statement No. 34, much of the information previously included in the letter of transmittal must now be incorporated into the required management's discussion and analysis, an element of the CAFR's financial section. Because governments have only recently adopted Statement No. 34, it is uncertain what role the letter of transmittal will play in the future.

The introductory section would generally contain a *certificate of achievement for excellence in financial reporting*, if one has been awarded by the Government Finance Officers Association (GFOA) for the report of the previous year. This certificate is awarded to governments whose annual reports conform to GFOA standards for both content and display. The GFOA does not, however, vouch for the accuracy of the underlying information.

FINANCIAL SECTION The financial section consists of

- auditors' report
- management's discussion and analysis (MD&A)
- basic financial statements
- required supplementary information other than the MD&A
- combining statements, individual statements, and schedules

Auditors' Report The auditors' report serves the same general function for government financial statements as it does for those of businesses: it provides assurance that the statements are presented fairly in accordance with generally accepted accounting principles (GAAP). The typical audit is undertaken to express an opinion on the basic financial statements taken as a whole. It is not designed to cover all information included in the CAFR. Accordingly, auditors do not always subject statistical data, individual funds (if presented), and supplementary information to the same range of audit procedures as the basic financial statements.

Management's Discussion and Analysis (MD&A) Although it might be easy to dismiss the MD&A as little more than a reembodiment of the letter of transmittal, it has the potential to become one of the most informative elements of the CAFR. As was noted in Chapter 1 and is emphasized again later in this chapter and in Chapter 14, the basic financial statements, no matter how comprehensive and detailed, can never, by themselves, provide adequate information as to a government's financial standing. In large part, this is because a government's fiscal health is as much dependent on the economic environment from which it draws its resources as on the resources already within its control. It is also, however, because the statements fail to provide sufficient information on the nature and extent of services that the government will be expected to provide in the future. Although governments have long been required to include in the statistical section of the CAFR extensive data on both demographic and economic trends, it was left to the statement users to interpret them and place them in perspective.

The MD&A contains a wealth of information and insights that was not available in the CAFR prior to Statement No. 34. Equally important, it provides government officials the opportunity to present the government's economic condition in a way that is understandable to the average citizen. Table 11-2 highlights the main features of the MD&A as required by the GASB.

Basic Financial Statements The basic financial statements, as emphasized throughout this text, are of two types: government-wide and fund. There are only two government-wide statements: the statement of net assets (balance sheet) and the statement of activities (statement of revenues and expenses).

TABLE 11-2
Key Types of Information that Must Be Included in the MD&A

- A brief description of the required financial statements
- Condensed financial information derived from government-wide statements
- An analysis of the government's overall financial position and results of operations, including impact of important economic factors
- An analysis of balances and transactions of individual funds
- An analysis of differences between original and final budget amounts and between actual and budgeted amounts
- A description of changes in capital assets and long-term debt during the year
- A discussion of the condition of infrastructure assets (for governments using the modified approach)
- A description of currently known facts, decisions, or conditions that have, or are expected to have, a material effect on financial position or results of operations

Source: Summarized from GASB Statement No. 34, para. 11.

Fund statements must be prepared for each of the three categories of funds—a total of seven statements:

- governmental funds (general, special revenue, capital projects, debt service, and permanent funds)
  - balance sheet
  - statement of revenues, expenditures, and changes in fund balances
- proprietary funds (enterprise and internal service funds)
  - statement of net assets (balance sheet)
  - statement of revenues, expenses, and changes in fund net assets
  - statement of cash flows
- fiduciary funds (pension and other employee benefit trust, investment trust, private-purpose trust, and agency funds)
  - statement of fiduciary net assets
  - statement of changes in fiduciary net assets (not applicable to agency funds)

The governmental and proprietary fund statements focus on major funds; nonmajor funds are aggregated into a single column. The *major funds* concept does not apply to fiduciary funds, which should be aggregated into a separate column for each fund type.

As noted in the discussion of component units, governments may elect to provide detailed information about their major discretely presented component units in combining statements. If they choose this option, those statements (one column for each unit) should be included after the fund statements.

Required notes are an essential element of the basic financial statements. Similar to notes to the financial statements of businesses, they describe significant accounting policies and disclose details of various accounts, commitments, and contingencies. Most significantly, the notes must include the schedules of capital assets and long-term liabilities. These schedules reconcile, by type of asset and liability, beginning and ending balances and indicate the amount of depreciation allocated to each of the government's main functions. The notes also should include a summary reconciliation of the governmental fund statements to the government-wide statements, unless this information is provided at the bottom of the fund statements.

Required Supplementary Information (RSI)

Required Supplementary Information (RSI)   RSI comprises schedules, statistical data, and other information designed to supplement the basic financial statements. Examples include

- actual-to-budget comparisons for the general fund and for special revenue funds that have legally adopted budgets
- information about infrastructure condition (for those governments that elect not to depreciate these types of assets)
- details of pension actuarial valuations

The notes and RSI are similar in that both present GASB-mandated disclosures. However, whereas notes are considered part of the basic financial statements, RSI is not. As a consequence, RSI might be subject to a lower level of auditor scrutiny than the notes.

Combining Statements, Individual Statements, and Schedules   The combining statements supplement the basic statements by providing the details of the nonmajor funds, one column for each fund. The totals columns tie into the amounts reported in the nonmajor funds columns of the basic fund statements. Combining statements for nonmajor funds are optional, not required by Statement No. 34.

Internal service funds, as indicated in Chapter 9, are presented in the basic proprietary fund statements in a single column that combines all funds of that type. They do not have to be separately reported in the basic fund statements even if they meet the criteria of major funds. Therefore, individual internal service funds may be reported on in the combining statements.

Governments may also include in this part of the financial section more detailed statements of individual funds necessary to demonstrate compliance with legal and contractual provisions. For example, a government might present a statement of a nonmajor enterprise fund so as to show that it has made proper use of cash or other assets that secure outstanding revenue bonds. Similarly, this part of the financial section may include schedules that tie together data dispersed among several statements. For example, a government might present a table that summarizes all its investments, irrespective of the funds in which they are held.

STATISTICAL SECTION The GASB *Codification* lists fifteen statistical tables (see Table 11-3) that a government should include in its CAFR, unless the information is clearly inapplicable. The statistical data are of value because of a key limitation of government financial statements that was pointed to in Chapter 1: Governments have the power to tax. They can thereby command the resources of their constituents. The fiscal wherewithal of a government cannot be assessed merely by examining the resources actually within the government's control; those potentially within its control must also be taken into account.

Both Orange County, California, and Bridgeport, Connecticut, sought the protection of bankruptcy courts in the 1990s. The financial statements of both governments were equally dismal. Yet their overall fiscal conditions were dramatically different. Orange County was one of the wealthiest communities in the country, whereas Bridgeport was one of the poorest. If Orange County defaulted on its debts or reduced public services, it did so not because it lacked access to the necessary resources, but because the citizenry elected not to draw upon them.

TABLE 11-3
Statistical Tables Required for the CAFR

- General Governmental Expenditures by Function—Last Ten Fiscal Years
- General Revenues by Source—Last Ten Fiscal Years
- Property Tax Levies and Collections—Last Ten Fiscal Years
- Assessed and Estimated Actual Value of Taxable Property—Last Ten Fiscal Years
- Property Tax Rates—All Overlapping Governments—Last Ten Fiscal Years
- Special Assessment Billings and Collections—Last Ten Fiscal Years (if the government is obligated in some manner for related special assessment debt)
- Ratio of Net General Bonded Debt to Assessed Value and Net Bonded Debt per Capita—Last Ten Fiscal Years
- Computation of Legal Debt Margin (if not disclosed in the basic financial statements)
- Computation of Overlapping Debt (if not disclosed in the basic financial statements)
- Ratio of Annual Debt Service for General Bonded Debt to Total General Expenditures—Last Ten Fiscal Years
- Revenue Bond Coverage—Last Ten Fiscal Years
- Demographic Statistics
- Property Value, Construction, and Bank Deposits—Last Ten Fiscal Years
- Principal Taxpayers
- Miscellaneous Statistics

Source: GASB *Codification*, Section 2800.103.

The statistical section supplements the financial statements. The required tables fall into two broad categories. The first category provides additional information or insights into data reported in current or previous financial statements. These include, for example, tables that show ten-year trends in expenditures, revenues, tax collections, and bond coverage.

The second category reports on economic conditions within the government's jurisdiction. These include tables that indicate the largest taxpayers, overlapping debt, and trends in the value of property, construction, and bank deposits. They provide insight into the government's **fiscal capacity**—the economic base that the government can draw upon for its resources.

WHAT ARE THE REPORTING REQUIREMENTS FOR COLLEGES, UNIVERSITIES, AND OTHER SPECIAL PURPOSE GOVERNMENTS?

To this point, the text has focused mainly on general purpose governments, such as towns, cities, counties, and states. However, many (perhaps most) governments serve only a single, well-defined purpose. These include universities and special districts that provide utility, health, and educational services. These governments are legal entities in their own right, but may be component units of other governments. If so, as discussed earlier in this chapter, their financial statements would be included in those of the primary government. Nevertheless, they often are required, or elect, to issue their own (stand-alone) financial statements.

GENERAL REQUIREMENTS Broadly speaking, per Statement No. 34, special purpose governments that issue stand-alone financial statements must adhere to the same reporting and disclosure requirements as general purpose governments, unless they engage in such a narrow range of activities that a complete set of financial statements would be unwarranted. Thus, if they engage in more than one program or in both business-type and governmental activities, they must prepare both government-wide and fund statements.

By contrast, special purpose governments that engage in only a single governmental activity (e.g., a park or road district) have two options. First, they may combine their government-wide and fund statements into a single statement. That is, in one column they can present the government-wide full accrual data and in one or more columns (one for each fund) they can present the fund, modified accrual, data. However, in another column, they must show the differences for each line item between the fund and the government-wide data. These reconciling differences must be explained either on the face of the financial statements or in an accompanying schedule.

The other option is to present separate government-wide and fund statements, but adopt a simpler format for their government-wide statement of activities than that required for general purpose governments. For example, instead of a multicolumn statement (e.g., Table 3-2 in Chapter 3), they can show both revenues and expenses in two or more rows within a single column. However, in keeping with the spirit of the statement required of general purpose governments, the program revenues must be deducted from the program expenses, not the reverse. The difference—the net expenses to be covered from other sources—should be followed by contributions to endowments, transfers, and extraordinary items.

Special purpose governments engaged in only business-type activities need present only the statements required for enterprise funds—a statement of net assets, a statement of revenues, expenses, and changes in net assets, and a statement of cash flows. However, like all governments, they must also present an MD&A, notes, and RSI.

REQUIREMENTS FOR COLLEGES AND UNIVERSITIES U.S. higher education is characterized by a diversity unparalleled in other countries. Not only is our system dichotomized between public and private institutions, but they range in size from small liberal arts colleges of a few hundred students to multicampus systems of a hundred thousand or more students. As a consequence, standard setting has been beset by controversy, not only over specific accounting and reporting standards, but even as to which bodies should have rule-making authority.

When the GASB was being established, constituents of private institutions contended that the FASB should have jurisdiction over all colleges and universities, whereas those of the GASB asserted that GASB should have responsibility for at least government-operated institutions. The issue was resolved by granting the FASB jurisdiction over all private institutions and the GASB over all public institutions. Today, therefore, private colleges and universities follow the FASB pronouncements pertaining to not-for-profit organizations. These will be discussed in the following chapter. Public colleges and universities must adhere to the same GASB pronouncements as other types of governments.

Accounting and reporting by colleges and universities posed especially thorny issues to the GASB, owing to several considerations:

- Public and private institutions have much in common, so comparability is clearly desirable.

- Most colleges and universities have a long tradition of using an accounting and reporting model especially designed for them and set forth in recent years by the AICPA. Some institutions, however, most notably community colleges, have used the standard government model.

- Colleges and universities differ from other governments in how they are funded and managed. For example, although they have both restricted funds and auxiliary enterprises, most do not budget by fund. Therefore, statement users may have only limited interest in fund-by-fund information.

After much debate, the GASB decided that colleges and universities should be subject to the same reporting requirements as other special purpose governments—but with a loophole.[3] The loophole is that most public institutions satisfy the GASB's criteria for entities engaging exclusively in business-type activities. The reason is that, per Statement 34, a government may use an enterprise fund for any activity that charges fees to external users for goods or services.[4] Therefore, public colleges and universities have a choice: they may elect to report as special purpose entities engaging (1) only in business-type activities, (2) only in governmental activities, or (3) in both.

Most colleges and universities will probably choose the first option, in that they lobbied the GASB to be able to report as business-type entities. If so, they need prepare only a statement of net assets, a statement of revenues, expenses, and changes in net assets (both on the full accrual basis), and a statement of cash flows. They need not present detailed fund statements but should include an MD&A, notes, and RSI. The required statements for the first option are illustrated in Table 11-4.

---

[3]GASB Statement No. 35, *Basic Financial Statements—and Management's Discussion and Analysis—for Public Colleges and Universities* (an amendment of GASB Statement No. 34), 1999.

[4]GASB Statement No. 34, *Basic Financial Statements—and Management's Discussion and Analysis—for State and Local Governments*, para. 67.

TABLE 11-4

**Financial Statements of a Public University Engaged
in only Business-Type Activities
ABC University
Statement of Net Assets
June 30, 2002**

	Primary Institution	Component Unit Hospital
Assets		
Current Assets		
Cash and Cash Equivalents	$ 4,571,218	$ 977,694
Short-term Investments	15,278,981	2,248,884
Accounts Receivable, Net	6,412,520	9,529,196
Inventories	585,874	1,268,045
Deposit with Bond Trustee	4,254,341	—
Notes and Mortgages Receivable, Net	359,175	—
Other Assets	32,263	426,427
Total Current Assets	31,894,372	14,450,246
Noncurrent Assets		
Restricted Cash and Cash Equivalents	24,200	18,500
Endowment Investments	21,548,723	—
Notes and Mortgages Receivable, Net	2,035,323	—
Other Long-term Investments	—	6,441,710
Investments in Real Estate	6,426,555	—
Capital Assets, Net	158,977,329	32,602,940
Total Noncurrent Assets	189,012,130	39,063,150
Total Assets	220,906,502	53,513,396
Liabilities		
Current Liabilities		
Accounts Payable and Accrued Liabilities	4,897,470	2,911,419
Deferred Revenue	3,070,213	—
Long-term Liabilities—Current Portion	4,082,486	989,321
Total Current Liabilities	12,050,169	3,900,740
Noncurrent Liabilities		
Deposits	1,124,128	—
Deferred Revenue	1,500,000	—
Long-term Liabilities	31,611,427	2,194,236
Total Noncurrent Liabilities	34,235,555	2,194,236
Total Liabilities	46,285,724	6,094,976
Net Assets		
Invested in Capital Assets, Net of Related Debt	126,861,400	32,199,938
Restricted for		
Nonexpendable		
Scholarships and Fellowships	10,839,473	—
Research	3,767,564	2,286,865
Expendable		
Scholarships and Fellowships	2,803,756	—
Research	5,202,732	—
Instructional Department Uses	938,571	—
Loans	2,417,101	—
Capital Projects	4,952,101	913,758
Debt Service	4,254,341	152,947
Other	403,632	—
Unrestricted	12,180,107	11,864,912
Total Net Assets	$174,620,778	$47,418,420

(*continued*)

TABLE 11-4 *(continued)*
ABC University
Statement of Revenues, Expenses, and Changes in Net Assets
For the Year Ended June 30, 2002

	Primary Institution	Component Unit Hospital
Revenues		
Operating Revenues		
Student Tuition and Fees (net of scholarship allowances of $3,214,454)	$ 36,913,194	$ —
Patient Services (net of charity care of $5,114,352)	—	46,296,957
Federal Grants and Contracts	10,614,660	—
State and Local Grants and Contracts	3,036,953	7,475,987
Nongovernmental Grants and Contracts	873,740	—
Sales and Services of Educational Departments	19,802	—
Auxiliary Enterprises:		
Residential Life (net of scholarship allowances of $428,641)	28,079,274	—
Bookstore (net of scholarship allowances of $166,279)	9,092,363	—
Other Operating Revenues	143,357	421,571
Total Operating Revenues	88,773,343	54,194,515
Expenses		
Operating Expenses		
Salaries:		
Faculty (physicians for the hospital)	34,829,499	16,703,805
Exempt Staff	29,597,676	8,209,882
Nonexempt Wages	5,913,762	2,065,267
Benefits	18,486,559	7,752,067
Scholarships and Fellowships	3,809,374	—
Utilities	16,463,492	9,121,352
Supplies and Other Services	12,451,064	7,342,009
Depreciation	6,847,377	2,976,212
Total Operating Expenses	128,398,803	54,170,594
Operating Income (Loss)	(39,625,460)	23,921
Nonoperating Revenues (Expenses)		
State Appropriations	39,760,508	—
Gifts	1,822,442	—
Investment Income (net of investment expense of $87,316 for the primary institution and $19,823 for the hospital)	2,182,921	495,594
Interest on Capital Asset-related Debt	(1,330,126)	(34,538)
Other Nonoperating Revenues	313,001	321,449
Net Nonoperating Revenues (expenses)	42,748,746	782,505
Income before other revenues, expenses, gains or losses	3,123,286	806,426
Capital Appropriations	2,075,750	—
Capital Grants and Gifts	690,813	711,619
Additions to Permanent Endowments	85,203	—
Increase in Net Assets	5,975,052	1,518,045
Net Assets		
Net Assets—Beginning of Year	168,645,726	45,900,375
Net Assets—End of Year	$174,620,778	$47,418,420

TABLE 11-4 (*continued*)
ABC University
Statement of Cash Flows
For the Year Ended June 30, 2002

	Primary Institution	Component Unit Hospital
CASH FLOWS FROM OPERATING ACTIVITIES		
Tuition and Fees	$ 33,628,945	$ —
Research Grants and Contracts	13,884,747	—
Payments from Insurance and Patients	—	18,582,530
Medicaid and Medicare	—	31,640,524
Payments to Suppliers	(28,175,500)	(13,084,643)
Payments to Employees	(87,233,881)	(32,988,044)
Loans Issued to Students and Employees	(384,628)	—
Collection of Loans to Students and Employees	291,642	—
Auxiliary Enterprise Charges:		
Residence Halls	26,327,644	—
Bookstore	8,463,939	—
Other Receipts (payments)	1,415,502	(997,502)
Net Cash Provided (used) by Operating Activities	$(31,781,590)	3,152,865
CASH FLOWS FROM NONCAPITAL FINANCING ACTIVITIES		
State Appropriations	39,388,534	—
Gifts and Grants Received for Other Than Capital Purposes:		
Private Gifts for Endowment Purposes	85,203	—
Net Cash Flows Provided by Noncapital Financing Activities	$ 39,473,737	—
CASH FLOWS FROM CAPITAL AND RELATED FINANCING ACTIVITIES		
Proceeds from Capital Debt	4,125,000	—
Capital Appropriations	1,918,750	—
Capital Grants and Gifts Received	640,813	711,619
Proceeds from Sale and Capital Assets	22,335	5,066
Purchases of Capital Assets	(8,420,247)	(1,950,410)
Principal Paid on Capital Debt and Lease	(3,788,102)	(134,095)
Interest Paid on Capital Debt and Lease	(1,330,126)	(34,538)
Net Cash Used by Capital and Related Financing Activities	(6,831,577)	(1,402,358)
CASH FLOWS FROM INVESTING ACTIVITIES		
Proceeds from Sales and Maturities of Investments	16,741,252	2,843,124
Interest on Investments	2,111,597	70,501
Purchase of Investments	(17,680,113)	(4,546,278)
Net Cash Provided (Used) by Investing Activities	(1,172,736)	(1,632,653)
Net Increase in Cash	2,033,306	117,854
Cash—Beginning of Year	2,562,112	878,340
Cash—End of Year	$ 4,595,418	$ 996,194

(*continued*)

TABLE 11-4 *(continued)*
ABC University
Statement of Cash Flows *(continued)*
For the Year Ended June 30, 2002

	Primary Institution	Component Unit Hospital
Reconciliation of Net Operating Revenues (Expenses) to Net Cash Provided (Used) by Operating Activities		
Operating Income (Loss)	$ (39,625,460)	$ 23,921
Adjustments to Reconcile Net Income (Loss) to Net Cash Provided (used) by Operating Activities:		
Depreciation Expense	6,847,377	2,976,212
Change in Assets and Liabilities:		
Receivables, Net	1,295,704	330,414
Inventories	37,284	(160,922)
Deposit with Bond Trustee	67,115	—
Other Assets	(136,229)	75,456
Accounts Payable	(323,989)	(75,973)
Deferred Revenue	217,630	—
Deposits Held for Others	(299,428)	—
Compensated Absences	138,406	(16,243)
Net Cash Provided (used) by Operating Activities	$(31,781,590)	$(3,152,865)

Source: GASB Statement No. 35, para 59.

As shown in Table 11-4 (page 284), expenses would usually be classified by object (e.g., salaries, utilities, and supplies). To supplement this information the GASB encourages (but does not require) colleges and universities to present cost information about their various programs and activities.

SEGMENT INFORMATION Statement No. 34 requires all governments that report enterprise funds or use enterprise fund (i.e., business-type) accounting to present segment information in notes to the financial statements. As amended by Statement No. 37,[5] it defines a segment as any activity or group of activities for which revenue bonds have been issued and that has an identifiable (i.e., accounted for separately) revenue stream and related expenses and gains and losses pledged in support of those bonds. For colleges and universities, segments are likely to include auxiliary enterprises, such as dormitories, bookstores, and intercollegiate athletics. The segment information would include key elements of the financial statements.

---

[5]GASB Statement No. 37, *Basic Financial Statements—and Management's Discussion and Analysis—for State and Local Governments: Omnibus* (an amendment of GASB Statements No. 21 and No. 34), para. 17.

QUESTIONS FOR REVIEW AND DISCUSSION

1. Per GASB Statement No. 14, what is the key criterion as to whether a government should be included as a *component unit* in the reporting entity of another government?

2. How does *discrete presentation* differ from *blending*? When is each appropriate?

3. What is the primary deficiency of discrete presentation as it must be applied in government-wide statements?

4. What are the three main sections of the Comprehensive Annual Financial Report (CAFR)? What are the main components of the financial section?

5. Provide five examples of the type of information to be addressed by management in its discussion and analysis (MD&A).

6. What are the main reporting options available to government colleges and universities? Do they have to prepare fund statements? Explain.

7. Why are the basic financial statements of a government—more so than those of a business—inadequate as a basis for assessing the entity's fiscal health?

8. Many public universities are quite similar to their private counterparts. Indeed, some large state universities receive less than 25 percent of their resources from the state. How, then, can you account for the substantial differences in their reporting practices?

9. Both notes to the financial statements and required supplementary information (RSI) must be included in a government's CAFR. What, then, does it matter if information is provided in notes as opposed to RSI?

10. True or false? Since public universities are permitted to report as business-type activities, they no longer have to provide information on individual auxiliary enterprises, such as those for athletics and housing facilities. Explain.

EXERCISES AND PROBLEMS

11-1

Select the *best* answer.

1. New York State has unlimited authority to control and regulate Yonkers, New York, as well as all other municipalities within its jurisdiction. Consistent with GASB Statement No. 14,
   a. both New York State and Yonkers could be considered primary governments
   b. only New York State could be considered a primary government
   c. Yonkers could be considered a primary government only if the State has explicitly passed legislation ceding key fiscal controls to local governments such as Yonkers
   d. Yonkers could be considered a primary government only if the State opts not to account for Yonkers as a component unit

2. Which of the following is *not* a power that a municipality must have to be considered fiscally independent of other governments?
   a. to determine its budget
   b. to levy taxes and set rates
   c. to establish debt limitations
   d. to issue bonds

3. Carson City appoints a voting majority of the Carson City Housing Authority's governing board. Which of the following additional criteria would *not* be sufficient evidence that Carson City is financially accountable for the Carson City Housing Authority?
   a. The mayor of Carson City must approve the Housing Authority's budget.
   b. Two of the five members of the Housing Authority's governing board are also members of the Carson City council.

c. Carson City guarantees any debt incurred by the Housing Authority.

d. The Carson City council can appoint the managing director of the Housing Authority.

4. The Sierra Library District satisfies the criteria to be blended into the financial statements of Sierra County. Which of the following fund types of the two governments would not be combined in the blended statements?

   a. pension trust funds

   b. general funds

   c. permanent funds

   d. proprietary funds

5. A primary government could "blend" its financial statements with those of a component unit as long as

   a. the governing boards of the two governments are substantively the same

   b. there is a financial benefit/burden relationship between the two governments

   c. the primary government provides services exclusively to the component unit

   d. the two governments satisfy GASB Statement No. 14 criteria for "economic inseparability"

6. With respect to a *nonmajor* component unit, a government

   a. must disclose key financial data about the unit in either the financial statements themselves or in notes thereto

   b. must, in its combining fund statements, present detailed financial statements of the unit in a separate column

   c. may, in its government-wide statements, exclude data pertaining to the unit from its component units column

   d. is not required to provide even summary financial data of the individual unit

7. Which of the following is *incorrect* with respect to a joint venture?

   a. It must be reported as a component unit of each government that has an interest of 20 percent or more in the venture.

   b. It may be accounted for in a proprietary fund on the equity basis.

   c. It may be reported in a schedule of capital assets.

   d. It must be accounted for in government-wide statements on an equity basis.

8. A *related organization*

   a. must be reported in the combining statements of the government to which it is related, but must not be incorporated into the government-wide statements of that government

   b. may be reported as a component unit of the reporting government to which it is related if the reporting government so elects

   c. must be described in notes to the financial statements of the reporting government to which it is related but must not be incorporated into the financial statements of that government

   d. may either be described in notes to the financial statements of the reporting government to which it is related or be incorporated into the financial statements of that government

9. The James City school system, although not a separate legal entity, maintains its own set of financial records. It is administered by a board, the members of which are appointed by the James City mayor. The system receives 70 percent of its funds from city appropriations and the balance from state and federal grants. The James City council has the authority to approve the school system's budget and to veto any decisions of its administering board. James City

   a. should account for the system as a component unit and blend its financial statements with its own

   b. should account for the system as a component unit and report it "discretely"

   c. should account for, and report, the system as it does other city departments

   d. should account for the system as a component unit only if the system does not prepare its own stand-alone financial statements

10. If a primary government has several component units, none of which satisfies the criteria for blending, then in its government-wide statements it

   a. must report governmental component units in one column and business-type component units in another

   b. must combine all component units into a single column

   c. must present each major component unit in a separate column but may combine all nonmajor component units into a single column

d. must incorporate data of all component units, whether major or nonmajor, into one or more columns

11-2

Select the *best* answer.

1. Which of the following should *not* be included in the introductory section of a city's CAFR?

   a. Management's discussion and analysis

   b. Letter of transmittal

   c. Government Finance Officers' certificate of achievement

   d. Photos of city officials

2. Which of the following should *not* be included in a city's management's discussion and analysis?

   a. condensed financial information drawn from government-wide statements

   b. a ten-year forecast of future sales tax revenues

   c. a discussion of the condition of the city's road system

   d. an explanation of the decrease during the past year in the unrestricted general fund balance

3. A city's general fund actual-to-budget comparisons should be included as part of a CAFR's

   a. introductory section

   b. notes to the basic financial statements

   c. required supplementary information

   d. statistical section

4. Internal service funds

   a. should be presented in the governmental fund statements in a single column

   b. should be presented in the proprietary fund statements in a single column

   c. should be presented in multiple columns (one for each major fund) in a separate set of fund statements

   d. need not be reported in the fund statements

5. Which of the following tables would be least likely to be found in the statistical section of a city's CAFR?

   a. General revenues by source—last ten years

   b. Computation of overlapping debt

   c. Property values—last ten years

   d. Salaries of key government officials—last ten years

6. For purposes of external reporting, private colleges and universities

   a. must adhere to all FASB pronouncements

   b. must adhere to all GASB pronouncements

   c. can opt to follow either all FASB or all GASB pronouncements

   d. must follow all FASB pronouncements issued prior to November 30, 1989, and either all or none of the GASB pronouncements subsequent to that date

7. For purposes of external reporting, a public college or university

   a. must report as if it were a general purpose government

   b. may report as if it were a comparable private college or university

   c. may report as a special purpose government engaged exclusively in business-type activities

   d. may report in accordance with the AICPA college and university model if it had adhered to that model prior to the issuance of GASB Statement No. 35

8. Which if the following would *not* be reported as required supplementary information?

   a. management's discussion and analysis

   b. details of pension actuarial valuations

   c. the condition of infrastructure

   d. the GFOA certificate of achievement (if earned)

9. Which of the following is least likely to be included in the CAFR of New Jersey State University, a public university that reports as a business-type entity?

   a. government-wide statement of activities

   b. management's discussion and analysis

   c. statement of cash flows

   d. required supplementary information

10. A special purpose government, such as an independent school district, that carries out multiple programs

   a. may opt to report as if it were a single purpose government engaged in only governmental activities

   b. may opt to report as if it were a single purpose government engaged in only business-type activities

   c. must report as if it were a general purpose government

d. must report as if it were a general purpose government, except that it need not prepare government-wide statements

11-3

A government must apply the criteria of GASB Statement No. 14 in determining whether and how to include a related entity in its reporting entity.

Frost city is considering whether and how it should include the following related entities in its reporting entity.

1. Its school system, although not a legally separate government, is managed by a school board elected by city residents. The system is financed with general tax revenues of the city and its budget is incorporated into that of the city at large (and thereby is subject to the same approval and appropriation process as other city expenditures).
2. Its capital asset financing authority is a legally separate government that leases equipment to the city. To finance the equipment, the authority issues bonds that are guaranteed by the city and expected to be paid from the rents received from the city. The authority leases equipment exclusively to the city.
3. Its housing authority provides loans to low-income families within the city and is governed by a five-person board appointed by the city's mayor.
4. Its hospital is owned by the city but managed under contract by a private hospital management firm.
5. Its water purification plant is owned in equal shares by the city and two neighboring counties. The city's interest in the plant was acquired with resources from its water utility (enterprise) fund.
6. Its community college, a separate legal entity, is governed by a board of governors elected by city residents and has its own taxing and budgetary authority.

Based on the information provided, indicate whether and how the city should report the related entity.

11-4

Some component units are presented "discretely"; others are "blended."

Elba City's reporting entity includes the following component units.

- A "capital projects financing authority" purchases capital assets and leases them exclusively to the city. It finances the acquisitions by issuing revenue bonds, which are payable out of the lease payments collected from the city.
- A "housing finance authority" is governed by a board, the majority of whose members are ap-

pointed by the city council. The authority purchases houses and leases them to low-income city residents. It finances the acquisitions by issuing revenue bonds, which are payable out of the lease payments collected from the residents.

- A "housing finance authority" is governed by a board, the members of which are also members of the city council. The authority purchases houses and leases them to low-income city residents. It finances the acquisitions by issuing revenue bonds, which are payable out of the lease payments collected from the residents.
- A "sanitation authority" is governed by a board, the majority of whose members are appointed by the city council. The authority provides trash collection services exclusively to city residents. It finances its capital assets with bonds that are guaranteed by the city. It obtains all of its revenues from user charges.

1. Based on the information provided, indicate whether each of the component units described above should be presented discretely or should be blended. Justify your responses.
2. Explain what is meant by *blending.* How is the general fund of a blended component unit reported on the primary government's financial statements?

11-5

A series of questions can be used to guide decisions as to whether and how to incorporate a potential component unit.

Apple County's library system is a legally constituted government entity governed by a ten-person board. Six of the members are appointed by the county council; four are selected by the other board members. The members serve staggered terms of three years and, once appointed, they can be removed from office only for illegal activities.

The county provides 95 percent of the library system's resources and thereby can control the total amount spent by the system. However, the governing board adopts the system's budget, which need not be approved by the county. The board also controls the day-to-day operations of the system.

By asking, and answering, a series of questions (as was done in the chapter) indicate whether and, if so, how the county should incorporate the library system into its reporting entity.

11-6

Public housing authorities are typical of the related entities toward which GASB Statement No. 14 is directed.

Hull City established a public housing authority (PHA) to fund the construction of low-income residential homes within city limits. The PHA is governed by a nine-person board of trustees. New trustees are nominated by the board, but must be formally appointed by the city council. However, the council has never rejected a board nominee. The trustees have complete responsibility for the PHA's day-to-day operations, but are required to obtain city council endorsement of the PHA's annual budget and must submit audited annual financial statements to the council. The PHA is permitted to issue its own debt, which is guaranteed by the federal government.

Approximately 90 percent of the PHA's day-to-day operating costs are paid by the Department of Housing and Urban Development (HUD, a federal agency) and 10 percent are paid by the city.

The sources of the funds used by the PHA to perform its functions are as follows:

- Authority-issued bonds (which will be repaid by tenant rents)—60 percent
- Direct federal subsidies—30 percent
- Direct city subsidies—10 percent

1. Should the city include the PHA in its reporting entity as a component unit per the provisions of GASB Statement No. 14? If so, how? Explain your response.

2. Assume the same facts except that the PHA does not directly fund the construction of homes. Instead, it lends money to the city's housing department, which, in turn, lends the funds to home buyers. How, if at all, would your response to question 1 differ?

3. Assume the same facts as for question 1, except that the city council serves as the PHA's board of trustees. How, if at all, would your response to question 1 differ? Explain.

11-7

Discrete presentation, unlike blending, may combine two or more major component units into a single column.

Hawkins Township has two component units that it is required to include in its reporting entity. The first, a housing authority, maintains two funds: a general fund and a special revenue fund. The second, a transportation authority, has only one fund: an enterprise fund. The township itself has only a general fund.

Condensed fund balance sheets for all three entities are shown below (in millions). Also presented, as appropriate, are general capital assets and long-term obligations that are not recognized on the governmental fund statements, since the statements are on a modified accrual basis.

Hawkins Township

	General Fund	General Capital Assets and Long-Term Obligations
Cash and Investments	$800	
Capital Assets	—	$140
Less: Accumulated Depreciation	—	40
Net Capital Assets		$100
Total Assets	$800	$100
Long-Term Obligations	—	$ 30
Fund Balance	$800	—
Total Long-Term Obligations and Fund Balance	$800	$ 30

Transportation Authority

Cash and Investments	$ 50
Capital Assets	800
Less: Accumulated Depreciation	200
Net Capital Assets	600
Total Assets	$650
Long-Term Obligations	$200
Fund Balance	$450
Total Long-Term Obligations and Fund Balance	$650

Housing Authority

	General Fund	Special Revenue Fund	General Capital Assets and Long-Term Obligations
Cash and Investments	$10	$5	—
Capital Assets	—	—	$45
Less: Accumulated Depreciation	—	—	20
Net Capital Assets	—	—	$25
Total Assets	$10	$5	$25
Long-Term Obligations	—	—	$ 5
Fund Balance	$10	$5	—
Total Long-Term Obligations and Fund Balance	$10	$5	$ 5

1. Assume that both component units qualify for *discrete presentation*. On its government-wide

statements, the township elects to combine the two units into a single column.

a. Prepare a government-wide statement of net assets (on a full accrual basis) that presents both the township and its component units.

b. Comment on the significance of the column in which the two component units are presented.

2. Suppose instead that the town is required to *blend* the two component units.

a. Prepare a government-wide statement of net assets. Be sure to show the transportation authority as a business-type activity.

b. In its fund statements, how would the township report the housing authority's special revenue fund? How would it report the authority's general fund?

11-8

A government's Comprehensive Annual Financial Report (CAFR) is divided into three main sections.

For each of these items from a municipality's CAFR, indicate whether it would be found in the introductory, financial, or statistical section. If the item would be found in the financial section, then specify whether it would be included in:

- the management's discussion and analysis (MD&A)
- the basic financial statements
- required supplementary information other than the MD&A
- combining statements and schedules

1. A balance sheet of nonmajor special revenue funds

2. A GFOA certificate of achievement for excellence in financial reporting

3. Data on general revenues, by source, for the past ten years

4. A letter of transmittal

5. An analysis of balances of individual funds

6. A government-wide statement of activities

7. The total unfunded actuarial liability of a pension plan for the past three years

8. Data on property tax collections for the past ten years

9. A statement of revenues, expenses, and changes in fund net assets for the city's utility fund (one of two major enterprise funds)

10. A statement comparing budgeted and actual revenues and expenditures for a special revenue fund

11. A statement of cash flows for a nonmajor enterprise fund

11-9

Colleges and universities may report as entities engaged only in business-type activities.

Review the financial statements of ABC University in Table 11-4.

1. For purposes of internal accounting, the university maintains several funds. Based on the information provided, indicate the names (or types) of as many funds as you can identify. Why would the university maintain so many funds?

2. What is the most likely distinction between the net assets classified as "expendable" and those as "nonexpendable?"

3. Suppose that the university financed the construction of its dormitories by issuing bonds secured by revenues from student room fees. What financial statements in addition to the three statements included in Table 11–4 would the university have to include in its CAFR? Why?

4. Suppose that the university elected to report as a special purpose government engaged in both governmental and business-type activities. How would the financial statements differ from those presented in Table 11-4? Which set of financial statements would provide the more comprehensive information? Explain.

5. The university attributes some of its revenues to "auxiliary enterprises." Although some examples were given, auxiliary enterprises were not addressed in detail in this chapter. Nevertheless, what is the most likely distinction between auxiliary enterprises and other academic or service units of the university?

6. The university hospital is reported as a discretely presented component unit. What is the most likely reason that it is not blended and reported as an integral part of the university (as are, for example, the college bookstore and its dormitories)?

7. The university reports unrestricted net assets of more than $12 million. Suppose that a faculty member complained in a letter to the university president that the institution is holding back resources that should properly be used to increase faculty salaries, acquire computers and library books, and improve classroom facilities. What might be an obvious response to the faculty member's complaint?

11-10

The fund balance sheet of a public university can be recast so that it conforms to GAAP.

The fund balance sheet of Sundown State University, a public institution, is presented on p. 295. For external reporting, the university has opted to

		Sundown State University			
		Fund Balance Sheet			
		(in thousands)			
	Current	Loan	Endowment	Plant	Total
Assets:					
Cash and temporary investments	$18,567	$22,108	$29,611	$ 10,853	$ 81,139
Accounts receivable	—	2,736	—	45,974	48,710
Inventories	1,990	—	—	—	1,990
Loans to other funds	8,557	—	6,879	—	15,436
Land, buildings and equipment, net of accumulated depreciation	—	—	—	283,181	283,181
Total assets	29,114	24,844	36,490	340,008	430,456
Liabilities:					
Accounts payable	23,024	—	—	1,704	24,728
Loans from other funds	—	32	—	15,404	15,436
Bonds payable	—	24,505	—	188,466	212,971
Total liabilities	23,024	24,537	0	205,574	253,135
Net assets	$ 6,090	$ 307	$36,490	$134,434	$177,321
Fund balances:					
Restricted	$ 4,102	$ —	$20,346	$134,434	$158,882
Designated by the university	1,002	—	10,000	—	11,002
Unrestricted	986	307	6,144	0	7,437
Total fund balance	$ 6,090	$ 307	$36,490	$134,434	$177,321

report as a special purpose entity that engages only in business-type activities. As best the data permit, recast the balance sheet into one that conforms to generally accepted accounting principles.

11-11

Exploring Orlando's financial report

Refer to the financial statements of the City of Orlando in Chapter 3 and to Tables 11-1, 11-2, and 11-3 in this chapter.

1. Is Orlando a primary government? Explain.
2. Which of the component units of Orlando's reporting entity are discretely presented? In which financial statements and where in those statements is information about these component units presented?
3. Why is the Civic Facilities Authority included as a component unit of Orlando's reporting entity when (per the notes in Table 11-1) the City does not appoint a voting majority of its board? Isn't appointment of a voting majority the key criterion for financial accountability, and thus for inclusion of a component unit in the reporting entity under Statement No. 14? Explain.
4. In which financial statements and where on those statements is Orlando's Community

Redevelopment Agency reported? Why is it reported differently from the Downtown Development Board and the Civic Facilities Authority?

5. Orlando's comprehensive annual financial report (CAFR) for fiscal year 2001 includes the following selected information. Indicate in which section of the CAFR you would expect to find this information: introductory section (IS), financial section (FS), or statistical section (SS).

   a. Auditor's report
   b. Combining statements for nonmajor governmental funds
   c. Tax revenues by source—last ten fiscal years
   d. Computation of direct and overlapping debt
   e. GFOA Certificate of Achievement for Excellence in Financial Reporting
   f. Budget-to-actual comparison for the general fund
   g. Description of the reporting entity
   h. Condensed statement of the government-wide statement of net assets
   i. Schedule of the ten largest taxpayers
   j. Brief description of the required financial statements

CHAPTER 12

Not-for-Profit Organizations

Governments and private-sector not-for-profit organizations confront similar accounting and reporting issues, but they do not necessarily follow the same standards. The differences can be justified in part by differences in the entities' characteristics and their constituents' information needs. For example, unlike governments, not-for-profits lack the authority of law to generate revenues and they have greater flexibility in administering their budgets. Different standards also result from dissimilarities in the composition and perspectives of the standard-setting authorities. This chapter will address accounting and reporting issues that affect all private not-for-profits in general. Chapter 13 considers issues specific to health care entities and universities. In Chapter 14 we shall discuss the elements of financial statement analysis for both governments and not-for-profits.

WHO'S IN CHARGE?

Whereas the GASB has standard-setting jurisdiction over all state and local governments, including government-owned not-for-profits, the FASB has jurisdiction over all private not-for-profits. Thus, for example, a state university or a city hospital or museum would be under the GASB's authority, whereas comparable nongovernmental entities would be under the FASB's control.

Although the FASB began operations in 1973, it did not establish standards specifically for not-for-profit organizations until 1987, when it issued a pronouncement on depreciation of their fixed assets. Until then, the AICPA articulated the accounting and reporting practices of not-for-profits through four industry audit guides—one each for colleges and universities, hospitals and other health care providers, voluntary health and welfare organizations, and other not-for-profit entities. Inasmuch as each publication was prepared by a different committee, there were inconsistencies in the guidelines. However, in 1996, because the FASB pronouncements were now common to all not-for-profits, the AICPA eliminated the inconsistencies and consolidated its audit guides into two:

1. *Health Care Organizations* covers hospitals, clinics, health maintenance organizations, nursing homes, and home health organizations.

2. *Not-for-Profit Organizations* covers all other not-for-profits, including colleges and universities.

These guides are updated periodically and incorporate the latest FASB pronouncements. They also provide guidance as to issues not addressed by the FASB.

Not-for-profit accounting is closer to business than to government accounting. Like their GASB counterparts, the FASB and AICPA pronouncements emphasize the superiority of the accrual basis of accounting, but they allow far fewer modifications and exceptions. External reporting is entirely on the full accrual basis. Irrespective of how not-for-profits maintain their records internally, the modified accrual basis has no place in their publicly issued statements. Thus, not-for-profits do not distinguish between expenses and expenditures; they have only expenses.

WHAT SHOULD BE THE FORM AND CONTENT OF FINANCIAL STATEMENTS?

As emphasized in Chapter 2, not-for-profits, like governments, account for their resources in funds, each of which is a separate accounting entity. As in governments, most entities maintain an unrestricted operating (or general) fund, as well as one or more restricted funds. Accordingly, the journal entries in this chapter will be made in the individual funds. However, the FASB is concerned with how entities report their overall financial position and operating results, not with the specific funds they maintain. A key issue, therefore, is whether not-for-profits should display each fund separately, aggregate them into groups of funds, or consolidate them into a single-column presentation. Although this chapter directs considerable attention to revenue and expense recognition in the funds, it will soon be apparent that how funds are aggregated impacts how and when certain types of revenues and expenses are reported in the basic financial statements.

REPORTING ASSETS AND LIABILITIES In its Statement No. 117, *Financial Statements of Not-for-Profit Organizations*, the FASB requires that not-for-profits issue three primary financial statements:

1. A statement of financial position (balance sheet)
2. A statement of activities
3. A statement of cash flows

Not-for-profits must classify their **net assets** into three categories based on the existence or absence of *donor-imposed* restrictions:

- **Unrestricted net assets**
- **Temporarily restricted net assets**—mainly resources that must be used either for specific purposes, in specific periods, or when specified events have occurred
- **Permanently restricted net assets**—ordinarily endowments, the principal of which must permanently remain intact, with only the income available for expenditure

Temporarily restricted net assets can take several forms. Resources that must be used for research, specific programs, or the acquisition of plant and equipment would be temporarily restricted as to *purpose*. The restriction would be removed when the organization incurred expenses that satisfied the donor's stipulations. A **term endowment** would be temporarily restricted as to *time*. A term endowment is a gift from which only the income is available for expenditure for a specified period of time. After that period, the gift principal is also available for expenditure. Pledges that will not be received until future periods may also be seen as subject to time restrictions. They are unavailable for expenditure until then. An **annuity** would be temporarily restricted, pending the occurrence of a *specified event*. An annuity is a gift that provides the donor with income until his or her death. Upon death, the balance of the gift reverts to the donee for either restricted or unrestricted purposes.

Even assets classified as unrestricted are not necessarily free of all restrictions—only those imposed by donors. Restrictions imposed by the organization's members, its own governing board, or by outside parties other than donors, such as bondholders and regulatory authorities, do not affect how net assets should be classified.

TABLE 12-1
American Health Association, Local Affiliate
Statement of Financial Position as of June 30, 2004

	Unrestricted	Temporarily Restricted	Permanently Restricted	Total
Assets				
Current Assets:				
Cash and Cash Equivalents	$ 806,383	$ —	$ —	$ 806,383
Short-Term Investments	8,884,309	288,073	—	9,172,382
Accrued Investment Income	192,427	—	—	192,427
Accounts Receivable—				
Federated and Nonfederated	—	694,382	—	694,382
National Center	20,382	—	—	20,382
Bequest Receivable	—	286,000	—	286,000
Pledges	84,601	19,000	—	103,601
Other	70,719	—	—	70,719
Educational and Campaign				
Material Inventory	250,670	—	—	250,670
Prepaid Expenses	79,410	—	—	79,410
Total Current Assets	10,388,901	1,287,455	—	11,676,356
Noncurrent Assets:				
Accounts Receivable—				
Pledges, Net of Discount of $1,000	—	19,000	—	19,000
Charitable Gift Annuity—				
National Center	40,500	—	—	40,500
Long-Term Investments	6,622,538	331,695	2,383,620	9,337,853
Beneficial Interest in Perpetual Trust	—	—	2,767,900	2,767,900
Contributions Receivable from Charitable				
Remainder Trust	—	4,963,216	—	4,963,216
Land, Buildings and Equipment, at Cost				
Less Accumulated Depreciation				
of $2,344,393	3,921,690	—	—	3,921,690
Total Noncurrent Assets	10,584,728	5,313,911	5,151,520	21,050,159
TOTAL ASSETS	$20,973,629	$6,601,366	$5,151,520	$32,726,515
Liabilities and Net Assets				
Current Liabilities:				
Payable to the National Center—				
Campaign Share	$ 3,181,641	$ 414,241	$ —	$ 3,595,882
Purchased Material	137,781	—	—	137,781
Accounts Payable and Accrued Expenses	585,896	—	—	585,896
Research Awards Payable				
Within One Year	3,315,845	—	—	3,315,845
Total Current Liabilities	7,221,163	414,241	—	7,635,404
Noncurrent Liabilities:				
Payable to the National Center—				
Campaign Share	—	1,240,804	—	1,240,804
Annuity Obligation	19,640	—	—	19,640
Research Awards Payable After One Year,				
Net of Discount of $50,000	1,983,172	—	—	1,983,172
Post Retirement Benefit Obligation	932,246	—	—	932,246
Total Noncurrent Liabilities	2,935,058	1,240,804	—	4,175,862
Total Liabilities	10,156,221	1,655,045	—	11,811,266

TABLE 12-1 *(continued)*
American Health Association, Local Affiliate
Statement of Financial Position as of June 30, 2004

	Unrestricted	Temporarily Restricted	Permanently Restricted	Total
Net Assets:				
Unrestricted				
Net Investment in Land, Building and Equipment	3,921,690	—	—	3,921,690
Designated by the Governing Board for Programs and Operations for the Ensuing Fiscal Year	6,697,513	—	—	6,697,513
Research Designated to Future Years	177,345	—	—	177,345
Charitable Gift Annuity—National Center	20,860	—	—	20,860
Temporarily Restricted				
Land, Buildings, and Equipment	—	168,953	—	168,953
Research	—	232,759	—	232,759
Public Health Education	—	354,341	—	354,341
Community Services	—	467,856	—	467,856
Charitable Remainder Trust	—	3,722,412	—	3,722,412
Permanently Restricted				
Endowment Funds	—	—	2,383,620	2,383,620
Beneficial Interest in Perpetual Trust	—	—	2,767,900	2,767,900
Total Net Assets	10,817,408	4,946,321	5,151,520	20,915,249
TOTAL LIABILITIES AND NET ASSETS	$20,973,629	$6,601,366	$5,151,520	$32,726,515

Statement No. 117 does not mandate a particular format for the statement of financial position but it requires six totals: total assets, total liabilities, total net assets, total unrestricted net assets, total temporarily restricted net assets, and total permanently restricted net assets. An illustrative statement shows the organization's assets, liabilities, and net assets (i.e., fund balances) from all funds in a single column. Net assets are then broken down into the three required categories of restrictiveness. Information as to the nature and amount of restrictions may be shown on the face of the statement or in the notes. For example, the two categories of restricted net assets may be subdivided by purpose, such as "restricted for acquisition of plant" or "restricted for scholarships." Another of several possibilities is to present the three categories of net assets in separate columns, with specific resources, as well as net assets, assigned to each category.

The FASB also directs that data as to liquidity be reported either on the face of the statement or in the notes. Most organizations satisfy this requirement by categorizing assets and liabilities as either current or noncurrent. For not-for-profits (unlike governments), there is little ambiguity as to what constitutes a current asset or liability; business standards apply. That is, current assets are resources reasonably expected to be realized in cash or sold or consumed during the normal operating cycle of the business.[1] Current liabilities are obligations whose liquidation is expected to require the use of current assets, or the creation of other current liabilities. Table 12–1 presents

---

[1]AICPA, Accounting Research Bulletin No. 43, *Restatement and Revision of Accounting Research Bulletins*, Chapter 3A.

the statement of financial position of the American Health Association, a voluntary health and welfare organization.

REPORTING REVENUES AND EXPENSES Statement No. 117 directs that revenues and expenses be reported in a statement of activities. Like the statement of financial position, it should focus on the organization as a whole. Further, it should report the changes in each of the three categories of net assets. The FASB specifies that the statement of activities must break out gains and losses recognized on investments and other assets from revenues and expenses, but otherwise leaves the form and content of the statement to the individual organization. Therefore, as in the statement of financial position, organizations can present the information in respect to the three categories of net assets in separate sections of the statement of activities (several rows each for the different categories) or in three separate columns.

Revenues are to be reported as increases in one of the three categories of net assets, depending on donor-imposed restrictions. However, in a controversial decision, the Board concluded that *all expenses should be reported as decreases in unrestricted net assets*. The Board reasoned that the organization's management selects the activities to be carried out, as well as how and when particular resources are to be used. The donors dictate only which of the activities their contributions will support.

As a result, a not-for-profit must make two sets of journal entries whenever it spends restricted resources. The first, in a restricted fund, records the decrease in cash or other assets and the release of the restrictions (decrease in restricted net assets); the second, in an unrestricted fund, records the expense and the resources released from restrictions (increase in unrestricted net assets). This entry has no effect on total unrestricted net assets, inasmuch as it consists of an expense (a debit) offset by the bookkeeping equivalent of an internal transfer-in (a credit) of the expended resources.

E X A M P L E   *Reporting Revenues and Expenses*
● ●

The Professional Accountants' Association receives a $50,000 contribution to promote truth in budgeting among governments. In the same year it spends the funds for the stipulated purpose.

The contribution is restricted as to purpose and would be recorded in a temporarily restricted fund:

Cash	$50,000	
Revenue from contributions		$50,000

To record the receipt of a temporarily restricted contribution (restricted fund)

When the association expends the resources for the stipulated purpose, it would account for the reduction in cash as follows:

Resources released from restriction	$50,000	
Cash		$50,000

To record the disbursement of cash in satisfaction of contributor restrictions (restricted fund)

"Resources released from restriction" is comparable to "other financing sources (or uses)," such as nonreciprocal transfers, in government accounting. It would be reported in the statement of activities as negative revenue, rather than an expense, because, as indicated, restricted funds do not report expenses.

At the same time, an unrestricted fund would recognize the expense and a corresponding increase in net assets:

Program expense	$50,000	
Resources released from restriction		$50,000

To record an expense and the release of contributor restrictions (unrestricted fund)

To be sure, the FASB's approach is complex. However, it permits not-for-profits to report all expenses in a single column and thereby show more clearly the full cost of organizational operations. In that regard, the result is similar to a government-wide statement of activities, which shows all expenses in one column, albeit grouped into those of governmental activities versus those of business-type activities.

The FASB permits an important exception to the requirement that all restricted contributions be classified upon receipt as restricted. It gives not-for-profits the option of reporting restricted contributions as unrestricted if the restriction has been met in the same period as the contribution is made. Table 12–2 presents the statement of activities of the American Health Association.

To fulfill its stated goal, financial reporting should provide information as to an organization's service efforts. (See excerpts from the FASB's statement of objectives in Table 1–4 of Chapter 1.) The FASB mandates that either the statement of activities or the accompanying notes report expenses by *function*—that is, by program services or supporting activities. As a result, the statement indicates to users not only the activities on which the organization is spending its resources, but more importantly the proportion of resources that are being directed toward service, as opposed to administrative, undertakings.

Voluntary health and welfare organizations must also report expenses by "natural" (i.e., object) classification, such as salaries, rent, electricity, and interest. The dual classification should be presented in matrix form in a separate financial statement of functional expenses. Other not-for-profits are encouraged, but not required, to provide similar information. Voluntary health and welfare organizations are organizations other than hospitals and colleges or universities that are formed to provide services to a community rather than to their own members. Examples include the United Way, Boy and Girl Scouts, the American Heart Association, and most social service agencies.

REPORTING CASH FLOWS As discussed in Chapter 9 pertaining to business-type activities, the GASB requires that governments report their cash flows in four categories:

1. Cash flows from operating activities
2. Cash flows from noncapital financing activities
3. Cash flows from capital and related financing activities
4. Cash flows from investing activities

By contrast, the FASB, in Statement No. 95, *Statement of Cash Flows*, directs that businesses classify their cash flows into three categories:

1. Cash flows from operating activities
2. Cash flows from financing activities
3. Cash flows from investing activities

In requiring a statement of cash flows for not-for-profits the FASB faced a dilemma. On the one hand, many experts, including a task force of the AICPA, asserted that, with respect to cash flows, the operations of not-for-profits more closely parallel those of governments than of businesses. Not-for-profits, like governments, draw the distinction between cash flows attributable to operations and those that are restricted

TABLE 12-2
American Health Association, Local Affiliate
Statement of Activities for the Year Ended June 30, 2004

	Unrestricted	Temporarily Restricted	Permanently Restricted	Total
Revenue:				
Public Support				
Received Directly				
Contributions	$ 2,603,328	$ 263,759	$ —	$ 2,867,087
Contributed Services	85,160	—	—	85,160
Capital Campaign	—	9,486	—	9,486
Special Events	10,528,221	12,500	—	10,540,721
Special Event Incentives	(1,802,014)	—	—	(1,802,014)
Net Special Events	8,726,207	12,500	—	8,738,707
Legacies and Bequests	1,327,126	788,844	270,000	2,385,970
Total Received Directly	12,741,821	1,074,589	270,000	14,086,410
Received Indirectly				
Allocated by Federated Fund-Raising				
Organizations	—	694,382	—	694,382
Allocated by Unassociated				
and Nonfederated				
Fund-Raising Organizations	142,472	—	—	142,472
Total Received Indirectly	142,472	694,382	—	836,854
Total Public Support	12,884,293	1,768,971	270,000	14,923,264
Other Revenue				
Grants from National Center	87,180	—	—	87,180
Program Fees	302,530	—	—	302,530
Sales of Educational Materials	1,106,074	—	—	1,106,074
Membership Dues	68,103	—	—	68,103
Investment Income	806,041	107,433	—	913,474
Perpetual Trust Revenue	—	64,732	—	64,732
Gains on Sale of Fixed Assets	6,468	—	—	6,468
Unrealized Gain on Perpetual				
Trust Contribution	—	—	308,100	308,100
Gains on Investment Transactions	—	103,544	—	103,544
Miscellaneous Revenue	96,296	—	—	96,296
Total Other Revenue	2,472,692	275,709	308,100	3,056,501
Net Assets Released from Restrictions:				
Satisfaction of Research Restrictions	704,264	(704,264)	—	—
Satisfaction of Program Restrictions	118,256	(118,256)	—	—
Satisfaction of Equipment Acquisition				
Restrictions	20,298	(20,298)	—	—
Satisfaction of Geographic Restrictions	266,000	(266,000)	—	—
Expiration of Time Restrictions	513,898	(513,898)	—	—
Total Net Assets Released				
from Restrictions	1,622,716	(1,622,716)	—	—
Total Public Support				
and Other Revenue	$16,979,701	$ 421,964	$ 578,100	$17,979,765

TABLE 12–2 *(continued)*			
American Health Association, Local Affiliate			
Statement of Activities for the Year Ended June 30, 2004			
	Unrestricted	**Temporarily Restricted**	**Permanently Restricted**	**Total**
---	---	---	---	---
Expenses:				
Program Services				
Research—to Acquire New Knowledge Through Biomedical Investigation	$ 3,659,784	$ —	$ —	$ 3,659,784
Public Health Education—to Inform the Public About the Prevention and Treatment of Cardiovascular Diseases and Stroke	3,565,704	—	—	3,565,704
Professional Education and Training—to Improve the Knowledge, Skills, and Techniques of Health Professionals	971,708	—	—	971,708
Community Services—to Provide Organized Training in Emergency Aid, Blood Pressure Screening, and Other Community-Wide Activities	2,050,768	—	—	2,050,768
Total Program Services	10,247,964	—	—	10,247,964
Supporting Services				
Management and General—Providing Executive Direction, Financial Management, Overall Planning, and Coordination of the Association's Activities	1,069,084	—	—	1,069,084
Fund Raising—Activities to Secure Vital Financial Support from the Public	2,487,090	—	—	2,487,090
Total Supporting Services	3,556,174	—	—	3,556,174
Total Program and Supporting Services Expenses	13,804,138	—	—	13,804,138
Allocation to the American Health Association, Inc. (National Center) for National Research and Other Activities	3,467,527	—	—	3,467,527
Total Expenses and Allocation to National Center	17,271,665	—	—	17,271,665
Change in Net Assets before Cumulative Effect of Changes in Accounting Principles	(291,964)	421,964	578,100	708,100
Cumulative Effect of Changes in Accounting Principles	(520,508)	3,844,838	2,459,800	5,784,130
Change in Net Assets	(812,472)	4,266,802	3,037,900	6,492,230
Net Assets, Beginning of Year	11,629,880	679,519	2,113,620	14,423,019
Net Assets, End of Year	$10,817,408	$4,946,321	$5,151,520	$20,915,249

for capital and comparable long-term purposes, such as permanent endowment funds. Accordingly, the experts contended, the FASB should adopt a four-way classification scheme similar to that established by the GASB. On the other hand, by requiring a four-way scheme the FASB would be widening the gulf between business and not-for-profit reporting, thereby countering a trend, and apparent objective, of narrowing it.

Emphasizing the importance of comparability between businesses and not-for-profits, the FASB elected to apply the three-way scheme to not-for-profits. However, in Statement No. 117 it modified Statement No. 95 so that it would be more germane to not-for-profits. For example, it stipulated that cash flows from financing activities should include both contributions restricted for long-term purposes and interest and dividends from investments restricted for long-term purposes. Other contributions and interest and dividends on investments not restricted for long-term purposes could be classified as operating cash flows. Table 12–3 sets forth the main types of cash flows included in each category.

TABLE 12–3
Classification of Cash Receipts and Disbursements Per FASB Statement No. 95, *Statement of Cash Flows*, as Modified by FASB Statement No. 117, *Financial Statements of Not-for-Profit Organizations*

Cash Flows from Operating Activities

Inflows
- Contributions that are either unrestricted or restricted for short-term purposes
- Sales of goods and services
- Interest and dividends not restricted for long-term purposes, for acquisition of capital assets, or for additions to endowments

Outflows
- Payments to employees
- Payments for supplies
- Payments of interest
- Payments of taxes
- Grants to other organizations

Cash Flows from Investing Activities

Inflows
- Proceeds from sale of facilities
- Payments received on notes from sale of capital assets
- Receipts from sale of stocks and bonds

Outflows
- Purchases of stocks and bonds
- Acquisitions of capital assets

Cash Flows from Financing Activities

Inflows
- Contributions restricted for long-term purposes
- Interest and dividends from investments restricted for long-term purposes
- Contributions restricted to the acquisition of capital assets
- Interest and dividends restricted to the acquisition of capital assets
- Contributions to endowments
- Proceeds of borrowing

Outflows
- Repayment of debt
- Lease payments under capital leases

In another notable difference between the GASB and FASB approaches to reporting cash flows, the GASB (per Statement No. 34) mandates that governments use the direct, as opposed to the indirect, method. The FASB only encourages, but does not require, use of the direct method. Table 12–4 presents the statement of cash flows of the American Health Association, prepared using the indirect method.

TABLE 12–4
American Health Association, Local Affiliate
Statement of Cash Flows for the Year Ended June 30, 2004

Cash Flows from Operating Activities	
Change in Net Assets	$ 6,492,230
Adjustments to Reconcile Change in Net Assets to Net Cash	
Provided by Operating Activities	
Depreciation and Amortization	386,056
Unrealized Gain on Perpetual Trust Contributions	(308,100)
Gains on Investment Transactions	(103,544)
Gain on Sale of Fixed Assets	(6,468)
Contributions Restricted to Investment in Property	(9,486)
Contributions to Endowment Funds	(270,000)
Increase in Accrued Investment Income	(57,260)
Increase in Federated and Nonfederated Receivable	(13,516)
Increase in National Center Receivable	(20,382)
Decrease in Other Receivables	116,532
Decrease in Bequest Receivable	314,000
Decrease in Pledges Receivable	2,812
Decrease in Educational and Campaign Material Inventory	78,454
Increase in Other Assets	(21,255)
Increase in Perpetual Trust	(2,459,800)
Increase in Charitable Gift Annuity	(40,500)
Increase in Charitable Remainder Trust	(4,963,216)
Increase in Payable to National Center	1,332,258
Increase in Accounts Payable and Accrued Expenses	808,360
Increase in Research Awards Payable	225,508
Increase in Annuity Obligation	19,640
Decrease in Deferred Revenue and Support	(413,959)
Net Cash Provided by Operating Activities	$ 1,088,364
Cash Flows from Investing Activities	
Purchase of Equipment	$ (724,492)
Proceeds from Sale of Equipment	200,217
Proceeds from Maturities of Investments	7,730,368
Purchase of Investments	(8,216,079)
Net Cash Used in Investing Activities	$(1,009,986)
Cash Flows from Financing Activities	
Contributions to Endowment Funds	$ 270,000
Proceeds from Contributions Restricted to Investment in Property	9,486
Net Cash Provided by Financing Activities	$ 279,486
Net Increase in Cash and Cash Equivalents	$ 357,864
Cash and Cash Equivalents (at Beginning of Year)	448,519
Cash and Cash Equivalents (at End of Year)	$ 806,383
Supplemental Data	
Noncash Investing and Financing Activities—Gifts of Equipment	$30,000

What are Contributions, and How Should Pledges be Accounted for?

Contributions, a mainstay of support for many not-for-profits, encompass all *nonreciprocal* receipts of assets or services. In FASB standards, a nonreciprocal receipt is one for which the recipient gives nothing in exchange. Thus, it is equivalent to a nonexchange revenue of a government.

As defined by the FASB in Statement No. 116, *Accounting for Contributions Received and Contributions Made,* contributions may be made in cash, marketable securities, property and equipment, utilities, supplies, intangible assets (such as patents and copyrights) and the services of professionals and craftsmen.[2] Contributions also include **unconditional promises,** that is, **pledges,** to give those items in the future. They exclude, however, **conditional promises.** A conditional promise depends on a specified future event to bind the donor. For example, a university alumnus might promise funds to construct a new physics laboratory *if* the university wins a government research grant.

CONTRIBUTIONS VERSUS EXCHANGE TRANSACTIONS Contributions must be distinguished from exchange transactions. A contribution is a transfer of assets in which the donor does not expect to receive equal value in return. An exchange transaction is one in which each party receives and gives up resources of commensurate value. For example, if a private corporation were to give a not-for-profit research foundation funds to study the cause of a disease, with the expectation only that the results would be published in a scientific journal, the transaction would be considered a contribution. If, on the other hand, it gave the funds with the contractual agreement that it would have the rights to resultant patents, then the transaction would be considered an exchange transaction.

Distinguishing between exchange transactions and contributions requires the exercise of judgment. When people join the Friends of the Library Association, do they do so to support the library's scholarly activities or to obtain the right to attend members-only lectures? Do they send money to their local public radio station to promote classical music or to receive the coffee mugs offered as a premium? Factors to be taken into account in making a decision include the recipient's intent in soliciting the resources, whether the transferor or the transferee establishes the amount of the transfer, and the penalties if either party fails to deliver on its promise.

As previously discussed, the classification of resources into the three categories of restrictiveness is based on *donor* stipulation. Hence, restrictions apply only to contributions. Exchange transactions are always unrestricted and should be accounted for as ordinary commercial transactions.

PLEDGES Not-for-profits have traditionally recognized gifts of cash and other assets not preceded by a pledge as revenue upon receipt. Gifts of assets other than cash have been measured at their fair (i.e., market) value.

But when should not-for-profits recognize pledges to donate cash or other assets in the future? Organizations generally lack legally enforceable claims against fickle donors. Even if they do have legally enforceable claims, they may be reluctant to act upon them because of the associated costs in both goodwill and legal fees. A pledge may be legally enforceable when the organization has acted on it and thereby incurred costs. Suppose, for example, that an organization, relying on a donor's

---

[2]FASB Statement No. 116, para. 5.

promise to finance a new building, engages an architect to draw up plans. The donor reneges. The organization may have a valid claim upon the donor for its losses but may decide that the potential benefit is not worth the cost of pursuing the claim.

More importantly, pledges receivable, albeit assets, are not available for expenditure. They cannot be used to pay employees or suppliers. Recognition of pledges might give the unwarranted impression that the organization has excess spendable funds and thereby has less need for further financial assistance.

On the other hand, many organizations have sufficient experience to reliably estimate the percentage of pledges that will be uncollectible and, like merchants, can establish appropriate allowances for uncollectibles. Further, they can borrow against the pledges and spend the proceeds. Arguably, therefore, there is no more justification for a not-for-profit than for a merchant to delay revenue recognition until cash is in hand.

Until the FASB standardized practice, some not-for-profits recognized revenue upon receipt of a pledge. Most, however, consistent with their conservative accounting traditions, chose to wait until cash had been collected.

Businesses measure receivables at the present value of anticipated cash flows (except for short-term receivables for which the impact of discounting would be immaterial). They adjust the stated amount of a receivable to take into account both anticipated defaults and the time value of money. Prior to the FASB pronouncement on contributions, not-for-profits that recorded pledges reduced their carrying value to take into account anticipated defaults. They did not, however, discount the face value to take into account the time value of money.

EXAMPLE   *Pledges*

In November 2004, a public broadcasting station conducts its annual pledge drive and receives telephone pledges of $700,000. By year-end December 31, it has collected $400,000 of the pledges. Based on previous experience, it estimates that $60,000 of the balance will be uncollectible. In addition, it receives a pledge from a local foundation to contribute $100,000 at the end of each of the next three years.

FASB Standards

In Statement No. 116, the FASB, over the vociferous objections of many not-for-profits, decided that unrestricted pledges should be reported as revenue upon receipt of the pledge. The amount of revenue reported should take into account both anticipated bad debts and the time value of money, using a discount rate commensurate with the risk involved. However, not-for-profits need not discount pledges to be collected within one year.

To avoid recognizing contributions as unrestricted revenue before they are available for expenditure, not-for-profits should consider pledges of cash to be received in future periods as subject to *time restrictions.* The FASB concluded that by promising to make payments in the future, donors implicitly restrict the donated resources to support future, not current, activities. Hence, the recipient organizations should classify them as *temporarily restricted.* When the cash is received and available for expenditure, they transfer resources from the temporarily restricted to the unrestricted category. However, the standard allows an option to recognize pledges that are restricted, either as to time or use, as unrestricted if the restriction has been met in the same period as the donation is made.

The following entries, in both unrestricted and temporarily restricted funds, summarize the results of the year's pledge drive:

Pledges receivable	$400,000	
Revenues from contributions		$400,000

To record the pledges of cash to be paid in the current year (unrestricted fund)

Cash	$400,000	
Pledges receivable		$400,000

To record the collection of cash (in an unrestricted fund)

These pledges fall under the exception that, when time restrictions are satisfied within the same year, the revenue may be reported as unrestricted.

Pledges receivable	$300,000	
Pledges receivable—allowance for uncollectibles		$ 60,000
Revenues from contributions		240,000

To record the pledges expected to be collected in future periods (temporarily restricted fund)

As the pledges are collected in subsequent years, the resources would be released from the temporarily restricted category and added to the unrestricted category. Thus, if $75,000 were collected:

Resources released from restriction	$75,000	
Pledges receivable		$75,000

To release the resources from restriction upon collection of cash (temporarily restricted fund)

Cash	$75,000	
Resources released from restriction		$75,000

To record the collection of cash (unrestricted fund)

Were the station to determine that 10 percent is an appropriate discount rate, then the present value of the annuity of $100,000 per year for three years would be $248,690. (The present value of an annuity of $1 for three periods, discounted at a rate of 10 percent, is $2.4869. Hence, the present value of the annuity of $100,000 is $100,000 × 2.4869.) The appropriate discount rate is the prevailing *risk-free* interest rate. The risk-free rate should be used because, by establishing an allowance for uncollectibles, the organization will have already factored in the risk of loss from bad debts.

Pledges receivable	$248,690	
Revenues from contributions		$248,690

To record a pledge of three annual payments of $100,000, the present value of which, discounted at 10 percent, is $248,690 (temporarily restricted fund)

Each year, as the $100,000 is received, the station would recognize interest at a rate of 10 percent on the net balance of the pledge (the pledge receivable less the remaining discount) and record the excess as a reduction of the pledges receivable. Interest for the first year would be 10 percent of $248,690, or $24,869. Thus, when the first installment is received:

Resources released from restriction	$75,131	
Pledges receivable		$75,131

To release the resources upon collection of cash in the first year (temporarily restricted fund)— $100,000 cash received less interest at a rate of 10 percent on the pledge balance of $248,690

Cash	$100,000	
Contributions—interest revenue		$24,869
Resources released from restriction		75,131

To record the first year's payment of $100,000 (unrestricted fund)

In the two subsequent years, as the balance in pledges receivable is reduced, greater proportions of the $100,000 would be assigned to principal and lesser proportions to interest. By the end of the third year the balance in the pledges receivable account would be reduced to zero. The interest should be reported as additional contributions.

WHEN SHOULD USE-RESTRICTED CONTRIBUTIONS BE RECOGNIZED?

Contributions to not-for-profits that are subject to **use restrictions** are equivalent, in concept, to a government's restricted grants; they can be used only for donor-specified purposes. Before the FASB issued its pronouncement on contributions, most not-for-profits recognized revenue from restricted grants as they expended the funds for the specified purpose. In that way, they matched the revenues to the expenses to which they were related.

As a consequence of this practice, organizations failed to give timely recognition to transactions that, it could be argued, clearly enhanced their welfare. A restricted gift, no less than an unrestricted gift, provides an economic benefit; it helps the organization to carry out its mission.

EXAMPLE   *Use-Restricted Contributions*

In 2004, the Lyric Opera Society receives a $150,000 contribution to fund a production of Gilbert and Sullivan's *H.M.S. Pinafore*, to be performed in 2005.

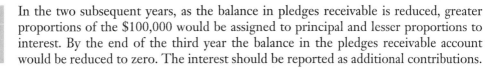

FASB Standards

Per Statement No. 116, restricted contributions, including pledges, are recognized as revenues in the period received or promised, irrespective of when the resources will be expended. As discussed previously, for reporting purposes, distinctions must be drawn among resources that are unrestricted, temporarily restricted, and permanently restricted.

Thus, the Lyric Opera Society would report its gift in a temporarily restricted fund:

Cash	$150,000	
Revenues from contributions		$150,000

To record a temporarily restricted gift (temporarily restricted fund)

When, in 2005, the Society expends the resources, it would record the release of the funds in the restricted fund and the expense in its current operating fund:

Resources released from restriction	$150,000	
Cash (or payables)		$150,000

To record the release of restrictions (temporarily restricted fund)

Production expenses	$150,000	
Resources released from restriction		$150,000

To record the expenditure of funds previously restricted (unrestricted fund)

The expenditure of the funds raises a related issue. Suppose the society budgeted an additional $150,000 or more of its own resources to finance the production. When it spent the first $150,000, was it spending its own resources or the donated resources?

Per the FASB, as long as the organization incurs an expense for a purpose for which the restricted resources are available, it should consider the restriction as having been released. The only exception is that if the organization receives resources from two external donors, both of which restrict resources for the same purpose, then it cannot release the two restrictions with the expenditure of the same resources.

The FASB approach is similar to that of the GASB in that pledges subject to use restrictions should be recognized as revenue upon receipt of the pledge. Recall from Chapter 4 that GASB standards require governments to give immediate recognition to grants or other revenues subject to purpose restrictions. The recipients should not delay recognition until they have satisfied the restrictions.

SHOULD CONTRIBUTIONS OF SERVICES BE RECOGNIZED?

Not-for-profits benefit from the services of volunteers, ranging from professional assistance that would otherwise have to be paid for at commercial rates to normal activities carried out by an organization's members. Consider some examples:

- An advertising agency develops a fund-raising campaign for a not-for-profit welfare agency.
- An attorney provides free legal counsel to a hospital.
- Nurses are paid considerably less than the prevailing wage by a hospital maintained by a religious order of which they are members.
- Community members perform odd jobs at a local hospital, such as carrying meals to patients, staffing the reception desk, and maintaining the hospital's library and recreation area.
- Church members paint the church facilities and construct a children's play center.

In each example, the organization receives an economic benefit from the contributed services. Correspondingly, it incurs a cost in that it "consumes" the services provided. Yet it is not obvious whether the values of these contributed services can be reliably measured and, if they can, whether they should be accorded financial statement recognition.

EXAMPLE   *Service Contributions*

The Northern New Mexico Clinic, a not-for-profit health care provider, recruits a local contractor to repave its parking lot. Had the contractor billed the clinic at standard rates, the cost would have been $12,000.

FASB Standards

Recognizing the diverse nature of contributed services, the FASB in Statement No. 116 prescribes that they should be recognized only if they are of a *professional nature* and of the type that the *entity would ordinarily have had to pay for*

(continued)

FASB Standards (*continued*)

had they not been donated. It establishes two conditions, either of which must be met, for recognition:

- The services create or enhance nonfinancial assets.
- The services require specialized skills, are provided by individuals possessing those skills, and would typically need to be purchased if not provided by donation. Services requiring specialized skills, according to the FASB, are those provided by accountants, architects, carpenters, doctors, electricians, lawyers, nurses, plumbers, teachers, and other professionals and craftsmen.[3]

The services received by the Northern New Mexico Clinic satisfy both of these conditions. Hence, the clinic should recognize both a revenue and a corresponding expense of $12,000.

SHOULD CONTRIBUTIONS OF COLLECTION ITEMS BE RECOGNIZED?

In Chapter 7, pertaining to capital assets, we addressed the issue of whether governments should capitalize the collectibles that they hold in museums, universities, libraries, and similar institutions. We noted that the GASB adopted the basic position of the FASB as set forth in FASB Statement No. 116. A notable difference between the FASB and GASB positions, however, is that the GASB requires that governments recognize the receipt of all collectibles as revenues. If they capitalize the collectibles they would offset the revenues with a capital asset. If not, they would offset the revenues with an expense. The FASB, by contrast, does not permit not-for-profits to recognize as revenues the receipt of collectibles that they do not capitalize.

FASB Standards

Statement No. 116 encourages not-for-profits to recognize contributions of collectibles as revenues and to capitalize their entire collections. However, it states that entities *need* not (*Note*: not *cannot*) recognize contributions of collectibles as long as the items satisfy all of the following conditions:

- They are held for public exhibition, education, or research in furtherance of public service rather than financial gain.
- They are protected, kept unencumbered, cared for, and preserved.
- They are subject to an organizational policy that requires proceeds from sales of collection items be used to acquire other items for collections.

If not-for-profits elect not to capitalize their collections, then they must disclose, in notes to the statements, the details of items both purchased and "deaccessed." If they capitalize their collections, they must recognize contributions of collection items as revenues; if not, they should not recognize them as revenues.[4]

---

[3]FASB Statement No. 116, para. 9.
[4]FASB Statement No. 116, paras. 11 and 13.

WHEN SHOULD CONDITIONAL PROMISES BE RECOGNIZED?

Donors may promise to contribute to a not-for-profit on condition that a specified event take place or that the entity take specified actions. **Conditional promises to give** must be distinguished from *restricted* contributions. A restricted gift is one that must be used for a particular purpose. A conditional promise, by contrast, is one in which the donor will provide the resources only if the specified condition is satisfied. The resources to be provided may be either restricted or unrestricted.

In practice, the distinction between a restricted gift and a conditional gift may be ambiguous. A donor may pledge resources that can be used only to support a particular activity, such as a conference. Although the promise is not explicitly conditioned upon the entity holding the conference, the donor is not likely to provide the resources if the conference is not held. Such a restricted gift is not much different from a conditional gift—one in which the donor promises to provide resources to the organization if and when it holds the conference.

A conditional promise unquestionably is an economic benefit to a not-for-profit entity, as long as there is a probability that the conditions can be met. Yet, if there is reasonable uncertainty, the entity may be premature in recognizing revenue before it has "earned" the right to the contribution by satisfying the conditions.

EXAMPLE *Conditional Promises*

The City Symphony is conducting a campaign to provide financing for a new auditorium. In 2004, a private foundation agrees to match 50 percent of all other contributions up to $1 million (i.e., each $1 of its gift is conditioned upon the symphony raising $2 from other sources). During the year, the symphony receives $500,000 in other donations.

FASB Standards

Statement No. 116 stipulates that conditional promises to give shall be recognized when the conditions on which they depend are substantially met.

In 2004, the symphony satisfied the conditions to receive $250,000 of the foundation's donation. Thus, it should recognize pledges receivable and contributions revenue in that amount. It would delay recognition of any further contributions from the foundation until it raised additional funds from other parties.

Reimbursement grants generally fall within the category of conditional promises. Either implicitly or explicitly, the grantor pledges to reimburse the grantee for allowable costs conditioned upon the grantee incurring, and providing documentation of, those costs.

How Should "Pass-Through" Contributions Be Accounted For?

In Chapter 4, we raised the issue of how governments should account for pass-through grants. These are grants that a recipient is required to distribute to other parties—for example, when a state receives a federal grant that it must pass through to local governments. The GASB's position is that the original recipient of the grant should recognize it as revenue (and the subsequent distribution as an expenditure or expense) unless the original recipient is nothing more than a *cash conduit*—an entity that has no administrative involvement with the grant, such as selecting the ultimate beneficiaries or monitoring compliance with grant requirements.

Not-for-profits face similar issues with regard to contributions. Consider, for example, the following three situations.

EXAMPLE   *A Federated Fund-Raising Organization*

The United Campaign of Springfield distributes all contributions received to numerous local, regional, and national organizations, including entities as diverse as local food distribution centers and the Red Cross. Donors have three choices as to how their contributions may be used:

- They can give without restriction, in which case the distribution of their gifts is left to a committee of United Campaign board members.
- They can specify that their gifts be designated for one of several groups of organizations, each of which targets a specific community need (e.g., health care, youth activities, poverty, education, or cultural organizations).
- They can designate a gift to one or more *specific* organizations.

EXAMPLE   *A Foundation that Transfers Assets to a Specified Organization*

The Foundation for Classical Music, which is governed by an independent board of trustees, was established to benefit a local opera company. The foundation's charter states that all contributions will be added to its permanent endowment. Endowment income will be transferred to the opera company, subject to the right of the foundation's trustees to redirect funds to other arts-related organizations, without donor approvals, if and when, in the trustees' judgment, the opera company becomes self-supporting.

EXAMPLE   *A Foundation that Supports a Related Organization*

The Friends of the Museum Foundation, which is governed by a board of trustees selected by the museum's board of governors, was established to stimulate private contributions from the community to assist the museum in acquiring works of art and carrying out various cultural activities. Although all funds collected by the foundation will eventually benefit the museum, the foundation's trustees can choose the timing of transfers from the foundation and the specific purposes for which they will be used.

FASB Standards

In its Statement No. 136, *Transfers of Assets to a Not-For-Profit Organization or Charitable Trust that Raises or Holds Contributions for Others*, the FASB took a position similar in spirit, but different in approach, to that of the GASB. The FASB held that when an organization accepts contributions from a donor and agrees to transfer the assets to, or use them on behalf of, a specific beneficiary, then it should not recognize the donation as revenue (or the subsequent distribution as an expense). Instead, the recipient organization should offset the assets received with a liability—a payable to the ultimate beneficiary. There are, however, two main exceptions:

1. If the donor has explicitly granted the recipient organization **variance power,** then the organization must recognize the contribution as revenue. *Variance power* is the right to unilaterally redirect the use of the assets received to another beneficiary. The rationale for this exception is that an organization that has variance power is not merely an agent, but has substantive decision-making authority and discretion over how the donation may be used.

2. If the recipient and beneficiary organizations are *financially interrelated*, then the recipient organization must recognize the contribution as revenue. Correspondingly, the beneficiary organization must recognize an interest in the net assets of the recipient organization (an asset) and periodically adjust that interest for its share in the change in the net assets of the recipient organization. This type of accounting is similar to the equity method of accounting for a business's interest in a subsidiary. Organizations are considered to be "financially interrelated" when

   - One organization has the ability to influence the operating and financial decisions of the other (as when one organization has "considerable" representation on the governing board of the other) *and*

   - One organization has an ongoing economic interest in the net assets of the other characterized by *residual rights* (as when the beneficiary organization profits from the investment, fund-raising, or operating activities of the recipient organization).

The second exception is based on the premise that when two organizations have a close cooperative relationship, the recipient organization is unlikely to have an obligation to transfer its assets to the beneficiary organization at any specific time. Instead, the beneficiary organization is content to leave the resources with the recipient organization, knowing that it will have access to them whenever it needs them. Typically, however, this exception may be moot. If one of the entities can control the other, then the two will most probably be required to consolidate their financial statements (an issue to be commented on later in this chapter). Then, of course, the contribution would be recognized as revenue by the consolidated entity when received.

In the first example, the United Campaign would recognize as unrestricted revenue the contributions on which the donors did not place restrictions. Those donations designated for one of several groups of organizations would be recorded as *temporarily restricted revenue*, inasmuch as they must be used for specified purposes. United Campaign could not, however, recognize as revenue the contributions of the donors who designated *specific* organizations. The receipt of these contributions would have to be recorded as a liability to those organizations; the United Campaign does not have variance power, and it is not financially affiliated with the beneficiary organizations.

In the second example, the Foundation for Classical Music has been granted variance power; it can redirect endowment income to arts organizations other than the local opera company. Therefore, it can recognize contributions as revenue (permanently restricted since they must be added to a permanent endowment) upon receipt.

In the third example, the foundation and the museum are related organizations. Upon receipt of contributions, the foundation can recognize them as revenue (restricted or unrestricted depending on the donors' stipulations). In the same period, the museum would recognize an asset (e.g., interest in net assets of museum foundation), offset by a revenue (e.g., increase in interest in net assets of museum). However, assuming that the two entities are so tightly intertwined that they will have to prepare consolidated financial statements, the foundation's interest in the net assets of the museum (and the offsetting increase in the net assets) will be eliminated in the consolidation process.

WHEN SHOULD GAINS AND LOSSES ON INVESTMENTS BE RECOGNIZED?

The FASB standards for not-for-profits on investment valuation are generally consistent with those of the GASB for governments. Both require that investments be marked to market.

FASB Standards

The FASB, in Statement No. 124, *Accounting for Certain Investments Held by Not-for-Profit Organizations*, prescribed that not-for-profits, like businesses, must report their investments at fair value and recognize the changes in fair value as they occur. They need not, however, classify the investments into the three categories (trading, available-for-sale, and held-to-maturity) required of businesses. Therefore, even debt securities that are expected to be held to maturity must be stated at fair value. The only exempt securities are investments accounted for under the equity method, investments in consolidated subsidiaries, and those for which the fair value is not readily determinable. The fair value of an equity security is generally considered to be readily determinable if the security is traded on a major exchange or over the counter.

Per Statement No. 124, interest, dividends, and gains and losses from changes in the fair value of securities should be reported on the statement of activities as increases or decreases in *unrestricted* net assets—unless their use is temporarily or permanently restricted by explicit donor stipulation or law. However, even investment income and gains from restricted assets may be recognized as increases in unrestricted assets if the restrictions are met in the same reporting period and the organization follows the same policy with respect to contributions received.

EXAMPLE *Investment Gains*

In June 2004, the Children's Welfare Association receives a grant of $100,000, which it classifies as temporarily restricted. To earn a return until it needs the funds, the Association invests the proceeds in Treasury notes. As of December 31, 2004, the fair market value of the notes is $103,000. The following entry in an *unrestricted* fund would be appropriate:

Investments	$3,000	
Investment earnings—appreciation in fair value		$3,000

To record the increase in fair value

The earnings would be reported in an unrestricted fund because only the grant, not the earnings from the grant, is restricted.

The investments would now be divided into the two fund categories:

Unrestricted	$ 3,000
Temporarily restricted	100,000
Total	$103,000

If the securities were subsequently sold for $103,000, entries in both an unrestricted and restricted fund would be needed:

Cash	$100,000	
Investments		$100,000

To record the sale of securities in a temporarily restricted fund

Cash	$3,000	
Investments		$3,000

To record the sale of securities in an unrestricted fund

The toughest investment decision for managers of many not-for-profits is whether they should place their cash in a checking or a savings account. Others, however, must manage multibillion dollar portfolios. The Ford Foundation, for example, has investments that are worth more than $14 billion; the endowment portfolio of Harvard University is over $6 billion.

Many not-for-profits face the same pressures as governments and businesses to maximize their investment returns. As a result, they sometimes place their funds in sophisticated financial instruments, such as derivatives, and engage in complex transactions, such as interest-rate swaps. Financial reporting standards do not address the suitability of particular instruments. Rather, they ensure that reporting entities disclose information as to the value of their investments and the nature of the transactions in which they engage. The requirements for not-for-profits are generally the same as those for businesses.

How Should Organizations Account for Gains and Losses on Endowments?

ENDOWMENT GAINS In Chapter 10, we noted that, in the absence of specific donor or legal stipulations to the contrary, the GASB permits governments to account for gains on the investments of endowment funds in accordance with the decision of the endowment trustees. Thus, they may be accounted for as additions to (nonexpendable) principal or (expendable) income. The FASB is more precise as to its criteria for the expenditure of gains, but the resultant practices are similar to those of governments.

FASB Standards

Statement No. 117 says: "A statement of activities shall report gains and losses recognized on investments and other assets (or liabilities) as increases or decreases in *unrestricted* net assets unless their use is temporarily or permanently restricted by explicit donor stipulations or by law."[5] If, by donor stipulation or law, investment gains were permanently restricted (i.e., not expendable), then they would be reported as additions to *permanently restricted* net assets. If they were expendable, but had to be used for a specific purpose, then they would be reported as additions to *temporarily restricted* net assets.

ENDOWMENT LOSSES The differences between the investment practices of governments and not-for-profits are more significant with respect to endowment losses than gains. As discussed in Chapter 10, the GASB has not specifically addressed the issue of losses and most governments apportion them to the funds (whether expendable or nonexpendable) that account for the securities on which the losses were sustained. Thus, losses recorded on the (nonexpendable) principal of an endowment could reduce its balance below the amount contributed by donors and which they expected to be preserved in perpetuity. The FASB requirements would prevent this result.

FASB Standards

Per FASB Statement No. 124, unless a not-for-profit is required by donor or legal stipulation to do otherwise, it should first charge investment losses (both realized and unrealized) to temporarily restricted net assets to the extent that donor-imposed restrictions on previously recognized net appreciation have not yet been met. It should charge any remaining losses to unrestricted net assets. If, in a subsequent year, investment gains restore the value of the investments to their original value, then organizations should credit the gains first to unrestricted net assets (to the extent previously deducted) and then to temporarily restricted net assets.

Thus, absent alternative donor or legal stipulations, a not-for-profit's endowment principal (permanently restricted net assets) would not be affected by either gains or losses on investments.

---

[5]FASB Statement No. 117, para. 22, emphasis added.

HOW CAN ORGANIZATIONS PROTECT AGAINST INFLATION, YET REAP THE BENEFITS OF CURRENT INCOME?

Not-for-profits, as well as governments, can readily protect against inflation, yet simultaneously reap the benefits of current income, by taking a *fixed rate of return* (often referred to as a *total return*) approach to the distribution of income. The fixed rate of return approach requires the organization to make available for current expenditure a fixed percentage of its endowment portfolio, irrespective of actual interest and dividends. The fixed (or *spending*) rate would be based on long-term estimates of anticipated appreciation, inflation, dividends, and interest.

EXAMPLE   *Fixed Rate of Return Approach*

A university expects to earn an annual return of 10 percent on its $1 million portfolio, divided as follows:

Interest and dividends	$ 40,000
Appreciation	60,000
Total Return	$100,000

It anticipates an annual inflation rate of 3 percent per year. Thus, it expects its real (inflation-adjusted) return to be only 7 percent (10 percent less 3 percent). Consistent with the fixed rate of return concept, the university permits annual spending of only 7 percent of its endowment principal—$70,000 the first year. The first-year excess of $30,000 is to be added to the principal and reinvested.

The apparent—and one-time controversial—accounting issue faced by organizations that take a total return approach is whether the fund in which the endowment *income* is reported should recognize as investment revenue the amount *transferred* to it or the amount *actually earned* by the endowment fund. However, under Statement No. 117 for not-for-profits (and current practice for governments), the answer is now clear. A fixed rate of return approach has no special accounting standing. Both not-for-profits and governments should account for investment income, including appreciation, as previously described.

In the example, therefore, if endowment income does not legally have to be added to principal, then, irrespective of whether the university were private or public, the entire $100,000 should be accounted for as ordinary investment revenue. The university could authorize the expenditure of only $70,000, opting to retain $30,000 as if it were permanently restricted. If it were to do so, however, then it should record the $30,000 in the same fund as other investment earnings and report the amount as temporarily restricted or unrestricted net assets.

HOW SHOULD DEPRECIATION BE REPORTED?

As emphasized in previous chapters, governments charge depreciation in their government-wide, proprietary, and fiduciary fund statements, but not in their governmental fund statements owing to their focus on budgets. Not-for-profits, like governments, generally budget on a cash or near-cash basis, and governing boards, managers, and external constituents are vitally concerned with actual-to-budget comparisons. The major challenge faced by managers and governing boards of most not-for-profits is meeting day-to-day cash demands. Inasmuch as depreciation is not a cost that requires cash, they have little or no interest in it; it does not enter into their financial deliberations or decisions.

On the other hand, as important as the budget is to not-for-profits, it does not have the same force of law as it does for governments. Therefore, not-for-profit statement users (particularly outsiders to whom basic financial statements are directed) may place greater weight on reporting objectives calling for information on the cost of services than on budgetary compliance. Depreciation represents the cost of consuming assets; in any comparison of service efforts with accomplishments, it may be too significant to ignore.

EXAMPLE   *Depreciation*

A not-for-profit job placement service acquires a personal computer for $3,000. It pays for the computer out of a fund restricted for the acquisition of equipment. Estimated useful life is three years.

FASB Standards

The FASB, in its Statement No. 93, *Recognition of Depreciation by Not-for-Profit Organizations*, mandates that not-for-profits recognize depreciation on their long-lived tangible assets and disclose depreciation expense and accumulated depreciation. For purposes of internal control and reporting, some not-for-profits account for capital assets, and charge depreciation, in their current operating funds; others maintain special plant funds. However, as discussed previously, Statement No. 117 requires that all expenses be reported as decreases in *unrestricted* net assets. Thus, irrespective of the fund in which the depreciation is recorded, it would still be reported in the unrestricted column or section of the statement of activities.

The following entries would record the acquisition of the computer and first-year depreciation:

Resources released from restriction	$3,000	
Cash		$3,000

To record the release of restricted assets to acquire the computer (restricted fund)

Equipment	$3,000	
Resources released from restriction		$3,000

To record the purchase of the computer (unrestricted fund)

Depreciation expense	$1,000	
Accumulated depreciation		$1,000

To record first-year depreciation (unrestricted fund)

What Issues Does a Not-for-Profit Face in Establishing Its Reporting Entity?

Not-for-profits, no less than governments, can own or be integrally affiliated with either businesses or other not-for-profits. Indeed, these relationships among not-for-profits can be quite varied. For the most part, however, they manifest three basic (though overlapping) characteristics:

- *Ownership.* An organization may own all or part of another entity. For example, a hospital may own another hospital or a physicians' group practice; a college may own a research laboratory.

- *Control.* An organization may control another entity by having the power to appoint the majority of its governing board. For example, a health care organization may establish a fund-raising foundation, specifying that the foundation's governing board be composed of the organization's own officers. Alternatively, per affiliation agreements a national fraternal organization may have the authority to establish operating policies and standards for its local chapters; a religious "judicatory," such as an archdiocese, presbytery, or synod, may have certain supervisory powers over local churches that are members of its denomination.

- *Economic interest.* An organization may have an economic interest in another entity because the entity holds or utilizes resources on its behalf, the entity produces income or provides services to it, or the organization guarantees the entity's debt. For example, a professional association may provide 100 percent of the funding for a political action committee that lobbies on its behalf; a legally independent, self-governing, fund-raising foundation may support the activities of a university or hospital.

It would be as misleading for a not-for-profit as for a business or government to exclude certain affiliated organizations from its reporting entity.

FASB Standards (proposed)

In a 1999 exposure draft, *Consolidated Financial Statements: Purpose and Policy*, the FASB proposed that organizations consolidate all entities that they control, unless that control were merely temporary. The draft defined control as "the ability of an entity to direct the policies and management that guide the ongoing activities of another entity so as to increase its benefits and limit its losses from that of the other entity's activities." It indicated that "for purposes of consolidated financial statements, control involves decision-making ability that is not shared with others."

As this text went to press, the FASB was still wrestling with the question of how to characterize control more precisely. The difficulty is that even seemingly obvious manifestations of control, such as the ability to appoint a majority of directors, may not ensure that an organization can use another entity's resources for its own benefit. The charter or other governing instruments, for example, might provide that the other entity's resources be used exclusively to support third parties (e.g., a university appoints the trustees of a research foundation established to distribute grants to scientists seeking a cure for a specified

(continued)

FASB Standards (continued)

disease). At the same time, an organization may be able to direct the resources of another entity for its own benefit, even in the absence of the authority to appoint a majority of directors or formal legal powers of control (e.g., a university's athletic director may have de facto command over the funds collected by the football team's booster club).

Most probably, the FASB will decide that for some relationships (e.g., when a not-for-profit owns a majority interest in a corporation) the "parent" should consolidate the "subsidiary," just as if the entities were businesses. For others, however, those in which one organization does not own the other, the FASB will have to specify approaches that are unique to the not-for-profit sector.

Control is multidimensional and not subject to precise measurement. In light of the myriad relationships among not-for-profit organizations, any standards the FASB eventually establishes are certain to be controversial.

COMPREHENSIVE EXAMPLE   *Museum of American Culture*

This example synthesizes several of the principles presented so far. We start with the statement of financial position of the Museum of American Culture as of December 31, 2004 (presented in Table 12–5). Then we account for the museum's transactions during 2005 (journalized in the body of the text), and prepare selected financial statements as of December 31, 2005 (presented in Table 12–6).

The museum engages in two main programs: curatorial and exhibits, and education. These are backed by two support functions: fund raising and administration.

The AICPA's audit and accounting guide, *Not-For-Profit Organizations*, provides the most comprehensive and authoritative accounting guidance for museums. It covers not-for-profits as diverse as colleges and universities, cemetery associations, civic organizations, fraternal associations, labor unions, professional associations, religious organizations, and performing arts organizations. It does not, however, cover health care organizations, which are addressed in a separate guide.

The key transactions in which the museum engaged during 2005 (in summary form) follow (000s omitted).

Accrual of Wages and Salaries   Museum employees earned wages and salaries of $1,045. During the year the museum paid employees $1,039, including $8 from the previous year. At year-end it owed employees $14, which was slated to be paid in early 2006. Hence, an adjustment of $6 must be made to accrued wages and salaries payable.

FASB Statement No. 117 provides that the statement of activities set forth expenses by *function*. The museum allocated the wages and salaries to its functions as indicated in the following entry:

Wages and salaries—curatorial and exhibits	$780	
Wages and salaries—education	85	
Wages and salaries—fund raising	50	
Wages and salaries—administration	130	
Cash		$1,039
Accrued wages and salaries payable		6

To record wages and salaries (unrestricted fund)

TABLE 12-5
Museum of American Culture
Statement of Financial Position
December 31, 2004
(in Thousands)

Assets

Current Assets:

Cash	$ 120
Investments	4,210
Pledges Receivable	165
Less: Allowance for Uncollectibles	(15)
	150
Supplies Inventory	20
Prepaid Expenses	50
Total Current Assets	4,550
Property, Plant, and Equipment	2,100
Less: Accumulated Depreciation	(540)
	1,560
Total Assets	$6,110

Liabilities

Current Liabilities:

Wages and Salaries Payable	$ 8
Accounts Payable	250
Total Liabilities	258

Net Assets

Unrestricted	2,002
Temporarily Restricted	850
Permanently Restricted (Endowments)	3,000
Total Net Assets	$5,852

Other Operating Expenses; Inventory   The museum incurred other operating expenses of $280 ($200 in curatorial and exhibit costs, $30 for education, $10 for fund raising, and $40 for administration). Consistent with the accrual basis, the museum accounts for supplies inventory and prepaid items on the *consumption basis.* During the period, the museum purchased $5 more of supplies than it used and, as a consequence, inventory increased by the same amount. Moreover, it reduced its balances in accounts payable by $3 and in prepaid expenses by $7. It disbursed a total of $281 in cash relating to the operating expenses:

Other operating expenses—curatorial and exhibits	$200	
Other operating expenses—education	30	
Other operating expenses—fund raising	10	
Other operating expenses—administration	40	
Accounts payable	3	
Inventory	5	
Cash		$281
Prepaid expenses		7

To record other operating expenses (unrestricted fund)

Acquisition of Fixed Assets; Long-Term Debt   The museum acquired $20 of new furniture and fixtures in exchange for a long-term note. Although many not-for-profits account for both their capital assets and related long-term debt in a plant fund, this museum accounts for them in its operating fund. For reporting purposes, the results would be the same. The assets are reported in the unrestricted fund along with other unrestricted resources:

Property, plant, and equipment	$20	
Notes payable		$20

To record the acquisition of capital assets (unrestricted fund)

Unlike governments (in their governmental fund statements), not-for-profits must account for interest on long-term notes on the accrual basis.

TABLE 12–6
Museum of American Culture
Statement of Activities
For the Year Ending December 31, 2005 (in Thousands)

	Unrestricted	Temporarily Restricted	Endowment Fund	Total
Support and Revenues				
Admissions and Memberships	$ 505			$ 505
Investments—Dividends and Interest	280			280
Investments—Appreciation	100			100
Revenue from Auxiliary Enterprises	470			470
Unrestricted Contributions, Including Pledges	338	$160		498
Restricted Contributions		90		90
Total Support and Revenues	1,693	250		1,943
Expenses				
Program:				
Curatorial and Exhibits	1,140			1,140
Education	130			130
Support Services:				
Fund Raising	65			65
Administration	200			200
Acquisition of Art	710			710
Expenses of Auxiliary Enterprises	350			350
Total Expenses	2,595			2,595
Excess (Deficiency) of Support and Revenue over Expenses	(902)	250		(652)
Resources Released from Restrictions	855	(855)		
Net (Decrease) in Fund Balances	(47)	(605)		(652)
Net Assets, Beginning of Period	2,002	850	$3,000	5,852
Net Assets, End of Period	$1,955	$245	$3,000	$5,200

(continued)

TABLE 12-6 *(continued)*
Museum of American Culture
Statement of Financial Position
December 31, 2005
(in Thousands)

Assets
Current Assets:

Cash	$ 68
Investments	3,810
Pledges Receivable	190
Less: Allowance for Uncollectibles	(25)
	165
Supplies Inventory	25
Prepaid Expenses	43
Total Current Assets	4,111
Property, Plant, and Equipment	2,120
Less: Accumulated Depreciation	(750)
	1,370
Total Assets	5,481

Liabilities
Current Liabilities:

Wages and Salaries Payable	14
Accounts Payable	247
Total Current Liabilities	261
Note Payable	20
Total Liabilities	281

Net Assets:

Unrestricted	1,955
Temporarily Restricted	245
Permanently Restricted (Endowments)	3,000
Total Net Assets	$5,200

Museum of American Culture
Schedule of Program and Support Expenses
For the Year Ending December 31, 2005
(in Thousands)

	Curatorial & Exhibits	Education	Fund Raising	Administration and Other	Total
Wages and Salaries	$ 780	$ 85	$50	$ 130	$1,045
Other Operating Expenses	200	30	10	40	280
Depreciation	160	15	5	30	210
Acquisition of Art				710	710
Auxiliary Enterprise				350	350
Total	$1,140	$130	$65	$1,260	$2,595

TABLE 12-6 *(continued)* *Museum of American Culture* *Statement of Cash Flows* *For the Year Ending December 31, 2005*	
Cash Flows from Operating Activities	
Contributions	$ 573
Admissions and Memberships	505
Interest and Dividends	280
Cash from Auxiliary Enterprises	120
Cash from Sale of Art	500
Wages and Salaries Paid	(1,039)
Purchases of Art	(710)
Payments for Other Operating Expenses	(281)
Net Cash Provided by Operating Activities; Net Increase (Decrease) **in Cash**	(52)
Cash on Hand, Beginning of Year	120
Cash on Hand, End of Year	$ 68
Supplemental Data	
Noncash Investing and Financing Activity—Acquisition of Property, Plant, and Equipment in Exchange for a Note Payable	$ 20

Depreciation   The museum recognized depreciation of $210 in the fund it used to account for capital assets:

Depreciation expense—curatorial and exhibits	$160	
Depreciation expense—education	15	
Depreciation expense—fund raising	5	
Depreciation expense—administration	30	
Accumulated depreciation		$210

To record depreciation (unrestricted fund)

Admissions and Memberships   The museum's main operating revenues ($505) are derived from admissions and membership fees.

Cash	$505	
Revenues—admissions and memberships		$505

To record revenues from admissions and members (unrestricted fund)

Interest and Dividends   The museum earned $280 in interest and dividends on its investments, most of which are held in an endowment fund. For this particular museum, the endowment income is unrestricted and thereby should be recorded in the operating fund and reported as unrestricted income. Were it restricted for a specific purpose, it would be recorded in a temporarily restricted fund and reported as temporarily restricted income. The endowment principal is accounted for in a permanently restricted fund. For internal bookkeeping purposes, many not-for-profits initially account for endowment interest and dividends in the endowment fund and then transfer them to the beneficiary funds. For external reporting purposes, however, the investment income should be reported as revenue of the beneficiary fund:

Cash	$280	
Investment earnings—interest and dividends		$280

To record dividends and interest (unrestricted fund)

Changes in Fair Values   During the year, the fair value of the museum's investments increased by $100. Assuming that there are no explicit legal or donor-imposed restrictions requiring that gains from the appreciation of the endowment portfolios be added to the principal of the endowment, the increase in fair value would be recognized as unrestricted investment earnings—the same as dividends and interest.

Investments	$100	
Investment earnings—appreciation in fair value		$100

To record appreciation in fair value (unrestricted fund)

Revenues and Expenses of Auxiliary Enterprises   The museum operates a gift shop. In 2005, revenues and expenses totaled $470 and $350, respectively.

Governments account for their business-type activities in enterprise funds. These funds are accounted for on the full accrual basis and are not combined with governmental funds in either the government-wide or the fund statements. Since not-for-profits account for their general operations on the full accrual basis, there is less need to separate their business from their nonbusiness activities. Although it is usually convenient to account for *auxiliary* (i.e., business-type) activities in separate funds, for external purposes they are usually reported along with other operations and the resources are classified as unrestricted. Many not-for-profits aggregate their auxiliary revenues on one line and their auxiliary expenses on another. Others break out the revenues and expenses by individual, or types of, enterprises. The following summary entry would capture the museum's 2005 auxiliary activities:

Expenses applicable to auxiliary activities	$350	
Cash	120	
Revenues from auxiliary activities		$470

To record the activities of auxiliary activities (unrestricted fund)

Insofar as the revenues and expenses affected balance sheet accounts other than cash, such as inventory, prepaid expenses, and accumulated depreciation, then those accounts, rather than cash, would be debited or credited.

Unrestricted and Time-Restricted Pledges   During the year, the museum conducted a fund-raising campaign. As of year-end it had received cash of $338 and pledges for an additional $180. It estimates that $20 of the pledges will be uncollectible.

Contributions, including unconditional promises to give, should be recognized as revenue upon receipt. However, the pledges outstanding, inasmuch as they are unavailable for expenditure (and thereby subject to time restrictions), should be recorded as an increase in restricted resources.

Cash	$338	
Revenue from unrestricted contributions		$338

To record unrestricted contributions (unrestricted fund)

Pledges receivable	$180	
Allowance for uncollectible pledges		$ 20
Revenue from unrestricted contributions		160

To record pledges subject to time restrictions (temporarily restricted fund)

For convenience, "revenue from unrestricted contributions" has been reduced by the "allowance for uncollectible pledges." Many not-for-profits would record this estimate as bad debt expense rather than as a reduction of revenues.

During the year, the museum collected $145 of time-restricted pledges receivable outstanding from prior years and wrote off $10 as uncollectible:

Cash	$145	
Resources released from restriction		$145

To record cash collected on outstanding pledges (unrestricted fund)

Allowance for uncollectible pledges	$ 10	
Resources released from restriction	145	
Pledges receivable		$155

To release resources from time restrictions and to write off uncollectible pledges (temporarily restricted fund)

Use-Restricted Contributions

The museum received a $90 contribution from a patron who required that the gift be used to acquire additional works of art. During the year, the museum used the gift, along with $620 of resources that had previously been restricted, to add to its collection.

Because the gift is restricted (and the museum did not expect to expend it in the current year), the museum accounted for the gift in a temporarily restricted fund:

Cash	$90	
Revenue from restricted contributions		$90

To record contributions restricted for acquisition of art (temporarily restricted fund)

This museum, like most others, elects *not* to capitalize its art collection. Therefore, the costs to acquire the new art would be reported as an expense. However, because not-for-profits must report all expenses in an unrestricted fund, the resources must be released from the restricted fund to the unrestricted fund:

Resources released from restriction	$710	
Cash		$710

To record the release of restricted resources upon acquiring new art (temporarily restricted fund)

Acquisition of art—expense	$710	
Resources released from restriction		$710

To record the acquisition of art (unrestricted fund)

To pay for the art, the museum sold $500 of unrestricted investments. There was no gain or loss on sale, inasmuch as the museum carried the investments at fair value:

Cash	$500	
Investments		$500

To record the sale of investments (unrestricted fund)

Volunteer Services

The museum benefits from the services of volunteer guides. Guides are essential to operations and, were it not able to attract volunteers, the museum would have to hire them. Nevertheless, the guides do not have to possess specialized skills (those characteristic of craftsmen or professionals), and therefore the museum need not recognize the value of their services as either revenues or expenses.

Table 12–6 summarizes the 2005 transactions in a statement of activities, a year-end statement of financial position, a schedule of program and support expenses, and a statement of cash flows.

Questions for Review and Discussion

1. Provide an example of resources that are temporarily restricted as to (a) purpose, (b) time, and (c) occurrence of a specific event. Provide an example of permanently restricted resources.

2. A not-for-profit organization receives a restricted gift. When, and in which type of fund, should it recognize the revenue? When, and in which type of fund, should it recognize the related expense? What is the reason for the apparent inconsistency between the fund types in which the revenues and expenses are reported?

3. A foundation pledges to donate $1 million to an art institute one year in the future. When, and in what amount, should the institute recognize revenue? The institute applies a discount rate of 10 percent to all pledges. Would your response be the same if the foundation promised to donate the funds only if and when the institute held an exhibition of nineteenth century American photography? Why do many not-for-profits object to the standards pertaining to revenue recognition of pledges?

4. Members of the National Accounting Association, a not-for-profit organization, are charged annual dues of $150. Of this amount, $50 is restricted, per association policy, to covering the cost of the association's journal, which every member receives. In what category of restrictiveness should the association report the portion of revenues associated with the journal? Explain.

5. In what significant way do not-for-profits account for investments differently than do businesses?

6. In a recent month a CPA provided ten hours of volunteer time to the Society for the Visually Impaired. He devoted seven hours to maintaining the organization's financial records and three to recording tapes of newspapers and magazine articles. If volunteers had not provided these services, the organization would have had to hire others. Should the organization give accounting recognition to the CPA's services?

7. A museum received gifts of two valuable paintings. It recorded the value of one as an asset and recognized the corresponding revenue. It gave no accounting recognition to the other. What might be a legitimate explanation for such an apparent inconsistency?

8. How do not-for-profits differ from governments in the way they account for business-type activities, such as dining halls, gift shops, and admission fees?

9. What is meant by *variance power?* Suppose that a charitable foundation receives a gift that the donor specifies must be used to support the college education of a particular individual. Of what relevance is variance power to how the foundation accounts for the gift?

10. In what significant ways do the FASB standards differ from those of the GASB with respect to the statement of cash flows?

Exercises and Problems

12–1

Select the *best* answer.

1. A *term endowment* is a gift
   a. the principal of which must be returned to the donor after a specified period of time
   b. the principal of which is available for expenditure after a specified period of time
   c. the income from which must be expended within a specified period of time
   d. the income of which must be added to the principal for a specified period of time

2. A not-for-profit organization maintains an endowment of $1 million, the income from which must be used for research into substance abuse. In a particular year, the endowment had income of $60,000, all of which was expended in accord with the donor's specifications. The expense should be reported as a decrease in
   a. permanently restricted net assets
   b. temporarily restricted net assets
   c. unrestricted net assets
   d. any of the above

3. A private think tank receives a gift of $100,000 that must be used to fund a symposium on federal accounting. When the institution conducts the symposium, which of the following accounts should be debited in a temporarily restricted fund?

   a. program expense

   b. deferred revenue

   c. resources released from restriction

   d. deferred program expense

4. The statement of cash flows of a not-for-profit should be divided into which of the following categories of cash flows?

   a. operating activities, noncapital financing activities, capital and related financing activities, investing activities

   b. operating activities, capital activities, investing activities

   c. operating activities, financing activities, capital activities

   d. operating activities, financing activities, investing activities

5. The Senior League, a not-for-profit welfare agency, redeemed a $100,000 bond that it had held as an investment of unrestricted resources. It also received an interest payment of $6,000. In its statement of cash flows the league should report

   a. $106,000 as a cash flow from investing activities

   b. $106,000 as a cash flow from operating activities

   c. $100,000 as a cash flow from investing activities and $6,000 as a cash flow from financing activities

   d. $100,000 as a cash flow from investing activities and $6,000 as a cash flow from operating activities

6. Enrex Corporation gave a not-for-profit research foundation $500,000 to conduct research relating to the development of a new type of battery. Per the terms of the gift, Enrex had the rights to any patents issued as a consequence of the research and could control when and where the research results were published. At the time of receipt of the $500,000, the foundation should recognize

   a. revenue of $500,000 in a temporarily restricted fund

   b. revenue of $500,000 in an unrestricted fund

   c. deferred revenue of $500,000 in a temporarily restricted fund

   d. deferred revenue of $500,000 in an unrestricted fund

7. Harley Safe-Place, a not-for-profit organization, received an unrestricted pledge of $600,000. The donor promised to make payment within six months (which would be in the organization's next fiscal year). At the time of the pledge, the organization should recognize

   a. revenue of $600,000 in a temporarily restricted fund

   b. revenue of $600,000 in an unrestricted fund

   c. deferred revenue of $600,000 in a temporarily restricted fund

   d. deferred revenue of $600,000 in an unrestricted fund

8. Walden Institute, a not-for-profit, politically oriented association, was promised a $1 million endowment on condition that it establish a program in entrepreneurial studies and hire a leading scholar to lead it. Upon receiving the pledge the institute should recognize

   a. zero revenue

   b. revenue of $1 million in a permanently restricted fund

   c. revenue of $1 million in a temporarily restricted fund

   d. deferred revenue of $1 million in a permanently restricted fund

9. Emerson Museum received a cash gift of $7 million. The board of trustees decided that the gift should be used to establish a permanent endowment, the income from which would be used to provide research grants to impressionist art historians. The museum should report the gift as an increase in

   a. unrestricted resources

   b. temporarily restricted resources

   c. permanently restricted resources

   d. board restricted resources

10. The Fellowship Church of America issues $10 million of bonds that must be used to construct new facilities. Included in the bond indenture is a provision that the church must maintain $400,000 in a specially designated bank account to ensure timely payment of principal and interest. Upon receiving the $10 million in bond proceeds and placing the $400,000 in the designated bank account, the church should report

    a. cash of $9.6 million in an unrestricted fund and $400,000 in a temporarily restricted fund

    b. cash of $10 million in an unrestricted fund

   c. cash of $10 million in a temporarily restricted fund

   d. cash of $9.6 million in a temporarily restricted fund and $400,000 in a permanently restricted fund

12–2

Select the *best* answer.

1. A local chapter of the Society for Protection of the Environment benefited from the voluntary services of two attorneys. One served as a member of the society's board of directors, performing tasks comparable to other directors. During the year he attended twenty hours of meetings. The other drew up a lease agreement with a tenant in a building owned by the society. She spent five hours on the project. The billing rate of both attorneys is $200 per hour. In the year in which the services were provided, the society should recognize revenues from contributed services of

   a. $0

   b. $1,000

   c. $4,000

   d. $5,000

2. The Museum of Contemporary Art received two valuable paintings. The museum has determined that one, with a market value of $7,000, is inappropriate for display and therefore will be sold. The other, with a market value of $10,000, will be placed on exhibit. The museum has a policy of not capitalizing its art collection. In the year that it receives the two paintings it should recognize contribution revenues of

   a. $0

   b. $7,000

   c. $10,000

   d. $17,000

3. The United Way of Lano County distributes all contributions to not-for-profit organizations within its county. Donors have a choice. They can either designate the organization to which their contributions will be given or they can permit the United Way to distribute their contributions as it deems appropriate. During the current year, the United Way received $1 million of specifically designated contributions and $6 million of undesignated contributions. It should recognize contribution revenue of

   a. $0

   b. $1 million

   c. $6 million

   d. $7 million

4. *Variance power* refers to the ability

   a. of a not-for-profit organization to use property for commercial purposes even though it was zoned for residential purposes

   b. of a charitable organization to unilaterally direct the use of donated assets to a beneficiary other than that specified by the donor

   c. of a donor to change the beneficiary of a gift from that which was initially specified

   d. of a not-for-profit organization to alter the terms of any purpose restrictions associated with a contribution that it received

5. The Association for Educational Enrichment receives a contribution of $400,000 that must be used for student scholarships. Prior to granting any scholarships, the association invests the funds received in marketable securities. During the year, the securities pay dividends of $10,000 and increase in market value to $440,000. The association should report

   a. unrestricted investment earnings of $50,000

   b. temporarily restricted investment earnings of $50,000

   c. unrestricted investment earnings of $10,000 and temporarily restricted investment earnings of $40,000

   d. temporarily restricted investment earnings of $10,000

6. Carter Research Center, a not-for-profit entity, acquires $50,000 of laboratory instruments with funds that were donated and restricted for the purchase of equipment. The instruments have a useful life of five years and no salvage value. During each of the five years of the instruments' useful life, the center should recognize depreciation expense of

   a. $0

   b. $10,000 in a temporarily restricted fund

   c. $10,000 in an unrestricted fund

   d. $10,000 in either a temporarily restricted fund or an unrestricted fund, depending on which fund is used to account for the instruments

7. With respect to the statement of cash flows

   a. both the FASB and the GASB encourage entities to use the direct method

   b. the GASB, but not the FASB, requires entities to use the direct method

c. the FASB, but not the GASB, requires entities to use the direct method

d. both the FASB and the GASB require entities to use the direct method

8. The Friends of the Opera, a financially interrelated fund-raising support group for the City Opera Company, receives $100,000 in donations, all of which will eventually be transferred to the City Opera Company. When Friends of the Opera receives the gift

   a. Friends of the Opera should recognize revenue of $100,000 and the City Opera company should make no journal entries

   b. Friends of the Opera should recognize a liability of $100,000 and the City Opera Company should recognize a receivable

   c. Friends of the Opera should recognize revenue of $100,000 and the City Opera Company should recognize an increase of $100,000 in the net assets of Friends of the Opera

   d. Friends of the Opera should recognize a liability of $100,000 and the City Opera Company should make no entry

9. At the start of the year, the permanent endowment fund of the State Performing Arts Festival Association reported net assets of $1 million. During the year, it earned $40,000 in interest and dividends but its investments lost $60,000 in market value. The association spent the entire $40,000 in interest and dividends. At year-end the permanent endowment fund should report net assets of

   a. $1,000,000
   b. $980,000
   c. $960,000
   d. $940,000

10. The Mountain Research Institute began the year with net assets in its permanent endowment fund of $1 million. During the year it earned $70,000, and the market value of its investments increased by $20,000. However, the institute's policy is to permit earnings to be spent only to the extent that they exceed an amount necessary to cover inflation. The inflation rate for the year was 3 percent. During the year, the institute spent none of the $70,000. At year-end, the permanent endowment fund should report net assets of

    a. $1,000,000
    b. $1,020,000
    c. $1,030,000
    d $1,090,000

12–3

Minor differences in the terms of a contribution may justify major differences in revenue recognition.

Upon meeting with the executive director of the Crime Victims Advocacy Group, the president of a private foundation agreed to contribute, in the following year, $100,000 in support of the group's proposed program to provide legal assistance to victims of violent crimes. Suppose that the foundation's formal letter acknowledging its pledge was worded in three different ways:

   a. "We are pleased to pledge $100,000 in support of your group's efforts to assist victims of violent crimes."

   b. "We are pleased to pledge $100,000 in support of your group's efforts to develop a new program to provide legal assistance to victims of violent crimes."

   c. We are pleased to pledge $100,000 upon your developing a new program to provide legal assistance to victims of violent crimes."

For each of the three options:

1. Prepare the journal entries that should be made upon receipt of the letter from the foundation. Assume that it was unlikely that the pledge would be fulfilled in the same period that it was made.

2. Prepare the journal entries that should be made to record the expenditure of $100,000 on activities related to the legal assistance program.

3. Prepare the journal entries that should be made upon receipt of the $100,000 check, assuming that it was received shortly after the legal assistance program was established and the group spent the $100,000 on program-related activities.

4. Comment on why minor differences in wording might justify major differences in accounting.

Be sure to indicate the type of fund in which your entries would be made.

12–4

Some, but not all, contributions of goods and services are given accounting recognition.

In each of the following scenarios, an organization receives a contribution in kind. Prepare journal entries, as necessary, to give them accounting recognition. For each, tell why you made an entry or why you did not.

1. A local not-for-profit art museum receives free advertising for its yearly benefit from radio station WLOU. The air time would have cost the museum $1,000.

2. Volunteers for "Breakfast on Bikes," a voluntary health and welfare organization, deliver hot meals to the elderly three times a week. Each of the ten volunteers works about six hours per week. All of the volunteers have permanent jobs with pay averaging $16.10 an hour.

3. Lynn Simms, a local CPA, maintains the books and records of her church. Although her normal billing rate is $60 per hour, she accepts no payment from the church. She works on church matters approximately four hours a week.

4. A construction company allows a not-for-profit community association to use its bulldozer, at no cost, to clear land for a new baseball park. It would have cost $1,400 to rent the bulldozer.

12–5

Investment gains and losses have to be recognized as they occur—and have to be assigned to the appropriate category of net assets.

During 2004, the Pulmonary Disease Foundation received a contribution of marketable securities that were to be placed in a permanent endowment fund. Neither donor stipulations nor applicable state law requires that capital gains or increases in value be added to the endowment principal. The income from the securities was to be restricted for research in pulmonary diseases. The following schedule indicates the value of the securities as of the date of receipt (labeled "cost"), the fair value on December 31, 2004, and the unrealized gains and losses of the year.

Endowment Portfolio as of December 31, 2004 (in thousands)		
	Cost	**Fair Value**	**Unrealized Gain (Loss)**
Northwest Industries	$260	$275	$15
Campbell Corp.	317	304	(13)
St. Regis, Inc.	141	171	30
	$718	$750	$32

1. Prepare a journal entry to record the unrealized net gain during the year. Be sure to indicate the type of fund (e.g., unrestricted, temporarily restricted, permanently restricted) in which the entry would be made. Assuming no other transactions and no other assets in the relevant funds,

show how the investments would be reported on the foundation's year-end 2004 statement of financial position.

2. During 2005, the foundation sold the Northwest Industries securities for $280. Prepare appropriate journal entries to record the sale. Credit the gain to the same account in which you credited the unrealized appreciation of 2004.

3. As of December 31, 2005, the market value of the Campbell Corp. securities had increased to $320; that of the St. Regis, Inc. securities to $180. Prepare a journal entry to record the unrealized gain during the year. Show how the foundation would report the investment portfolio on its December 31, 2005, statement of financial position. You may combine the cash and securities of each type of fund into a single account.

12–6

The distinction between contributed services that warrant financial statement recognition and those that do not is not always clear.

For each of the following situations, indicate whether the organization should recognize the described contributed services as revenue (offset by a corresponding expense). Briefly justify your response or identify key issues.

1. Nellie Wilson, the noted country-western singer, performs a benefit concert for the Save-Our-Farms Association, a political advocacy group. Wilson, who would normally charge $60,000 per concert, did not accept a fee.

2. Camp Chi-Wan-Da, a summer camp for disadvantaged youth, benefits from the services of four physicians, each of whom spends two weeks at the camp providing medical services to the campers. The doctors receive free room and board but no salary. Camp association standards require that a camp of Chi-Wan-Da's size either have a physician on the premises or one on call.

3. The Taconic Music Festival, a performing arts association, needed new practice facilities. The architecture firm of Lloyd-Wright designed the facilities for the association without charge, and local merchants provided the building materials. All construction work was carried out by community volunteers, only a few of whom had professional experience in the building trades.

4. A neurologist serves on the board of trustees of the Neurological Disease Foundation, an organization that funds clinical research. He was asked to serve because of his expertise in the

area of neurological research and he chairs the board's committee that selects grant recipients.

5. The Museum of Natural History benefits from the volunteer services of twenty docents (museum guides), who provide approximately 10,000 hours of service per year. The docents give tours, staff the information desk, and assist in the museum gift shop. Were it not for their voluntary services, the museum would have to hire employees, who would be paid at least $10 per hour.

12–7

Should exchange transactions be accounted for differently than contributions?

In December 2005, the Consumer Association of America (CAA), a not-for-profit research organization, received notification of a $6 million grant from the Sporting Goods Manufacturers Association (SGMA) to develop a football helmet that will provide better protection against head injuries. The grant was intended to cover $4 million of direct costs and $2 million of indirect (overhead) costs. The grant contract stipulated that the SGMA would make its payment to the CAA upon receiving invoices from CAA for the actual direct costs incurred. It further required that the research results be reported only to the SGMA and not be made publicly available. Each reimbursement payment for direct costs incurred would also include an appropriate proportion of indirect costs (i.e., an additional $.50 for each $1 of direct costs).

In 2006, the CAA carried out and completed the research for which it contracted. Direct costs were, as estimated, $4 million. It submitted the necessary invoices and received payment in full.

1. Prepare required journal entries for 2005 and 2006. Be sure to indicate whether each entry should be made to an unrestricted or temporarily restricted fund. You need not, however, record the indirect costs themselves (inasmuch as, by their nature, they are not tied directly to the grant).

2. Assume, instead, that in December 2005 the CAA received from the National Sports Association (NSA) a pledge of $6 million. The donation is for research relating to football helmets. The NSA is a not-for-profit agency and the results of any research will be in the public domain. In January 2006, the CAA received the contribution. Throughout the remainder of 2006, it carried out its football-related research (incurring $4 million of direct costs). Prepare the required journal entries for 2005 and 2006 and indicate whether each entry should be made

to an unrestricted or a temporarily restricted fund.

3. Comment on any differences between the two awards that might justify differences in revenue recognition.

4. Suppose instead that the NSA promised to make its contribution only upon receiving a report that the research had actually been completed. Would your approach be different? Explain.

12–8

Contributions of fixed assets may affect more than one type of fund.

Discovery Barn, a not-for-profit science center for children, received a contribution of $30,000 explicitly designated for the acquisition of computers. During the year, it acquired $21,000 of computers, which it estimated have a useful life of three years. It is the policy of the organization to charge an entire year's depreciation in the year of acquisition.

Prepare all required journal entries, being certain to indicate the type of fund in which each entry would be made.

12–9

For purposes of external reporting, not-for-profits, unlike governments in their governmental fund statements, do not distinguish between plant and other types of resources.

In 2004, the Northwest Ballet Association (NBA), a not-for-profit performing arts organization, undertook a major capital campaign to fund a new theater, expected to cost $10 million. It was quickly able to raise $6 million, all of which was donor restricted. It borrowed the balance, issuing a five-year, 8 percent, term note for $4 million.

During the year, the NBA broke ground on the project and incurred construction costs of $3.4 million. It earned $0.52 million in interest on temporary investments. It incurred and paid $0.32 million in interest on the note. In addition, as required by the note, it placed $0.7 million in a reserve fund (a specially dedicated bank account) for the repayment of the debt.

1. To show how these transactions would be reflected on the NBA's financial statements, prepare a December 31, 2004, statement of financial position and statement of activities. Assume that these were the only transactions in which the organization engaged and that all available cash, except that in the reserve fund, had been invested in short-term marketable securities. Be sure to properly classify all resources as to whether they are temporarily restricted or unrestricted.

2. Comment briefly on whether the contributions from donors and the proceeds from the bonds should be reported as restricted or unrestricted.

3. Comment briefly on whether the $0.7 million in the reserve fund should be reported as restricted or unrestricted.

12–10

Investment losses need not impair the principal of not-for-profits' endowment funds.

In 2005, the Rubin Center for the Arts received a $2 million endowment, the income of which was to be used to support local artists. The center invested the proceeds in securities. In 2005, owing to interest, dividends, and changes in market prices, the value of the endowment increased by $120,000. Of this amount, the center spent $80,000 on programs that were consistent with the endowment's restrictions. In 2006, owing to a market downturn, the portfolio incurred net losses of $60,000. In 2007, it had net gains of $70,000. In neither 2006 nor 2007 did the center use any endowment resources to support its programs.

In the absence of donor specifications and applicable statutes, what would be the balances, at the end of 2005, 2006, and 2007, in the center's (1) permanently restricted endowment fund and (2) related temporarily restricted fund? Indicate also any impact on unrestricted funds.

12–11

Investment losses cannot be accounted for as the mirror image of investment gains.

On December 31, 2004, The Child Crisis Center establishes an endowment fund with a $5 million gift of securities. Income from the endowment is to be used exclusively to support a nutrition program. Expendable income is defined in the indenture agreement so as to include all investment gains, both realized and unrealized. Investment gains and losses are to be accounted for as recommended by the FASB.

During 2005, the endowment earns $100,000 in interest and dividends and spends the entire amount on the nutrition program. The value of its securities portfolio increases by $500,000—from $5 million to $5.5 million.

During 2006, the endowment again earns $100,000 in interest and dividends and spends the entire amount on the nutrition program. This year, however, the value of its securities portfolio decreases by $800,000—from $5.5 million to $4.7 million.

During 2007, the endowment continues to earn and spend $100,000 in interest and dividends. This year the portfolio recovers $400,000 of its investment losses and at year-end is worth $5.1 million.

At the start of 2005, the center had a cash balance of $600,000 in an unrestricted fund. Over the three-year period, this balance was unaffected by transactions other than those just described.

1. Prepare a schedule for each of the three years (2005 through 2007) in which you summarize the transactions as they affect permanently restricted, temporarily restricted, and unrestricted net assets.

2. At the beginning of 2006, the year of the loss, the total value of the security portfolio was $5.5 million. Of this amount, the initial $5 million was classified as permanently restricted; the balance as temporarily restricted. Assuming that you adhered to the FASB pronouncement, how much of the loss did you assign to the permanently restricted assets and how much to the temporarily restricted assets? How can you justify this division of the loss?

CHAPTER 13

Special Issues for Not-for-Profit Health Care Providers and Institutions of Higher Education

Health care in the United States is in the midst of a massive economic reorganization in which the divisions between business, not-for-profit, and government providers are becoming increasingly blurred. The accounting distinctions among health care providers in the three sectors are also becoming less significant. Similarly, as noted in Chapter 11, most government colleges and universities can be expected to report as special purpose entities engaged in only business-type activities. Therefore, inasmuch as both government and not-for-profit institutions will account for their activities on a full accrual basis and present only consolidated financial statements, the differences are likely to be less pronounced than in the past.

Moreover, as discussed in Chapter 12, with the FASB's issuance of Statement No. 117, *Financial Statements of Not-for-Profit Organizations*, the differences in financial reporting among all types of not-for-profits are now only minimal. Therefore, in this chapter, we limit our discussion to transactions that are either unique, or of special importance, to health care providers and institutions of higher education. Although our focus is on not-for-profit entities, the industry guidance we discuss is available to government entities when it does not conflict with GASB standards. We also point out some of the more notable differences between FASB and GASB reporting standards on similar issues.

WHAT UNIQUE ISSUES DO NOT-FOR-PROFIT HEALTH CARE PROVIDERS FACE?

The accounting and reporting practices of health care organizations have been strongly influenced by the Healthcare Financial Management Association and the American Hospital Association, both of which are industry associations, and the AICPA. Until recently, external financial reporting was governed mainly by separate AICPA industry audit guides pertaining to hospitals and other types of health care organizations. Many of those guides' directives have been superseded by FASB pronouncements, such as Statement No. 116, *Accounting for Contributions Received and Contributions Made*, and Statement No. 117. Nevertheless, the AICPA's current industry audit guide, *Health*

Care Organizations (which, unlike earlier versions, deals with both hospitals and other types of health care providers) is the primary authoritative source for issues not addressed by the FASB. Similarly, it is a source of guidance for government health care providers for issues not addressed in GASB pronouncements.

Health care may be provided by individual practitioners (including physicians, therapists, and counselors), hospitals, out-patient clinics, medical service and retirement institutions, and a wide range of not-for-profit specialty organizations (such as screening clinics, support organizations, and research institutes). At one time, most health care organizations billed their patients (or third-party payers such as insurance companies) for services actually rendered. Today, an increasing percentage of medical care is provided through health maintenance organizations (HMOs) or related types of health plans that provide services to members in return for fixed, periodic payments. These HMOs or health plans may subcontract with hospitals, physicians' associations, or other medical groups to provide specialized services in exchange for *capitation* (per person) fees. The capitation fees are generally based on the number of persons covered and expected costs to be incurred rather than actual services provided.

More than most other not-for-profits, health care organizations must be concerned with their costs. Many other not-for-profits focus mainly on fund raising; they then adjust the level of services to available revenues. Health care organizations charge for their services. Often the amount of fees charged is limited by competition or preestablished reimbursement rates. Therefore, they must be vitally interested both in determining and controlling the cost of their services.

FUND STRUCTURE   The basic financial statements of not-for-profit health care organizations are similar in all major respects to those of the museum illustrated in the previous chapter. The statement of financial position and statement of activities should distinguish among unrestricted, temporarily restricted, and permanently restricted resources. The statement of activities should classify the revenues as unrestricted, temporarily restricted, or permanently restricted, but should report expenses only as decreases in unrestricted resources.

Hospitals and other health care providers typically maintain one or more unrestricted operating funds, as well as several temporarily and permanently restricted funds. The general operating funds record both financial resources and property, plant, and equipment. Temporarily restricted funds typically account for donated resources received for particular purposes, including specified programs or services (e.g., geriatric care, research, community education) as well as replacement of, or additions to, plant and equipment. In addition, temporarily restricted funds include term endowment funds, annuity funds, and life income funds.

Two points regarding temporarily restricted funds warrant emphasis:

- Temporarily restricted funds related to plant and equipment generally account only for *resources* restricted to their purchase or construction, not for the plant and equipment itself, which are typically reported in the general operating fund. (A notable exception involves capital assets acquired by gift. These assets may be subject to restrictions that expire as the asset is depreciated, and hence, they may be accounted for in temporarily restricted funds.)

- An organization may opt to establish temporarily restricted funds to account for resources designated by its governing board for specific purposes (e.g., to replace plant and equipment). For purposes of external reporting, however, board-designated resources are *not* considered restricted and should be reported with other unrestricted operating resources. They may, however, be classified within the unrestricted fund as "assets whose use is limited" (or a similar category).

As with other not-for-profits, permanently restricted funds of health care organizations encompass mainly endowments, the principal of which must remain intact; only the earnings are expendable.

Like other not-for-profits (as well as governments), health care organizations may maintain numerous funds in each of the three categories of restrictiveness. For reporting purposes, however, the funds should be aggregated by category.

CLASSIFICATION OF REVENUES AND EXPENSES The statement of activities of a health care organization is relatively straightforward. Revenues are displayed by category (often in columns): unrestricted, temporarily restricted, and permanently restricted. They are divided into at least two classifications (usually rows): patient care revenues and other revenues. Patient care revenues include

- Routine services (such as room, board, and general nursing)
- Other nursing services (such as operating room services)
- Professional services (such as physicians' services, laboratories, and pharmacy)

Other revenues include

- Contributions
- Educational services
- Miscellaneous sources (such as rental of space, auxiliary enterprises, and fees charged for medical records)

In addition, revenues from capitation fees should generally be shown apart from other types of revenues.

Expenses are reported exclusively within the unrestricted category. They may be classified either by function or by object. However, per Statement No. 117, if the expenses are classified by object, then the functional classification must be presented in the notes.

The statement of activities must also indicate resources released from restriction and any transfers between funds. Likely functional and natural (object) classifications of expenditures include the following:

Functional	*Natural*
Nursing services	Salaries and wages
Other professional services	Employee benefits
General services	Fees to individuals and organizations
Fiscal services	Supplies and other expense
Administrative services	Purchased services
Bad debts	Bad debts
Depreciation	Depreciation
Interest	Interest

RECOGNIZING FEE-FOR-SERVICE PATIENT-CARE REVENUES Health care organizations may provide patient services over an extended period of time. Yet patients are often billed only at the conclusion of their stay at the facility.

In reality, most patients pay either none, or only a small portion, of their bills themselves. Health care organizations derive most of their revenues from third parties, such as Medicare, Medicaid, Blue Cross, and other insurance companies and health plans. These third parties pay the hospital or other health care provider based on contractual or other predetermined rates. For example, in most circumstances,

Medicare reimburses hospitals based on the nature of patients' illnesses. Under its Prospective Payment System (PPS), it classifies patient care into diagnosis-related groups (DRGs) and allows a specified rate for each group. In some circumstances, however, it reimburses specified allowable costs. The amounts paid by the third-party payers are almost always less than the provider's standard billing rate.

At the time they provide patient care, hospitals and other health care providers cannot be certain as to the portion of their standard charges that ultimately will be paid. Usually the amount is known for certain only when they receive payment. In fact, under some retrospective payment arrangements, payments are based on total costs incurred during a particular period. Although the third-party payer makes interim payments, a final determination might not be reached until after the end of the period.

Inasmuch as many patients who are uninsured cannot afford the costs of an extended hospital stay or expensive medical procedures, health care providers may face high rates of bad debts. Moreover, unlike businesses, providers often serve patients who they know will be unable to pay the amounts billed.

Owing to the uncertainty of the amounts that they will actually collect for their services, hospitals face salient issues of when and how to report their patient-care revenues and value their related receivables.

EXAMPLE *Patient-Care Revenues*
....

During a particular week a hospital records $400,000 in patient charges. The charges applicable to patients that were actually discharged from the hospital (including charges incurred in prior weeks) were $395,000.

The hospital estimates that 80 percent of the charges will be billed to third-party payers, who will, on average, pay only 75 percent of the invoiced amounts. The remaining 20 percent will be billed to patients who are uninsured. Of this 20 percent, 60 percent will be uncollectible.

AICPA Guidance

According to the AICPA audit guide, *Health Care Organizations*, revenue from health care services is usually recorded "when coverage is provided to an enrollee or the service is provided to a patient or resident."[1] Thus, the patient discharge method (at one time a popular basis for revenue recognition) is *inappropriate*.

Further, the guide advises:

> Revenue and the related receivables for health care services are usually recorded in the accounting records on an accrual basis at the provider's *full established rates*. The provision for contractual adjustments (that is, the difference between established rates and third-party payer payments) and discounts (that is, the difference between established rates and the amount collectible) are recognized on an *accrual basis* and deducted from gross revenue to determine net patient service revenue. Contractual adjustments, discounts, and an allowance for uncollectibles are recorded to report the receivables for health care services at net realizable value. [emphasis added][2]

Bad debts, as implied in the recommended classification of expenses, should be reported as an expense, not a deduction from revenues.

---

[1]AICPA, *Health Care Organizations*, para. 10.04.

[2]AICPA, *Health Care Organizations*, para. 5.03.

The following entries would be consistent with these guidelines:

Patient accounts receivable	$400,000	
Patient revenues		$400,000

To record one week's patient revenues

Revenue from patient services—		
estimated contractual adjustments	$80,000	
Patient accounts receivable—allowance		
for contractual adjustments		$80,000

To establish an allowance for contractual adjustments (25 percent of the 80 percent of the $400,000 that will be paid by third parties)

Bad debt expense	$48,000	
Patient accounts receivable—allowance		
for bad debts		$48,000

To establish an allowance for bad debts (60 percent of the 20 percent of the $400,000 that will be paid directly by patients)

RECOGNIZING CAPITATION FEE REVENUES Health care organizations receive capitation fees when they contract either with an individual or with an insurance company or other third-party payer to provide covered services during a specified period of time. Typically, an organization receives the payments at the beginning of each month and is obligated to provide the services during the month. Sometimes the organization also assumes the risk of having to refer a patient to other organizations for diagnosis or treatment and to pay for those services.

EXAMPLE   *Capitation Fee Revenues*
• •

A physicians' group receives $300,000 in capitation fees from the Hartford Insurance Company to provide comprehensive health care to members of the company's health plan. During the month it provides services for which it would bill, at standard rates, $240,000. In addition, it refers patients to hospitals and other health care providers, for which it expects to be billed $18,000.

AICPA Guidance

Per the AICPA audit guide, revenue from capitation fees "is earned as a result of agreeing to provide services to qualified beneficiaries and not as a result of actually providing the care."[3]

Therefore, the physicians' group should recognize revenue in the period covered by the capitation fees. Correspondingly, it should establish a liability for any related costs for which it has not yet paid. Thus:

Cash	$300,000	
Revenue from capitation fees		$300,000

To record capitation fees received

---

[3] AICPA, *Health Care Organizations*, para. 1.19.

Patient referrals (expense) $18,000
    Obligations for patient referrals $18,000
To record liability for patient referrals

The amount for which it would have billed at standard rates is therefore irrelevant.

ACCOUNTING FOR AND REPORTING CHARITY CARE Health care organizations provide uncompensated patient care as a matter of both policy and law. The *Hospital Survey and Construction Act of 1946* (Public Law 79–725, usually referred to as the *Hill–Burton Act*) stipulates that hospitals receiving federal construction funds must provide a certain amount of charity care. This care does not result in cash inflows and consequently, it can be argued, should not qualify for recognition either as revenue or as receivables. On the other hand, charity care is conceptually similar to patient care for which third parties will reimburse the hospital or other provider at less than full rates (in the case of charity care, at zero) or patient care in which substantial bad debts are anticipated.

EXAMPLE   *Charity Care*
•••

A hospital values care provided to indigent patients at $300,000, based on standard billing rates. However, it anticipates collecting for none of its services.

AICPA Guidance

The AICPA audit guide specifies that gross revenue should *exclude* charity care. However, it also makes clear that health care organizations are obligated to disclose their policies for providing charity care and should indicate the amounts provided based on the provider's "rates, costs, units of service, or other statistics."[4]

The guide recognizes that distinguishing bad debt expense from charity care requires judgment. However, it notes that "charity care represents health care services that are provided but are never expected to result in cash flows," whereas it defines bad debt expense as "the provision for actual or expected uncollectibles resulting from the extension of credit."[5] The key distinction is that an entity provides charity care in the expectation that it will not receive compensation, but it incurs bad debts by providing service in the hope of at least partial payment.

Thus, in the example, the hospital need not make an entry to record the value of the charity care. It should, however, explain its policies and report the total value of the care provided in notes to the financial statements.

---

[4]AICPA, *Health Care Organizations*, paras. 10.03 and 10.20.

[5]AICPA, *Health Care Organizations*, para. 7.2 and glossary.

ACCOUNTING FOR TIMING DIFFERENCES BETWEEN COSTS INCURRED AND COSTS REIMBURSED Under Medicare and other arrangements with third-party payers, health care organizations may be entitled to reimbursement for allowable costs. For example, a county government might agree to share the cost of a not-for-profit hospital's emergency room. The government would reimburse the hospital for an established percentage of all direct costs (including depreciation) as well as allocated overhead costs. The third-party payers, however, might not necessarily reimburse the allowable costs in the same period in which the organization expenses the costs in its financial statements. The differences would arise when an organization

- Uses straight-line depreciation for reporting purposes but claims reimbursement on an accelerated basis
- Reports gains and losses from the early extinguishment of debt in the year of extinguishment for purposes of financial reporting (per FASB Statement No. 76, *Extinguishment of Debt*), but must delay recognition for purposes of reimbursement
- Capitalizes certain interest costs for purposes of financial reporting (per FASB Statement No. 34, *Capitalization of Interest*) but recognizes them as expenses for purposes of reimbursement

If the organization were to recognize an expense in one period and the reimbursement in another, then there would be a clear mismatch of revenue and expenses. However, if it were to recognize reimbursement revenue in a period before (or after) it were actually reimbursed, it would be recognizing revenue in a period before (or after) it actually had use of the resources.

Reimbursement timing differences are conceptually similar to a business's income tax timing differences. Such differences occur when a revenue or expense is recognized in one period for reporting purposes, but in another for tax purposes. Current FASB standards require that these differences be accounted for so that the reported tax expense is tied to reported income, irrespective of when the taxes actually have to be paid.

EXAMPLE *Timing Differences*

In 2004, a hospital acquires $600,000 of medical equipment with an estimated useful life of three years. For purposes of financial reporting, it charges depreciation on a straight-line basis—$200,000 per year. A third-party payer, however, allows reimbursement on a double-declining balance basis—$400,000 in 2004, $133,333 in 2005, and $66,667 in 2006.

Consistent with the FASB's approach to other types of timing differences, reimbursement revenues should be matched to related expenses. The differences between revenue recognized and amounts actually reimbursed should be debited or credited to a balance sheet account comparable to deferred income taxes.

In this example, the hospital should record straight-line depreciation in the usual way in each of the three years:

Depreciation expense	$200,000	
Allowance for depreciation		$200,000

To record depreciation in 2004 (Identical entries would also be made in 2005 and 2006.)

The hospital should recognize reimbursement revenue in the amount of the expense to be reported on its current-year financial statements, even if this expense differs from the actual amount to be reimbursed. Thus, in this example, even though the reimbursement will differ each year, the amount recognized as revenue should be the same. The difference between the amount of the reimbursement and the amount recognized as revenue should be either debited or credited to a balance sheet account—deferred (or advanced) reimbursement. The amount recognized as the deferred (or advanced) reimbursement in the first year would automatically be reversed by the last. Thus:

2004

Cash	$400,000	
Reimbursement revenue		$200,000
Reimbursements received in advance of		
the related depreciation charge (a liability)		200,000

To record the reimbursement for equipment acquired in 2004

2005

Cash	$133,333	
Reimbursements received in advance of		
the related depreciation charge	66,667	
Reimbursement revenue		$200,000

To record the reimbursement for equipment acquired in 2004

2006

Cash	$ 66,667	
Reimbursements received in advance of		
the related depreciation charge	133,333	
Reimbursement revenue		$200,000

To record the reimbursement for equipment acquired in 2004

Timing differences must be distinguished from *permanent* differences. Suppose the hospital bought the same $600,000 of equipment as in the example, but the third-party would reimburse only 80 percent of the costs. Assume further (to avoid complicating the issue) that the third party would reimburse depreciation charges on the same basis used by the hospital (the straight-line basis). Thus, the hospital would be reimbursed for $160,000 each year (80 percent of $200,000). In these circumstances the difference between what the hospital charges as an expense and the amount for which it will be reimbursed is not a temporary (or timing) difference but a permanent difference. The hospital would recognize revenue of $160,000 per year—the amount actually received. No special adjustments would be necessary.

ACCOUNTING FOR AND REPORTING MALPRACTICE CLAIMS Malpractice claims have become an accepted, if unwanted, concern of health care organizations and a routine element of their financial reports. Potential losses arising from malpractice claims are obviously consequential, so most entities transfer a portion of their risk to independent insurers. However, even if all or a portion of the risk is insured, litigation costs can still be daunting. The key accounting and reporting issues relate to when and how much of a loss should be recognized, owing to both unsettled claims and claims that have not yet been filed.

EXAMPLE *Malpractice Claims*

A hospital has been charged with negligence in the death of a patient. Although no claim has yet been filed, past experience indicates that the hospital is almost certain to be sued.

FASB Standards

FASB standards for malpractice and other claims are drawn from FASB Statement No. 5, *Accounting for Contingencies*, and are therefore the same as for businesses. They provide that a health care organization should accrue an estimated loss by a charge to operations as soon as both of the following conditions are met:

- It is probable that an asset has been impaired or a liability has been incurred.
- The amount of the loss can be reasonably estimated.

If neither of these conditions is met, but there is at least a *reasonable possibility* that a loss will be incurred, then the organization should disclose the nature of the contingency and estimate the possible loss or the range of the loss (or state that an estimate cannot be made).

Thus, the cost of a malpractice claim should be accrued when the incident giving rise to the claim occurs, as long as the eventual loss can be reasonably estimated. Obviously, health care organizations face considerable practical difficulties in estimating the amounts for which claims will eventually be settled, particularly those that have not yet been asserted. Nevertheless, the organization can draw upon both its own past experience and industry data. Moreover, it does not have to assess each incident individually. It can group together similar incidents and thereby take advantage of statistical relationships. The total accrued cost should take into account litigation fees, but should be reduced by anticipated insurance recoveries.

In the example, the hospital would be required to charge an expense (a loss) in the period of the incident if it were able to make a reasonable estimate of the amount. If it were unable to estimate the amount, then it would be required to disclose the details of the incident. Assuming the best estimate of the loss was $300,000, the following entry would be appropriate:

Anticipated legal claims (expense)	$300,000	
Commitments and contingencies (liability)		$300,000

To record the estimated cost of settling a potential malpractice claim

REPORTING RETROSPECTIVE INSURANCE PREMIUMS Another aspect of the question as to when and how malpractice claims should be reported is that of reporting malpractice insurance expense. Some insurance policies make provisions for *retrospectively rated premiums*. These policies require that, at the expiration of the policy, the premium costs be adjusted to take into account actual loss experience. Thus, if claims during the period are greater than anticipated, the insured will have to pay more; if claims are less, then it will receive a refund. As a consequence, the insured does not always know by year-end what that year's actual insurance costs will be.

These types of policies do not provide true insurance coverage (except, perhaps, for claims above a specified amount), since the insured is being charged for all, or a portion, of actual losses.

EXAMPLE   *Retrospective Premiums*

In June 2004, a health maintenance organization (HMO) entered into an insurance contract for the period July 1, 2004, through June 30, 2005. The basic premium was $120,000 for the year, which the HMO paid in June 2004. However, the policy also contained a complex formula for premium adjustments upon termination of the policy. Prior to preparing its financial statements for the year ended December 31, 2004, the HMO estimated, based on both asserted and unasserted claims, that it would have to pay an additional $50,000 in premiums resulting from incidents in the last six months of 2004.

AICPA Guidance

The AICPA audit guide indicates that the insured entity should charge the basic premium as an expense pro rata over the term of the policy. In addition, it should accrue additional premiums or refunds based on the FASB Statement No. 5 criteria for recognition of losses. If it is unable to estimate losses from claims, then it should disclose the contingencies in the notes.

The following entry would summarize insurance activity for 2004:

Malpractice insurance expense	$110,000	
Prepaid insurance (basic premium)	60,000	
Cash		$120,000
Commitments and contingencies (liability		
to insurance company)		50,000

To record 2004 malpractice insurance expense (basic premium of $60,000 for six months plus anticipated claims adjustment of $50,000) and prepaid insurance for 2005 (basic premium of $60,000 for six months)

DIFFERENT STANDARDS FOR GOVERNMENT VERSUS NOT-FOR-PROFIT HEALTH CARE PROVIDERS Government hospitals and other health care providers are within the GASB's jurisdiction. However, most of them (the notable exception being those financed entirely with nonexchange revenues) follow similar accounting practices to comparable business and not-for-profit entities, including the guidance in the AICPA's health care audit guide. As special purpose entities engaged in only business-type activities, they would present only government-wide financial statements and would not be required to present fund statements, thus enhancing comparability with their not-for-profit counterparts.

Nevertheless, there are differences between the FASB's reporting model under Statement No. 117 and the GASB's under Statement No. 34. Most notably, the FASB requires that net assets (and revenues) be presented in three categories of restrictiveness—permanently restricted, temporarily restricted, and unrestricted—whereas the GASB's required categories are: invested in capital assets net of related debt, restricted net assets, and unrestricted net assets. Moreover, whereas the FASB's categories of restrictiveness are based on donor specification, the GASB draws no distinction between resources restricted by donors and those restricted by other outside parties, such as bondholders. These and other differences between FASB and GASB standards limit the comparability of the financial statements of government and not-for-profit health care providers.

WHAT UNIQUE ISSUES DO COLLEGES AND UNIVERSITIES FACE?

Not-for-profit colleges and universities are subject to the same FASB standards as other not-for-profit entities. As noted earlier and in Chapter 11, most government institutions can be expected to report as special purpose entities engaged only in business-type activities. They would present only government-wide statements, whereas prior to the issuance of GASB Statements No. 34 and 35, they were required to present only fund statements. Therefore, inasmuch as both government and not-for-profit institutions will account for their activities on a full accrual basis and report them in consolidated financial statements, the differences are likely to be less pronounced than in the past. Nevertheless, as previously noted with respect to health care organizations, FASB and GASB standards applicable to colleges and universities differ in significant ways. Thus, users' ability to compare the financial statements of public and private institutions continues to be limited.

Although the FASB pronouncements for not-for-profits apply to colleges and universities, they do not address the unique accounting and reporting issues of these entities. The same is true of the GASB pronouncements applicable to government institutions. In 1973, the AICPA issued an industry audit guide, *Audits of Colleges and Universities*, that dealt exclusively with colleges and universities. It supplemented this guide, in 1974, with Statement of Position (SOP) 74-8, *Financial Accounting and Reporting By Colleges and Universities*. However, the AICPA has now superseded these publications with its more inclusive industry audit guide, *Not-for-profit Organizations*, that covers all not-for-profits (except health care organizations), but does not deal with the specific issues facing colleges and universities.

For guidance on specific questions, both government and not-for-profit institutions can look to the superseded AICPA publications, to the literature of the National Association of College and University Business Officers (the leading association of university accounting and financial managers), and to prevalent practice.

The current AICPA industry audit guide on not-for-profits carried forward from the superseded publications a description of what is referred to as the "AICPA model" for colleges and universities. This model establishes a fund structure, summarized in Table 13–1, that many institutions, both public and private, continue to maintain for purposes of internal accounting and control. However, for purposes of external reporting, not-for-profit institutions must now group their funds into the three categories of restrictiveness established in FASB Statement No. 117. Similarly, government colleges and universities that report as entities engaged only in business-type activities must consolidate their funds into government-wide statements

TABLE 13–1 **AICPA Model Fund Structure** **for Colleges and Universities** **(for Internal Accounting and Reporting Only)**

Current Operating Funds

The current funds are equivalent to a general purpose government's general fund and special revenue funds. Like a government, a university maintains a single current unrestricted fund plus as many current restricted funds as needed.

Loan Funds

Loan funds account for resources dedicated for student loans. A type of restricted fund, their assets are principally loans receivable and investments. They do not typically have liabilities of consequence, except if the university has borrowed the funds that it lends. Fund balances are ordinarily increased by gifts, grants, and investment earnings. They are decreased by administrative costs and provisions for bad debts.

Endowment Funds

Endowment funds are analogous to a government's permanent funds (i.e., nonexpendable funds). Most commonly they account for gifts that specify that the donated amount is to be invested and that only the income from the investments may be expended. The donors may either stipulate the purpose for which the income must be expended or leave it to the university's discretion.

Annuity and Life Income Funds

These funds are special types of endowment funds. They account for gifts that provide a return to the donor (or a person designated by the donor) for a specified term or for the remainder of his or her life. Thereafter, what remains of the gift will revert to the university. For example, a donor might want to contribute her fortune to a university while she is alive, but still reap all or a portion of the earnings from it. She can accomplish this (and perhaps also be rewarded with advantageous tax treatment) by attaching to the gift the stipulation that she receive either a stated annual sum (an annuity) or a percentage of the investment earnings from the gift (life income) until her death.

Plant Funds

Universities divide their plant funds into four categories:

* *Plant funds—unexpended.* These are the university version of capital projects funds. They account for resources reserved for the construction or purchase of plant and equipment. Universities finance the construction of capital projects by issuing bonds, accepting gifts or grants, or setting aside general operating revenues.
* *Plant fund—renewals and replacements.* These are, in essence, additional capital projects funds. Their resources, however, are committed to the renewal and replacement of existing plant and equipment rather than the acquisition of new facilities.
* *Plant funds—retirement of indebtedness.* These funds correspond to a government's debt service funds. Their assets, mostly cash and investments, are held for the retirement of debt and the payment of interest.
* *Plant funds—investment in plant.* These funds report the university's capital assets, including land, buildings, construction in progress, improvements other than buildings, equipment, and library books.

Plant funds report both assets and related debt. Thus, if proceeds from issuing bonds are initially reported in an unexpended plant fund, then the cash received would be recognized as an asset; the bonds payable as a liability. If the bond money was subsequently used to construct a building, then both the cash and the bonds payable would be removed from the unexpended plant fund. In the investment in plant fund, the new building would be reported as an asset; the related bonds payable as a liability. The excess of plant fund assets over liabilities in each of the categories is generally reported as either *fund balance* or *investment in plant.*

Agency Funds

The agency funds of a university are virtually identical to those of a government. They account for resources that the institution holds as a custodian or fiscal agent for "outsiders," such as student organizations and employees. Like a government's agency funds, they have only assets and liabilities—no fund balances.

and need not present fund statements. In contrast, government institutions that elect to report as entities engaged only in governmental activities, or engaged in both governmental and business-type activities, must present fund statements using the fund structure specified in GASB Statement No. 34, as well as government-wide statements.

CLASSIFICATION OF REVENUES AND EXPENSES FASB Statement No. 117 does not specify how revenues and expenses should be classified. But most colleges and universities, both government and private, classify revenues by source and expenses by function. Common categories of revenues include

- Tuition and fees
- Government appropriations
- Government grants and contracts
- Gifts and private grants
- Endowment income
- Revenues from auxiliary enterprises
- Gains (or losses) on sales of investments

Common categories of expenses include

- Education and general
  - instruction and departmental research
  - extension and public service
  - libraries
  - student services
- Sponsored research
- Operation and maintenance of plant
- General administration
- Expenses of auxiliary enterprises
- Depreciation
- Interest
- Provision for uncollectible student loans

RECOGNIZING TUITION AND FEE REVENUES AND RELATED EXPENSES The issue of when tuition and fee revenues should be recognized arises mainly because most colleges and universities end their fiscal year in the summer months, their "slow" season. Therefore, summer semesters or quarters may overlap fiscal years, whereas fall and spring terms generally take place entirely within a single fiscal year.

Several events or transactions could be justified as a point of revenue recognition for tuition and fees:

- As students pay their tuition or fees (i.e., a cash collection basis)
- The start of a semester
- The last date at which refunds can be claimed
- The passage of time (i.e., if a semester overlaps two fiscal years, then the revenue could be allocated between the years based on the number of semester days in each year)

EXAMPLE   *Tuition and Fee Revenues*

The fiscal year of a college ends July 31. In June 2004, a college collects $6 million in tuition and fees for its summer semester that begins on June 1 and ends on August 15. It also collects $9 million for the following fall semester, which begins on September 6. Faculty salaries applicable to summer session courses are $500,000. Of this amount, $400,000 is paid in June and July and $100,000 in August.

Neither the FASB nor the GASB pronouncements, nor the current AICPA not-for-profit audit guide, addresses the issue of tuition revenue. Thus, the 1973 AICPA college and university guide remains the most authoritative source of guidance for both government and not-for-profit institutions.

AICPA Guidance

The 1973 AICPA audit guide states that "revenues and expenditures of an academic term, such as a summer session, which is conducted over a fiscal year-end, should be reported totally within the fiscal year in which the program is predominantly conducted."

Thus, in the example, the entire summer semester tuition and fees, as well as the related faculty salaries, should be recognized in the year ending July 31, 2004:

Cash	$6,000,000	
Revenue from tuition and fees		$6,000,000

To record revenue for the summer semester beginning June 1, 2004

Faculty salaries relating to the summer semester—expense	$500,000	
Cash		$400,000
Deferred faculty salaries relating to the summer semester (liability)		100,000

To record the faculty salaries applicable to the summer semester beginning June 1, 2004

In this example it is assumed that faculty salaries, but not other operating costs, can be tied directly to summer courses. Therefore, the faculty salaries have been matched to the tuition revenues and fees. The other operating costs would be accounted for as "period" costs and expensed as incurred.

The $9 million in tuition and fees applicable to the fall semester should be recognized as revenue in the year ending July 31, 2005, and should therefore be reported as deferred revenue when received in June 2004:

Cash	$9,000,000	
Deferred revenue—fall semester tuition and fees (liability)		$9,000,000

To record tuition and fees applicable to the fall semester beginning September 5, 2004

ACCOUNTING FOR AND REPORTING GRANTS For many colleges and universities, reimbursement grants for research and related activities are a mainstay of financial support. Grantors, especially the federal government, do not expect recipients to earn a profit from their grants; they expect the grants merely to cover the costs of the specified research or other activities. Nonetheless, almost all grants provide reimbursement for indirect costs or overhead, and Office of Management and Budget rules detail how overhead allowances on federal grants should be computed.[6]

The most controversial accounting issue as to research grants is the same as that discussed in Chapter 4 pertaining to government grants: When should revenue and expenses be recognized, inasmuch as the various stages in the grant process (award, fulfillment of terms, and payment) may occur in different accounting periods?

EXAMPLE   *Grants*

••

In 2004, a private university's accounting department received a $300,000 federal grant to carry out research in government budgeting. Of this amount, $180,000 was to cover faculty salaries and $120,000 was to cover overhead. During 2004, the department began the research and paid faculty members $45,000. It was reimbursed by the federal government for $75,000 (the direct costs incurred plus a proportionate share of the overhead).

FASB Standards

Per Statement No. 116, grants (excluding those that are exchange transactions in which the grantors expect to receive reciprocal value) are a form of contributions and should be accounted for as such. Reimbursement grants are conditioned upon the grantee's incurring qualifying costs. Therefore, they should be accounted for as conditional grants. They should be recognized as revenue only as the grantee incurs qualifying costs.

The following entries would be appropriate in 2004:

Sponsored research—expense	$45,000	
Cash		$45,000

To record faculty salaries (in an unrestricted fund)

The overhead costs incurred are not broken out separately because, by their nature, they cannot be. They are subsumed in categories such as maintenance, administration, and library costs.

Due from federal government	$75,000	
Government grants and contracts—direct		
reimbursement (revenue)		$45,000
Government grants and contracts—reimbursement		
for overhead (revenue)		30,000

To record the amount due from the federal government for reimbursement of direct costs and overhead (in an unrestricted fund)

Cash	$75,000	
Due from federal government		$75,000

To record the collection of cash from the federal government (in an unrestricted fund)

In this illustration, the resources received from the federal government are restricted for specified research. Nevertheless, the transactions are recorded entirely in the

---

[6]Office of Management and Budget Circular A-21, *Cost Principles for Educational Institutions.*

unrestricted category because it is assumed that the university will exercise its option to report restricted contributions as unrestricted if the restriction has been met in the same period as the donation is made.

Given the same circumstances for a government university, the entries would be essentially the same, except that, due to the purpose restriction, a restricted fund would be used. As discussed in Chapter 4 GASB Statement No. 33, *Accounting and Financial Reporting for Nonexchange Transactions*, requires governments to recognize revenue from a reimbursement grant only as allowable costs under the grant are incurred. In the example, the

TABLE 13-2
Financial Statements of a Private College or University

Oberlin College
Statements of Financial Position
as of June 30, 2004 and 2003
(in thousands)

	2004	2003
Current Assets		
Cash and Cash Equivalents	$ 6,219	$ 2,701
Short-term Investments	340	7,408
Accounts Receivable, Net	4,119	2,240
Inventories	560	596
Deposits and Prepaid Expenses	1,967	1,212
Total Current Assets	13,205	14,157
Pledges Receivable and Bequests in Probate	10,806	10,371
Long-term Receivables		
Student Loans	11,249	11,101
Allowance for Doubtful Loans	(1,273)	(1,266)
Total Long-term Receivables	9,976	9,835
Long-term Investments		
Assets Restricted to Investment in Land, Buildings, and Equipment	19,498	18,335
Endowment Funds	441,383	392,475
Annuity and Life Income Funds	19,801	17,946
Funds Held in Trust by Others	18,424	15,261
Total Long-term Investments	499,106	444,017
Property, Plant, and Equipment		
Land, Buildings, and Equipment	195,242	187,214
Construction in Progress	4,039	746
Less: Accumulated Depreciation	(95,268)	(87,489)
Total Property, Plant, and Equipment	104,013	100,471
Total Assets	$637,106	$578,851
Liabilities and Net Assets		
Current Liabilities		
Accounts Payable	$ 10,438	$ 9,335
Current Portion of Bonds Payable	1,335	1,275
Deposits and Agency Funds	2,827	2,248
Accrued Payroll and Other Liabilities	1,777	1,032
Total Current Liabilities	16,377	13,890

resources received would offset expenses incurred. Thus, there would be no change in the net assets reported on the institution's government-wide statements. Financial resources received in advance of incurring the related allowable costs would be reported as deferred revenues in a restricted fund. Revenue would be recognized as the costs are incurred.

Table 13–2 contains the statement of financial position and statement of activities for Oberlin College, a private institution. These statements may be contrasted with the statement of net assets and statement of revenues, expenses, and changes in net assets for ABC University, a public institution, in Table 11–4 of Chapter 11.

TABLE 13–2 (*continued*)
Financial Statements of a Private College or University

Oberlin College
Statements of Financial Position
as of June 30, 2004 and 2003
(in thousands)

	2004	2003
Other Liabilities		
Accruals for Staff Benefit Programs	17,269	17,048
Annuity Obligations	11,679	10,654
Federal Student Loan Funds	5,954	5,890
Notes Payable	477	976
Bonds Payable, Net	49,179	50,457
Total Liabilities	100,935	98,915
Net Assets		
Unrestricted		
Current Operations	(15,540)	(12,628)
Designated for Specific Purposes	1,474	1,077
Unexpended Plant and Facility Funds	5,371	5,613
Invested in Plant Facilities	41,902	38,875
Quasi-endowment Funds	201,477	181,166
Total Unrestricted	234,684	214,103
Temporarily Restricted		
Donor Designated for Specific Purposes	7,907	6,763
Annuity and Life Income Funds	3,926	4,001
Unexpended Plant and Facility Funds	14,578	12,451
Unamortized Contributions for Long-lived Assets	12,761	13,094
Quasi-endowment Funds	135,935	115,864
Total Temporarily Restricted	175,107	152,173
Permanently Restricted		
Student Loan Funds	1,313	1,181
Annuity and Life Income Funds	2,443	2,215
Funds Held in Trust by Others	18,424	15,261
Endowment Funds	104,200	95,003
Total Permanently Restricted	126,380	113,660
Total Net Assets	536,171	479,936
Total Liabilities and Net Assets	$637,106	$578,851

(*continued*)

TABLE 13–2 (*continued*)
Financial Statements of a Private
College or University

Oberlin College
Statements of Activities
For the year ended June 30, 2004, with summarized totals for 2003
(in thousands)

	2004				2003
	Unrestricted	Temporarily Restricted	Permanently Restricted	Total	Total
Operating Revenues					
Tuition and Fees	$ 63,479			$ 63,917	$ 60,717
Auxiliary Enterprises	17,682			17,682	16,988
Government Grants and Contributions		$ 2,698		2,260	2,031
Private Gifts and Grants	5,619	2,963		8,582	13,739
Investment Earnings and Gain	9,651	9,221	$ 469	19,341	17,698
Other Sources	2,315	35		2,350	1,898
Net Assets Released from Restrictions	12,722	(12,722)			
Total Operating Revenues	111,468	2,195	469	114,132	113,071
Operating Expenses					
Instruction	30,552			30,552	29,104
Research	339			339	417
Student Aid	25,730			25,730	22,022
Academic Support	6,679			6,679	6,117
Student Services	7,765			7,765	7,206
Institutional Support	11,267			11,267	9,670
Facilities:					
Operations	5,385			5,385	5,496
Depreciation	5,753			5,753	5,295
Interest Expense	1,627			1,627	1,704
Auxiliary Enterprises:					
Operations	12,898			12,898	12,621
Depreciation	2,026			2,026	2,046
Interest Expense	1,334			1,334	1,367
Total Operating Expenses	111,355			111,355	103,065
Increase in Net Assets from Operating Activities	113	2,195	469	2,777	10,006
Nonoperating Activities					
Investment Earnings and Gain	24,373	22,757	920	48,050	20,657
Unrealized Gain	(4,180)	(1,384)	2,610	(2,954)	33,772
Matured Life Income Agreements	13	(13)			
Capital and Deferred Gifts	368	3,429	8,080	11,877	7,334
Pledges and Bequests	794	(1,397)	1,038	435	5,916
Change in Annuity Obligations	(91)	(397)	(537)	(1,025)	(2,823)
Payments to Beneficiaries		(1,308)		(1,308)	(1,132)
Other	(1,267)	(373)	23	(1,617)	(1,172)
Redesignated Funds	34	(151)	117		
Net Assets Released from Restrictions	424	(424)			
Increase in Net Assets from Nonoperating Activities	20,468	20,739	12,251	53,458	62,552
Net Increase in Net Assets	20,581	22,934	12,720	56,235	72,558
Net Assets at Beginning of Year	214,103	152,173	113,660	479,936	407,378
Net Assets at End of Year	$234,684	$175,107	$126,380	$536,171	$479,936

QUESTIONS FOR REVIEW AND DISCUSSION

1. A hospital receives a donation that must be used to acquire plant and equipment. In which type of fund would it account for the donation? In which type of fund would it likely account for the plant and equipment that it acquires with the donated funds? Are there any circumstances in which it should not account for the plant and equipment in that fund?

2. A hospital board of governors votes to set aside resources to acquire plant and equipment. In which type of fund should these resources be accounted for?

3. Hospitals and other health care organizations provide services knowing that they will collect from third-party payers, such as insurance companies, considerably less than their established billing rates. In addition, they provide services to uninsured patients, aware that they will collect either none or only a small portion of the amounts to be billed. Comment on how these organizations distinguish between charity care, bad debts, and contractual adjustments, and indicate how each affects the amount of revenue from patient care that they should report.

4. What is meant by *retrospective* insurance premiums, and how should they be reported?

5. How can a hospital or other not-for-profit avoid a mismatch of revenues and expenses when it recognizes expenses in one period for purposes of financial reporting but in another for purposes of obtaining reimbursement from an outside party? Give an example of how this situation can arise.

6. What is meant by *capitation fees*? When should they be recognized as revenues?

7. A hospital controller is informed that a patient suffered serious injury as a result of the hospital's negligence. The patient is sure to sue the hospital, but the amount of any judgment or settlement cannot be reasonably estimated. If you were the controller, how, if at all, would you recommend the hospital report the incident in its financial statements?

8. Recent pronouncements of the GASB and the FASB have considerably narrowed the differences in accounting and reporting practices between government and not-for-profit colleges and universities. Do you agree? Are there any remaining distinguishing features?

9. What is meant by the *AICPA model* for colleges and universities? What are its main features? In what way is the model still relevant for both government and not-for-profit institutions?

10. Colleges and universities face special issues in accounting for revenues and expenses of summer sessions. Why? How have these issues been resolved?

EXERCISES AND PROBLEMS

13–1

Select the *best* answer.

1. In a particular year, a not-for-profit hospital provides free care to charity patients, which, if billed at standard rates, have a value of $3 million. During the same period, it bills patients for $100 million. However, owing to contractual adjustments with insurance companies and other third-party payers, it expects to collect only $80 million. The hospital should report gross revenues of

   a. $80 million
   b. $83 million
   c. $100 million
   d. $103 million

2. In a particular year, owing to arrangements with an insurance company, a not-for-profit hospital receives $600,000 in *capitation fees*.

During the year, however, it provides covered services, which, if billed at standard rates, have a value of only $500,000. The fees received from the insurance company are based on what the parties expect will be the average value of services provided. Hence, in some years, the amount received from the insurance company will exceed the value of services provided; in some years it will be less. The hospital should report

a. revenue of $500,000 and deferred revenue of $100,000
b. revenue of $600,000, less an allowance of $100,000 for contractual adjustments
c. revenue of $500,000 and a liability of $100,000
d. revenue of $600,000

3. The fiscal year of Baker College ends on June 30. However, the college conducts a summer session that begins on June 1 and concludes on August 30. In May 2004 the college collects $1,800,000 in summer session tuition. For the year ending June 30, 2004, the college should recognize summer session tuition revenue of

a. $0
b. $600,000
c. $900,000
d. $1,800,000

4. Several days prior to the end of its fiscal year, physicians at Healthy Heart Hospital negligently treated a patient, resulting in the patient's death. Although the patient's family has not yet asserted a claim against the hospital, it is likely to do so. Hospital officials are unable to make a reliable estimate of the magnitude of any eventual costs to the hospital, but they believe that they will be in the range of $400,000 to $500,000. In its financial statements for the year in which the incident occurred, the hospital

a. need not report the incident
b. should report an expense and a liability equal to the hospital's best estimate of the eventual costs
c. should disclose the incident in notes to the financial statements, indicating the hospital's best estimate of the range of eventual costs
d. should disclose the incident in notes to the financial statements, without placing an estimate on the eventual costs

5. In their external financial statements, government colleges and universities
a. may opt to adhere to the standards of the FASB
b. may opt to report as special purpose governments engaged in only business-type activities
c. are not required to prepare government-wide statements
d. may opt to adhere to the AIPCA model

6. In its statement of activities, a not-for-profit hospital
a. must classify all expenses by object
b. must classify all expenses by function
c. may classify all expenses by object, but if it does so must present a functional classification in notes
d. may classify all expenses by function, but if it does so must present an object classification in notes

7. Depreciation on a not-for-profit hospital's plant and equipment may be reported in a temporarily restricted fund if the plant and equipment
a. were acquired with proceeds of bonds that were restricted to the acquisition of equipment
b. were acquired with proceeds of donations that were restricted to the acquisition of equipment
c. will be replaced with proceeds from bonds restricted to the acquisition of equipment
d. will be replaced with proceeds from donations restricted to the acquisition of equipment

8. A government hospital, unlike a not-for-profit hospital,
a. would report on a modified accrual basis
b. would have to report all investments at cost
c. would have to report its cash flows in four categories rather than three
d. would report charity care as an expense rather than a deduction from revenues

9. A not-for-profit hospital acquires $800,000 in equipment having a useful life of four years. For purposes of reporting it charges depreciation on a straight-line basis. A third-party payer, however, agrees to reimburse the hospital on a double declining balance basis, but for only 75 percent of the equipment cost. In the first year that the hospital charges deprecia-

tion, it should recognize depreciation expense of $200,000 and reimbursement revenue of

a. $150,000
b. $200,000
c. $300,000
d. $400,000

10. A not-for-profit university accounts for its athletic department as an auxiliary enterprise. The operations of the department should be accounted for in a

a. proprietary fund
b. auxiliary fund
c. temporarily restricted fund
d. unrestricted fund

13–2

Select the *best* answer.

1. A government university opts to report as a special purpose government engaged in only business-type activities. Therefore, it need not present a

a. government-wide statement of net assets
b. statement of revenues and expenses for major funds
c. management's discussion and analysis
d. statement of cash flows

2. In reporting gross revenue, a hospital should include

a. both charity care and third-party discounts
b. charity care but not third-party discounts
c. third party discounts but not charity care
d. neither charity care nor third-party discounts

3. A not-for-profit college receives a $1 million endowment, the income from which is restricted to student scholarships. During a particular year the endowment earns $60,000 in income and dividends, none of which has been spent by year-end. However, the market value of the endowment declines by $45,000. At year-end, the university should report permanently and temporarily restricted net assets, respectively, of

	Permanently Restricted	Temporarily Restricted
a.	$1,000,000	$60,000
b.	$955,000	$60,000
c.	$1,000,000	$15,000
d.	$955,000	$60,000

4. A not-for-profit hospital agrees to pay $480,000 for a malpractice insurance policy that covers the period April 1, 2003 to March 31, 2004. In January 2004, prior to preparing its 2003 financial statements, it is notified by its insurance company that, in accord with provisions of the policy, it will have to pay an additional $80,000 in premiums owing to unexpectedly high claims in October and November. For its fiscal year ending December 31, 2003, the hospital should report insurance expense relating to this policy of

a. $360,000
b. $440,000
c. $480,000
d. $560,000

5. In October 2004, the sociology department of a not-for-profit university is awarded a grant by the U.S. Science Foundation to conduct research on rural poverty. The foundation agrees to reimburse the department for all direct expenses incurred, up to $1 million, plus overhead of 40 percent—a total of $1,400,000. During 2004, the department incurs $100,000 in allowable direct expenses and is reimbursed a total of $60,000. For the year ending December 31, 2004, the university should recognize grant revenue of

a. $60,000
b. $100,000
c. $140,000
d. $1,400,000

6. Which of the following expenses would be least likely to be found on the statement of activities of a not-for-profit college that reports expenses by function?

a. sponsored research
b. student services
c. operation and maintenance of plant
d. faculty salaries

7. A not-for-profit hospital held the following endowments:

- $4 million specified by the donor as permanently nonexpendable
- $2 million specified by a donor as expendable only upon his death
- $1 million specified by the hospital's governing board as permanently nonexpendable

The amount that the hospital should report as permanently nonexpendable is

a. $3 million

b. $4 million

c. $6 million

d. $7 million

8. The plant funds (maintained for internal accounting purposes only) of a not-for-profit college include plant and equipment of $500 million and cash and investments of $40 million. The cash and investments represent the proceeds from bonds issued to renovate classroom and lab facilities. The amount that the college should report as unrestricted funds is

a. $0

b. $40 million

c. $500 million

d. $540 million

9. A government university, in contrast to a not-for-profit university,

a. does not have to divide its resources into three categories of donor restrictiveness

b. recognizes reimbursement grants as revenue when the grant is received rather than when allowable costs are incurred

c. does not have to depreciate capital assets

d. is not permitted to capitalize collectibles, such as artwork and rare books

10. A not-for-profit university receives a $4 million cash grant from an automobile manufacturer to carry out research on long-lived batteries. Per the terms of the grant, the automobile manufacturer has the exclusive rights to any patents, and must approve any publications, that may result from the research. Upon receiving the grant, the university should credit a

a. revenue account in an unrestricted fund

b. deferred revenue account in an unrestricted fund

c. revenue account in a temporarily restricted fund

d. deferred revenue account in a temporarily restricted fund

13–3

The basis for recognizing patient care revenue is not always obvious.

In a particular month, Northwest Medical Clinic, a not-for-profit entity, reported the following:

1. It provided direct care services to patients, billing them $400,000. Of this amount it received $120,000 in cash, but as a consequence of bad debts it expects to collect a total of only $330,000.

2. It provided direct care to patients who are covered by insurance and are members of various group health plans. At standard rates, it would have billed $650,000. However, owing to contractual arrangements with the payers, it actually billed them for, and expects to collect, only $480,000.

3. It provided charity care, for which it would have billed, at standard rates, $82,000.

4. It received capitation fees of $1,400,000 from health care plans and provided services to members of those plans, for which it would have billed, at standard rates, $1,600,000.

Prepare appropriate journal entries to recognize revenue.

13–4

A multifund balance sheet can readily be recast so that it conforms with FASB standards.

A balance sheet of Blue University, a not-for-profit institution, is shown on page 357. It was drawn from the university's internal accounts, which are maintained according to the "old" (1973) AICPA model fund structure.

Recast the fund balances (net assets) section of the balance sheet so that it conforms to the net assets section of a balance sheet per FASB Statement No. 117. Assume that the new balance sheet reports all amounts in a single column (i.e., as in the totals column of the balance sheet presented). However, divide the net assets section into three separate sections, each of which conforms to one of the three categories of restrictiveness required by Statement No. 117. Report each fund balance (category of net assets) on the new balance sheet within one of the three categories. Make appropriate assumptions as to the type of restriction that applies to each of the funds.

		Current	Loan	Endowment	Plant
	Total	Funds	Funds	Funds	Funds

Blue University
Balance Sheet as of June 30, 2004
(in Thousands)

	Total	Current Funds	Loan Funds	Endowment Funds	Plant Funds
Assets:					
Cash	$110,922	$45,268	$ 590	$ 61,555	$ 3,509
Investments	507,503	9,042		456,126	42,335
Accounts Receivable	15,070	14,499	426		145
Notes Receivable	26,000		26,000		
Inventories and Pre-Paid Expenses	5,047	5,047			
Land, Buildings, and Equipment (Less Accumulated Depreciation)	196,897				196,897
Due From (to) Other Funds		11,338	(3,376)	3,323	(11,285)
Total Assets	$861,439	$85,194	$23,640	$521,004	$231,601
Liabilities and Fund Balances:					
Liabilities:					
Accounts Payable—Accrued Liabilities	$ 29,788	$20,836		$ 6,597	$ 2,355
Deferred Revenues	5,424	5,424			
Agency Accounts	10,375	10,375			
Bonds Payable	88,399				88,399
Total Liabilities	133,986	36,635		6,597	90,754
Fund Balances:					
Current Funds					
Designated	20,445	20,445			
Restricted	28,114	28,114			
Student Loans Funds Established by Gift and Grants	23,640		23,640		
Endowment and Similar Funds					
Unrestricted Quasi-Endowment Funds	59,644			59,644	
Restricted Endowment Funds	68,352			68,352	
Other Endowment Funds	369,399			369,399	
Life Income Funds	17,012			17,012	
Plant Funds					
Unexpended	19,452				19,452
Retirement of Indebtedness	6,306				6,306
Net Investment in Plant	115,089				115,089
Total Fund Balances	727,453	48,559	23,640	514,407	140,847
Total Liabilities and Fund Balances	$861,439	$85,194	$23,640	$521,004	$231,601

13–5

University plant funds can readily be recast from an AICPA to an FASB presentation.

A not-for-profit university maintains several plant funds as shown in the condensed balance sheets that follow. The fund structure and presentation are consistent with the (1973) AICPA college and university reporting model. Although this model has been superseded by FASB Statement No. 117, it might still be used by colleges and universities for internal purposes.

Plant Funds (in Thousands)		
Unexpended Plant Funds		
Assets:		
Cash		$ 9,000
Investments		27,000
Total Assets		$ 36,000
Liabilities and Fund Balances:		
Bonds Payable		$ 24,000
Fund Balance		
Restricted by Donors for		
Specified Projects	$4,000	
Unrestricted	8,000	12,000
Total Liabilities		
and Fund Balances		$ 36,000
Funds for Renewals and Replacements		
Assets:		
Cash		$ 4,500
Investments		85,100
Total Assets		$ 89,600
Liabilities and Fund Balances:		
Fund Balance		$ 89,600
Funds for Retirement of Indebtedness		
Assets:		
Cash		$ 21,600
Investments		25,600
Total Assets		$ 47,200
Liabilities and Fund Balances:		
Fund Balance		$ 47,200
Investment in Plant		
Assets:		
Construction in Process		$ 3,500
Equipment		39,300
Land		12,000
Buildings		127,800
Total Plant		182,600
Less: Accumulated Depreciation		(78,200)
Total Investment in Plant		$104,400
Liabilities and Fund Balances:		
Notes Payable		$ 20,000
Bonds Payable		39,000
Capital Lease Obligations		8,500
Net Investment in Plant		36,900
Total Investment in Plant		$104,400

1. Recast the plant funds as they would appear in external financial statements in accord with Statement No. 117. Allocate the cash ($9,000) and investments ($27,000) of the unexpended plant funds between the donor-restricted and unrestricted categories based on the ratio of donor-restricted fund balance to total liabilities and fund balances (i.e., $4,000/$36,000).

2. Comment briefly on the advantages and disadvantages of each presentation.

13–6

Pledges must be distinguished by the extent to which they are restricted.

Abel College, a private institution, receives the following pledges of support:

1. As part of its annual fund drive, alumni and friends of the college pledge $8 million. The college estimates that about 15 percent of the pledges will prove uncollectible.

2. A CPA firm promises to establish an endowed chair in the accounting department by donating $500,000. The chair agreement provides that the funds be used to purchase investment-grade securities and that the income from the securities be used to supplement the salary of the chairholder and support his or her academic activities.

3. A private foundation promises to donate $100,000 to be used to support a major revision of the college's public administration curriculum.

4. An alumnus pledges $25,000 to the college's loan fund, which is used to make loans to students requiring financial assistance.

5. The college is seeking support for construction of a new athletic field house. A local real estate investor promises to donate ten acres of land on which a fieldhouse could be built if the college is able to raise the funds required to construct the building. The land has a market value of $1 million.

Indicate the category of net assets (unrestricted, temporarily restricted, or permanently restricted) in which each of the contributions should be recorded and the amount of revenue, if any, that should be recognized when the pledge was made. Briefly explain your response.

13–7

Not-for-profits must account for timing differences in reimbursements, just as businesses must account for timing differences in taxes.

The Round Hill Health Clinic, a not-for-profit medical center that serves a rural population, is reimbursed by Williams County for 60 percent of certain allowable costs.

In each of the three years, 2003 through 2005, the clinic incurs $600,000 of allowable, reimbursable costs. In addition, the following two items affected the clinic:

- The 2003 purchase of $60,000 of equipment. For purposes of external reporting, the clinic depreciates this equipment over three years. The county, however, reimburses the clinic (at the 60 percent rate) entirely in the year of acquisition.
- The 2003 loss of $10,000 on early extinguishment of debt. For purposes of external reporting, the clinic recognizes the entire loss in the year the debt is extinguished. The county, however, reimburses the clinic (at the 60 percent rate) over what would have been the remaining life of the debt—in this instance, two years.

1. Prepare a schedule in which you compare, for each of the three years, the expenses that the clinic would report on its financial statements with those for which it would be reimbursed. (Use two columns—reportable and reimbursable.)
2. Prepare journal entries for each of the three years to record the reimbursements.

13–8

The statement of cash flows of a government hospital would differ from that of a not-for-profit hospital.

The following represent a hospital's inflows and outflows of cash:

- Patient service fees received
- Government grants for operating purposes
- Government grants for specific research programs
- Contribution restricted for construction of a new building
- Salaries and wages
- Supplies
- Interest paid on long-term debt
- Interest paid on short-term operating debt
- Acquisition of capital assets
- Purchases of marketable securities
- Proceeds from sale of marketable securities
- Interest received from investments
- Dividends received from investments
- Proceeds of long-term debt to finance a new building
- Proceeds of short-term borrowings for operating purposes

1. Categorize the cash inflows and outflows as they would be reported in a statement of cash flows, assuming that the hospital is government-owned.
2. Do the same, this time assuming that the hospital is a not-for-profit.
3. Why did the GASB opt for a four-way classification, whereas the FASB retained for not-for-profits the three-way classification developed for businesses?

13–9

This example, drawn from the actual financial statements of a major urban not-for-profit hospital, illustrates the main types of transactions (in summary form) in which hospitals engage.

The December 31, 2004, statement of financial position of Mosholu Medical Center, a major urban not-for-profit hospital and research center, is shown on page 360. All amounts are in thousands.

The following transactions and events occurred in 2005 (all dollar amounts in thousands):

a. The hospital provided $705,943 in patient care at standard rates. On average, it expects to collect approximately 75 percent ($529,457) of this amount, owing mainly to discounts by third-party providers. Further, it expects that 5 percent of the 75 percent ($26,473) will have to be written off as bad debts.

b. It collected $480,125 in patient accounts and it wrote off $50,000 of bad debts.

c. It also provided $52,000 in charity care, which it never expected to collect.

d. It earned $15,040 in investment income, of which $10,080 is unrestricted and $4,960 is temporarily restricted.

e. It purchased plant and equipment of $242, all of which was paid for with restricted resources.

f. It charged depreciation of $29,262.

g. It received unrestricted pledges of $2,070 and temporarily restricted pledges of $120. It collected all of the unrestricted pledges and $100 of the temporarily restricted pledges.

h. It earned other operating revenues (including those from auxiliary enterprises) of $135,000.

i. It incurred $430,650 in wages and salaries, of which it paid $425,000. The balance was accrued. It also incurred $200,000 in other operating expenses (including those of auxiliary enterprises), of which it paid $198,500. The balance was vouchered (and thereby credited to accounts payable).

j. It incurred and paid $210,200 in costs related to restricted contracts and grants (amounts that were not included in any other expense category). It was reimbursed for $206,800 and expects to be reimbursed for the balance in the future. In addition, it received $3,000 in advances on other grants.

k. The other operating expenses include insurance costs. However, under "retrospective" in-

surance policies, the hospital anticipates having to pay an additional $3,500 in premiums.

1. Prepare journal entries to record the transactions. Be sure to indicate whether each entry would affect unrestricted, temporarily restricted, or permanently restricted funds.

2. Prepare a statement of activities for 2005 and a statement of financial position as of December 31, 2005.

Mosholu Medical Center
Statement of Financial Position
as of December 31, 2004
(in Thousands)

	Unrestricted	Temporarily Restricted	Permanently Restricted
Assets:			
Current Assets			
Cash	$ 2,449	$ 252	$ 3
Receivables for Patient Care ($110,465 Less Allowance for Contractual Adjustments and Doubtful Accounts of $45,755)	64,710		
Other Receivables	13,059	11,343	
Marketable Securities	109,085	61,691	17,133
Other Current Assets	27,853		
Total Current Assets	217,156	73,286	17,136
Noncurrent Assets			
Property, Plant, and Equipment ($512,184 Less Accumulated Depreciation of $223,259)	$288,925		
Other Assets	11,522		
Total Noncurrent Assets	300,447		
Total Assets	517,603	$73,286	$17,136
Liabilities and Net Assets:			
Current Liabilities			
Accounts Payable	$ 55,960		
Accrued Wages and Salaries	56,942		
Total Current Liabilities	112,902		
Noncurrent Liabilities			
Long-Term Debt	292,370		
Deferred Revenue and Other Noncurrent Liabilities	96,609	10,323	
Total Noncurrent Liabilities	388,979	10,323	
Total Liabilities	501,881	10,323	
Net Assets	15,722	62,963	17,136
Total Liabilities and Net Assets	$517,603	$73,286	$17,136

13–10

The distinction between contributed services that should be recognized as revenue and those that should not be is subtle.

Daughters of Charity Hospital draws its nursing staff from members of its religious order. The nurses are not paid a salary. Instead, they receive free room and board and a living allowance. The total cost to the hospital is about 60 percent of the approximately $10 million it would have to pay in salary and benefits in the open market.

In addition, the hospital benefits from the services of candy stripers and other volunteers, who staff the hospital's gift shop, carry meals to patients, and perform a variety of other important functions. Were it not for these volunteers, the hospital would have to hire additional personnel to carry out many of their duties. The approximate cost would be $400,000.

1. How much should the hospital recognize as revenue from contributed services?

2. How do you distinguish between the services of the nurses and those of the candy stripers?

13–11

Is there a sound reason for accounting for contributions to a not-for-profit university differently than those to a government university?

In January 2004, Kirkland University receives a pledge of $200,000, to be used exclusively to support research in a specialized area of communication disorders. The university's fiscal year ends on July 31.

In December 2004 (the following fiscal year), Kirkland receives the pledged contribution of $200,000 and spends $150,000 on qualifying research.

1. Prepare journal entries to record the transactions described, based on the assumptions indicated. Name the type of fund in which the entries would be made.

   a. Assume first that Kirkland is a private, not-for-profit, university.

   b. Assume instead that Kirkland is a public university that elects to report as a special purpose government engaged in only business-type activities.

   c. Finally, assume that Kirkland is a public university that elects to report as a general purpose government that accounts for the contribution in a governmental fund.

2. On what grounds, if any, can you justify different accounting principles for the same transaction depending on the type of institution (public or private) or the assumption as to type of public institution?

CHAPTER 14

Financial Analysis

In Chapter 1, we discussed the objectives of financial reporting for governments and not-for-profits. A primary objective of the basic financial statements is to provide information that resource providers—including taxpayers, grantors, donors, and legislative and other governing bodies—need to make resource allocation decisions. These groups, as well as beneficiaries of the services of governments and not-for-profits and the public at large, also need information to help them hold governments and not-for-profits accountable for their use of the resources provided and for their service efforts and accomplishments.

However, financial statements alone cannot provide all the information that resource providers and other interested parties need. An entity's financial position and its results of operations, as portrayed in the financial statements, are affected by its economic environment and by social, political, and demographic influences. Thus, financial analysis is complex. Analysts must combine financial statement information with both financial and nonfinancial information from other sources.

In this final chapter, we present an approach to analyzing the economic condition of both governments and selected not-for-profits.

HOW CAN A GOVERNMENT'S ECONOMIC CONDITION BE ASSESSED?

A government's *economic condition* is a broader concept than its *financial position* (i.e., the status of its assets, liabilities, and net assets, as portrayed in its statement of net assets or balance sheet). Economic condition comprises the government's ability and willingness, on a continuing basis, to meet its commitments to provide services at the levels agreed upon with its citizenry, as well as to satisfy its financial obligations. Not only is a government's economic condition directly dependent upon economic, political, social, and demographic factors within its jurisdiction, it is also intertwined with those of other governments that provide financial aid or serve the same constituents. Thus, assessing economic condition is a daunting task.

Table 14–1 presents one approach to the task. As the outline makes clear, financial statements are but one, albeit critical, source of information. Nonfinancial considerations are at least as important, although they may be less subject to quantification as ratios or other numerical measures.

In the business sector, the ability of ratios and similar indicators to predict fiscal stress can be evaluated statistically by constructing regression or similar models in which the ratios and other indicators are associated with actual failures. In the public sector, owing to the small number of bankruptcies and defaults, there is considerably less evidence as to which indicators actually point to impending failure. Hence, the indicators presented in this section, while widely accepted, have not been statistically validated.

| TABLE 14-1 |
| A City's Economic Condition: A Comprehensive Analysis |

I. General Approach
  A. Review the current economic, political, and social environment in which the city operates
  B. Identify and assess the impact of key factors likely to affect the city's economic, political, and social environment in the future (e.g., the next five years)
  C. Assess the city's current status as revealed in its comprehensive annual financial report (taking into account the city's reporting practices and policies)
  D. Forecast the city's fiscal status for the next five years taking into account the previously identified environmental changes and the city's likely response to them
II. Current state of, and trends in, the government's operating environment
  A. Population
    1. Age of population
    2. Income level
    3. Educational and skill level
    4. Other relevant demographic factors
  B. Economic environment
    1. Wealth and income of citizenry (e.g., per capita net worth and income)
    2. Major industries (and stability)
    3. Unemployment rates
    4. Value of property per capita
    5. Sales tax base
    6. Elasticity of revenues
  C. Political climate
    1. Formal structure of government
    2. Extent of political competition
    3. Competence of government officials
    4. Overall citizen satisfaction with and expectations of government
    5. "Liberal" or "conservative" citizen view as to role of government
    6. Relations with state government and other local governments (e.g., those of surrounding and overlapping entities)
  D. Social conditions
    1. Crime rates
    2. Other measures of social well-being
III. Changes likely to affect the government's operating environment and its finances
  A. Demographics and geographical boundaries
    1. Impact on infrastructure
      a. Highways and streets
      b. Utilities
    2. Impact on operating revenues
    3. Impact on operating expenses
  B. Nature and scope of government services to be performed
  C. Nature and scope of enterprise activities carried out (e.g., future of electric utility)
  D. Political climate (e.g., pro- or anti-growth; pro- or anti-business)
  E. Form and organization of government (e.g., possibility of single-member election districts)
  F. Political attitudes and intergovernmental relationships
    1. Changing views toward the role of government
    2. Relations with legislature
    3. Extent of state and federal assistance
    4. Additional costs imposed by overlapping governments (e.g., school districts)

(continued)

TABLE 14-1 (*continued*)
A City's Economic Condition: A Comprehensive Analysis

    G. Technology (i.e., changes that will affect the government both directly—such as increased use of computers—and indirectly—such as interactive TV and means of transmitting electricity)

    H. Social changes (e.g., changes in family structure resulting in need for more government facilities to provide care for elderly)

    I. Commerce and industry
       1. Major employers (including stability and likelihood of relocating)
       2. Impact on revenues (e.g., property taxes) and expenditures (e.g., infrastructure improvements)

    J. Wealth and income of population

    K. Other economic changes (e.g., those affecting the electric power and health care industries)

IV. Insight into city's financial position, as revealed by accounting and reporting practices
    A. Overall quality of disclosure
    B. Auditor's opinion
    C. Management's discussion and analysis
    D. GFOA certificate
    E. Key accounting policies
       1. Reporting entity
       2. Number, type, and character of (reason for) funds
       3. Revenue and expenditure or expense recognition
       4. Accounting changes
    F. Budget-related and accounting-related practices
       1. One-shot additions to revenues or reductions in expenditures
       2. Unusual budget-balancing transactions (e.g., certain interfund transfers)
       3. Changes in budget-related practices (such as delaying payments or speeding up tax collections)
       4. Use of off-the-balance-sheet debt (e.g., leases, long-term contracts) and of revenue debt
       5. Use of long-term debt to finance operating expenditures
       6. Increased use of short-term debt to cover temporary cash shortages

V. Calculating and interpreting financial and economic indicators
    A. Fiscal capacity and effort
       1. Revenues from own sources/median family income
       2. Revenue from own sources/total appraised value of property
       3. Total sales subject to tax/total retail sales
       4. Sales and property tax rates
    B. Trends in fund balance
    C. Trends in mix of revenues and expenditures and reasons for trends
    D. Trends in stability of revenues
       1. Intergovernmental revenues/total operating revenues
       2. Property tax revenues/total operating revenues
       3. Restricted revenues/total operating revenues
       4. One-time revenues/total operating revenues
       5. Uncollected property taxes
    E. Trends in spending patterns
       1. Number of employees per capita
       2. Nondiscretionary expenditures/total expenditures
       3. Percentage breakdown of total expenditures by function
    F. Trends in liquidity
       1. Adequacy of fund balance—unreserved fund balance/operating revenues
       2. Adequacy of working capital—cash, short-term investments, and receivables/current liabilities

T A B L E 1 4 – 1 (*continued*)
A City's Economic Condition: A Comprehensive Analysis

    G. Trends in burden of debt
       1. Debt margin
       2. Debt service as a percentage of total general fund and debt service expenditures
       3. Debt per capita
       4. Debt as a percentage of taxable property
       5. Maturity structure
    H. Trends in pension and other postemployment benefits
       1. Unfunded actuarial accrued liabilities
          a. Funded ratios (pension assets compared to actuarial liabilities)
          b. Unfunded liabilities compared to values of property, annual payroll
       2. Percent of annual pension costs actually contributed
    I. Bond ratings
    J. Trends in amounts of new borrowing
    K. Overlapping debt
    L. Trends in capital expenditures
       1. By type
       2. By geographic area
       3. Reasons behind trends
       4. Commitments and planned expenditures per the capital improvements plan
VI. Fiscal forecasts
    A. Overview of how trends and exogenous variables will affect key fiscal indicators in the next five years (taking into account how city will likely respond to them)
    B. Pro forma financial statements of general and other key funds
VII. Summary and conclusion
    A. Will the city have the financial wherewithal to provide the services expected of it in the future (e.g., the next five years)?
    B. What are the key risks and uncertainties facing the city that might impair its ability to provide these services?
       1. How can the city best manage these risks?
       2. What should be the key concerns of city managers, especially those directly concerned with finances?

The discussion that follows expands upon the key elements of the outline, concentrating mainly on data that are reported in the CAFR, as discussed in Chapter 11. Although the outline is specific in some respects to cities, the general approach can readily be adapted to special purpose governments, such as school districts, as well as to private not-for-profits.

The approach described in the outline is to first assess the current economic, political, and social environment in which the government operates and then to identify the changes that are likely to occur in the future (e.g., the next five years). The accounting information can then be examined within the framework of the current and future available resources and claims upon those resources.

THE CAFR IS AN IMPORTANT, BUT NOT EXCLUSIVE, SOURCE OF INFORMA- TION The CAFR is probably the single richest source of data as to a government's economic condition. But the data of any one period, by themselves, are little more than a collection of numbers. They provide a scant basis on which to assess past performance or make predictions as to its future. They are useful only when related to other data in the form of ratios, trends, and comparisons. Although the CAFR reports some of these relationships, it is mainly a source of raw data. The burden of analysis and interpretation falls upon individual users, who must custom tailor the data to meet their own needs.

The CAFR is intended to provide information that is relevant to a wide range of decisions; it is not designed to be the sole source of information for any particular decision. Bond rating agencies, for example, require governments to supplement their CAFRs with additional documents, such as budgets, long-range forecasts and plans, biographical summaries of key officials, and economic reports. Analysts are not bound by these documents. They should also look to newspaper and magazine articles, economic reports and forecasts by government agencies, private research services, knowledgeable business people, and community representatives.

EVALUATING FISCAL CAPACITY   The ultimate ability of a government to provide the services expected of it and to meet its financial obligations will be determined not by the resources currently on hand, but by those within the government's command, often referred to as its *fiscal capacity*. Thus, the demographic, economic, and social bases of the community that the government serves are of prime importance in assessing the government's economic condition.

Demographic Factors   Population size and composition have a major impact on a community's economic base. Composition is as critical as size. There are several significant factors. For example:

- *Age.* The elderly require extensive medical care; the young, education.
- *Income distribution.* The poor require more social services; the wealthy may demand more recreational and cultural services as well as a higher level of basic services.
- *Education level.* Better-educated populations make it easier to attract technologically oriented industries; they are also likely to demand higher quality schools for their children.
- *Native born vs. immigrant.* New arrivals require different types of services than native born.

Economic Conditions   The potential of an economy to generate tax and other revenues depends on the composition of its taxpayers. If the leading taxpayers are in a variety of industries rather than concentrated in just a few, the government's revenue stream is less likely to be adversely affected by recessions, technological developments, changes in consumer tastes, or similar factors. In addition, some industries may be riding a wave of expansion, whereas others are caught in an undertow of decline. Some companies, perhaps because of high capital investments or historical ties, are likely to remain in a community. Others, maybe because their facilities are aging or they can reduce operating costs by relocating abroad, may be candidates for early departure.

Political and Leadership Characteristics   The ability and willingness of a government to exercise decisive leadership both in planning for the future and in responding to crises adds strength to its economic condition. Several factors may be influential:

- *Formal structure of the government and the powers granted to key officials.* In some governments, the chief executive officers have the authority to make major spending decisions without legislative approval. In others, even minor decisions are subject to lengthy administrative or legislative processes.

- *Degree of political competition.* In the absence of political competition (e.g., evidenced by closely contested elections), the chief executive officer may be able to act swiftly and forcefully irrespective of requirements for formal legislative approval.

- *Competence and integrity of government officials.* Bright, experienced, and honest officials are a necessary, if not always a sufficient, condition for economic well-being.

- *Relations with other governments.* These are affected not only by the power of home rule (the authority to act without the approval of the state or some other government) but also by personal and political relationships among the officials of the various levels of government.

- *Political climate.* Politics and economics go hand-in-hand. Albeit a highly subjective factor, a favorable political climate makes it easier for a community to achieve its social, environmental, or educational goals while assuring that the costs are distributed equitably.

Social Considerations   Closely tied to demographic considerations are sociological factors such as crime rates, percentage of citizens requiring public assistance, and the percentage of residents owning their own homes. These factors affect the extent and level of services that the government will have to provide, as well as its ability to raise revenues.

WHY IS IT IMPORTANT TO ASSESS LIKELY FUTURE CHANGES?

Analysts are concerned with both the past and the present, mainly because they help predict the future. Analysts are not seers, but the essence of financial analysis is forecasting. They must try to identify the changes that will likely affect the government's environment within the time horizon they are considering. The outline (Table 14–1) sets forth a few specific factors that must be considered in addition to those presented in the previous section.

POPULATION Population increases are often associated with expanding economies and the creation of new businesses. Growth, however, may have its fiscal downside, especially in the short term. As new housing developments are constructed and families with young children move into a community, the government may have to extend infrastructure, construct new schools, and enhance social services.

ENTERPRISES The nature of government services will undoubtedly change in the next decade. Many governments will be under pressure to privatize (outsource) some of the functions that they carry out today. Perhaps the most financially significant of these is electric service, which may constitute the major portion of a city's revenues, expenses, assets, and liabilities. Until recently, electric utilities were the quintessential example of a regulated monopoly. The 1990s, however, witnessed a trend toward both competition and deregulation, and the continued "profitability" of municipal utilities is now problematic. In response to similar developments and the resultant economic uncertainty, many cities are also considering privatizing their hospitals and sanitation facilities. Further, some governments are outsourcing clerical operations (such as processing welfare or payroll checks) and repair and maintenance services.

TECHNOLOGY *E-commerce* and related means of electronic communication will almost certainly affect governments, just as they are transforming businesses. Activities such as reading electric and water meters and issuing purchase orders will soon be performed electronically. These changes may enhance efficiency and thereby reduce operating costs. They will also require enormous investments in computer hardware and software.

WHY IS IT IMPORTANT TO EVALUATE ACCOUNTING AND REPORTING PRACTICES?

The computation of ratios and statistical measures appropriate to the decision to be made is central to financial analysis. However, key clues to a government's financial health can be obtained as much from its accounting and reporting practices as from its ratios or the underlying numbers.

THE BUDGET A government's plans are most explicitly revealed in future-oriented documents, such as its operating and capital budgets and long-term capital improvement plans. As indicated in Chapter 1, governments (and not-for-profits) are "governed" by their budgets as opposed to the marketplace. The budget is a detailed map of the fiscal path the government is following.

Analysts must test the integrity of the budget by comparing previous budgets with actual results. They must also assess whether the estimated revenues are attainable and the amounts budgeted for nondiscretionary expenditures are reasonable. Further, they must ascertain whether the budget provides for foreseeable changes in population and other conditions, as well as for contingencies and unanticipated events.

Budgets are generally on a cash or near-cash basis. Consequently, governments can engage in any number of measures to increase revenues or decrease expenditures, even in the absence of substantive changes in economic resources. For example, they can delay payments to suppliers or employees, speed up collections from taxpayers, or transfer resources from one fund to another. These and other one-shot infusions to fund balance may provide compelling evidence of fiscal stress—that the government is unable to balance its budget by legitimate means.

THE FINANCIAL STATEMENTS Financial statements must adhere to GAAP. Therefore, governments have far less opportunity to manipulate their reported than their budgeted revenues and expenditures. Nevertheless, as observed in previous chapters, they can influence the reported amounts in numerous ways:

- They can account for certain transactions in internal service or enterprise funds rather than in the general fund.
- They can finance capital acquisitions by incurring off-the-balance-sheet obligations (e.g., through leases or service contracts) rather than general obligation debt.
- They can opt for "liberal" accounting practices and policies (e.g., change the period after year-end during which cash receipts satisfy the available criterion for governmental fund revenue recognition; reduce estimates of uncollectible taxes; adjust actuarial assumptions in determining required pension contributions).

Analysts should take note of an entity's reporting practices for at least two reasons. First, and more importantly, they (like the budget practices) may be a symptom of underlying financial deficiencies. If a government can produce a reported surplus only by stretching the limits of GAAP and taking advantage of available reporting loopholes, then it may be masking a true economic deficit. Second, when analysts compare governments, they need to consider differences in accounting practices.

WHAT RATIOS AND OTHER INDICATORS MAY BE USEFUL?

In calculating and interpreting financial indicators, analysts face a difficult issue. Should ratios and other measures be based on (1) the government-wide statements, (2) the general fund only, or (3) some analyst-selected combination of funds?

Measures based on the government-wide statements capture the totality of the government's resources. They do not show which specific assets are restricted and may therefore be used for only specified purposes; for that information, analysts must look to the fund financial statements. On the other hand, over the long term, all resources, whether restricted or not, benefit the government and can be used to provide government services or to satisfy its obligations.

Thus, the answer to the question must depend on *why* the measure is being calculated and *how* it will be interpreted. For example, if analysts are interested in the overall financial position of the government; the net (accrual-basis) cost to taxpayers of all governmental activities or of a particular function, such as public safety; or totals for specific government assets or liabilities, such as investments or general long-term debt, they can find this information in the government-wide statements. If analysts seek the total amount of government resources restricted for specific functions (e.g., road repair), then it makes sense to examine the funds used to account for those resources. By contrast, if they are concerned with the ability of the government to meet its short-term obligations from a specific fund, such as the general fund or an enterprise fund, then they should probably take into account only the resources of that fund.

FISCAL EFFORT A government's fiscal effort is the extent to which it is taking advantage of its fiscal capacity—its ability to access resources within its jurisdiction. Fiscal effort may be measured by comparing the government's total revenues, excluding grants from other governments, with either the wealth or income of its taxpayers. Income can be captured by measures such as median family income; wealth by indicators such as total appraised (market) value of property. Thus, fiscal effort equals:

$$\frac{\text{Revenue from own sources}}{\text{Median family income}}$$

or

$$\frac{\text{Revenue from own sources}}{\text{Total appraised value of property}}$$

As these ratios increase, the government exerts greater fiscal effort and thereby uses a greater portion of its fiscal capacity. It has less ability to raise taxes in the future.

OPERATING DEFICITS Operating deficits (revenues less than expenditures or expenses) should be to financial analysts what red flags are to bulls. They should get their attention, but should not distract them from other, more consequential, targets. A widely used rule of thumb holds that two consecutive years of operating deficits connote serious fiscal stress. But operating deficits as a measure of financial performance have inherent limitations and must be interpreted with considerable caution.

First, reported operating deficits (as well as all other accounting measures) are measured by GAAP. Accounting principles represent compromises among competing objectives and were not developed to facilitate any particular decisions. Thus, reported revenues and expenditures or expenses might not necessarily have been determined on the most appropriate basis for the purpose at hand.

Second, operating deficits, whether government-wide or of individual funds, even for two or more years, do not necessarily signify deteriorating financial position. A government that has accumulated excessive surpluses in the past might elect, quite sensibly, to draw them down by running planned deficits over the following several years.

ANALYZING REVENUE AND EXPENDITURE TRENDS In governments, more revenue is not necessarily preferable to less. Revenues need only—but at the same time must—be sufficient to cover expenditures. A key step in assessing the adequacy of revenues, therefore, is to associate trends in revenues with those in expenditures.

Revenues and expenditures are closely correlated with the size of the constituency. To compare those of the same government over time, or of one government with another, it is necessary to take into account differences in population. For many analytical purposes, revenues and expenditures are best expressed per capita.

Revenues   A stable revenue base is generally characterized by several diverse sources of revenues, so that a decline in one source will not necessarily be contemporaneous with declines in others. Moreover, the revenues should be linked to population, so that the costs of providing for a larger population are automatically offset by a broader revenue base. For example, a state government that generates its revenue from a mix of property, income, and sales taxes; user fees; and intergovernmental aid is less likely to suffer from a recession or downturn in the price of a single commodity than a state government that relies primarily on taxes on oil production.

The following ratios spotlight the stability of a government's revenues:

- *Intergovernmental revenues/Total operating revenues.* Governments generally want to maximize the amount of resources received from other governments. Failure to take advantage of intergovernmental grants can rightfully be interpreted as a sign of poor management. But what a granting government gives, it can also take away. Therefore, a high, or increasing, ratio of intergovernmental revenues to total revenues is a sign of risk and is generally considered a negative fiscal characteristic.

- *Restricted revenues/Total operating revenues.* Restricted revenues decrease the flexibility of governments to respond to changing conditions and may lead to a misallocation of resources. State gasoline taxes, for example, might be dedicated to highway construction and thereby be unavailable to meet pressing needs for new schools. Therefore, lower percentages of restricted revenues are preferred to high percentages.

- *One-time revenues/Total operating revenues.* As suggested earlier in the text, one-time revenues may result from substantive measures, such as sales of assets, or merely one-shot technical adjustments, such as changes in the due date of taxes or license fees. Some can be motivated by opportunities to enhance productivity; others by a need to artificially balance the budget. A high proportion of one-time revenues is generally viewed as a decidedly negative characteristic.

- *Property tax revenues/Total operating revenues.* Property taxes are considered a stable revenue source, and a high ratio of property tax revenues to other, less stable, revenues is a positive attribute.

- *Uncollected property taxes/Total property taxes levied.* A high rate of uncollected property taxes may signal an underlying weakness in the economy. It may be a warning of an impending reduction in revenues, not only from property taxes, but from other sources as well.[1]

Expenditures   Expenditures (and expenses) are measures of the costs of services provided. Changes in per capita amounts can be the result of several factors, some positive, some negative, and some neutral. For example, increases can be attributable to

- *Decreases in productivity or increases in prices.* For example, the government provides the same services but at greater cost.
- *Changes in the number, quality, or mix of services owing to favorable or unfavorable economic conditions.* This might include new housing developments or new industries that require a city to enhance its infrastructure, or increases in unemployment that require a city to provide free medical care for a larger number of citizens.
- *Factors beyond the control of the government.* Weather is a prime example.

Ratios that may be used to identify changes in spending patterns, and thereby signal the need for an investigation into the cause of the change, include the following:

- *Number of employees/Population* or *Payroll expenditures/Total expenditures.* Without evidence of corresponding increases in the level or quality of services, increases in payroll costs may be a consequence of decreased productivity.
- *Expenditures for specific functions/Total expenditures.* Disproportionate increases in expenditures for specific functions (such as public safety or health and welfare) may indicate new policies or circumstances that presage additional increases in the future.
- *Nondiscretionary expenditures/Total expenditures.* Governments typically have control over only a limited percentage of their total costs. Others are dictated by contractual agreements (such as leases), debt commitments, and mandates from higher levels of government. The higher the percentage of nondiscretionary expenditures, the less flexibility the government has to reduce (or limit increases in) spending.

ASSESSING THE BALANCE SHEET (OR STATEMENT OF NET ASSETS)   A government's balance sheets or statements of net assets report on its resources and the claims against them. Therefore they provide an indication of a government's ability to provide the services expected of it and to fulfill its obligations. Key issues in assessing the burden of long-term obligations and the adequacy of long-term assets have already been addressed in the chapters dealing with the long-term debt and capital assets.

Fund Balance   Of all a government's balance sheet accounts—particularly those of its governmental funds—fund balance typically draws the greatest attention. In large part, fund balance is so highly visible because it embodies all other balance sheet accounts and, in governmental funds, is an indicator of net available financial resources.

---

[1]These and several of the other ratios presented in this chapter have been adapted from Sanford M. Groves and Maureen Godsey Valente, *Evaluating Financial Condition, A Handbook for Local Government* (Washington, D.C.: International City Management Association, 1986).

Most governments try to maintain a positive general fund balance so as to be better able to cope with unforeseen expenditures or revenue shortfalls. The adequacy of a fund balance is often measured by the ratio:

$$\frac{\text{Unreserved fund balance}}{\text{Operating revenues}}$$

Other factors being equal, a declining trend in the ratio is seen as a sign of deteriorating financial position.

However, the significance of the general fund balance can easily be overstated. It is nothing more than the accumulation of annual surpluses and deficits and is therefore subject to the limitations ascribed earlier to operating deficits. If, as is common, the budgetary principles applicable to a particular government differ from GAAP, the reported general fund balance may not necessarily denote the resources legally available for expenditure. In addition, since it is established by the application of modified accrual accounting principles, the general fund balance (or any governmental fund balance) excludes the government's equity in both capital assets and receivables not expected to be collected in time to satisfy current obligations—resources that obviously affect financial position. Similarly, the reported governmental fund balances fail to take into account long-term obligations, which are not accorded balance sheet recognition.

The fund balances of proprietary funds, on the other hand, reflect values based on historical costs, which have little or no bearing on economic condition. The net assets on a government-wide statement of net assets—especially the portion denoting the investment in capital assets; net of related debt—suffer from similar limitations.

Liquidity Liquidity in governments can be measured just as in businesses—by comparing some or all current assets to current liabilities. Because a government's inventories are not usually for sale and will not be a source of cash, most analysts exclude them from their liquidity ratios. Thus, the current ratio takes the form:

$$\frac{\text{Cash, short-term investments, and receivables}}{\text{Current liabilities}}$$

A more rigorous form of the ratio excludes receivables:

$$\frac{\text{Cash and short-term investments}}{\text{Current liabilities}}$$

Other Ratios As in businesses, analysts can key in on a specific balance sheet account by comparing it to the revenue or expenditure (or a similar inflow or outflow measure) with which it is associated. For example, the extent to which property taxes are being collected on a timely basis can be evaluated by dividing *property taxes receivable* (or uncollected property taxes) by the *total property tax levy for the year*. Similarly, a build-up in unfunded pension obligations can be detected by examining trends in pension ratios, such as *actuarial value of assets/actuarial accrued liabilities* and *unfunded actuarial accrued liabilities/covered payroll*. As discussed in Chapter 10, these ratios are reported in the schedule of funding progress, which is included as required supplementary information after the basic financial statements.

Analysts must, of course, pay particular attention to trends in the burden of debt. Of special concern are *debt margin, per capita debt*, and *overlapping debt*, as well as the ratings assigned to the government's bonds by independent rating services. These and other considerations relating to debt were addressed in Chapter 8 pertaining to long-term obligations.

No analysis of a government's economic condition can be meaningful if it fails to consider the condition of the entity's infrastructure—information that is not required to be included in the CAFR, unless the government has adopted the "modified approach" to accounting for infrastructure (discussed in Chapter 7). Analysts may, therefore, need to obtain from other sources information on the age, condition, and capacity of infrastructure and assess the demands that its maintenance and improvement will place on future revenues.

How Can the Economic Condition of a Not-for-Profit Be Assessed?

In the previous sections, we emphasized that the economic condition of a government can be assessed only by taking into account a wide range of economic, demographic, and social factors, many of which might not be incorporated into a complete CAFR, let alone the basic financial statements. The same is true of assessments of the economic condition of not-for-profit organizations.

In a broad sense, the outline in Table 14–1 and the related discussion are as applicable to not-for-profits as they are to governments. Obviously, however, every type of organization has unique characteristics, and an analysis must be custom-crafted to take them into account. This is particularly true of nonfinancial data, such as performance ratios and other statistics, including information about constituent demand for the not-for-profit's services and the extent of competition from similar entities. Indeed, these factors tend to have as much influence on a not-for-profit's economic condition as on that of a general purpose government.

IDENTIFYING KEY FACTORS Tables 14–2 and 14–3 outline the key factors that Standard & Poor's takes into account in rating the debt instruments of private colleges and universities and of health care organizations. Creditors are interested primarily in the ability of a not-for-profit to pay interest and repay debt principal. That ability is affected not only by financial factors, such as the entity's financial position and operating results, but also by the efficiency of the entity's management, its compliance with restrictions on the use of resources, and its effectiveness in meeting and increasing the demand for its services, which will affect its future financial viability. Thus, as illustrated in the tables, analysts need to combine the information reported in the basic financial statements with a range of nonfinancial ratios and other statistical information.

Other external parties also have an interest in assessing the economic condition and service results of not-for-profits. These parties include donors, accreditation agencies, legislative and oversight bodies, associations of educational and health professionals, consumers of not-for-profit services (e.g., students, parents, and patients), and the general public. They are interested in a not-for-profit's operational efficiency, compliance, and effectiveness—perhaps even more than creditors are, and often on a more personal basis.

Some of the nonfinancial information that analysts need may be provided by the entity itself, either with the financial statements or in separate reports of accomplishments that may accompany the financial statements—for example, fund-raising appeals and similar publications about the entity. Philanthopic Research, Inc., itself a not-for-profit organization, provides a treasure-trove of statistical data about

TABLE 14-2
Factors Focused on by Standard & Poor's in Evaluating the Revenue Bonds of Private Colleges and Universities

I. Student demand
   A. Enrollment trends, including the reasons for upward or downward cycles
   B. Flexibility in admissions and programs
      1. The acceptance rate (a college that accepts almost all applicants is more vulnerable to a decline in demand than one that is highly selective and admits only a small percentage)
      2. Geographic diversity (the wider the geographic diversity, the less likely that an economic downturn will affect enrollment)
      3. Student quality (strong student quality, as measured by class rank, standardized test scores, and other factors, enhances a school's ability to withstand a decline in enrollment)
      4. Faculty (the higher the percentage of tenured faculty, the less likely that the university's program offerings can change to reflect current demand)
      5. Program offerings (the more specialized the programs, the greater the risk of an enrollment decline owing to changes in the work force)
      6. Competition (schools that are the first choice of their students are less threatened by widespread enrollment declines than those that are their second or third selections)
      7. Attrition (high attrition might be a sign of student dissatisfaction and a precursor to declining demand)
II. Finances
   A. Revenues
      1. Diversification (a diverse revenue base, in which a substantial portion of revenue is from grants, endowment income, dormitories, and other sources in addition to tuition, tends to mitigate shortfalls in any single revenue stream)
      2. Ability to raise revenues through tuition adjustments (low rates in comparison with competitors indicate room for increases)
   B. Expenses
      1. Ability to reduce costs if revenues decline (a high ratio of fixed to variable costs limits flexibility)
      2. Amounts being retained to build up plant and endowment (large amounts of resources being transferred to plant and endowment funds signify the availability of resources that could be redirected to debt service)
   C. Operating results (modest surpluses convey that revenues are sufficient to meet expenses, but one- or two-year deficits are not necessarily a problem)
   D. Endowment
      1. Comparison with debt level
      2. Amount per student
      3. Proportion that is unrestricted (the greater the proportion, the greater the flexibility)
   E. Debt (a ratio of maximum annual debt service to unrestricted current fund expenditures that is greater than 10 percent generally indicates an excessive debt burden)
III. Management
   A. Ability to foresee and plan for potential challenges
   B. Strategies and policies that appear realistic and attainable
   C. A track record indicative of an ability to deal with new situations and problems
   D. A history of management continuity
IV. Legal provisions
   A. Security pledges (debt secured by enterprise revenues, such as dormitory rentals, is seen as weaker than that backed by general revenues or tuition revenues)
   B. Covenants (provisions requiring the institution to set certain rates and fees at specified levels may enhance the security of the bonds)
   C. Debt service reserve policies (the existence of reserve funds enhances the security of the bonds, especially those that are backed strictly by enterprise revenues)
   D. Credit enhancements, such as loan guarantees or bond insurance

Source: Drawn from *Standard & Poor's Public Finance Criteria* (New York: Standard & Poor's, 2000), pp. 178–184.

TABLE 14–3
Factors Focused on by Standard & Poor's in Evaluating the Revenue Bonds of Health Care Organizations

   I. Demand and service area characteristics
      A. Trends in volume, such as number of outpatient procedures, number of inpatient and outpatient surgeries, and number of observation days
      B. Utilization rates
      C. Demographic factors, including age distribution
      D. Economic factors, such as unemployment rates and local wealth levels
  II. Institutional characteristics and competitive profile
      A. Size, age, and level of board certification of medical staff
      B. Ability to attract and retain new doctors
      C. Relationships with physicians' groups that may provide financial incentives for doctors to remain loyal to the organization
 III. Management and administrative factors
      A. Depth and experience of management team and ability to deal effectively with hospital staff, to promote sound budgeting, to control financial and personnel resources, and to provide strong leadership
      B. The strength of management information systems
 IV. Financial factors
      A. Trends in revenue growth and profitability
      B. Financial flexibility as indicated by the ratio of fixed to variable costs
      C. Market position
      D. Costs in comparison with competitors
      E. Strength of income statement as indicated by operating margins, debt service coverage, and debt burden
      F. Strength of balance sheet as indicated by number of days' cash on hand, cash flow to total debt ratio, and debt to capitalization ratio

Source: Drawn from *Standard & Poor's Public Finance Rating Criteria* (New York: Standard & Poor's, 2000), pp. 161–163.

not-for-profits on its "Guidestar" Web site (*http://www.Guidestar.org).* Federal agencies, such as the National Center for Educational Statistics and the National Center for Health Statistics, provide information about educational and health care not-for-profits. Moreover, publications of industry associations, such as the National Association of College and University Business Officers and the Healthcare Financial Management Association are also useful data sources.

ANALYZING REVENUES AND EXPENSES

Revenues   Many types of not-for-profit entities—colleges and universities and health care organizations in particular—obtain a significant proportion of their operating revenues from user charges. These might include ticket sales (e.g., for a theater company), student tuition and fees, and payments from patients and third-party payors. They also, of course, receive operating resources from private donations, government grants, and, sometimes, government appropriations.

    As noted previously in the discussion related to governments, analysts must assess trends in the composition of revenues. Of particular significance is the proportion of resources generated by the entity itself to those provided by outside parties such as grantors and donors. For a university, for example, the trend in the ratio of revenues from student tuition and fees and from auxiliary enterprises (e.g., bookstores and dormitories) to total unrestricted revenues may indicate whether the demand for the institution's services is increasing or decreasing.

On the other hand, as indicated in Table 14–2, the diversity of the revenue base—the extent to which shortfalls in tuition, fees, and other charges for services may be offset by revenues from other sources—is also important. A diverse revenue base enhances the institution's ability to respond to institutional and environmental changes and unforeseen circumstances. Also, the ability to attract grants and donations is an indicator of constituent support for the institution's programs and its ability to continue operations. Not-for-profits' statements of activities generally provide information by major revenue sources to facilitate these kinds of analyses. (See, for example, the classification in Chapter 13 of revenue sources for health care organizations and for colleges and universities and the composition of the statement of activities in Table 13–2.)

Expenses The analysis of expenses, similar to that for revenues, should be aided by the entity's statement of activities, which, as discussed in Chapter 13, should provide information about expenses by functional area. For a university, service-related expenses are primarily those for instruction and research; for a health care organization, they comprise primarily nursing and other professional services. For other not-for-profits, they are typically the costs that relate to the organization's main mission. Analysts also should assess the adequacy of user charges, such as tuition and fee revenues, to service-related expenses, such as instruction expenses. From this analysis, they can determine the extent to which the entity's service activities must be financed from other sources, including grants, donations, and debt.

Analysts should pay special attention to the percentage of program-related expenses to general administrative and fund-raising expenses. Whereas the former are often variable costs (i.e., proportional to the services provided by the organization), administrative and fund-raising expenses may be generally fixed in nature (the amount must be met regardless of the level of services provided and related revenues). Relatively high administrative and fund-raising expenses may indicate a lack of flexibility or even an inability to respond to reductions in demand or other adverse circumstances.

More significantly, donors may be reluctant to contribute to organizations that consume a substantial portion of their resources for activities that are not directly related to the mission of the entity, especially fund-raising activities. Donors, as well as other financial statement users, want assurance that their donations are being used mainly to support substantive programs and activities. Private foundations, umbrella agencies such the United Way, and major donors almost always demand detailed financial data prior to making a commitment of resources. Moreover, state and local government regulatory authorities established to deter fraud may require that organizations permitted to solicit funds in their jurisdictions furnish information as to the proportion of funds raised that goes to substantive programs.

Fund-Raising Expenses The proportion of fund-raising expenses to program-related expenses is often a particular concern of donors as well as regulators. However, fund-raising activities are often carried out in conjunction with programmatic or administrative activities. Thus, fund-raising expenses may not be easily distinguishable from other expenses. For example, suppose that the American Cancer Society takes out newspaper advertisements alerting readers to the seven danger signals of cancer and appropriate responses. The ads include a plea for funds, accompanied by a coupon asking for the donor's name, address, and amount of contribution. Should the costs of this activity be apportioned between fund-raising and mission-related programs? If so, on what basis should they be apportioned?

Left to their own devices, many organizations would prefer to assign costs to progammatic rather than to fund-raising efforts. In that way, they would appear to be spending more of their funds fulfilling their mission. However, the AICPA has provided guidance on this issue in its 1998 Statement of Position (SOP 98–2), *Accounting for Costs of Activities of Not-For-Profit Organizations and State and Local Governmental Entities that Include Fund-Raising*. The AICPA directs that not-for-profit organizations classify as fund-raising *all* costs of activities that include fund-raising as well as programmatic, management, or general functions, *unless* the activities satisfy three broad criteria:

- *Purpose*. The purpose of a joint activity includes accomplishing program or management and general functions. Moreover, the majority of the compensation or fees paid to outside contractors, such as consultants, must be based on criteria other than the amount of contributions raised.

- *Audience*. The audience for the materials or activities is selected principally based on its need for the program or for its ability to advance program goals in ways other than by financial support.

- *Content*. The materials or activities call for specific actions that will help accomplish the entity's mission beyond providing financial support.

When an activity meets these criteria, the costs may be allocated between programmatic and fund-raising expenses, using a rational and systematic allocation method.

In the example, the American Cancer Society would satisfy all three criteria because the ads include educational material about the danger signals of cancer and actions to be taken, and they are directed to a broad segment of society, all members of which are potential cancer victims.

ANALYZING OPERATIONAL EFFICIENCY AND EFFECTIVENESS

Operational Efficiency Analysts can make assessments about a not-for-profit's operational efficiency by comparing operating (unrestricted) revenues with operating expenses. Although an occasional operating deficit should not be a significant concern, a continued excess for several years of expenses over revenues should raise questions about the entity's ability to continue operations. On the other hand, continual, significant excesses of revenues over expenses may indicate that the number or quality of programs is less than optimal. If so, demand for the entity's services may be expected to decline in the future, with a resulting decline in its ability to meet its obligations and continue operations.

Other evidence of the trend in demand may be provided by nonfinancial information, such as, for colleges and universities, enrollment statistics, admissions versus applications, student credit hours, and degrees granted, and, for health care entities, admissions, number of rooms, and average room-occupancy rates. Some of these statistics can also contribute to efficiency assessments by relating them to expenses—for example, educational expenses per student credit hour and per degree granted; health care operating expenses per available room, per average occupancy, and per admission.

Operational Effectiveness Effectiveness of operations means the extent to which the organization is meeting its stated objectives. As with assessing efficiency, analysts need statistical data to assess effectiveness. More importantly, they must understand the entity's mission and its short-, medium-, and long-term goals. Examples of relevant statistical information for colleges and universities include graduation rates, admission rates to graduate schools, number of students that pass standardized exams, such as the CPA exam or medical boards, and number of faculty publications in top-tier research journals. For health care entities, useful statistics include length of stay, cure-rates, and average cost per specific type of service performed. For both types of entities, assessments of effectiveness may also be aided by information about accreditations sought and obtained and other evidence of external recognition of the entity's quality and achievements.

HOW CAN CONCLUSIONS BE DRAWN?

The goal of financial analysis is to draw conclusions regarding the ability of a government or not-for-profit to meet its financial obligations and to provide the services expected of it in the future. One means of capturing the financial factors discussed in the previous sections is to prepare **pro forma financial statements.** Based on forecasts of revenues, expenditures (or expenses), capital outlays, and debt proceeds, analysts can prepare statements of revenues and expenditures or expenses, balance sheets, and statements of cash flows for each year covered by the projections. These will provide evidence as to whether revenues will be sufficient to cover expenditures or expenses, and even more importantly, whether cash inflows will be adequate to cover outflows or whether the initial projections will need to be adjusted.

Analysts not blessed with the power of prophesy will be unable to foresee all events and circumstances that will affect the government or not-for-profit in the future. Nevertheless, they must do their best to identify key risks and uncertainties and assess the ability of the entity to cope with them. Indeed, one of the advantages of computer spreadsheets is that they enable analysts to examine any number of "what if" situations. These should always include bad-case and even worst-case scenarios. Clearly, no government or not-for-profit will have the resources to cover all potential calamities, but analysts should look for evidence that the entity is taking no imprudent risks.

QUESTIONS FOR REVIEW AND DISCUSSION

1. Why must a financial analysis of a city focus upon the entity's *economic condition* as opposed to merely its *financial position*?

2. You are comparing two cities. In one, the average age of the population is considerably below the average age for the country; in the other, it is considerably above. What are the financial implications of the differences?

3. The text notes that two consecutive years of operating deficits are generally seen by analysts as a sign of fiscal stress. Suppose that a government has had several years of *general fund* surpluses. Are they necessarily a sign of financial strength?

4. Why might analysts be concerned if a government has an unusually high ratio of intergovernmental revenues to total revenues, relative to a comparable government? Why might they be concerned if the same ratio is unusually low?

5. What is meant by *fiscal capacity* and *fiscal effort*? Why are they of significance in assessing a government's economic condition?

6. Why do some analysts see the budget of a government as being of no less importance than its CAFR in assessing economic condition?

7. Governments list their principal taxpayers in their CAFR's statistical section. In what way does this information contribute to an analysis of economic condition?

8. Why are *one-shots* and other financial gimmicks of special concern to analysts?

9. Why is the ratio of administrative expenses to total expenses expecially important for not-for-profit organizations?

10. You are comparing two colleges. In one, the average SAT score is 1400; in the other, only 1000. Why might this seemingly nonfinancial statistic, in fact, have financial implications?

EXERCISES AND PROBLEMS

14–1

Select the *best* answer.

1. Which of the following is least likely to be found in a city's CAFR?

   a. population data for ten years

   b. ten largest employers

   c. biographical summaries of key officials

   d. property tax collections for ten years

2. Which of the following would you, as an analyst, consider a positive characteristic in assessing a city's fiscal health?

   a. the city's major employer is a U.S. military base

   b. no single employer employs more than 2 percent of the work force

   c. the city's five largest employers are in the textile industry; no single employer employs more than 20 percent of the work force

   d. the city's major taxpayer is a well-known theme park that attracts tourists from throughout the world

3. A ratio that compares revenue from own sources to either median family income or total appraised value of property measures

   a. fiscal effort

   b. liquidity

   c. fiscal elasticity

   d. economic effort

4. A high ratio of intergovernmental revenues to total revenues might indicate that the government

   a. is not taking advantage of available state and federal grants

   b. is relying too heavily on state and federal grants

   c. faces the risk that revenues may decline owing to factors beyond its control

   d. is not sufficiently taxing its population

5. Which of the following revenue sources is generally considered the most stable?

   a. property taxes

   b. sales taxes

   c. mineral taxes

   d. income taxes

6. A large percentage of restricted to unrestricted revenues is generally viewed as

   a. favorable because restricted revenues cannot be used for frivolous purposes

   b. favorable because restricted revenues are typically not subject to as much fluctuation as unrestricted revenues

   c. unfavorable because restricted revenues reduce a government's flexibility to respond to changing conditions

   d. unfavorable because restricted revenues are inherently inequitable

7. A common indicator of the adequacy of fund balance is the ratio of unreserved fund balance to

   a. total assets

   b. net assets

   c. revenues

   d. assessed value of property

8. A common measure of a government's liquidity is the ratio of

   a. cash and short-term investments to current liabilities

   b. cash and investments to total liabilities

   c. cash and short-term investments to net assets

   d. all assets (excluding capital assets) to all liabilities (excluding capital debt)

9. One indicator of the health of a government pension plan is to examine the trend in the unfunded actuarial accrued liability compared with

   a. number of employees

   b. total pension assets

   c. actuarially adjusted payroll

   d. covered payroll

10. Which of the following should be viewed favorably in assessing the fiscal health of a not-for-profit college?

    a. policy of admitting virtually all applicants

    b. history of restricting admissions to students in the top 10 percent of their class

    c. high percentage of tenured faculty

    d. narrow range of highly specialized programs

14–2

Ratios can help users in assessing economic condition.

The data that follow were taken from the CAFR of Chaseville, a mid-sized midwestern city with a population of 82,000. All dollar amounts are in thousands.

Total assessed value of property	$2,300,000
Total property tax levy	42,500
Direct debt	70,000
Overlapping debt	46,486
General fund:	
• Cash and investments	3,120
• Total assets	19,500
• Total liabilities	16,230
• Reserved fund balance	780
• Unreserved fund balance	5,789
• Total tax revenues	38,756
• Total expenditures	44,600
• Debt service expenditures	4,500
• Revenue from own sources	46,500
• Total revenues	48,865
• Intergovernmental revenue	2,003
• Public safety expenditures	9,321
• Health and welfare expenditures	4,567

Indicate and calculate the ratios that would best be used to compare Chaseville with similar cities as to whether the following statements are true.

1. Chaseville is more dependent on revenues from other governments.
2. It is directing a greater share of its expenditures toward public safety.
3. It has the necessary liquid resources to be better able to meet its short-term obligations as they come due.
4. It has a greater available general fund balance relative to revenues, to meet future needs.
5. Its citizens pay a higher tax rate.
6. Its citizens pay more in taxes per person.
7. It is a wealthier city, in that its citizens own relatively more property.
8. It exerts greater fiscal effort.

14–3

Citizens of wealthier cities might not only have a lighter tax burden, but they might receive more intergovernmental assistance.

The following data are drawn from the CAFRs of two northern Virginia cities.

(dollars in thousands)	Fairfax	Manassas
Population	20,200	27,856
Value of taxable property	$1,933,472	$1,948,337
Property tax levy	18,664	24,534
Total general fund revenues	38,397	36,092
General fund tax revenues	31,861	29,706
Intergovernmental revenues	5,050	2,351

1. Based on the limited data provided, which city has the greater resources upon which to draw?
2. Which city imposes the greater tax burden on its population based on
   a. per capita total general fund taxes?
   b. per capita property taxes?
   c. tax rate (i.e., property taxes as a percent of property value)?
3. Which city receives a greater amount of assistance from other governments
   a. as a percentage of its total general fund revenues?
   b. per capita?

14–4

Environmental regulators see the financial forests, but not the trees.

The U.S. Environmental Protection Agency (EPA) requires owners of municipal solid waste landfills to demonstrate that they have the financial capability of satisfying the costs of closing and subsequently caring for the landfills that they operate. Per EPA regulations, one way for a local government to demonstrate financial capability is by satisfying certain financial standards. In particular, a government must meet the following four ratios:

- Cash plus marketable securities to total expenditures greater than or equal to 0.05
- Annual debt service to total expenditures less than or equal to 0.20
- Long-term debt issued and outstanding to capital expenditures less than or equal to 2.00
- Current cost estimates for closure and postclosure corrective action to total revenue less than or equal to 0.43

The regulations provide no interpretative guidance, except to imply that the ratios are to be based on financial statements prepared in accordance with GAAP.

Suppose you are engaged as a consultant to a state agency that has to administer the regulations. In the course of examining the evidence of financial capability supplied by municipal landfill operators, state officials raised the following questions as to how the ratios should be calculated:

a. Should the ratios be based only on a government's general fund, or should they encompass funds in addition to the general fund (e.g., should they be based on government-wide statements)?

b. Assuming the ratios should not be based exclusively on the general fund, should they include proprietary funds (i.e., does use of the term *expenditures* imply that expenses should be excluded)?

c. Should the ratios incorporate restricted as well as unrestricted funds?

d. Should capital expenditures include only those for the year in question, or an average of capital expenditures for several years?

Propose answers to these questions that you believe are most consistent with the EPA's objective of assuring financial capability. For each question, recommend an appropriate policy, justify it, and cite any potential limitations.

Suggest at least three additional questions that you believe need to be addressed in order to assess financial capability.

14–5

Changes in the mix of revenues and expenditures must be interpreted with care.

The data that follow were drawn from the city of Boulder, Colorado's CAFR. Dates have been changed. They are from two statistical-section schedules showing the mix of revenues and expenditures for a ten-year period. They include amounts only from the general fund, special revenue funds, and debt service funds.

Revenues	2003	1994
	(Amounts in thousands)	
Sales and Use Taxes	$41,941	$18,750
General Property Taxes	9,501	4,900
Other Taxes	9,673	3,756
Charges for Services	5,004	2,524
Intergovernmental	10,114	6,840

	2003	1994
	(Amounts in thousands)	
Proceeds from Bonds and Notes	—	16,330
Other	8,246	5,692
Total Revenues	$84,479	$58,792

Expenditures		
General Government and Administration	$10,222	$3,975
Public Safety	17,466	10,786
Public Works	16,472	7,499
Housing and Human Services	6,195	4,093
Culture and Recreation	16,764	9,016
Acquisition of Real Estate and Open Spaces	11,315	11,706
Debt Service	10,816	2,886
Other	2,323	—
Total Expenditures	$91,573	$49,961

1. As a consultant for a citizens' association, you have been asked to determine whether there have been significant changes in the way the city acquires and spends its resources. Prepare a schedule in which you compare 2003 and 1994 in terms of the mix of revenues and the mix of expenditures for each year. Note and comment on any items that might distort a straightforward comparison of revenues or of expenditures for the two years.

2. Comment on any changes between the two years that you consider significant.

3. Expenditures for debt service increased significantly. What are the most likely reasons for the increase? Is it necessarily a sign of increased financial stress?

14–6

Strong financial statements are not necessarily indicative of strong economic condition.

The following information was taken from the CAFRs of two cities of approximately the same size in the same state.

	Riverside	Lakeview
	(Dollar amounts in thousands)	
Population	92,000	96,000
Number of Employees	1,050	1,420
Total Operating Revenues	$120,000	$170,000
Property Tax Levy	83,000	102,000

(continued)

	Riverside	Lakeview
	(Dollar amounts in thousands)	
Total Operating Expenditures	112,000	174,000
Cash, Investments, and Receivables	27,000	15,000
Current Liabilities	9,000	12,000
Unreserved General Fund Balance	7,000	1,000
General Obligation Debt	21,000	32,000
Total Appraised Value of Property	965,000	1,620,000

1. Compare the economic condition of the two cities based on the following indicators:
   a. Per capita operating expenditures
   b. Per capita general obligation debt
   c. Operating surplus (deficit)
   d. Liquid assets/Current liabilities
   e. Unreserved general fund balance/Total operating revenues
   f. Number of employees per capita
2. Compare the economic condition of the two cities based on the following additional measures:
   a. Operating revenues/Total appraised value of property
   b. Property taxes/Total appraised value of property
   c. Total appraised value of property per capita
3. What conclusions can be drawn from the two sets of measures? Comment on the apparent discrepancy between them.

14–7

Qualitative factors may be as important as quantitative factors in assessing a government's fiscal health.

You are a CPA in charge of auditing a mid-sized school district. You recognize that the risk of financial failure is as much dependent on factors not reported in the basic financial statements as on factors that are reported. Accordingly, you conduct a comprehensive analysis of the district. Some of your findings are summarized below. For each, indicate how it might affect the ability of the district to service its outstanding debt and provide the services that its constituents expect.

1. Owing to an influx of new high-tech firms into a nearby community (which is not within the jurisdiction of the school district), the population within the district is increasing by approximately 8 percent per year. Most of the new arrivals are young engineers and other professionals.

2. A developer has under construction within the jurisdiction of the school district a senior citizens' retirement village. The village is expected to increase both the district's population and its land value by approximately 4 percent.

3. During the year, the district changed the pay date of its employees. Previously, employees were paid on the last day of the month; now they are paid on the first day of the following month.

4. The district's largest taxpayer, representing 10 percent of its property tax revenues, manufactures blue jeans and other clothing made of denim.

5. The district's superintendent recently resigned in the wake of charges that he falsified student scores on statewide achievement tests.

6. School district elections are hotly contested. The current school board is composed of three members who are committed to "traditional" educational methods and four who are considered "progressives." Board meetings are almost always contentious.

7. Voters of the county in which the school district is located recently approved the largest general obligation bond issue in the county's history.

8. One of two candidates for governor of the state in which the school district is located is a strong advocate of a school voucher plan. The plan would provide financial assistance to students who elect to attend private schools.

14–8

One of the challenges of financial analysis in government is that it is not always obvious whether an increase in a financial ratio is a sign of increasing or decreasing fiscal strength.

Explain the significance of each of the following ratios.

For each ratio indicate whether an increase can be interpreted as a sign of (1) increasing or (2) decreasing fiscal strength. Where appropriate, show how an increase in the ratio can be interpreted as a sign of either. Explain and justify your response.

1. Cash, short-term investments and receivables/Current liabilities
2. Revenue from own sources/Median family income
3. Number of employees/Population
4. Property tax revenues/Total operating revenues
5. Nondiscretionary expenditures/Total expenditures
6. Unreserved general fund balance/Total operating revenues

7. Intergovernmental revenues/Total operating revenues

8. Expenditures for public safety/Total expenditures

14–9

Some sources of revenue, and some types of expenses, may be more conducive to fiscal health than others.

The following financial statements relate to the American Wildlife Fund (AWF) and the National Wildlife Fund (NWF), two real not-for-profits devoted to the protection of wildlife and other natural resources. The data were taken from reports prepared by a not-for-profit organization that evaluates other not-for-profit organizations. The data are obviously not presented in a format that is in accord with GAAP, including the classification of revenues.

	American Wildlife Association	National Wildlife Fund
	(Dollar amounts in millions)	
Revenue		
Contributions	$ 36.2	$ 56.3
In-kind contributions	0	11.2
Bequests and endowments	0	10.4
Sales of publications	49.9	0
Government grants and contracts	0	23.4
Income from investments	24.3	13.0
Increase in net unrealized gains on investments	14.0	0
Royalties	2.3	4.0
Revenue from local chapters	0	11.9
Other	2.1	0
Total revenues	$128.8	$130.2
Expenses		
Program expenses	$100.0	$ 93.5
Fund-raising expenses	8.5	12.7
Administrative expenses	6.3	4.9
Total expenses	$114.8	$111.1
Revenues in excess of expenses	$ 14.0	$ 19.1

1. Compare the two organizations. Indicate which organization you would rate more favorably with respect to the following revenues. That is, which of the revenues are likely to be more sta-

ble and thereby indicative of a more fiscally sound organization? Explain your response. You must use your own judgment; there is no specific guidance in the text for this type of organization. Comment on which organization you think, on balance, has the preferable mix of revenues.

a. Contributions and in-kind contributions

b. Sales of publications

c. Investment income, including that derived from unrealized gains

d. Government grants and contracts

e. Bequests and endowments

2. Which of the two organizations would you rate more favorably with respect to fund-raising expenses? Explain.

14–10

Exploring Orlando's financial report

Refer to the financial statements of the City of Orlando in Chapter 3 and to Tables 11–2 and 11–3 in Chapter 11.

Where, in Orlando's CAFR, would you look for information about the following items that might contribute to assessing Orlando's economic condition? Cite the appropriate section of the CAFR and be as specific as you can about the location (financial statements, notes, supplementary tables, etc.) of the information that you would seek.

1. An analysis of Orlando's overall financial position and results of operations, including the impact of important economic factors

2. Demographic statistics

3. Whether property tax revenues have been an increasing or decreasing proportion of general revenues in recent years

4. Key accounting policies

5. Current percentage of total operating revenues of all governmental activities that is from intergovernmental revenues

6. Net general obligation bonded debt per capita

7. Trends in pension plan assets compared with actuarial accrued liabilities for benefits

8. A description of currently known facts, decisions, or conditions that have, or are expected to have, a material effect on financial position or results of operations

9. Total revenues from gas taxes

14–11

Exploring Orlando's financial report

Refer to the financial statements of the City of Orlando in Chapter 3.

1. Calculate the following ratios for Orlando or the indicated fund as of September 30, 2001, and comment briefly on what each ratio indicates. Most of the information needed can be found in the financial statements included in the text. The following additional information was obtained from the statistical section of the CAFR:

- City population: 192,152
- Total appraised (estimated) value of real property: $10,401,534,347
- Total property tax levy—City: $70,660,149

a. Fiscal effort—primary government

b. Intergovernmental revenue/Total operating revenue (general fund)

c. Property tax revenue/Total operating revenues (general fund)

d. Property tax collection rate (general fund) (*Hint:* Assume that reported general fund property tax revenues were collected in full.)

e. Fire service expenditures/Total expenditures (general fund)

f. Unreserved fund balance/Total operating revenues (general fund)

g. Net bonded debt per capita (governmental activities)

h. Liquidity of the Orlando Centroplex

2. What kinds of additional information should you seek before drawing conclusions from these ratios?

GLOSSARY

A

Accrual basis—A method of accounting that recognizes revenues when earned and expenses when incurred, regardless of when cash is received or paid.

Accrued expenses—Expenses that have been incurred and recorded, but have not yet been paid.

Accrued revenue—Revenue that has been earned and recorded, but not yet received.

Actuarial accrued liability—Employee pension benefits earned to date as determined by an appropriate actuarial cost method.

Actuarial cost method—A means of allocating the total cost of expected pension benefits over the total years of employee service.

Advance refunding—Issuance of debt to retire outstanding bonds or other debt instruments prior to their maturity or call date.

Agency fund—A fund used to account for assets that a government or not-for-profit holds temporarily for other parties (e.g., for taxes or fees collected on their behalf).

Agent—A party that acts on behalf of another—for example, a government that collects taxes for another government.

Allocated costs—Costs that cannot be associated directly with specific products or services, but are assigned to them according to a predetermined formula or algorithm.

American Institute of Certified Public Accountants (AICPA)—A professional organization for certified public accountants (CPAs) that is responsible for establishing auditing and related professional standards.

Amortization—(1) The process of allocating the cost of an intangible asset over its useful life. (2) The reduction of debt by regular payments of principal and interest sufficient to retire the debt by maturity.

Annual pension cost—A measure of a government's annual cost of maintaining or participating in a defined benefit pension plan. Per GASB Statement No. 27, the annual pension cost is the annual required contribution adjusted to remove the actuarial amortization of the principal of a net pension obligation.

Annual report—The financial report of a business, government, or not-for-profit. Typically consists of financial statements, such as a balance sheet, operating statement, and statement of cash flows, and other supplementary information.

Annual required contribution (ARC)—An employer's annual required contribution to a defined benefit pension plan as determined in accordance with GASB requirements.

Annuity—A series of equal payments over a specified number of equal time periods.

Annuity fund—An endowment fund maintained by a college or university or other not-for-profit to account for gifts that provide fixed payments to the donor (or a person designated by the donor) for a specified term or for the remainder of his or her life. Thereafter, what remains of the gift will typically revert to the recipient organization.

Appropriation—An amount authorized by a legislative body for a department or other governmental unit to make expenditures and incur liabilities for a specified purpose.

Appropriations budget—The legislatively approved budget that grants expenditure authority to departments and other governmental units in accordance with applicable laws.

Arbitrage—The concurrent purchase and sale of the same or an equivalent security in order to profit from differences in interest rates. Generally, as it relates to state and local governments, the issuance of debt at relatively low, tax-exempt, rates of interest and the investment of the proceeds in taxable securities yielding a higher rate of return.

Assessed value—A value set upon real estate or other property by a government as a basis for levying taxes.

Audit—A systematic investigation or review to corroborate the assertions of others or to determine whether operations have conformed to prescribed criteria or standards. An examination of records to check their accuracy.

Available criterion—Principle of the modified accrual basis of accounting applicable to governmental funds whereby revenues may only be recognized when they are collectible within the current period or soon enough thereafter to be used to pay liabilities of the current period.

Available "window" or period—A specified period after year-end by the end of which cash must be collected in order for related revenue to be recognized for the period just ended in accord with the available criterion of modified accrual accounting. For property taxes, the available window is sixty days. For other revenues, governments may select the period and must disclose it.

B

Balance sheet—A financial statement that reports the balances in an entity's asset and liability accounts and the difference between the two (equity, net assets, or fund balance) as of a point in time.

Basic financial statements—The set of financial statements, including notes thereto, required for conformity to generally accepted accounting principles (GAAP).

Basis of accounting—The means of determining the timing of revenue and expenditure or expense recognition. See also *Cash basis*, *accrual basis*, and *modified accrual basis*.

Blending—One of two methods of reporting component units required by GASB Statement No. 14. (See *Discrete presentation* for a description of the other method). This method combines a component unit's transactions and balances with the data of the primary government, in both the fund statements and the government-wide statements, as if the component unit were a part of that government.

Bond anticipation note (BAN)—A short-term, interest-bearing note issued by a lender in the expectation that long-term bonds will soon replace it.

Bond discount—At issue date, the excess of a bond's stated (par) value over the bond's initial sales (issue) price. Bonds are issued at a discount so that the return to investors will be equal to the prevailing market interest rate, even though that rate might be higher than the interest rate stated on the bond (the stated or coupon rate). At later dates, bond discount is the excess of a bond's stated value over the bond's initial price plus the portion of the discount already amortized.

Bond premium—The converse of a bond discount; that is, the bond's initial sales price exceeds the bond's stated (par) value.

Bond rating agency—A company, the leading ones being Standard & Poor's (S&P), Moody's Investors Service, and Fitch IBCA, that evaluates bonds or other securities based on the likelihood that the issuer will not default on payments of principal or interest.

Bond refunding—The issuance of new bonds to replace bonds already outstanding, usually with the intent of reducing debt service costs.

Budget—A plan of financial operations embodying an estimate of proposed expenditures for a given period and the proposed means of financing them.

Budgetary control—The control or management of a government or enterprise in accordance with an approved budget to keep expenditures within the limitations of available appropriations and available revenues.

Business-type activities—Activities engaged in by a government or not-for-profit that are similar in nature to those carried out by businesses; activities that are financed in whole or in part by fees charged to external parties for goods or services.

C

CAFR—See *Comprehensive Annual Financial Report*.

Call price—A predetermined price at which the issuer of bonds may redeem (call) the bonds irrespective of the current market price.

Callable bond—A bond that permits the issuer to redeem the obligation at a specified price before the stated maturity date.

Capital asset—A long-lived asset, such as a building, equipment, and infrastructure, used in operations.

Capital budget—A plan of proposed capital outlays, such as for infrastructure, buildings, equipment, and other long-lived assets, and of the means of financing them.

Capital debt—Long-term debt issued to finance capital assets.

Capital expenditure—An expenditure to acquire or construct capital assets.

Capital improvement program (CIP)—A plan for the acquisition of capital assets over several (typically five) years.

Capital lease—A lease that is essentially an installment purchase and meets the criteria for capitalization of FASB Statement No. 13. The lessee ("purchaser") records the acquired property as an asset and correspondingly recognizes the present value of the agreed-upon lease payments as a liability.

Capital projects fund—A fund to account for financial resources set aside for the acquisition or construction of major capital facilities.

Cash basis—A method of accounting in which revenues and expenses are recognized and recorded only when received or paid, not necessarily when earned or incurred.

Cash equivalent—A short-term (usually three months or less), highly liquid investment that is both readily convertible to cash and so close to its maturity that the risk of changes in value because of changes in interest rates is insignificant.

Codification of the Government Accounting Standards Board—*Governmental Accounting and Financial Reporting Standards*, a compendium of GASB promulgated accounting principles, including those adopted from predecessor standard-setting organizations.

Collateral—Assets pledged to secure deposits, investments, or loans.

Collectibles—Works of art, rare books, and historical artifacts.

Combined statement—A financial statement, usually with multiple columns, each of which reports data for two or more separate funds that have been aggregated without eliminating interfund activity or balances.

Combining statement—A financial statement that provides the details of individual funds (e.g., nonmajor funds or internal service funds) that are combined or consolidated in higher-level statements. Each fund is displayed in a separate column and a "totals" column ties into amounts reported in another statement.

Compensated absence—An absence, such as for vacation, illness, and holidays, for which it is expected that employees will be paid. The term does not encompass severance or termination pay, pensions or other postretirement benefits, deferred compensation, or other long-term fringe benefits, such as group insurance and long-term disability pay.

Component unit—Per GASB Statement No. 14, a legally separate government for which the elected officials of a primary government are financially accountable, and either can impose their will, or there is the potential for the organization to provide specific financial benefits to, or impose specific financial burdens on, the primary government.

Comprehensive annual financial report (CAFR)— The official annual report of a state or local government. It includes introductory materials (such as a letter of transmittal and organization chart), financial statements (and supporting notes and supplementary schedules), and statistical data.

Conditional promise to give—Per FASB Statement No. 116, a promise to donate an asset or provide a service in the future that is contingent on a specified future event.

Conduit debt—An obligation issued in the name of a government on behalf of a nongovernmental entity. The debt is expected to be serviced entirely by the nongovernmental entity.

Consolidated statement—A statement in which two or more funds are aggregated, and most interfund activity and balances are eliminated, so that they are reported as if they were a single economic entity.

Constant dollar cost—The cost of goods or services in dollars that have been adjusted to take into account changes in the general level of prices (i.e., inflation).

Contingent grant—A grant that is conditioned upon a specified occurrence or action on the part of the recipient (e.g., the ability of the recipient to raise resources from other parties).

Contracting out—Engaging an outside, private-sector firm to provide services that have previously been performed in-house; also known as outsourcing or privatizing.

Consumption method—A method of accounting for inventories and prepaid expenses, such as rent, in which goods or services are recorded as expenditures or expenses when used rather than when purchased; differentiated from the purchases method.

Contingent liability—An obligation that will become payable only if a specified future event occurs.

Contributed capital—The permanent capital of a proprietary fund, generally resulting from transfers from other funds, or from grants or customer fees restricted to capital acquisition or construction. Per GASB Statement No. 34, contributed capital should be reported in a separate section of the operating statement from other revenues.

Coupon rate—The stated interest rate on the face of a bond; a bond's nominal interest rate.

Credit risk—The risk that a counterparty to an investment will not fulfill its obligations.

Current asset—Cash and other resources expected to be converted into cash during the normal operating cycle of the entity or within one year, whichever is longer.

Current financial resources measurement focus—Measurement focus on near-term (current) inflows, outflows, and balances of expendable (spendable) financial resources. The measurement focus of the governmental funds.

Current fund—The general or main operating fund of a not-for-profit organization.

Current liability—A financial obligation that is reasonably expected to be paid using current assets or by creating other current liabilities within one year or the entity's operating cycle, whichever is longer.

D

Debt margin—The difference between outstanding debt, computed according to applicable legal provisions, and the maximum amount of debt that can legally be issued.

Debt refunding—See *Bond refunding.*

Debt service fund—A fund to account for financial resources set aside for the payment of interest and principal on long-term debt; a sinking fund.

Deferred maintenance cost—A cost that an entity avoided in a current year or past years by failing to perform required routine maintenance and repairs on a capital asset, but that will have to be incurred in the future.

Deferred revenue—A receipt of cash or other assets for which asset recognition criteria have been met, but for which revenue recognition criteria have not been met; for example, property taxes received in the period prior to that for which they were levied (i.e., intended to finance).

Deficit—(1) The excess of liabilities and reserved fund balance of a fund over its assets. (2) The excess of expenditures or expenses over revenues during an accounting period.

Defined benefit pension plan—A plan that specifies the pension benefits to be paid to retirees, usually as a function of factors such as age, years of service, and compensation.

Defined contribution plan—A plan that specifies the amount of contributions to an individual's retirement account instead of the amount of benefits the individual is to receive. Under a defined contribution plan, the benefits a participant will receive depend only on the amount contributed to the participant's account and the returns earned on investments of those contributions.

Demand bond—A long-term debt instrument with demand ("put") provisions that require the issuer to repurchase the bonds, upon notice from the bondholder, at a specified price that is usually equal to the principal plus accrued interest. To ensure their ability to redeem the bonds, issuers of demand bonds frequently enter into standby liquidity agreements ("takeout" agreements) with banks or other financial institutions.

Depreciation—The systematic and rational allocation of the cost of tangible noncurrent operating assets (capital assets) over the periods benefited by the use of the assets.

Derivative—A financial asset whose value is derived from the shift in the price of an underlying asset, such as a bond, or an index of asset values, such as the Standard & Poor's index of 500 stocks, or an index of interest rates.

Derived tax revenue—A tax revenue that is based on an exchange transaction between parties other than the taxing government. Examples include sales taxes and income taxes.

Direct cost—A cost, such as for labor and materials, directly associated with specific products or activities of an organization. Distinguished from indirect (overhead) costs.

Discrete presentation—One of two methods of reporting component units required by GASB Statement No. 14. (See *Blending* for a description of the other method). This method reports component units in the government-wide statements only, in one or more columns to the right of (and thus not included in) the "total" column for the primary government. For example, a state government might report its state-owned power authorities in a single column and other component units in a separate column, or it might report all component units in a single column.

Donated services—A service provided at no charge to an organization by an individual volunteer or business.

Due from (to) other funds—An asset (liability) account used to indicate amounts owed to (by) one fund by (to) another.

E

Economic cost—The full cost of goods or services, as opposed to that which might be recognized for financial accounting. For example, the full amount of compensation to be paid by a government, including that of pensions and compensated absences, rather than merely the amount paid to the employees in a current period.

Economic gain (loss)—In the context of an advance refunding, the difference between the present value of the old debt service requirements and the present value of the new debt service requirements, discounted at the effective interest rate and adjusted for additional cash paid.

Economic resources measurement focus—Measurement focus on all inflows, outflows, and balances affecting or reflecting an entity's net assets, including capital assets and long-term debt. The measurement focus of the government-wide, proprietary, and fiduciary fund statements of governments, per GASB Statement No. 34, and of the financial statements of not-for-profits and businesses.

Eligibility requirement—In relation to government-mandated and voluntary nonexchange transactions, a condition established by a donor or grantor, such as qualifying characteristics, time requirements, allowable costs, and other contingencies.

Encumbrance—A government's commitment to purchase goods or services authorized by the budget; for example, an unfilled purchase order or contract.

Endowment fund—A nonexpendable fund used to account for contributions that the donor specifies are to be invested and that only the income from the investments may be expended.

Enterprise fund—A proprietary fund established to account for operations financed and operated in a manner similar to a private business (e.g., water, gas and electric utilities; airports; parking garages; and transit systems). Per GASB Statement No. 34, an enterprise fund may be used to account for any activity for which a fee is charged to external users for goods or services. It must be used to account for an activity financed with revenue debt, when laws or regulations require that an activity's costs be recovered with fees and charges, or when pricing policies dictate that fees and charges be established to cover the activity's costs.

Entitlement—A payment, usually from a higher-level government, to which a state or local government or an individual is entitled as a matter of law in an amount determined by a specified formula.

Escheat property—Private property that has reverted to a government owing to lack of heirs or claimants or because of a breach of a condition.

Exchange revenue—A revenue that arises from a sale transaction in which each party receives benefits and incurs costs.

Exchange transaction—A sales-type transaction in which goods and services are exchanged for consideration of approximately equal value.

Expendable fund—A governmental fund whose resources are received from taxes, fees, or other sources and may be expended (spent); the governmental as opposed to the proprietary funds of a government.

Expenditure—In government accounting, a decrease in net financial resources under the modified accrual basis of accounting.

Expenditure-driven grant—See *Reimbursement grant*.

Expense—A decrease in overall net assets from delivering services or producing goods under the full accrual basis of accounting.

Exposure draft—A preliminary version of a standard-setting authority's official pronouncement, issued as a means of obtaining public comment.

External report—A report issued for use by parties outside the reporting entity, such as citizens, investors, and creditors, as opposed to inside parties, such as managers.

Extraordinary item—A transaction or other event that is both unusual in nature and infrequent in occurrence. Per GASB Statement No. 34, these items, unlike special items, are outside the control of management. (See also *Special item*.)

F

Face value—As applied to securities, the amount indicated on the face of a bond that will have to be paid at maturity.

FASAB—See *Federal Accounting Standards Advisory Board*.

FASB—See *Financial Accounting Standards Board*.

Federal Accounting Standards Advisory Board (FASAB)—The federal board charged with establishing federal accounting standards.

Fiduciary activity—Per GASB Statement No. 34, an activity for which the government acts as a trustee or agent for individuals, external organizations, or other governments.

Fiduciary fund—A trust or agency fund used to account for assets held by a government as a trustee or agent for individuals, private organizations, other governments, or other funds.

Financial accountability—The key criterion, per GASB Statement No. 14, for inclusion of an organization in the financial reporting entity of a primary government; demonstrated by the primary government's appointment of a voting majority of the organization's governing body and either (1) the primary government's ability to impose its will on the organization or (2) the potential for the organization to provide (impose) specific financial benefits (burdens) on the primary government. Financial accountability may also be indicated by fiscal dependence. (See *Fiscally independent*.)

Financial Accounting Standards Board (FASB)—The authoritative accounting and financial reporting standard-setting body for all nongovernment entities.

Financial resources—Cash, investments and receivables, and other assets expected to become cash in the normal course of operations. Financial resources minus the current claims against them equals net financial resources.

Financial statement audit—An examination that determines whether an entity's financial statements are presented fairly in accordance with generally accepted accounting principles (GAAP) and whether the entity has complied with laws and regulations that might have a material effect on the financial statements.

Fiscal—Of or relating to (1) taxation, public revenues, or public debt or (2) financial matters.

Fiscal capacity—The economic base that the government can draw upon for the resources necessary to provide the goods or services expected of it and to meet its financial obligations.

Fiscal effort—The extent to which a government is taking advantage of its fiscal capacity. Generally measured by comparing the revenues that the government generates from its own sources (i.e., total revenue excluding grants from other governments) with either the wealth or income of its taxpayers.

Fiscal funding clause—A clause in a lease agreement providing that the lease is cancelable if the legislature or other funding authority does not appropriate the funds necessary for the government to fulfill its obligations under the lease agreement.

Fiscal period (year)—Any period at the end of which a government determines its financial position and the results of its operations: also accounting period.

Fiscally independent—Per GASB Statement No. 14, a special purpose government is fiscally independent if it can determine its budget, levy taxes, or set rates or charges, and issue bonded debt without another government's approval.

Fixed asset—A long-lived tangible asset, such as a building, equipment, an improvement other than a building, and land. (See also *Capital asset.*)

Fixed cost—A cost of goods or services that does not vary with the volume of goods or services provided (e.g., rent, interest, executive salaries, and air-conditioning costs.

Full cost—The cost of goods or services that includes both direct and indirect (overhead) costs.

Functional classification—Expenditures that are grouped according to the purpose for which they are made, such as public safety, general administration, or recreation.

Fund—A fiscal and accounting entity, with a self-balancing set of accounts, used to account for resources, and claims against them, that are segregated in accord with legal or contractual restrictions or to carry out specific activities.

Fund accounting—An accounting system in which an entity's resources are divided between two or more accounting entities known as funds.

Fund financial statements—Part of the basic financial statements required by GASB Statement No. 34, the other part being the government-wide financial statements. Three sets of fund financial statements report, respectively, on governmental, proprietary, and fiduciary funds and also include blended component units and fiduciary component units, if any. Governmental fund statements are on a modified accrual basis; proprietary and fiduciary fund statements are on a full accrual basis.

Funded pension plan—A pension plan in which contributions are made and assets are accumulated to pay benefits to potential recipients before cash payments to recipients actually are required; as opposed to a pay-as-you-go plan.

Funded ratio—The actuarial value of the assets of a defined benefit pension plan divided by the actuarial accrued liability for benefits earned to date. An increasing funded ratio is a sign of fiscal health.

Funding policy—In the context of pension plans, the policy that determines the amounts and timing of contributions to be made by plan members (employees), employers, and other parties to accumulate the resources required to pay retirees their specified benefits.

Fund type—A fund classification. In government accounting, the governmental fund types are the general, special revenue, debt service, capital projects, and permanent funds; the proprietary fund types are enterprise and internal service funds; the fiduciary fund types are pension and other employee benefit trust funds, investment trust funds, private-purpose trust funds, and agency funds.

G

GAAP—See *Generally accepted accounting principles.*

GASB—See *Governmental Accounting Standards Board.*

General capital asset—A capital asset that is not an asset of any particular fund, but of the government (governmental activities) as a whole. Most often these assets arise from the expenditure of the financial resources of governmental (as opposed to proprietary or fiduciary) funds.

General fund—A fund used to account for unrestricted resources. The fund that accounts for resources not required to be accounted for in other funds.

General obligation debt—Debt that is secured by the full faith and credit of the issuing body.

General purpose government—A government, such as a state, city, town, or county, that provides a variety of services. Contrast with *Special purpose government.*

General revenue—Per GASB Statement No. 34, any revenue that is not required to be reported as a program revenue in the government-wide statement of activities; includes all tax revenues, even those levied for a specific purpose, as well as interest, grants, and contributions that do not meet the criteria for reporting as program revenues.

Generally accepted accounting principles (GAAP)—Uniform minimum standards and guidelines for financial accounting and reporting that govern the form and content of financial statements. They encompass the conventions, rules, and procedures necessary to define accepted accounting practice at a particular time.

Government-assessed tax—A tax, such as a property tax, in which the government determines the amount owed. Distinguished from a taxpayer-assessed tax, such as an income tax, in which parties other than the government determine the amount owed.

Government-wide financial statements—Part of the basic financial statements required by GASB Statement No. 34, the other part being the fund financial statements. Government-wide statements report on a government's governmental and business-type activities (including its discretely presented governmental and business-type component units, if any), without subdividing the information into funds. Government-wide statements are on a full accrual basis.

Government accounting—The composite activity of analyzing, recording, summarizing, reporting, and interpreting the financial transactions of governments.

Governmental Accounting Standards Board (GASB)—The authoritative accounting and financial reporting standard-setting body for all state and local government entities, including government not-for-profits, such as public colleges and universities, hospitals and other health care organizations, museums, and libraries.

Govermental activity—An activity of a government that is financed predominantly through taxes and intergovernmental revenue.

Government-mandated nonexchange transaction—A transaction that occurs when a government at one level (e.g., the federal or a state government) provides resources to a government at another level (e.g., a local government or school district) and requires that the recipient use the resources for a specific purpose; for example, a state might grant funds to a county stipulating that the resources be used for road improvements. Acceptance and use of the resources are mandatory.

Government Finance Officers Association (GFOA)—An association of state and local governments and officials and other individuals interested in state and local government finance.

Governmental funds—A category of funds used to account for the acquisition, use, and balances of expendable financial resources and the related current liabilities, except those accounted for in proprietary funds and fiduciary funds; the five governmental fund types are general, special revenue, debt service, capital projects, and permanent funds.

Grant—A contribution from one party to another to be used or expended for a specified purpose, activity, or facility; ordinarily distinguished from an exchange transaction in that the grantor does not receive compensation in return for the resources contributed.

H–I–J

Historical cost—The original purchase price or construction cost of an asset, plus any additional costs incurred in placing the asset in its intended location and condition to fulfill its intended purpose.

Impact fee—A fee charged to developers by a government for costs of anticipated improvements, such as sidewalks and parks, which will be necessary as a result of a development.

Imposed nonexchange revenue—An assessment imposed by a government on individuals and business entities, the most prominent of which are property taxes and fines.

Independent sector—The sector of the economy that is composed of not-for-profit organizations (as opposed to government and business entities).

Indirect cost—A cost that is related to an activity or object but cannot be directly traced to that activity; an overhead cost; distinguished from a direct cost.

Industrial development bond—A bond issued by a government at low interest rates to encourage private development. Repayment of the debt is expected to be the responsibility of the beneficiary of the bond.

Infrastructure asset—Per GASB Statement No. 34, a long-lived capital asset that normally is stationary in nature and normally can be preserved for a significantly greater number of years than most capital assets. Examples include roads, bridges, tunnels, drainage systems, water and sewer systems, dams, and lighting systems. Buildings are not considered infrastructure assets unless they are an ancillary part of a network of infrastructure assets.

Inputs—The resources applied to a service, such as dollar cost, number of labor hours, and amount of material.

In-substance defeasance—An advance refunding (retirement) of bonds in which the government places sufficient resources in a trust account to cover all required principal and interest payments on the defeased debt. Although the government is not legally released from being the primary obligor on the refunded bonds, the possibility of it having to make additional payments is considered remote.

Intangible asset—An asset that has a future benefit, but cannot be physically seen—for example, a patent or copyright.

Intergenerational equity—See *Interperiod equity*.

Interfund services provided and used—Sales and purchases of goods and services between funds of the same government for a price approximating their external exchange value. They should be reported as revenues in seller funds and expenditures or expenses in purchaser funds.

Interfund transfers—See *Nonreciprocal interfund activity (transfers and reimbursements)*.

Internal service fund—A fund used to account for activities that provide goods or services to other funds, departments, or agencies of the primary government or its component units, or to other governments, on a cost-reimbursement basis.

Interperiod equity—The extent to which current-year revenues are sufficient to pay for current-year services (as opposed to whether the costs of current-year services are being shifted to future years or were paid in past years).

Insolvency—The condition of being unable to meet debts or discharge liabilities owing to a deficiency of available financial resources.

Issue costs—Costs incurred to issue bonds, such as amounts paid to underwriters, attorneys, accountants, and printers.

Invested in capital assets, net of related debt—A government's capital assets, less outstanding associated debt; per GASB Statement No. 34, one of three categories in which net assets must be reported on the government-wide statement of net assets.

Investment in plant fund—A fund maintained mainly by colleges and universities and other not-for-profits to account for capital assets and the liabilities incurred to acquire them.

Investment pool—A fiscal entity established to invest the resources of two or more funds or independent entities; comparable to a mutual fund.

Investment trust fund—A fiduciary fund maintained by a government to account for an investment pool maintained for other governments.

Joint venture—A contractual arrangement whereby two or more participants agree to carry out a common activity, with each sharing in both risks and rewards.

Journal—A book of original entry in which transactions or events are recorded.

K–L

Lessee—The entity that rents an asset from the asset's owner (the lessor).

Lessor—The owner of rental property who transfers the right to use the property to the user (the lessee).

Levy—To impose or collect a tax; also the tax itself.

Lien—In relation to delinquent property taxes and special assessments, a government's right to seize and sell the real or personal property on which the taxes were assessed, in accordance with applicable law.

Life income fund—An endowment fund maintained by colleges and universities and other not-for-profits to account for gifts that provide a return to the donor (or a person designated by the donor) for the remainder of his or her life. Thereafter, what remains of the gift will typically revert to the recipient entity.

Liquidity—The ability of an entity to meet its financial obligations as they come due.

Loan fund—A fund maintained by colleges and universities and other not-for-profits to account for resources that will provide loans to a designated class of beneficiaries, such as students or small businesses.

Long-term debt—In government, an obligation that the government does not expect to pay with currently available financial resources. In not-for-profits, an obligation that the entity does not expect to pay in cash or other operating assets within one year or the entity's normal operating cycle.

M

Major fund—Per GASB Statement No. 34, the general fund and any other governmental or enterprise fund whose revenues, expenditures/expenses, assets, or liabilities are at least 10 percent of the corresponding element total for all governmental or enterprise funds (excluding extraordinary items) and at least 5 percent of the aggregate amount for all governmental and enterprise funds for the same element. Each major fund is reported in a separate column on the fund financial statements. Nonmajor funds are aggregated and reported in a single column on the appropriate financial statements.

Management's discussion and analysis (MD&A)—a component of an annual report in which management provides an analysis of the entity's financial activities. Per GASB Statement No. 34, the MD&A is required supplementary information that is to be presented before the basic financial statements.

Matching concept—The principle that expenses or expenditures should be recognized in the same accounting period as related revenues.

Measurement focus—The accounting convention that determines which assets and liabilities are included on an entity's balance sheet and will thereby affect the determination of revenues and expenses (or expenditures) to be reported on the entity's operating statement. Measurement focus determines what is being measured—for example, net profits or flows of financial resources. See also *Current financial resources measurement focus* and *Economic resources measurement focus*.

Modified accrual basis—The accrual basis of accounting adapted to the measurement focus of governmental funds on current financial resources. Revenues are recognized in the period in which they become available and measurable. Most expenditures are recognized on an accrual basis but some are on a cash basis.

Modified approach—In the context of accounting for infrastructure assets, a government's election not to depreciate those assets. Election of the modified approach entails compliance with specific requirements of GASB Statement No. 34, including the disclosure of asset condition levels.

Moral obligation debt—A bond or note issued by one entity (usually a state agency), but backed by the implied (not legally binding) promise of another entity (usually the stare itself) to make up any debt service deficiencies.

Municipality—A city or town or other area incorporated for self-government; also, in its broadest sense, any state or local government, including states, counties, cities, towns, and special districts.

Municipal bond—A bond issued by a municipality.

N

National Council on Governmental Accounting (NCGA)—The governmental accounting standard-setting authority that preceded the GASB.

Natural classification—Expenditures or expenses that are grouped according to an object, such as salaries and wages.

Net assets—The residual of assets minus liabilities.

Net cost (or net expense or revenue)—On the government-wide statement of activities, per GASB Statement No. 34, the difference between functional expenses (or program expenses) and program revenues; that is, the net cost of the function or program to the taxpayers.

Net pension obligation (NPO)—The cumulative difference between an employer's annual pension costs (based on its annual required contribution determined per the requirements of applicable accounting and actuarial standards) and the employer's actual contributions to a pension plan.

Nominal interest rate—The contractual interest rate shown on the face of a bond and used to compute the amount of interest to be paid; the stated or coupon rate; differentiated from the yield (effective interest) rate.

Nonappropriation clause—See *Fiscal funding clause*.

Nonexchange revenue—Revenue that arises when a government receives resources but gives nothing in exchange (at least not directly). Examples include taxes, duties, fines, penalties, donations, and most grants.

Nonexchange transaction—A transaction in which one party provides resources to another without receiving consideration of approximately equal value in return; includes derived tax revenue transactions (such as sales and income taxes), imposed nonexchange transactions (such as property taxes, duties, and fines), and government-mandated and voluntary nonexchange transactions (such as grants and donations).

No-commitment debt—See *Conduit debt*.

Nonexpendable funds—(1) Proprietary funds that "pay their own way" through customer charges. Contrast with expendable funds, the resources of which are provided by taxes, fees, or other revenues and are expected to be spent each year. (2) Endowment funds, the principal of which must be maintained intact and only the income can be expended.

Nonreciprocal interfund activity (transfers and reimbursements)—Per GASB Statement No. 34, the internal equivalent of nonexchange transactions. (1) Includes interfund transfers of cash or goods without equivalent flows of assets in return and without a requirement for repayment. Examples include when the general fund transfers cash to a debt service fund for payment of principal or interest on long-term debt, or when the general fund transfers cash to a newly established internal service fund for start-up capital. In governmental funds, transfers should be reported as other financing sources and uses (not revenues and expenses); in proprietary funds, they should be reported as nonoperating revenues and expenses. (2) Also includes interfund reimbursements; that is, repayments from the funds responsible for particular expenditures or expenses to the funds that initially paid for them. Reimbursements should not be displayed in the financial statements.

Nonreciprocal receipt—A contribution for which the recipient gives nothing in exchange. Per FASB Statement No. 116, contributions may be made in cash, marketable securities, property and equipment, utilities, supplies, intangible assets, and the services of professionals and craftsmen.

Normal cost—With respect to defined benefit pension plans, the portion of the present value of pension benefits that is allocated to a particular year by an appropriate actuarial cost method; also known as current service cost.

Note disclosure—Information disclosed in the notes to the financial statements.

O–P

Object—An item in an expenditure classification that relates to the type of goods or services obtained rather than to the purpose of the expenditure or the nature of the activity that it supports. Examples of objects include wages and salaries, supplies, and contractual services.

Off-balance-sheet financing—An obligation, such as from an operating lease, that does not satisfy the accounting criteria of a reportable liability and, therefore, is not displayed on an entity's balance sheet.

Operating debt—Debt issued to cover general operating, as opposed to capital, expenditures.

Operating lease—A rental agreement that permits an entity to use an asset for a specified period of time, but does not meet the criteria set forth in FASB Statement No. 13 of a capital lease.

Operating statement—A statement that shows an entity's revenues, expenditures or expenses, and transfers over a specified period of time.

Outcomes—The results (accomplishments) of a service, generally measured so as to take into account the quality of performance.

Outputs—The quantity, or units of service, provided by an activity.

Overhead—Indirect costs; those elements of cost necessary in the production of a good or service that are not directly traceable to the product or service, such as rent, heat, light, supplies, management, and supervision.

Overlapping debt—The proportionate share that property within a reporting government's jurisdiction must bear of the debts of all other governments located wholly or partly within its geographic boundaries.

Pass-through grant—A grant that a government or not-for-profit must transfer to, or spend on behalf of, a secondary recipient or beneficiary. For example, a federal grant for education that states must distribute to local school districts.

Pay-as-you-go basis—In the context of pension accounting and risk management, the practice of accumulating resources only when the benefits or obligations become due and payable; differentiated from financing them when or as the transaction or event occurs using an acceptable actuarial funding method.

Payment in lieu of taxes—An amount paid by one government to another in place of property taxes that it is not required to pay. Generally occurs when a jurisdiction contains a substantial amount of facilities of other governments; for example, a payment that the federal government makes to a local school district instead of paying property taxes that, if federal property were not tax-exempt, it would be required to pay on a military base within the district.

Pension—A sum of money paid periodically (usually monthly) to a retired or disabled employee or a surviving spouse owing to his or her years of employment.

Pension contribution—The amount paid into a pension plan by an employer, employee, or other entity, pursuant to the terms of the plan, state law, actuarial calculations, or some other basis for determination.

Pension obligation—See (1) *Actuarial accrued liability* and (2) *Net pension obligation*.

Pension trust fund—A fiduciary fund used to account for the assets accumulated by a government pension plan; accounted for on an accrual basis.

Per capita debt—The amount of a government's debt divided by its population.

Permanent fund—Per GASB Statement No. 34, an endowment fund in which the beneficiary is the government itself rather than outside parties. Examples are endowments where the donor specified that the income only be used to help maintain a city park, public cemetery, or library. Permanent funds are classified and accounted for as governmental funds.

Permanently restricted net assets—Endowments of which the principal must permanently remain intact and only the income is available for expenditure. Per FASB Statement No. 117, one of the three main categories into which resources of not-for-profits must be classified.

Plant fund—A fund maintained by colleges and universities and other not-for-profits to account for capital assets and the resources set aside to acquire or replace them. As used by colleges and universities, plant funds may be of four types: unexpended plant, renewal and replacement, retirement of indebtedness, and investment in plant.

Pledge—A promise by a donor to make a donation of cash or other assets in the future.

Present value—The amount that a buyer is willing to pay for one or a series of payments to be received in the future. Computed by discounting the future cash flows at an appropriate rate of interest and for an appropriate period of time.

Primary government—Per GASB Statement No. 14, a state government, a general purpose local government, such as a municipality or a county, or a special purpose government, such as a school district, that has a separately elected governing body, is legally separate from other primary governments, and is fiscally independent of other governments.

Private-purpose trust fund—A fiduciary fund maintained by a government to account for assets held for the benefit of outside parties (e.g., individuals, private organizations, or other governments).

Privatization—See *Contracting out.*

Proforma financial statement—A projected financial statement of an organization for a future period.

Program—A series of related activities intended to fulfill a common function or objective.

Program revenue—Per GASB Statement No. 34, a revenue generated by and, thus, directly attributable to a function or program; includes charges for services and directly attributable operating and capital grants; distinguished from general revenues.

Proprietary fund—An income-determination fund used to account for a government's business-type activities (enterprise funds) and its internal services provided on a cost-reimbursement basis (internal service funds); both fund types use the full accrual basis of accounting.

Purchases method—A method of accounting for inventories and prepaid expenses, such as rent, in which goods or services are recorded as expenses or expenditures when purchased, rather than when consumed; differentiated from the consumption method.

Purpose restriction—A stipulation, usually as part of a grant or donation, as to the purpose for which the resources must be used.

Q–R

Qualified opinion—An audit opinion stating that "except for" the effect of the matter to which the qualification relates, the financial statements present fairly the financial position, results of operations and (when applicable), changes in financial position in conformity with GAAP. Generally expressed when auditors cannot obtain adequate information to express an unqualified opinion, when there are significant uncertainties as to the value of assets or liabilities, or when there are material departures from GAAP.

Quasi-endowment fund—A fund maintained by colleges and universities and other not-for-profits to account for assets to be retained and invested as if they were contractually required endowments; for example, earnings (and only the earnings) from investments acquired with the resources are to be used for a specified purpose.

Realized gain or loss—The difference between the proceeds of sale of an investment and its cost.

Reciprocal interfund activity—Per GASB Statement No. 34, the internal equivalent of exchange transactions (those in which the parties receive and surrender consideration of approximately equal value); for example, interfund sales and purchases of goods and services (See *Interfund services provided and used*), and loans and repayments of loans.

Redemption value—In the context of investment pools and mutual funds, the amount that the pool or fund will pay per share to an investor electing to withdraw its funds; generally based on the current market value of the underlying securities.

Refinance—To replace existing debt with new debt, generally to take advantage of lower interest rates or to shorten or lengthen the debt payout period.

Refunding—See *Bond refunding.*

Reimbursement grant—A grant for which a potential recipient must first incur qualifying expenditures (allowable costs) to be eligible; an expenditure-driven grant.

Related organization—Per GASB Statement No. 14, an entity that satisfies the criteria of financial accountability, but not other necessary criteria, and therefore does not qualify as a component unit.

Renewal and replacement fund—A plant fund used by colleges and universities and other not-for-profits to account for resources set aside to restore and replace existing buildings, equipment, and other capital assets.

Replacement cost—The cost of acquiring or constructing an asset today that is identical to or has the same service potential as an asset already owned. An indicator of an asset's current value.

Reporting entity—The organizational unit covered by a set of financial statements. In government, it includes the primary government and all of its component units, if any, defined per the requirements of GASB Statement No. 14, as amended.

Repurchase agreement ("Repo")—An investment instrument in which an investor (buyer-lender) transfers cash to a broker-dealer or financial institution (seller-borrower). The broker-dealer or financial institution transfers securities to the investor and promises to repay the cash plus interest in exchange for the same securities or for different securities. Contrast with a reverse repurchase agreement.

Required supplementary information (RSI)— Statements, schedules, statistical data, or other information not included in, but required to be presented with, the basic financial statements. Per GASB Statement No. 34, it includes management's discussion and analysis, budget-to-actual comparisons, details of actuarial valuations of pension plans, and for governments that use the modified approach, information about the condition of infrastructure.

Reserved fund balance—That portion of a governmental fund balance that either represents resources that are not of a type that can be appropriated (e.g., reserves for inventory) or that are legally segregated for a specific future use (reserves for encumbrances).

Restricted grant—A payment that the grantor stipulates must be used for a specified purpose, project, or activity. (See *Purpose restriction*.)

Restricted net assets—Net assets that are restricted as to when and how they can be used; per GASB Statement No. 34, one of three categories in which net assets must be classified on the government-wide statement of net assets.

Retirement of indebtedness fund—A fund maintained by colleges and universities and other not-for-profits that is comparable to a debt service fund of a government and is used to account for resources set aside for the repayment of debt.

Revenue anticipation note (RAN)—A short-term note, issued in anticipation of the collection of revenues, and that will not be converted into a long-term instrument.

Revenue debt—A bond or other obligation whose principal and interest are payable exclusively from earnings of a specific enterprise, such as an electric utility, toll road, or dormitory, and are thereby not backed by the full faith and credit of the issuer. Contrast with general obligation debt.

Reverse repurchase agreement ("Reverse repo")—A borrowing instrument by which a borrower (seller) receives cash from a broker-dealer or financial institution (buyer-lender); in exchange, the borrower (seller) transfers securities to the broker-dealer or financial institution and promises to repay the cash plus interest in exchange for the same or different securities. Contrast with a repurchase agreement.

RSI—See *Required supplementary information*.

Rule 203 (of the AICPA's Code of Professional Conduct)—The provision that auditors should not express an unqualified opinion on financial statements that are in violation of the standards established by organizations designated by the AICPA's Council.

S

SEA—See *Service efforts and accomplishments indicators*.

Self-insurance—The retention of a risk by an entity, as opposed to the transfer of the risk to an independent third party through the purchase of an insurance policy.

Serial bond—A bond issue that matures in a series of installments at future dates—for example, a portion matures in five years, a portion in six years, a portion in seven years, and so on. Contrast with *Term bond*.

Service efforts and accomplishments (SEA) indicators—Measures of an entity's inputs, outputs, outcomes, and efficiency in carrying out its activities.

Shared revenue—Revenue levied by one government, such as a state, but shared on a predetermined basis with other governments, such as cities.

Short-term debt—An obligation that an entity expects to pay within one year or the entity's operating cycle.

Special assessment—A compulsory tax levy on certain properties to defray all or part of the cost of a specific capital improvement or service deemed to benefit primarily those properties or their owners.

Special assessment bond—A bond payable from the proceeds of special assessments.

Special item—Per GASB Statement No. 34, a significant transaction or other event that is within the control of management and is either unusual in nature or infrequent in occurrence. Contrast with *Extraordinary item*.

Special purpose government—A government that serves only a single, well-defined purpose, such as a university, utility district, or library district. Contrast with general purpose government.

Special revenue fund—A governmental fund used to account for the proceeds of specific revenue sources that are legally restricted to expenditure for specific purposes.

Stated interest rate (on bonds)—See *Coupon rate* or *Nominal rate*.

Sunk cost—A cost that has already been incurred and cannot be recovered.

T–U–V

Take-out agreement—An agreement between an issuer of demand bonds and a financial institution per which the financial institution will provide funding for the issuer in the event that bondholders demand redemption of their bonds.

Tangible asset—An asset that is used in the normal operations of an organization and that can be physically seen.

Tap fee—A fee charged by a government utility to new customers to hook up to its system.

Tax anticipation note (TAN)—A short-term note that a government does not expect to convert into long-term debt, issued in anticipation of the future collection of taxes.

Taxpayer-assessed tax—A tax, such as a sales or income tax, the amount of which is determined by parties other than the government. Distinguished from a government-assessed tax, such as a property tax.

Temporarily restricted net assets—Resources that must be used either for a specified purpose or when specified events have occurred. Per FASB Statement No. 117, one of three categories into which not-for-profit resources must be classified.

Term bond—A bond that matures in one lump sum at a specified future date. Contrast with *Serial bond*.

Term endowment—An endowment in which the principal may be expended after a specified number of years.

Time requirement—Per GASB Statement No. 33, a stipulation, usually as part of a grant, as to the time period in which the resources must be used or when use may begin.

Trustee—A party that administers property for a beneficiary.

Trust fund—A fund used to account for assets over which the entity acts as a trustee or that must be invested and the income only, not the principal, may be expended. Examples include pension trust funds, investment trust funds, private-purpose trust funds, and endowments.

Unconditional promise to give—A pledge or promise to give an asset or provide a service in the future that is not dependent on a certain event occurring.

Unfunded actuarial accrued liability—The excess of a pension plan's actuarial accrued liability over the actuarial value of its assets.

Unqualified opinion—An auditor's opinion stating that the financial statements present fairly the financial position, results of operations, and (when applicable) changes in financial position in conformity with GAAP.

Unrealized gain or loss—Cumulative change in the fair (market) value of an investment prior to its disposition.

Unrestricted grant—A grant that is unrestricted as to purpose, project, or activity.

Unrestricted net assets—Net assets that are not restricted as to when and how they can be used. Per GASB Statement No. 34, one of three categories in which net assets must be classified on the government-wide statement of net assets. Per FASB Statement No. 117, one of three categories into which not-for-profit resources must be classified.

Use restriction—See *Purpose restriction*.

User charge—A charge for the use of a service, such as for parking or trash collection, as opposed to a tax that is not directly related to services received.

Variable cost—A cost that changes in direct proportion to volume.

Variance power—Per FASB Statement No. 136, the ability of a not-for-profit to unilaterally redirect donated resources to a beneficiary other than that specified by the donor.

Vested benefit—A benefit for which an employer has an obligation to make payment even if an employee is terminated. Thus, the benefit is not contingent on an employee's future service.

Voluntary health and welfare organization—A not-for-profit formed to provide services to a community, rather than to its own members. Examples include the United Way, Boy and Girl Scouts, the American Heart Association, and most social service agencies.

Voluntary nonexchange transaction—A transaction that results from a legislative or contractual agreement entered into willingly by two or more parties. These transactions include grants given by one government to another and contributions from individuals (e.g., gifts to public universities).

W–X–Y–Z

Yield rate—The actual (effective), as distinguished from the nominal (coupon or stated), rate of return on a bond or other investment.

Zero coupon bond—A bond with a stated annual interest rate of zero. It provides a return to investors in that it is issued at a price considerably less than the bond's face value and sufficiently low so that the difference between face value and issue price will equal a return comparable to that on conventional bonds.